Biogeography in the Sub-Arctic

Biogeography in the Sub-Arctic

The Past and Future of North Atlantic Biota

Edited by

Eva Panagiotakopulu
University of Edinburgh
UK

Jon P. Sadler
University of Birmingham
UK

This edition first published 2021

© 2021 John Wiley & Sons Ltd

The right of Eva Panagiotakopulu and Jon P. Sadler to be identified as the authors of the editorial material in this work has been asserted in accordance with law.

Registered Offices
John Wiley & Sons, Inc., 111 River Street, Hoboken, NJ 07030, USA
John Wiley & Sons Ltd, The Atrium, Southern Gate, Chichester, West Sussex, PO19 8SQ, UK

Editorial Office
9600 Garsington Road, Oxford, OX4 2DQ, UK

For details of our global editorial offices, customer services, and more information about Wiley products visit us at www.wiley.com.

Wiley also publishes its books in a variety of electronic formats and by print-on-demand. Some content that appears in standard print versions of this book may not be available in other formats.

Library of Congress Cataloging-in-Publication Data is applied for

ISBN 9781118561478

Cover Design: Wiley
Cover Image: © Eva Panagiotakopulu

Set in 9.5/12.5pt STIXTwoText by SPi Global, Pondicherry, India
Printed and bound by CPI Group (UK) Ltd, Croydon, CR0 4YY

C9781118561478_040521

Contents

List of Contributors

Inger G. Alsos
The Arctic University Museum of Norway
Tromsø
Norway

Ole Bennike
Geological Survey of Denmark and Greenland
Copenhagen
Denmark

Jens Böcher
Zoological Museum
Copenhagen
Denmark

Christian Brochmann
The Natural History Museum
University of Oslo
Oslo
Norway

Thomas Denk
Department of Palaeobiology
Swedish Museum of Natural History
Stockholm
Sweden

Gaston R. Demarée
Royal Meteorological Institute of Belgium
Brussels
Belgium

Kevin J. Edwards
Department of Geography and Environment and
Department of Archaeology
School of Geosciences, University of Aberdeen
Aberdeen
UK
Scott Polar Research Institute and McDonald
Institute for Archaeological Research
University of Cambridge
Cambridge
UK

Egill Erlendsson
Department of Geography and Tourism
Faculty of Life and Environmental Sciences
University of Iceland
Reykjavík
Iceland

Anna Maria Fosaa
Faroese Museum of Natural History
Tórshavn
Faroe Islands

Gísli Már Gíslason
Institute of Life and Environmental Sciences
University of Iceland
Reykjavík
Iceland

Friðgeir Grímsson
Department of Botany and Biodiversity
Research
University of Vienna
Vienna
Austria

Jennifer Harland
Archaeology Institute
University of the Highlands and Islands
Orkney College
Kirkwall
UK

Erlingur Hauksson
Fornistekkur 14
Reykjavík
Iceland

Henning Heide-Jørgensen
Department of Biology
University of Copenhagen
Copenhagen
Denmark

Brian T. Hill
Institute for Ocean Technology
National Research Council
Canada

Ib Johnsen
Department of Biology
University of Copenhagen
Copenhagen
Denmark

Ingrid Mainland
Archaeology Institute
University of the Highlands and Islands
Orkney College
Kirkwall
UK

Astrid E. J. Ogilvie
Stefansson Arctic Institute
Akureyri
Iceland
Institute of Arctic and Alpine Research
(INSTAAR)
University of Colorado
Boulder
CO
USA

Bergur Olsen
Faroe Marine Research Institutre
Faroe Islands

Eva Panagiotakopulu
School of GeoSciences
University of Edinburgh
Edinburgh
UK

Aevar Petersen
Brautarland 2
Reykjavík
Iceland

Jon P. Sadler
School of Geography
Earth and Environmental Sciences
The University of Birmingham
Birmingham
UK

J. Edward Schofield
Department of Geography and Environment
School of Geosciences
University of Aberdeen
Aberdeen
UK

Thóra Ellen Thórhallsdóttir
Institute of Life and Environmental Sciences
University of Iceland
Reykjavík
Iceland

Brian G. J. Upton
School of GeoSciences
University of Edinburgh
Edinburgh
UK

Bernd Wagner
Institute of Geology and Mineralogy
University of Cologne
Cologne
Germany

Reinhard Zetter
Department of Palaeontology
University of Vienna
Vienna
Austria

Introduction

Jon P. Sadler[1] and Eva Panagiotakopulu[2]

[1] *School of Geography, Earth and Environmental Sciences, The University of Birmingham, Birmingham, UK*
[2] *School of GeoSciences, University of Edinburgh, Edinburgh, UK*

There is no escaping the fact that the island bioge-ography of the North Atlantic Region is singularly peculiar. While it has aspects of the characteristics of many island groups in terms of disharmonic and impoverished species pools (Coope 1986), it lacks true endemics (Buckland 1988; Downes 1988, but cf. Böcher 1988), although it is home to a wide number of putative subspecies and races (e.g. Lindroth 1968; Löve and Löve 1963). Sitting in the north of the Atlantic Ocean these islands have been subjected to large-scale shifts in climate over the last few million years, unlike the other island groups further south which were likely buff-ered from the vicissitudes of Quaternary climate changes (Sadler 2001). Unlike island groups else-where, there is only one documented extinction on these island groups (the Great Auk) and those in the insects are local events relating to species that are distributed throughout the Palaearctic region. Over half the insect species in Iceland and Greenland are non-indigenous and many of these were first introduced to the islands by the Norse colonists (Buckland 1988; Panagiotakopulu 2014; Sadler 1990). The faunas, excluding Greenland (Böcher 1988, are predominantly Palaearctic

(Buckland 1988; Downes 1988; Lindroth 1931), and have close affinities with the faunas of the British Isles and Scandinavia. These unique physical and biological characteristics have inter-ested biologists and biogeographers for centuries (Hooker 1862).

In their seminal book *North Atlantic Biota and Their History*, Löve and Löve (1963) concluded that plants survived the heavily glaciated Atlantic areas, in 'glacial refuges' or 'nunataks', dismiss-ing the earlier 'now merely historical' *tabula rasa* idea – the hypothesis that the current Atlantic flo-ras were established following postglacial immi-gration from source areas situated outside the ice sheets. The virtually complete consensus among plant biogeographers (with notable exceptions among some palaeoecologists) at that time was based on two main arguments, the occurrence of (a) disjunct and (b) endemic taxa in the North Atlantic region. Firstly, the presence of disjuncts was believed to necessitate in situ glacial survival because long-distance dispersal in general and trans-oceanic dispersal in particular was con-sidered to be extremely rare, if not impossible, because many amphi-Atlantic disjuncts lacked adaptations for long-distance dispersal. Secondly, the occurrence of endemics was believed to necessitate in situ glacial survival because the postglacial period was considered to be far too short to allow for evolution of endemic taxa, an argument that has been supported in later studies (e.g. Dahl 1987). The pervading view was to postulate in situ glacial survival not only during the last glaciation but throughout the entire Pleistocene, to explain the occurrence of disjuncts and endemics in the North Atlantic region. Other research on insects, principally by Lindroth (1957), also argued for early immigration via landbridges and glacial refugia to explain the biogeographical affinities of the biota. More recent work also supports the refugial hypothesis (Maggs et al. 2008).

Löve and Löve (1963) perceptively pointed to the fact that conclusive tests of these varying colonization hypotheses must await a more extensive fossil record. Indeed, recent investigations of a rich plant fossil record seem to support the view that a North Atlantic Land Bridge facilitated plant migration between North America and Europe until the late Miocene (e.g. Brochmann et al. 2003). The Quaternary fossil record is now very extensive and has been used by many to support tabula rasa and post-glacial colonization via ice rafting at the terminal phase of the last glaciation (Buckland et al. 1988; Coope 1986). Moreover, the fossil beetle fauna demonstrates that even at the beginning of the previous interglacial period a similar situation might have occurred, capable of transporting European taxa over the North Atlantic to Greenland (Bennike and Böcher 1994; Böcher 2012).

Unlike several island archipelagos (e.g. Pacific and Indian oceans) and continental shelf islands (e.g. Magascar), Pre-European settlement in the North Atlantic was restricted to Greenland where Inuit settlers colonized the islands in the mid-Holocene (Andreasen 1996; Jensen 2006). Although some scholars have consistently argued for pre-Viking settlement of the Faroe and Iceland (e.g. Church et al. 2013; Hermanns-Audardóttir 1991),

the first major European settlement of the North Atlantic region was undertaken by Norse or Viking colonists who reached Faroe by CE 850, Iceland by CE 870, Greenland by CE 986 and ultimately America (Newfoundland) by CE 1000 (Fitzhugh and Ward 2000). In Greenland, however, European settlements were abandoned by the sixteenth century (Arneborg 2003), although the island was recolonized by Norwegians some 200 years later. The role that these human colonists played in shaping biogeographical patterns shows pulses of European introductions linked to Norse arrival (e.g. Panagiotakopulu 2014). The impact of the settlers on the island ecosystems also had an indirect influence in shaping habitats and therefore assemblage dynamics. Palynological work has tracked the Landnám 'footprints' of the Norse settlers in the region (Edwards et al. 2008, 2011) and Dugmore et al. (2012) have recently presented a comprehensive review of the environmental impact of Norse farming practices on ecosystem management, soils and pasture management. Wholescale environmental modification of this magnitude has left its mark on the biota in terms of assemblage changes and local extinctions (Buckland and Panagiotakopulu 2010; McGovern et al. 2007).

Some 40 years have elapsed since Löve and Löve's (1963) volume was published and the key debates concerning the biogeography of the North Atlantic islands still rumble on. Was it cryptic refugia (Stuart and Lister 2001) or otherwise (Willis and Whittaker 2000), or tabula rasa and recolonization (Buckland and Dugmore 2010)? How important were human communities in shaping the existing biota and biogeographical patterns? Throw into this mix current concerns over global warming, we can now add how resilient is the biota to change, either natural or anthropogenic? This volume draws together a range of researchers with longstanding research interests in the region, from diverse academic backgrounds, to evaluate these questions.

This book is organized into sections each examining a particular theme. Section I focuses on the remote origins of the islands, diving deep into the early history of the region. Upton (Chapter 1) examines the opening of the North Atlantic from a geological perspective, charting its origin from super-continent in the lower Palaeozoic, approximately 420–430 million years (Ma) ago, to the development of the North Atlantic Ocean as a late product of the disintegration of Laurasia, a part of Pangaea, which split to form North America, Greenland, Europe and Asia. The Cenozoic vegetation and phytogeography of the sub-arctic areas are discussed by Grímsson et al. (Chapter 2). They examine the *'Arcto-Tertiary element' hypothesis* and present data that demonstrate that several north temperate tree taxa thrived in the sub-arctic during the Paleogene, while also noting evidence for the presence of several 'Arcto-Tertiary elements' in Greenland. They then go on to evaluate the possible role for the 'The North Atlantic Land Bridge', reviewing recent investigations of the rich plant fossil record, and demonstrate that the NALB facilitated plant migration between North America and Europe until the late Miocene. Moving forward in time, Bennike and Böcher (Chapter 3) examine the biotal record from the last interglacial period. They review the refugia-tabula rasa debate in light of this record and point to areas where knowledge is lacking, such as the role of microclimate and insolation in supporting the former. They illustrate that during the interglacials there was a rich biota in suitable biotopes on the North Atlantic.

Section II of the volume examines the contentious issue of biotal origins. Brochmann and Alsos (Chapter 4) present new genetic evidence based on a total of 9018 plants from 1140 populations to re-evaluate their earlier conclusions (Brochmann et al. 2003) on the origins and dispersal of the North Atlantic vascular plant floras. The data point towards postglacial immigration of a highly dispersive flora, although they note convincing molecular evidence suggesting in situ glacial persistence of some elements of the 'west-arctic' species group. Gíslason (Chapter 5)

examines the aquatic fauna of the North Atlantic islands with a particular emphasis on Iceland. He notes that the islands have few aquatic species, almost no aquatic endemics, but their faunas are closely related. He goes on to discuss how the proportion of continental (Norway and Britain) species present on the islands is much higher among crustaceans than other groups. Despite low levels of endemism found amongst crustaceans in subterranean groundwater systems, the patterns indicate a Holocene (post glacial) origin for the biota.

Thórhallsdóttir (Chapter 6) evaluates and analyses data on the vascular floras of high-latitude islands, again with special reference to Iceland, corralling independent lines of evidence that all favour the view that the Icelandic flora is young, i.e. of Holocene descent. In Quaternary vertebrates from the North Atlantic islands, Bennike and Wagner (Chapter 7) review the meagre fossil record of mammals from the main islands of Greenland, Iceland and Faroe, pointing out the incomplete record and the need for other independent lines of evidence such as genetic analyses. Panagiotakopulu (Chapter 8) reviews the North Atlantic insect fauna data revealing the effect of climate change and their early immigration to the islands but emphasizing the importance of the arrival of Europeans in the North Atlantic region in terms of introduction of species to the region but also the biological impact that they have had on the fauna.

Section III picks up on this key theme of human impact on the islands. Edwards et al. (Chapter 9) use the archaeological and palaeoecological records to examine the impact of Landnám and the North Atlantic flora. The review highlights the fact that the impacts of *landnám* on vegetation were broadly similar across that region, but that there are subtle differences in the Norse 'footprint' when examined at finer spatial scales which varied according to the interplay of the climatic, pedogenic, topographic and anthropogenic factors at each location.

Petersen and Olsen (Chapter 10) review the status of the bird fauna of Iceland and Faroe and discuss its colonization and Mainland and Harland (Chapter 11) explore the profound impact of farming on North Atlantic vertebrate biota, reviewing evidence for the introduction of domesticated faunas and rapid and widespread changes to the island landscapes and environments as a result of pastoralism and the exploitation of marine resources. The former (Chapter 10) characterizes the patterns in bird dispersal and extinctions and extirpations and its conservation significance of the avian fauna, while the latter (Chapter 11) presents comprehensive evidence showing that farming and fishing were vital to subsistence and trade as well as being core to island and community identity in the past, roles they continue to play out to the current day.

The prospects for the future environmental systems of the region is addressed in Section IV. Ogilvie et al. (Chapter 12) use a rich historical dataset to provide an elegant perspective on the significance and importance of sea ice patterns and flows to both historical and contemporary communities. Fosaa (Chapter 13) returns to a biodiversity theme and reviews the influence of both climate change and direct human impact on the flora of Faroe, including the threats posed by introduced species pointing to elements in Faroese flora that are of some conservation concern. The policy and legislative frameworks for biodiversity and conservation in Iceland under a changing climate is evaluated in considerable detail by Hauksson (Chapter 13). Johnsen and Heide-Jørgensen (Chapter 14) examine the natural environment and its biodiversity in Greenland during the present climate change, presenting observations of the biological response related to an increasing greenhouse effect and stratospheric ozone depletion with an emphasis on terrestrial plant ecology.

It is appropriate that we conclude this introduction with a tribute to one of the region's leading scientists for whom this volume was conceived. Professor Paul C. Buckland blended his early (doctoral) training from the related fields of archaeology and geology, work on tephrochronology of East Africa lakes, a detailed evaluation of the value of insect fossils in the interpretations of archaeological deposits across the world, into a unique, innovative and complementary skillset for examining the biological conundrum that was (and to some extent still is) the biogeography of the North Atlantic. Like many researchers and colleagues (several authors of chapters in this volume), both editors of this book have been small cogs in this body of research and benefitted greatly from Paul Buckland's supervision and tutorage as doctoral researchers. Having developed a love for the environments, plants, animals and people of the North Atlantic region in a research career spanning some four decades, this book and contributions within it are a fitting tribute to his unique contribution to our understanding of the biogeography of the region.

References

Andreasen, C. (1996). A survey of paleoeskimo sites in Northern East Greenland. In: *The Paleo-Eskimo Cultures of Greenland – New Perspectives in Greenlandic Archaeology* (ed. B. Grønnow), 177–190. Copenhagen: Danish Polar Center Publications No. 1.

Arneborg, J. (2003). Norse Greenland: reflections on settlement and depopulation. In: *Contact, Continuity, and Collapse. The Norse Colonization of the North Atlantic* (ed. J.H. Barrett), 163–181. Turnhout: Brepols.

Bennike, O. and Böcher, J. (1994). Land biotas of the last interglacial/glacial cycle on Jameson Land, East Greenland. *Boreas* 23: 479–487.

Böcher, J. (1988). *The Coleoptera of Greenland*, vol. 26. *Meddelelser om Grønland (Bioscience)*, 100 pp.

Böcher, J. (2012). Interglacial insects and their possible survival in Greenland during the last glacial stage. *Boreas* 41: 644–659.

Brochmann, C., Gabrielsen, T.M., Nordal, I. et al. (2003). Glacial survival or *tabula rasa*? The history of North Atlantic biota revisited. *Taxon* 52: 417–450.

Buckland, P.C. (1986). North Atlantic faunal connections – introduction or endemics? *Entomologica Scandinavica* 32: 7–29.

Buckland, P.C. and Dugmore, A. (1991). If this is a refugium, why are my feet so bloody cold? The origins of the Icelandic biota in the light of recent research. In: *Environmental Change in Iceland Past and Present* (eds. J.K. Maizels and C. Caseldine), 107–125. Dordrecht: Kluwer.

Buckland, P.C. and Panagiotakopulu, E. (2010). Reflections on North Atlantic Island Biogeography: a Quaternary entomological view. In: *Dorete – Her Book:– Being a Tribute to Dorete Bloch and to Faroese Nature*, Annales Societatis *Scientiarum Færoensis Supplementum*, vol. 52 (eds. S.-A. Bengtson, P. Buckland, P.H. Enckell and A.M. Fosaa), 187–215. Tórshavn: Faroe University Press.

Buckland, P.C., Perry, D.W., Gíslason, G.M., and Dugmore, A.J. (1986). The pre-landnám fauna of Iceland: a palaeontological contribution. *Boreas* 15: 173–184.

Church, M.J., Arge, S.V., Edwards, K.J. et al. (2013). The Vikings were not the first colonizers of the Faroe Islands. *Quaternary Science Reviews* 77: 228–232.

Coope, G.R. (1986). The invasion and colonization of the North Atlantic islands: a palaeoecological solution to a biogeographical problem. *Philosophical Transactions of the Royal Society of London, B* 314: 619–635.

Dahl, E. (1987). The nunatak theory reconsidered. *Ecological Bulletin* 38: 77–94.

Downes, J.A. (1988). The postglacial colonisation of the North Atlantic islands. *Memoirs of the Entomological Society of Canada* 144: 55–92.

Dugmore, A.J., McGovern, T.H., Vésteinsson, O. et al. (2012). Cultural adaptation, compounding vulnerabilities and conjunctures in Norse Greenland. *Proceedings of the National Academy of Sciences of the United States of America* 109: 3658–3663.

Edwards, K.J., Schofield, E., and Mauquoy, D. (2008). High resolution paleoenvironmental and chronological investigations of Norse landnám at Tasiusaq, Eastern Settlement, Greenland. *Quaternary Research* 69: 1–15.

Edwards, K.J., Erlendsson, E., and Schofield, J.E. (2011). Is there a Norse 'footprint' in North Atlantic pollen records? In: *Viking Settlements and Society: Papers from the Sixteenth Viking Congress, Reykjavík and Reykholt, 16–23 August 2009* (eds. S. Sigmundsson, A. Holt, G. Sigurðsson, et al.), 65–82. Reykjavík: Hið íslenska fornleifafélag and University of Iceland Press.

Fitzhugh, W.W. and Ward, E.I. (2000). *Vikings. The North Atlantic Saga*. Washington: Smithsonian Institute.

Hermanns-Audardóttir, M. (1991). The early settlement of Iceland. *Norwegian Archaeological Review* 24 (1): 1–9.

Hooker, J.D. (1862). Outline of the distribution of Arctic plants. *Transactions of the Linnean Society of London* 23: 251–348.

Jensen, J. F. 2006. Stone Age of Qeqertarsuup Tunua (Disko Bugt) a regional analysis of the Saqqaq and Dorset cultures of Central West Greenland. *Meddelelser om Grønland/ Monographs on Greenland, Man & Society*, Vol. 32, 272 pp.

Lindroth, C.H. (1931). Die Insekfauna Islands und ihre probleme. *Zoologiska bidrag från Uppsala* 13: 105–600.

Lindroth, C.H. (1957). *The Faunal Connections between Europe and North America*. New York: Wiley.

Lindroth, C.H. (1968). The Icelandic form of *Carabus problematicus* Hbst (Col. Carabidae) – A statistical treatment. *Opscula Entomologica* 33: 157–182.

Löve, A. and Löve, D. (eds.) (1963). *North Atlantic Biota and Their History*. Oxford: Pergamon Press, 430 pp.

Maggs, C.A., Castilho, R., Foltz, D. et al. (2008). Evaluating signatures of glacial refugia from North Atlantic benthic marine taxa. *Ecology* 89 (Suppl): S108–S122.

McGovern, T.H., Fridriksson, A., Church, M. et al. (2007). Landscapes of settlement in northern Iceland: historical ecology of human impact and climate fluctuations on the millennial scale. *American Anthropologist* 109: 27–51.

Panagiotakopulu, E. (2014). Hitchhiking across the North Atlantic – insect immigrants, origins, introductions and extinctions. *Quaternary International* 341: 59–68.

Sadler, J.P. (1990). Beetles, boats and biogeography: insect invaders of the North Atlantic Islands. *Acta Archaeologica* 61: 199–211.

Sadler, J.P. (2001). Biodiversity on oceanic islands: a palaeoecological assessment. *Journal of Biogeography* 26: 75–87.

Stuart, J.R. and Lister, A.M. (2001). Cryptic northern refugia and the origins of the modern biota. *Trends in Ecology and Evolution* 16 (11): 608–613.

Willis, K.J. and Whittaker, R.J. (2000). The refugial debate. *Science* 287 (5457): 1406–1407.

Section I

Remote Origins

1

The Opening of the North Atlantic

Brian G. J. Upton

School of GeoSciences, University of Edinburgh, UK

The northern landmasses, namely North America, Greenland and Europe/Asia were part of one global super-continent in the lower Palaeozoic, approximately 420–430 million years (Ma) ago. This super-continent (Pangaea) resulted from continental collisions. Driven by convective flow deep in the interior of the Earth it is the nature of continents to break apart, re-join and to come apart again. Such a separation and amalgamation constitutes 'the Wilson Cycle', which takes several hundred million years to run its full course. No sooner had Pangaea come into existence than it became subject to tectonic stresses that tended to disrupt it. The North Atlantic Ocean is a late product of the disintegration of Laurasia, a part of Pangaea, which split to form North America, Greenland, Europe and Asia. Continental separation had begun in the south Atlantic region at *ca* 130 Ma and spread north by 60–50 Ma.

Plate Tectonic Résumé

Before considering the birth and growth of the North Atlantic, a brief résumé concerning plate tectonics is in order. Volumetrically the greater bulk of the planet is composed of the mantle. The latter, itself covered by thin veneers of crust, hydrosphere and atmosphere, extends down to a depth of 2885 km, i.e. to the outer boundary of the core from which it receives heat. The mantle is composed of various magnesium-rich silicates and oxides and is deduced to behave as a ductile material that is in constant slow convective motion, flowing whilst remaining (almost entirely) in the solid state. The flowage is due to variations in its composition and temperature (principally the latter) that confer different densities to some parts. Consequently, the relative buoyancy of those parts with lower density causes them to rise while, simultaneously, other denser parts sink to take their place.

Whereas most of the mantle is thought to behave in a ductile manner, a relatively thin outer layer differs in being mechanically rigid and is known as the lithosphere. The lower and larger part of this comprises the lithospheric mantle whilst the upper layer (the crust) consists of less magnesian and more siliceous and aluminium-rich rocks. The lithosphere is sub-divided into some 30 major tectonic plates and a host of micro-plates. These tectonic plates, floating on the convecting

Biogeography in the Sub-Arctic: The Past and Future of North Atlantic Biota, First Edition.
Edited by Eva Panagiotakopulu and Jon P. Sadler.

underlying mantle, move relative to each other in one of three ways. They may (a) slide past each other without colliding, (b) collide and under- or over-ride another plate or (c) just move apart. Typically, the continental lithosphere has a thickness of >100 km but under the oceans the lithosphere is much thinner, ranging from zero (at the mid-ocean ridges) to ~100 km. Older, colder and thicker parts of the oceanic lithosphere sink back into the deeper mantle at subduction zones where they undergo re-cycling. This loss of oceanic lithosphere is counterbalanced by continuous growth of new lithosphere along the 'mid-ocean ridges' or 'constructive plate boundaries', where the plates move apart. This juvenile lithosphere is formed from material arising from the underlying ductile mantle. In the context of oceanic lithosphere, 'old' means having ages of up to ~200 Ma whereas the rocks of the continental lithosphere have ages of anything up to 4000 Ma.

Continental lithosphere differs from its oceanic counterpart not only in being older and thicker but in composition, complexity and overall lower density. The last of these causes it to 'float' higher so that most rises above sea-level and the remainder is covered only by shallow seas and constitutes the continental shelves. By contrast, because of its higher density, the oceanic lithosphere lies at lower levels than its continental counterpart and its surface is almost invariably submarine, with the ocean floors generally lying at depths of ~4 km. The oceanic lithosphere, with its constructive plate boundaries (mid-ocean ridges) and corresponding destructive plate boundaries (along subduction zones, generally demarcated by deep ocean trenches), covers some 5/7th of the Earth's surface. The continental shelves slope steeply down from depths of ~2 km to the deep ocean floors. Consequently, the submarine 2 km contour approximates the change-over from one type of lithosphere to the other. On the western side of the North Atlantic the continental shelf is very narrow, contrasting with the European side where it is much broader.

The first mid-ocean 'ridge' to be recognized was the 'mid-Atlantic Ridge' along the Atlantic axis (Heezen et al. 1959: Figure 1, see Plate section). This was subsequently shown to be merely a part of a great circum-global ridge system, some ~80 000 km long, rising to heights of 3 km or more from the deep ('abyssal') oceanic plains. Typically, these ridges bear a rift-valley along their crests that can be up to 10–20 km wide and with a relief of ~1 km (Bown and White 1994).

The ocean floor moves away symmetrically on either side of the mid-ocean ridges as new lithosphere is generated along them. The process of ocean-floor spreading causes a reduction of pressure along the axes which in turn promotes partial melting, to the extent of some 10–15%, of the asthenospheric mantle that underlies the lithosphere. The melt product is basaltic magma that, being less dense than the residual solid mantle, ascends towards the surface. Losing heat as it does so, most crystallizes to form intrusive rocks within the oceanic crust and the remainder erupts as lava on the ocean floor. Although the volume of lava erupted from the mid-ocean ridges is estimated to be between 2 and 3 km³/year, a much greater volume is estimated to crystallize to form the underlying intrusions.

The spreading process confers bilateral symmetry to the mid-ocean ridges as juvenile material is welded on either side to the pre-existing lithosphere. The mantle rocks that are not consumed in the melting remain behind, contributing to the lower part of the oceanic lithosphere. Sea-floor spreading occurs at rates that can exceed 100 mm/year, whilst that in the North Atlantic is roughly 25 mm/year (Bown and White 1994).

When extensional stresses acting on a ridge sector become too great, rupturing (rifting) occurs along its crest and the new-formed magma rises up a vertical fissure to form an intrusive 'dyke'. The dykes cool to form tabular, near-vertical intrusions, typically not more than a few metres wide. Their repeated generation produces a 'sheeted

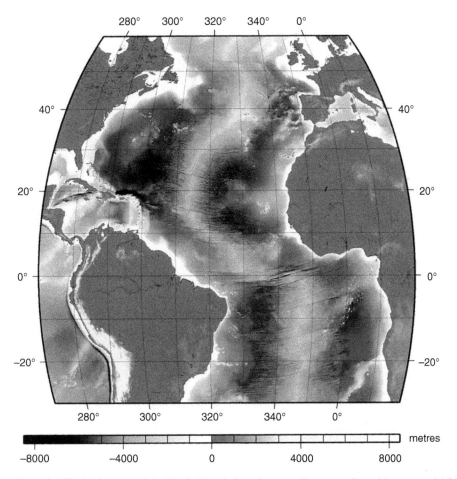

Figure 1 The bathymetry of the North Atlantic, based on satellite sea-surface altimetry, model DNSC08. The symmetrical disposition of the mid-Atlantic ridge relative to the bounding continents is well exhibited. *Source:* Based on Anderson, O.B. & Knudsen, P. 2009. (See colour plate section for colour representation of this figure.)

complex' in which the youngest are those newly formed along the spreading axis and the oldest are those furthest away. Dykes can compose virtually the entirety of the sheeted complexes lying beneath the lavas extruded on the ocean floor.

Because of this mechanism the spreading (and thus growth of the oceanic plate) does not take place continuously but in a jerky, spasmodic manner. For example, generation of a new fissure 1 m wide every 50 years would correspond to an averaged spreading rate of 20 mm/year. Hence,

whilst the spreading ocean floors can be crudely considered as analogous to moving walkways, it is intermittent with intervals of tens to hundreds of years intervening between the intrusion of one dyke and the next. The relatively hot rocks composing the axial region have a lower density so that they rise to form the mid-ocean ridges. With age and cooling they subside to the depths of the abyssal plains.

The mid-ocean ridges are offset by faults of a type known as transform faults. The motions along these fractures (which can have offsets ranging up to hundreds of kilometres) are dominantly horizontal. In the North Atlantic there are several of these major fractures that subdivide the mid-ocean ridge between Greenland and Norway. The most prominent are the Senja fracture zone to the south of Spitzbergen and the Jan Mayen fracture zone at ~52°N.

Magnetic Anomalies

As a result of processes in the Earth's core, the magnetic field spontaneously reverses at irregular intervals averaging at 500,000 years. The direction of magnetization is recorded within the oxide minerals that crystallize from the magmas, much as in a compass needle. As they cool, these minerals retain a memory of the field at the time of their formation. As sea-floor spreading proceeds, alternating strips of 'normally magnetized' (i.e. with the magnetic field as it is currently) and those with 'reversed magnetization' are left on the ocean floor (Figure 2, see Plate section). It was the discovery of these ocean floor magnetic anomalies by Vine and Matthews (1963) that provided confirmation of Hess's (1962) ocean-floor spreading hypothesis. Vine and Matthews demonstrated that continuous growth of the ocean floor, in conjunction with the periodic reversals, produces distinct magnetic stripes, developed as mirror-images on either side of the spreading ridge.

These magnetic signatures record the past positions of the ridge axis and, since specific ages can now be assigned to the reversals, the age of the ocean floor from new-formed crust to oldest (first-formed) crust can be determined.

Mantle Plumes

Masses of mantle rock rise convectively when their composition and/or temperature confers buoyancy. Temperature, however, is regarded as the dominant factor and great volumes of abnormally hot rock are thought to detach periodically from deeper parts of the mantle to rise as so-called mantle plumes. Although the concept of mantle plumes dates back to the early 1970s, it remains controversial with opponents of the idea referring simply to foci of high temperature phenomena as 'hot-spots' and denying that such plumes arise from the deep mantle (e.g. Anderson 2005).

The idea that mantle plumes have a mushroom-like shape, with a massive plume head and an extremely hot tail, is based on fluid-dynamical studies. The most voluminous magmatic events during the Earth's history have been related in space and time to an impact at the base of the lithosphere by such a plume head. Such a 'hot-spot' model was outlined for the North Atlantic by White (1988), postulating a central plume causing raised asthenospheric temperatures across a wide region. A review of conflicting hypotheses with respect to the North Atlantic by Meyer et al. (2007) concluded that it would be difficult to present a model explaining both the records of igneous activity and associated uplift (discussed below) without appealing to an up-rise of hot mantle beneath the lithosphere. Because the various arguments cannot be rehearsed in this chapter the author adopts a partisan attitude, regarding the plume model as the more robust and better supported by evidence.

The Iceland Plume

The sudden and massive onset of magmatic activity in what may be broadly termed the north Atlantic region during the early Cenozoic (i.e. in the Palaeocene and Eocene epochs, between 66 and 34 Ma) has been attributed to a dramatic increase in the temperature of the underlying mantle starting at around 62 Ma. The most plausible explanation for this is that it was due to the

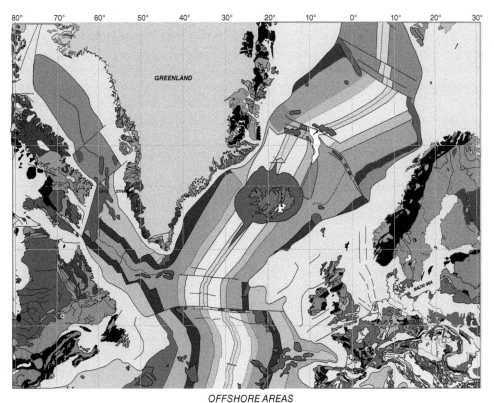

OFFSHORE AREAS

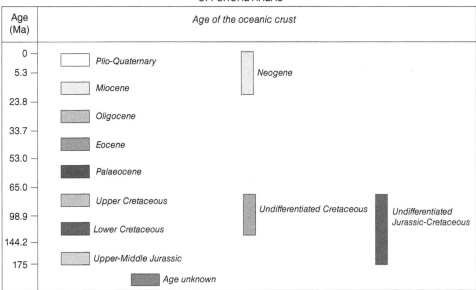

Figure 2 The pattern of magnetic stripes in the North Atlantic, 2005. Geological Map of the World. Scale: 1 : 50 000 000. *Source:* Published by CGMW & UNESCO. (See colour plate section for colour representation of this figure.)

arrival at shallow levels of an abnormally hot mantle body, namely a mantle plume. However, some sea-mounts in the Rockall Trough, dated at 70+/−1 Ma, may indicate some precursor plume activity commencing in the Cretaceous (O'Connor et al. 2000).

The opening of the North Atlantic (and the subsidiary opening of Baffin Bay west of Greenland) is believed to have involved complex interaction between this plume (the proto-Iceland plume evolving to the Iceland plume) and 'normal' sea-floor spreading processes (White 1997; White and McKenzie 1989; Fitton and Larsen 2001; Smallwood and White 2002). The abundant generation of magma gave rise to a great igneous province prior to and accompanying the sundering of Laurussia and the creation of the embryonic North Atlantic Ocean. This province embraced a large region including eastern Greenland, a large part of the Norwegian shelf (the Vøring Plateau), the Faeroes and the Hebridean and Northern Irish parts of the British Isles. The cause of this magmatic activity is held to be partial melting generated by the proto-Iceland plume as is the, approximately contemporaneous, activity that occurred across part of western Greenland and eastern Baffin Island. The magmatism commenced abruptly and was also relatively short-lived, being mostly confined within 2–3 million years (White 1988). Not only were prodigious quantities of basaltic magma produced but also unusually magnesian ('picritic') magmas signifying exceptionally high temperatures were erupted, mainly in the opening stages of the activity. The time interval between the start of continental lithosphere stretching and creation of embryonic ocean was short, perhaps only 4–6 Ma (Smallwood and White 2002). This suggests that injection of great volumes of magma into the continental lithosphere weakened it, facilitating rapid thinning leading to its eventual failure.

Evidence of continental uplift preceding the magmatism is plausibly attributed to the arrival ('impact') of the buoyant and abnormally hot mantle plume. Uplift and magmatism preceded the continental rupturing that marked the genesis of a new ocean floor. At its earliest arrival the plume axis is inferred to have lain beneath west-central Greenland but, as Greenland drifted westwards across the axis of the plume, the latter came to underlie a more central site under Greenland by 55 Ma (Lawver and Müller 1994; Saunders et al. 1997).

After first encountering the continental lithosphere the plume, with a temperature some 150 °C hotter than the normal mantle, spread out rapidly beneath the lithosphere in a crudely circular disposition ~2500 km diameter (White and McKenzie 1995; Smallwood and White 2002). It caused transient crustal uplift, large-scale volcanism and complementary intrusive activity in conjunction with stretching and thinning of the continental lithosphere. Eventually the continental lithosphere parted, sea-floor spreading commenced and the North Atlantic Ocean was born.

The Kangerdlugssuaq area of East Greenland is believed to have lain above the plume head at some stage (Brooks 2011). Striking evidence relating to the East Greenland uplift is provided by a horizon of conglomerate a few metres thick (Figure 3a and b, see Plate section). This distinctive conglomerate was noted by Maync (1942) and Koch and Haller (1971) and was referred to as 'the breakup unconformity' (Larsen and Saunders 1998). It crops out at intervals along the east Greenland coast from Wollaston Forland (76°N) and the Hold with Hope peninsula (73–74°N: Upton et al. 1980) to the Kangerdlugssuaq region (67°N; Soper et al. 1976) and abruptly overlies fine-grained marine Cretaceous sediments. It indicates change to a high-energy sedimentary environment and reflects significant tectonic uplift of the source region, inferentially at no great distance to the west (Upton et al. 1980). Although this unconformity is merely one of a number of Palaeogene unconformities spread in time and place over the

(a)

(b)

Figure 3 (a) Conglomerate from a 2–3 m thick stratum separating Cretaceous shales from the base of the overlying plateau lavas on Wollaston Forland, East Greenland (75° N). Cobbles are of quartzite and muscovite granite. (b) Aerial photograph of the same (white) stratum on Kap Broer Ruys, East Greenland (73°30′N). Well-stratified dark grey Cretaceous shales beneath and brown/black lavas above. *Source:* B.G.J. Upton. (See colour plate section for colour representation of this figure.)

North Atlantic region, now regarded as reflecting variations in flux of the Iceland plume, its position immediately beneath the volcanic sequence suggests that its description as 'the' break-up unconformity may not be inept.

Early in the Eocene mantle temperatures in the head of the plume may have fallen rapidly (Smallwood and White 2002) and the plume is inferred to have assumed a narrower subcylindrical form with a 'central core' about a 100 km across. Magmatism due to this 'plume tail' marked out the shallow submarine welt of the Greenland–Iceland–Faeroes ridge as the Greenland/American tectonic plate migrated westwards. This ridge is characterized by an abnormal thickness (30–40 km) of oceanic crust and rises to shallow depths. The plume tail itself (the Iceland plume) is now considered to underlie eastern Iceland.

Early Palaeocene Before the North Atlantic Opening

Before the arrival of the postulated mantle plume, the landscapes of Greenland, Norway and Britain largely consisted of relatively high ground composed of early Palaeozoic and Precambrian metamorphic rocks transected by low-lying faulted basins. The latter, developed during Mesozoic extensional tectonics, were subject to occasional marine inundation. The faulting had structurally preconditioned a tract of the Laurasian continent to a state ripe for exploitation by later rifting and magmatism in the Palaeocene. The embryonic ocean first appeared at approximately 56 Ma around the Palaeocene–Eocene boundary (currently defined at 55.8 ± 0.2 Ma). For the previous 10 Ma we may visualize rifted landscapes roughly comparable to those of Kenya and Ethiopia at present and which appears to have been well vegetated with an equable climate (Walker 1979).

Figure 4 presents a reconstruction of the geography of Greenland, Norway and the British Isles before the ocean opening and shows the pattern of faulting (Jolley and Bell 2002). These 'normal faults', generally dipping away from what were to become the Greenland and European hinterlands, presented barriers so that the Mesozoic marine transgressions rarely extended much to the west of the Greenland coastline nor much to the east of the western European coasts. Some of these fault escarpments were rejuvenated to play a role in the Palaeocene–Eocene when they prevented the floods of basaltic lavas from spreading west and east onto what were to become the continental hinterlands.

Figure 5 (see Plate section) shows that the eventual localization of the new ocean approximately followed the axis of the early Palaeozoic Caledonide Orogeny.

Episodes of raised Mesozoic sea-levels saw the transgression of shallow seas across these low-lying rifted basins. Whilst there is an abundant environmental and ecological record within the accompanying marine sediments, we can only surmise that during the millions of years between the transgressions there were widespread forested landscapes and little hindrance to intermixing of flora and fauna between North America/Greenland and Eurasia. In the early Palaeocene, before volcanism commenced, shallow non-marine lakes or swamps formed in these rifts and sedimentary deposits accumulated. Fossil plants in the latter (occasionally forming thin coals) testify to the proximity of vegetated shores. Accordingly, when the first magmas reached surface levels they frequently encountered water or wet sediments and high-pressure steam generation led to explosive (phreatomagmatic) eruptions. The resultant disrupted particles of basalt magma from these eruptions cooled rapidly to glassy material, the accumulations of which are called hyaloclastites. These are typically accompanied by

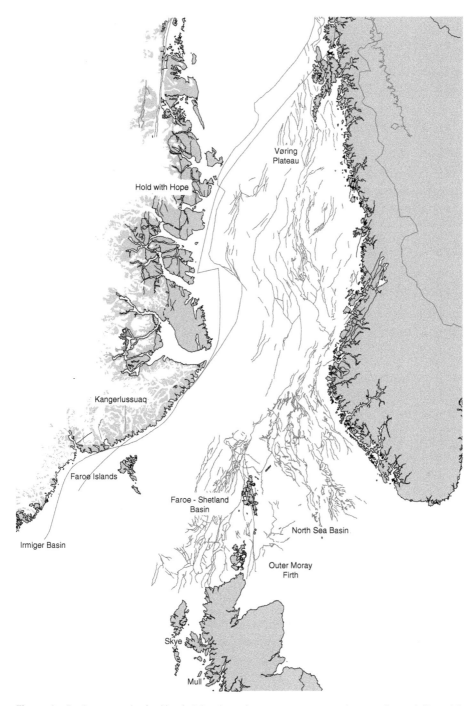

Vøring
Plateau

Hold with Hope

Kangerlussuaq

Faroe Islands

Faroe - Shetland
Basin

North Sea Basin

Irmiger Basin

Outer Moray
Firth

Skye

Mull

Figure 4 Fault pattern in the North Atlantic region on a map restored to continental dispositions prior to ocean opening. *Source:* Jolley and Bell (2002).

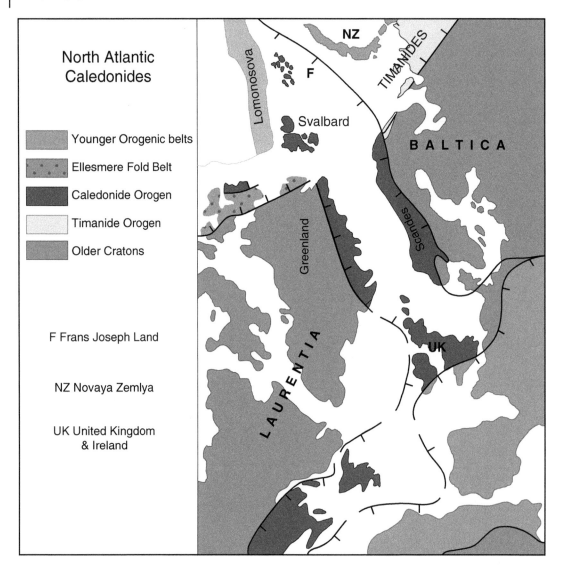

Figure 5 Map showing the orogenic belts on either side of the North Atlantic. Note that between Greenland and Norway the North Atlantic is approximately bilaterally symmetrical through the Caledonian Orogenic belt. *Source:* Gee et al. 2008. (See colour plate section for colour representation of this figure.)

characteristic sub-aqueous lava forms, referred to as pillow-lavas on account of their rounded, tube-like pillowy forms. As the rates of magma outflow increased and the crust inflated, the waters were expelled and there was evolution from sub-aqueous to sub-aerial eruptions.

Figure 6 (see Plate section), a coastal section in Baffin Island (East Canada), shows a rift-related sequence of sediments followed by sub-aqueous and sub-aerial volcanic rocks that is broadly similar to the successions generated along the East Greenland coast.

Figure 6 A coastal section on Cape Searle Island, Baffin Island, Canada, showing a succession similar to that of parts of the East Greenland coast. Palaeocene non-marine sediments form the basal third, with white sandstones and dark coals and organic-rich shales. The central part (pale brownish and not well stratified) is of sub-aqueous volcanic rocks (picritic hyaloclastites and pillow breccias). The upper third consists of subaerially erupted picritic lavas. *Source:* B.G.J.Upton (See colour plate section for colour representation of this figure.)

The Geographical Pattern of Break-Up

The bathymetry of the ocean shows that the continental shelf alongside east Greenland is narrow compared with that on the European side. Spreading started in the south and propagated northwards at a rate of ~1 m/year (Larsen 1988). Initially the line of opening lay close to the present East Greenland coastline, apart from the region between Kangerdlugssuaq and Hold with Hope where it had a large deflection, convex to the east. Thus, the line of parting was divided into three (Figure 7). To the north and south of this easterly deflection spreading has been simple and continuous up to the present. By contrast, in the deflected mid-section spreading was complex, with repeated shifts in position of the spreading axis. The mid-section produced the lavas of central East Greenland and, after continental breaking, the lavas of Iceland and the now extinct Ægir Ridge–Jan Mayen spreading axis (Larsen et al. 1989).

Micro-continent Formation

The initial separation of the western and eastern plates lay close to the present east Greenland coastline. Continental separation often results in formation of micro-continents, representing 'splinters'

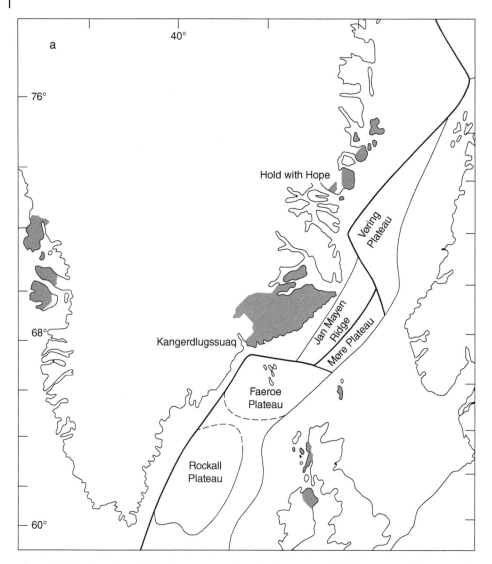

Figure 7 Map showing the break-up pattern showing the eastward displacement of the central section separating the Vøring Plateau and the Faeroe Plateaux. The shading indicates the outcrop of the flood basalts on Greenland. *Source:* Larsen et al. (1989).

that remain isolated. The Rockall Plateau became such a micro-continent, as did also a fragment further north between Iceland and Jan Mayen.

Evolution of the oceanic lithosphere was attended by development of the transform faults. At least some of these were probably inherited from faulting on the continents prior to separation. Such faults not only separate different crustal segments, but the rifting style and average magma characteristics are liable to change across them. To the north of one of these, the Jan Mayen Fracture Zone, the mid-ocean ridge is called the Mohns Ridge. The active Kolbeinsey and the extinct Ægir Ridge lay between this and the evolving Iceland–Faeroe Fracture Zone, whilst south of that (and Iceland) the mid-ocean ridge is called the Reykjanes Ridge.

Magmatism Heralding the Birth of the New Ocean

Volcanism preceding continental break-up is generally confined to a narrow zone along which new oceanic crust is generated and is typically subdued. Although phenomena comparable to that of the North Atlantic area are known from some other oceanic openings (e.g. the Red Sea), such voluminous magmatism is the exception rather than the rule. For the North Atlantic the huge quantities of intrusive and extrusive igneous rocks that heralded the opening of the new ocean are now attributed to the ascent within a few million years of abnormally hot proto-Icelandic plume.

The contrast between the much smaller degree of magmatism attending the southern parts of the Atlantic and that attending the North Atlantic opening is ascribed to the major influence of a mantle plume in the latter. The opening of the North Atlantic, and Baffin Bay, was presaged by magma generation along the zones attenuated as a result of Mesozoic continental extension. Whilst the surviving volcanic products can be seen in the eastern coastal regions of Greenland, the Faeroes, north-western UK as well as in central West Greenland and eastern Baffin, most of the basaltic rocks are submerged and lie off the Greenland and Norwegian shelves, the Faeroe and Rockall

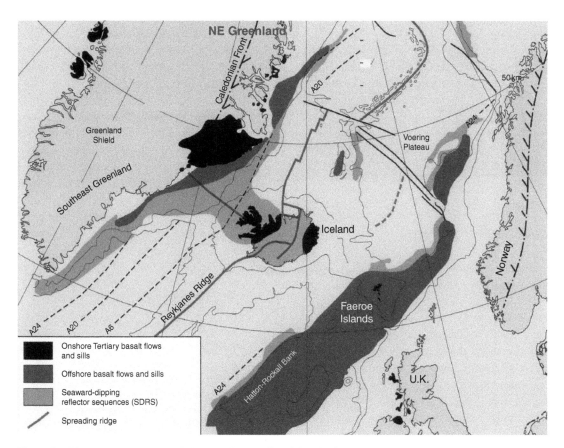

Figure 8 Distribution of the early Paleogene lavas, subaerial and submarine. The current spreading centres are marked in red. *Source:* Based on Larsen et al. (1994). (See colour plate section for colour representation of this figure.)

plateaux and the Jan Mayen ridge (Figure 8, see Plate section).

The magmatism occurred in two principal periods, (a) 62–58 Ma and (b) 56–52 Ma (Saunders et al. 1997; Fitton and Larsen 2001). The latter period was characterized by higher eruption rates and greater magmatic volumes, accompanied by rapid thinning and rupture of the continental lithosphere. The bulk of the magmatism may have been accomplished within only two to three million years (White 1988).

The start of magmatism in the early stages of the first period typically involved sediments rich in volcanic particles (i.e. volcanogenic sedimentation) and the accumulation of sequences of pillow lavas and hyaloclastite breccias in shallow (non-marine) waters. Subsequently, sub-aerial eruptions dominated. During the earlier period a large volume of basalt lavas was erupted in West Greenland and Baffin Island, but within the Northern Irish and Hebridean region activity was more subdued. Eroded remnants of the prodigious quantities of lavas erupted in the second period are preserved along much of the coastal region of East Greenland between latitudes 67.5° and 75°N (Figure 8) and on the Faeroe Islands.

Flood Basalt Eruptions

The lavas were erupted at elevations little above sea-level and the typical magma channels are inferred to have been fissures up to tens of kilometres long. However, in other cases the magma conduits became more highly localized and, rather than producing an elongate fissure volcano, a 'shield volcano' of more or less circular geometry provided the lava source. In both cases the highly fluid lavas flowed widely and sub-horizontally, in some cases for many tens

of kilometres. In East Greenland the lavas cover over 65,000 km^2 with sequences up to 7 km thick (Brooks 2011; Figures 8 and 9, see Plate section). Lavas in the Faeroes, approximately coeval with those of East Greenland, are at least 5.5 km thick (Larsen 1988).

Lavas in the British Isles were far less voluminous and rarely built up successions more than 1.5 km thick. What were considered to be the earliest lavas attributable to the proto-Icelandic plume are the (Danian) basaltic lavas and trachytic tuffs of the Eigg Lava Formation in the Hebridean 'Small Isles' (Pearson et al. 1996). However, the Lower Basalt Formation in Antrim (Northern Ireland) appears to be still older, being dated at 62.6 ± 0.3 Ma (Ganerød et al. 2010). Since the chemical composition of the Hebridean–Irish basalts differs significantly from that of the younger lavas of Faeroes and Greenland it is surmised that they arose from mantle with a composition distinct from those of other parts of the North Atlantic.

A central-type volcano developed early at Rum (Inner Hebrides), in which high-temperature (picritic) magmas attained shallow crustal levels. It has been argued that these came from a hot outer sheath of mantle that surrounded the plume itself although geochemical characteristics suggest that it arose from a compositionally distinctive part of the plume (Upton et al. 2002). Rapid erosion of the Rum volcano (Emeleus et al. 1996; Emeleus and Bell 2005) was followed by eruption of the Skye lava field (Hamilton et al. 1998).

In response to loading by the lava successions there was synchronous subsidence of the underlying crust. Thus, it appears that successive eruptions could build up lava sequences kilometres thick while each eruptive site was never far from sea-level. The intervals between one eruption and the next are inferred to have

(a)

(b)

Figure 9 (a) Flat-lying basalts of the Geikie Plateau Formation, Gåseland, East Greenland, looking towards 1980 m summit. *Source:* Photo by W.S. Watt. (b) View of the steep east coast of Greenland (the Blosseville coast) between ca. 67° and 69° N, composed of horizontal basalt lavas, west of the seaward flexing. *Source:* Photo by B.G.J. Upton. (See colour plate section for colour representation of this figure.)

lasted hundreds to thousands of years. With relatively fast weathering under warm, humid conditions, surface features of the lavas were rarely preserved. However, dendritic drainage patterns of river systems developed on the lava plains and inter-flow fluviatile sediments are preserved (e.g. in the Hebrides). After each eruption, colonization of the lava surface by plants would have been rapid, probably ferns in the first stages followed by forest growth. Jointing patterns in the lavas provide evidence for chilling against trees; some relic fossils of these remain vertical as with the celebrated McCulloch's Tree in the south west of Mull in the Hebrides.

Seaward Dipping Reflectors

In the Kangerdlugssuaq region of East Greenland transition from flat-lying lavas into a zone in which the lavas acquire increasingly steep dips towards the coast was first recorded by Wager (1934, 1947) and described by Larsen and Jakobsdottir (1988) (Figure 10, see Plate section). The zone of downwarping is accompanied by an increase in the intensity of the coast-parallel dyke swarm, culminating in an underlying 'sheeted complex' comparable to those seen in ophiolite occurrences regarded as uplift portions of oceanic crust (Nielsen and Brooks 1981; Muttervet al. 1982;

Figure 10 Kap Hammer on the East Greenland coast (67°40′N), within the zone showing maximum seaward flexing. The cliffs here consist almost entirely of dykes, thus composing a 'sheeted complex'. Since the flexure here is eastwards, the dykes have a corresponding westward dip. The greater the inclination, the older the dyke. A few (young) near-vertical dykes are seen in the near cliffs. *Source:* Photo by B.G.J. Upton. (See colour plate section for colour representation of this figure.)

Brooks 2011). It came to be realized that what marine seismologic surveyors referred to as 'seaward-dipping reflectors', occurring as belts up to 150 km wide, occur on both sides of the Atlantic and also in west Greenland, were the off-shore equivalents of these down-warped lavas.

The lavas acquired their seaward dips long after the time of their eruption, which had been subaerial (Brooks 2011). Since the total thickness of lavas and their associated intrusions on the rifted margins reaches 25–35 km (Reid et al. 1997; Smallwood and White 2002), these great quantities of basaltic materials on the thinned continental lithosphere would have very significantly increased its bulk density causing the down-warping. Figure 11 (see Plate section) shows subaerial

exposures in West Greenland analogous to those of East Greenland where initially sub-horizontal lavas were down-warped towards a new ocean floor in Baffin Bay. As demonstrated in East Greenland, the down-warping was achieved, not by ductile folding but by displacements along a myriad normal faults dipping away from the developing ocean (Nielsen 1975; Nielsen and Brooks 1981).

Ash Beds of Western and Central Europe

Palaeocene–Eocene basaltic ashes occur widely across north-west and central Europe (Knox

Figure 11   Sub-aerial (picritic) lavas on the Svartenhuk peninsula, West Greenland (71° 30′N). These lie within the flexed zone, dipping westwards towards the Baffin Bay spreading centre. Such 'seaward-dipping reflectors' are generally sunk below sea-level but in this instance they are well seen sub-aerially. *Source:* Photo by T.C.R. Pulvertaft. (See colour plate section for colour representation of this figure.)

and Morton 1988; Egger et al. 2000). It has been concluded that the ashes were the products of extremely energetic fountaining of magma close to the time of ocean-opening (Fitton and Larsen 2001; Larsen et al. 2003). The continental crust thinned and subsided, eventually sinking beneath sea-level as it became ever more laden with lavas and mafic intrusions. At this critical stage, close to parting and formation of the embryonic ocean, the rising magmas interacted with shallow sea waters, producing cataclysmic steam-driven ash eruptions.

Ashes from these eruptions travelled hundreds of kilometres eastwards and are reported from as far away as Austria (Egger et al. 2000). Those falling into the shallow seas that covered much

of western Europe were generally diluted by normal terrestrial sedimentation and are thus hard to recognize. However, in western Denmark in a shallow marine basin in which diatomite sediment was being very slowly accumulated, some two hundred ash layers contrast strikingly with the intervening white sediments (Figure 12, see Plate section). The alternation of the 'ash' beds and white clay reflects the repose periods between eruptions (Fitton and Larsen 2001; Larsen et al. 2003).

Whilst the older ash layers are inferred to have come from sub-aerial volcanoes on the thinning continental lithosphere, the climactic ('Stage 4') ashes are attributed to a time when the locus of the proto-Iceland plume had shifted away from

Figure 12 Dark ash layers contrasting with white diatomite sediments on the island of Fur, Limfjord, Jutland. Originally deposited sub-horizontally, the sequence was later severely deformed by Pleistocene ice sheets. *Source:* Photo by B.G.J. Upton. (See colour plate section for colour representation of this figure.)

the Greenland continent into the sea-covered opening rift. Interaction of incandescent magmas and sea water caused the change from relatively quietly effusive to violently explosive eruptions.

The Palaeocene–Eocene Thermal Maximum

A prolonged period of global warming commencing at 55 Ma (Palaeocene–Eocene thermal maximum) is attributed to the effects of the proto-Iceland plume. This was 'a period of climatic turmoil' that lasted for over 100,000 years during which ocean temperatures increased by 3–10 °C (Nisbet et al. 2009). On land, this period saw the extinction of a large number of mammalian groups that had been dominant in the Palaeocene and the appearance of three modern mammalian orders. These evolutionary changes have been linked to diversification and dispersal in response to rapid environmental changes at this time (Hallam 2004). In the oceans the principal casualties were the benthic foraminifera, the most abundant deep-water organisms. At ~55 Ma about half of all benthic Foraminifera species were wiped out (a greater loss than had occurred at the Cretaceous–Palaeocene boundary (best known for the extinction of the dinosaurs). This calamity for the foraminiferans has been ascribed to ocean warming and acidification as a result of rising CO_2 content (Hallam 2004; Lovell 2010).

Methane hydrates (clathrates) are solids resembling ice, composed of water + gas and stable at high pressures and low temperatures that occur beneath the sea floor. Destabilization of these compounds yields free methane, which is a more efficacious 'greenhouse gas' for absorption of solar heat than CO_2 (Svenson et al. 2004). There are numerous hypotheses regarding the actual process by which the 'greenhouse' gases were emitted. It has been suggested that arrival of the mantle plume resulted in short-term sea-floor uplift that caused both a sea-temperature rise, pressure reduction and consequent dissociation of the hydrates (MacLennan and Jones 2006). Yet another hypothesis is that a great emission of methane came from an enclosed marine basin in which enormous amounts of methane briefly existed. One such basin, specifically suggested, between Norway and Greenland (called 'the Kilda Basin) and the triggering of gas was related to a rise of the Iceland Plume (Nisbet et al. 2009).

Iceland

The volcanic activity in Iceland over the past 16 Ma is a direct continuation of the magmatism that commenced at 56–55 Ma in East Greenland (Figure 13, see Plate section). The North Atlantic spreading axis can be observed in the Icelandic eastern neo-volcanic zone at the present day where the plume axis is presently inferred to underlie the Vatnajökull ice-cap (Wolfe et al. 1997). Rift volcanism re-commenced in October 2014 in the Bárðarbunga volcanic system and is currently active as I write. Volcanic cycles in Iceland are connected to rift-jumping, thought to occur in order to bring the spreading centre over the plume axis. These cycles have an approximate life-span of 8–12 Ma (Brooks 2011 and references therein).

Evidence for Plume Pulsing

That the plume tail arose in pulses of varying temperature was suggested by White et al. (1995) following Vogt (1971), from consideration of the strength of the V-shaped ridges of the ocean floor south of Iceland. These ridges, signifying thickened oceanic crust, straddle the mid-ocean ridge on either side of Iceland. The thickenings are held to be due to fluctuating temperatures as unusually hot pulses in the underlying asthenospheric

Figure 13 Lava fountaining along a fissure (Krafla volcano) northern Iceland 1980, during an episode of extension and rift opening. *Source:* Photo by Halldór Ólafsson. (See colour plate section for colour representation of this figure.)

mantle radiate away from Iceland (Poore et al. 2009, 2011). These authors propose that the hot pulses, with a temperature some 25 °C hotter than that of the back-ground plume temperature, arise intermittently through a plume conduit (with a radius of ~150 km) under Iceland. The upwelling rate in the conduit is estimated at 27 cm/year with the rate of radial spreading beneath the lithosphere being ~40 cm/year (Poore et al. 2011). Since the varying temperature of the out-flowing mantle causes elevation or subsidence of the overlying crust (White et al. 1995; Wright and Miller 1996; White and Lovell 1997), it has important stratigraphical implications; hot pulses are responsible for sea-floor elevation, leading in turn to increased erosion. Consequently, the stratigraphic sequences in the sedimentary basins

retain records of intermittent uplifts (White and Lovell 1997; Hartley et al. 2011).

At times during the Cenozoic parts of the European continental shelf were so markedly elevated as to be raised above sea-level and river systems were established. The reconstructed history of one of these ancient landscapes, dating from the Palaeocene–Eocene thermal maximum, has shown that it was lifted above sea-level in three distinct steps, each of 200–400 m. After about one million years of sub-aerial erosion, it sank again beneath the sea. Thus the asthenospheric mantle radiating from the Iceland plume was inferred not to have had a constant temperature but to have involved a number of pulses that were exceptionally hot, i.e. that the temperature of the plume fluctuates over time intervals of a few million years (White and Lovell 1997). The size and duration of the shelf uplifts were used to constrain the magnitude and velocity of these pulses (Shaw Champion et al. 2008; Hartley et al. 2011). Thus, the stratigraphy of sedimentary rocks on the ocean retains a record of the mantle pulsing (White and Lovell 1997; Hartley et al. 2011).

Where uplift raises continental margins above sea-level, their consequent sub-aerial erosion causes relatively coarse-grained sediments to be deposited on adjacent sub-marine shelves. These pulse-drive uplifts can have significant commercial consequences: for example, the Forties oilfield is dependent on sandy reservoir rocks that resulted from continental lithosphere uplift at ~55 Ma, marking the arrival of a major thermal input (Lovell 2010). Furthermore, the changes in the elevation of the Greenland–Faeroes–Iceland and Scotland ridge over millions of years have controlled the deep-water overflow of the Denmark Straits (Wright and Miller 1996; Nisbet et al. 2009; Poore et al. 2009, 2011).

Continental Uplift after Ocean Formation

In the aftermath of the ocean opening there was notable uplift of the adjacent 'trailing' continental margins. The uplift is noteworthy in, for example, western Scotland and Norway, but is most extreme in eastern Greenland where 'plateau lavas' erupted close to sea-level (and which were preceded by marine Mesozoic strata) have been raised, while remaining essentially horizontal. Among the uplifted rocks are those of Gunnbjørns Fjeld, which at 3693 m is the highest mountain in the Arctic. How much strata have been eroded from above it is unknown.

The pre-opening loading, by up to 7 km of basaltic lavas, would be expected to have depressed rather than elevated surfaces. However, the uplift is inferred to be the consequence of intrusion of igneous rocks deep in the crust that more than compensate for the surface loading (Larsen et al. 1998). Despite the huge volume of erupted lavas a much larger volume of magma crystallized deep in the crust as 'underplating'. The east coast of Greenland presents an elongate area of uplift centred on that part (Kangerdlugssuaq) where the plume axis is deduced to have passed from continent to ocean (Lawver and Müller 1994).

The tilting of the topography in northern Britain from west to east is also attributed to the process of magmatic underplating (Brodie and White 1994). Consequently, the Iceland plume has been instrumental in shaping the landscapes on either side of the ocean (Fitton and Larsen 2001).

Summary

No serious discussion of the Atlantic opening was possible before adoption of the plate tectonic theory some 50 years ago. Since then studies have demonstrated that sea-floor spreading has not been simple and that the concept of a mantle plume appears critical to its understanding. Opening of the ocean was a continuation of earlier continental rifting brought about by extension. The close proximity of much of the igneous activity and rifting 'to the old orogenic sutures and/or fronts suggests that lithospheric control was an important factor in the embryonic stages of magmatism and rifting' (Hansen et al. 2009).

It has become realized that the Iceland plume is a dynamic phenomenon that has controlled the vertical movements of European, Greenlandic and Canadian continental rocks. Its arrival was responsible for the high heat-flux and the consequent large-scale magmatism around the Palaeocene/Eocene boundary. Furthermore, it has had a major influence on the ocean and the atmosphere. Indeed, the plume can be figuratively envisaged as a vigorous organism that, at an age of ~60 Ma, not only has the potential for continued ocean widening but, as we are reminded by the recent Eyjafjalljökull eruption (a very minor one in the Icelandic record for the past millennium), can have a considerable impact on society.

Acknowledgements

The author is very grateful to J.G. Fitton, R. Meyer and B. Lovell for help in improving the manuscript.

References

Anderson, D.L. 2005. Scoring hotspots: The Plume and Plate Paradigms, In: *Plates, Plumes and Paradigms*. G.R. Foulger, J.H. Natland, D.C. Presnall and D.L. Anderson (eds). Geological Society of America, Special Paper 388, 31–54.

Anderson, O.B. and Knudsen, P. (2009). DNSC08 mean sea-surface and mean dynamic topography models. *Journal of Geophysical Research* 114: 1–12.

Bown, J.W. and White, R.S. (1994). Variation with spreading rate of oceanic crustal thickness and geochemistry. *Earth and Planetary Science Letters* 121: 435–449.

Brodie, J. and White, N. (1994). Sedimentary basin inversion caused by igneous underplating: Northwest European continental shelf. *Geology* 22: 147–150.

Brooks, C.K. (1973). Rifting and doming in southern East Greenland. *Nature Physical Science* 244: 23–25.

Brooks, C.K. (2011). The East Greenland rifted volcanic margin. *Geological Survey of Denmark and Greenland Bulletin* 24: 92.

Egger, H., Heilman-Clauren, C., and Schmitz, B. (2000). The Paleocene–Eocene boundary interval of a Tethyan deep-sea section (Austria) and its correlation with the North Sea Basin. *Bulletin Societé Géologique de France* 171: 207–216.

Emeleus, C.H. and Bell, B.R. (2005). The Palaeogene Volcanic Districts of Scotland, 4e, 212. Nottingham: British Geological Survey.

Emeleus, C.H., Cheadle, M.J., Hunter, R.H. et al. (1996). The rum layered intrusion. In: Layered Intrusions (ed. C.G. Cawthorn), 403–439. Elsevier Science B.V.

Fitton, G. and Larsen, L.M. (2001). The geological history of the North Atlantic Ocean. *Det Kongelige Danske Videnskabernes Selskab, Historisk-filosofiske Meddelelser* 82: 9–27.

Ganerød, M., Smethurst, M.A., Torsvik, T.H. et al. (2010). The North Atlantic Igneous Province reconstructed and its relation to the Plume Generation Zone: the Antrim Lava Group revisited. *Geophysical Journal International* 182: 183–202.

Gee, D.G., Fossen, H., Henriksen, N., and Higgins, A.K. (2008). From the Early Paleozoic platforms of Baltica and Laurentia to the Caledonide Orogen of Scandinavia and Greenland. Episodes 31, No. 1: 44–51.

Hallam, T. (2004). Catastrophes and Lesser Calamities. The cause of mass extinctions., 226. Oxford University Press.

Hamilton, M.A., Pearson, D.G., Thompson, R.N. et al. (1998). Rapid erosion of Skye lavas inferred from precise U–Pb and Ar–Ar dating of the Rum and Cuillin plutonic complexes. *Nature* 394: 260–263.

Hansen, J., Jerram, D.A., McCaffrey, K., and Passey, S.R. (2009). The onset of the North Atlantic Igneous Province in a rifting perspective. *Geological Magazine* 146: 309–325.

Hartley, R.A., Roberts, G.G., White, N., and Richardson, C. (2011). Transient convective uplift of an ancient buried landscape. *Nature Geoscience* 4: 562–565.

Heezen, B.C., Tharp, M., and Ewing, M. (1959). The floors of the oceans. l. The North Atlantic. *Geological Society of America, Special Paper, vol.* 65: 122.

Hess, H.H. (1962). History of ocean basins. In: Petrologic Studies: A Volume to Honor A. F. Buddington (eds. A.E.J. Engel, H.L. James and B.F. Leonard), 599–620. New York: Geological Society of America.

Jolley, D.W. & Bell, B.R. 2002. The evolution of the North Atlantic Igneous Province and the opening of the NE Atlantic rift. In: *The North Atlantic Igneous Stratigraphy, Tectonic, Volcanic and Magmatic Processes*. D.W. Jolley and B.R. Bell (eds). Geological Society of London Special Publication, No. 197, 1–13.

Knox, R.W.O.'.R. and Morton, A.C. (1988). The record of early tertiary N. Atlantic volcanism in sediments of the North Sea Basin. In: Early Tertiary Volcanism and the Opening of the N.E. Atlantic. Special Publication **39** (eds. A.C. Morton and L.M. Parson), 407–419. London: Geological Society.

Koch, L. and Haller, J. (1971). Geological ap of East Greenland 72°-76°N lat. (1:250,000). *Medellelser om Grønland* 183.

Larsen, H.C. 1988. A multiple and propagating rift model for the NE Atlantic (extended abstract). In: *Early Tertiary Volcanism and the Opening of the NE Atlantic*, A.C. Morton and L.M. Parson (eds), Geological Society of London Special Publication No. 39, 157–158

Larsen, H.C. & Jakobsdottir, S. 1988. Distribution, crustal properties and significance of seawards dipping sub-basement reflectors off E. Greenland. In: *Early Tertiary Volcanism and the Opening of the NE Atlantic*. A.C. Morton and L.M. Parson (eds), Geological Society of London Special Publication No. 39, 95–114.

Larsen, H.C. and Saunders, A.D. (1998). Tectonism and volcanism at the southeast Greenland rifted margin; A record of plume impact and later continental rupture. In: *Proceedings of the Ocean Drilling Program*, vol. 152 (eds. A.D. Saunders, H.C. Larsen and R.J. Wise Jr.), 503–533. College Station, Texas (Ocean Drilling Program),: Scientific Results.

Larsen, H.C., Saunders, A.D., Clift, P.D. and the Shipboard Party. (1994). 1. Introduction: breakup of the Southeast Greenland margin and the formation of the Irminger Basin: background and scientific objectives. *Proceedings of the Ocean Drilling Programme, Initial Reports* 152: 5–16.

Larsen, L.-M., Watt, W.S., and Watt, M. (1989). Geology of the lower tertiary plateau basalts of the Scoresby Sund region, East Greenland. *Grønlands Geologiske Undersøgelse, Bulletin* 157: 164.

Larsen, L.-M., Waagstein, R., Pedersen, A.K., and Storey, M. (1999). Transatlantic correlation of the Palaeogene volcanic successions in the Faroe Islands and East Greenland. *Journal of the Geological Society, London* 156: 1081–1095.

Larsen, L.-M., Fitton, J.G., and Pedersen, A.K. (2003). Paleogene volcanic ash layers in the Danish Basin: compositions and source areas in the North Atlantic Igneous Province. *Lithos* 71: 47–80.

Lawver, L.A. and Müller, R.D. (1994). Iceland hotspot track. *Geology* 22: 311–314.

Lovell, B. (2010). Challenged by Carbon. The Oil Industry and Climate Change, 212. Cambridge University Press.

MacLennan, J. and Jones, S.M. (2006). Regional uplift, gas hydrate dissociation and the origin of the Paleocene–Eocene thermal maximum. *Earth & Planetary Science Letters* 245: 65–80.

Maync, W. (1942). Stratigraphie und Fazieverhältnisse der oberpermischen Ablagerungen östgrönlands (olim "Oberkarbon-Unterperm") zwischen Wollaston Forland und dem Kejser Franz Josephs Fjord. *Meddelelser om Grønland* 115: 128.

Meyer, R., van Wijk, J., and Gernignon, L. (2007). The North Atlantic Igneous Province: a review of models for its formation. *The Geological Society of America, Special Paper* 430: 525–552.

Mutter, J.C., Talwani, M., and Stoffa, A. (1982). Origin of the seaward dipping reflectors in oceanic crust off the Norwegian margin by subaerial sea-floor spreading. *Geology* 10: 353–357.

Nielsen, T.F.D. (1975). Possible mechanism of continental break-up in the North Atlantic. *Nature* 253: 182–184.

Nielsen, T.F.D. and Brooks, C.K. (1981). The E. Greenland continental margin: an explanation of the coastal flexure. *Journal of the Geological Society, London* 38: 559–568.

Nisbet, E.G., Jones, S.M., Maclennan, J. et al. (2009). Kick-starting ancient warming. *Nature Geoscience* 2: 156–159.

O'Connor, J.M., Stoffers, P., Wijbrans, J.R., Shannon, P.M. & Morrissey, T. 2000. Evidence from episodic seamount volcanism for pulsing of the Iceland plume in the past 70 Myr. Nature, **408**. 21/28 Dec. 2000. www.Nature.com.

Pearson, D.G., Emeleus, C.H., and Kelley, S.P. (1996). Precise ^{40}Ar/^{39}Ar dating for the initiation of Palaeogene volcanism in the inner Hebrides and its regional significance. *Journal of the Geological Society, London* 153: 815–818.

Poore, H.R., White, N., and Jones, S. (2009). A Neogene chronology of Iceland plume activity from V-shaped ridges. *Earth and Planetary Science Letters* 283: 1–13.

Poore, H., White, N. & Maclennan, J. 2011. Ocean circulation and mantle melting controlled by radial flow of hot pulses in the Iceland plume. *Nature Geoscience*, **4** August 2011. 558–561. http://www.nature.com/naturegeoscience.

Reid, J.D., Dahl-Jensen, T., Holbrook, W.S. et al. (1997). 32-38km thick mafic igneous crust beneath the Greenland-Iceland Ridge. *Eos, Transactions of the American Geophysical Union* 78: 656.

Saunders, A.D., Fitton, J.G., Kerr, A.C. et al. (1997). The North Atlantic Igneous Province. In: Large Igneous Provinces: Continental, Oceanic and Planetary Flood Volcanism, American Geophysical Union, Geophysical Monograph, vol. 100 (eds. M.F. Coffin and J.J. Mahoney), 45–93.

Shaw Champion, M.E., White, N.J., Jones, S.M., and Lovell, J.P.B. (2008). Quantifying transient mantle convective uplift: an example from the Faroe-Shetland basin. *Tectonics* 27: 1–18.

Smallwood, J.R. & White, R.S. 2002. Ridge-plume interaction in the North Atlantic and its influence on continental break-up and sea-floor spreading. In: D.W. Jolley & B.R. Bell (eds) *The North Atlantic Igneous Stratigraphy, Tectonic, Volcanic and Magmatic Processes*. Geological Society of London Special Publications, No. 197, 15–18.

Soper, N.J., Higgins, A.C., Downie, C. et al. (1976). Late Cretaceous-early Tertiary stratigraphy of the Kangerdlugssuaq area, East Greenland and the age of opening of the north-east Atlantic. *Journal of the Geological Society, London*, 132: 85–104.

Svenson, H.S., Planke, A., Malthe-Sorenssen, B. et al. (2004). Release of methane from a volcanic basin as a mechanism for initial Eocene global-warming. *Nature* 429: 542–545.

Thompson, R. (1993). Sea-floor spreading and plate-tectonics. In: P. McLeod Duff. (ed.),. In: Holmes' Principles of Physical Geology, 4e, 641–663. London: Chapman Hall.

Upton, B.G.J., Emeleus, C.H., and Hald, N. (1980). Tertiary volcanism between 74° and 76°N, NE Greenland: Hold with Hope and Gauss Halvø. *Journal of the Geological Society, London* 137: 491–508.

Upton, B.G.J., Skovgard, A.C., McClurg, J. et al. (2002). Picritic magmas and the Rum ultramafic complex. *Geological Magazine* 139: 437–452.

Vann, J.R. 1978. The siting of Tertiary vulcanicity. In: Bowes, D.R. & Leake, B.E. (eds). *Crustal Evolution in North-Western Britain and Adjacent Regions*. Geological Journal Special Issue, 10, 393–414.

Vine, F.J. and Matthews, D.H. (1963). Magnetic anomalies over ocean ridges. *Nature* 199: 947–949.

Vink, G.E. (1984). A hotspot model for Iceland and the Vøring plateau. *Journal of Geophysical Research* 89: 9949–9959.

Vogt, P. (1971). Asthenospheric motion recorded by the ocean floor south of Iceland. *Earth and Planetary Science Letters* 13: 153–160.

Wager, L.R. (1934). Geological investigations in East Greenland part 1. General Geology from Angmasalik to Kap Dalton. *Meddelelser om Grønland* 105 (2): 46.

Wager, L.R. (1947). Geological investigations in East Greenland part lV. The stratigraphy and tectonics of Knud Rasmussens land and the Kangerdlugssuaq region. *Meddelelser om Grønland* 134 (3): 64.

Walker, G.P.L. (1979). The environment of tertiary volcanism in Britain. (abstract). *Bulletin of the Geological Survey of Great Britain* 70: 5–6.

White, R.S. 1988. A hot-spot model for early Tertiary volcanism in the N. Atlantic. In: *Early Tertiary Volcanism and the Opening of the NE Atlantic.* A.C. Morton & L.M. Parson (eds), Geological Society of London Special Publication No. 39, 157–160.

White, R.S. (1997). Rift-plume interaction in the North Atlantic. *Philosophical Transactions of the Royal Society, London, Series A* 355: 319–339.

White, N. and Lovell, B. (1997). Measuring the pulse of a plume with the sedimentary record. *Nature* 387: 888–891.

White, R.S. and McKenzie, D.P. (1989). Magmatism at rift zones: the generation of volcanic continental margins and flood basalts. *Journal of Geophysical Research* 94: 7685–7729.

White, R.S. and McKenzie, D.P. (1995). Mantle plumes and flood basalts. *Journal of Geophysical Research* 100: 17,543–17,585.

White, R.S., Bown, J.W., and Smallwood, J.R. (1995). The temperature of the Iceland plume and origin of outward propagating V-shaped ridges. *Journal of the Geological Society, London* 152: 1039–1045.

Wolfe, C.J., Bjarnason, I.T., van Decar, J.C., and Soloman, S.C. (1997). Seismic structure of the Icelandic mantle plume. *Nature* 385: 245–247.

Wright, J.D. and Miller, K.G. (1996). Control of North Atlantic deep water circulation by the Greenland–Scotland ridge. *Palaeoceanography* 11 (21): 157–170.

2

Cenozoic Vegetation and Phytogeography of the Sub-arctic North Atlantic

Friðgeir Grímsson[1], Thomas Denk[2] and Reinhard Zetter[3]

[1] Department of Botany and Biodiversity Research, University of Vienna, Vienna, Austria
[2] Department of Palaeobiology, Swedish Museum of Natural History, Stockholm, Sweden
[3] Department of Palaeontology, University of Vienna, Vienna, Austria

This chapter provides a review of Cenozoic plant assemblages from the sub-arctic North Atlantic region and their biogeographic implications. Previous work is reviewed and new data are presented that considerably change our understanding of the role of the northern North Atlantic for plant dispersal and evolution of plant lineages during the Paleogene and Neogene. Paleogene plant fossils in this region are known from West and East Greenland, the Faroe Islands and Scotland. In contrast to the widely held view that most Paleogene plant taxa of Greenland belong to extinct lineages, we provide evidence for the presence of several extant genera in these floras (e.g. *Fagus, Quercus*). Thus, Engler's hypothesis about the 'Arcto-Tertiary element' remains a fundamental hypothesis about the origin of northern temperate tree genera. In general, a remarkable diversity of extinct and modern lineages of Fagaceae is documented for Palaeocene and Eocene floras. Neogene fossils are found in Iceland and provide records of climate evolution in the sub-arctic North Atlantic and of the duration of a functioning land bridge for plant migration between North America and Europe. Counter to the traditional view suggesting a functioning land bridge only during the Paleogene, there is now convincing evidence that this link was available for plants until the latest Miocene. This has important implications for understanding low genetic differentiation documented in extant plant groups having a disjunct distribution in northern temperate regions of Europe, North America and East Asia. Relatively warm conditions persisted in the sub-arctic North Atlantic until the end of the Zanclean (early Pliocene) based on plant fossil evidence from Iceland. The shift to modern tundra conditions occurred during the Piacenzian (late Pliocene) and is documented in the Pliocene and Pleistocene fossil plant assemblages of Iceland.

Introduction

Palaeobotanical investigations in the sub-arctic regions of the North Atlantic date back to the middle nineteenth century (Heer 1859 et seq., Iceland, Greenland, Svalbard; Gardner 1887, Island of Mull; Hartz 1903, Faroe Islands). The first mention of fossil plants in this region dates back to

Biogeography in the Sub-Arctic: The Past and Future of North Atlantic Biota, First Edition.
Edited by Eva Panagiotakopulu and Jon P. Sadler.

1772 (Ólafsson 1772). Heer believed all the Arctic floras to be of Miocene age (e.g. Heer 1868), based on comparison with the (truly) Miocene flora of Öhningen. This age estimate was questioned by Gardner (1884), who suggested an Eocene age for the floras of Mull, Spitsbergen and Greenland based on the presence of *Macclintockia* in these floras. Gardner's assessment was later corroborated by evidence from molluscs (Ravn 1922). With the general acceptance of plate tectonics in the early 1960s and subsequent first radiometric dating of basalts bordering the North Atlantic basin (e.g. Moorbath and Bell 1965), the modern picture of the evolution of the North Atlantic region emerged. The Cenozoic floras of the northern North Atlantic region belong to the Brito-Arctic Igneous (floral) Province (BIP; Figure 1) according to Boulter and Manum (1989). The BIP floras are the result of the initial break-up of the northern North Atlantic during the early Cenozoic and the widening of the North Atlantic during the Neogene (cf. Denk et al. 2011). Whereas the floras at the western (Greenland) and eastern (Scotland, Faroe Islands) margins of the North Atlantic are of Paleogene age, the intra-basaltic plant-bearing sedimentary rocks of Iceland are of Neogene age (Figure 2). As such, all these palaeofloral assemblages provide a unique and almost continuous

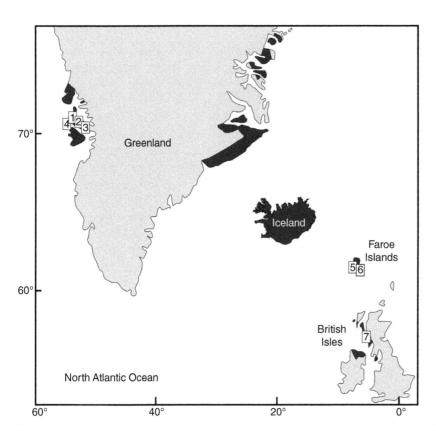

Figure 1　The northern North Atlantic part of the Brito-Arctic Igneous (floral) Province (BIP). Volcanics (dark grey) and sedimentary rocks on West and East Greenland, the Faroe Islands and the British Isles are of Paleogene age, while the rocks on Iceland are of Neogene age. Paleogene BIP-floras discussed in the text are indicated.
1 – Agatdalen flora; 2 – Upper Atanikerluk A flora; 3 – Upper Atanikerluk B flora; 4 – Hareø flora; 5 – Mykines flora; 6 – Prestfjall flora; 7 – Mull flora.

archive of Cenozoic vegetation development in the sub-arctic North Atlantic region.

In early accounts of Paleogene plant fossils from high latitudes angiosperm plant remains were mainly ascribed to modern genera (e.g. *Alnus, Castanea, Fagus, Laurus, Populus,* etc.; Heer 1868 et seq.). This assessment of high-latitude fossil plants, and their alleged close relationship to the modern northern temperate woody flora, brought Engler (1879) to establish the term 'Arcto-Tertiary element', used for plant groups that today dominate temperate forest regions and have prominent fossil representatives in Paleogene floras at high latitudes. Later authors considered many of the fossils to represent extinct taxa, commonly with unknown botanical affinities (Koch 1963; Boulter and Kvaček 1989; Kvaček et al. 1994; Mai 1995; Manchester 1999). In contrast, Budantsev

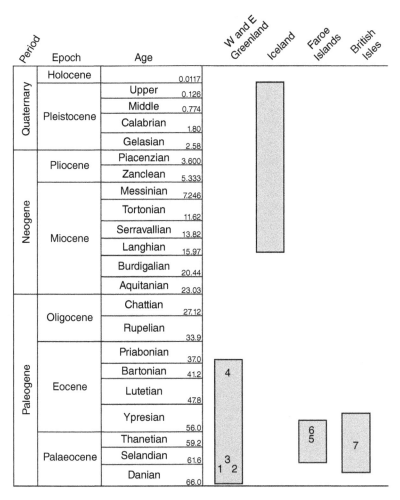

Figure 2   Relative age of Cenozoic (pre-Holocene) volcanics and sedimentary rocks of the Brito-Arctic Igneous (floral) Province (BIP). Stratigraphic occurrences of Paleogene floras of West Greenland, the Faroe Islands and the British Isles (Scotland) discussed in the text are indicated. 1 – Agatdalen flora; 2 – Upper Atanikerluk A flora; 3 – Upper Atanikerluk B flora; 4 – Hareø flora; 5 – Mykines flora; 6 – Prestfjall flora; 7 – Mull flora. Geological time scale based on ICS (2020).

and Golovneva (2009) and Grímsson et al. (2015, 2016a) suggested that a substantial number of alleged extinct taxa actually belong to modern genera (*Aesculus*, *Alnus*, *Betula*, *Carpinus*, *Fagus*, *Quercus* and *Ulmus*), thus supporting Engler's hypothesis about the 'Arcto-Tertiary element'.

Neogene plant fossils from the sub-arctic North Atlantic have recently been shown to be important for understanding modern biogeographic patterns in northern temperate plant groups and assessing the subsidence history of the Greenland-Scotland Transverse Ridge (Tiffney and Manchester 2001; Grímsson and Denk 2007; Tiffney 2008; Denk et al. 2010a, 2011). Biogeographic inferences from plant fossils have also important implications for understanding molecular differentiation in plants and animals (e.g. Denk and Grimm 2010; Kornobis et al. 2011).

In this chapter, we review previous work on the plant fossil record from Palaeocene to Pleistocene sedimentary formations of the sub-arctic North Atlantic region. This includes Paleogene plant assemblages from Greenland, the Faroe Islands and Scotland, as well as Neogene floras from Iceland (Figures 1 and 2). In addition, we present revised macro-fossil and new palynological data from Palaeocene to Eocene sediments of Greenland and the Faroe Islands, which considerably change our understanding of the biogeographic history of several northern temperate woody plant taxa that are among the most ecologically important tree species in the mid-latitudes of North America, Europe and East Asia.

Paleogene Floras and Vegetation

Greenland

Palaeocene to Eocene plant-bearing sedimentary rocks are exposed in the Disco–Nuussuaq–Svartenhuk Halvø area (at 69 to 72°N), West Greenland, and in the Kap Gustav Holm–Scoresby Sund–Shannon area (at 69 to 74°N), East Greenland (Figure 1). Extensive fossil plant collections exist from the Paleogene sediments of West Greenland (e.g. Heer 1868 et seq.; Seward and Conway 1935; Koch 1963), whereas material from East Greenland is sparse (e.g. Mathiesen 1932; Seward and Edwards 1941), rendering these floras less informative.

The Cretaceous–Cenozoic lithostratigraphy in the Disco–Nuussuaq–Svartenhuk Halvø area, West Greenland, including the plant-bearing Paleogene sediments, has recently been revised by Dam et al. (2009). The strata of the Nuussuaq peninsula are divided into two major units, the Nuussuaq Group and the younger Western Greenland Basalt Group (WGBG). The Nuussuaq Group is composed of five Cretaceous formations (Kome, Slibestensfjeldet, Upernivik Næs, Atane, Itilli), one Cretaceous/Palaeocene formation (Kangilia), and four Palaeocene formations (Agatdal, Quikavsak, Eqalulik, Atanikerluk). Some formations extend over vast areas, whereas others are local and contemporaneous with formations in neighbouring regions (for details see Dam et al. 2009). The Agatdal Formation comprising the 'Agatdalen flora' of Koch (1963, 1972a, b) and the Quikavsak Formation (Nuuk Qiterleq Member) comprising the 'Upper Atanikerluk A flora' of Heer (1868, 1869, 1874, 1880, 1883) are believed to be partly contemporaneous and resulting from the same tectonic event prior to accumulation of the overlying so-called Naajaat palaeo-lake sedimentary rocks (e.g. Pedersen et al. 1998; Dam et al. 2009; Grímsson et al. 2016b). The Quikavsak Formation is followed by the Atanikerluk Formation (Naujât Member), which comprises the 'Upper Atanikerluk B flora' of Heer (1880, 1883). Radiometric ages of contemporaneous volcanic structures give an age between 62 and 60 Ma (Selandian age; Storey et al. 1998; Dam et al. 2009) for the Atanikerluk Formation (Upper Atanikerluk B flora; Figure 2). The older Agatdal Formation (Agatdalen flora) and Quikavsak Formation (Upper Atanikerluk A flora) are between 64 and 62 Ma (late Danian age; see Figure 7 in Grímsson et al. 2016b).

The Paleogene strata on the island of Hareø (west of Disco; Figure 1) are divided into the Maligât Formation and the younger Hareøen Formation, both of which are part of the WGBG. The Hareøen Formation is divided into two successive members, the Aamaruutissaa Member (clastic) and the Talerua Member (volcanic; Hald 1976, 1977; see Figure 2 in Grímsson et al. 2015). The Aamaruutissaa Member comprises the 'Hareø flora' of Heer (1883) and Nathorst (1885). Lavas of the overlying Talerua Member have been radiometrically dated at ca. 39 Ma (cf. Schmidt et al. 2005) and are of late Bartonian age (late Eocene). This suggests that the underlying sedimentary rocks comprising the Hareø flora are of late Lutetian to early Bartonian age, ca. 42–40 Ma old (Figure 2); this is also supported by palynological data (Grímsson et al. 2015).

The first comprehensive treatment of fossil plants from the Cenozoic of Greenland was by Heer (1868, 1869, 1874, 1883), who studied plant fossils from 20 localities in Greenland. Heer described 143 plant species from Upper Atanikerluk A and 78 from the younger Upper Atanikerluk B horizon; from Hareø, 53 plant species were described (Heer 1883). Taxa recovered from nearly all localities were *Metasequoia* [as *Sequoia langsdorfii*, *Taxodium*] and *Trochodendroides* [as *Populus arctica*]. From the Upper Atanikerluk A flora, 12 species of Fagaceae were identified, among which nine were *Quercus*. In addition, four species of (evergreen) *Laurus* were recognized by Heer in this horizon. The latter were missing in the Upper Atanikerluk B flora (Heer 1883). From Upper Atanikerluk B, 10 species of Fagaceae were recorded and two species of *Ilex* (Aquifoliaceae) indicating the presence of evergreen angiosperms in the lower Palaeocene. From Hareø, the most characteristic elements reported by Heer were *Ginkgo*, Cupressaceae (incl. Taxodiaceae), *Pinus*, *Acer*, Fagaceae (three species of *Fagus* and *Castanea*, four species of *Quercus*) and *Platanus* (Heer 1883). Some of Heer's original taxa have later been revised

and lumped, resulting in many less species for the individual floras (cf. Koch 1963; Kvaček et al. 1994). Other of Heer's taxa are in need of revision (Figure 3A as *Paliurus pusillus* and 3D as *Cissites steenstrupi* Heer).

A few studies briefly summarized the Palaeocene floras of (West) Greenland (Pedersen 1976; Mai 1995; Kvaček 2010) but did not provide new data or comprehensive revisions of the Greenland floras. However, Mai (1995) pointed to the presence of the extinct Fagaceae *Eotrigonobalanus* in the early Palaeocene flora of Atanikerluk, along with several other extinct types of Fagaceae. This observation has recently been confirmed by both pollen and leaf fossils from Agatdalen (Grímsson et al. 2016a, 2016b).

Koch (1963) collected and described plant fossils from the late Palaeocene Agatdalen Formation, Nuussuaq Peninsula. Most common macrofossil elements of the Agatdalen flora are *Metasequoia* (locally), *Trochodendroides* [as *Cercidiphyllum*], *Macclintockia*, and *Platanus bella* (Heer) Kvaček, Manchester and Guo [as *Dicotylophyllum bellum* (Heer) Seward and Conway]. Koch (1963) recognized the extant genus *Liriodendron* (Figure 3B) but placed leaf imprints similar to modern *Sassafras* (Figure 3C) within the extinct genus *Lauraceaephyllum* based on subtle differences in venation between the fossil and the modern genus. Revision of the Agatdalen macroflora by Grímsson et al. (2016a) reduces the ca. 38 taxa by Koch (1963) down to ca. 32. Still, the newly studied palynoflora from the same formation is relatively rich, comprising at least 145 angiosperms, 25 gymnosperms and around 30 different spore types (Grímsson et al. 2016a, 2016b). Overall, the palaeovegetation of the Agatdalen area appears to have been dominated by riparian elements (ferns, Taxodioideae, *Trochodendroides*, *Platanus*, Figure 4C and D), and Fagaceae, Betulaceae, Hamamelidaceae and *Vitis* (Figure 4A) as elements of the well-drained hinterland. The enigmatic plant *Macclintockia* also played a significant role in the palaeofloral assemblages.

(a)   (b)   (c)

(d)   (e)

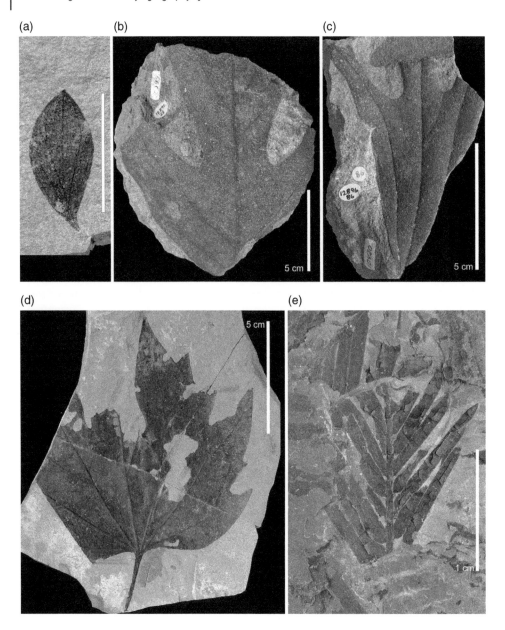

Figure 3 Palaeocene fossil leaves from West Greenland (Agatdalen, Atanikerluk) and the Faroe Islands (Mykines). (A) Small acrodromous leaf from Upper Atanikerluk B, MGUH 6443 [as *Paliurus pusillus* Heer in Heer (1883; Pl. LXXXI, figs 9 and 10)]. (B) *Liriodendron* sp., from Agatdalen, MGUH 10393 [as cfr. *Liriodendron* sp. in Koch (1963; Pl. 16, fig. 1)]. (C) *Sassafras* sp., from Agatdalen, MGUH 10420 [as *Lauraceaephyllum stenolobatus* Koch in Koch (1963; Pl. 30, fig. 2)]. (D) Large actinodromous leaf from Upper Atanikerluk B, MGUH 6435 [as *Cissites steenstrupi* Heer in Heer (1883; Pl. LXXXI, fig. 1)]. (E) *Metasequoia occidentalis* (Newb.) Chaney, from Mykines (Beinisvørð Formation), S134471. (See colour plate section for colour representation of this figure.)

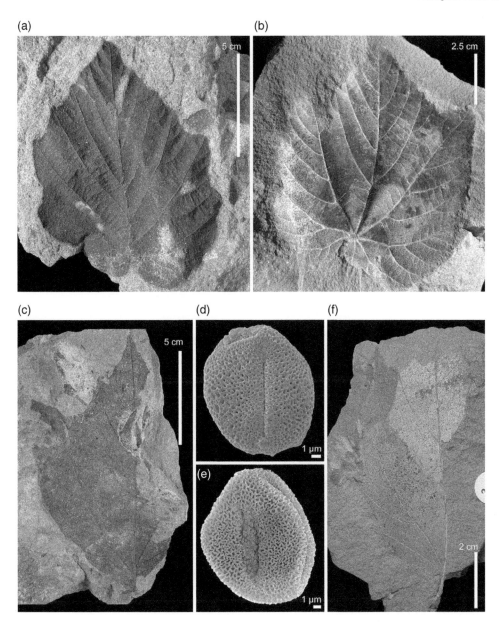

Figure 4 Palaeocene leaves and Eocene pollen from West Greenland (Agatdalen, Hareø) and the Miocene of Iceland (Selárdalur, Botn). (A) *Vitis* sp., from Agatdalen, MGUH 10421 [as cfr. *Vitis olriki* Heer in Koch (1963; Pl. 30, fig. 3)]. (B) *Tilia selardalense* Grímsson, Denk & Símonarson, from Selárdalur. (C) *Platanus* sp., from Agatdalen, MGUH 10412 [as *Platanus* sp. cfr. *aceroides* Goepp. in Koch (1963; Pl. 26, fig. 1)]. (D) *Platanus* sp., from Hareø. (E) *Platanus* sp., from Botn. (F) *Platanus leucophylla* (Unger) Knobloch, from Selárdalur, IMNH 302.

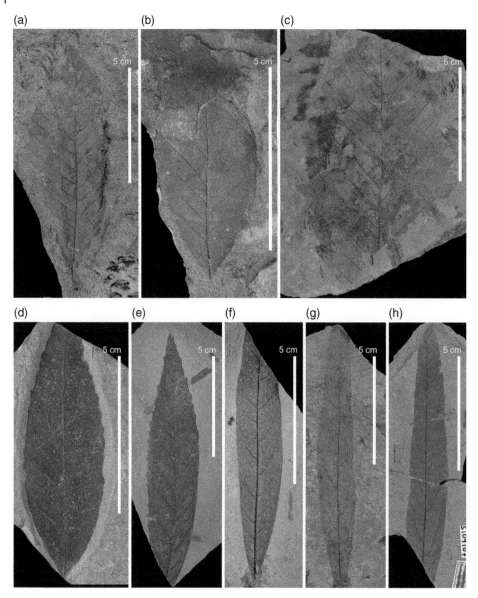

Figure 5 Palaeocene fossil leaves from Atanikerluk, West Greenland. (A) *Fagopsiphyllum groenlandicum* (Heer) Manchester, from Upper Atanikerluk A, MGUH 6894 [as *Fagus castaneaefolia* Ung. in Heer (1868; Pl. XLVI, fig. 3a)]. (B) *Fagopsiphyllum groenlandicum* (Heer) Manchester, from Upper Atanikerluk A, MGUH 6269 [as *Castanea ungeri* Heer in Heer (1883; Pl. LXIX, fig. 3)]. (C) *Fagopsiphyllum groenlandicum* (Heer) Manchester, from Upper Atanikerluk A, MGUH 6270 [as *Quercus grönlandica* Heer in Heer (1883; Pl. LXIX, fig. 4)]. (D) *Eotrigonobalanus* sp., from Upper Atanikerluk B, MGUH 6349 [as *Quercus laharpii* Gaud. in Heer (1883; Pl. LXXIV, fig. 2)]. (E) *Eotrigonobalanus* sp., from Upper Atanikerluk B, MGUH 6372 [as *Pterocarya denticulata* Web in Heer (1883; Pl. LXXVI, fig. 1)]. (F) *Eotrigonobalanus* sp., from Upper Atanikerluk B, MGUH 6390 [as *Laurus reussii* Ettingsh. in Heer (1883; Pl. LXXVII, fig. 7)]. (G) *Eotrigonobalanus* sp., from Upper Atanikerluk B, S109006 [as *Laurus primigenia* Ung. in Heer (1880; Pl. III, fig. 8a)]. (H) *Eotrigonobalanus* sp., from Upper Atanikerluk B, S109107. (See colour plate section for colour representation of this figure.)

Macrofossils of the Upper Atanikerluk A flora comprise a large number of leaves resembling various modern genera of Fagaceae. Among these, *Fagopsiphyllum* is fairly abundant (Figure 5A to C, see Plate section). Figure 5C shows a typical leaf of *Fagopsiphyllum*; in contrast, the leaves shown in Figure 5A and B, although falling into the morphological variability of *Fagopsiphyllum*, clearly are reminiscent of leaf types encountered in modern taxa of *Quercus* section *Cyclobalanopsis*, and of the castaneoid genera *Lithocarpus* and *Castanopsis* (see illustrations in Camus 1929 et seq.). Another distinct leaf type is morphologically similar to both leaves from the Paleogene of North America (*Dryophyllum*-like leaves; Jones and Dilcher 1988) and to *Eotrigonobalanus* from Europe (Kvaček and Walther 1989; Figure 5D to H). The pollen spectrum of the Upper Atanikerluk A flora has not yet been studied with high resolution scanning electron microscopy (SEM). However, the contemporaneous Agatdalen flora and the middle Eocene Hareø flora have recently been investigated and yield a remarkably high diversity of Fagaceae pollen (Grímsson et al. 2015, 2016a). Pollen unambiguously referable to *Fagus*, along with macrofossils of this genus, provide reliable evidence of this genus in the Cenozoic of Greenland (Figure 6A and B and Figure 7A). In addition, pollen of various Castaneoideae (according to Ørsted; see Praglowski 1984) is documented (Figure 6C and D). Numerous types of *Quercus* pollen represent various sections within the genus: Sect. *Lobatae* (Figure 6I and J), *Lobatae/Quercus* (white or red oaks; Figure 6K and L) and sect. *Protobalanus* (see Grímsson et al. 2015). Apart from this, additional Fagaceae pollen types represent extinct or ancestral lineages, *Eotrigonobalanus* (Figure 6G and H), *Paraquercus* (see pl. 12, Figures 1 to 5 in Grímsson et al. 2016b), and the pollen shown in Figure 6E and F. The latter is indistinguishable from pollen of the modern *Quercus* sect. *Ilex* (according to Denk and Grimm 2010;

Denk et al. 2017; synonymous with subgenus *Heterobalanus* according to Menitsky 1984, 2005). This type of pollen has been suggested to be plesiomorphic within oaks (Denk and Grimm 2009a). In the Neogene of Europe, pollen of this type co-occurs with leaves of *Quercus drymeja* Unger and *Q. mediterranea* Unger belonging to *Quercus* sect. *Ilex* (Denk et al. 2010b). Based on the modern distribution of this group of oaks from the Mediterranean area to south of the Himalayas and Southeast Asia (Menitsky 1984; Denk and Grimm 2010) and of the absence of foliage indicative of this group, the pollen encountered in the Eocene Hareø flora of Greenland may originate from an extinct and ancestral member of *Quercus* that had retained the plesiomorphic pollen. This would be in accordance with the presence of Fagaceae foliage with unclear generic/infrageneric affinities in the Palaeocene to Eocene of Greenland.

The presence of *Aponogeton* in the Eocene of West Greenland (Grímsson et al. 2014) is recorded both in the palynological (Figure 6O and P) and macrofossil records of Hareø (Figure 7B and C). The foliage associated with the pollen partly recalls foliage from the Eocene/Oligocene Renardodden Formation of Svalbard ascribed to the extinct genus *Haemantophyllum* by Budantsev and Golovneva (2009, plate 88, Figures 5 and 6) and originally described as *Alsima macrophylla* by Heer (1876). The fossil pollen from Hareø clearly suggests closer affinities to *Aponogeton* than to any other members of the Alismatales (Grímsson et al. 2014).

Faroe Islands

The Faroe Islands are patchy sub-aerial remnants of a previously extensive Paleogene lava sequence that is considered part of the Brito-Arctic Igneous (floral) Province (BIP; Figure 1). The strata composing the Faroes are named the Faroe Islands Basalt Group (Passey and Jolley 2009). The

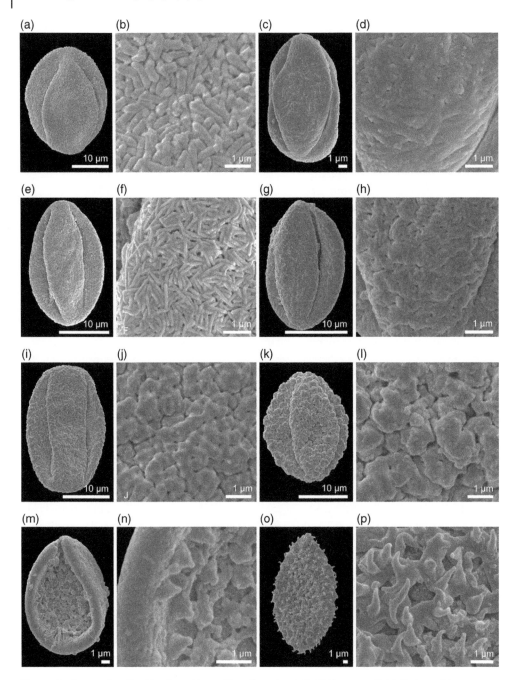

Figure 6 Eocene fossil pollen from Hareø, West Greenland. (A, B) *Fagus* sp. (C, D) Castaneoideae gen. et spec. indet. (E, F) *Quercus* plesiomorphic pollen type of *Quercus*; identical to extant pollen of *Quercus* sect. *Ilex*. (G, H) aff. *Eotrigonobalanus* sp. (I, J) *Quercus* sp. (K, L) *Quercus* sect. *Lobatae/Quercus*. (M, N) *Spirematospermum* sp. (O, P) *Aponogeton* sp.

(a)

(b)　　　　　　　　(c)

Figure 7　Eocene fossil leaves from Hareø, West Greenland. (A) *Fagus* sp., S110238. (B) *Aponogeton* sp., S110339. (C) *Aponogeton* sp., S110337.

stratigraphic thickness of exposed rock is ca. 3.2 km, with additional ca. 3.4 km thick subsurface units documented from boreholes. Recently, the stratigraphy and age of the Faroe Islands has been summarized and revised (cf. Riisager et al. 2002; Passey and Jolley 2009). The strata are subdivided into seven formations. The Lopra Formation is the basal volcanic construction, known only from boreholes, and is succeeded by the geochemically different Beinisvørð Formation. Most of the few

reported plant macrofossils from the Faroe Islands (e.g. Hartz 1903; Rasmussen and Koch 1963) originate from the upper half of this formation, in an outcrop on the island Mykines (Mykines flora). The lavas of the Beinisvørð Formation are overlain by sedimentary rocks of the Prestfjall Formation. These sedimentary rocks contain two coal seams and associated silt and sandstones (Rasmussen and Noe-Nygaard 1969). The palynological content of this formation (Prestfjall flora) has been studied by Laufeld (1965) and Lund (1989) from outcrops on the island Suðuroy. The sedimentary rocks of the Prestfjall Formation are succeeded by pyroclastics and lavas of the Hvannhagi and Malistindur Formations and the volcaniclastics and lavas of the Sneis and Enni Formations (e.g. Passey and Jolley 2009). Radiometric dating of lavas from the Faroe Islands and corresponding lavas on Greenland show that basalts below the Prestfjall Formation are ca. 60–56 Ma and volcanics above the Prestfjall Formation are ca. 56–54 Ma (e.g. Waagstein et al. 2002; Storey et al. 2007; Passey and Jolley 2009). Stratigraphic correlation of the plant-bearing sedimentary rock units on Mykines with Waagstein et al. (2002) suggest they are ca. 58 Ma and of late Palaeocene age (late Thanetian), but those of the Prestfjall Formation are just under 56 Ma and of early Eocene age (earliest Ypresian; Figure 2).

Plant macrofossils have been known from the Faroe Islands since 1901 (see Hartz 1903). Until now the only detailed description is of *Metasequoia* vegetative long and short shoots (Rasmussen and Koch 1963; Figure 3E). Remains of other Cupressaceae have also been recorded and believed to represent *Sequoia*, *Taxodium* and *Juniperus*. The few fragmentary angiosperm leaf fossils recovered have been considered unidentifiable (Hartz 1903; Rasmussen 1925; Rasmussen and Koch 1963). Despite the current lack of macrofossils from the Faroe Island, two previous light microscopic palynological studies by Laufeld (1965) and Lund (1989) suggest that a rather diverse palaeovegetation existed during the accumulation of the early Eocene coal-bearing Prestfjall Formation.

The early Eocene palynological assemblage was characterized by swamp forests and riparian elements comprising several ferns, taxodiaceous Cupressaceae (intermittently amounting to over 30% of the palynological assemblage), Juglandaceae and Betulaceae. On more mesic sites Fagaceae, Juglandaceae and other eudicots may have thrived along with *Pinus*, *Sciadopitys* and possibly *Sequoia*.

Island of Mull

The Palaeocene flora of Mull, Scotland, originally described by Gardner (1887) is the only Paleogene BIP flora that has been revised in more recent years (Boulter and Manum 1989; Figures 1 and 2). The age of the intrabasaltic plant-bearing sediments of Mull has been radiometrically dated at 60–58 Ma (Chambers and Pringle 2001).

Among riparian and wetland elements, the ferns *Dennstaedtia*, *Onoclea* and *Osmunda* were widespread in Paleogene Arctic plant assemblages, commonly co-occurring with *Metasequoia*. Among the diverse gymnosperms, *Ginkgo gardneri* Florin represents a lineage more closely related to Mesozoic ginkgoes than to the Cenozoic *Ginkgo adiantoides* (Ung.) Heer from Europe and Svalbard (Denk and Velitzelos 2002). Further, *Amentotaxus*, cf. *Cephalotaxus*, *Glyptostrobus*, *Elatocladus* (with affinities to modern *Taxodium* and *Sequoia*), *Metasequoia* and *Pinus* and cf. *Tsuga* are recorded (Boulter and Kvaček 1989; Kvaček 2010). *Platanites hebridicus* Forbes is an extinct Platanaceae distinct from the coeval *Platanus schimperi* (Heer) Saporta and Marion of Gelinden (Belgium; Mai 1995) and *Platanus* aff. *leucophylla* (Unger) Knobloch from western Greenland. The genus *Platanites* has also been recorded from the Paleogene of Saskatchewan (Canada; McIver and Basinger 1993) and possibly from the Eocene of north-western Wyoming (Crane et al. 1988). In addition, few pentafoliate leaves and leaflets belong to the extinct *Platanus* subgenus *Glandulosa* Kvaček, Manchester and Guo. These were assigned to *Platanus fraxinifolia* (Johnson and Gilmore) Walther by Boulter and Kvaček (1989) in contrast to the trifoliate leaves of *P. bella* from Greenland.

Common elements of Mull, mostly shared with the floras of Greenland, are *Trochodendroides* (and rare *Ziziphoides*), betulaceous leaves of *Corylites* [shared with Svalbard], *Fagopsiphyllum groenlandicum* (Heer) Manchester [as *Fagopsis groenlandica* (Heer) Wolfe; shared with the floras of Greenland and Svalbard], *Ushia olafsenii* (Heer) Boulter and Kvaček, *Juglandiphyllites* spp., foliage with affinity to Fagaceae (*Castanopsis, Lithocarpus, Quercus* sect. *Cyclobalanopsis* [as *Camptodromites* spp.] and *Macclintockia*. A number of taxa not found in other BIP floras are the distinct foliage of *Davidoidea* (similar to Platanaceae, Hamamelidaceae and *Euptelea*) and of *Vitiphyllum* with affinities to *Vitis* along with a flower of unclear taxonomic relationships (*Calycites*).

Similar floras are known from Isle of Skye, Scotland (Poulter et al. 2008, 2010) and Ballypalady (County Antrim, Ireland; Mai 1995). In the latter flora, cones of *Pinus plutonis* Baily are abundant and biogeographically interesting. According to Mai (1995), *P. plutonis* belongs to section *Sylvestres* subsection *Resinosae* and provides another potential link between Europe and North America.

Neogene Floras and Vegetation

Iceland

Iceland is a volcanic island with several intra-basaltic plant-bearing sedimentary rock formations. The oldest sedimentary rocks are found in Northwest Iceland (ca. 15 Ma) and East Iceland (ca. 14 Ma) and are of Miocene age (Figures 1 and 2). In a simplified version the strata become progressively younger towards the volcanic zones crossing the centre of the island from southwest to northeast (for a recent review of the geology of Iceland see contributions in Sigmundsson et al. 2008). Sedimentary rock formations occur in Miocene to Pleistocene strata and often contain

plant fossils. The palaeo-floras of Iceland have been comprehensively studied in recent years (e.g. Denk et al. 2011; see also Denk et al. 2005; Grímsson et al. 2005, 2008; Grímsson and Símonarson 2006, 2008a, 2008b).

The middle Miocene plant assemblages of Iceland (15–12 Ma) record vegetation thriving under a warm and moist climate. Wetlands and riparian vegetation of the lowlands was characterized by warmth-loving taxa, such as taxodiaceous Cupressaceae, Magnoliaceae (*Magnolia, Liriodendron*), Lauraceae (*Sassafras*), Platanaceae (Figure 4E and F) and others, whereas the well-drained vegetation of the hinterland comprised forests dominated by *Fagus* with evergreen trees and shrubs in the understorey (*Rhododendron, Ilex*). The endemic linden tree, *Tilia selardalense* Grímsson, Denk and Símonarson (Figure 4B) was confined to these forests (Grímsson and Denk 2005; Grímsson et al. 2007a, 2007b; Denk et al. 2011). The oldest floras of Iceland share a few taxa with the Paleogene floras of Greenland and/or Svalbard: *Glyptostrobus, Platanus, Fagus*, and *Tilia*.

A major change is seen in the early Tortonian (10 Ma) floras of Iceland, both in the palynological and the macrofossil record. Whereas herbaceous taxa did not play a significant role in the older floras, they amount to 30% of all recorded plant taxa in the 10 Ma floras. This increase in herbaceous plants is accompanied by the first occurrence of small-leaved Ericaceae typical of the modern tundra vegetation in Iceland (*Vaccinium, Arctostaphylos*) and boreal conifers such as *Larix*. Nevertheless, several warmth-loving elements persisted and new elements are recorded (*Ginkgo*; Denk et al. 2005, 2011). Floras preserved in strata between 10 and 3.6 Ma reflect stepwise cooling; *Fagus* persisted until 7–6 Ma and *Quercus* until 5.5 Ma, whereas the evergreen, large-leaved *Rhododendron* aff. *ponticum* L. ranges from the oldest to the 3.8–3.6 Ma floras. At 4.4–3.6 Ma, small-leaved Salicaceae occur for the first time. The second major reorganization of the vegetation is recorded in floras from the Pliocene–Pleistocene transition. Temperate woody elements are not found in any of the Pleistocene floras, which are essentially similar to the modern flora of Iceland (Denk et al. 2011).

Biogeographic Implications

Paleogene Links

The importance of the early Paleogene North Atlantic Land Bridge (NALB) for intercontinental flora and fauna exchange has been underscored by many authors (e.g. McKenna 1983; Tiffney 1985, 2008). In his classic paper from 1985, Tiffney mentions plant genera that are shared between the early Miocene Brandon Lignite Flora of eastern North America and Paleogene and Neogene floras of western Eurasia to illustrate the importance of the NALB. Subsequently, the shared North American–European fossil record of numerous additional plant genera suggest the same migration route (reviewed in Manchester 1999; Manchester et al. 2009; *Amentotaxus, Cedrelospermum, Cercidiphyllum, Corylopsis, Gordonia, Koelreuteria, Mastixia, Phellodendron, Platycarya, Tapiscia, Tilia* and *Toricellia*). Most recently, Paleogene disjunctions involving the NALB have been suggested for *Decodon* (Grímsson et al. 2012), *Castanopsis* (Sadowski et al. 2018, 2020), *Eotrigonobalanus* (Denk et al. 2012), *Mahonia* (Güner and Denk 2012) and *Spirematospermum* (Fischer et al. 2009). Notably, most of these taxa have not been recorded in the Paleogene fossil record of the sub-arctic northern North Atlantic region and Svalbard. Until now it was assumed that the NALB played a crucial role for inter-continental plant and animal migration via Greenland and the Faroe Islands (the so-called Thulean route; McKenna 1983), but fossils from Greenland

and the Faroe Islands that proved such a link were absent. Palynological data now provide direct evidence for a number of genera with a Paleogene transatlantic distribution to have thrived on Greenland, suggesting that they actually migrated via the NALB. For instance, *Quercus* sect. *Quercus/Lobatae* has previously been known from the middle Eocene of Axel Heiberg Island (McIntyre 1991, pollen; McIver and Basinger 1999, foliage) and Baltic amber deposits (Crepet 1989; Sadowski et al. 2020); Grímsson et al. (2015) provided unambiguous evidence for the presence of this type of *Quercus* in the Eocene of Greenland. Similarly, *Fagus* has previously been known from the middle Eocene of Axel Heiberg Island (McIntyre 1991, pollen). Recently, Grímsson et al. (2015, 2016a) provided the first record of *Fagus* pollen for the late Palaeocene (Agatdalen) and middle Eocene of West Greenland (Hareø; incl. leaves), complementing the records from Axel Heiberg Island (McIntyre 1991; Denk and Grimm 2009b). However, in view of the lack of *Fagus* in Eocene sediments of western Eurasia, there is currently no evidence for a transatlantic migration of *Fagus* during the Palaeocene or Eocene (Denk and Grimm 2009b).

Among extinct lineages of Fagaceae, foliage and pollen of the genus *Eotrigonobalanus* are reported from Palaeocene and Eocene sediments of West Greenland (Grímsson et al. 2016a; Figures 5 and 6). *Eotrigonobalanus* had a wide distribution in Eurasia (Kvaček and Walther 1989; Hofmann et al. 2011) from the Palaeocene/Eocene onwards and extending until the Miocene (Kvaček and Walther 1989). Foliage traditionally assigned to *Dryophyllum* from Paleogene sediments of the North American Gulf Coastal Plain (Jones and Dilcher 1988) co-occurs with pollen closely similar to *Eotrigonobalanus* (Denk et al. 2012). The fossils from Europe, North America and Greenland may all belong to the same extinct lineage that had a wide distribution across the sub-arctic North Atlantic in the Paleogene. Another extinct genus with a transatlantic Paleogene distribution is *Platanites* (Boulter and Kvaček 1989, Isle of Mull; McIver and Basinger 1999, Canada). Another member of Platanaceae, *Platanus* subgenus *Glandulosa*, is represented with two species in the BIP floras. Boulter and Kvaček (1989) reported *P. fraxini-folia* (Johnson and Gilmore) Walther from the Palaeocene of Mull, whereas *P. bella* is known from the Palaeocene of Greenland (Koch 1963; Kvaček et al. 2001). This has interesting biogeographic implications, as *P. fraxinifolia* essentially is a Central European species. However, Boulter and Kvaček (1989) also speculated that the specimens from Mull could be conspecific with *P. bella* but because of the insufficient informative characters in the infructescences of the Mull material did not assign the specimens from Mull to *P. bella*.

In summary, these examples demonstrate a variety of possible migration routes during the Paleogene. Widespread taxa, such as the lineage comprising *Eotrigonobalanus*, might have migrated over the North Atlantic from both directions and migration from North America to Eurasia or vice versa may also have involved the Bering Land Bridge (see also, Tiffney and Manchester 2001). Taxa that migrated across the NALB either from the west or from the east are *Cedrelospermum*, *Cercidiphyllum*, *Corylopsis*, *Mastixia*, *Platanites*, *Quercus* and possibly *Spirematospermum* (Figure 6M and N) among others. A few taxa clearly have an earlier fossil record from North America and might have migrated to Europe from the west (*Amentotaxus*, *Decodon*, *Koelreuteria*, *Mahonia* and possibly *Tilia*). In rare cases, plant lineages may have reached Greenland but not crossed over to Europe or North America (*Fagus* is known from the Palaeocene of Greenland, the Eocene of North America, including Axel Heiberg Island, and Greenland, but has no Eocene fossil record in

Europe). *P. fraxinifolia* may have been restricted to Europe and Scotland.

Neogene Links

It has traditionally been suggested that the NALB had become unavailable for animal and plant migration in the course of the Oligocene (McKenna 1983). However, both new subsidence models (e.g. Poore et al. 2006) and palaeobotanical data (Denk et al. 2011 and references in their Chapter 12) suggest that this link persisted much longer than previously thought, providing a functioning 'land bridge' particularly for plants (see also recent reviews by Tiffney and Manchester 2001; Tiffney 2000, 2008). The exceptionally rich Neogene record of Iceland allows distinguishing directions of transatlantic migration during the Miocene and Pliocene. The oldest floras of Iceland are characterized by taxa that had a markedly widespread northern hemispheric distribution during large parts of the Cenozoic (*Glyprostrobus*, *Sequoia*, *Cercidiphyllum*, *Platanus*, *Liriodendron*, *Sassafras*, etc.). These taxa may have migrated to Iceland either from the east or from the west. A similar pattern is seen in the early late Miocene floras, where less common taxa such as *Rhododendron* section *Pontica* have closely similar related taxa in the modern floras of eastern North America and western Eurasia. At the same time, a number of late Miocene taxa recovered from Iceland clearly migrated from Europe (*Fagus gussonii* Massalongo emend. Knobloch and Velitzelos, *Trigonobalanopsis*). Similarly, the pollen record suggests that *Quercus* sect. *Quercus/Lobatae* migrated to Iceland from the west as late as between 7 and 6 and 5.5 Ma (Denk et al. 2010a). Younger floras record a stepwise loss of 'exotic' taxa until the complete extinction of the (warm) temperate elements of the ancient Icelandic flora during the cold phases of the Pleistocene. Interglacial and postglacial plant colonization of Iceland occurred predominantly from the east.

Conclusion and Future Research

In this chapter we briefly summarized current knowledge about the Cenozoic floras of the sub-arctic North Atlantic. From the biogeographic point of view, two issues are of major importance within this temporal and geographical frame. First, how timely is the 'Arcto-Tertiary element' (biogeographic) hypothesis of Engler? And second, how long into the Neogene did the NALB provide a functioning link for plant migration across the North Atlantic?

The 'Arcto-Tertiary element' Hypothesis

The present data demonstrate that several modern north temperate tree taxa did actually thrive in the sub-arctic during the Paleogene. Also, there is unequivocal evidence for the presence of several 'Arcto-Tertiary elements' in Greenland (for example *Fagus*). Some of these records are, however, not the oldest for these temperate taxa (for example *Acer*). Future palynological investigations of Palaeocene sediments are on their way and will provide final clues to solving whether the 'Arcto-Tertiary element' represents a secondary radiation of taxa that originated in mid-latitudes to high latitudes or whether they actually originated

at high latitudes. Nevertheless, the present data demonstrate that this biogeographic concept is all open for discussion.

The North Atlantic Land Bridge

Most recent investigations of an exceptionally rich plant fossil record demonstrate that the NALB facilitated plant migration between North America and Europe until the late Miocene. This finding is in agreement with low molecular divergences found both for animal and plant lineages with a transatlantic distribution. Little genetic differentiation of these lineages strongly suggests that gene exchange via the NALB must have occurred long into the Neogene (Denk and Grimm 2010; Kornobis et al. 2011). The improved understanding of the history of the NALB is crucial for basic biogeographic assumptions. For example, Donoghue and Smith (2004) based on molecular divergence times between transatlantic sister lineages (erroneously) suggested that taxa with an inferred divergence time of less than 30 million years ago must have migrated from North America via the Bering Strait (and via East and Central Asia) to Europe. The quality of future biogeographic studies using modern plants and molecular differentiation patterns to infer historical biogeography will largely depend on revised fossil data in order to arrive at meaningful biogeographic scenarios.

References

Boulter, M.C. and Kvaček, Z. (1989). The Palaeocene flora of the Isle of Mull. *Special Papers in Palaeontology* 42: 1–149.

Boulter, R.D. and Manum, S.B. (1989). The Brito-Arctic Igneous Province flora around the Palaeocene/Eocene boundary. *Proceedings of the Ocean Drilling Program* 104B: 663–680.

Budantsev, L.Y. and Golovneva, L.B. (2009). Fossil Flora of Arctic, II. Paleogene Flora of Spitsbergen. St. Petersburg: Russian

Academy of Sciences, Komarov Botanical Institute.

Camus, A. (1929). Les châtaigniers. Monographie des genres *Castanea et Castanopsis*. Paris: Lechevalier.

Camus, A. (1936–1938). Les Chênes. Monographie du genre Quercus. Tome I. Genre Quercus, sous-genre Cyclobalanopsis, sous-genre Euquercus (sections Cerris et Mesobalanus). Paris: Lechevalier.

Camus, A. (1938–1939). Les Chênes. Monographie du genre Quercus. Tome II. Genre Quercus, sous-genre Euquercus (sections Lepidobalanus et Macrobalanus). Paris: Lechevalier.

Camus, A. (1952–1954). Les Chênes. Monographie du genre Quercus. Tome III. Genre Quercus, sous-genre Euquercus (sections Protobalanus et Erythrobalanus) et genre Lithocarpus. Paris: Lechevalier.

Chambers, L.M. and Pringle, M.S. (2001). Age and duration of activity at the Isle of Mull Tertiary igneous centre, Scotland, and confirmation of the existence of subchrons during Anomaly 26r. *Earth and Planetary Science Letters* 193: 333–345.

Crane, P.R., Manchester, S.R., and Dilcher, D.L. (1988). Morphology and phylogenetic significance of the angiosperm *Platanites hebridicus* from the Palaeocene of Scotland. *Palaeontology* 31: 503–517.

Crepet, W.L. (1989). History and implications of the early North American fossil record of Fagaceae. In: Evolution, Systematics, and Fossil History of the Hamamelidae. Volume 2: 'Higher' Hamamelidae (eds. P.R. Crane and S. Blackmore), 45–66. Oxford: Oxford Science Publications.

Dam, G., Pedersen, G.K., Sønderholm, M. et al. (2009). Lithostratigraphy of the Cretaceous-Palaeocene Nuussuaq Group, Nuussuaq Basin, West Greenland. *Geological Survey of Denmark and Greenland Bulletin* 19: 1–171.

Denk, T. and Grimm, G.W. (2009a). Significance of pollen characteristics for infrageneric classification and phylogeny in *Quercus* (Fagaceae). *International Journal of Plant Sciences* 170: 926–940.

Denk, T. and Grimm, G.W. (2009b). The biogeographic history of beech trees. *Review of Palaeobotany and Palynology* 158: 83–100.

Denk, T. and Grimm, G.W. (2010). The oaks of western Eurasia: traditional classifications and evidence from two nuclear markers. *Taxon* 59: 351–366.

Denk, T. and Velitzelos, D. (2002). First evidence of epidermal structures of *Ginkgo* from the Mediterranean tertiary. *Review of Palaeobotany and Palynology* 120: 1–15.

Denk, T., Grímsson, F., and Kvaček, Z. (2005). The Miocene floras of Iceland and their significance for late Cainozoic North Atlantic biogeography. *Botanical Journal of the Linnean Society* 149: 369–417.

Denk, T., Grímsson, F., and Zetter, R. (2010a). Episodic migration of oaks to Iceland: evidence for a North Atlantic "land bridge" in the latest Miocene. *American Journal of Botany* 97: 276–287.

Denk, T., Tekleva, M.V., Zetter, R. & Hofmann, C.-C. 2010b. Importance of pollen characteristics for systematics of living and fossil oaks (*Quercus*, Fagaceae). *8th European Palaeobotany-Palynology Conference*, Budapest, Program and Abstracts, p. 78.

Denk, T., Grímsson, F., Zetter, R., and Símonarson, L.A. (2011). Late Cainozoic Floras of Iceland – 15 Million Years of Vegetation and Climate History in the Northern North Atlantic. Dordrecht: Springer.

Denk, T., Grímsson, F., and Zetter, R. (2012). Fagaceae from the early Oligocene of Central Europe: persisting New World and emerging Old World biogeographic links. *Review of Palaeobotany and Palynology* 169: 7–20.

Denk, T., Velitzelos, D., Güner, T.H. et al. (2017). Taxonomy and palaeoecology of two widespread western Eurasian sclerophyllous oak species: *Quercus drymeja* Unger and *Q. mediterranea* Unger. *Review of Palaeobotany and Palynology* 241: 98–128.

Donoghue, M.J. and Smith, S.A. (2004). Patterns in the assembly of temperate forests around the Northern Hemisphere. *Philosophical Transactions of the Royal Society of London Series B –Biological Sciences* 359 (1450): 1633–1644.

Engler, A. 1879. Versuch einer Entwicklungsgeschichte der Pflanzenwelt, insbesondere der Florengebiete seit der Tertiärperiode. 1. Theil. *Die extratropischen Gebiete der nördlichen Hemisphäre*. Wilhelm Engelmann, Leipzig.

Fischer, T.C., Butzmann, R., Meller, B. et al. (2009). The morphology, systematic position and inferred biology of *Spirematospermum* – an extinct genus of Zingiberales. *Review of Palaeobotany and Palynology* 157: 391–426.

Gardner, J.S. (1884). On the evidence of fossil plants regarding the age of the tertiary basalts of the north-East Atlantic. *Proceedings of the Royal Society of London* 38: 14–23.

Gardner, J.S. (1887). On the leaf-beds and gravels of Ardtun, Carsaig, etc. in Mull, with notes by G.A.C. Cole. *Quaternary Journal of the Geological Society London* 43: 270–301.

Grímsson, F. and Denk, T. (2005). *Fagus* from the Miocene of Iceland: systematics and biogeographical considerations. *Review of Palaeobotany and Palynology* 134: 27–54.

Grímsson, F. and Denk, T. (2007). Floristic turnover in Iceland from 15 to 6 Ma – extracting biogeographic signals from fossil floral assemblages. *Journal of Biogeography* 34: 1490–1504.

Grímsson, F. and Símonarson, L.A. (2006). Beyki úr íslenskum setlögum. *Náttúrufræðingurinn* 74: 81–102.

Grímsson, F. and Símonarson, L.A. (2008a). Íslands fornu skógar. *Skógræktarritið* 2: 14–30.

Grímsson, F. and Símonarson, L.A. (2008b). Upper tertiary non-marine environments and climatic changes in Iceland. *Jökull* 58: 303–314.

Grímsson, F., Símonarson, L.A., and Friedrich, W.L. (2005). Kynlega stór aldin úr síðtertíerum setlögum á Íslandi. *Náttúrufræðingurinn* 73: 15–29.

Grímsson, F., Denk, T., and Símonarson, L.A. (2007a). Middle Miocene floras of Iceland – the early colonization of an island? *Review of Palaeobotany and Palynology* 144: 181–219.

Grímsson, F., Símonarson, L.A., and Denk, T. (2007b). Elstu flórur Íslands. *Náttúrufræðingurinn* 75: 85–106.

Grímsson, F., Denk, T., and Zetter, R. (2008). Pollen, fruits, and leaves of *Tetracentron* (Trochodendraceae) from the Cainozoic of Iceland and western North America and their palaeobiogeographic implications. *Grana* 47: 1–14.

Grímsson, F., Ferguson, D.K., and Zetter, R. (2012). Morphological trends in the fossil pollen of *Decodon* and the palaeobiogeographic history of the genus. *International Journal of Plant Sciences* 173: 297–317.

Grímsson, F., Zetter, R., Halbritter, H., and Grimm, G.W. (2014). *Aponogeton* pollen from the Cretaceous and Paleogene of North America and West Greenland: Implications for the origin and palaeobiogeography of the genus. *Review of Palaeobotany and Palynology* 200: 161–187.

Grímsson, F., Zetter, R., Grimm, G.W. et al. (2015). Fagaceae pollen from the early Cenozoic of West Greenland: revisiting Engler's and Chaney's Arcto-tertiary hypotheses. *Plant Systematics and Evolution* 301: 809–832.

Grímsson, F., Grimm, G.W., Zetter, R., and Denk, T. (2016a). Cretaceous and Paleogene Fagaceae from North America and Greenland: evidence for a Late Cretaceous split between *Fagus* and the remaining Fagaceae. *Acta Palaeobotanica* 56: 247–305.

Grímsson, F., Pedersen, G.K., Grimm, G.W., and Zetter, R. (2016b). A revised stratigraphy for the Palaeocene Agatdalen flora (Nuussuaq Peninsula, western Greenland): correlating fossiliferous outcrops, macrofossils, and palynological samples from phosphoritic nodules. *Acta Palaeobotanica* 56: 307–327.

Güner, T. and Denk, T. (2012). The genus *Mahonia* in the Miocene of Turkey: taxonomy and biogeographic implications. *Review of Palaeobotany and Palynology* 175: 32–46.

Hald, N. (1976). Early tertiary flood basalts from Hareøen and western Nûgssuaq, West Greenland. *Bulletin Grønlands Geologiske Undersøgelse* 120: 1–36.

Hald, N. (1977). Lithostratigraphy of the Maligât and Hareøen Formations, West Greenland Basalt

Group, on Hareøen and western Nûgssuaq. *Rapport Grønlands Geologiske Undersøgelse* 79: 9–16.

Hartz, N. (1903). Planteforsteninger fra Færøerne. *Meddelelser fra Dansk Geologisk Forening* 2 (9): 61–66.

Heer, O. (1859). Flora Tertiaria Helvetica – Die tertiäre Flora der Schweiz, vol. 3. Winterthur: J. Wurster & Compagnie.

Heer, O. (1868). Flora fossilis arctica 1. Die Fossile Flora der Polarländer enthaltend die in Nordgrönland, auf der Melville-Insel, im Banksland, am Mackenzie, in Island und in Spitzbergen entdeckten fossilen Pflanzen. Zürich: F. Schulthess.

Heer, O. (1869). Contributions to the fossil flora of North Greenland, being a description of the plants collected by Mr. Edward Whimper during the summer of 1867. *Philosophical Transactions of the Royal Society of London* 159: 445–488.

Heer, O. (1874). Nachträge zur Miocene Flora Grönlands, enthaltend die von der Schwedischen Expedition im Sommer 1870 gesammelten miocenen Pflanzen. *Kongliga Svenska Vetenskaps-Akademiens Handlingar* 13 (2): 1–29.

Heer, O. (1876). Flora fossilis arctica 4. Beiträge zur fossilen Flora Spitzbergens. Stockholm: P. A. Norstedt & Söner.

Heer, O. (1880). Nachträge zur fossilen Flora Grönlands. *Kongliga Svenska Vetenskaps-Akademiens Handlingar* 18 (2): 1–17.

Heer, O. (1883). Flora fossilis arctica 7. Die fossile Flora der Polarländer, enthaltend: Den zweiten Theil der fossilen Flora Grönlands. Zürich: J. Wurster & Comp.

Hofmann, C.-C., Mohamed, O., and Egger, H. (2011). A new terrestrial palynoflora from the Palaeocene/Eocene boundary in the northwestern Tethyan realm (St. Pankraz, Austria). *Review of Palaeobotany and Palynology* 166: 295–310.

ICS 2020. International Chronostratigraphic Chart v2020/01. Available from: https://stratigraphy.org/ICSchart/ChronostratChart2020-01.pdf.

Jones, J.H. and Dilcher, D.L. (1988). A study of the "*Dryophyllum*" leaf forms from the Paleogene of southeastern North America. *Palaeontographica B* 208: 53–80.

Koch, B.E. (1963). Fossil plants from the lower Palaeocene of the Agatdalen (Angmârtussut) area, central Nûgssuaq peninsula, northwest Greenland. *Bulletin Grønlands Geologiske Undersøgelse* 38 (also *Meddelelser om Grønland* **172/5**): 1–120.

Koch, B.E. (1972a). Fossil picrodendroid fruit from the upper Danian of Nûgssuaq, West Greenland. *Bulletin Grønlands Geologiske Undersøgelse* 98 (also *Meddelelser om Grønland* **193/3**): 1–33.

Koch, B.E. (1972b). Coryphoid palm fruits and seeds from the Danian of Nûgssuaq, West Greenland. *Bulletin Grønlands Geologiske Undersøgelse* 99 (also *Meddelelser om Grønland* **193/4**): 1–38.

Kornobis, E., Pálsson, S., Sidorov, D.A. et al. (2011). Molecular taxonomy and phylogenetic affinities of two groundwater amphipods, *Crangonyx islandicus* and *Crymostygius thingvallensis*, endemic to Iceland. *Molecular Phylogenetics and Evolution* 58: 527–539.

Kvaček, Z. (2010). Forest flora and vegetation of the European early Palaeogene – a review. *Bulletin of Geosciences* 85 (1): 3–16.

Kvaček, Z. and Walther, H. (1989). Revision der mitteleuropäischen tertiären Fagaceen nach blattepidermalen Charakteristiken III. Teil *Dryophyllum* Debey ex Saporta und *Eotrigonobalanus* Walther & Kvaček gen. nov. *Feddes Repertorium* 100: 575–601.

Kvaček, Z., Manum, S.B., and Boulter, M.C. (1994). Angiosperms from the Palaeogene of Spitsbergen, including an unfinished work by A. G. Nathorst. *Palaeontographica B* 232: 103–128.

Kvaček, Z., Manchester, S.R., and Guo, S.-X. (2001). Trifoliolate leaves of *Platanus bella* (Heer) comb. n. from the Palaeocene of North America, Greenland, and Asia and their relationships among extinct and extant Platanaceae. *International Journal of Plant Sciences* 162: 441–458.

Laufeld, S. (1965). Sporomorphs in tertiary coal from the Faeroe Islands. *Geologiska Föreningen i Stockholm Förhandlinger* 87: 231–238.

Lund, J. (1989). A late Palaeocene non-marine microflora from the interbasaltic coals of the Faeroe Islands, North Atlantic. *Bulletin of the Geological Society of Denmark* 37: 181–203.

Mai, H.D. (1995). Tertiäre Vegetationsgeschichte Europas. Jena: Gustav Fischer.

Manchester, S.R. (1999). Biogeographical relationships of North American tertiary floras. *Annals of the Missouri Botanical Garden* 86: 472–522.

Manchester, S.R., Chen, Z.-D., Lu, A.-M., and Uemura, K. (2009). Eastern Asian endemic seed plant genera and their paleogeographic history throughout the Northern Hemisphere. *Journal of Systematics and Evolution* 47: 1–42.

Mathiesen, J. (1932). Notes on some fossil plants from East Greenland (Cape Dalton, Turner Sound, Cape Brewster, and Sabine Island). *Meddelelser om Grønland* 85 (4): 1–62.

McIntyre, D.J. (1991). Pollen and spore flora of an Eocene forest, eastern Axel Heiberg Island, N.W.T. *Geological Survey of Canada Bulletin* 403: 83–97.

McIver, E.E. and Basinger, J.F. (1993). Flora of the Ravenscrag formation (Palaeocene), southwestern Saskatchewan, Canada. *Palaeontographica Canadiana* 10: 1–167.

McIver, E.E. and Basinger, J.F. (1999). Early tertiary floral evolution in the Canadian high Arctic. *Annals of the Missouri Botanical Garden* 86: 523–545.

McKenna, M.C. (1983). Cenozoic paleogeography of North Atlantic land bridges. In: Structure and Development of the Greenland-Scotland Ridge (eds. M.H.P. Bott, S. Saxov, M. Talwani and J. Thiede), 351–399. New York: Plenum Press.

Menitsky, J.L. (1984). Duby Asii. Leningrad: Nauka.

Menitsky, J.L. (2005). Oaks of Asia. New Hampshire: Science Publishers.

Moorbath, S. and Bell, J.D. (1965). Strontium isotope abundance studies and Rubidium-Strontium age determinations on Tertiary igneous rocks from the Isle of Skye North-West Scotland. *Journal of Petrology* 6: 37–66.

Nathorst, A.G. (1885). Sjunde kapitlet. In: Den andra Dicksonska Expeditionen til Grönland (ed. A.E. Nordenskiöld), 302–348. Stockholm: F. & G. Beijers Förlag.

Ólafsson, E. (1772). Vice-Lavmand Eggert Olafsens og Land-Physici Biarne Povelsen Reise igiennem Island, foranstaltet af Videnskabernes Sælskab i København 1–2 Sorø. Videnskabernes Sælskap.

Passey, S.R. and Jolley, D.W. (2009). A revised lithostratigraphic nomenclature for the Palaeogene Faroe Islands Basalt Group, NE Atlantic Ocean. *Earth and Environmental Science Transactions of the Royal Society of Edinburgh* 99: 127–158.

Pedersen, K.R. (1976). Fossil floras of Greenland. In: Geology of Greenland (eds. A. Escher and W.S. Watt), 519–535. Andelsbogtrykkeriet, Odense: The Geological Survey of Greenland.

Pedersen, G.K., Larsen, L.M., Pedersen, A.K., and Hjortkjær, B.F. (1998). The syn-volcanic Naajaat lake, Palaeocene of West Greenland. *Palaeogeography, Palaeoclimatology, Palaeoecology* 140: 271–287.

Poore, H.R., Samworth, R., White, N.J. et al. (2006). Neogene overflow of northern component water at the Greenland-Scotland ridge. *Geochemistry Geophysics Geosystems* 7: Q06010. https://doi.org/10.1029/2005GC001085.

Poulter, J., Francis, J., Wilson, M., Candela, Y. & Anderson, L. 2008. Deciphering floral diversity and palaeoclimate signals from the mid Palaeocene floras of the Isle of Skye, Scotland. [52nd] *Annual Meeting of the Palaeontological Association*, Glasgow. Abstracts, pp. 74–75.

Poulter, J., Francis, J., Wilson, M. & Candela, Y. 2010. Mid Palaeocene floras and climate of the Isles of Skye and Mull, Scotland. *8th European Palaeobotany–Palynology Conference, 2010, Budapest, Hungary. Program and Abstracts*, p. 197.

Praglowski, J. (1984). Fagaceae Dumort. Castaneoideae Oerst. *World Pollen Spore Flora* 13: 1–21.

Rasmussen, R. (1925). Um skógir í Føroyum í forðum. *Varðin* 5: 153–163.

Rasmussen, J. and Koch, B.E. (1963). Fossil *Metasequoia* from Mikines, Faroe Islands. *Fróðskaparrit* 12: 83–96.

Rasmussen, J. and Noe-Nygaard, A. (1969). Beskrivelse til geologisk kort over Færøerne i målestok 1:50.000. *Geological Survey of Denmark* I/24: 1–370.

Ravn, J.P.J. (1922). On the Mollusca of the Tertiary of Spitsbergen. *Resultater av de Norske statsunderstøttede Spitsbergenekspedisjoner* 1 (2): 1–28.

Riisager, P., Riisager, J., Abrahamsen, N., and Waagstein, R. (2002). New paleomagnetic pole and magnetostratigraphy of Faroe Islands flood volcanics, North Atlantic igneous province. *Earth and Planetary Science Letters* 201: 261–276.

Sadowski, E.-M., Hammel, J.U., and Denk, T. (2018). Synchrotron X-ray imaging of a dichasium cupule of *Castanopsis* from Eocene Baltic amber. *American Journal of Botany* 105 (12): 1–12.

Sadowski, M., Schmidt, A.R., and Denk, T. (2020). Staminate inflorescences with in-situ pollen from Eocene Baltic amber reveal high diversity in Fagaceae (oak family). *Willdenowia* 50 (3): 405–517.

Schmidt, A.G., Riisager, P., Abrahamsen, N. et al. (2005). Palaeomagnetism of Eocene Talerua member lavas on Hareøen, West Greenland. *Bulletin of the Geological Society of Denmark* 52: 27–38.

Seward, A.C. and Conway, V.M. (1935). Fossil plants from Kingigtok and Kagdlunguak,

West Greenland. *Meddelelser om Grønland* 93 (5): 1–41.

Seward, A.C. and Edwards, W.N. (1941). Fossil plants from East Greenland. *Annals and Magazine of Natural History* 11 (8): 169–176.

Sigmundsson, F., Símonarson, L.A., Sigmundsson, O., and Ingólfsson, Ó. (eds.) (2008). The dynamic geology of Iceland. *Jökull* 58: 1–422.

Storey, M., Duncan, R.A., Pedersen, A.K. et al. (1998). ^{40}Ar/^{39}Ar geochronology of West Greenland Tertiary volcanic province. *Earth and Planetary Science Letters* 160: 569–586.

Storey, M., Duncan, R.A., and Tegner, C. (2007). Timing and duration of volcanism in the North Atlantic Igneous Province: Implications for geodynamics and links to the Iceland hotspot. *Chemical Geology* 241: 264–281.

Tiffney, B.H. (1985). The Eocene North Atlantic land bridge: Its importance in Tertiary and modern phytogeography of the Northern Hemisphere. *Journal of the Arnold Arboretum* 66: 243–273.

Tiffney, B.H. (2000). Geographic and climatic influences on the Cretaceous and Tertiary history of Euramerican floristic similarity. *Acta Universitatis Carolinae Geologica* 44: 5–16.

Tiffney, B.H. (2008). Phylogeography, fossils, and Northern Hemisphere biogeography: The role of physiological uniformitarianism. *Annals of the Missouri Botanical Garden* 95: 135–143.

Tiffney, B.H. and Manchester, S.R. (2001). The use of geological and paleontological evidence in evaluating plant phylogeographic hypotheses in the northern hemisphere Tertiary. *International Journal of Plant Sciences* 162: S3–S17.

Waagstein, R., Guise, P., and Rex, D. (2002). K/Ar and 39Ar/40Ar whole-rock dating of zeolite facies metamorphosed flood basalts: The upper Palaeocene basalts of the Faroe Islands, NE Atlantic. *Geological Society London Special Publications* 197: 219–252.

3

Interglacial Biotas from the North Atlantic Islands

Ole Bennike[1] and Jens Böcher[2]

[1] *Geological Survey of Denmark and Greenland, Copenhagen, Denmark*
[2] *Zoological Museum, Copenhagen, Denmark*

Introduction

The North Atlantic Islands comprise from south to north, the Faroe Islands, Iceland and Greenland (Figure 1, see Plate section). They span almost 30° of latitude from temperate to high arctic climates, from North-West Europe to North America. The Faroe Islands are a group of small islands with an area of 1400 km², whereas Greenland is the largest island on Earth, covering an area of 2 166 086 km², of which 410 449 km² are ice free. Iceland with an area of 103 100 km² is intermediate in size.

Large parts of the North Atlantic islands are mountainous, with the highest peak at 3693 m found in East Greenland. In addition to the Inland Ice, numerous local ice caps and other types of glaciers are found in Greenland and Iceland, whereas the Faroe Islands are unglaciated. Fjords and straits are common.

The mean temperature for the warmest month shows a fall from 10 to 12 °C in the Faroe Islands, Iceland and southern-most Greenland to 2 °C in the far north and the mean temperature for the coldest month shows a fall from 4 to −34 °C. The precipitation also falls towards the north, from ~4000 mm/year locally on the Faroe Islands and on ice caps in south-western Iceland to below 200 mm/year in some areas of northern Greenland. The Faroe Islands, Iceland and south-west Greenland are influenced by northward flowing relatively warm ocean currents, whereas North and East Greenland as well as northern Iceland are influenced by cold, southward flowing currents. The sea off northern Greenland is covered by ice all year round, whereas sea ice is not found in the Faroe Islands, which are characterized by a strongly maritime climate.

The number of native vascular plants is ~520 in Greenland, ~460 in Iceland and ~250 in the Faroe Islands, which reflects the different areas of ice-free land. Scrubs, heaths, grasslands, and mires are the main vegetation types, but in the Faroe Islands, Iceland and southernmost Greenland forested areas are also found. In these areas farming is also widespread. Farthest to the north, at 83°N, areas of polar desert, where no woody plants can survive, are found. Fell fields with scattered plants are found on windy places where the snow is blown away during the winter. The number of

Biogeography in the Sub-Arctic: The Past and Future of North Atlantic Biota, First Edition.
Edited by Eva Panagiotakopulu and Jon P. Sadler.
© 2021 John Wiley & Sons Ltd. Published 2021 by John Wiley & Sons Ltd.

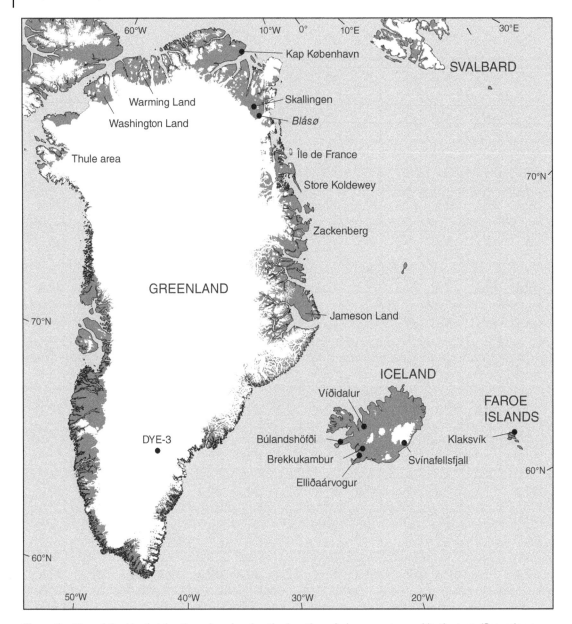

Figure 1 Map of the North Atlantic region showing the location of place names used in the text. (See colour plate section for colour representation of this figure.)

indigenous beetles is ~36 in Greenland, ~ 150 in Iceland and ~ 160 in the Faroe Islands.

The famous, deep ice cores from the Greenland ice sheet have provided a wealth of detailed information about regional climate history during the past 123 000 years. However, the ice cores have only provided little information about past plant and animal life. The only exception is the basal ice from DYE3 which contains ancient DNA. Most information on interglacial biotas in the North Atlantic Islands comes from open geological sections formed by river erosion or coastal erosion. In contrast, interglacial sediments have been discovered in a number of lakes on Baffin Island in eastern arctic Canada (e.g. Miller et al. 1999). Most of these lake records are confined to the last interglacial stage, but in one lake succession, sediments from several interglacial stages are found (Briner et al. 2007).

The North Atlantic Islands were repeatedly glaciated during the Quaternary glacial stages and only glimpses of the pre-Holocene history are available. Nevertheless, the scattered occurrences of interglacial deposits give a fairly detailed picture of plant and animal life as well as climatic changes. Holocene deposits are much more widespread than pre-Holocene deposits, and detailed studies of changes of climate, vegetation history as well as flora and fauna history have been conducted. Late glacial lake deposits have been found in northern Iceland and in southernmost Greenland.

This review focuses on non-marine biotas. We present data for the Quaternary, the last 2.6 million years (Ma), and cover the Faroe Islands, Iceland and Greenland. In a geological sense the postglacial, or Holocene, is also an interglacial stage, and we include some notes on Early and Middle Holocene biotas. We focus on vascular plants and beetles but also summarize data on other taxa where available. Pollen, spores, plant macro-fossils and animal fossils have been studied. Figure 1 shows the location of place names used in the text and Figure 2 provides a chronological overview. When discussing radiocarbon ages we use ages calibrated to calendar years BP.

Marine interglacial deposits in the North Atlantic Islands were first described in the 1800s, but description of non-marine deposits followed later. In the Faroe Islands only a single interglacial

Age (Ma)	FAEROE ISLANDS	ICELAND	GREENLAND
0	Klaksvik	Elliðaárvogur	Last Interglacial
			Stage 11
		Svínafellsfjall Fm	
1		Búlandshöfði Fm	
		Víðidalur Fm	
2			Île de France Fm, Store Koldewey Fm Kap København Fm, member B
		Brekkukambur Fm	
			Kap København Fm, member A

(Left axis labels: Quaternary, Pliocene)

Figure 2 Stratigraphical overview of the Quaternary (the last 2.6 Ma) showing ages of interglacial deposits from the North Atlantic islands. Fm: formation.

deposit has been located, which was studied by Rasmussen (1972), Jóhansen (1985), Wastegård et al. (2005) and recently by Bennike et al. (2018). Data on the Early to Mid-Holocene biotic history were presented by Jóhansen (1985), Bennike et al. (1998) and Hannon et al. (2003, 2010). So far, no late glacial deposits have been recovered in the Faroe Islands.

In Iceland, plant fossils from interglacial deposits were first described in the 1930s (Áskelsson 1938; Líndal 1939) and a review of the palaeobotany of Pleistocene deposits in Iceland was recently provided by Grímsson (2011). The oldest interglacial plant-bearing deposits are from the Early Quaternary, and the youngest interglacial deposits with plant and invertebrate remains probably date from the last interglacial period. Pollen analyses and macro-fossil analyses of late glacial and Early Holocene deposits in Iceland were conducted by Rundgren (1995, 1998) and Rundgren and Ingólfsson (1999). Studies of the Early to Mid-Holocene vegetation history of Iceland have been published by, for example, Caseldine (2001), Wastl et al. (2001), Hallsdóttir (1995), Hallsdóttir and Caseldine (2005) and Caseldine et al. (2006).

In Greenland non-marine interglacial biotas were not documented until 1979, when the Kap København Formation was discovered (Funder and Hjort 1980; Funder et al. 1984, 1985, 2001; Bennike 1990; Böcher 1995). The first description of Late Quaternary interglacial biotas in Greenland was published by Meldgaard and Bennike (1989). Later on, near-shore marine deposits with washed-out remains of plants and invertebrates were discovered in North-West and East Greenland in the 1990s (Funder 1990; Bennike and Böcher 1992, 1994; Funder et al. 1994, 1998; Hedenäs 1994; Hedenäs and Bennike 2003; Böcher 2012). Remains of southern extra-limital plants and beetles have been discovered at several sites. Southern extra-limital species are species that only occur south of the fossil locality at

present. Interglacial deposits in Greenland with non-marine biotas are mainly dated to the Early Quaternary and to the last interglacial stage, the Eemian. Analyses of Holocene non-marine floras and faunas were initiated by Iversen (1954) and followed up by Fredskild, Funder and Bennike (e.g. Fredskild 1973, 1983, 1985; Funder 1978, 1979; Bennike et al. 1999, 2008a,b; Bennike 2000a; Wagner et al. 2008; Bennike and Wagner 2012; Wagner and Bennike 2012). In addition to pollen, plant macro-fossils and insect remains have been studied. Arthropod remains from Early to Mid-Holocene deposits have been reported by, for example, Fredskild et al. (1975), Böcher and Fredskild (1993), Böcher and Bennike (1996), Bennike et al. (2000, 2004) and Böcher et al. (2012).

The Faroe Islands

At Borðoyarvík near Klaksvík in the northeastern part of the Faroe Islands, an interglacial deposit is exposed in a coastal cliff section (Rasmussen 1972; Wastegård et al. 2005). The deposit is ~1 m thick and dominated by clay with a content of total organic carbon that decreases from 6% in the lower part to 2% in the upper part. The diatom flora comprises some marine or brackish taxa, but the common presence of statoblasts of the freshwater bryozoan *Cristatella mucedo*, especially in the lower part of the unit, may contradict a brackish water environment, because the species usually does not occur in brackish water (but see Økland and Økland 2000).

Notes on the pollen flora are found in Rasmussen (1972; sample analysed by Johs. Iversen), in Jóhansen (1985, p. 12) and in Wastegård et al. (2005). Iversen reported a dominance of *Empetrum* and Poaceae, with some *Betula* and rare grains of *Pinus* and *Corylus*. Jóhansen reported pollen of *Buxus*, *Betula*, *Lonicera*, *Plantago lanceolata*, *Nymphaea*, Poaceae, Cyperaceae and Ericales.

Wastegård et al. (2005) found *Alnus, Betula, Carpinus, Picea, Pinus*, Ericaceae, Apiaceae and Asteraceae. A more recent study (Bennike et al. 2018) indicates accumulation in a coastal lagoon in a landscape and climate similar to that of the Mid-Holocene.

Plant macrofossils are represented by a few pieces of wood. One of them was identified to *Pinus* and another to *Picea* or *Larix* (Rasmussen 1972; Jóhansen 1985). However, it is possible that the wood is driftwood (Wastegård et al. 2005) and if so it may not provide information on the local flora. *Betula* remains were referred to as *Betula* sp. by Wastegård et al. (2005), but the remains come from tree birches (*Betula* sect. *Albae*, Bennike et al. 2018). *Cristatella mucedo, Betula* sect. *Albae* and *Ajuga* are fairly thermophilous and may indicate summer temperatures slightly higher than at present. The interglacial deposit at Borðoyarvík can be referred to the Eemian, based on tephrochronological studies (Wastegård et al. 2005).

The Faroe Islands were covered by a local ice cap during the last glacial stage (Jørgensen and Rasmussen 1986; Sejrup et al. 2005), and the oldest minimum dates for the deglaciation are ~11.3 ka (Jóhansen 1985; Hannon et al. 2010). The Early Holocene vegetation history of the Faroe Islands is best documented from a high-resolution study of lake sediments from Lykkjuvøtn on Sandøy (Hannon et al. 2010). Some information is also available from sub-marine lake deposits from Skálafjørður (Bennike et al. 1998; Tendal 2004; Bennike 2010). Plants documented by macrofossil finds from Early Holocene deposits include the shrubs *Salix herbacea, Betula nana, Empetrum nigrum*, the herbs *Stellaria alsine, Oxyria digyna, Rumex acetosa, Ranunculus flammula, Ranunculus acris, Cardaminopsis petraea, Filipendula ulmaria, Viola palustris, Caltha palustris*, the club moss *Selaginella selaginoides* and the water plants *Isoetes lacustris, Potamogeton pusillus, Potamogeton filiformis,*

Myriophyllum alterniflorum and *Sparganium angustifolium* (Jóhansen 1985; Bennike et al. 1998; Hannon et al. 2010). The invertebrate fauna from Skálafjørður includes the sponge *Racekiela ryderi*, an amphi-Atlantic species that probably arrived by long distance chance dispersal by birds. The same probably applies to the bryozoans *Plumatella* sp. and *C. mucedo*. The coleopteran fauna includes the ground beetle *Nebria rufescens* that is common and widespread in the islands today. The Early Holocene flora and fauna from the Faroe Islands indicate a climate similar to the present.

Iceland

This short review on interglacial biotas in Iceland is mainly based on the excellent and richly illustrated review by Grímsson (2011). Five occurrences with plant remains and one with arthropod remains have been described from Iceland, and exposures of two of them are shown in Figure 3 (see Plate section). The ages of the older formations are relatively well constrained from palaeomagnetic studies and by Ar/Ar age determinations of underlying or overlying volcanic rocks. *Alnus* fossils, referred to *Alnaster viridis fossilis, Alnus* aff. *viridis* and *Alnus* cf. *viridis* are found in deposits from the four oldest formations (Figure 4). During the Holocene, *Alnus* did not reach Iceland.

The Brekkukambur Formation

The Brekkukambur Formation consists of sedimentary rocks that are exposed in south-west Iceland. The age of the succession is estimated to 2.4–2.1 Ma, and it is dominated by fluvial conglomerate and sandstone with some siltstone and claystone deposited in a lake. Macrofossils of *Alnaster viridis fossilis, Betula* sp., *Vaccinium uliginosum, Dryas octopetala, Salix glauca, Salix*

(a)   (b)

Figure 3 (a) Mt. Stöð with an outcrop of the Búlandshöfði Formation showing lagoonal mud overlain by deltaic sandstones. (b) Svínafell with the Svínafellsfjall Formation showing exposed lake sediments. *Source:* Photographs kindly provided by Friðgeir Grímsson. (See colour plate section for colour representation of this figure.)

lanata and *Salix phylicifolia fossilis* have been recorded. The pollen flora is dominated by *Alnus*, *Salix* and *Betula*, and the flora can be characterized as boreal with some arctic elements, notably *D. octopetala*.

The Víðidalur Formation

The Víðidalur Formation (~ 1.7 Ma) is found in north-western Iceland and consists of tillite, conglomerate, sandstone, siltstone and claystone. The macrofossil assemblage is dominated by *Alnus* aff. *viridis* and *Polygonum viviparum* but also includes *B. nana* × *pubescens*, *Vaccinium* cf. *uliginosum*, *D. octopetala* and *Salix* sp. The pollen and spore flora are species-rich and include *Pinus*, *Menyanthes*, *Myrica*, *Trollius*, *Fragaria* and *Sanguisorba*. Overall, the fossil flora indicates forest-tundra vegetation on uplands in the region.

The Búlandshöfði Formation

This formation is found in western Iceland; it is covered by lavas that are dated to ~1.1 Ma. The lower part of the formation is a glaciomarine deposit with arctic molluscs such as the small

bivalve *Portlandia arctica*. The upper part is dominated by shallow-water marine deposits with an interglacial fauna that includes the gastropods *Littorina littorea* and *Nucella lapillus*, the blue mussel *Mytilus edulis* and the barnacle *Balanus balanoides*. The upper part of the formation includes a lacustrine succession with sandstone and siltstone with plant fossils (Figure 4).

Macrofossils of *E. nigrum*, *Vaccinium* cf. *uliginosum*, *Potentilla* sp., *Salix arctica* tp., *S. herbacea* and *Valeriana* sp. have been recorded. Again, the pollen and spore flora are more diverse than the macroflora and include *Pinus*, *Alnus* and *Betula*, *Mercurialis perennis*, *Plantago coronopus* and *Polygonum aviculare* and overall the fossil flora indicates forest-tundra vegetation on uplands in the region and an interglacial type of climate similar to that of the Holocene.

The Svínafellsfjall Formation

The Svínafellsfjall Formation in south-eastern Iceland is approximately 0.8 Ma old and comprises lacustrine siltstone and sandstone with numerous dropstones. Plant macrofossils include *Thelypteris limbosperma*, *Alnus* cf. *viridis*, *Vaccinium* cf.

Figure 4 Examples of leaf imprints of vascular plants from interglacial deposits in Iceland. (a) *Dryas octopetala* from the Víðidalur Formation. (b) *Salix herbacea* from the Búlandshöfði Formation. (c) *Salix arctica* type from the Búlandshöfði Formation. (d) *Thelypteris limbosperma* from the Svínafellsfjall Formation. (e) *Alnus* cf. *viridis* from the Svínafellsfjall Formation. (f) *Dryas octopetala* from the Svínafellsfjall Formation. (g, h) *Salix arctica* type from the Svínafellsfjall Formation. (h) *Salix herbacea* from the Svínafellsfjall Formation. Scale bars 5 mm.
Source: Photographs kindly provided by Friðgeir Grímsson.

uliginosum, P. viviparum, Alchemilla sp., *D. octo-petala, Sorbus* aff. *aucuparia, S. arctica* tp. and *S. herbacea* (Figure 4). The pollen flora includes *Pinus, Artemisia, Betula, Menyanthes, Thalictrum* and *Galium.* Except for *T. limbosperma, Pinus* and *Alnus* cf. *viridis,* all taxa are part of the modern-day flora of Iceland, and again the fossil flora point to forest tundra and an interglacial type of climate, which is surprising because of the frequent occurrence of dropstones in the sediments.

Succession at Elliðaárvogur Near Reykjavík

About 5 km east of Reykjavík an interglacial succession comprises layers of sand and fine gravel with shells of marine shallow water molluscs. Lake deposits with organic remains are also found (Thorkelsson 1935; Einarsson 1981). Seeds and fruits were identified by K. Jessen who recorded *E. nigrum, Menyanthes trifoliata, M. alterniflorum, Potamogeton* sp., *Carex* sp. and *Scirpus* sp. He also found spicules of *Spongilla lacustris.* K.L. Henriksen identified insect remains and recorded the beetles *N. rufescens, Patrobus septentrionis, Pterostichus diligens, Hydroporus* sp., *Agabus solieri, Tachinus collaris* and *Byrrhus fasciatus.* Fossil cladocerans were identified by Einarsson (1981) who found seven to eight species that all occur in Iceland at present. In contrast, one of the beetles (*Hydroporus* sp. non *Hydroporus nigrita*) and one of the vascular plants (*Scirpus* sp.) do not occur in Iceland at present. The age of the Elliðaárvogur beds is uncertain, but a last interglacial age is possible (LIGA members 1991; Leifur Símonarson and Jón Eiriksson, personal communication, 2013).

Late Glacial and Early Holocene

During the last ice age Iceland was covered by an ice cap, the margin of which extended out on to the edge of the shelf (Andrews et al. 2000). Some parts of Iceland were deglaciated during the late glacial, and late glacial raised marine deposits are known from several sites. Late glacial lake deposits have been recovered from the Skagi peninsula in northern Iceland. Studies of late glacial and Early Holocene deposits were conducted in the 1990s (Rundgren 1995, 1998; Rundgren and Ingólfsson 1999).

Sediments from the Allerød chronozone contain a fairly diverse pollen flora with woody plants such as *B. nana, Salix, Juniperus* and *Empetrum* that formed a significant part of the vegetation, which also included various herbs, grasses and sedges. Prior to the Allerød and during the Younger Dryas, a vegetation with pioneer plants dominated (Rundgren 1995).

The Early Holocene sediments contain plant macro-fossils in addition to pollen. Macro-fossils of *B. nana, S. herbacea, Salix* cf. *phylicifolia, E. nigrum, Vaccinium* sp., *D. octopetala, C. palustris, Angelica sylvestris* and *Armeria maritima* are recorded. Pollen and plant macrofossil records reflect progressive closing of the vegetation cover, from herb tundra over a dwarf-shrub phase to a shrub and dwarf-shrub phase (Rundgren 1998).

Pollen from tree birch are rare in Early Holocene deposits in northern Iceland and it has been suggested that they represent long-distance transport, either from outside Iceland or from limited areas in Iceland with local tree birch growth (Caseldine 2001). Birch woodland began to develop in Iceland in lowlands along fjords and in valleys ~2000–4000 years after the beginning of the Holocene, and reached their maximum before 7000 years BP. During the Mid- and Late Holocene heaths and mires expanded and woodlands became more open (Hallsdóttir and Caseldine 2005).

Rundgren and Ingólfsson (1999) contended that many plant species survived the Younger Dryas in northern Iceland and that these species also could have survived the last glacial maximum in Iceland. In contrast, Buckland et al. (1986), updated in Buckland and Panagiotakopulu (2010), argued that the virtual absence of endemic species supports a model of late glacial or Early Holocene immigration, and maintained that most species of vascular plants and beetles, including heavy flightless beetles, arrived by ice-rafting from North-West Europe at the Pleistocene–Holocene transition, an idea first put forward by Coope (1969).

Greenland

The Kap København Formation

The Kap København Formation is a succession of clay, silt and sand in eastern North Greenland. The formation was discovered in 1979 and the sequence has been the focus of several subsequent visits (Funder and Hjort 1980). This short review on the Kap København Formation and its flora and fauna is based on Funder et al. (1984, 1985, 2001), Bennike (1990), Böcher (1995) and Símonarson et al. (1998).

The formation covers an area of ~300 km^2 and is exposed at numerous places along rivers. It has been divided into members A and B. Member A is at least 50 m thick and is dominated by finely laminated clay and silt with rare stones. This member contains rare shells of bivalves and more frequent tests of foraminifers and valves of ostracods. Member B is 40–50 m thick and is dominated by two sandy units (units B1 and B2), which are separated by a more fine-grained unit (B2). B1 is dominated by horizontally laminated fine and medium grained sand, but cross bedding and other types of sedimentary structures also occur. The sand is texturally and mineralogically mature quartz sand with heavy mineral concentrations in some places. In the upper part large scour-and-fill structures are found, these contain large amounts of organic detritus. The sediments in unit B1 were deposited in coastal environments during rising water depth. Unit B2 is characterized by bioturbated clay and silt that was deposited on the inner

shelf. Unit B3 is heterogeneous, but it is dominated by horizontally laminated sand. Logs of small trees (Figure 5a, see Plate section) as well as lenses and layers of organic detritus (Figure 5b) is a characteristic feature for unit B3, which is interpreted as deposited in coastal parts of delta environments. In the western part of the Kap København area unit B2 is missing and unit B3 is devoid of plant and animal remains. Member B in this area is interpreted as fluvial.

Member A and unit B2 contain relatively rich marine faunas. Member A contains an element of warmth demanding Foraminifera species. Unit B2 has a fairly diverse mollusc fauna that includes the bivalves *Cyrtodaria kurriana* and *Macoma balthica*, in addition to rich faunas of foraminifers and ostracods. The highest sea water temperatures probably prevailed during deposition of unit B2, with summer temperatures at the sea bottom 7–8 °C higher than at present. Both members A and B show sign of lowered salinity and influence from freshwater. On the surface of member A exposures strongly abraded shell fragments are rather common. They have been designated the allochthonous fauna; it comprises the bivalve *Arctica islandica*. The allochthonous fauna is assumed to be older than member A, and *A. islandica* is one of the most warmth-demanding mollusc species found in the area.

Unit B1 and especially B3 contain a wealth of well-preserved remains of non-marine plants and animals, with many different groups represented. Vascular plants include a mixture of boreal and arctic species (Figure 6). Taxa such as *Larix groenlandii*, *Picea mariana*, *Thuja occidentalis* and *Taxus* sp., *Betula* sect. *Albae*, *Myrica arctogale*, *Cornus stolonifera*, *Viburnum* cf. *edule* and *Scirpus microcarpus* belong to the first group, whereas *D. octopetala*, *O. digyna* and *Papaver* sect. *Scapiflora* belong to the second. All remains of wood come from small trees or shrubs, and the largest log that was found had a diameter of 18 cm. Growth rings are narrow to extremely

Figure 5 (a) A log of *Larix* sitting in sandy deposits of the Kap København Formation (member B) in North Greenland. The light part has been bleached by the sun. Note the contrasting modern treeless landscape. (b) Organic-rich layers of the Kap København Formation (member B). (c) Excavation of last interglacial deposits on Jameson Land, central East Greenland. (d) Sandy interglacial deposits on Jameson Land with organic-rich sediments in the bottom of a trough. (e) Archaeological excavation of a Mid-Holocene midden in central West Greenland. (See colour plate section for colour representation of this figure.)

narrow, which may indicate that the mean temperature for the warmest month of the year was ~10–11 °C. *Thuja* and *Taxus* cannot tolerate very cold winters, and the mean temperature for the coldest month was probably not below −17 °C. Thus, it appears that the area was dominated by forest tundra, which grew in an oceanic type of sub-arctic climate.

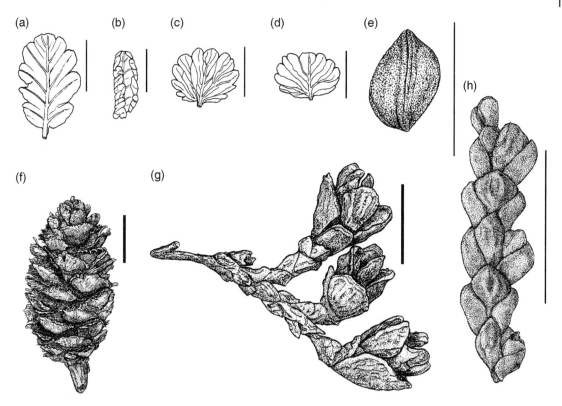

Figure 6 Drawings of plant remains from the Kap København Formation in North Greenland. (a-b) Leaves of *Dryas octopetala*. Leaf that comes from a plant that grew on a protected site (a) and a narrow leaf with recurved leaf margin, which comes from a plant that grew on a wind-exposed site (b). (c, d) Leaves of *Betula nana*. (e) Fruit stone of *Cornus stolonifera*. (f) Cone of *Larix groenlandii*. (g) Twig of *Thuja occidentalis* with three small cones. (h) Twig of *Thuja occidentalis* with scaly leaves. Thick scale bars: 10 mm, thin bars: 5 mm. *Source:* From Bennike (1990).

By far the most diverse group of invertebrates is beetles, of which at least 210 species are present, an impressive and surprising number when compared with the modern day beetle fauna of Greenland that comprises ~36 species (Böcher 1988, 2012). The fossil insect fauna comprise 155 named species, of which 142 species are Coleoptera, mostly Carabidae, Staphylinidae, and Curculionidae. Ants are absent from modern Greenland, so it is remarkable that four species of ants (*Formica* and *Camponotus*) are represented in the Kap København fauna. Trichoptera (caddis flies) include nine named species and 12 genera, indicating the existence of a great variety of freshwater biotopes, which is confirmed by the presence of various chironomids, water beetles, macro-limnophytes, crustaceans and bryozoans. Some examples of insect remains from the Kap København Formation are shown in Figure 7.

The insect fauna of the Kap København Formation allows a detailed palaeoecological reconstruction of a highly diverse environment. Freshwater, freshwater shores, humid terrestrial biotopes, forests and alpine biotopes each contributes about equal numbers of species, with somewhat fewer taxa from dry environments, including steppe and saline ponds (Böcher 1995).

Figure 7 Scanning electron microscope photographs of beetle and ant remains from the Kap København Formation in North Greenland. (a) Head of *Cicindela* cf. *hybrida*. (b-d) Elytra of *Aegialia terminalis*, *Scolytus piceae* and *Kalissus nitidus*. (e) Head of *Formica* sp. (f) Elytron of *Litodactylus leucogaster*. Scale bars: 0.5 mm. *Source:* From Böcher (1995).

Biogeographically the Kap København fossil flora is dominated by taxa with a modern Holarctic or Nearctic range (Figure 8, see Plate section; Bennike 1990), whereas the fossil insect fauna has an equal share of what are today Nearctic and Palaearctic elements (Böcher 1995). Nine of the beetles from the Kap København Formation are found in Greenland today; most of these are widespread Holarctic, low arctic–subarctic species such as the boreo-alpine carabid *N. rufescens*. The

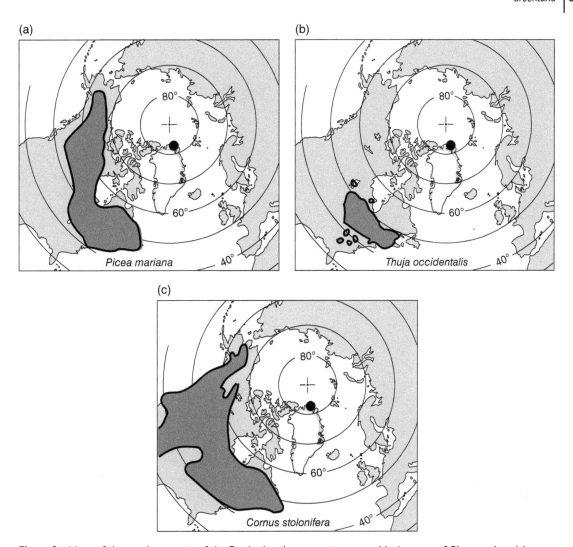

Figure 8 Maps of the northern parts of the Earth, showing present geographical ranges of *Picea mariana* (a), *Thuja occidentalis* (b) and *Cornus stolonifera* (c). Remains of these species have been found in the Kap København Formation (black dot in North Greenland). *Source:* From Bennike (1990).(See colour plate section for colour representation of this figure.)

greater part of the insects points to temperate conditions, but heterogeneous compositions of some of the insect assemblages indicate either subarctic or temperate summer temperatures (Böcher 1995).

Except in a few cases – the carabid *Diacheila matthewsi* (Böcher 1995) and a couple of undescribed staphylinids, which probably represent extinct species – all the named insect taxa have been referred to living species. Thus once more the longevity of insect species is demonstrated (Coope 1970, 1978, 1979; Buckland and Coope 1991). A few of the vascular plant remains are referred to extinct species: *L. groenlandii, M. arctogale* and *Aracites globosa* (Figure 9). The

(a)   (b)

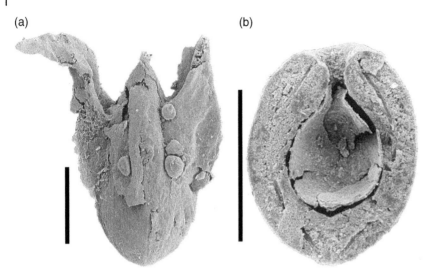

Figure 9 Scanning electron microscope photographs of fruits from extinct plants from the Kap København Formation in North Greenland. (a) *Myrica arctogale*. (b) *Aracites globosa*. Scale bars: 1 mm. *Source:* From Bennike (1990).

latter is an enigmatic species that may belong to the family Araceae (Aalto et al. 1992).

The insect fauna and the flora of the Kap København Formation show a high degree of similarity with that from the 0.5–1 million years older Beaufort Formation on Meighen Island, Arctic Canadian Archipelago (Matthews, 1977, 1979a, 1979b; Matthews and Telka 1977; Matthews and Fyles 2000; Elias and Matthews 2002; Elias et al. 2006). For instance, at both sites the genus *Bembidion* and the subgenus *Cryobius* of *Pterostichus* (Carabidae) are predominant. There are, however, important differences as well. For instance, the genus *Carabus* is represented by several species on Meighen Island but not found in the Kap København sediments. These, in return, contain a species of *Cicindela*, a genus not represented in the Beaufort Formation. A strange absence in the Kap København Formation is that of *Amara alpina*, so common both in last interglacial sites from Greenland and in the Beaufort Formation (Matthews and Fyles 2000; Elias and Matthews 2002).

The dating of the Kap København Formation is based on a number of different methods, of which the most important are biostratigraphy, palaeomagnetic analyses and amino acid analyses. The biostratigraphically most important groups are foraminifers, ostracods, molluscs and mammals. The occurrence of the extinct rabbit *Hypolagus* sp. and the extant hare *Lepus* sp. in member B3 is particularly important. These genera co-occurred in North America during the time period from ~2.3 to 2.0 million years BP (Repenning et al. 1987). This is in good agreement with the latest age estimate based on benthic foraminifera, which indicate an age for member B of ~2 Ma (Bennike et al. 2010), perhaps corresponding to marine isotope stage 77 and one of the so-called super interglacials that have been documented in Arctic Russia (Melles et al. 2012).

The Île de France Formation

At the type locality the lower part of the Île de France Formation in North-East Greenland is heterogeneous, consisting of diamicton, fine-grained sand, homogenous silt and rhythmically layered silt and sand. This part contains no macro-fossils and was presumably laid down in a glaciomarine environment. The upper part of the sequence is more homogenous and consists of bioturbated silt and fine sand with scattered shell fragments of marine molluscs. At a few sites on northern Île de France sand with organic detritus is found (Bennike et al. 2002a).

Twenty-four species of marine molluscs have been found and the fauna includes *Trichotropis bicarinata*, which formerly as a fossil in Greenland has only been reported from the Kap København Formation (Bennike 1989), and *Astarte alaskensis*, which is not known from other sites in Greenland. Diatoms are represented by 99 species, of which the vast majority are marine species, but the diatom flora also includes some freshwater taxa. The latter as well as colonies of the fresh water algae *Pediastrum* sp. and *Botryococcus* sp. indicate some outflow of freshwater. The diatom flora comprises *Fossula arctica*, which is associated with sea ice and is only known from the Arctic.

The marine fauna show that the sediments were deposited at sub-littoral water depths on the inner shelf. The molluscs comprise warmth demanding species such as *A. islandica*, which shows that the water temperature was considerably higher than at present. The dinoflagellate cysts indicate polar to sub-polar environments.

In addition to remains of marine organisms and microscopic freshwater algae scattered fragments of wood and bark are found, as well as rare seeds and fruits. This material comprises *Picea*, probably *P. mariana*, *Thuja* sp. and *M. trifoliata*. These sparse remains may imply that the adjoining land areas were covered by coniferous forest or forest tundra.

The Île de France Formation may have been deposited during the Olduvai normal polarity subchron at 1.95–1.78 Ma, based on palaeomagnetic studies and data from benthic foraminifera (Bennike et al. 2010). This means that it is slightly younger than member B of the Kap København Formation.

The Store Koldewey Formation

The Store Koldewey Formation is found at ~120 m above sea level and consists of bioturbated marine silt and fine sand (Bennike et al. 2010). The marine mollusc fauna comprises 13 species of bivalves and 5–6 species of gastropods. The presence of *M. balthica* and *C. kurriana* indicates lowered salinity, perhaps near a river outlet.

At two localities thin layers with species-rich, well-preserved remains of non-marine macrofossils were found. The fossil flora comprises remains of trees (*Larix* sp., *Betula* sect. *Albae* sp. and *Alnus* sp.), shrubs and dwarf-shrubs (*Arctostaphylos uva-ursi*, *Andromeda polifolia* and *E. nigrum*) and herbs (*Viola* sp., *Saxifraga oppositifolia* and *S. microcarpus*), which indicate the presence of forest-tundra vegetation in the region. The presence of several species of macro-limnophytes and statoblasts of the freshwater bryozoan *C. mucedo* testifies to the presence of various freshwater biotopes. Coleoptera remains were scarce and represented by five taxa that are also found in the Kap København Formation. Only a single taxon, the circumpolar, low arctic-temperate rove beetle *Tachinus elongatus* was identified to species level.

The moss remains from Store Koldewey were discussed by Hedenäs and Bennike (2009). A total of ~50 species were found, of which several are southern extralimital species. Two of them, *Hamatocaulis vernicosus* and *Hygrohypnum montanum*, do not occur in Greenland at present. They are the only examples of non-Greenland moss species found as fossils in Greenland.

It was suggested that the age of the Store Koldewey Formation is similar to the age of the Île de France Formation by Bennike et al. (2010), mainly based on palaeo-magnetic studies and data from benthic foraminifera.

Other Possible Early Quaternary Occurrences

At several sites in northern Greenland occurrences of reworked wood that have yielded non-finite radiocarbon ages have been located (Bennike 1990, 1998, 2000b). These occurrences may represent remains of Early Quaternary interglacial forests. The largest concentrations of wood are found in Washington Land, where wood is found at elevations up to 600 m above sea level (Bennike 2000b). At none of these sites have sedimentary deposits been found in connection with the wood.

Marine Oxygen Isotope Stage 13

Analyses of pollen and spores from a marine sediment core (ODP 646) indicate that southern Greenland was characterized by shrub-tundra vegetation (de Vernal and Hillaire-Marcel 2008) during marine oxygen isotope stage 13, which is dated to ~500 ka.

Marine Oxygen Isotope Stage 11

Analyses of samples from core ODP 646 indicate that marine oxygen isotope stage 11 was characterized by a much reduced, nearly vanished Greenland ice sheet, with boreal coniferous forest with abundant *Picea* and some *Abies* in southern Greenland (de Vernal and Hillaire-Marcel 2008). The MIS 11 interglacial is different from other Middle Quaternary interglacials because of its near 50 000-year duration. It is dated to ~400 ka. The dominance of *Picea* from the beginning to the end of the interglacial period suggests the presence of forest vegetation throughout the entire interval, at least over southern Greenland. The base of MIS 11 is marked by higher proportions of shrub and herb pollen, indicating more open vegetation and a cooler climate, but *Picea* was probably already present regionally. Detailed examination of the *Picea* pollen indicates the occurrence of several species, among which *Picea*

abies dominated. *Picea abies* is presently common in northern Europe.

Studies of the basal silty-rich ice from the 2 km long DYE-3 ice core from south-central Greenland showed that the ice contains remains of DNA molecules that could be assigned to *Picea*, *Pinus*, *Alnus*, Taxaceae, Poaceae, Asteraceae and Fabaceae. The presence of these plant taxa indicates open northern boreal forests, very different from today's Arctic environment (Willerslev et al. 2007). These taxa were identified by independent laboratories; in addition, *Achillea*, *Betula*, *Cerastium*, *Festuca*, *Luzula*, *Plantago*, *Poa*, *Saxifraga*, *Symphoricarpos* and *Populus* were recorded but lacked identity between independent laboratories. Most of these genera are common in northern boreal forests. The ice also contained arthropod DNA from Lepidoptera and probably Coleoptera, Diptera, Arachnida and Nymphalidae. The age of the DNA molecules from DYE-3 is uncertain, but it is possible that they correlate with marine oxygen isotope stage 11.

Marine Oxygen Isotope Stage 7

During MIS 7, the penultimate interglacial period, sea-surface temperatures off southern Greenland were lower than those of MIS 13, and the pollen and spore content of sediment remained lower. The pollen assemblages are dominated by herb taxa, notably Poaceae and Cyperaceae, suggesting the development of tundra in southern Greenland (de Vernal and Hillaire-Marcel 2008).

Marine Oxygen Isotope Stage 5e, the Last Interglacial

Southern Greenland. Pollen concentrations in samples from MIS 5e from core ODP 646 are five times higher than in Holocene samples, and the concentrations of fern spores are also higher. The assemblages are characterized by dominant *Alnus* and abundant spores of *Osmunda*. In samples from sediment core HU-90-013-013 collected near ODP 646, more detailed analyses of MIS 5e document the pollen succession. A rapid increase of *Alnus* occurred during an early phase of MIS 5e, which suggests rapid development of shrub tundra after ice retreat. A subsequent increase of *Osmunda* represents a unique event in the last million years. It suggests the development of dense fern vegetation over southern Greenland under climatic conditions not unlike those of the modern boreal forest. Towards the end of MIS 5e, pollen and spore influxes decreased and at the same time herb percentages increased, indicating a change to herb tundra resulting from regional cooling at the onset of ice growth (de Vernal and Hillaire-Marcel 2008).

Jameson Land. Deposits from the last interglacial are found along the south and west coast of Jameson Land in central East Greenland (Figures 1 and 5c and d). Most widespread are sandy, silty and clayey sediments, which were deposited in shallow marine water along the coast, partly in connection with deltas, in the coastal zone and in rivers. The deposits often contain shells of marine molluscs, and the fauna includes *M. edulis*, a warmth-demanding southern extralimital species (Vosgerau et al. 1994). At many sites layers and lenses rich in organic detritus are found. The detritus consists mainly of washed together remains of plants that grew in the catchment area, but it also contains remains of insects and other invertebrates. The plant and animal remains give a regional picture of the non-marine biotas.

The fossil flora includes many species of dwarf shrubs and other woody plants (Figure 10). Most noteworthy are common remains of *Betula pubescens*, which probably formed shrub or low forest on sheltered sites. At present, *B. pubescens* is confined to southernmost Greenland, whereas *B. nana*, today common in Jameson Land, has not been found in interglacial deposits in East Greenland. Samples from many localities contain remains of *Alnus* cf. *crispa*, which grows in southwestern Greenland and North America at present. Another woody plant that grows in southernmost Greenland at present is *Cornus canadensis*, fruits of which are rare in the fossil assemblages. Dwarf shrubs are represented by no less than 11 species, of which the majority is ericaceous. Remains of *E. nigrum*, *V. uliginosum*, *Arctostaphylos alpina* and *D. octopetala* are particularly common, whereas remains of *Cassiope tetragona* and *Harrimanella hypnoides* are rarer. Leaves of *S. herbacea* are common; this tiny woody plant is characteristic of snow beds. Herbaceous plants

Figure 10 Scanning electron microscope photographs of plant remains from last interglacial deposits in Jameson Land, East Greenland. (a) Catkin scale of *Alnus* cf. *crispa*. (b) Leaf of *Dryas octopetala*. (c) Leaf of *Vaccinium uliginosum*. (d) Endocarp of *Arctostaphylos alpina*. (e) Leaf of *Phyllodoce coerulea*. Scale bars: 1 mm. *Source:* From Bennike and Böcher (1994).

are represented by, for example, *Melandrium apetalum* and *O. digyna*, which are typical arctic plants that are common in the region today.

The fossil interglacial flora from Jameson Land is also rich in remains of bryophytes. The bryophyte flora is diverse with more than 60 identified taxa and it includes some southern extralimital species such as *Climacium dendroides* and *Sphagnum warnstorfii* (Hedenäs 1994). Abundant remains of Polytrichaceae and *Racomitrium* show that unstable soil with sparse vascular plant cover was important.

The fossil interglacial fauna of Coleoptera comprises almost 25 taxa of beetles, which is highly surprising considering that Jameson Land's present beetle fauna only comprises three species. In contrast to the flora of vascular plants, the beetle fauna comprised several species that are absent from the modern fauna of Greenland. On the other hand, many of Greenland's extant species are not represented as fossils in the interglacial fauna. The fauna comprises *A. alpina* (see below) and *Otiorhynchus nodosus* (Figure 11).

The latter is a typical example of a Palaearctic species (Figure 12, see Plate section) that lived in Greenland during the last interglacial and the Holocene. The same applies to, for example, *B. fasciatus* and *Simplocaria metallica*.

All beetle species recorded live in the sub-arctic bioclimatic zone (Bennike and Böcher 1994; Böcher 2012). The difference between the interglacial and the Holocene fauna indicates that chance dispersal plays a large role in determining which species colonized Greenland during the last and the present interglacial period. Half of the species are Palaearctic, and hence they must have immigrated to Greenland from Europe.

At a single site head capsules of midges were found. Some of these head capsules come from species that live in rivers – a biotope that is otherwise unrepresented in the palaeoecological data (Bennike et al. 2000). Furthermore, it may be mentioned that the fauna includes the freshwater bryozoan *C. mucedo*, which probably lives in south-west Greenland at present (Fredskild 1983).

(a)   (b)   (c)

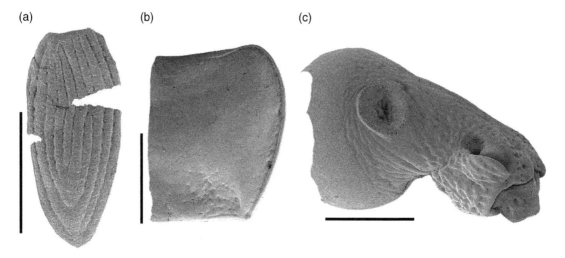

Figure 11 Scanning electron microscope photographs of beetle remains from last interglacial deposits at Narsaarssuk near Thule air base, North-West Greenland (a, b) and Jameson Land in East Greenland (c). (a) Elytron of *Isochnus arcticus*. (b) Half pronotum of *Amara alpina*. (c) Head of *Otiorhynchus nodosus*. Scale bars: 1 mm. *Source:* From Böcher (1989) and Bennike and Böcher (1992).

(a)

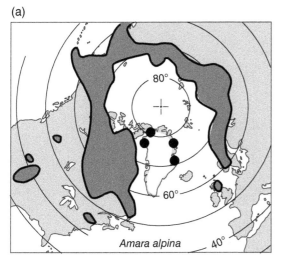

(b)

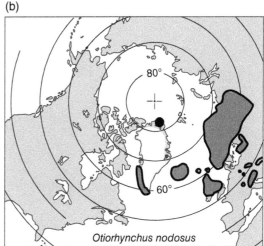

Figure 12 Maps of the northern part of the Earth, showing the present-day range of the ground beetle *Amara alpina* and the weevil *Otiorhynchus nodosus*. The dots show fossil finds in Greenland, assumed to come from the last interglacial. Modern distributions according to Böcher (1989) and Bennike and Böcher (1994). (See colour plate section for colour representation of this figure.)

Some of the most warmth-demanding plant species from the interglacial layers are *B. pubescens*, *Alnus* cf. *crispa* and *C. canadensis* (Figure 13, see Plate section), and the flora and insect fauna indicate sub-arctic conditions, implying a mean summer temperature at least 5 °C higher than today and a displacement of the sub-arctic bioclimatic zone from southernmost Greenland at least 1000 km northwards. The temperature estimate corresponds with results from studies of an ice core from Renland Ice Cap, an isolated ice cap west of Jameson Land (Johnsen et al. 1992; Vinther et al. 2009).

The deposits from Jameson Land have been dated using a number of different methods, the most important being luminescence dating, which shows that the deposits can be referred to the last interglacial stage, or marine isotope stage 5e, which has been dated to the time interval 115 to 130 000 years BP (Funder et al. 1998).

The Thule area. Deposits from the last interglacial period are also fairly widespread in the Thule area, where marine, coastal-near deposits

consisting of gravel, sand, silt and clay are found. The marine fauna includes the barnacle *B. balanoides* that does not occur so far north today (Kelly et al. 1999). Last interglacial lake sediments with the southern extralimital midge *Chaoborus* have also been found in the area (McFarlin et al. 2018).

One of the coastal cliff sections contains remains of non-marine plants and animals (Böcher 1989, 2012; Bennike and Böcher 1992; Brodersen and Bennike 2003; Hedenäs and Bennike 2003). Some of these species, such as the mosses *Pleurozium schreberi* and *Conardia compacta*, the shrub *Betula* sect. *Nanae*, the clubmoss *S. selaginoides* and the invertebrates *Simocephalus vetulus* and *C. mucedo*, are southern extralimital (Bennike and Böcher 1992; Hedenäs and Bennike 2003). The mean temperature for the warmest month of the year was ~4 °C higher than at present. The layers at Thule are primarily dated by means of luminescence dating.

Remains of the arctic/alpine carabid beetle *A. alpina* have been reported from last interglacial layers from both the Thule area (Figure 11)

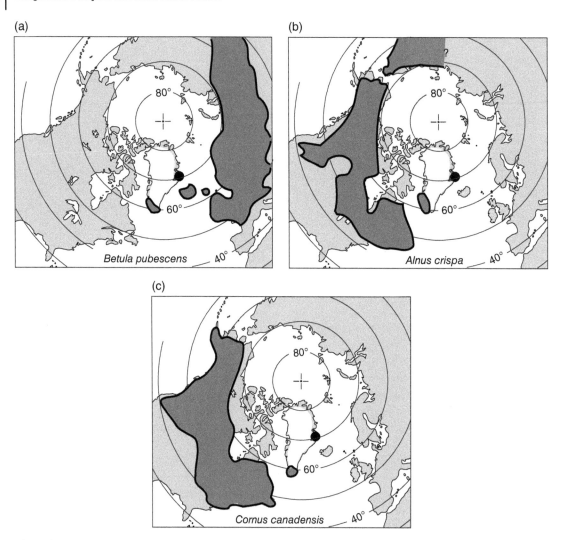

Figure 13 Maps of the northern parts of the Earth, showing the present-day geographical ranges of (a) *Betula pubescens*, (b) *Alnus crispa* and (c) *Cornus canadensis*. Remains of these species have been found in layers from the last interglacial stage in Jameson Land, East Greenland (black dots). *Source:* From Bennike and Böcher (1994; 1996). (See colour plate section for colour representation of this figure.)

and from Jameson Land; in addition, fragments believed to be reworked from last interglacial layers have been recorded from Zackenberg (Christiansen et al. 2002) and Washington Land (Bennike et al. 2000; Bennike 2002). The finds indicate a wide geographical range of *A. alpina* in Greenland at that time. The species is absent

from Greenland today, but has otherwise a wide circumpolar distribution, and it is found as close to North-West Greenland as Devon Island in high arctic Canada (Figure 12; Lindroth 1957, 1968; Böcher 1989; Allan V. Morgan, personal communication). It is difficult to understand why the species is missing in modern Greenland.

One explanation could be that temperatures during the Holocene thermal maximum were not high enough to allow the species to migrate from Canada (Böcher 1989). The occurrence of another Holarctic species, *Isochnus arcticus* (Curculionidae; Figures 11 and 12) in sediments from both the Thule area and Jameson Land also favours this explanation (Bennike and Böcher 1992). Remains of the seed-bug *Nysius groenlandicus* have also been found in last interglacial sediments from North-West, North and East Greenland (Bennike and Böcher 1992, 1994; Bennike et al. 2000).

The most remarkable zoogeographical characteristic of the interglacial beetle fauna is the total absence of exclusively Nearctic taxa of today, whereas Palaearctic and circumpolar species account for 67 and 33%, respectively. This is the same situation as found in modern Greenland, but in an even more extreme version. Accordingly, the fossil beetle fauna demonstrates that even at the beginning of the previous interglacial a similar situation (ice-rafting?) might have occurred, capable of transporting European taxa over the North Atlantic to Greenland (Bennike and Böcher 1994; Böcher 2012).

The composition of the interglacial fauna deviated strongly from the modern. For instance, two species of Coccinellidae are found both as fossils and living, but the species are different. Four species of Carabidae are found today, but three different species are recorded as interglacial fossils. This striking dissimilarity presumably reflects the small chance of successful long-distance dispersal from Europe.

Warming Land. Dating of a *Salix* twig from a sample of organic detritus found in Warming Land, North Greenland yielded a non-finite radiocarbon age. The fossil flora includes *D. octopetala*, *S. arctica*, *S. oppositifolia*, *O. digyna* and *M. apetalum* and is similar to the present flora of the region. In addition to plant remains, the assemblage comprises a mandible of *Lepidurus arcticus* and five droppings of a small rodent, probably lemming (Meldgaard and Bennike 1989). The plant and animal remains imply interglacial conditions and they may date from the last interglacial period.

Washington Land. Dating of leaves of *Dryas integrifolia* from a peat deposit in southern Washington Land gave non-finite ages (Bennike and Jepsen 2000). Radiocarbon dating and optically stimulated luminescence dating of further samples from what is believed to be the same deposits gave Holocene ages, and it is possible that both interglacial and Holocene material is present at the site (Bennike 2002). Further work is needed to clarify this issue. The fossil flora comprises *E. nigrum* that does not grow this far north at present. Herbaceous plants are represented by, for example, *S. oppositifolia*, *P. viviparum*, *O. digyna* and *Ranunculus hyperboreus*, which are all found in the region today (Bennike and Jepsen 2000).

From Lafayette Bugt, western Washington Land, dating of a sample of *D. integrifolia* leaves from thin layers rich in organic detritus gave an age of ~4000 ka BP. In addition to *D. integrifolia* the sample was dominated by *S. arctica*, *Potentilla* sp., *S. oppositifolia* and *Carex stans*, all common in the region today. However, the sample also comprised two achenes of the macrolimnophyte *P. filiformis*, which does not occur so far north today, and a few fragments of the ground beetle *A. alpina*, which does not occur in Greenland today. The remains of *P. filiformis* and *A. alpina* may originate from unknown interglacial deposits in the area and a last interglacial age has been proposed (Bennike et al. 2000; Bennike 2002).

Blåsø, Kronprins Christian Land. Another site with organic detritus has been reported from North-east Greenland (Bennike and Weidick 2001). A sample of *D. integrifolia* was dated to the Mid-Holocene, but the fossil assemblage comprised oospores of the charophyte *Nitella* sp. and achenes of *P. filiformis*, which do not occur this far north today. The remains of these taxa may have been reworked from unknown interglacial deposits.

Skallingen, Kronprins Christian Land. In Lille Sneha Sø north of Blåsø interglacial plant and animal remains have been discovered. The interglacial flora and fauna include several species that do not live so far north today, such as *Tolypella* cf. *nidifica*, *P. filiformis*, the ostracod *Bradleystrandesia reticulata*, the tad-pole shrimp *L. arcticus*, an unidentified dytiscid water beetle and the small bivalve *Pisidium* sp. Several age determinations of *Scorpidium scorpioides* gave pre-Holocene ages (Wagner and Bennike 2015). In nearby Trifna Sø a similar flora and fauna was found and a radiocarbon age determination of stems of the bryophyte *S. scorpioides* gave an age > 52 ka (Kusch et al. 2019). We suggest that the remains from Skallingen are of last interglacial age.

Kap København, Peary Land. A fragment of a strongly weathered reindeer *Rangifer tarandus* antler found at the ground near Kap København gave a non-finite age, and a last interglacial age has been proposed (Meldgaard and Bennike 1989).

Zackenberg. A fragment of a mesosternum of *A. alpina* from an Early Holocene delta deposit at Zackenberg must have been reworked from interglacial, possibly Eemian, sediments (Christiansen et al. 2002).

Early Weichselian Interstadial Deposits

In addition to interglacial deposits, glacial and non-glacial deposits that are referred to marine isotope stages 5d to 5a are also found along the coast of Jameson Land in East Greenland (Funder et al. 1998). The Hugin Sø Interstadial, which is correlated with marine isotope stade 5c, represents an ice-free period during the early part of the Weichselian. The vegetation appears to have consisted of herbs and bryophytes only. Remains of *S. oppositifolia* are common, and seeds of *Papaver* sect. *Scapiflora* also occur (Bennike

and Böcher 1994). These species are found all over Greenland, but play an increasingly larger role towards the north, and none of them have been found in deposits from the last interglacial. The only beetle species found is *A. alpina*, one of the most cold-adapted ground beetles on Earth. It has been proposed that the mean temperature for the warmest month of the year was 3–4 °C lower than at present (Bennike and Böcher 1994), which is in accordance with the marine mollusc fauna that shows similarities to modern faunas from North Greenland (Funder et al. 1998). In contrast, the fossil bryophyte flora from the Hugin Sø Interstadial comprises several warmth-demanding species such as *Amphidium mougeotii* and *Polytrichastrum longisetum*, which indicate a slightly warmer climate than at present (Hedenäs 1994). However, it is possible that some of the bryophyte material is reworked from Eemian deposits.

The Last Glacial Maximum in Greenland

During the past decades it has become clear that the Greenland Ice Sheet was much larger than at present during the last glacial maximum, at ~21 ka BP. In the north-west, the Greenland ice sheet coalesced with the Innuitian Ice Sheet that covered the Canadian Arctic Archipelago (Blake et al. 1992; Kelly and Bennike 1992; Bennike and Björck 2002). Studies of sediment cores and detailed bathymetrical surveys show that the margin of the Greenland Ice Sheet reached the edge of the continental shelf both in South-East Greenland (Mienert et al. 1992), in central West Greenland (Ó Cofaigh et al. 2013), in North-West Greenland (Dowdeswell et al. 2014; Slabon et al. 2016) and probably also in East Greenland (Winkelmann et al. 2010; Arndt et al. 2017; Laberg et al. 2017; Arndt 2018). In South Greenland, geophysical modelling implies that the margin of the ice sheet reached the shelf edge and even the highest mountains were glaciated (Bennike et al. 2002b).

Jameson Land in central East Greenland is characterized by deep weathering and little glacial scouring, and Funder (1979) suggested that this area was ice free during the last glacial maximum. On the basis of surface exposure dating of glacial erratics, Håkansson et al. (2009) questioned this restricted extent, but Funder et al. (2011) maintained that Jameson Land was ice free. New surface exposure dating of bedrock surfaces in Jameson Land indicates that the area was ice-covered during the last glacial maximum, but it was deglaciated already at ~18–21 ka (Håkansson et al. 2011). A major expansion of the Greenland ice sheet during the last glacial maximum is in accordance with results from ice core studies (Vinther et al. 2009; Simonsen et al. 2019). The temperature minimum during the last ice age is dated to ~25 ka BP in Greenland, at which time the mean annual temperature was ~23° lower than today (Dahl-Jensen et al. 1998).

Chronology of the Last Deglaciation

A lot of data has been acquired that throw light on the chronology of the deglaciation of the ice-free land parts of Greenland and a chronology for the last recession of the Inland Ice was proposed by Bennike and Björck et al. (2002). Their chronology was mainly based on radiocarbon dated shells from raised marine deposits. In addition to shell dates, the ages of algae, basal peat, basal gyttja, remains of land plants and drift wood were used. Most of the ice-free parts of Greenland were deglaciated in the Early Holocene, between 11.5 and 8 ka BP, but in the far south some small areas became ice free during the late glacial period. During the past years, a number of studies have used surface exposure dating, which has improved our understanding of the patterns of ice retreat (e.g. Kelley et al. 2015; Sinclair et al. 2016), but the chronology suggested by Bennike and Björck et al. (2002) is still valid.

Another surprising result of surface exposure dating is that Greenland was apparently nearly ice free for extended periods during the Quaternary (Schaefer et al. 2016).

Late Glacial and Early to Mid-Holocene Flora and Fauna

Late glacial sediments from a locality in southernmost Greenland have been analysed for pollen (Björck et al. 2002). Not surprisingly, the concentration of pollen is extremely low and a large proportion of the pollen grains must be regarded as being long-distance transported. Pollen of Poaceae, *Sagina* type, *Saxifraga caespitosa* type and *Saxifraga stellaris* type presumably come from the local vegetation, and the same apply to a few seeds of *Minuartia* sp. and *Saxifraga* cf. *oppositifolia*. The vegetation probably consisted of mosses and scattered pioneer herbs.

Deposits from the earlier Holocene from West and East Greenland also contain remains of bryophytes and herbs only, and the herbs represented are species that can tolerate low summer temperatures and unstable soils (Fredskild 1985; Bennike et al. 1999; Bennike 2000a; Wagner et al. 2010; Bennike and Wagner 2012; Wagner and Bennike 2012). The first woody plant that appears to have immigrated to Greenland is *E. nigrum*, which was present from ~11000 years BP. It was soon followed by *S. herbacea*, known from 10800 years BP, and *V. uliginosum*, known from 10500 years BP. *Betula nana* arrived in Greenland at ~8800 years BP, *S. glauca* at ~8700 years BP and *Juniperus communis* at ~8400 years BP.

Chydorus arcticus is the most common and widespread cladoceran in Greenland, and the first species to immigrate after the last deglaciation, with the oldest remains dated to ~13800 years BP. The species lived in South Greenland during the Younger Dryas. *Daphnia* arrived in South Greenland ~12500 years ago. *Acroperus harpae* was also an early immigrant to South Greenland, but it disappeared during the Younger Dryas, and reappeared in the Early Holocene (Bennike and Björck 2000).

Among insects, head capsules of chironomid larvae are found in late glacial deposits (Bennike and Björck 2000) and remains of the caddis fly *Apatania zonella* are found in Early Holocene deposits (Bennike et al. 2000). Remains of the seed bug *N. groenlandicus* have been found in a fairly large number of deposits, and the species was an early immigrant to Greenland (Bennike et al. 2000; Böcher et al. 2012), although it has not been recorded from earliest Holocene deposits. Remains of water beetles are quite common in lake deposits and *Colymbetes dolabratus* remains have been recovered from Early Holocene deposits in both West and East Greenland. The ground beetle *Bembidion grapii* is widespread in southern Greenland and remains of it have been found in Early Holocene deposits in both East and West Greenland (Böcher and Bennike 1996; Böcher et al. 2012). The pill beetle *S. metallica* has also been found in Early Holocene deposits in West Greenland. A find dated to ~9920 years BP is the oldest record of a terrestrial beetle from Holocene Greenland (Böcher et al. 2012). From Mid-Holocene deposits specimens of *Rutidosoma globulus* have recently been recorded; this is a species that is extremely rare in nowadays Greenland

(Böcher et al. 2012). Finds in East Greenland of the leaf beetle *Phratora* cf. *polaris* in deposits dated to between 8700 and 7900 years BP are most surprising. This species, which is unknown in present day Greenland, is probably extinct (Böcher and Bennike 1996; Bennike et al. 1999). Mid-Holocene insect faunas are well known from a few investigations of midden layers in central West Greenland, with remarkably well-preserved remains (Figures 5e and 14; Böcher and Fredskild 1993).

Among vertebrates, the known temporal range of the small fish *Gasterosteus aculeatus* extends back to ~10 ka, that of reindeer *R. tarandus* to ~9 ka, that of wolf *Canis lupus* to ~8 ka and that of musk-ox *Ovibos moschatus* to ~5 ka (Meldgaard 1986; Bennike 1997, 2013; Bennike and Björck 2002; Campos et al. 2010).

Discussion and Conclusions

For over 100 years an intense debate has been going on among biologists and geologists about the history of the plants and animals on the North Atlantic islands. The question is whether the species survived the last ice age in ice-free areas, or

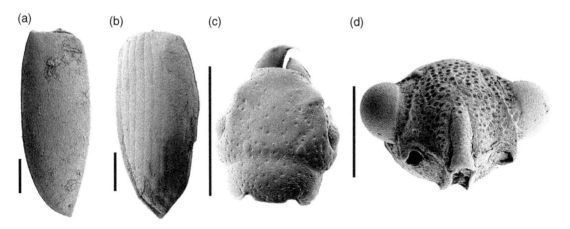

(a) (b) (c) (d)

Figure 14 Scanning electron microscope photographs of remains of insect remains from Mid-Holocene midden deposits from Qeqertasussuk, West Greenland. (a, b) Elytra of *Hydroporus morio* and *S. metallica*. (c, d) Heads of *Micralymna brevilingue* and *Nysius groenlandicus*. Scale bars: 0.5 mm. *Source:* From Böcher and Fredskild (1993).

if they arrived after the last deglaciation. The discussion was opened by the Danish botanist Eugen Warming when he proposed that most vascular plants could have survived the ice age in Greenland (Warming 1888). This was strongly opposed by the Swedish geologist A.G. Nathorst, who believed that most species of vascular plants immigrated after the last ice age (Nathorst 1892).

The debate is still very much alive. Among the botanists who in more recent times have advocated most warmly for survival is Tyge Böcher. Thus he wrote: 'Is it a too daring assumption that the (tree) birch held its own . . . in the lowlands on sunny sides of the mountains during the last Glacial Age? If the Greenland birch (*Betula pubescens* coll.) demonstrably constitutes a special form cycle which is not identical with Icelandic or American races, this will highly strengthen such a survival hypothesis' (Böcher 1956). Tree birch is one of the most warmth demanding plant species in Greenland, and is only found in the far south of Greenland. If it survived the last ice age in Greenland, this would mean that ice-free areas were present and that the climate was not much different from the present. Tyge Böcher also proposed that the dwarf birch could be an ice age survivor. Even though dwarf birch is far less warmth demanding than tree birch, it also has a northern range limit in Greenland, and from a Greenland point of view it cannot be considered a cold adapted plant. *Betula* species are prolific pollen producers and their former arrival at a certain area in Greenland is usually marked by an abrupt increase in pollen values. It is now clear from palaeobotanical studies of lake deposits that all three Greenlandic birch species are Holocene immigrants (Fredskild 1991).

Among zoologists that have advocated for survival on the North Atlantic Islands the Swedish entomologist Carl Lindroth must be mentioned. Originally Lindroth suggested that many beetle species had colonized the Faroe Islands, Iceland and Greenland over a land bridge, which he suggested had existed after the last ice age. When geological investigations in the North Atlantic showed that such a land bridge could not have existed this late, Lindroth proposed that the beetles had colonized the North Atlantic Islands in interglacial time and survived the last ice age (Lindroth 1957, 1973).

Most palaeoecologists have opposed the idea of survival. Johs Iversen, who worked out the first pollen diagram from Greenland, proposed that only the most hardy plants survived (Iversen 1954), a point of view followed by Fredskild who continued Iversen's work (Fredskild 1973) and by Ole Bennike (Figure 15,

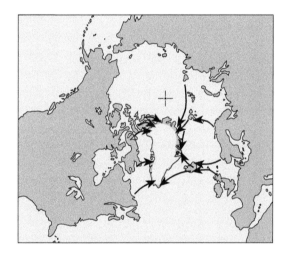

Figure 15 Maps of the Earth's northern parts with arrows that show immigration routes to the North Atlantic islands. The routes are mainly suggested from the modern-day geographical ranges of the species. However, we know from historical sources that Norse people sailed to the North Atlantic islands from North-West Europe and hunters travelled with their families to Greenland from Canada as late as the 1860s. In 1937 large flocks of migrating fieldfares *Turdus pilaris* were blown from Norway to Greenland where they established a small breeding population. Surprisingly many species have colonized the North Atlantic islands from North-West Europe. The distance between the islands is long, but the islands form stepping stones along the route *Source:* From Bennike (1999). (See colour plate section for colour representation of this figure.)

see Plate section; Bennike 1999). Among zoologists, Russell Coope and Paul Buckland from Britain opposed Lindroth's ideas about survival, as almost all the Greenland beetle species are warmth demanding and could hardly survive the last ice age in Greenland (Coope 1986). Thus they concluded that most beetle species immigrated after the last ice age. In a recent paper, Jens Böcher suggested that the importance of microclimate and the number of sun hours during the Arctic summer have not been sufficiently considered when discussing survival contra immigration, and he contended that some hardy beetle species and the seed bug *N. groenlandicus* could be survivors (Böcher 2012).

With respect to Iceland, Rundgren and Ingólfsson (1999) suggested that survival was supplemented by renewed immigration during each interglacial period. The interglacial floras and faunas show that rich biota existed in suitable biotopes on the North Atlantic islands during the Quaternary interglacials. However, the interglacial occurrences do not prove continuity, as pointed out by Buckland and Panagiotakopulu (2010). Anyway, it is clear that the old discussion about survival contra immigration is far from dead.

References

Aalto, M., Eriksson, B., and Hirvas, H. (1992). Naakenavaara interglacial – a till covered peat deposit in western Finnish Lapland. *Bulletin of the Geological Society of Finland* 64: 169–181.

Andrews, J.T., Hardarsdóttir, J., Helgadóttir, G. et al. (2000). The N and W Iceland shelf: insights into the Last Glacial Maximum ice extent and deglaciation based on acoustic stratigraphy and basal radiocarbon AMS dates. *Quaternary Science Reviews* 19: 619–631.

Arndt, J.E. (2018). Marine geomorphological record of Ice Sheet development in East Greenland since the Last Glacial Maximum. *Journal of Quaternary Science* 33: 853–864.

Arndt, J.E., Jokat, W., and Dorschel, B. (2017). The last glaciation and deglaciation of the Northeast Greenland continental shelf revealed by hydroacoustic data. *Quaternary Science Reviews* 160: 45–56.

Áskelsson, J. (1938). Kvartärgeologischen Studien auf Island II. Interglaziale Pflanzenablagerungen. *Meddelelser fra Dansk Geologisk Forening* 9: 300–319.

Bennike, O. (1989). *Trichotropis bicarinata* (Gastropoda) from the Plio-Pleistocene Kap København Formation, new to the fossil fauna of Greenland. *Mededelingen van de Werkgroep voor Tertiaire en Kwartaire Geologie* 26: 137–143.

Bennike, O. (1990). The Kap København Formation: stratigraphy and palaeobotany of a Plio-Pleistocene sequence in Peary Land, North Greenland. *Meddelelser om Grønland, Geoscience* 23: 85.

Bennike, O. (1997). Quaternary vertebrates from Greenland: a review. *Quaternary Science Reviews* 16: 899–909.

Bennike, O. (1998). Late Cenozoic wood from Washington Land, North Greenland. *Geology of Greenland Survey Bulletin* 180: 155–158.

Bennike, O. (1999). Colonisation of Greenland after the last ice age: a review. *Polar Record* 35: 323–336.

Bennike, O. (2000a). Palaeoecological studies of Holocene lake sediments from West Greenland. *Palaeogeography, Palaeoclimatology, Palaeoecology* 155: 285–304.

Bennike, O. (2000b). Notes on the late Cenozoic history of the Washington Land area, western North Greenland. *Geology of Greenland Survey Bulletin* 186: 29–34.

Bennike, O. (2002). Late Quaternary history of Washington land, North Greenland. *Boreas* 31: 260–272.

Bennike, O. (2010). Palaeoecology of Skálafjørður, the Faroe Islands. *Annales Societatis Scientiarum Færoensis, Supplementum* 52: 244–258.

Bennike, O. (2013). Radiocarbon dating of musk-ox (*Ovibos moschatus*) bones from the Thule region, North-West Greenland. *Polar Record* https://doi.org/10.1017/S0032247413000193.

Bennike, O. and Björck, S. (2000). Lake sediment coring in South Greenland in 1999. *Geology of Greenland Survey Bulletin* 186: 60–64.

Bennike, O. and Björck, S. (2002). Chronology of the last recession of the Greenland Ice Sheet. *Journal of Quaternary Science* 17: 211–217.

Bennike, O. and Böcher, J. (1992). Early Weichselian interstadial land biotas at Thule, Northwest Greenland. *Boreas* 21: 111–117.

Bennike, O. and Böcher, J. (1994). Land biotas of the last interglacial/glacial cycle on Jameson Land, East Greenland. *Boreas* 23: 479–487.

Bennike, O. and Jepsen, H.F. (2000). A new interglacial sequence from Washington Land, North Greenland. *Polar Research* 19: 267–270.

Bennike, O. and Wagner, B. (2012). Deglaciation chronology, sea-level changes and environmental changes from Holocene lake sediments of Germania Havn Sø, Sabine Ø, northeast Greenland. *Quaternary Research* 78: 103–109.

Bennike, O. and Weidick, A. (2001). Late Quaternary history around Nioghalvfjerdsfjorden and Jøkelbugten, North-East Greenland. *Boreas* 30: 205–227.

Bennike, O., Böcher, J., Konradi, P. et al. (1998). Macrofossil studies of lacustrine sediments from Skálafjørður, the Faroe Islands: preliminary results. *Fróðskaparrit* 46: 267–275.

Bennike, O., Björck, S., Böcher, J. et al. (1999). Early Holocene plant and animal remains from North-east Greenland. *Journal of Biogeography* 26: 667–677.

Bennike, O., Björck, S., Böcher, J., and Walker, I. (2000). The Quaternary arthropod fauna of Greenland: a review with new data. *Bulletin of the Geological Society of Denmark* 47: 111–134.

Bennike, O., Abrahamsen, N., Israelson, C. et al. (2002a). A multi-proxy study of Pliocene sediments from Île de France, North-East Greenland. *Palaeogeography, Palaeoclimatology, Palaeoecology* 186: 1–23.

Bennike, O., Björck, S., and Lambeck, K. (2002b). Estimates of South Greenland late-glacial ice limits from a new relative sea level curve. *Earth and Planetary Science Letters* 197: 171–186.

Bennike, O., Brodersen, K.P., Jeppesen, E., and Walker, I.R. (2004). Aquatic invertebrates and high-latitude palaeolimnology. In: Long-Term Environmental Change in Arctic and Antarctic Lakes (eds. R. Pienitz, M.S.V. Douglas and J.P. Smol), 159–186. Dordrecht: Springer.

Bennike, O., Sørensen, M., Fredskild, B. et al. (2008a). Late Quaternary environmental and cultural changes in the Wollaston Forland region, Northeast Greenland. *Advances in Ecological Research* 40: 45–79.

Bennike, O., Goodsite, M., and Heinemeier, J. (2008b). Palaeoecology of Holocene peat deposits from Nordvestø, north-west Greenland. *Journal of Paleolimnology* 40: 575–565.

Bennike, O., Knudsen, K.L., Abrahamsen, N. et al. (2010). Early Pleistocene sediments on Store Koldewey, northeast Greenland. *Boreas* 39: 603–619.

Bennike, O., Hedenäs, L., Lemdahl, G., and Wiberg-Larsen, P. (2018). A multiproxy study of Eemian deposits from Klaksvík, the Faroe Islands. *Boreas* 47: 106–113.

Björck, S., Bennike, O., Rosén, P. et al. (2002). Anomalously mild Younger Dryas summer conditions in South Greenland. *Geology* 30: 427–430.

Blake, W. Jr., Boucherle, M.M., Fredskild, B. et al. (1992). The geomorphological setting, glacial history and Holocene development of 'Kap Inglefield Sø', Inglefield Land, North-west Greenland. *Meddelelser om Grønland, Geoscience* 27: 42.

Böcher, T.W. (1956). Area limits and isolations of plants in relation to the physiography of the southern part of Greenland. *Meddelelser om Grønland* 124 (8): 40.

Böcher, J. (1988). The Coleoptera of Greenland. *Meddelelser om Grønland, Bioscience* 26: 100.

Böcher, J. (1989). First record of an interstadial insect from Greenland: *Amara alpina* (Paykull, 1790) (Coleoptera: Carabidae). *Boreas* 18: 1–4.

Böcher, J. (1995). Palaeoentomology of the Kap København Formation, a Plio-Pleistocene sequence in Peary Land, North Greenland. *Meddelelser om Grønland, Geoscience* 33: 82.

Böcher, J. (2012). Interglacial insects and their possible survival in Greenland during the last glacial stage. *Boreas* 41: 644–659.

Böcher, J. and Bennike, O. (1996). Early Holocene insect and plant remains from Jameson Land, East Greenland. *Boreas* 25: 187–193.

Böcher, J. and Fredskild, B. (1993). Plant and arthropod remains from the palaeo-Eskimo site on Qeqertasussuk, West Greenland. *Meddelelser om Grønland, Geoscience* 30: 35.

Böcher, J., Bennike, O., and Wagner, B. (2012). Holocene insect remains from South-Western Greenland. *Polar Research* 31: 18367.

Briner, J.P., Axford, Y., Forman, S.L. et al. (2007). Multiple generations of interglacial lake sediment preserved beneath the Laurentide ice sheet. *Geology* 35: 887–890.

Brodersen, K. and Bennike, O. (2003). Interglacial Chironomidae (Diptera) from Thule, Northwest Greenland: matching modern analogues to fossil assemblages. *Boreas* 32: 560–565.

Buckland, P.C. and Coope, G.R. (1991). A Bibliography and Literature Review of Quaternary Entomology, 85. Department of Archaeology and Prehistory, University of Sheffield: J.R. Collis Publications.

Buckland, P.C. and Panagiotakopulu, E. (2010). Reflections on North Atlantic island biogeography: a quaternary entomological view. *Annales Societas Scientarum Færoensis Supplementum* 52: 187–215.

Buckland, P.C., Perry, D.W., Gíslason, G.M., and Dugmore, A.J. (1986). The pre-Landnám Fauna of Iceland: a palaeontological contribution. *Boreas* 15: 173–184.

Campos, P.F., Willerslev, E., Sher, A. et al. (2010). Ancient DNA analyses exclude humans as the driving force behind late Pleistocene musk ox (*Ovibos*) population dynamics. *Proceedings of the National Academy of Sciences of the United States of America* 107: 5675–5680.

Caseldine, C. (2001). Changes in *Betula* in the Holocene record from Iceland – a palaeoclimatic record or evidence for early Holocene hybridisation? *Review of Palaeobotany and Palynology* 117: 139–152.

Caseldine, C., Langdon, P., and Holmes, N. (2006). Early Holocene climate variability and the timing of the Holocene thermal maximum (HTM) in northern Iceland. *Quaternary Science Reviews* 25: 2314–2331.

Christiansen, H.H., Bennike, O., Böcher, J. et al. (2002). Holocene environmental evidence from the Zackenberg Delta, NE Greenland. *Journal of Quaternary Science* 17: 145–160.

Coope, G.R. (1969). The contribution that the Coleoptera of Glacial Britain could have made to the subsequent colonisation of Scandinavia. *Opuscula Entomologica* 34: 95–108.

Coope, G.R. (1970). Interpretation of Quaternary insect fossils. *Annual Review of Entomology* 15: 97–120.

Coope, G.R. (1978). Constancy of insect species versus inconstancy of Quaternary environments. In: Diversity of Insect Faunas, Symposia of the Royal Society of London, vol. 9 (eds. L.A. Mound and N. Waloff), 176–187. Oxford: Blackwell.

Coope, G.R. (1979). Late Cenozoic fossil Coleoptera: evolution, biogeography and ecology. *Annual Review of Ecology and Systematics* 10: 247–257.

Coope, G.R. (1986). The invasion and colonisation of the North Atlantic islands: a palaeoecological solution to a biogeographic problem. *Philosophical Transactions of the Royal Society of London* B314: 619–635.

Dahl-Jensen, D., Mosegaard, K., Gundestrup, N. et al. (1998). Past temperatures directly from the Greenland ice sheet. *Science* 282: 268–271.

Dowdeswell, J.A., Hogan, K.A., Cofaigh, C.Ó. et al. (2014). Late Quaternary ice flow in a West Greenland fjord and cross-shelf trough system: submarine landforms from Rink Isbrae to Uummannaq shelf and slope. *Quaternary Science Reviews* 92: 292–309.

Einarsson, Á. (1981). Krabbadýr frá hlýskeiði ísaldar. *Náttúrufræðingurinn* 51: 47–53.

Elias, S.A. and Matthews, J.V. Jr. (2002). Arctic North American seasonal temperatures from the latest Miocene to the early Pleistocene, based on mutual climatic range analysis of fossil beetle assemblages. *Canadian Journal of Earth Sciences* 39: 911–920.

Elias, S.A., Kuzmina, S., and Kiselyov, S. (2006). Late Tertiary origins of the Arctic beetle fauna. *Palaeogeography, Palaeoclimatology, Palaeoecology* 241: 373–392.

Fredskild, B. (1973). Studies in the vegetational history of Greenland. Palaeobotanical investigations of some Holocene lake and .bog deposits. *Meddelelser om Grønland* 198 (4): 245.

Fredskild, B. (1983). The Holocene vegetational development of the Godthåbsfjord area, West Greenland. *Meddelelser om Grønland, Geoscience* 10: 28.

Fredskild, B. (1985). The Holocene vegetational development of Tugtuligssuaq and Qeqertat, Northwest Greenland. *Meddelelser om Grønland, Geoscience* 14: 20.

Fredskild, B. (1991). The genus *Betula* in Greenland – Holocene history, present distribution and synecology. *Nordic Journal of Botany* 11: 393–412.

Fredskild, B., Jacobsen, N., and Røen, U. (1975). Remains of mosses and freshwater animals in some Holocene lake and bog sediments from Greenland. *Meddelelser om Grønland* 198 (5): 44.

Funder, S. (1978). Holocene stratigraphy and vegetation history in the Scoresby Sund area, East Greenland. *Bulletin Grønlands Geologiske Undersøgelse* 129: 66.

Funder, S. (1979). Ice-age plant refugia in East Greenland. *Palaeogeography, Palaeoclimatology, Palaeoecology* 28: 279–295.

Funder, S. (ed.) (1990). Late Quaternary stratigraphy and glaciology in the Thule area. *Meddelelser om Grønland, Geoscience* 22: 63.

Funder, S. and Hjort, C. (1980). A reconnaissance of the Quaternary geology of eastern North Greenland. *Rapport Grønlands Geologiske Undersøgelse* 99: 99–105.

Funder, S., Bennike, O., Mogensen, G.S. et al. (1984). The Kap København Formation, a Late Cainozoic sedimentary sequence in North Greenland. *Rapport Grønlands Geologiske Undersøgelse* 120: 9–18.

Funder, S., Abrahamsen, N., Bennike, O., and Feyling-Hanssen, R.W. (1985). Forested Arctic: evidence from North Greenland. *Geology* 13: 542–546.

Funder, S., Hjort, C., and Landvik, J.Y. (1994). The last glacial cycles in East Greenland, an overview. *Boreas* 23: 283–289.

Funder, S., Hjort, C., Landvik, J.Y. et al. (1998). History of a stable ice margin. – East Greenland during the Middle and Upper Pleistocene. *Quaternary Science Reviews* 17: 77–125.

Funder, S., Bennike, O., Böcher, J. et al. (2001). Late Pliocene Greenland – the Kap København Formation in North Greenland. *Bulletin of the Geological Society of Denmark* 48: 117–134.

Funder, S., Kjellerup, K., Kjær, K.H., and Cofaigh, C.Ó. (2011). The Greenland ice sheet, the last 300,000 years: a review. In: Quaternary Glaciations – Extent and Chronology. Part IV:

A Closer Look (eds. E. Ehlers and P. Gibbard), 699–713. Amsterdam: Elsevier.

Grímsson, F. (2011). The Pleistocene floras (2.4–0.8 Ma) – shaping the modern vegetation of Iceland. In: Late Cainozoic Floras of Iceland, *Topics in Geobiology*, vol. 35 (eds. T. Denk, F. Grímsson, R. Zetter and L.A. Símonarson), 555–645.

Håkansson, L., Alexanderson, H., Hjort, C. et al. (2009). Late Pleistocene glacial history of Jameson Land, central East Greenland. *Boreas* 38: 244–260.

Håkansson, L., Briner, J., Alhadan, A., and Possnert, G. (2011). [10]Be data from meltwater channels suggest that Jameson Land, East Greenland, was ice-covered during the last glacial maximum. *Quaternary Research* 76: 452–459.

Hallsdóttir, M. (1995). On the pre-settlement history of Icelandic vegetation. *Buvisindi* 9: 17–29.

Hallsdóttir, M. and Caseldine, C.J. (2005). The Holocene vegetation history of Iceland, state-of-the-art and future research. *Developments in Quaternary Sciences* 5: 319–334.

Hannon, G., Bradshaw, R.H., and Wastegård, S. (2003). Rapid vegetation change during the early Holocene in the Faroe Islands detected in terrestrial and aquatic ecosystems. *Journal of Quaternary Science* 18: 615–619.

Hannon, G., Rundgren, M., and Jessen, C.A. (2010). Dynamic early Holocene vegetation development on the Faroe Islands inferred from high-resolution plant macrofossil and pollen data. *Quaternary Research* 73: 163–172.

Hedenäs, L. (1994). Bryophytes from the last interglacial/glacial cycle, Jameson Land, East Greenland. *Boreas* 23: 488–494.

Hedenäs, L. and Bennike, O. (2003). Moss remains from the last interglacial at Thule, Northwest Greenland. *Lindbergia* 28: 52–58.

Hedenäs, L. and Bennike, O. (2009). A Plio-Pleistocene moss assemblage from Store Koldewey, NE Greenland. *Lindbergia* 33: 23–37.

Iversen, J. (1954). Origin of the flora of western Greenland in the light of pollen analysis. *Oikos* 4: 85–103.

Jóhansen, J. (1985). Studies in the vegetational history of the Faroe and Shetland Islands. In: Annales Societas Scientarum Færoensis Supplementum, vol. 11, 117.

Johnsen, S.J., Clausen, H.B., Dansgaard, W. et al. (1992). A 'deep' ice core from East Greenland. *Meddelelser om Grønland, Geoscience* 29: 22.

Jørgensen, G. and Rasmussen, J. (1986). Glacial striae, roches moutonnees and ice movements in the Faroe Islands. *Danmarks Geologiske Undersøgelse Serie* C7: 114.

Kelley, S.E., Briner, J.P., and Young, N.E. (2015). Rapid ice retreat in Disko Bugt supported by 10Be dating of the last recession of the western Greenland Ice Sheet. *Journal of Quaternary Science* 30: 271–280.

Kelly, M. and Bennike, O. (1992). Quaternary geology of western and central North Greenland. *Rapport Grønlands Geologiske Undersøgelse* 153: 34.

Kelly, M., Funder, S., Houmark-Nielsen, M. et al. (1999). Quaternary glacial and marine environmental history of Northwest Greenland: a review and reappraisal. *Quaternary Science Reviews* 18: 373–392.

Kusch, S., Bennike, O., Wagner, B. et al. (2019). Holocene environmental history in high-Arctic North Greenland revealed by a combined biomarker and macrofossil approach. *Boreas* 48: 273–286.

Laberg, J.S., Forwick, M., and Husum, K. (2017). New geophysical evidence for a revised maximum position of part of the NE sector of the Greenland ice sheet during the last glacial maximum. *Arktos* 3: 3.

LIGA members (1991). Report of 1st discussion group: the last interglacial in high latitudes of the northern hemisphere: terrestrial and marine evidence. *Quaternary International* 10–12: 9–28.

Líndal, J.H. (1939). The interglacial formation in Viðidal, northern Iceland. *Quarterly Journal of the Geological Society* 95: 261–273.

Lindroth, C.H. (1957). The Faunal Connection Between Europe and North America, 344. Stockholm: Almquist and Wiksell.

Lindroth, C.H. (1968). The ground-beetles (Carabidae, excl. Cicindelinae) of Canada and Alaska, part 5. In: Opuscula Entomologica, Supplementum, vol. 33, 649–944.

Lindroth, C.H. (1973). Survival of animals and plants on ice-free refugia during the Pleistocene glaciations. *Endeavor* 29: 129–134.

Matthews, J.V. Jr. (1979b). Fossil beetles and the Late Cenozoic history of the tundra environment. In: Historical Biogeography, Plate Tectonics, and the Changing Environment (eds. J. Gray and A.J. Boucot), 371–376. Oregon: Oregon State University Press.

Matthews, J.V. Jr. and Fyles, J.G. (2000). Late Tertiary plant and arthropod fossils from the high-terrace sediments on Fosheim Peninsula, Ellesmere Island, Nunavut. *Geological Survey of Canada Bulletin* 529: 295–317.

Matthews, J.V. Jr. (1977). Tertiary Coleoptera fossils from the North American Arctic. *The Coleopterists Bulletin* 31: 297–308.

Matthews, J.V. Jr. (1979a). Late Tertiary carabid fossils from Alaska and the Canadian Archipelago. In: Carabid Beetles, Their Evolution, Natural History and Classification (eds. T.L. Erwin, G.E. Ball and D.R. Whitehead), 425–445. The Hague: Junk.

Matthews, J.V. Jr. and Telka, A. (1977). Insect fossils from the Yukon. In: Insects of the Yukon (eds. H.V. Danks and J.A. Downes). Ottawa.

McFarlin, J.M., Axford, Y., Osburn, M.R. et al. (2018). Pronounced summer warming in Northwest Greenland during the Holocene and Last Interglacial. *Proceedings of the National Academy of Sciences – PNAS* 115: 6357–6362.

Meldgaard, M. (1986). The Greenland caribou – zoogeography, taxonomy, and population dynamics. *Meddelelser om Grønland, Bioscience* 20: 88.

Meldgaard, M. and Bennike, O. (1989). Interglacial remains of caribou (*Rangifer tarandus*) and lemming (*Dicrostonyx torquatus* [?]) from North Greenland. *Boreas* 18: 359–366.

Melles, M., Brigham-Grette, J., Minyuk, P.S. et al. (2012). 2.8 million years of Arctic climate change from Lake El'gygytgyn, NE Russia. *Science* 337: 315–320.

Mienert, J., Andrews, J.T., and Milliman, J.D. (1992). The East Greenland continental margin (65°N) since the last deglaciation: changes in seafloor properties and ocean circulation. *Marine Geology* 106: 217–238.

Miller, G.H., Mode, W.N., Wolfe, A.P. et al. (1999). Stratified interglacial lacustrine sediments from Baffin Island, Arctic Canada: chronology and paleoenvironmental implications. *Quaternary Science Reviews* 18: 789–810.

Nathorst, A.G. (1892). Kritische Bemerkungen über die Geschichte der Vegetation Grönlands. *Englers Botanische Jahrbücher* 14: 183–221.

Ó Cofaigh, C., Dowdeswell, J.A., Jennings, A.E. et al. (2013). An extensive and dynamic ice sheet on the West Greenland shelf during the last glacial cycle. *Geology* 41: 219–222.

Økland, K.A. and Økland, J. (2000). Freshwater bryozoans (Bryozoa) of Norway: distribution and ecology of *Cristatella mucedo* and *Paludicella articulata*. *Hydrobiologia* 421: 1–24.

Rasmussen, J. (1972). Mórena á Bordoyarvík, som bendir á eitt millumbil íglersetingini har norduri. *Fróðskaparrit* 20: 54–70.

Repenning, C.A., Brouwers, E.M., Carter, L.D., Marincovoch Jr., L. & Ager, T.A. 1987. The Beringian ancestry of *Phenacomys* (Rodentia: Cricetidae) and the beginning of the modern Arctic Ocean borderland biota. *U.S. Geological Survey Bulletin* 1687, Ottawa: Biological Survey of Canada (terrestrial arthropods).

Rundgren, M. (1995). Biostratigraphic evidence of the Allerød–Younger Dryas–Preboreal oscillation in northern Iceland. *Quaternary Research* 44: 405–416.

Rundgren, M. (1998). Early Holocene vegetation of northern Iceland: pollen and plant macrofossil evidence from the Skagi peninsula. *The Holocene* 8: 553–564.

Rundgren, M. and Ingólfsson, Ó. (1999). Plant survival in Iceland during periods of glaciation? *Journal of Biogeography* 26: 387–396.

Schaefer, J.M., Finkel, R.C., Balco, G. et al. (2016). Greenland was nearly ice-free for extended periods during the Pleistocene. *Nature* 540: 20146.

Sejrup, H.P., Hjelstuen, B.O., Dahlgren, K.I.T. et al. (2005). Pleistocene glacial history of the NW European margin. *Marine and Petroleum Geology* 22: 1111–1129.

Símonarson, L.A., Petersen, K.S., and Funder, S. (1998). Molluscan palaeontology of the Pliocene-Pleistocene Kap København Formation, North Greenland. *Meddelelser om Grønland, Geoscience* 36: 103.

Sinclair, G., Carlson, A.E., Mix, A.C. et al. (2016). Diachronous retreat of the Greenland ice sheet during the last deglaciation. *Quaternary Science Reviews* 145: 243–258.

Slabon, P., Dorschel, B., Jokat, W. et al. (2016). Greenland ice sheet retreat history in the northeast Baffin Bay based on high-resolution bathymetry. *Quaternary Science Reviews* 154: 182–198.

Tendal, O.S. (2004). Freshwater sponges (Porifera: Spongillidae) in the Faroe Islands. *Fróðskaparrit* 51: 298–303.

Thorkelsson, T. (1935). A fossiliferous interglacial layer at Elliðaárvogur, Reykjavík. *Visindafélag Íslands, Greinar* 1: 78–91.

de Vernal, A. and Hillaire-Marcel, C. (2008). Natural variability of Greenland climate, vegetation, and ice volume during the past million years. *Science* 320: 1622–1625.

Vinther, B.M., Buchardt, S.L., Clausen, H.B. et al. (2009). Holocene thinning of the Greenland ice sheet. *Nature* 461: 385–388.

Vosgerau, H., Funder, S., Kelly, M. et al. (1994). Palaeoenvironments and changes in relative sea level during the last interglaciation at Langelandselv, Jameson Land, East Greenland. *Boreas* 23: 398–411.

Wagner, B. and Bennike, O. (2012). Chronology of the last deglaciation and Holocene environmental change in the Sisimiut area, south-west Greenland based on lacustrine records. *Boreas* 41: 481–493.

Wagner, B. and Bennike, O. (2015). Holocene environmental changes in the Skallingen area, eastern North Greenland, based on a lacustrine record. *Boreas* 44: 45–59.

Wagner, B., Bennike, O., Bos, J.A.A. et al. (2008). A multidisciplinary study of Holocene sediment records from Hjort Sø on Store Koldewey, Northeast Greenland. *Journal of Paleolimnology* 39: 381–398.

Wagner, B., Bennike, O., Cremer, H., and Klug, M. (2010). Late Quaternary history of the Kap Mackenzie area, Northeast Greenland. *Boreas* 39: 492–504.

Warming, E. (1888). Om Grønlands vegetation. *Meddelelser om Grønland* 12: 245.

Wastegård, S., Björck, S., Greve, C., and Rasmussen, T.L. (2005). A tephra-based correlation between the Faroe Islands and the Norwegian Sea raises questions about chronological relationships during the last interglacial. *Terra Nova* 17: 7–12.

Wastl, M., Stötter, J., and Caseldine, C. (2001). Reconstruction of Holocene variations of the upper limit of tree or shrub birch growth in northern Iceland based on evidence from Vesturárdalur-Skiðadalur, Tröllaskagi. *Arctic, Antarctic and Alpine Research* 33: 191–203.

Willerslev, E., Cappellini, E., Boomsma, W. et al. (2007). Ancient biomolecules from deep ice cores reveal a forested southern Greenland. *Science* 317: 111–114.

Winkelmann, D., Jokat, W., Jensen, L., and Schenke, H.-W. (2010). Submarine end moraines on the continental shelf off NE Greenland – implications for lateglacial dynamics. *Quaternary Science Reviews* 29: 1069–1077.

Section II

Origins of the Present Biota

4

Origin and Dispersal of the North Atlantic Vascular Plant Floras

Christian Brochmann[1] and Inger G. Alsos[2]

[1] *The Natural History Museum, University of Oslo, Oslo, Norway*
[2] *The Arctic University Museum of Norway, Tromsø, Norway*

In the 1963 book *North Atlantic Biota and their History*, Á. Löve concluded that the theory of the survival of plants within the heavily glaciated Atlantic areas, the 'glacial survival' or 'nunatak' theory, replaces 'the now merely historical *tabula rasa* idea' – the hypothesis that the current Atlantic floras were established following postglacial immigration from source areas situated outside the ice sheets (Löve and Löve 1963). The virtually complete consensus among plant biogeographers (with notable exceptions among palaeoecologists) at that time was based on two main arguments, the occurrences of disjunct taxa and endemic taxa in the North Atlantic region. Firstly, the occurrence of disjuncts was believed to *necessitate in situ* glacial survival because long-distance dispersal in general and trans-oceanic dispersal in particular were considered to be extremely rare, if not impossible, at least for the many disjuncts that lack typical adaptations to long-distance dispersal (e.g. Hultén 1937; Dahl 1963). Most attention was paid to the amphi-Atlantic disjuncts, especially the 'west-arctic' subgroup that consists of species with their main range in northeastern North America and with their European occurrences restricted to formerly glaciated areas. Secondly, the occurrence of endemics was believed to *necessitate in situ* glacial survival because the postglacial period was considered to be far too short to allow for evolution of endemic taxa (e.g. Nordhagen 1936, 1963; Dahl 1955, 1987; Knaben 1959a, 1959b, 1982). It was commonly thought that it was necessary to postulate *in situ* glacial survival not only during the last glaciation, but throughout the entire Pleistocene, to explain the occurrence of disjuncts and endemics in the North Atlantic region.

Forty years later, we reviewed and analysed the geological, molecular, biogeographical and taxonomic evidence accumulated since the 1963 book was published (Brochmann et al. 2003). New geological evidence, in particular from exposure age dating that had provided a break-through in distinguishing formerly glaciated areas from unglaciated ones, suggests that several ice-free areas such as nunataks and ice-free uplands indeed did exist within the maximum limits of the ice sheets in the North Atlantic region (Figure 1). However, no fossils have so far been found in such areas to prove continuous *in situ* existence of life throughout the

Biogeography in the Sub-Arctic: The Past and Future of North Atlantic Biota, First Edition.
Edited by Eva Panagiotakopulu and Jon P. Sadler.

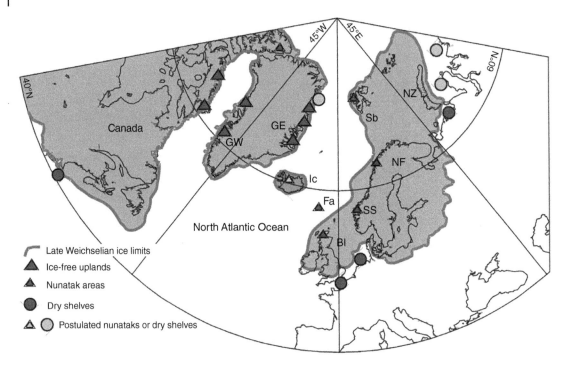

Figure 1 Reconstruction of the Late Weichselian (25 000–10 000 years ago) maximum ice limits in the North Atlantic region. Ice-free areas are indicated (red symbols: strong geological evidence). The nine Atlantic subregions analysed for endemism are indicated: GW – Greenland, West and South (SE to Lindenowfjord); GE – Greenland, East (N of Lindenowfjord); Sb – Svalbard including Bear Island and Franz Josef Land; NZ – Novaya Zemlya (excl. Vaigach); Ic – Iceland; Fa – The Faroes; BI – Northern British Isles; SS – Scandes, southern part; NF – Fennoscandia, northern part including the Kola Peninsula. A nunatak may also have existed in Jan Mayen, but there are no recent studies of glaciation in this island. Reproduced with permission from Brochmann et al. (2003). (See colour plate section for colour representation of this figure)

last glaciation (c. 110 000–11 700 BP) and, based on the new molecular and taxonomic evidence, we concluded that invoking *in situ* glacial survival could not be considered a *necessity* after all. We considered North Atlantic floras to be essentially formed in the postglacial period, following immigration from extra-glacial source areas. Although we could not exclude the possibility that some 'intra-glacial' ice-free areas might have provided continuous support for some life, our review concluded that the glacial survival hypothesis was superfluous for all examined species. The molecular data showed beyond reasonable doubt that trans-oceanic dispersal occurs much more

frequently than traditionally thought, even across the entire North Atlantic and even in species lacking typical adaptations to long-distance dispersal. The occurrence of very similar, in some cases even identical, multilocus genotypes across isolated Atlantic areas provided strong evidence for recent dispersal, most likely with wind across sea ice or with birds (Brochmann et al. 2003).

We concluded our 2003 review with the notion that there is not one single nunatak hypothesis versus one single *tabula rasa* hypothesis to test in future work, but numerous – one for each species (cf. Berg 1963). In this chapter, we first provide a synopsis of our 2003 analysis of North Atlantic endemism, which was based on a detailed updating of taxonomic and experimental data. Next, we review molecular studies of North Atlantic vascular plants carried out during the last decades, as well as studies of genetic and floristic relationships of some isolated North Atlantic island floras. The new data strengthen our 2003 scenario of massive postglacial immigration, rendering the glacial survival theory *superfluous* for most species. However, we also present some studies providing quite convincing molecular evidence suggesting *in situ* glacial persistence of three rare 'west-arctic' species, northern single-spike sedge *Carex scirpoidea,* tufted pearlwort *Sagina caespitosa* and low sandwort *Arenaria humifusa* (Westergaard et al. 2011; 2019). Much more unexpected and still controversial is the report of ancient DNA of pine *Pinus sylvestris* and spruce *Picea abies* in northern Scandinavia dated to the last glacial maximum (Parducci et al. 2012b; see also Birks et al. 2012 and Parducci et al. 2012a), an issue that still has not been solved (Alsos et al. 2020).

North Atlantic Endemics – A History of Over-Description and Rapid Hybrid Speciation

Only a few of the many endemic vascular plant taxa described from the North Atlantic region have survived the critical eyes of modern taxonomists, and several of those remaining have not yet been studied in detail. Detailed comparisons of postulated endemic taxa with material from wider geographic areas have often shown that the morphological variation in the North Atlantic falls within that observed at larger spatial scales. In our 2003 analysis, we tentatively accepted 77 endemic taxa at the species or subspecies level in the north boreal/alpine/arctic flora in the North Atlantic (excluding eastern Canada; Brochmann et al. 2003). More than half of them (40 taxa) occur in more than one of the nine Atlantic subregions

considered by us (Figure 1), and thus in most cases provide evidence for trans-oceanic dispersal (more often the case between North Greenland and Svalbard/Novaja Zemlja, between East Greenland and northern Fennoscandia, and between Iceland, Scotland and southern Scandinavia). Among the remaining 37 taxa endemic to a single Atlantic subregion, the vast majority (31) occur in areas directly or closely connected to large continental areas (Scandinavia, the British Isles and West Greenland). We were only left with two taxa endemic to East Greenland and three taxa endemic to Svalbard, whereas one poppy *Papaver* subspecies listed by us in 2003 as endemic to Novaja Zemlja no longer is accepted (Elven et al. 2011, based on new morphological and molecular analyses by Solstad 2009). Notably, we did not accept a single species or subspecies endemic to Iceland or the Faroes (see Brochmann et al. 2003 for details; note that this analysis only concerned taxa belonging to the north boreal/alpine/arctic flora of the North Atlantic, i.e. the most likely glacial survivors). Surveys published after 2003 (e.g. Elven et al. 2011; Alsos et al. 2015; Wasowicz 2020) have only resulted in minor adjustments to the taxonomy outlined in Brochmann et al. (2003).

Thus, the level of endemism in the North Atlantic as accepted in modern taxonomy is extremely low compared to alpine areas situated outside the northern ice sheets, whereas endemism in each Atlantic subregion (Figure 1) amounts to 0.0–1.9% among its north boreal/alpine/arctic taxa, the level of endemism is 32% in the Alps, 34% in the Balkan Mountains, 25% in Caucasus and 8% in the Ural Mountains (Brochmann et al. 2003). This pattern testifies to the much younger age of the North Atlantic floras and suggests they were essentially formed via postglacial immigration.

Where, when and how did the currently accepted North Atlantic endemics originate? Most of them are polyploids, i.e. they may have formed during a few generations following hybridisation and chromosome doubling (allopolyploidy). The two endemics in East Greenland, low northern-rockcress *Braya intermedia* and East Greenland saxifrage *Saxifraga nathorstii*, are sexual and morphologically distinct, and probably originated recently as allopolyploids, the latter from the hybrid yellow mountain saxifrage × purple saxifrage *S. aizoides × oppositifolia* (Böcher 1966, 1983; Ferguson 1972). Two of the Svalbard endemics, Svalbard cinquefoil *Potentilla insularis* and Svalbard saxifrage *S. svalbardensis*, are asexual polyploids and probably of postglacial hybrid origin, the latter from nodding saxifrage × alpine brook saxifrage *S. cernua × rivularis* (Brochmann et al. 1998; Hansen et al. 2000; Steen et al. 2000; Brochmann and Håpnes 2001; Nyléhn and Hamre 2002). All four progenitor species of the two island endemics for which the parentage has been clarified in detail (*S. nathorstii* and *S. svalbardensis*) are widespread in the Arctic. Notably, *S. rivularis* and the morphologically and genetically variable polyploid *S. cernua* have also hybridized in Scandinavia, probably several times, and have given rise to the Scandinavian endemic Oppdal saxifrage *S. opdalensis*. This species is morphologically and genetically distinct from *S. svalbardensis* in spite of having originated from populations belonging to the same two progenitor species (Steen et al. 2000). The third Svalbard endemic, Svalbard saltmarsh grass *Puccinellia svalbardensis*, is also polyploid but its distinctivity and relationships are not well known (Rønning 1962; Elven et al. 2011).

Quite a few of the endemics listed by Brochmann et al. (2003) for the other North Atlantic subregions, which are directly or closely connected to large continental areas, are probably older species. In Northern Fennoscandia, for example, such species may either have persisted more or less *in situ* in ice-free areas or immigrated after the last glaciation from non-glaciated, vast eastern source areas, where they subsequently became extinct or are still not discovered. Notably, among the 43 North Atlantic endemics we considered as potentially hardy enough for nunatak survival, there is not a single outcrossing diploid that could suggest long-term evolution (Brochmann et al. 2003).

Colonisation History of North Atlantic Plants

The phylogeographic histories of many plant species that occur in the North Atlantic region are now known to some degree (see also Brochmann et al. 2003, 2013; Brochmann and Brysting 2008; Alsos et al. 2015; Birkeland et al. 2017). In a recent synopsis, we used AFLP fingerprinting of ~8000 individual plants of 17 widespread species to assess major patterns of genetic variation across the entire circumpolar area by constructing GIS-based composite maps (Eidesen et al. 2013). Although the Pleistocene glaciations were found to have had a major impact on overall genetic diversity, gene flow has been most severely hampered by longstanding physical barriers, i.e. the Atlantic Ocean, the Greenlandic Ice cap, the Ural Mountains and the lowlands between the European Arctic and southern alpine areas. Much more genetic diversity was found around the Bering Strait than in the North Atlantic region, a pattern also confirmed in further analyses of 23 species (Stewart et al. 2016). This corroborates the role of unglaciated Beringia as a major refugium during the Pleistocene (Hultén 1937; Abbott and Brochmann 2003). The genetically most distinct populations were, however, located in unglaciated Siberia, suggesting that this refugium has contributed less as a source for postglacial expansion than Beringia.

The geographic locations of the glacial source populations resulting in the contemporary North Atlantic populations vary. In some species, only a single or a few very similar multilocus genotypes have colonised the entire North Atlantic range of the species after the last glaciation. For example, the populations of the alpine rock-cress *Arabis alpina* (Ehrich et al. 2007) and the glacier butter-cup *Ranunculus glacialis* (Schönswetter et al. 2003) in the European Alps contain considerable diversity and only a depauperate fraction of this diversity served as a source for northward postglacial colonisation. The genetically depauperate North Atlantic populations of the pygmy butter-cup *Ranunculus pygmaeus* originated from variable source populations in the Polar Urals, and this species is genetically diverse also in other arctic areas (Schönswetter et al. 2006). In these species, postglacial colonisation followed the leading-edge model (Hewitt 1996), resulting in genetic depauperation through repeated bottlenecks. Other species, which are likely to have persisted in large populations during the glaciations, appear to have colonised deglaciated areas along broad northwards fronts, and thus retained much more genetic diversity (e.g. the dwarf willow *Salix her-bacea*; Alsos et al. 2009). Finally, the current north Atlantic populations of some cold-adapted species are genetically more variable than the southern ones, where they are restricted to refugia under the current climate (e.g. nodding saxifrage *Saxifraga cernua*, Bauert et al. 1998, Gabrielsen and Brochmann 1998; Kjølner et al. 2004; mountain avens *Dryas octopetala*, Skrede et al. 2006; bilberry *Vaccinium uliginosum*, Alsos et al. 2005; Eidesen et al. 2007a). The colonisation histories vary among such species. For *Dryas octopetala*, for example, the eastern parts of the North Atlantic were colonised both from refugia situated south of the main ice sheets (the Alpine lineage) and east of them (the Russian lineage). This species can serve to illustrate that high genetic diversity is not only found in areas little affected by the major ice sheets, such as Beringia, but also in areas that were colonised postglacially by several lineages. *Dryas octopetala* has high diversity in northern Siberia and the Urals, but also in secondary contact zones in northern Scandinavia, Svalbard and East Greenland (Skrede et al. 2006; see also Vik et al. 2010).

The traditional view of low dispersal ability of most northern plants (e.g. Hultén 1937; Dahl 1963) has now been rejected based on several types of molecular data and for many species. This is in agreement with the fossil record, which suggests rapid range shifts following climate changes (e.g. Birks 1994; Birks and Willis 2008). Although there is less gene flow across the North Atlantic Ocean than across continuous land masses (Eidesen et al. 2013), the sea does certainly not represent an impermeable barrier. Alsos et al. (2007) showed, for example, that long-distance colonisation of Svalbard has occurred frequently and from several source regions (Figure 2). The genetic effect of restricted colonisation (the founder effect) was strongly correlated with the temperature requirements of the nine species analysed, implying that hardy species have established in the archipelago more frequently than less hardy ones, regardless of their dispersal adaptations. The fact that Svalbard was almost completely glaciated during the last glaciation (Landvik et al. 1998, 2003; Ingólfsson and Landvik 2013) in itself suggests that most plant species occurring there today immigrated via cross-oceanic dispersal after the last glaciation (but see Westergaard et al. 2011; discussed below). Alsos et al. (2007) found that the major source for colonisation of Svalbard is north-western Russia (Figure 2). In eight of the nine species investigated by AFLP fingerprinting, multiple propagules resulting in successful establishment (a minimum of 6–38) were necessary to bring the observed genetic diversity to Svalbard, implying that many more propagules actually must have reached the archipelago. In *Dryas octopetala*, for example, the genetic diversity in Svalbard was similar to that in the source regions and it is likely that thousands of seeds have been spread by wind and/or sea ice to the islands. In *Vaccinium uliginosum*, there are two genetically distinct types of Svalbard populations, one originating from northwestern Russia and one originating from East Greenland.

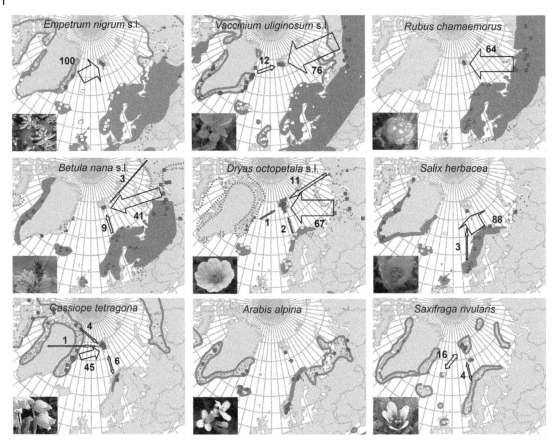

Figure 2 Colonisation of the Svalbard archipelago with source regions inferred from statistical assignment analyses of AFLP multilocus genotypes. The geographical distribution of each species is shaded (that of closely related species is indicated by dotted lines for *Betula nana* (*B. exilis*) and *Dryas octopetala* (*D. integrifolia*). Colours represent main genetic groups and symbols represent subgroups. Numbers on the arrows indicate the percentage allocation of Svalbard genotypes to a source region (using a log-likelihood difference of 1; i.e. 10 times as likely from that source region as from any other source regions). For *C. tetragona*, the direction of dispersal between Svalbard and Scandinavia is uncertain because of low diversity in Scandinavia. The source for the Svalbard populations of *A. alpina* could not be determined because of lack of genetic variation. In *S. rivularis*, the highest levels of genetic variation and most private markers were observed in the Svalbard populations, which also were clearly separated from the two amphi-Atlantic genetic groups. Thus, survival in Svalbard during the last glacial maximum cannot be excluded for this high-arctic species. Reproduced with permission from Alsos et al. (2007). (See colour plate section for colour representation of this figure)

An analysis of the genetic (AFLP) relationships of the rare and vulnerable alpine plants occurring in Scotland was presented by Westergaard et al. (2008). The Scottish populations of most species belong to widespread (European/Eurasian) genetic groups and show little genetic distinctiveness, suggesting postglacial immigration to Scotland from glacial refugia situated outside the major ice sheets.

While AFLP fingerprinting data do not allow for dating of dispersal events (Ehrich et al. 2009), it is possible to obtain reasonable estimates of divergence time among populations based on DNA sequencing data. In the circumpolar species alpine cress *Cardamine bellidifolia*, which has no obvious adaptations to long-distance dispersal, molecular dating has now been carried out based on sequencing of eight nuclear genes (Gustafsson, Brochmann, Ikeda et al., unpublished). Phylogenetic analyses show that the variation in these genes is poorly structured geographically and two different methods (the isolation with migration model (IM) and *BEAST) estimated that this species expanded recently, most likely in the current interglacial, across the entire circumarctic area. The most recent divergence was found between the populations in Svalbard and those in Alaska/Yukon (IM: mean 2600 years before present (BP), *BEAST: 21 200 years BP), whereas the mainland Scandinavian populations showed a somewhat older divergence time. A similar DNA sequence analysis of trailing azalea *Kalmia procumbens* (syn. *Loiseleuria procumbens*) suggests that eastward, postglacial colonisation from Beringia has resulted in its current circumarctic distribution (Ikeda et al. 2017).

Similar inferences have been made for other species at the circumpolar scale, although without explicit dating. Notably, white arctic bell-heather *Cassiope tetragona* and cloudberry *Rubus chamaemorus* have been found as early macrofossils in northern Greenland (2.5–2.0 million years old; Bennike and Böcher 1990), which might be taken as evidence for Hultén's (1937) hypothesis of pre-Pleistocene expansion from Beringia and subsequent refugial survival throughout the glaciations. However, no plastid DNA variation was found in *Cassiope tetragona* at the circumpolar scale, suggesting a more recent history of the contemporary populations (Eidesen et al. 2007b). The data are consistent with a Beringian origin of subspecies *tetragona* and westward expansion into northern Siberia at least one glacial cycle ago, but eastward expansion probably occurred as late as in the current interglacial period. The AFLP data show a conspicuous leading-edge model pattern, suggesting recent colonisation from Beringia

throughout Canada and Greenland and across the Atlantic into Svalbard and Scandinavia. Similar results were obtained for *Rubus chamaemorus* (Ehrich et al. 2008). Thus, it seems that these two species have expanded from Beringia several times, but that the early immigrants to the Atlantic region left the fossils in North Greenland and later went extinct. There are no similar fossil finds of *Saxifraga rivularis*, but the extreme Beringian–Atlantic disjunction in this species appears to have formed at least twice (Westergaard et al. 2010). The first expansion, presumably from Beringia where the species seems to have originated via allopolyploidy, occurred at least one glacial cycle ago, followed by allopatric differentiation into one Beringian and one Atlantic subspecies. A new expansion from Beringia most likely occurred via several long-distance dispersals in the current interglacial period, resulting in colonisation of the western Atlantic region by the Beringian subspecies. We note, however, that *S. rivularis* has high levels of genetic diversity in Svalbard, which could indicate either glacial survival or immigration from Russia; no samples were analysed from the latter region.

Genetic and Floristic Relationships Among Five Atlantic Floras

Similar to our analyses for Svalbard and Scotland (see above), we recently assembled published and unpublished AFLP datasets on intraspecific diversity in 25 North Atlantic plant species (8932 plants from 1110 populations). We subjected this assembled dataset to a meta-analysis for inference of the source areas for the current populations occurring in five North Atlantic 'target' areas (East Greenland, Iceland, Svalbard, the Faroe Islands and Jan Mayen; Alsos et al. 2015). This dataset was analysed to identify genetic groups within each species and for statistic assignment of genotypes to identify source regions. We complemented this genetic meta-analysis by a new analysis of the floristic relationships among north Atlantic areas based on updated taxonomy and recent floras (Alsos et al. 2015).

The vascular plant floras in the target areas in East Greenland, Iceland, Svalbard, the Faroes and Jan Mayen contain a total of 369–388, 428–430, 180–181, 282–293 and 65 taxa, respectively (the exact numbers are unknown because there are some remaining taxonomic problems). We calculated the proportion (%) of species found in each target area that also occurred in each potential source area (Figure 3). All target areas showed high floristic similarity with several source areas, but with a clear east–west pattern. In East Greenland 70% of the taxa were found both in the west (West Greenland and Northeast Canada)

and in the east (Scandinavia). Similarly, ~80% of the taxa in Svalbard were found both in East Greenland and Northwest Russia. Iceland showed the highest similarity to Scandinavia (94%), but also to the British Isles (74%). The Faroes showed high similarity to the British Isles (94%), Scandinavia (97%) and Iceland (77%). The relationships of the Jan Mayen flora were not clear (Figure 3).

Based on the new assembled genetic dataset, immigration to East Greenland appears to have occurred both from the west and the east, in agreement with the floristic analysis. The East Greenlandic populations of the 12 species sampled there belonged to amphi-Atlantic (5 spp.), West-Atlantic (3 spp.), Greenlandic–Icelandic (3 spp.), unique (1 sp.) and both western and eastern genetic groups (1 sp.). Overall, the highest

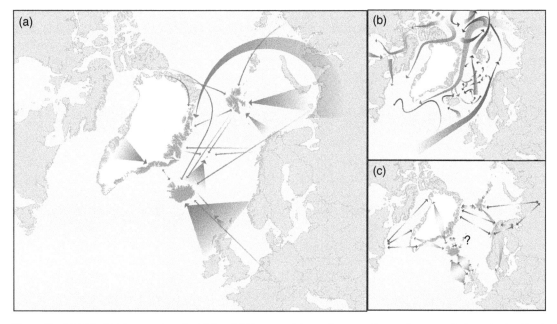

Figure 3 (a) Main (thick arrows) and additional (thin arrows) long-distance dispersal routes of plants in the North Atlantic area inferred from genetic and floristic data (cf. Figure 1). (b) Sea surface circulation patterns in the North Atlantic area (blue: cold water, red: warm water). (c) Main migration routes for geese species (thick blue arrows) and the supposedly efficient seed disperser *Plectrophenax nivalis* (snow bunting, thin red arrows) in the North Atlantic area. Reproduced with permission from Alsos et al. (2015). (See colour plate section for colour representation of this figure)

proportion of genetic groups was shared with West Greenland (80%) whereas a genetic assignment test showed high assignment to both Canada/West Greenland and Northwest Russia.

Also for Iceland, the genetic results were consistent with the floristic analysis, suggesting that its flora mainly immigrated from the east. Most Icelandic populations (21 species) belonged to eastern or amphi-Atlantic genetic groups, and contact zones for eastern and western groups were observed in dwarf birch *Betula nana* and rosebay willowherb (fireweed) *Chamerion angustifolium*. The assignment tests identified eastern main source areas for 14 species and the allocations to eastern source areas were eight times higher than to western ones. This is also consistent with previous genetic studies of marsh saxifrage *Saxifraga hirculus* (Oliver et al. 2006) and northern rock cress *Arabidopsis lyrata* (Schmickl et al. 2010).

Among the 11 species analysed from Svalbard, the populations of five species belonged to amphi-Atlantic genetic groups (*Saxifraga rivularis* having a unique group in addition), four to East-Atlantic groups, one to West-Atlantic groups and one had both a western and an eastern genetic group. The highest proportion of genetic groups was shared with the Ural Mountains (88%) followed by Norway (50%) and East and West Greenland (~40%). This was in accordance with the assignment test, which indicated the Urals as the most important source region (88%) followed by Norway (38%) and East Greenland (13%). Among the five species sampled in the Faroe Islands, four appeared to have immigrated mainly from the east and one from Iceland, in accordance with the floristic analysis. Whereas the floristic relationships of Jan Mayen were unclear, the genetic data clearly indicate that Iceland was the most important source area for immigration to this island.

Potential dispersal agents are birds, sea currents, wind and drift ice, or a combination of these (Figure 3). Sea ice has been suggested as an important dispersal agent as it may act both as a ferry for transport of organisms as well as a smooth surface for dispersal by wind (Savile 1972; Johansen and Hytteborn 2001). To test the role of sea ice for dispersal in the amphi-Atlantic region, we added a compilation of the Late Glacial and Holocene fossil records of the species as well as a reconstruction of past sea ice conditions to the genetic and floristic data described above (Alsos et al. 2016). For each fossil record, we compared the most likely past dispersal routes based on floristic and genetic data with sea ice at the time of the earliest record. Our results showed that sea ice was more prevalent along the most likely dispersal route at the time of first colonisation than along other possible routes. Thus, we conclude that sea ice may have facilitated high dispersal frequency in the region.

Some Glacial Survivors After All?

Some 'extreme' supporters of the glacial survival theory thought that most or at least large parts of the floras in various Atlantic areas persisted *in situ* throughout the last, or even several, glaciations (e.g. Warming 1888; Nordhagen 1936, 1963; Dahl 1955, 1963; Böcher 1956; Hadač 1963; Rønning 1963; Steindórsson 1963). Although this appears very unlikely to us given the vast accumulated body of taxonomic and molecular evidence, two studies provide quite convincing evidence for glacial persistence of three species belonging to the 'west-arctic element' of the amphi-Atlantic disjuncts, having their few and only European occurrences well within the maximum limits of the last glaciation (Westergaard et al. 2011; 2019). In each of *Sagina caespitosa* and *Arenaria humifusa*, two very distinct and partly diverse genetic groups, one East Atlantic and one West Atlantic, were identified based on AFLP fingerprinting

(Figure 4). These findings exclude with reasonable certainty postglacial dispersal from North America as an explanation for their European occurrences, in accordance with the prediction of the glacial survival theory. The patterns we observed in genetic diversity and distinctiveness rather indicate that glacial populations existed in East Greenland and/or Svalbard (*A. humifusa*) and in southern Scandinavia (*S. caespitosa*).

However, in spite of their presumed lack of long-distance dispersal capacity, these two species have recently spread over large distances in the Atlantic: populations with mixed ancestry from the East and West Atlantic genetic groups were observed in West Greenland and Iceland, indicating postglacial contact zones (Figure 4). So why did they not spread across the entire Atlantic, as previously documented for other west-arctic, amphi-Atlantic and circumpolar species? The reason may simply be a matter of seed production. *Sagina caespitosa* and *Arenaria humifusa* are small plants typically occurring in small and fragmented populations, producing only a few seeds available for occasional, chance-based long-distance dispersal (cf. Berg 1983), in contrast to massive seed-producers such as *Saxifraga oppositifolia*, *S. cespitosa*, and *Cassiope tetragona* (Gabrielsen et al. 1997; Tollefsrud et al. 1998; Abbott et al. 2000; Eidesen et al. 2007b).

We cannot exclude with certainty, however, the possibility that *Sagina caespitosa* and *Arenaria humifusa* rather persisted in glacial populations situated south or east of the North European ice sheets, serving as sources for postglacial establishment of the current East Atlantic populations but later went extinct. In both species, the phylogeographical structure was shallow in the East Atlantic genetic group, which can be taken as evidence for a single glacial source population. In *A. humifusa*, however, the geographical patterns of genetic diversity and distinctiveness suggest that this source population was indeed situated within the maximum ice limits in the East Atlantic

region. The Svalbard and East Greenland populations of this species were more diverse and had more exclusive AFLP markers than populations in the Norwegian mainland (Figure 4), a pattern contrary to predictions from a hypothesis of postglacial immigration from a source located south or east of the North European ice sheets. The most likely glacial source population for the East Atlantic group in *A. humifusa* was therefore located in Svalbard or East Greenland. In *S. caespitosa*, the pattern observed suggests glacial survival in Southern Norway (Figure 4), from where northwards and westwards colonisation resulted in decreasing diversity via repeated bottlenecks. However, for this species we would expect a similar genetic pattern if the actual source population was situated south of the ice margin.

The most convincing evidence for glacial survival comes from a recent range-wide study of single nucleotide polymorphisms in *Carex scirpoidea* ssp. *scirpoidea*. This is a dioecious, amphi-Atlantic arctic-alpine sedge which is widely distributed in North America, but only has three highly disjunct populations in Norway, all well within the limits of the Scandinavian Ice Sheet (Westergaard et al. 2019). The three Norwegian populations had low levels of within-population genetic diversity but high numbers of private alleles. They were highly divergent from the populations in Greenland and North America, and demographic analyses supported a pre-Weichselian colonisation of Norway from East Greenland. As this species has its only European populations well within the maximum limits of the Weichselian Ice Sheet, postglacial colonisation from areas outside the ice sheet is highly unlikely. This is a robust, genome-wide study, and we regard it to provide the most solid proof for glacial survival in Norway.

Molecular evidence suggesting *in situ* glacial survival has also been found for *Saxifraga rivularis*, but postglacial immigration from its current range in northwestern Russia could not be excluded because samples were lacking from this

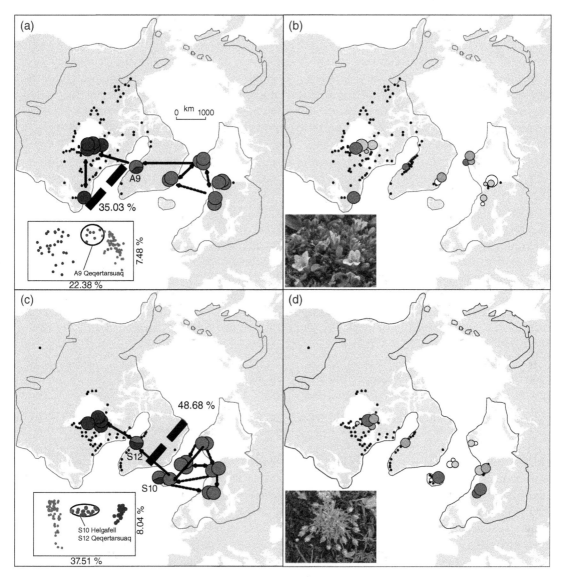

Figure 4 Genetic patterns detected in two west-arctic species, providing quite convincing evidence of glacial persistence in East Greenland/Svalbard (*Arenaria humifusa*) and southern Scandinavia (*Sagina caespitosa*). Each species contains two distinct genetic (AFLP) groups, one East Atlantic (red) and one West Atlantic (blue), excluding with reasonable certainty postglacial dispersal from North America as an explanation for their rare European occurrences. The maps show total geographical distribution (black dots), sampling sites and the Last Glacial Maximum ice extent (blue line). Reproduced with permission from Westergaard et al. (2011). (a, c) Genetic groups (blue and red) identified by structure analysis; pie diagrams with both colours indicate mixed ancestry, probably resulting from postglacial long-distance dispersal. Arrows represent dispersal routes inferred from assignment to geographic regions. The dashed black line shows division between the two main groups with the percentage of genetic variation assigned to between-group variation. The variation among all individual plants analysed, coloured according to genetic group, are depicted in the ordination analysis placed in the lower left corner of each map. (b, d) Geographical distribution of genetic diversity and distinctiveness. The size of the circles is proportional to gene diversity within populations, and the colours of the circles represent the four quartiles of genetic distinctiveness measured by occurrence of rare alleles (red – upper quartile, orange and yellow – intermediate quartiles, white – the lower quartile). The geographical positions of Svalbard (S) and Jan Mayen (JM) are indicated in (d). Photos: I. G. Alsos (*A. humifusa*; Svalbard, Bockfjorden) and K. I. Flatberg (*S. caespitosa*; S Norway, Knutshø Mts). (See colour plate section for colour representation of this figure)

area (Westergaard et al. 2010). The moss campion *Silene acaulis* shows a complex history of vicariance, long-distance dispersal and regional extinction–recolonisation dynamics throughout its disjunct circumpolar distribution (Gussarova et al. 2015). In this species, there is some molecular evidence pointing to glacial persistence as well as abundant cross-oceanic dispersal in the East Atlantic, but potential source populations in the European Alps remain to be examined.

While contemporary genetic patterns may provide indirect evidence for glacial survival, direct evidence may be obtained from dated fossils or ancient DNA. Several of our recent studies clearly demonstrate the emerging power of exploring the vast ancient DNA archives preserved in permafrost and lake sediments (e.g. Sønstebø et al. 2010; Parducci et al. 2012b, 2017; Willerslev et al. 2014; Epp et al. 2015; Paus et al. 2015; Clarke et al. 2019). In a lake at Andøya in northern Norway, we found DNA of *Pinus sylvestris* and *Picea abies* in sediment layers dated to 22 000 and 17 700 years BP (Parducci et al. 2012b). The origin of these DNAs has, however, been disputed. Drift wood, contamination, leaching of DNA and re-sedimentation have been suggested as alternative explanations to local occurrence at this time (Parducci et al. 2012a; Birks et al. 2012). However, it is also possible that previous reconstructions of glacial assemblages based on pollen records may have been carried out too conservatively; small amounts of tree pollen have typically been discarded as likely long-distance dispersed from remote sources. Notably, there are numerous macrofossils and pollen finds from the same site, indicating a climate that could have been suitable even for tree species (Parducci et al. 2012a, 2012b). We recently studied pollen, macrofossils and ancient DNA from three new cores from a neighboring lake, combined with a review of all previous records from the region, and confirmed an overall rich and varied flora with a total of 94 plant taxa from the period before 14.7 cal BP

(Alsos et al. 2020). We found exceptionally high organic matter content and high isotopic values of nitrogen and carbon, suggesting that carbon and nitrogen were derived from marine sources via birds. The finding of bones of the little auk gave further evidence suggesting nutrient input from a bird colony. Unfortunately, it was difficult to obtain high-quality DNA data from the lake sediments at this site, and although pine and spruce DNA was found, the amounts were only marginally above the background contamination. Thus, whereas the new and improved environmental reconstruction of this site did not preclude local growth of pine or spruce, their presence still remains to be confirmed. We did confirm, however, the less disputed survival of high arctic poppies *Papaver* by findings of seeds and by obtaining new AMS dates, showing that this area was ice-free from ca. 26 000 cal. BP (Alsos et al. 2020).

Concluding Remarks

Most of the new data accumulated since our 2003 review strengthen the scenario of massive postglacial immigration, rendering the glacial survival theory in its original sense *superfluous* for most species (Brochmann et al. 2003). It is no longer *necessary* to postulate glacial survival in the East Atlantic to explain biogeographic disjunctions in species, because their dispersal capacity generally turns out be much higher than previously thought, nor to explain endemic species or subspecies, because the level of endemism turns out to be extremely low in the light of modern taxonomy and new data. Nevertheless, new data revealing 'endemic genetic groups' and patterns of genetic diversity within species (Westergaard et al. 2011, 2019), as well as more favorable conditions than previously thought at the LGM ice-free area on Andøya (Alsos et al. 2020), suggest that some populations of some species did persist in ice-free areas within mainly glaciated regions. It is likely that several ongoing projects using next-generation sequencing techniques for both modern and ancient DNA, combined with traditional palaeoecological methods, soon will shed new light on the glacial survival debate.

Acknowledgements

We are indebted to our former university teachers and supervisors, our own research groups and our colleagues for numerous discussions of this topic during many years.

References

Abbott, R.J., Smith, L.C., Milne, R.I. et al. (2000). Molecular analysis of plant migration and refugia in the Arctic. *Science* 289: 1343–1346.

Abbott, R.J. and Brochmann, C. (2003). History and evolution of the arctic flora: in the footsteps of Eric Hultén. *Molecular Ecology* 12: 299–313.

Alsos, I., Engelskjøn, T., Gielly, L. et al. (2005). Impact of ice ages on circumpolar molecular diversity: insight from an ecological key species. *Molecular Ecology* 14: 2739–2753.

Alsos, I.G., Eidesen, P.B., Ehrich, D. et al. (2007). Frequent long-distance colonisation in the changing Arctic. *Science* 316: 1606–1609.

Alsos, I.G., Alm, T., Normand, S., and Brochmann, C. (2009). Past and future range shift and loss of genetic diverstity in dwarf willow (*Salix herbacea* L.) inferred from genetics, fossils, and modelling. *Global Ecology and Biogeography* 18: 223–239.

Alsos, I.G., Ehrich, D., Eidesen, P.B. et al. (2015). Long-distance plant dispersal to North Atlantic islands: colonisation routes and founder effect. *AoB Plants* 7: plv036. https://doi.org/10.1093/aobpla/plv036.

Alsos, I.G., Ehrich, D., Seidenkrantz, M.-S. et al. (2016). The role of sea ice for vascular plant dispersal in the Arctic. *Biology Letters* 12: 20160264.

Alsos, I.G., Sjögren, P., Brown, A.G. et al. (2020). Last Glacial Maximum environmental conditions at Andøya, northern Norway: evidence for a northern ice-edge ecological 'hotspot. *Quaternary Science Reviews* 239: 106364.

Bauert, M.R., Kalin, M., Baltisberger, M., and Edwards, P.J. (1998). No genetic variation detected within isolated relict populations of *Saxifraga cernua* in the Alps using RAPD markers. *Molecular Ecology* 7: 1519–1527.

Bennike, O. and Böcher, J. (1990). Forest-tundra neighboring the North Pole: plant and insect remains from the Plio-Pleistocene Kap København formation, North Greenland. *Arctic* 43: 331–338.

Berg, R.Y. (1963). Disjunksjoner i Norges fjellflora og de teorier som er framsatt til forklaring av dem. *Blyttia* 21: 133–177. (In Norwegian with English summary).

Berg, R.Y. (1983). Plant distribution as seen from plant dispersal. General prinsiples and basic modes of plan dispersal. In: *Dispersal and Distribution* (ed. K. Kubitzki), 13–36. Hamburg: Verlag Paul Parley.

Birkeland, S., Skjetne, E.B., Brysting, A.K. et al. (2017). Living on the edge: conservation genetics of seven thermophilous plant species in a High Arctic archipelago. *AoB Plants* https://doi.org/10.1093/aobpla/plx001.

Birks, H.H., Giesecke, T., Hewitt, G.M. et al. (2012). Comment on 'Glacial survival of boreal trees in northern Scandinavia'. *Science* 338: 742.

Birks, H.H. (1994). Plant macrofossils and the nunatak theory of per-glacial survival. *Dissertations in Botany* 234: 129–143.

Birks, H.J.B. and Willis, K.J. (2008). Alpines, trees, and refugia in Europe. *Plant Ecology and Diversity* 1: 147–160.

Böcher, T. (1956). Area-limits and isolation of plants in relation to the physiography of the southern parts of Greenland. *Meddeleser om Grønland* 124: 1–40.

Böcher, T.W. (1966). Experimental and cytological studies on plant species. *IX. Some arctic and montane crucifers. Biologiske Skrifter* 14 (7): 1–74.

Böcher, T.W. (1983). The allotetraploid *Saxifraga nathorstii* and its diploid probale progenitors *S. aizoides* and *S. oppositifolia. BioScience* 11: 1–22.

Brochmann, C., Xiang, Q.Y., Brunsfeld, S.J. et al. (1998). Molecular evidence for polyploid origins in *Saxifraga* (Saxifragaceae): the narrow arctic endemic *S. svalbardensis* and its widespread allies. *American Journal of Botany* 85: 135–143.

Brochmann, C. and Håpnes, A. (2001). Reproductive strategies in some arctic *Saxifraga* (Saxifragaceae), with emphasis on the narrow endemic *S. svalbardensis* and its parental species. *Botanical Journal of the Linnean Society* 137: 31–49.

Brochmann, C., Gabrielsen, T.M., Nordal, I. et al. (2003). Glacial survival or *tabula rasa*? The history of North Atlantic biota revisited. *Taxon* 52: 417–450.

Brochmann, C. and Brysting, A.K. (2008). The Arctic – An evolutionary freezer? *Plant Ecology and Diversity* 1: 181–195.

Brochmann, C., Edwards, M., and Alsos, I.G. (2013). The dynamic past and future of arctic plants: climate change, spatial variation, and genetic diversity. In: *The Balance of Nature and Human Impact* (ed. K. Rhode), 133–152. Cambridge: Cambridge University Press.

Clarke, C.L., Edwards, M.E., Gielly, L. et al. (2019). Persistence of arctic-alpine flora during 24,000 years of environmental change in the Polar Urals. *Scientific Reports* 9 (1): 19613.

Dahl, E. (1955). Biogeographic and geologic indications of unglaciated areas in Scandinavia during the Ice Ages. *Bulletin of the Geological Society of America* 66: 1499–1519.

Dahl, E. (1963). Plant migrations across the North Atlantic Ocean and their importance for the palaeogeography of the region. In: *North Atlantic Biota and Their History* (eds. Á. Löve and D. Löve), 173–188. Oxford: Pergamon.

Dahl, E. (1987). The nunatak theory reconsidered. *Ecological Bulletins* 38: 77–94.

Ehrich, D., Gaudeul, M., Assefa, A. et al. (2007). Genetic consequences of Pleistocene range shifts: contrast between the Arctic, the Alps and the East African mountains. *Molecular Ecology* 16: 2542–2559.

Ehrich, D., Alsos, I.G., and Brochmann, C. (2008). Where did the northern peatland species survive the dry glacials: cloudberry (*Rubus chamaemorus*) as an example? *Journal of Biogeography* 35: 801814.

Ehrich, D., Eidesen, P.B., Alsos, I.G., and Brochmann, C. (2009). An AFLP clock for absolute dating of shallow-time evolutionary history – Too good to be true? *Molecular Ecology* 18: 4526–4532.

Eidesen, P.B., Alsos, I.G., Popp, M. et al. (2007a). Nuclear versus plastid data: complex Pleistocene history of a circumpolar key species. *Molecular Ecology* 16: 3902–3925.

Eidesen, P.B., Carlsen, T., Molau, U., and Brochmann, C. (2007b). Repeatedly out of Beringia: *Cassiope tetragona* embraces the Arctic. *Journal of Biogeography* 34: 1559–1574.

Eidesen, P.B., Ehrich, D., Bakkestuen, V. et al. (2013). Genetic roadmap of the Arctic: plant dispersal highways, traffic barriers and capitals of diversity. *New Phytologist* 200: 898–910.

Elven, R., Murray, D.F., Razzhivin, V.Y., and Yurtsev, B.A. (eds.) (2011). *Annotated Checklist of the Panarctic Flora (PAF)*. University of Oslo: Vascular plants. Natural History Museum http://nhm2.uio.no/paf/.

Epp, L.S., Gussarova, G., Boessenkool, S. et al. (2015). Lake sediment multi-taxon DNA from North Greenland records early post-glacial appearance of vascular plants and accurately tracks environmental changes. *Quaternary Science Reviews* 117: 152–163.

Ferguson, I.K. (1972). Notes on the pollen morphology of *Saxifraga nathorstii* and its putative parents, *S. aizoides* and *S. oppositifolia*. *Kew Bulletin* 27: 475–481.

Gabrielsen, T.M., Bachmann, K., Jakobsen, K.S., and Brochmann, C. (1997). Glacial survival does not matter: RAPD phylogeography of Nordic *Saxifraga oppositifolia*. *Molecular Ecology* 6: 831–842.

Gabrielsen, T.M. and Brochmann, C. (1998). Sex after all: high levels of diversity detected in the arctic clonal plant *Saxifraga cernua* using RAPD markers. *Molecular Ecology* 7: 1701–1708.

Gussarova, G., Allen, G.A., Mikhaylova, Y. et al. (2015). Vicariance, long-distance dispersal, and regional extinction-recolonisation dynamics explain the disjunct circumpolar distribution of the arctic-alpine plant *Silene acaulis*. *American Journal of Botany* 102: 1703–1720.

Hadač, E. (1963). On the history and age of some arctic plant species. In: *North Atlantic Biota and Their History* (eds. Á. Löve and D. Löve), 207–219. Oxford: Pergamon.

Hansen, K.T., Elven, R., and Brochmann, C. (2000). Molecules and morphology in concert: tests of some hypotheses in Arctic *Potentilla* (Rosaceae). *American Journal of Botany* 87: 1466–1479.

Hewitt, G.M. (1996). Some genetic consequences of ice ages, and their role in divergence and speciation. *Biological Journal of the Linnean Society* 58: 247–276.

Hultén, E. (1937). *Outline of the History of Arctic and Boreal Biota during the Quarternary Period*. Cramer, New York: Lehre J.

Ikeda, H., Eidesen, P.B., Yakubov, V. et al. (2017). Late Pleistocene origin of the entire circumarctic range of the arctic-alpine plant *Kalmia procumbens*. *Molecular Ecology* 26: 5773–5783.

Ingólfsson, Ó. and Landvik, J.Y. (2013). The Svalbard–Barents Sea ice-sheet – Historical, current and future perspectives. *Quaternary Science Reviews* 64: 33–60.

Johansen, S. and Hytteborn, H. (2001). A contribution to the discussion of biota dispersal with drift ice and driftwood in the North Atlantic. *Journal of Biogeography* 28: 105–115.

Kjølner, S., Såstad, M., Taberlet, P., and Brochmann, C. (2004). Amplified fragment length polymorphism versus random amplified polymorphic DNA markers: clonal diversity in *Saxifraga cernua*. *Molecular Ecology* 13: 81–86.

Knaben, G. (1959a). On the evolution of the *radicatum*-group of the *Scapiflora* Papavers as studied in 70 and 56 chromosome species. *Part A. Cytotaxonomical aspects. Opera Botanica* 2 (3): 1–74.

Knaben, G. (1959b). On the evolution of the *radicatum*-group of the *Scapiflora* Papavers as studied in 70 and 56 chromosome species. *Part B. Experimental studies. Opera Botanica* 3 (3): 1–96.

Knaben, G. (1982). Om arts- og rasedannelse i Europa under Kvartærtiden 1. *Endemiske arter i Nord-Atlanteren. Blyttia* 40: 229–235. (in Norwegian with English summary).

Landvik, J.Y., Bondevik, S., Elverhøi, A. et al. (1998). The last glacial maximum of Svalbard and the Barents Sea area: ice sheet extent and configuration. *Quaternary Science Reviews* 17: 43–75.

Landvik, J.Y., Brook, E.J., Gualtieri, L. et al. (2003). Northwest Svalbard during the last glaciation: ice-free areas existed. *Geology* 31: 905–908.

Löve, Á. and Löve, D. (eds.) (1963). *North Atlantic Biota and their History*. Oxford: Pergamon.

Nordhagen, R. (1936). Skandinavias fjellflora og dens relasjoner til den siste istid. *Nordiska Naturforskarmöte i Helsingfors* 1936: 93–124.

Nordhagen, R. (1963). Recent discoveries in the south Norwegian flora and their significance for the understanding of the history of Scandinavian mountain flora during and after the last glaciation. In: *North Atlantic Biota and Their History* (eds. Á. Löve and D. Löve), 241–260. Oxford: Pergamon.

Nyléhn, J. & Hamre, E. 2002. Facultative apomixis and hybridization in arctic *Potentilla* section *Niveae* (Rosaceae). Contributions to an intricate taxonomy. PhD Thesis, University of Oslo.

Oliver, C., Hollingsworth, P.M., and Gornall, R.J. (2006). Chloroplast DNA phylogeography of the arctic-montane species *Saxifraga hirculus* (Saxifragaceae). *Heredity* 96: 222–231.

Parducci, L., Edwards, M.E., Bennett, K.D. et al. (2012a). Response to Comment on 'Glacial Survival of Boreal Trees in Northern Scandinavia'. *Science* 338: 742.

Parducci, L., Jørgensen, T., Tollefsrud, M.M. et al. (2012b). Glacial survival of boreal trees in northern Scandinavia. *Science* 335: 1083–1086.

Parducci, L., Bennett, K.D., Ficetola, G.F. et al. (2017). Transley Reviews: Ancient plant DNA from lake sediments. *New Phytologist* 214: 924–942.

Paus, A., Boessenkool, S., Brochmann, C. et al. (2015). Lake Store Finnsjøen – A key for understanding Late Glacial/Early Holocene vegetation and ice sheet dynamics in the central Scandes Mountains. *Quaternary Science Reviews* 121: 36–51.

Rijal, D.P., Heintzman, P.D., Lammers, Y. et al. (2020). Holocene plant diversity revealed by ancient DNA from 10 lakes in northern Fennoscandia. *bioRxiv* https://doi. org/10.1101/2020.11.16.384065.

Rønning, O.I. (1962). The Spitzbergen species of *Colpodium* Trin., *Pleuropogon* R. Br. and *Puccinellia* Parl. *Det Kongelige Norske Videnskabers Selskabs Skrifter* 4 (1961): 1–49.

Rønning, O.I. (1963). Phytogeographical problems in Svalbard. In: *North Atlantic Biota and Their History* (eds. Á. Löve and D. Löve), 99–107. Oxford: Pergamon Press.

Savile, D.B.O. (1972). Arctic adaptations in plants. *Canada Department of Agriculture Research Branch Monograph* 6: 1–81.

Schmickl, R., Jørgensen, M.H., Brysting, A.K., and Koch, M. (2010). The evolutionary history of the *Arabidopsis lyrata* complex: a hybrid in the amphi-Beringian area closes a large distribution gap and builds up a genetic barrier. *BMC Evolutionary Biology* 10: 98.

Schönswetter, P., Paun, O., Tribsch, A., and Niklfeld, H. (2003). Out of the Alps: colonisation of Northern Europe by East Alpine populations of the Glacier Buttercup *Ranunculus glacialis* L. (Ranunculaceae). *Molecular Ecology* 12: 3373–3381.

Schönswetter, P., Popp, M., and Brochmann, C. (2006). Rare arctic-alpine plants of the European Alps have different immigration histories: the snowbed species *Minuartia biflora* and *Ranunculus pygmaeus*. *Molecular Ecology* 15: 709–720.

Skrede, I., Eidesen, P.B., Portela, R.P., and Brochmann, C. (2006). Refugia, differentiation and postglacial migration in arctic-alpine Eurasia, exemplified by the mountain avens (*Dryas octopetala* L.). *Molecular Ecology* 15: 1827–1840.

Solstad, H. 2009. Taxonomy and evolution of the diploid and polyploid *Papaver* sect. *Meconella* (Papaveraceae). PhD Thesis, University of Oslo.

Sønstebø, J.H., Gielly, L., Brysting, A.K. et al. (2010). Using next-generation sequencing for molecular reconstruction of past arctic vegetation and climate. *Molecular Ecology Resources* 10: 1009–1018.

Steen, S.W., Gielly, L., Taberlet, P., and Brochmann, C. (2000). Same parental species but different taxa: molecular evidence for hybrid origins of the rare endemics *Saxifraga opdalensis* and *S. svalbardensis* (Saxifragaceae). *Botanical Journal of the Linnean Society* 132: 153–164.

Stewart, L., Alsos, I.G., Bay, C. et al. (2016). The regional species richness and genetic diversity of arctic vegetation reflect both past glaciations and current climate. *Global Ecology and Biogeography* 25: 430–442.

Steindórsson, S. (1963). Ice age refugia in Iceland as indicated by the present distribution of plant species. In: *North Atlantic Biota and Their History* (eds. Á. Löve and D. Löve), 303–320. Oxford: Pergamon.

Tollefsrud, M.M., Bachmann, K., Jakobsen, K.S., and Brochmann, C. (1998). Glacial survival does not matter – II: RAPD phylogeography of Nordic *Saxifraga cespitosa*. *Molecular Ecology* 7: 1217–1232.

Vik, U., Jørgensen, M.H., Kauserud, H. et al. (2010). Microsatellite markers show decreasing diversity but unchanged level of clonality in *Dryas octopetala* (Rosaceae) with increasing latitude. *American Journal of Botany* 97: 988–997.

Warming, E. (1888). Om Grønlands vegetation. *Meddelelser om Grønland* 12: 1–245.

Wasowicz, P. (2020). Annotated checklist of vascular plants of Iceland. *Fjölrit Náttúrufrœdistofnunar* 57: 1–193.

Westergaard, K.B., Alsos, I.G., Ehrich, D. et al. (2008). Genetic diversity and distinctiveness in Scottish alpine plants. *Plant Ecology and Diversity* 1: 329–338.

Westergaard, K.B., Jørgensen, M.H., Gabrielsen, T.M. et al. (2010). The extreme Beringian/Atlantic disjunction in *Saxifraga rivularis* (Saxifragaceae) has formed at least twice. *Journal of Biogeography* 37: 1262–1276.

Westergaard, K.B., Alsos, I.G., Popp, M. et al. (2011). Glacial survival may matter after all: nunatak signatures in the rare European populations of two west-arctic species. *Molecular Ecology* 20: 376–393.

Westergaard, K.B., Zemp, N., Bruederle L.P. et al. (2019). Population genomic evidence for plant glacial survival in Scandinavia. *Molecular Ecology* 28: 818–832.

Willerslev, E., Davison, J., Moora, M. et al. (2014). Fifty thousand years of Arctic vegetation and megafaunal diet. *Nature* 506: 47–51.

5

The Aquatic Fauna of the North Atlantic Islands with Emphasis on Iceland

Gísli Már Gíslason

Institute of Life and Environmental Sciences, University of Iceland, Reykjavík, Iceland

Introduction

This paper focuses on the island biogeography of aquatic invertebrates in the North Atlantic islands: Greenland, Svalbard, Iceland, Faroe Islands, Shetland and Orkney and adjacent larger regions, Norway and Britain. The islands have few aquatic species, almost no aquatic endemics, but their faunas are closely related. With the exception of the high arctic island of Svalbard, Iceland has the fewest number of insect species present, with 1606 species recorded (1240 in the last published species list; Ólafsson 1991, Ólafsson personal communication), compared to the 20 000 species in Norway and in Britain, the nearest larger regions to Iceland. This raises the biogeographical question as to when and how the colonization of Iceland and the other North Atlantic Islands took place.

The Tertiary climate was warm with relatively small latitudinal gradients. During the Palaeocene (66–57 Myr ago) and into the Eocene, most of the Earth enjoyed an equable and moist climate, and a tropical to subtropical flora and fauna flourished in Europe, reaching as far north as Svalbard and Ellesmere Island (Downes 1988). Towards the end of the Eocene (34 Myr ago), a cooling trend became evident, first at high latitudes. The climate warmed again during the Miocene but then progressive cooling set in, culminating in the onset of the Quaternary 'Ice Age' some 2.6 Myr ago. During the last glacial maximum (22 Kyr ago), ice covered almost all of Greenland, the present evidence indicating that only isolated nunataks and possibly fragments along coastal shelves remained ice-free (Brochmann et al. 2003). The late Weichselian ice sheet similarly covered virtually all of Svalbard, Iceland, Scandinavia, Scotland and the Scottish isles, extending as far as southern Ireland and southern England (CLIMAP 1976; Brochmann et al. 2003), but in the Antarctic only the south island of New Zealand and the small islands further south were affected.

The North Atlantic area was also the scene for major tectonic developments from the Tertiary onwards. Greenland began separating from Northern America about 80 Myr ago. Later, 65 Myr ago, the North Atlantic opened up with a rift between Greenland and Europe. The Norwegian Sea started expanding 47–50 Myr ago, initiating the isolation of the Faroes and this movement is still active today on the Reykjanes Ridge and

Biogeography in the Sub-Arctic: The Past and Future of North Atlantic Biota, First Edition.
Edited by Eva Panagiotakopulu and Jon P. Sadler.
© 2021 John Wiley & Sons Ltd. Published 2021 by John Wiley & Sons Ltd.

across central Iceland. Iceland seems to have separated from Greenland some 20–30 Myr ago and from the Faroes ca. 30–40 Myr ago. The age and timing of the final disappearance of a connecting land bridge is debated but it is generally agreed that it was at least non-existent at the onset of the Pleistocene, some 2.6 Myr (Downes 1988).

The Tertiary flora and fauna of the North Atlantic islands was very different from that of today. Exotic tree genera such as *Glyptostobus*, *Sequoia*, *Magnolia*, and *Cercidiphyllum* in addition to the northern hemisphere genera *Abies*, *Betula*, *Acer*, *Alnus* and *Populus* were common in West Iceland (Símonarson 1981, Grímsson et al. 2007), indicating warmer temperatures in Iceland. 'Proto-Iceland' was presumably connected to the mainland or accessible via a chain of islands (Grímsson et al. 2007). The late Tertiary fauna and flora of the North Atlantic islands, North America and Northern Europe showed a close relationship during this period (Friedrich et al. 1972).

Lindroth (1931, 1953, 1965) explained the present distribution of insects from land bridges between North-Western Europe to Greenland via Faroes and Iceland to Greenland.

Downes (1988) reviewed the formation of North Atlantic islands and the occurrence and dispersal of insects on the islands, with special emphasis on Lepidoptera. A more recent review (Buckland and Panagiotakopulu 2010) with special emphasis on the Faroe Islands indicates that most or all insects colonized the North Atlantic Islands after the Ice Age.

The coldest period was 25k years ago, when no boreal species could have survived, even if ice-free areas did exist in Iceland or on other ice-covered islands in the North Atlantic. However, the extent of the ice cover in Iceland was up to 100 nautical miles off the present coastline (Geirsdóttir et al. 2009, 2013), indicating no ice-free areas on the island. The Ice Age ended abruptly 11k years ago, when the temperature rose from severe coldness in the North Atlantic islands to a climate warmer than today in a few decades (Dansgaard et al. 1993; Geirsdóttir et al. 2013).

Aquatic Invertebrates

The distance from the mainland of Norway or from Britain to the North Atlantic islands differs, with Iceland and Greenland furthest away (Table 1). If colonization occurred from the mainland, the distance the organisms had to travel is considerable. Ecological studies on invertebrates with emphasis on their origin have focused on aquatic insects and crustaceans (Gíslason 2005). From a preliminary investigation of checklists of insects (Ólafsson 1991) and earlier studies (Lindroth 1931), aquatic crustaceans and insects

Table 1 Distances (km) between North Atlantic islands.

	Svalbard	Greenland	Iceland	Faroes	Norway	Shetland	Orkneys
Svalbard							
Greenland	400						
Iceland	1548	290					
Faroes	1790	1025	435				
Norway	823	1441	971	582			
Shetland	1876	1411	770	284	289		
Orkneys	2055	1492	850	320	419	78	
Britain	2120	1500	823	316	479	166	12

are good indicators of the origin of Icelandic invertebrates in general.

The number of species of Crustacea with diapausing stages that can withstand desiccation (Copepoda, Ostracoda) and insects on the North Atlantic islands decreases with the size of the islands and with the distance from Norway and Britain (Table 2, Figures 1 and 2). However, the number of Cladocera species, with diapausing eggs, that can be carried with birds is similar on the islands (Table 3) and represent 30% of the numbers in Britain and Norway.

Table 2 Number of species of aquatic insects on islands in the North Atlantic and Norway.

	Ephemeroptera	Plecoptera	Trichoptera	Simuliidae	Chironomidae
Svalbard	0	0	1	0	58
Greenland	1	0	7	5	117
Iceland	1	1	12	4	80
Faroes	0	0	20	2	72
Shetland	6	2	37	2	30
Orkney	15	13	73	2	?
Britain	47	34	198	34	439
Norway	46	35	193	45	505

Source: Based on King 1890; Crosskey 1965; Peterson 1977; Pinder 1978; Barry 1985; Andersen and Wiberg-Larsen 1987; Wallace et al. 1990; Edington and Hildrew 1995; Nilsson 1996, 1997; Hrafnsdóttir 2005; Andrew 2014; Naturhistoriska Riksmusset 2018; Pennington, 2018a, 2018b, Hansen and Gíslason 2020.

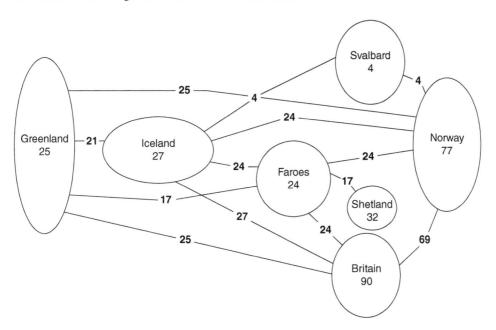

Figure 1 Numbers of Cladocera species on the North Atlantic islands and the numbers of species they have in common.

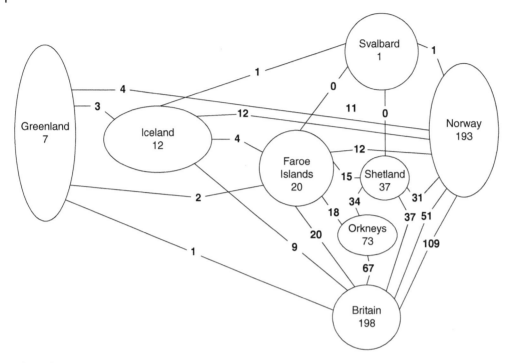

Figure 2 Numbers of Trichoptera species on the North Atlantic islands and the numbers of species they have in common.

Table 3 Number of species of freshwater Crustacea on islands in the North Atlantic and Norway.

	Ostracoda	Copepoda	Cladocera
Svalbard	4	6	4
Greenland	14	13	25
Iceland	14	48	27
Faroes	3	12	24
Shetland	?	20	32
Britain	80	91	90
Norway	62	67	77

Source: Based on Poulsen 1929, 1939; Scourfield and Harding 1966; Lindegaard 1979; Gíslason 2005; and own observations.

The same species of Cladocera occur on most of the islands, with numbers ranging between 24 and 32, except for Britain, where there are 90 species. In Norway, the number of species is 77. Svalbard is an exception, with only four recorded species of Cladocera (Table 3, Figure 1). The islands mostly share the same species.

Aquatic insect groups, such as Ephemeroptera and Plecoptera are non-existent on Svalbard and the Faroes and only a single ephmemeropteran taxon is found in Greenland. Iceland has a single species for each group (Table 2), but islands close to Britain, such as Orkney and Shetland have 6–15 species. Of the Diptera, only 2-5 species of Simuliidae are found on the islands, but Chironomidae are much better represented, with 30–117 species recorded on the islands, while 439 and 505 are recorded in Britain and Norway, respectively.

The number of Trichoptera species varied from 7 to 73 species on all the islands except Svalbard (1 species) and Britain (198 species)

(Gíslason 2005; Barnard and Ross 2012; Andrew 2014) (Table 2, Figure 2). All of the Icelandic species are found in Scandinavia but only nine in Britain, with none of the three circumpolar species found in Iceland occurring in the British Isles. In contrast to the distribution of Cladocera, the islands do not share the same Trichoptera fauna. For example, Iceland with 12 species, only shares four species with the Faroes, which in turn has 20 species (Figure 2) (Gíslason and Pálsson 2020, Hansen and Gíslason 2020). Greenland has a few species in common with the other islands and with Norway (Figure 2). All species occurring in Iceland are found in Norway but nine are shared with Britain. All 20 Faroese species are also found in Britain, but 12 in Norway (Hansen and Gíslason 2020). The species common to Greenland and Svalbard and found on the other islands and Norway have a circumpolar distribution. Other species found in Greenland are related to the North American fauna.

The number of aquatic cladocerans and copepods declines slightly with the distance from the mainlands, but the relationships are not statistically significant ($r = 0.5155$ and 0.8313, $n = 5$ for Norway and Britain, respectively) and Trichoptera on the North Atlantic islands decreases significantly with the distance from the mainland of Norway (Figure 3), with fewest numbers in Iceland and Greenland.

Most of the Trichoptera (and other insects) found on the North Atlantic islands are of Palaearctic origin (Gíslason 2005), but some species are circumpolar. Of the 12 Icelandic species, three are circumpolar and none are of Nearctic origin.

In a study of *Apatania zonella* (an arctic circumpolar, parthenogenetic trichopteran taxon with 1–2% males; Corbet 1966; Gíslason 1977; Raastad and Solem 1989), specimens were obtained from different parts of Iceland, Norway, Alaska, Northern USA and Canada and Greenland. The *A. zonella*

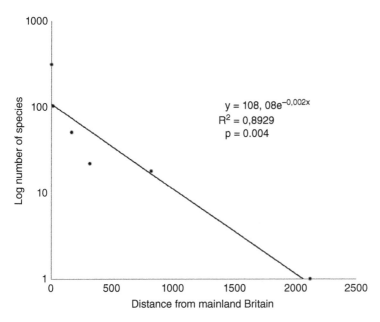

Figure 3 Number of species of Ephemeroptera, Plecoptera, Trichoptera, and Diptera: Simuliidae on the North Atlantic islands versus distance from the mainland of Britain (Greenland and Norway excluded).

specimens from Iceland originated from more than one colonization event, with at least one from North America through Greenland and one from Scandinavia (Pálsson et al. 2016). The specimens in North West Iceland are related to Scandinavian specimens, but specimens in South West and South Iceland are related to Greenland specimens. Some interbreeding has occurred in Iceland (Pálsson et al. 2016). Another Palaearctic trichopteran species, *Potamophylax cingulatus*, colonized Iceland in the twentieth century and was distributed in lowlands of East and Northeast Iceland until 1978 (Gíslason 1981; Gíslason et al. 2015). The species is now found in all lowland areas in Iceland (Gíslason et al. 2015). The species originated from southern middle Europe (Czech Republic) and dispersed in two directions, to the Iberian peninsula and to France, then northwards to the British Isles. From Britain, one group dispersed to Faroes and Iceland and another to Scandinavia (Gíslason et al. 2015). The Icelandic specimens are more related to the Faroes and British specimens than to those from Scandinavia (Gíslason et al. 2015).

Endemism

The only endemic species of aquatic invertebrates in Iceland are two subterranean amphipods. They live in the groundwater systems in the volcanic active zone. One species, *Crymostygius thingvallensis*, has only been found in two locations (Kristjánsson and Svavarsson 2004, 2007) and is of a distinct endemic family (Crymostygidae). The other species, *Cranonyx islandicus* (Svavarsson and Kristjánsson 2006), is widespread in the volcanic active zone crossing Iceland from south-west to north-east Iceland. Its populations have been isolated for differing lengths of time, and the oldest separation, on each side of the volcanic zone in North Iceland, occurred 5 million years ago (Kornobis et al. 2010), 2.5 million years before the onset of the Ice Age.

Discussion

The present occurrence and distribution of freshwater invertebrates on the North Atlantic islands can be explained according to the theory of island biography (MacArthur and Wilson 1967), where the number of species on islands decreases with increasing distance from continents (Figure 3), but in this case the number does not increase significantly with increasing size of islands. The number of planktonic crustaceans do not decline significantly from the mainlands (Britain or Norway) and the number between the islands are similar, with the exceptionally low numbers for Svalbard (Table 3, Figure 1). There is no evidence of land bridges between the islands during the last 20 million years (see, e.g., Heezen and Tharp 1963). The pre-Pleistocene fauna was similar to the present-day fauna of North America (Friedrich et al. 1972), while the contemporary fauna is mainly of Palaearctic origin. The present-day fauna of Iceland has a small proportion of arctic species, the Cladocera four species (Figure 1), and the Trichoptera of Iceland only has a single high arctic species, *A. zonella* (Zett.) (Figure 2) (Gíslason 1981).

The maximum extent of the ice sheet during the Late Weichselian limited ice-free areas and these were likely to be on Andøya in Lofoten and on south-west coast of Norway, with some in the Faroes, and on the Outer Hebrides and north-west Scotland. Southern England and Ireland were also ice-free. Iceland and Svalbard were most likely entirely covered by ice, but some nunataks in Greenland were ice free, according to Brochmann et al. (2003). The freshwater invertebrate fauna on the North Atlantic islands has a boreal distribution (Figures 1 and 2), related to the present fauna of continental Norway and Britain, but not related to the pre-Ice Age fauna; nor are there arctic species to any extent, except in the present high arctic (Svalbard and North Greenland), which would be expected if some species had survived the Ice Age.

The number of species of aquatic insects declines with distance from continental Europe and with island area (Figures 3), but the proportion of continental (Norway and Britain) species present on the islands is much higher among crustaceans than insects. This indicates that crustaceans are better equipped for long-distance dispersal, which may be related to their dry-resistant diapausing eggs (e.g. cladoceran *ephippia*), which can be transported in bird feathers or possibly in bird's stomachs. Their representation in Iceland, for example, is 33–77% compared with Norway and Britain. However, aquatic insects do not have life stages that can be transported by birds and usually disperse on the wing. It is also possible that at the end of the Ice Age, when pack ice covered the Arctic Ocean as far south as Iceland, a number of insect species were transported by floating ice from Norway and the British Isles to the North Atlantic islands (Buckland et al. 1986). Aquatic insect taxa are poorly represented in Iceland, making up only 0–16% of the total aquatic insect fauna of Norway and Britain.

Comparison with the Greenland fauna is difficult because of its Nearctic origins (Böcher 2002), but the other North Atlantic islands are dominated by Palaearctic species. The fauna of South Greenland has a boreal distribution, but arctic fauna, related to the fauna of northern Canadian islands, is to be found in North Greenland, north of 70°N (Downes 1988).

It is therefore likely that the only aquatic species to survive the Ice Age are those in subterranean groundwater, which may be influenced by geothermal water. The two Amphipoda species found in groundwater systems in Iceland are cold stenotherms (Kristjánsson and Svavarsson 2007), which must have existed during the Ice Ages. One of the species already existed in Iceland 5 million years ago (Kornobis et al. 2010) and may have had a wider distribution before the onset of the Ice Age.

Crustaceans with diapausing eggs that can be carried by waterfowl from the mainland to the islands show similarity in species composition. However, when comparing the species composition of crustaceans without resting eggs and aquatic insects on the North Atlantic islands, it reflects more the stochastic nature of the colonization rather than the survival of species reaching these islands. This is also supported by the fact that almost all invertebrate species in Iceland (>95%) have a boreal distribution in the Palaearctic region, with only a few species with a circumpolar distribution. Only the high arctic species would have survived the harsh arctic environment. Geological evidence (Geirsdóttir et al. 2009, 2013) strongly suggests that ice-free areas hardly existed in Iceland during the coldest period of the Ice Age, making it impossible for terrestrial invertebrates or invertebrates with a terrestrial life stage to survive.

This analysis, with the exception of the endemism found amongst crustaceans in subterranean groundwater systems, seems to fit well with the Holocene origin of higher plants in Iceland and on the other North Atlantic islands (Aegisdóttir and Thórhallsdóttir 2004).

References

Aegisdóttir, H.H. and Thórhallsdóttir, T.E. (2004). Theories on migration and history of the North-Atlantic flora: a review. *Jökull* 54: 1–16.

Andersen, T. and Wiberg-Larsen, P. (1987). Revised check-list of NW European Trichoptera. *Entomologica scandinavica* 18: 165–184.

Andrew, R.H. 2014. Orkney caddis (Trichoptera) species list with ecological notes: Part 1. *Orkney Field Club Bulletin* 2014: 43–52.

Barnard, P. and Ross, E. (2012). The adult Trichoptera (caddisflies) of Britain and Ireland. In: Handbooks for the Identification of British

Insects, vol. 1. Part 17, 192. St. Albans.: Royal Entomological Society.

Barry, J.R. (1985). The Natural History of Orkney, 300. London: Collins.

Böcher, J. (2002). Insekter og andre smådyr – I Grønlands fjeld og ferskvand, 302. Nuuk: Forlaget Atuagkat.

Brochmann, C., Gabrielsen, T.M., Nordal, I. et al. (2003). Glacial survival or tabula rasa? The history of North Atlantic biota revisited. *Taxon* 52: 417–450. https://doi.org/10.2307/3647444.

Buckland, P.C. and Panagiotakopulu, E. (2010). Reflections on North Atlantic Island biogeography: a quaternary entomological view. *Annales Societatis Scientiarum Færoensis Supplimentum* 52: 181–209.

Buckland, P.C., Perry, D.W., Gíslason, G.M., and Dugmore, A.J. (1986). The pre-Landnám fauna of Iceland: a palaeontological contribution. *Boreas* 15: 173–184. https://doi. org/10.1111/j.1502-3885.1986.tb00081.x.

CLIMAP (1976). The surface of the ice age earth. *Science* 191: 1131–1144. https://doi.org/10.1126/science.191.4232.1131.

Corbet, P.S. (1966). Parthenogenesis in caddisflies (Trichoptera). *Canadian Journal of Zoology* 44: 981–982. https://doi.org/10.1139/z66-100.

Crosskey, R.W. (1965). A new species of *Simulium* (*Eusimulium*) from St. Helena Island, South Atlantic (Diptera: Simuliidae). *Proceedings of the Royal Entomological Society of London, Series B Taxonomy* 34: 33–37. https://doi.org/10.1111/j.1365-3113.1965.tb01646x.

Dansgaard, W., Johnsen, S.J., Clausen, H.B. et al. (1993). Evidence for general instability of past climate from a 250-kyr ice-core record. *Nature* 364: 218–220. https://doi.org/10.1038/364218a0.

Downes, J.A. (1988). The post-glacial colonization of the North Atlantic islands. *Memoirs of the Entomological Society of Canada* 144: 55–92. https://doi.org/10.4039/entm120144055-1.

Edington, J.M. and Hildrew, A.G. (1995). A Revised Key to the Caseless Caddis Larvae of the British Isles, with Notes on Their Ecology, Freshwater Biological Association, 134. Scientific Publication No. 52.

Friedrich, W.L., Símonarson, L.A., and Heie, O.E. (1972). Steingervingar í millilögum í Mókollsdal (English summary: tertiary fossils from Mókollsdalur, NW-Iceland). *Náttúrufræðingurinn* 42: 4–17.

Geirsdóttir, Á., Miller, G.H., Axford, Y., and Ólafsdóttir, S. (2009). Holocene and latest Pleistocene climate and glacier flutctuations in Iceland. *Quaternary Science Reviews* 28: 2107–2118. https://doi.org/10.1016/j.quascirev.2009.03.013.

Geirsdóttir, Á., Miller, G.H., Larsen, D.J., and Ólafsdóttir, S. (2013). Abrupt Holocene climate transitions in the northern North Atlantic region recorded by synchronized laustrine records in Iceland. *Quaternary Science Reviews* 71: 48–62. https://doi.org/10.1016/j.quascirev.2013.03.010.

Gíslason, G.M. 1977. Aspects of the biology of Icelandic Trichoptera, with comparative studies on selected species from Northumberland, England. Department of Zoology, University of Newcastle upon Tyne. PhD Thesis. 412 pp.

Gíslason, G.M. 1981. Distribution and habitat preferences of Icelandic Trichoptera. In: *Proceedings of the 3rd International Symposium on Trichoptera* (ed. G.P. Moretti). Series Entomologia. 20, 99–109. Dr. W. Junk Publishers, Haag.

Gíslason, G.M. (2005). The origin of the freshwater fauna of the North-Atlantic Islands. Present distribution in relation to climate and possible migration routes. *Verhandlungen der Internationale Vereinigung für Theoretische und Angewandte Limnologie* 29: 198–203. https://doi.org/10.1080/03680770.2005.11901995.

Gíslason, G.M., Hannesdóttir, E.R., Munoz, S.S., and Pálsson, S. (2015). Origin and dispersal of *Potamophylax cingulatus* (Steph.) (Trichoptera: Limnephilidae) in Iceland. *Freshwater Biology* 60: 387–394. https://doi.org/10.1111/fwb.12501.

Gíslason, G.M. and Pálsson, S. (2020). Origin of the Trichoptera species in Iceland. *Zoosymposia* 18: 118–126. https://doi.org/10.11646/zoosymposia.18.1.15.

Grímsson, F., Denk, T., and Simonarsson, L.A. (2007). Middle Miocene floras of Iceland – the early colonization of an island? *Review of Paleobotany & Palynology* 144: 181–219. https://doi.org/10.1016/j.revpalbo.2006.07.003.

Harding, J.P. and Smith, W.A. (1960). A Key to the British Freshwater Cyclopid and Calanoid Copepods, Freshwater Biological Association, 56. Scientific Publication. No. 18.

Hansen, L.J. and Gíslason, G.M. (2020). Trichoptera of the Faroe Islands. *Zoosymposia* 18: 127–134. https://doi.org/10.11646/zoosymposia.18.1.16.

Heezen, B.C. and Tharp, M. (1963). The Atlantic floor. In: North Atlantic Biota and Their History (eds. A. Löve and D. Löve), 21–27. Oxford: Pergamon Press.

Hrafnsdóttir, T. (2005). Diptera 2 (Chironomidae). *Zoology of Iceland* 3 (48): 1–169.

Hynes, H.B.N. (1967). A Key to the Adults and Nymphs of the British Stoneflies (Plecoptera), with Notes on Their Ecology and Distribution, Freshwater Biological Association, 92. Scientific Publication No. 17.

King, J.J.F.X. (1890). Neuroptera from the island of Unst. *Entomologist's Monthly Magazine* 26: 176–180.

Kornobis, E., Pálsson, S., Kristjánsson, B.K., and Svavarsson, J. (2010). Molecular evidence of the survival of subterranean amphipods (Arthropoda) during Ice Age underneath glaciers in Iceland. *Molecular Ecology* 19: 2516–2530. https://doi.org/10.1111/j.1365-294X.2010.04663.x.

Kristjánsson, B.K. and Svavarsson, J. (2004). Crymostygidae, a new family of subterranean freshwater gammaridean amphipods (Crustacea) recorded from subarctic Europe. *Journal of Natural History* 38: 1881–1894. https://doi.org/10.1080/00222930310001597295.

Kristjánsson, B.K. and Svavarsson, J. (2007). Subglacial refugia in Iceland enabled groundwater amphipods to survive glaciations. *The American Naturalist* 170: 292–296. https://doi.org/10.1086/518951.

Lindegaard, C. (1979). The invertebrate fauna of Lake Mývatn, Iceland. *Oikos* 32: 151–161. https://doi.org/10.2307/3544225.

Lindroth, C. (1931). Die Insektenfauna Islands und ihre Probleme. *Zoologiska Bidrag från Uppsala* 13: 105–589.

Lindroth, C. (1953). Influence of Pleistocene climate change on the insect fauna of Northern Europe. *Transactions of the IX international Congress of Entomology* 2: 145–153.

Lindroth, C. (1965). Skaftafell, Iceland, a living glacial refugium. *Oikos* (Supplement 6): 1–142.

MacArthur, R.H. and Wilson, E.O. (1967). The Theory of Island Biogeography, 203. Princeton: Princeton University Press.

Naturhistoriska Riksmusset 2018. Check-list of Norwegian Trichoptera. http://www2.nrm.se/en/trichopteranorway.html (retrieved May 8th, 2018).

Nilsson, A. (ed.) (1996). Aquatic Insects of North Europe. A Taxonomic Handbook. Stenstrup, Denmark: Apollo Book.

Nilsson, A. (ed.) (1997). Aquatic Insects of North Europe 2. A Taxonomic Handbook. Stenstrup, Denmark: Apollo Book.

Ólafsson, E. 1991. Íslenskt skordýratal (A checklist of Icelandic insects). Icelandic Institute of Natural History Report no. 17, 69 pp (in Icelandic, with English summary).

Pálsson, S., Lecaudey, L.A., and Gíslason, G.M. (2016). Phylogeographic origin of *Apatania zonella* (Trichoptera) in Iceland. *Freshwater Science* 35: 65–79. https://doi.org/10.1086/684850.2015.

Pennington, M. 2018a. Trichoptera. http://www.nature-shetland.co.uk/entomology/caddis.htm (retrieved May 8th, 2018).

Pennington, M. 2018b. Diptera. http://www.nature-shetland.co.uk/entomology/diptera.htm (retrieved May 8th, 2018).

Peterson, B.V. (1977). The black flies of Iceland (Diptera: Simuliidae). *Canadian Entomologist* 109: 449–472. https://doi.org/10.4039/Ent109449-3.

Pinder, L.C.V. (1978). A Key to Adult Males of British Chironomidae, Freshwater Biological Association, vol. 1-2, 169. Scientific Publication No. 37.

Poulsen, E.M. (1929). Freshwater Crustacea. *Zoology of Faroes* 2 (1,31): 1–21.

Poulsen, E.M. (1939). Freshwater Crustacea. *Zoology of Iceland* 3 (35): 1–50.

Raastad, J.E. and Solem, J.O. (1989). Autogeny as successful reproductive strategy in high altitude blackflies (Diptera, Simuliidae). *Annales de Limnologie* 25: 243–249. https://doi.org/10.1051/limn/1989026.

Scourfield, D.J. and Harding, J.P. (1966). A Key to the British Freshwater Cladocera, Freshwater Biological Association, 55. Scientific Publication No. 5.

Símonarson, L. (1981). Íslenskir steingervingar. In: Náttúra Íslands, 2e (eds. V.T. Gíslason and S. Thórarinsson), 157–173. Reykjavík: Almenna bókafélagid. 475.

Svavarsson, J. and Kristjánsson, B. (2006). *Crangonyx islandicus* sp.nov., a subterranean freshwater amphipod (Crustacea, Amphipoda, Crangonyctidae) from springs in lava fields in Iceland. *Zootaxa* 1365: 1–17. https://doi.org/10.11646/zootaxa.1365.1.1.

Wallace, I.D., Wallace, B., and Philipson, G.N. (1990). A key to the case-bearing caddis larvae of Britain and Ireland, Freshwater Biological Association, 237. Scientific Publication No. 51.

6

The Vascular Floras of High-Latitude Islands with Special Reference to Iceland

Thóra Ellen Thórhallsdóttir

Institute of Life and Environmental Sciences, University of Iceland, Reykjavík, Iceland

Introduction

Isolated islands and archipelagos are found at high latitudes in both the northern and southern hemispheres. Some are close to a mainland but most are oceanic and include some of the most isolated terrestrial landmasses on earth. High-latitude islands are found in all major oceans and include representatives of all four sea-island types (oceanic, continental fragments, continental shelf and island continents; Whittaker and Fernández-Palacios 2007). Many volcanic islands have never been part of a larger mainland and, for others, such connections were severed millions of years ago. In addition to the inherent constraints of all isolated islands, i.e. low probabilities of dispersal and increasing risk of extinction with decreasing island area, the species richness of high-latitude islands is limited by at least two additional factors. One is a harsh climate, something that all the islands have in common, although the particulars may vary from cool, wet and windy to extremely cold and inhospitable. The second is history, but this varies greatly among the high-latitude islands. Some experienced complete ice-cover during the Pleistocene while others had limited or even no glaciation.

Since the publication of MacArthur and Wilson's seminal work (1967), a massive literature has built up on the biogeography of oceanic islands, their patterns of species richness and endemism. The bulk of these studies is concerned with tropical, sub-tropical or temperate islands. The biogeography and floristics of the sub-antarctic islands have attracted some attention (e.g. Chown et al. 1998; McDowell 2005; Michaux and Leschen 2005; Van der Putten et al. 2010), but there are few comparable studies of islands in sub-arctic or arctic climates and fewer still that encompass biogeography and endemism of high-latitude islands in both hemispheres. A comparative assessment of high-latitude islands, evaluating what they have in common and where they differ, may increase understanding of how different degrees of isolation, climate and past history have shaped the floras of these distinctive biotas. Such a comparison may also be useful for throwing light on the position of individual islands and here the focus is particularly on Iceland. The purpose of this paper is thus fourfold: (a) to evaluate and discuss

Biogeography in the Sub-Arctic: The Past and Future of North Atlantic Biota, First Edition.
Edited by Eva Panagiotakopulu and Jon P. Sadler.
© 2021 John Wiley & Sons Ltd. Published 2021 by John Wiley & Sons Ltd.

the richness and distinctiveness of high-latitude island vascular floras, with particular reference to Iceland, (b) to describe the composition and characteristics of the Icelandic vascular flora, (c) to discuss its richness and floristic distinctiveness in comparisons with other North-Atlantic islands, and (d) to present and evaluate arguments that may shed light on its age and origin.

A Survey of High-Latitude Islands

Seventeen islands and archipelagos were selected (Figure 1, Table 1). In the northern hemisphere (at 56–82°N), Iceland, the Faroe Islands, Jan Mayen, Bear Island and Svalbard are in the northeastern North Atlantic, Franz Josef Land and Wrangel in the Arctic ocean and Probilof islands in the Bering Sea in the north Pacific. Nine are at 44–54°S: the Falkland Islands and South Georgia in the Atlantic, Marion, Kerguelen and Heard in the Indian ocean and Chatham, Auckland, Campbell and Macquarie in the Pacific east or south of New Zealand. In addition, Iceland's nearest neighbour, the island continent of Greenland, is included for some comparisons. The islands encompass all the major oceans and island types (Whittaker and Fernández-Palacios 2007): island continent (Greenland), continental island (Wrangel), continental fragment (Falklands) and oceanic (the remaining 15 islands). They vary over almost three orders of magnitude in area and climatically from subarctic/subantarctic to high arctic and extremely cold. Two island groups actually enjoy milder climates, the cool-temperate Faroes and the still warmer Chatham Islands. Iceland, the Faroes, Greenland, Svalbard, Pribilof, Chatham and the Falklands are inhabited. On the remaining 11 islands, there is no permanent habitation (except sometimes scientific research stations, and Auckland was temporarily settled in the nineteenth century). Iceland, by far the largest island (excluding Greenland) resides

just below the Arctic Circle in the eastern North Atlantic, at the junction of hot and cold air masses and ocean currents, and almost 1000 km from the European continent. It is among the world's most volcanically active regions, with massive tephra falls accompanying some eruptions. About 10% of Iceland is covered by glaciers and the combination of volcanoes and large glaciers makes for a particularly destructive interaction.

The islands vary in almost all relevant environmental variables: size, degree of isolation, geological history, climate, topography and bedrock type. Therefore, several caveats must be borne in mind when undertaking comparisons. Most of the islands, including Iceland, are of volcanic origin and classified as oceanic. The definition of an oceanic island often includes two criteria, first that it is of oceanic crust (Nunn 2009) and second of never having been connected to a larger landmass (Whittaker and Fernández-Palacios 2007). In fact, the geological history of some islands may be more complex than is implied by their conventional classification as oceanic. In the early Tertiary, Iceland was part of a land bridge from Greenland to northwest Europe and connection to Greenland may have persisted until the mid Miocene (Grímsson et al. 2007). Some of the subantarctic oceanic islands may not have been isolated throughout their history either (Michaux and Leschen 2005). The continental shelf islands are typically composed of granite, lie close to a continent and were often connected during periods of lowered sea levels in the Pleistocene. Wrangel is slightly more isolated than the other continental islands off Siberia, but it is of particular interest here because, alone among the arctic and north Atlantic islands, it was ice free and part of Beringia during the last glacial period (Gualtieri et al. 2005). The granitic Falkland Islands are also of continental origin, being a fragment that broke away from Gondwanaland about a million years ago (Coffin 2009). Island age may be related to type of origin, with continental islands

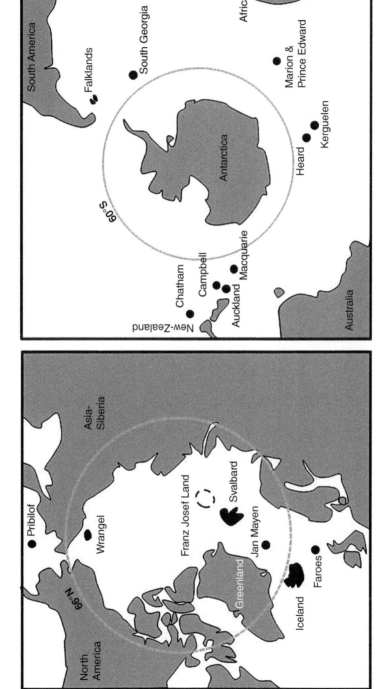

Figure 1 Location of the selected islands in the northern (left) and southern (right) hemispheres.

Table 1 A comparison of the selected northern and southern hemisphere islands, with Greenland included for some variables.

Island or archipelago	Latitude N/S	Isolation, km to nearest continent	Area, km² (largest in archipelago)	Ice-free, km² and %	Max. altitude, m	Origin	Mean °C of warmest month 1960–1990	N vascular spp. or taxa	N & % Endemic vascular taxa	Regional endemism
1 Iceland	63–67°N	810[a], 970[b]	103,000	93,000 90%	2,110	volcanic	10.6 Reykjavik 7.0 Hveravellir	443	0	}1
2 Faroes	62°N	330[a], 600[b], 450[c]	1,399 (373)	1,399 100%	882	volcanic	10.7	329	0	
3 Jan Mayen	70–71°N	950[a], 550[c]	377	264 70%	2,277	volcanic	4.9	75	0	
4 Svalbard	78–81°N	700	62,000 (37,673)	25,400 40%	1,717	orogenic, volcanic	5.9	165	4 2.4%	
5 Bear	74°N	400	178	178 100%	536	orogenic	5.0 (4.4)	54	0	
6 Franz Josef Land	80–82°N	850[d]	16,134 (2,900)	2,420 15%	507	volcanic	0.8–1.0	57	0	
7 Wrangel	71°N	140[d]	7,609	7,600 100%	1,093	continental	2.5	417	23 5.5%	
8 Greenland	60–84°N		2,170,000	326,340 15%	3,694	continental		515	12 (35) 2.3% (6.8%)	
9 Pribilof islands	56–57N	480	195 (104)	195 100%	203	volcanic	10.8	184	0?	
10 Chatham	44°S	863	970 (900)	970 100%	287	volcanic	14.8	441	≥41, ≥9%	
11 Auckland	50°S	465	626 (510)	626 100%	667	volcanic	11.2	187	4 2.1%	}Campbell province endemics = 35
12 Campbell	52°S	700	113	113 100%	569	volcanic	9.3	126	2 1.6%	
13 Macquarie	54°S	990	123	123/118 100%	433	tectonic	7.0	41 40	2 5%	

14	Falkland islands	51–53°S	530–550	12,200 (5,000)	12,200 100%	705	continental	9–10	159	13 8.2% } 1 fern shared by Falklands & S. Georgia
15	South Georgia	54°S	2,210	3,600	1481 42%	2,934	volcanic?	ca 6	25	0
16	Kerguelen	48–50°S	3.000	6,200 5,799	5,450 90%	1,850	volcanic	7.7	29	1 } Kerguelen province endemics = 6
17	Heard	53°S	3,850	367	91 25%	2,745	volcanic	4.2	11	0
18	Marion	46°S	1,900	290	>287 90%	1,230	volcanic	7.7	23	0

N and S refer to hemispherical location, latitude given to nearest degree. Distances to mainland: [a] Scotland, [b] Norway, [c] Iceland, [d] Siberia. For Chatham and the sub-antarctic islands, distance to New Zealand is used as a measure of isolation. References are cited for each island by reference number in the first column.

Glaciers and ice-free cover: 1. Statistics Iceland, http://www.statice.is; 3. Anda et al. (1985); 4. Hagen et al. (1993); 6. Lubinski et al. (1999). 8. Jensen and Christensen (2003), pp. 15–18; Hall (2002).

Climate: 1. Mean July *t*°C 1961–1990, Icelandic Meteorological Office, http://www.vedur.is/vedur/vedurfar/medaltalstoflur/#aa; 2. Mean July *t*°C 1961–1990 for Thórshavn, Danish Meteorological Office, http://www.dmi.dk 3. Mean August *t*°C 1961–1990, Norwegian Meteorological Office, http://home.online. no/~vteigen/klima.html; 4. Mean July *t*°C 1961–1990 for Svalbard Lufthavn, Norwegian Meteorological Office, http://home.online.no/~vteigen/klima.html; 5. Bear: http://www.theweathernetwork.com/forecasts/statistics/C00009, Lower figure from: http://www.npolar.no/en/the-arctic/svalbard/bjornoya; 6. Lubinski et al. (1999); 7. Climate Change Knowledge Portal, World Bank; 9. http://docs.lib.noaa.gov/noaa_documents/NOS/ORR/TM_NOS_ORR/TM_NOS-ORR_17/HTML/Pribilof_html/Pages/pribilof_island_climate.htm; 10–12. McGlone (2002); 13. Mean 1948–1986, Selkirk et al. (1990); 14. Climate Change Knowledge Portal, The World Bank, http://www.weatherbase.com/weather/weatherall.php3?s=98888&units; 15. Cook et al. (2010); 16. Frenot et al. (2001); 17. http://www.heardisland.aq; 18. Mean February *t*°C 1961–1990, ftp://dossier.ogp.noaa.gov/GCOS/WMO-Normals/RA-I/UA/68994.TXT.

Species richness and endemism: Species richness is the number of indigenous vascular species. An attempt was made to include only species-level endemism (but note two figures for Greenland). Microspecies of *Hieracium*, *Taraxacum* and *Pilosella* were not included in endemic taxa numbers. Where possible, Appendices 9.1 and 9.2 of the Arctic Biodiversity Assessment (2013) were used as sources for species richness and endemism (CAFF 2013). Additional sources: 1. Kristinsson (2010); 2. Fosaa (2014), Jóhansen (2000); 3. Norsk polarinstitutt (1997), Lid (1964); 4. http://svalbardflora.net/index. php?id=1; 5. Engelskjøn (1986); 6. Gjertz and Mørkved (1992); 7. UNESCO (2004), http://whc.unesco.org/en/list/1023/documents; 8. Jensen and Christensen 2003 (where the first number for endemism is species level, second includes all taxa); 9. Unpublished list of vascular species from St Mathew Island courtesy of S. Talbot (2013); 10. De Lange et al. (2011); 11–12. Wardle (1991), also Johnson and Campbell (1975); 13. Van der Putten et al. (2010), also Selkirk et al. (1990) and Wardle (1991); 14. McDowell (2005), also Moore (1968); 15. Chown et al. (1998); 16. Frenot et al. (2001); 17. Turneret al. (2006), http://www.heardisland.aq/nature/plants/vascular; 18. Chown et al. (1998) and for regional endemism, see Wardle (1991) (Campbell province), Hennion and Walton (1997) (Kerguelen Phytogeographic Zone) and McDowell (2005) (Falkland Islands, S. Georgia).

being older than those of volcanic origin. Small volcanic islands, in particular, may have a much shorter life span with accompanying ontological changes, becoming more eroded and topographically homogeneous with time (Nunn 2009).

Iceland is by far the largest island (excepting Greenland), having a glacier-free area over three times that of Svalbard and almost eight times that of the Falkland Islands. Half the sample is made up of islands less than one hundredth the area of Iceland. Most lie 400–1000 km from the nearest continent. Wrangel is only 140 km from Siberia, but at the other extreme are four small sub-antarctic islands (Heard, Kerguelen, South Georgia and Marion) that rank among the most isolated landmasses on earth. As a measure of isolation, distance to the nearest continent is only an approximation and is likely to be hemisphere-biased, with the probability of propagule dissemination significantly lower for a given distance in the southern hemisphere with its much smaller terrestrial landmasses and generally more unfavourable dominant wind directions (Fraser et al. 2012). Altitudinal range is not simply related to land area, as some of the small oceanic islands are simply enormously large volcanoes. Some islands are a single terrestrial landmass while the area figures for the archipelagos are the sum of many smaller islands (Table 1). This has implications for expected total species richness for which it is difficult to adjust in a general survey such as here, and this potential bias is disregarded in the following comparisons. The alternative was to use individual islands as units. The data for doing so were not always available and, furthermore, analyses may be then confounded by autocorrelations within archipelagos (cf. Selmi and Boulinier 2001).

Mean temperature of the warmest month is given as an indication of climatic severity. The quality of available climatic data is variable, but this is not regarded as a significant concern for present purposes where an approximation is considered sufficient. The islands can be roughly divided into four climatic groups. The high arctic Franz Josef Land, Wrangel and the north part of Svalbard have an extremely harsh climate. The second group includes islands with warmest month temperatures of 5–8 °C (mildest part of Svalbard, Jan Mayen, Bear, Macquarie, South Georgia, Kerguelen and Heard, as well as much of the central highland of Iceland). The third group (ca. 9–11 °C) encompasses the Faroes, Pribilof islands, Auckland, Campbell and the Falklands, plus most of the lowlands of Iceland. The fourth includes only the Chatham Islands, which are placed on the boundary between cool and warm temperate (Meurk 1984). In the Circumpolar Arctic Vegetation map, Franz Josef Land falls into bioclimatic subzone A, Wrangel into B, Svalbard into A, B and C and Bear and Jan Mayen into subzone C. Only the northernmost part of Iceland is included (in subzone E), while the Faroes and Pribilof Islands are placed outside the Arctic (CAVM Team 2003). In the southern hemisphere, Auckland and Campbell are classified as sub-antarctic in a cool temperate climate and Macquarie as low antarctic (Meurk 1984). The small sub-antarctic islands have extremely oceanic climates characterized by high cloud cover and small daily and annual temperature fluctuations. Unlike their arctic counterparts, permafrost is usually absent on the sub-antarctic islands. Nine islands are ice-free, but on four, glaciers cover more than half of the total land area (Svalbard, Franz Josef Land, South Georgia and Heard).

It is clear from Table 1 that no other high-latitude island is comparable to Iceland in all three relevant parameters: climate, size and degree of isolation. Some of the sub-antarctic islands and the Falklands are climatically similar to parts of Iceland, the Faroes being somewhat warmer. Several islands are at similar distances to New Zealand as Iceland is to Norway or Scotland, but, as mentioned earlier, actual isolation is probably greater in the southern hemisphere.

Patterns of Species Richness

The almost thousand-fold variation in island area is accompanied by a 40-fold difference in vascular species richness. Evidently, area *per se* is a poor indicator of species richness for these high-altitude islands as a whole (Figure 2a). For example, the warm but small (<100th the size of Iceland) Chatham Islands, the cold but not-so-isolated Wrangel and Iceland all have similar-sized floras. The regression of log species richness on log glacier-free area ($N = 17$, Greenland not included), is barely statistically significant ($p = 0.053$). As might be expected, the distribution of residuals against expected value (Figure 2b) reveals that the warm islands have relatively high positive residuals and the very isolated and cold south hemisphere islands have relatively high negative residuals. Wrangel is noticeable as the only cold island among the higher positive values. Iceland has a rather low residual but the highest leverage (0.34).

The 17 islands may be separated into three groups: four extremely isolated and cold, six relatively warm and not-so-isolated, and the remaining seven islands (Figure 2c). Again it is evident that the extremely isolated and cold sub-antarctic islands fall below the other two groups and the warm islands above. The regression is only significant for the middle group of islands, and the warm-and-not-so-isolated group hardly reflects any relationship of species richness with area.

How do the two fundamental features of the species–area relationship (z representing the slope and c the intercept on the log S axis) for the high-latitude islands compare to other island groups? For islands, z has been reported to lie in the region of 0.2–0.4 (Spiller and Schoener 2009). For 90 studies Connor and McCoy (1979) found a mean value of 0.31 and the mean of a global survey of vascular species richness on 488 islands was 0.33 (Kreft et al. 2008). The values here, $z = 0.26$

for the whole island sample ($N = 17$) and 0.33 for the group of seven islands (Figure 3), fall within the range. The present results thus support the general conclusion that z is actually rather invariant, which means that islands 'collect' species at similar rates with increasing area, irrespective of the environmental setting. It may be added that a selection of islands covering several biogeographical provinces is expected to yield a higher z-value than comparisons within provinces or archipelagos (Rosenzweig 2004).

In contrast to the small span of z, the intercept c varies over three to five orders of magnitude (Lomolino 2001) and has been shown to be correlated with latitude and productivity (Wright 1983). Here, the coefficient was 2.7 for the whole sample and 2.2 for the group including Iceland (Figure 3). This is very low compared to low-latitude islands, for example to the value of 28.6 for Galapagos land plants (Krebs 2001).

Five independent variables were included in a stepwise multiple regression for the 17 island samples. The best-fit model left out glaciation history and maximum altitude, but together, log island area, isolation and warmest-month mean temperature accounted for much of the variation in vascular species richness (R^2 adjusted = 0.786). All were significant (after applying Bonferroni correction for multiple comparisons). However, the regression coefficient for isolation ($p < 0.001$) was very low (95% confidence interval of -0.001–0.000), inferring that when the other two independent variables are kept constant, species richness declines extremely slowly with increasing isolation. The slope is steepest for the log glacier-free area (0.057–0.338, $p = 0.01$), followed by a warmest month mean temperature (0.029–0.195, $p = 0.012$). No outliers were identified. The highest studentized residuals were for Heard and Wrangel, both positive, followed by the Falklands with a rather high negative value.

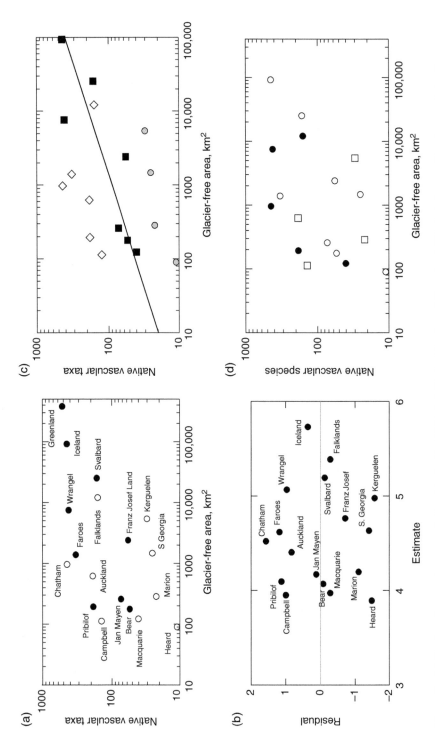

Figure 2 (a) The log–log species area relationship for the 17 high-latitude islands and Greenland. Filled circles are N and open circles S hemisphere islands. (b) The distribution of residuals against estimated value for the 17 islands. (c) The log–log species area relationship separating islands into three groups: filled circles = extremely isolated (≥1900 km) and cold (warmest month mean t <8 °C), open diamonds = not very isolated (≤700 km except for Chatham) and relatively warm (>8 °C) and black boxes with accompanying regression line = remaining islands. (d) The log–log species area relationship separating islands that were more or less completely glaciated (open circles), where glaciation was significant to extensive (filled boxes) or had little or no glaciation (black circles).

Comparisons to Global-Level and Other High-Latitude Island Studies

In a very large survey of vascular species richness of 488 islands, including high-latitude islands in both hemispheres, Kreft et al. (2008) selected the same or similar abiotic variables as here: area, isolation, mean annual air temperature and maximum elevation, but additionally geology (atolls, volcanic or continental origin) and precipitation. Area was by far the strongest predictor of species richness, explaining 66% of the variation in univariate analyses. In multivariate regression, the most significant predictors were in order of decreasing importance: area, isolation, temperature and precipitation. Their conclusions were therefore in line with the accepted paradigm that patterns of island species richness are most closely correlated with island area (Whittaker and Fernández-Palacios 2007).

Chown et al. (1998) investigated species–area relationships on 25 southern hemisphere islands, including nine of the same islands as here. They selected the same predictor variables (area, ice-free area, isolation, temperature, degree of glaciation and maximum altitude) plus three more (minimum age of surface rocks, date of human habitation and number of human occupants), a much wider latitudinal range (37–54°S) and very small islands in a more restricted size range (<2–7200 km^2). Their treatment differed in that their units were always individual islands; for example, East and West Falklands were treated as two separate units. As in the present data set, no single predictor variable reached statistical significance for explaining species richness. For vascular plants, area and temperature combined had the most explanatory power, although the model was sensitive to outliers. Once the small island of Bounty (1.35 km^2) had been removed, isolation explained most of the variance. Thus, their dataset revealed similar patterns as here, except that

their regression slope was higher for temperate than for colder islands. Isolation, which spanned 209–4570 km, was included in their multiple regression model for insects but not for vascular plants. Keeping in mind that the two surveys partly overlap (with nine islands in common), the similarity in results strengthens the conclusions reached here: (a) that area per se may be a weaker predictor of vascular species richness for high-latitude islands than for temperate or tropical islands; (b) that species richness declines very slowly with increasing isolation; and (c) that the regression model that best explains species richness includes area, temperature and isolation.

Glaciation History

The islands differ widely in degree of Pleistocene glaciation. Iceland is believed to have been completely glaciated at the last glacial maximum (LGM) with ice thickness of about 2000 m over most of the country (Norðdahl et al. 2008). The ice sheet extended far beyond the present shoreline towards the limits of the Iceland shelf with an estimated aerial extent of over three times the present land area (Norðdahl and Ingólfsson 2015). Empirical and modelling data do not indicate that there were ice-free coastal areas. The most likely regions for ice-free nunataks are in high mountains close to the coast in the north and northwest. However, the most recent models indicate that given the estimated thickness of the ice sheet and the glacio-isostatic subsidence (165 m at the edge to 600 m in the centre), no mountain tops may have risen above the ice at the LGM (Norðdahl and Ingólfsson 2015).

Wrangel was a part of Beringia and ice-free during the LGM (Gualtieri et al. 2005). Valley glaciers formed in the Faroes but the islands were never entirely ice covered (Hannon et al. 2009). The remaining, high-latitude North Atlantic islands and Franz Josef Land are believed to have been completely glaciated (Svendsen et al. 2004), although ice-free areas may have existed, notably in Svalbard (Landvik et al. 2003). Pribilof Islands were part of Beringia during the LGM (Guthrie 2004), but at least one island had limited Pleistocene glaciation (Hopkins and Einarsson 1966). Small glaciers are believed to have formed at high elevations in the Falklands (Wilson et al. 2002; McDowell 2005). South Georgia and Heard are believed to have been completely glaciated, Kerguelen heavily glaciated and some to extensive glaciation on Marion, Campbell and Auckland (Chown et al. 1998; McGlone 2002). The degree of glaciation on Macquarie is uncertain but glaciers did not cover the whole island and at least some vegetation remained (Selkirk et al. 1990; Van der Putten et al. 2010). Apart from a correlation with climate and latitude, glaciation history may be related to island size, such that some islands may have been too small to grow their own icecaps.

Perhaps surprisingly, glaciation history did not emerge as a significant predictor of vascular species richness in the multiple regression. Islands with little or no glaciation tend to be relatively species rich compared to other similar-sized islands (Figure 2d), but for most of them this is confounded by their lower latitudinal position and hence warmer climate. Still, the exception of the unglaciated and very species-rich Wrangel island among the high arctic islands must be regarded as significant (Figure 2d).

Habitat Diversity

The positive relationship between species number and island area may have several explanations: (a) lower extinction rates on large islands because they sustain bigger populations and (b) provide more refugia, (c) large islands may intercept a larger number of immigrants and (d) provide internal geographic isolation needed for *in situ* speciation, and large islands have (e) a greater diversity of habitats (Lomolino 2001). The simple island-area approach has long been criticized for failing to include what may be the most important determinant of species richness, habitat diversity (Triantis et al. 2003). It was not possible to include habitat diversity in this survey but separating it from the other predictors would certainly be illuminating for understanding the patterns of species richness on the high-latitude islands.

'One of the Most Striking Features of the Flora of Iceland Is Its Paucity of Species'

The above was the opening remark of botanist Steindór Steindórsson in his presentation at the 1962 Symposium and subsequent printed volume of the *North Atlantic Biota and Their History* (Steindórsson 1963, p. 303). A quarter century later, Einarsson (1987, p. 25) began a chapter on the Flora and Vegetation of Iceland in a similar vein: 'One of the main characteristics of the flora of Iceland is the small number of species of vascular plants'. Neither author justified his statement but is there any indication here that Iceland is species poorer than might be expected? Iceland was not identified as a statistical outlier in the regression analyses but how does Iceland compare to the other islands in terms of habitat diversity?

Iceland probably provides a far greater diversity of habitats than any of the other islands. Most small islands may have little surface freshwater and no lakes. Iceland has a wealth of lakes, glacial rivers, clear freshwater rivers and numerous cold, warm and hot springs. Small islands may be ringed by steep cliffs with little or no flat coastal areas. Iceland has a wide variety of coastal habitats, including cliffs, rocky and sandy shores, salt marshes and saline lagoons (Ólafsson 1998). Substrate diversity ranges from Tertiary basaltic bedrock to recent and old Holocene lava fields of basaltic, intermediate (andesitic) and more acidic (silicic) composition (Jakobsson et al. 2008). Some glacial rivers meander on wide sandy outwash plains (sandurs),

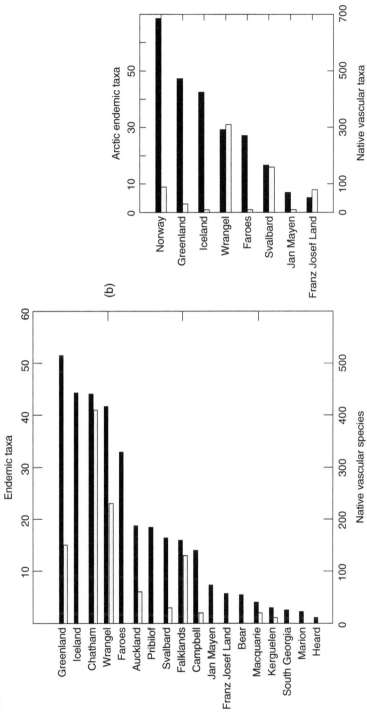

Figure 3 (a) Native vascular species richness (upper black columns) and endemism (lower light columns) in the sample of 17 high-latitude islands plus Greenland. (b) Arctic endemic taxa (lower light columns) and native species richness (upper black columns) for the Arctic islands, Greenland and Norway. Data on endemic taxa in (b) are from Arctic Biodiversity Assessment (CAFF 2013) and for sources in (a), see Table 1. Note different scales on the horizontal axes.

while others have associated riverine wetlands. Periglacial features abound with moraines, eskers, drumlins, patterned ground, palsas and the globally rare hyaloclastite mountains formed in subglacial eruptions (Einarsson 1994). In places, whole sections of landscape are partly or completely covered by tephra or sometimes coarse pumice. Other distinct types of volcanic substrates include cinder cones and rootless cones (Thordarson and Höskuldsson 2008). High alpine habitats include cliffs, narrow rims and flat plateaus. There are extensive peat mires, palsa mires with permafrost in the central highland (Thórhallsdóttir 1997), but true acidic bogs are poorly developed in Iceland and raised bogs are not found. The high-temperature geothermal fields have a distinctive flora with several red-listed species of bryophytes and vascular plants that in Iceland are completely or mostly restricted to those small habitat islands (Wasowicz and Heiðmarsson 2019). The lowlands of the mountainous peninsulas of the extreme northwest and north (the only regions classified as Arctic by the CAVM Team 2003) have exceptionally heavy and long-lasting snow cover, while the southern lowlands are characterized by light and mostly sporadic winter snow cover. Iceland's closest island neighbour, the Faroe Islands archipelago, is about 1.5% of the size of Iceland, but its vascular richness is equivalent to almost 75% of Iceland's flora. Given the above considerations, one may wonder whether a larger native flora might not have been expected in Iceland.

Endemism

Endemism varies widely between the high-latitude islands (Table 1, Figure 3a). It is clearly more prominent in the southern than in the northern hemisphere. Of the nine northern hemisphere islands, only three have endemic species, and on Greenland and Svalbard these account for <3% of the indigenous vascular flora. Six of nine southern hemisphere islands have endemic taxa and the endemic element is generally larger. When regional-scale endemism is included, the difference between the northern and southern hemisphere islands becomes even more pronounced (Table 1, last column). Wrangel island is a noticeable northern hemisphere exception, with the highest number of endemic taxa of all the Arctic and sub-arctic islands.

Most of the relatively species-rich islands have endemic taxa and their absence in Iceland is striking. After all, it is by far the largest island (excepting Greenland), its climate is relatively mild compared to many of the other islands and its degree of isolation is comparable to islands with a considerable endemic element (Table 1). Endemism in Iceland may also be examined over larger spatial scales, regionally and over the whole Arctic. The apomictic *Alchemilla faröensis* is the only species that can be regarded as a regional endemic, being restricted to East Iceland and the Faroes (Table 1). When endemism is evaluated in the context of the Arctic floristic province as a whole (Figure 3b), Iceland also appears to be singularly poor in endemics. It only has one species classified as endemic to the Arctic, *Cerastium arcticum*. This compares to 29 taxa in Greenland and 22 for Svalbard and Franz Josef Land together (Appendix 9.2 in Arctic Biodiversity Assessment, CAFF 2013).

While glacial history is not a good predictor of vascular species richness, there is a good correlation between glacial history and degree of endemism. Islands that remained more or less unglaciated throughout the Pleistocene have a strong endemic element, but endemism is weakly developed or absent on islands that were completely glaciated (Figure 4). This clearly indicates differences in the residence time of the biota, with the biota of the unglaciated islands having a long *in situ* history. In contrast, the flora of the completely glaciated islands is mostly or wholly of such recent descent that, in spite of isolation, endemic taxa have not had time to evolve.

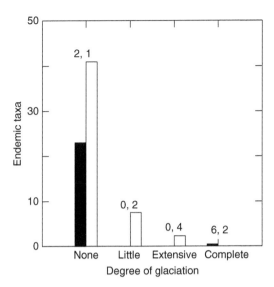

Figure 4 The relationship between the degree of Pleistocene glaciation (extent at LGM) and endemism for high-latitude islands in the northern (black columns) and southern (open columns) hemispheres. Numbers above the columns refer to the number of islands falling into each category: no glaciation, little, extensive and finally islands that were more or less completely covered with ice.

Floristic Characteristics of High-Latitude Islands: Woody Species and Megaherbs

While a detailed review of the floristic properties of the high-latitude islands is outside the scope of this chapter, two characteristics will be briefly addressed. A poor or even total lack of representation of woody species is characteristic of high-latitude islands, both in the northern and southern hemispheres. Their treeless state probably derives from a mixture of at least four causes: (a) Most of them are climatically beyond the treeline; (b) some have an extreme oceanic climate, wet and windy with a high cloud cover, which is not conducive to tree growth, even when the island may be temperature-wise within physiological limits for tree growth; (c) a very low probability of dispersal for tree seeds, which are larger and heavier

than those of herbs and grasses (e.g. Westoby et al. 1992); and (d) anthropogenic deforestation.

Betula pubescens is native to the small boreal enclave in southernmost Greenland (e.g. CAVM Team 2003), but is absent from the rest of the country. *Betula pubescens* macrofossils have been found in the Faroes, but the extent of pre-settlement shrub–woodland vegetation is unresolved, although it was almost certainly quite restricted at best (Hannon et al. 2001; Lawson et al. 2008). The Falkland Islands have no native tree species and probably have been treeless through the Holocene, but apparently both coniferous and deciduous forests grew there in the Tertiary (McDowell 2005). Among the sub-antarctic islands near New Zealand, the Chatham and Auckland islands have native forests and on Campbell Island the ericaceous scrub genus *Dracophyllum* forms dwarf forests up to 5 m tall (Wardle 1991). The remaining islands are treeless, – except for Iceland. Here, tall woody taxa are few and, at present, native forests and woodland only cover about 1.5% of the land area (Snorrason et al. 2019). Of the woody taxa, only *B. pubescens* has formed forests during the Holocene. Rowan (*Sorbus aucuparia*) is regionally widespread in the lowlands but only occurs as single trees in birch forest or woodland. *Populus tremula* has an extremely restricted distribution and of the four native *Salix* species, only *Salix phylicifolia* exceeds ca. 2.5 m in height. Birch forests and woodland and willow scrub may have covered 25–40% of the land area prior to settlement and the present very limited sparse forest and woodland cover is largely the result of direct and indirect human impact (e.g. Thorarinsson 1961; Erlendsson and Edwards 2009).

One of the peculiarities of the southern hemisphere, sub-antarctic islands are the endemic megaherbs: tall and lush perennial herbs, usually with large to very large leaves, long flowering stalks and often big and colourful flowers (e.g. Wardle 1991; Mitchell et al. 1999; Nicholls and Rapson 1999; Wagstaff et al. 2011). The megaherbs belong to at least six families: Asteraceae, Apiaceae, Brassicaceae, Gentianaceae and Liliaceae, with grasses (Poaceae) sometimes included. Megaherbs occur on Chatham, Campbell, Auckland and Macquarie, Kerguelen, Heard and Marion. The only two southern hemisphere islands (in Table 1) without megaherbs appear to be the Falklands and South Georgia, although the very tall tussock grass *Poa flabellata*, which grows on both, might possibly be included. The evolution of the sub-antarctic megaherbs has been linked to herbivore-free ecosystems, to nutrient harvesting from a maritime setting, and to maximizing heat capture in the diffuse radiation of the high cloud cover of these environments (Meurk et al. 1994). The megaherb growth form also occurs in high-alpine habitats, but as far as the author is aware, it has not been used to describe growth forms in the Arctic or subarctic. It is suggested here that while not endemic, *Angelica archangelica* may be regarded as Iceland's equivalent of the sub-antarctic megaherbs. Most of Iceland has been subjected to centuries of heavy sheep grazing and angelica is one of the most palatable plants in the flora. In the highland, sheep sometimes move through vegetation, eating only the angelica without even touching other favoured species such as *Rhodiola rosea*. In naturally protected areas or after exclusion of sheep, angelica often becomes very noticeable, by rivers and lakes in both lowland and highland, in the Western fjords, by cold springs and in the vegetated 'oases' of the central highlands. It may reach 1.8 m in height and is substantial enough to have strong visual impact on the landscape. Angelica may be a more significant part of the vegetation in these sites in Iceland than in other northern countries where it is native.

Iceland and Its Vascular Flora

Iceland is a large (103 000 km^2) island in the eastern North Atlantic, between about 63–67°N. It sits atop the boundary of two diverging tectonic plates (Einarsson 2008) and is one of the most volcanically active areas in the world with ≥20 eruption events per century (Thordarson and Höskuldsson 2008). Holocene lavas cover about 10% of the country (10 000 km^2) and include two of the Earth's largest lava flows in historical times. The active volcanic zone runs through the middle of Iceland, with a N–S orientation in the north but NE–SW in the south. Proximity to the active volcanic zone has profound implications for soil properties (e.g. rates of soil thickening, peat organic matter content and wetland pH) and soil fragility, disturbance regimes and the distribution of some groups of vascular plants and mosses. Vatnajökull is by far the largest ice-cap (>8000 km^2) but other major glaciers are Langjökull, Hofsjökull, Mýrdalsjökull and Eyjafjallajökull. Large rivers meandering on wide outlet plains flow from these glaciers, depositing sediments. Three of the above ice-caps lie above active volcanoes, intermittently generating large outburst floods (jökulhlaups), which are occasionally of catastrophic proportions (Björnsson and Pálsson 2008).

With 3.4 persons/km^2, Iceland is Europe's most sparsely inhabited country. Almost all inhabited areas, including farms, lie below 200 m a.s.l. but such land only accounts for about 25% of the total land area. In the northwest, central north and east, the lowlands are typically a narrow zone along fjords and inland valleys carved by Pleistocene glaciers. In the south and west there are wide lowland plains, largely on land that was below sea level in late glacial times. These plains, particularly in the south, are Iceland's largest and most important agricultural regions. Based on geological history, the uninhabited parts of Iceland can be roughly divided into two parts. In the northwest, central north and east, there are alpine landscapes with valleys and fjords carved into Tertiary basaltic bedrock, leaving 800 m (Western fjords) to 1500 m (central north) high mountains with steep scree slopes, cliffs and jagged peaks. About half of the area of Iceland is an interior high plateau, where isolated extinct or active volcanoes and extensive ice caps rise above a flat or undulating plain, which mostly lies at altitudes between 400 and 700 m. Most of this land has never been inhabited or at least not sustained long-term settlements.

The transition from lowland to highland vegetation is usually set at 300–400 m a.s.l. Outside the active volcanic zone on the central highland plateau, heathlands and wetlands form a transitional belt between the lowlands (<200 m) and more barren areas above ca. 450–500 m. On the active volcanic zone, continuous vegetation often ends close to the inhabited areas with mostly barren higher-lying inland areas. Much of the central highland is desert-like (2–5% plant cover) with continuous vegetation limited to fragmented islands in depressions and where the groundwater level is high and stable. Above about 600 m a.s.l., continuous vegetation becomes very patchy and above 700 m, plant cover is sparse.

Climate

The lowlands mostly have an oceanic climate with relatively cool summers and mild winters. July temperatures (1961–1990) range from about 7.6 °C in the northern part of the Western fjords (Hornbjargsviti) to over 10 °C in the lowland plains and valleys of the north and east, and exceeding 11 °C at Kirkjubæjarklaustur in the south. The only 30-year record available for the central highland is from Hveravellir (640 m a.s.l.), which had a July mean temperature of 7.0 °C. Lowland accumulated degree days >0 °C range from >1500 in the mild southern lowlands through 1000 in the exposed parts of the Western and Eastern fjords (May to September 1998–2013) to <900 at Hveravellir (data courtesy of the Icelandic Met Office 2014). There is a strong N–S gradient in precipitation. Mean annual precipitation (1961–1990) at Kirkjubæjarklaustur in the south was 1644 mm, while Akureyri almost due

north received 489 mm/year. North of the major icecaps, annual precipitation may fall below 400 mm/year.

Disturbance Regimes and Human History

Iceland was definitively settled in the ninth century CE, making it the second last large island in the world (after New Zealand) to be inhabited by people. A detailed assessment of the extent of continuously vegetated and forested/woody land at *landnám* (time of settlement) has not been carried out, but estimates range from about 50 to 65% for vegetated land and 25 to 40% for birch woodland and forest (Arnalds 1987; Óskarsdóttir 2011). Birch forest and woodland appears to have largely covered the lowlands (Hallsdóttir 1987; Kristinsson 1996), although pollen analyses have revealed open vegetation in areas that were either too wet or exposed in the south (Erlendsson et al. 2009; cf. Streeter et al. 2015) or possibly too xeric inland in the northeast (Hallsdóttir 1982). At present, only about 1.5% of Iceland has birch forest and woodland. Deforestation set in soon after the settlement (Hallsdóttir 1987; Kristinsson 1996) and this was followed by catastrophic erosion and desertification. Icelandic soils are Andosols, heavily impacted by active volcanism and massive tephra falls, as well as intense cryoturbation (Arnalds 2008). They are exceedingly friable once stripped of their protective vegetation cover and their fragility is exacerbated by the windy climate and frequent freeze–thaw cycles. Vegetated land not only lost its plant cover but virtually all organic soil (Arnalds et al. 2001). Presently, the large desert-like areas (37 000 km^2 of barrens +23 900 km^2 of patchily vegetated land; Árnason and Matthíasson 2009) are a mixture of natural deserts and land that can probably be regarded as more or less anthropogenically denuded. The exact causalities of the massive desertification over the past 1100 years continue to be a matter of debate. The interaction of deforestation with the environmental impact of tephra deposition may have been critical. The grasslands and heathlands created by the eradication of trees and shrubs were composed of herbs and dwarf shrubs, i.e. plants with their buds at, below or just above ground level (hemicryptophytes, chamaephytes, geophytes in the Raunkier 1934 scheme). Such plant communities are much more vulnerable to tephra deposition than tall, woody phanerophytes with buds above the ash layer, and these are much more likely to survive, stabilize the tephra deposited and facilitate ecosystem recovery (cf. Edwards et al. 2004).

In Iceland, the Little Ice Age (LIA) is now regarded as lasting from the late thirteenth to the early twentieth century (Geirsdóttir et al. 2009, 2013), which is longer than in most other European countries. In South Iceland, the firn line was depressed by 400 m during the latter part of the LIA (Björnsson and Pálsson 2008). Glaciers greatly expanded, reaching their Holocene maximum in the late nineteenth century when some outlet glaciers had advanced 10–15 km since the time of settlement (Björnsson and Pálsson 2008). Glacier rivers were larger and more destructive and beneath thicker glacier ice and subglacial eruptions and floods became more violent. Cold summers were often associated with extensive sea-ice coming from Greenland, and in the north especially this caused failure of the hay crop. Glacier retreat was marked after 1925 (Björnsson et al. 2013), slowing to a halt during a cold period after 1960. For all Icelandic glaciers, mass balance was negative for every year since 1996 to 2012 (Björnsson et al. 2013).

Land Cover and Land Use

Iceland was mapped in the Corine land cover project (Árnason and Matthíasson 2009). The largest land cover class (87.6% of the total area) was *forest and semi-natural areas*. Major surface types within this class were moors and heathland (35%), bare rocks (23%), sparsely vegetated land (13%) and glaciers (10.5%). Birch forest (with trees >2 m in height) covered only 0.3%. Wetlands occupied 7.2% and lakes about 2.3%. As defined in Corine, agricultural areas amounted to only 2.4% of the land area, of which 97% fell into the surface type *pastures*. Arable land was negligible (<0.02%). Artificial surfaces covered only 0.38% and based on the Corine specifications of a minimum mapping unit of 25 ha, continuous urban fabric does not exist in Iceland. Corine's allocation of almost 90% of Iceland's area into a single class is more a reflection of the poor fit of Icelandic land cover to the European classification system than a representation of the homogeneity of surface types in Iceland. On the most recent vegetation map of Iceland (Guðjónsson and Gíslason 1998), the major classes are sparsely vegetated land and barrens (41%), heathland, grassland and cultivated land (26%), glaciers (11%), moss-dominated vegetation (10%) and wetlands (8%). Most of Iceland is heavily marked by centuries of heavy livestock grazing and overexploitation.

Wholly, Partly or Hardly Arctic?

In many twentieth century publications, Iceland was placed wholly within the Arctic (e.g. Bliss 1979, Takhtajan 1986, Longton 1988, but see Yurtsev 1994). In the Circumpolar Arctic Vegetation Map, only the northernmost tips of Iceland are included in the Arctic (Bioclimate subzone E, CAVT team 2003, Walker et al. 2005), with the remainder of the country classified as boreal oceanic. The southern boundary of the arctic tundra is hard to define (e.g. ACIA 2005, p. 244), but the positioning of Iceland is complicated by at least three additional factors. One is that the criteria commonly used for defining the southern boundary of the Arctic are based on continental correlations that do not hold for an oceanic island. For example, mountain birch (*B. pubescens*) grows naturally (albeit very prostrate and low) in the northern part of the western fjords where mean July temperatures are <8 °C. Another is that, excepting low-growing juniper (*Juniperus communis*), there are no indigenous conifers. The third complicating factor is the great deforestation and subsequent desertification over the past 1100 years, which means that it is very difficult to draw the natural treeline. In terms of vegetation structure, canopy height, life forms and functional type composition, most of Iceland is much more akin to typical low-arctic rather than to boreal vegetation.

Composition of the Vascular Flora

Assessment and nomenclature of the vascular flora is based on Kristinsson (2008, updated web version 2010 in accordance with the Pan Arctic Flora Project [PAF 2014]). Species established prior to CE 1750 are regarded as native. Thus defined, the indigenous vascular flora includes 443 species, 7 clubmosses (Lycopodiophyta), 7 horsetails (Equisetopsida), 23 ferns and fern allies (Polypodiopsida), 1 conifer (Conferophyta) and 405 species of flowering plants (266 eudicots and 139 monocots).

The two largest families are Cyperaceae (53 spp.) and Poaceae (ca. 40), as is typical of low-arctic and sub-arctic floras. Other large families are Caryophyllaceae (26), Rosaceae (21), Juncaceae (20), Brassicaceae (20) and Asteraceae (16 species excluding *Hieracium* and *Taraxacum* microspecies). Only seven legumes (Fabaceae) are native. Several widespread arctic genera are absent in Iceland, e.g. *Oxytropis, Polygala, Polemonium, Androsace, Rhododendron* and *Artemisia*. Genera relatively well represented in Iceland include *Juncus* (14 of 16 arctic species), *Equisetum* (7 of 8), *Sagina* (all 6 spp.) and *Potamogeton* (7 of 9). Two species of *Betula* are native, dwarf birch (*Betula nana*) and mountain birch (*B. pubescens*), which has remained the only native forest-forming

species throughout the Holocene. Rowan (*Sorbus aucuparia*) is detected in pollen cores after about 5500 BP (Hallsdóttir 1995) and is widespread but only occurs as single trees in birch forest or woodland. *Populus tremula* was first identified in Iceland in 1911 (Davidsson 1957) and has since been found in eight locations. In some, the population appears to consist of a single clone (Sigurdsson et al. 1995). *Populus tremula* is dioecious and apparently does not flower in the wild. It has variously been suggested as the fragmented remains of a previously more widespread species, suppressed by livestock grazing after the settlement, or a recent addition to the flora through long-distance dispersal. Iceland has four of the 16 species of arctic willows (CAFF 2013), two of which may grow into tall shrubs, *S. phylicifolia* (up to 4–5 m) and *S. lanata* (ca. 2 m). All vascular species that occur on four of the five North Atlantic island groups (Faroes, Iceland, Svalbard/ Bear Island, Jan Mayen) and Greenland are in Iceland and of the 120 species that occur on the other three island groups, only two are not in Iceland, *Luzula nivalis* and *Draba alpina*.

Over 90% of the native vascular flora are listed as Arctic in the Arctic Biodiversity Assessment (CAFF 2013, Appendix 9.1). Eight species are classed as borderline Arctic. The remaining two dozen are a mixed group, but nearly all are rare in Iceland. Many are weedy (e.g. *Arrhenatherum elatius, Spergula arvensis*). Several others are likely to be human introductions, accidental (*Juncus gerardii*) or intentional, e.g. as food plants (*Allium oleraceum*, possibly *Glyceria fluitans*) or ornamentals (*Rosa dumalis*). The list includes a number of aquatic plants (e.g. *Tillaea aquatica, Veronica anagallis-aquatica, Callitriche brutia*). Finally, one of the most decorative of the Icelandic saxifrages is on the list. *Saxifraga cotyledon* is found in Fennoscandia, the Alps and Pyreneas, and the east and southeast of Iceland.

The revised 2008 Icelandic red list for vascular plants includes 45 species with one extinct

(*Primula egaliksensis*), five rated critically endangered and eight endangered (http://www.ni.is/grodur/valisti/). Four species are listed in Appendix I (Strictly protected flora species) of the Bern Convention (Convention on the Conservation of European Wildlife and Natural Habitats 1979): *Primula egaliksensis* (which is extinct, as already mentioned), *Botrychium simplex* (in Iceland both the European var. *simplex* and the North American var. *tenebrosum* are present), *Euphrasia calida* (species status remains to be verified) and *Saxifraga hirculus* (see Kristinsson et al. 2007). The golden saxifrage is common in Iceland, especially in the central highland. On joining the Bern Convention, Iceland made a special reservation, exempting *S. hirculus* from the protection specified in the Convention.

Floristic Affinities

The Icelandic vascular flora shows by far the closest affinities with the Fennoscandian flora with 98% of native vascular species (included for comparison in Table 2) also found in Norway. Of 407 native Icelandic species included in Table 2, only nine are not found in Norway. *Sesleria albicans* is actually listed as an alien species in Norway and as native in Sweden. It is very rare and local in Iceland where its native status may be questioned. The apomictic *Alchemilla faeroënsis* is found only in the Faroe Islands and eastern Iceland. The remaining seven species constitute the very small western element in the Icelandic flora.

Draba arctogena is found in North America, Greenland, Iceland (where its taxonomic status and distribution need further clarification), Svalbard and Bear Island. Two species extend from North America through Greenland to Iceland, but not further east, the orchid *Limnorchis hyperborea* and *P. egaliksensis* (the only vascular species known to have become extinct from its single known locality in Iceland, Wasowicz and Heiðmarsson 2019). The river beauty *Chamerion*

Table 2 Floristic affinities of the vascular flora of Iceland. Note that the apomictic microspecies of *Taraxacum, Hieracium* and *Pilosella* are not included.

Island	Native taxa	Common taxa with Iceland	Common taxa as % of Icelandic flora	Common taxa as % of other flora
Iceland[1]	407			
Norway[2]	Ca 1200	392/398*	96/98*	33
Greenland[3]	515	268	66	52
Faroes[4]	272	219	54	81
Svalbard[5]	166	90	22	54
Jan Mayen[6]	70	68	17	97
Wrangel[7]	292	63	15	22
Franz Josef Land[8]	52	26	6	50

Numbers are based on Appendix 9.1 of the Arctic Biodiversity Assessment (2013) and on: [1] Kristinsson 2010 and 2008. *Euphrasia calida* was excluded because of taxonomic uncertainty but *Potamogeton compressus*, discovered in 2012, has been added. [2] Native species for Norway refer to the mainland, based on Lid and Lid (2005). *The first number for the Norwegian flora refers to Northern Fennoscandia, i.e. the northernmost part assigned to the Arctic in the Pan Arctic Flora and the Arctic Biodiversity Assessment (2013). The second number refers to the whole mainland Norwegian flora. [3] Jensen and Christensen (2003). [4] Fosaa (2014). [5] The flora of Svalbard: http://svalbardflora.net/index.php?id=1. [6] Norsk Polarinstitutt (1997, updated 2003). [7] UNESCO (2004). [8] Gjertz and Mörkved (1992). Percentages are rounded to the nearest whole number.

latifolium is circumpolar-alpine (PAF 2014) and common in Iceland but absent from the rest of Europe. This leaves three western species with a highly disjunct distribution. *Carex lyngbyei* is chiefly Amphi-Pacific. It also occurs in Greenland (extremely local) and in the Faroes. The apomictic *Trisetum molle* extends from Taimyr east to Alaska, Canada, Greenland and Iceland. *Botrychium minganense* has a wide distribution in North America from eastern Canada and into the Russian Far

East although it has not been confirmed in the North East Atlantic or Europe except Iceland. Together, these seven species account for 1.7% of the native Icelandic flora. Jan Mayen shares all but two of its vascular species with Iceland and the Faroes share about 80% of their flora. In spite of being Iceland's nearest neighbour, floristic similarities are much lower between Greenland and Iceland than between Iceland and Norway. Among the native vascular flora, about one third is regarded as arctic/alpine and about half as boreal (Einarsson 1987). Of Dahl's 24 'west-Arctic species' (Dahl 1998), 13 are found in Iceland.

The High Arctic Element

In Table 3, the representation in Iceland of selected widespread high arctic genera is compared within the eastern North Atlantic and Arctic. The comparison is based on several sources that inevitably vary in degree of completeness and taxonomic categories may not be comparable across all the datasets. However, the table can be used for a general comparison of Iceland against the other islands, Fennoscandia and Greenland.

The data indicate that while the richness of some genera in Iceland (notably the saxifrages) is comparable to high-arctic islands and Fennoscandia, many appear to be poorly represented. For example, all 20 arctic species of Draba are found in Greenland, 13 are in Svalbard but only seven to eight in Iceland (presence/absence of *Draba norvegica sensu stricta* remaining to be verified). *Braya* does not occur in Iceland and only one species of *Pedicularis* (*P. flammaea*) is known. Arctic grass genera also appear to be modestly represented with *Arctophila*, *Arctagrostis* and *Dupontia* missing, and only three species of *Puccinellia* compared with Greenland's 13. This is not simply for lack of high-alpine habitats as there are 21 500 km^2 above 800 m altitude in Iceland, of which well over half is ice-free. At 1660 m a.s.l., *Saxifraga cespitosa* is the vascular species recorded

at the greatest elevation in Iceland (http://www.floraislands.is).

Large-Scale Disturbances as Regulators of Floristic Richness

Some parts of Iceland must rank among the Earth's most environmentally dynamic regions. In order of decreasing spatial scale, the most significant disturbances are: primary tephra deposition, the secondary movement of tephra, sand and soil particles by wind (in sandstorms), lava flows, glacier outburst floods and other floods associated with subglacial eruptions, and sand encroachment. Possibly, the impact of toxic gases (e.g. SO_2, HCl and HF) and ions emitted in some eruptions should be listed here as well because they affect plants (e.g. Witham et al. 2005; Frogner Kockum et al. 2006). Iceland is probably the only country in the world where all these types of disturbances occur and together they surpass most or even all other parts of the globe in diversity, frequency, spatial dimensions and severity of environmental impact.

Tephra refers to pyroclasts, fragments of mostly glass, crystals and lithics that are produced in volcanic eruptions and released through the air (Larsen and Eiríksson 2008). They characterize explosive eruptions. In Iceland, they are of two types: first when eruptions occur in gas-rich central volcanoes, where the explosive activity is related to the expansion of the gases, and second in sub-glacial eruptions when interaction between hot magma and meltwater produces tiny glassy particles, which may either solidify into hyaloclastite or be dispersed as tephra (Larsen and Eiríksson 2008). The tephra volumes produced by Icelandic volcanoes are staggering, an estimated 446 km^3 in postglacial times (Thordarson and Höskuldsson 2008). The largest Holocene tephra layers from mount Hekla are estimated to have had uncompacted volumes of 5–10 km^3 each and are recognizable in soil profiles over ca.

Table 3 A comparison of the species richness of arctic genera that are well represented in the North Atlantic and Arctic Oceans (first column) and in the high arctic (subzones A, B and C [Elvebakk et al. 1999], last column) for Iceland, selected other arctic islands, Greenland and Fennoscandia.

	Total spp/genus in N Atlantic & Arctic ocean	Greenland[1]	Iceland[2]	Faroes[3]	Jan Mayen[4]	Svalbard[5]	Franz Josef Land[6]	Wrangel[7]	Fennoscandia[8]	High-arctic in ABA
Braya	5	4	0	0	0	1	0	2	2	5
Draba	20	20	7-8	2	4	12	6	9	10	24
Pedicularis	17	8	1	1	0	2	0	10	3	14
Ranunculus	18	14	7	6	2	10	3	11	12	15
Saxifraga/Micranthes	25	16	14	7	7	13	9	16	14	23
Poa	10	7	6	4	3	6	5	5	8	7
Puccinellia	15	13	2	2	1	6	5	3	3	12
4 arctic grass genera *Arctophila, Arctagrostis, Dupontia, Phippsia*	(6)	6	1	0	1	6	6	4	4	5
Total species	116	88	29	20	18	56	33	60	56	105

The table includes vascular species regarded as native (by Pan Arctic Flora) in Greenland or one of the islands. Note that Fennoscandian species absent from the remaining islands and Greenland are not included. *Halerpestes* and *Coptidium* are included with *Ranunculus* and *Micranthes* is included with *Saxifraga*. The numbers are based on different sources and inevitably there will be some discrepancies. The last column is derived from Appendix 9.1 in ABA (2013) but the other columns are based on national floras as well as the Pan Arctic Flora (2014). [1] Böcher et al. (1978), [2] Kristinsson (2008), [3] Fosaa (2014), [4] Norsk Polarinstitutt (1997, updated 2003), [5] http://svalbardflora.net/index.php?id=1, [6] Gjertz and Mörkved (1992), [7] UNESCO (2004), [8] Lid (1979).

80% of the country (Larsen and Eiríksson 2008). Thordarson and Höskuldsson (2008) estimate that 156 explosive eruptions have taken place in Iceland since CE 1200, but tephra falls of the scale of the large Hekla eruptions have not taken place since *landnám*. Tephra thickness declines exponentially from the source but the patterns depend on wind direction and strength and the height of the plume. Immediately south of Grímsvötn volcano in Vatnajökull glacier, the tephra was 40 m thick following the 2011 eruption (H. Björnsson, personal communication). Deposition of aeolian materials appears to be greater in Iceland than in other major global dust areas, with erosion fluxes reaching 500–>2000 kg/m^2/day during storms and annual deposition rates exceeding 500 g/m^2 close to sand-source areas (Arnalds 2010). Historically, there is abundant evidence of the destructive power of the secondary movement of tephra, sand and denuded soil material on a regional scale. The best documented example may be the sandstorms in South Iceland towards the end of the nineteenth century, which led to the abandonment of over 30 farms, the transformation of hundreds of km^2 into a sandy wasteland and the complete disappearance of a lake that became sand-filled during a period of a few days (Sigurjónsson 1958).

The massive environmental changes initiated by human settlement, discussed earlier, have been known since the mid twentieth century, and during the past two decades much work has been done on mapping, classifying and understanding the processes of soil erosion and desertification (e.g. Arnalds et al. 2001). There has, however, been virtually no consideration of how Iceland's peculiar disturbance regimes might have affected floristic composition or species richness on a geological time scale. Preliminary analysis (Thórhallsdóttir in preparation) of the large-scale distribution of vascular diversity reveals lower species richness in the regions subjected to the most frequent and heaviest volcanic disturbances and higher species richness furthest away from the volcanic zone, even if the former includes the climatically most favourable parts of Iceland and the latter include the northernmost and Arctic zone.

The Age of the Icelandic Vascular Flora

Three events may have been crucial in shaping the richness and characteristics of the contemporary vascular flora of Iceland: the Pleistocene glaciations or at least the last glacial, Holocene trans-oceanic dispersal, and human-mediated accidental or deliberate introductions or post-landnam extinctions. Different scenarios can be constructed for the history of the flora based on: (a) the proportion of the flora that is ancient, or at least relatively ancient, ≥115 ka (NEEM community members 2013) to possibly ≥3 ma; (b) the proportion that is of the order of 10–15 ka in age; (c) the number of species first introduced in the past 1100 years, after *landnám*. Here, these scenarios are presented as four extreme hypotheses (Figure 5):

1) A significant part of the flora survived at least the last glacial and then possibly all of the Pleistocene in Iceland. Most of the remaining species arrived through long-distance Holocene dispersal. Few new species were added in the past 1100 years. The present flora is partly derived from ancient stock (≥115 ka to ≥3 ma) and partly from Holocene additions (10–15 ka).

2) A significant part of the flora survived at least the last glacial and then possibly all of the Pleistocene in Iceland. The probabilities of trans-oceanic dispersal were very low and through most of the Holocene, the flora was largely composed of ice-age relics. A lot of new species were introduced by humans. The present-day flora is a mixture of ancient stock (≥115 ka to ≥3 ma) and recent additions (≤1100 years) with a relatively small Holocene component.

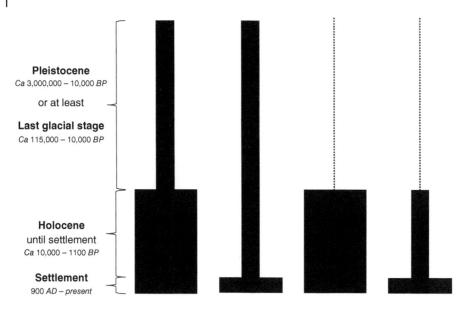

Pleistocene
Ca 3,000,000 – 10,000 BP

or at least

Last glacial stage
Ca 115,000 – 10,000 BP

Holocene
until settlement
Ca 10,000 – 1100 BP

Settlement
900 AD – present

Figure 5 Four hypothetical scenarios for the history of the Icelandic vascular flora. Bar thickness represents the proportion of the vascular flora derived from each period.

3) Populations of very few vascular species, perhaps none, survived the LGM in Iceland. At least during some period of the early Holocene there was considerable trans-oceanic dispersal. All or almost of the present flora is Holocene in age. The species composition of the vascular flora has not changed greatly since the time of initial settlement.

4) Populations of very few vascular species, perhaps none, survived the LGM in Iceland. The probabilities of long-distance dispersal remained very low during the Holocene. In pre-settlement in Iceland, the flora was very impoverished and largely composed of ice-age relicts. A great many species were first brought to Iceland accidentally or deliberately by humans in the last 1100 years. The present flora mostly has a short history in the country.

At the time of the publication of the first North Atlantic Biota volume, glacial survival was the dominant paradigm, not just in Iceland but

Scandinavia in general (Nordal 1987; Ægisdóttir and Thórhallsdóttir 2005). Steindórsson (1964) concluded that no less than 49% of the present vascular flora had survived the Ice Age. His arguments rested largely on discontinuities in the distribution patterns of certain species. In his 1963 paper, six refugia were identified (with additional single nunataks): the Western fjords, Breiðafjörður district (west Iceland), Eyjafjörður (central north), the Eastern fjords, Mýrdalur district (south) and Hvalfjörður (west). Some of these regions are among the more likely candidates to have harboured ice-free nunataks at the LGM, notably high mountains close to the north coast (Eyjafjörður), northern parts of the Western fjords, and possibly around Hvalfjörður in West Iceland. It is highly unlikely that there were ice-free areas in Mýrdalur and, in addition, the putative refugial species there are mostly thermophilic and their restricted distribution in Iceland is much more likely to reflect present-day climatic constraints. In line with other

Scandinavian botanists at the time (synthesis in Dahl 1998), Steindórsson (1963) placed emphasis on the distribution of the west-Arctic species, which he stated 'have been established with certainty as survivors in other northern countries' (p. 307). Of the 27 west-Arctic species recognized at the time, Steindórsson lists 13 in Iceland. Five are common all over the country (*Carex rufina, Draba rupestris, Epilobium lactiflorum, Euphrasia frigida* and *Festuca vivipara*). Of the remaining eight, seven turn out to be not restricted to the putative refugial regions (*Carex macloviana, C. nardina, Sagina caespitosa, Cerastium nigrescens, Stellaria borealis, Pedicularis flammea* and *Erigeron humilis*; for distribution maps see http://www.floraislands.is/index.html). The only west-Arctic species that is limited to putative nunatak areas of the refugial regions is *Campanula uniflora*. In Iceland, this high-Arctic species occurs in small or very small populations in the central-north mountains, with isolated occurrences in the Western fjords and two additional locations in the north. Five populations from Iceland were compared to populations from west (Qerqertarsuaq) and northeast Greenland (Zackenberg), Svalbard and north Norway by electrophoresis, using a six-enzyme system (Ægisdóttir 2003). Genetic diversity appeared low in all populations. Variability was detected within all populations sampled in Greenland, Svalbard and Norway, but none within or between any of the Icelandic populations. The biotically pollinated genus *Campanula* typically has a complex flowering phenology with secondary pollen presentation on the style, accompanied by an incompatibility system that breaks down towards the end of the flowering period when the stigmatic lobes bend backwards and may touch the pollen left on the style, thus facilitating self-fertilization of still-unfertilized ovules. This process was confirmed in Greenlandic populations of *C. uniflora* (Ægisdóttir and Thórhallsdóttir 2006). In the Icelandic populations, relative rates of anther and style elongation and maturation were

different, resulting in the pollen being deposited on the stigma before the flower opened and completely covering the receptive surfaces, thus prohibiting outbreeding (Ægisdóttir and Thórhallsdóttir 2006). The low genetic variation in the Icelandic populations may reflect this highly unusual breeding system (pre-anthesis cleistogamy) but the lack of variation between populations does not suggest long isolation in Iceland.

Opinion has also differed on how many species regarded as part of the native flora only arrived in Iceland in the past 1100 years through direct or indirect human agency (Thórhallsdóttir 1996). Steindórsson (1962, 1964) proposed that 92 species were such recent additions. According to his numbers, this then leaves only about 135 species (444 species in the total flora, 217 ice-age survivors and 92 recent introductions) that overcame what must have been formidable barriers to Holocene long-distance dispersal. Steindórsson's view of the history of the flora therefore seems to have been close to hypothesis 2 (Figure 5). Among the species listed by him as anthropogenic introductions are well known anthropochores, such as *Plantago major*, medical plants, such as *Valeriana* and *Achillea millefolium*, and valuable pasture plants, such as *Trifolium repens*. Steindórsson even proposed that some of the common pasture grasses were recent introductions, e.g. *Poa pratensis, Agrostis capillaris* and *Agrostis stolonifera*. While it is almost certain that seeds of fodder species, common ruderals and other plants that grew around the immigrants' habitations were carried accidentally (e.g. in hay) or adventitiously (externally on livestock, as part of packaging or bedding material, etc.), this has no bearing on the question of whether or not these species were already present in Iceland. The grasses listed above all have wide geographical, elevational and ecological distribution in Iceland. *Poa pratensis*, for example, occurs from sea level to high alpine habitats and is among only a handful of species found above

1350 m a.s.l. (http://www.floraislands.is/poaprate.html). *Agrostis stolonifera* has an unusually wide ecological amplitude, from seasonal ponds and wet mires to mesic grassland and even dry barrens. It is common from sea level to 800 m a.s.l. (http://www.floraislands.is/agrossto.html). Other species in the same grass genera (e.g. *Poa alpina, Poa glauca* and *Agrostis canina*) were not proposed as human introductions even if there is no reason to suppose that their probabilities of long-distance dispersal were any different from wild populations of the closely related pasture grasses.

Pollen analyses are, at least at the present level of resolution and in the absence of genetic support (cf. Gugerli et al. 2005), unlikely to provide definitive answers on which species first arrived after *landnám*. In the two largest vascular groups (sedges and grasses), pollen resolution is only to family level with the exception that the larger pollen grains of *Leymus arenarius* can be separated from other native grasses. Identification to species level is only possible for the minority of the flora. Two species or subspecies of *Valeriana* occur in Iceland but they have often not been distinguished (Kristinsson 2008). The wild populations have a restricted distribution in the lowlands of south, south-west and south-east Iceland but it remains to be verified if they are partly or wholly V. *sambucifolia* or *officinalis*. *Valeriana officinalis* is a garden plant and a well-known medical and spice plant at least since Roman times (Evans 1989) and *Valeriana* is therefore a likely candidate for deliberate human introduction. Steindórsson (1964) suggested it may have been brought by the Irish monks (*papar*) who are believed to have taken up residence in Iceland prior to the Norse. Since *Valeriana* is insect pollinated and has highly distinctive pollen grains, the presence of pollen grains in two locations in South Iceland (Hallsdóttir 1987) is strong evidence that it at least pre-dates the Norse *landnám*.

Some species may be composed of populations of different origin and age. *Plantago major* has two morphologically distinct populations in Iceland. It is common on disturbed ground in towns and by farms. It also grows by hot springs and geothermal areas and there it is often dwarfed. In South Iceland, *Trifolium repens* is mostly limited to lowland agricultural areas but in the north and east, it is common in natural vegetation and reaches much further inland and up to 500 m a.s.l. Similar conditions apply to *Achillea millefolium*. It is mostly found around farms and in disturbed ground in South Iceland, but has a very different distribution in the north, where it is common in the vast Ódáðahraun highland lava field and reaches 900 m a.s.l. in Eyjafjörður (http://www.floraislands.is/achilmil.html). Two subspecies of this apomictic species have been identified from Iceland, ssp. *millefolium* and ssp. *lanulosa* (http://nhm2.uio.no/paf/results?biogeographic=&bioclimatic=&region=&name=Achillea+millefolium#paf-861401). All three examples may suggest that some populations are descended from post-settlement introductions while others have a longer history in Iceland.

In general, pollen profiles do not indicate that the pre-settlement flora was particularly impoverished relative to the contemporary one. Pre-settlement groups include trees and shrubs (*Betula pubescens, B. nana, Salix, Sorbus aucuparius, Juniperus*), dwarf shrubs (e.g. *Empetrum, Calluna*) and a range of eudicots (Apiaceae including *Angelica*, Brassicaceae, Lamiaceae, Caryophyllaceae, Asteraceae, Rosaceae including *Filipendula ulmaria*, Polygonaceae including *Rumex, Koenigia, Oxyria* and *Bistorta vivipara*, Ranunculaceae including *Thalictrum alpinum, Saxifraga, Galium* type, *Rhinanthus* type, *Armeria, Pyrola, Gentianella, Lychnis, Silene, Thymus, Rubus, Trifolium, Sedum, Parnassia palustris* and *Geranium sylvaticum*). Wetland taxa include *Triglochin, Menyanthes, Caltha, Littorella, Hydrocharis, Myriophyllum, Potamogeton, Hippuris* and *Montia*. Seedless vascular taxa include *Lycopodium, Isoetes, Selaginella,*

Dryopteris, Polypodiaceae undiff., *Botrychium* and *Equisetum* (e.g. Hallsdóttir 1987, 1991, 1995; Caseldine et al. 2006; Vickers et al. 2011). In summary, the available data do not support a scenario of very limited Holocene pre-settlement dispersal with a large proportion of the present flora being <1100 years in age. This is notwithstanding the fact most pollen profiles show drastic vegetation changes following settlement, with deforestation and subsequent desertification and erosion, expansion of grasslands and open habitats, all of which led to changes in species' abundances and distributions (Thórhallsdóttir 1996). The distribution and population sizes of woodland species are likely to have contracted greatly, including woodland herbs such as *Paris quadrifolia*, *G. sylvaticum* and large ferns. Species typical of open ground and barrens increased, as exemplified by *T. alpinum* (Hallsdóttir 1987).

How likely is it that a part of the vascular flora survived at least the LGM? At present, there is no evidence for ice-free coastal areas around Iceland (Norðdahl et al. 2008). Ice-free areas would most likely have been high mountain nunataks close to the northern coast where the Pleistocene ice shield was thinner than in the central highland or in the south, which received much greater precipitation. However, extrapolating from the latest models of the Icelandic Ice Sheet that consider its thickness and glacio-isostatic subsidence, it appears that no nunataks may have extended above the ice at the LGM (Norðdahl and Ingólfsson 2015). The rapid appearance of plants in the wake of glacier retreat has been proposed as evidence for *in situ* survival of Icelandic vegetation (Rundgren and Ingólfsson 1999; Hallsdóttir and Caseldine 2005). In summary, the evidence reviewed here is circumstantial but, with the exception of rapid colonization, none of it can be interpreted as particularly favouring long isolation and Pleistocene survival.

The Icelandic vascular flora appears singularly poor in endemic species compared with other high latitude islands, and even within the Eastern North Atlantic, which is a noticeably endemics-poor part of the Arctic (CAFF 2001). The correlation between the degree of endemism and glaciation history (Figure 4) further supports the conclusion that the flora is Holocene in age. Iceland also seems relatively poor in hardy high-arctic taxa (Table 2), which, it may be argued, would be the most likely to survive in extremely hostile LGM environments. The molecular evidence for the age of the arctic North Atlantic flora is treated elsewhere (Brockmann and Alsos, Chapter 4 in this volume), but in almost all cases where Icelandic populations have been included, they do not exhibit geographical patterns that indicate long isolation. This includes *Arabis alpina* (Koch et al. 2006), *Betula nana* (Alsos et al. 2007), *Carex bigelowii* (Schönswetter et al. 2008), *Carex nigra* (Jimenez-Mejias et al. 2012), *Carex rufina* (Westergaard et al. 2011), *Cerastium arcticum* (Hagen et al. 2001), *Dryas octopetala* (Skrede et al. 2006), *J. communis* (Adams et al. 2003), *Phippsia algida* (Aares et al. 2000), *Ranunculus glacialis* (Schönswetter et al. 2003; Ronikier et al. 2012), *Salix herbacea* (Alsos et al. 2009), *Saxifraga hirculus* (Oliver et al. 2006), *Saxifraga oppositifolia* (Abbott et al. 1995; 2000), *Saxifraga paniculata* (Reisch 2008), *Saxifraga rivularis* (Westergaard et al. 2010), *Silene acaulis* (Abbott et al. 1995) and *Vaccinium uliginosum* (Alsos et al. 2005; Eidesen et al. 2007).

As for distinguishing between hypotheses 3 and 4, the available and again circumstantial evidence is much more compatible with a scenario of most of the flora being Holocene in age, with post-settlement species being a relatively small fraction of what is regarded as the native flora.

Views of the age of the North Atlantic flora have changed in the last half century, since the publication of the North Atlantic Biota volume in 1963. At that time, Ice-Age survival was the dominant paradigm for the North Atlantic, with small populations envisaged as persisting in many isolated refugia. The North Atlantic was regarded as a very strong barrier to dispersal and long-distance dispersal was discounted as the possible explanation for amphi-Atlantic distributions, i.e. for species occurring on either side of the Atlantic (Abbot and Brochmann 2003). Clearly, the biota of true oceanic islands can only have colonized through dispersal from distant terrestrial sources. Until recently, plant ecologists generally paid little attention to long-distance dispersal (Abbott et al. 2000), which was regarded as not amenable to experimentation and direct testing (Nathan et al. 2002). Lack of morphological adaptations for long-distance dispersal was sometimes invoked as an argument against long-distance propagule movement, but the rare, long-distance dispersal (ldd) events may have been brought about through other means than the plants' normal vectors (i.e. by 'non-standard means', Higgins et al. 2003). A wide variety of sources now indicate that this is more frequent and more important than previously assumed (de Queiroz 2005; Cowie and Holland 2006; Heany 2007; Gillespie et al. 2012). In some instances, direct evidence is available. For example, long-term monitoring showed that in seven out of 33 years, live insects were carried by winds to the Macquarie islands, both from New Zealand (990 km) and Australia (2000 km) (Greenslade et al. 1999). The wealth of genetic data now available provides very strong evidence for Holocene long-distance dispersal in the Arctic (Abbott and Brochmann 2003; Brochmann et al. 2003). Alsos et al. (2007) convincingly argued for the important role of long-distance dispersal for Svalbard. For eight of the nine species included in the assessment, they concluded that multiple dispersal events had been necessary to account for the present genetic diversity. In the sub-antarctic, Shepherd et al. (2009) found that the fern *Asplenianum hookerianum*, although rare on Chatham Islands, derives from at least two long-distance dispersal events from New Zealand.

Summary

The richness and composition of the vascular flora of Iceland reflects its latitude, its status as an isolated oceanic island and its geographical position in the North Atlantic. Grasses and sedges are the two largest families, which is typical of sub-arctic and low arctic environments, and woody species are few, as is characteristic of high-latitude islands. Floristically, Iceland is very strongly linked to NW Europe, particularly Norway. Evaluating the relative species richness of the flora is not a straightforward exercise and a comparison with other high-latitude islands fails to reveal the strong area correlations exhibited by lower-latitude archipelagos and island groups. Still, in comparing the species richness of Iceland with other much smaller islands, it is difficult to discount the notion that Iceland is at least on the relatively species-poor side of the range. Considering Iceland's area, climate and diversity of terrain, altitude and habitats, a greater number of species might have been expected.

Four independent lines of evidence, albeit circumstantial, all favour the view that the Icelandic flora is of young, i.e. Holocene, descent. (a) The high-latitude island survey revealed a correlation between glaciation history and endemism. Endemism is generally weakly developed in the eastern North Atlantic, but, even so, Iceland's complete lack of endemic vascular taxa is striking and must be regarded as a strong indication that the contemporary flora has not had a residence time long enough for the evolution of distinct taxa. (b) High-arctic taxa are generally not well represented in Iceland compared to its neighbours in the eastern North Atlantic, although there are high-alpine habitats that might be suitable for such plants. The extremely hardy high-arctic species would be more likely to survive glacial stages and their scarce representation also weighs against the hypothesis that a significant part of the flora survived the LGM. (c) While there is abundant evidence of the massive environmental transformation that was initiated by human settlement, deforestation, livestock grazing and other land uses, the available data do not indicate that a large part of the flora now regarded as native has a post-settlement origin. (d) The bulk of the now large body of molecular data that has been analysed has been interpreted to reflect a Holocene age of Icelandic populations. Of course, it is possible that small, glacial relict populations survived but had their genetic and possibly morphological signature swamped by later immigration. Rather, bearing in mind that a more complicated hypothesis should not be adopted until the simpler one has been rejected (Occam's razor), the conclusion to be drawn is that the present data are overwhelmingly compatible with the Icelandic vascular flora being of Holocene age.

Acknowledgements

I am grateful to Stephen Talbot for sharing the unpublished list of vascular species from St Mathew Island. I thank Hörður Kristinsson for reading the manuscript and for his useful comments and additions. The Icelandic part of this review largely rests on the great work done by him over the past 40 years. Finally, I thank Hreggviður Norðdahl for assistance with the glaciation history of Iceland.

References

Aares, E., Nurminiemi, M., and Brochmann, C. (2000). Incongruent phylogeographies in spite of similar morphology, ecology and distribution: *Phippsia algida* and *P. concinna* (Poaceae) in the North Atlantic region. *Plant Systematics and Evolution* 220: 241–261.

Abbott, R.J. and Brochmann, C. (2003). History and evolution of the arctic flora: in the footsteps of Eric Hultén. *Molecular Biology* 12: 299–313.

Abbott, R.J., Chapman, H.M., Crawford, R.M.M., and Forbes, D.G. (1995). Molecular diversity and derivations of populations of *Silene acaulis* and *Saxifraga oppositifolia* from the high Arctic and more southerly latitudes. *Molecular Ecology* 4: 199–208.

Abbott, R.J., Smith, L.C., Milne, R.I. et al. (2000). Molecular analysis of plant migration and refugia in the Arctic. *Science* 289: 1343–1346.

ACIA (2005). Arctic Climate Impact Assessment, 1042. Cambridge University Press.

Adams, R.P., Pandey, R.N., Leverenz, J.W. et al. (2003). Pan-arctic variation in *Juniperus communis*: historical biogeography based on DNA fingerprinting. *Biochemical Systematics and Ecology* 31: 181–192.

Ægisdóttir, H.H. 2003. Reproductive ecology, morphological and genetic variation in Campanula uniflora in Iceland, Greenland and Svalbard. MSc Thesis, Institute of Biology, University of Iceland, 89 pp.

Ægisdóttir, H.H. and Thórhallsdóttir, T.E. (2005). Theories on migration and history of the North-Atlantic flora: a review. *Jökull* 54: 1–16.

Ægisdóttir, H.H. and Thórhallsdóttir, T.E. (2006). Breeding system evolution in the Arctic: a comparative study of *Campanula uniflora* in Greenland and Iceland. *Arctic, Antarctic and Alpine Research* 38: 305–312.

Alsos, I.G., Engelskjøn, T., Gielly, L. et al. (2005). Impact of ice ages on cirumpolar molecular diversity: insights from an ecological key species. *Molecular Ecology* 14: 2739–2753.

Alsos, I.G., Eidesen, P.B., Ehrich, D. et al. (2007). Frequent long-distance plant colonization in the changing Arctic. *Science* 316: 1606–1609.

Alsos, I.G., Alm, T., Normand, S., and Brochmann, C. (2009). Past and future range shifts and loss of diversity in dwarf willow (*Salix herbacea* L.) inferred from genetics, fossils and modelling. *Global Ecology and Biogeography* 18: 223–239.

Anda, E., Orheim, O., and Mangerud, J. (1985). Late Holocene glacier variations and climate at Jan Mayen. *Polar Research* 3: 129–140.

Arnalds, A. (1987). Ecosystem disturbance in Iceland. *Arctic and Alpine Research* 19: 508–513.

Arnalds, Ó. (2008). Soils of Iceland. *Jökull* 58: 409–421.

Arnalds, Ó. (2010). Dust sources and deposition of aeolian materials in Iceland. *Icelandic Agricultural Sciences* 23: 3–21.

Arnalds, Ó., Þorarinsdottir, E.F., Metusalemsson, S. et al. (2001). Soil Erosion in Iceland, 121. Soil Conservation Service and Agricultural Research Institute.

Árnason, K. & Matthíasson, I.2009. *Corine-landflokkun á Íslandi*. CLC2006, CLC2000 og CLC-Change 2000–2006. National Land Survey of Iceland, 154 pp.

Björnsson, H. and Pálsson, F. (2008). Icelandic glaciers. *Jökull* 58: 365–386.

Björnsson, H., Pálsson, F., Gudmundsson, S. et al. (2013). Contribution of Icelandic ice caps to sea level rise: trends and variability since the Little Ice Age. *Geophysical Research Letters* 40: 1546–1550.

Bliss, L.C. (1979). Vascular plant vegetation of the southern circumpolar region in relation to antarctic, alpine, and arctic vegetation. *Canadian Journal of Botany* 57: 2167–2178.

Böcher, T.W., Fredskild, B., Holmen, K., and Jakobsen, K. (1978). Grönlands Flora, 326. Copenhagen: P. Haase & söns Forlag.

Brochmann, C., Gabrielsen, T.M., Nordal, I. et al. (2003). Glacial survival or *tabula rasa*? The history of North Atlantic biota revisited. *Taxon* 52: 417–450.

CAFF (2013). Arctic Biodiversity Assessment. Status and Trends in Arctic Biodiversity. Akureyri: Conservation of Arctic Flora and Fauna.

CAFF (Conservation of Arctic Flora and Fauna) (2001). Arctic Flora and Fauna: Status and Conservation, 272. Helsinki: Edita.

Caseldine, C., Langdon, P., and Holmes, N. (2006). Early Holocene climate variability and the timing and extent of the Holocene thermal maximum (HTM) in Northern Iceland. *Quaternary Science Reviews* 25: 2314–2331.

CAVM Team 2003. Circumpolar Arctic Vegetation Map. Scale 1:7,500,000. Conservation of Arctic Flora and Fauna (CAFF) Map No.1. US Fish and Wildlife Service, Anchorage, Alaska.

Chown, S.L., Gremmen, N.J.M., and Gaston, K.J. (1998). Ecological biogeography. *American Naturalist* 152: 562–575.

Climate Change Knowledge Portal, The World Bank, http://www.weatherbase.com/weather/weatherall.php3?s=98888&units.

Coffin, M.F. (2009). Granitic islands. In: Encyclopedia of Islands (eds. R.G. Gillespie and D.A. Clague), 380–382. Berkeley: University of California Press.

Connor, E.F. and McCoy, E.D. (1979). The statistics and biology of the species-area relationship. *The American Naturalist* 113: 791–833.

Convention on the Conservation of European Wildlife and Natural Habitats. Bern1979. Appendix 1: http://conventions.coe.int/Treaty/FR/Treaties/Html/104-1.htm.

Cook, A.J., Poncet, S., Cooper, A.P.R. et al. (2010). Glacier retreat on South Georgia and implications for the spread of rats. *Antarctic Science* 22: 255–263.

Cowie, R.H. and Holland, B.S. (2006). Dispersal is fundamental to biogeography and the evolution of biodiversity on oceanic islands. *Journal of Biogeography* 33: 193–198.

Dahl, E. (1998). The Phytogeography of Northern Europe, vol. 297. Cambridge: Cambridge University Press.

Davídsson, I. (1957). Nýir fundarstaðir jurta 1956. *Náttúrufræðingurinn* 26: 2.

De Lange, P.J., Heenan, P.B., and Rolfe, J.R. (2011). Checklist of Vascular Plants Recorded from Chatham Islands, 57. Wellington, New Zealand: Department of Conservation.

De Queiroz, A. (2005). The resurrection of oceanic dispersal in historical biogeography. *Trends in Ecology and Evolution* 20: 68–73.

Edwards, K.J., Dugmore, A.J., and Blackford, J.J. (2004). Vegetational response to tephra deposition and land use change in Iceland – a modern analogue and multiple working hypothesis approach to tephropalynology. *Polar Record* 40: 113–120.

Eidesen, P.B., Alsos, I.G., Popp, M. et al. (2007). Nuclear vs. plastid data: complex Pleistocene history of a circumpolar key species. *Molecular Ecology* 16: 3902–3925.

Einarsson, E. (1987). Flora and vegetation. In: Iceland 1986 (eds. J. Nordal and V. Kristinsson), 25–27. Reykjavík: The Central Bank of Iceland.

Einarsson, T. (1994). Geology of Iceland. Rocks and Landscape, 309. Reykjavík: Mál og menning.

Einarsson, P. (2008). Plate boundaries, rifts and transforms in Iceland. *Jökull* 58: 35–58.

Elvebakk, A., Elven, R., and Razzhivin, V.Y. (1999). Delimitation, zonal and sectorial subdivision of the arctic for the Panarctic Flora project. In: The Species Concept in the High North: A Panarctic Flora Initiative (eds. I. Nordal and V.Y. Razzihivin), 375–386. Oslo: The Norwegian Academy of Science and Letters.

Engelskjen, T. (1986). Eco-geographical relations of the Bjerneya vascular flora, Svalbard. *Polar Research* 5: 79–127.

Erlendsson, E. and Edwards, K.J. (2009). The timing and causes of the final pre-settlement expansion of *Betula pubescens* in Iceland. *The Holocene* 19: 1083–1091.

Erlendsson, E., Edwards, K.J., and Buckland, P.C. (2009). Vegetational response to human colonisation of the coastal and volcanic environments of Ketilstaðir, southern Iceland. *Quaternary Research* 72: 174–187.

Evans, W.C. (1989). Trease and Evans' Pharmacognosy, 13e, 832. London: Bailliére Tindall.

Fosaa, A.-M. 2014. Listi yvir plantur í Føroyum.

Fraser, C.I., Nikula, R., Ruzzante, D.E., and Waters, J.M. (2012). Poleward bound: biological impacts of Southern Hemisphere glaciation. *Trends in Ecology and Evolution* 27: 462–471.

Frenot, Y., Gloaguen, J.C., Massé, L., and Lebouvier, M. (2001). Human activities, ecosystem disturbance and plant invasions in subantarctic Crozet, Kerguelen and Amsterdam Islands. *Biological Conservation* 101: 33–50.

Frogner Kockum, P.C., Herbert, R.B., and Gislason, S.R. (2006). A diverse ecosystem response to volcanic aerosols. *Chemical Geology* 231: 57–66.

Geirsdóttir, Á., Miller, G.H., Axford, Y., and Ólafsdóttir, S. (2009). Holocene and latest Pleistocene climate and glacier flutctuations in Iceland. *Quaternary Science Reviews* 28: 2107–2118.

Geirsdóttir, Á., Miller, G.H., Larsen, D.J., and Ólafsdóttir, S. (2013). Abrupt Holocene climate transitions in the northern North Atlantic region recorded by synchronized laustrine records in Iceland. *Quaternary Science Reviews* 71: 48–62.

Gillespie, R.G., Baldwin, B.G., Waters, J.M. et al. (2012). Long-distance dispersal: a framework for hypothesis testing. *Trends in Ecology and Evolution* 27: 47–56.

Gjertz, I. & Mörkved, B. 1992. Environmental Studies from Franz Josef Land, with Emphasis on Tikhaia Bay, Hooker Island. Meddelelser nr. 120, Norsk Polarinstitutt, Oslo, 130 pp.

Greenslade, P., Farrow, R.A., and Smith, J.M.B. (1999). Long distance migration of insects to a subantarctic island. *Journal of Biogeography* 26: 1161–1167.

Grímsson, F., Denk, T., and Símonarson, L.A. (2007). Middle Miocene floras of Iceland – the early colonization of an island? *Review of Paleobotany and Palynology* 144: 181–219.

Gualtieri, L., Vartanyan, S.L., Brigham-Grette, J., and Anderson, P.M. (2005). Evidence for an ice-free Wrangel Island, Northeast Siberia during the Last Glacial Maximum. *Boreas* 34: 264–273.

Gudjónsson, G. & Gíslason, E. 1998. Gróðurkort af Íslandi 1:500.000. Icelandic Institute of Natural History, Reykjavík.

Gugerli, F., Parducci, L., and Petit, R.J. (2005). Ancient plant DNA: review and prospects. *New Phytologist* 166: 409–418.

Guthrie, R.D. (2004). Radiocarbon evidence of mid-Holocene mammoths stranded on an Alaskan Bering Sea Island. *Nature* 429: 746–749.

Hagen, J.O., Liestöl, O., Roland, E., and Jörgensen, T. (1993). Glacier Atlas of Svalbard and Jan Mayen. Norsk Polarinstitutt Meddelser, vol. 129. Oslo: Norwegian Polar Institute.

Hagen, A.R., Giese, H., and Brochmann, C. (2001). Trans-Atlantic dispersal and phylogeography of *Cerastium arcticum* (Caryophyllaceae) inferred from RAPD and SCAR markers. *American Journal of Botany* 88: 103–112.

Hall (2002). Review of present and quaternary periglacial processes and landforms of the maritime and sub-Antarctic region. *South African Journal of Science* 98: 71–81.

Hallsdóttir, M. 1982. Frjógreining tveggja jarðvegssniða úr Hrafnkelsdal – áhrif ábúðar á gróðurfar dalsins. (The pollen analysis of two soil profiles from Hrafnkelsdalur – the impact of settlement on the vegetation of the valley). In: *Eldur er í norðri. Afmælisrit helgað Sigurði Þórarinssyni sjötugum*, 8. janúar 1982 (eds. H. Þórarinsdóttir, Ó.H. Óskarsson, S. Steinþórsson & Þ. Einarsson. Sögufélag, Reykjavík, pp. 253–266.

Hallsdóttir, M. 1987. Pollen analytical studies of human influence on vegetation in relation to the Landnám Tephra Layer in Southwest Iceland. LUNDQUA Thesis, 18. Lund University, Department of Quaternary Geology, 46 pp.

Hallsdóttir, M. (1991). Studies in the vegetation history of North-Iceland. A radiocarbon-dated pollen diagram from Flateyjardalur. *Jökull* 40: 67–81.

Hallsdóttir, M. (1995). On the pre-settlment history of Icelandic vegetation. *Icelandic Agricultural Sciences* 9: 17–29.

Hallsdóttir, M. and Caseldine, C.J. (2005). The Holocene vegetation history of Iceland, state of the art and future research. In: Iceland – Modern Processes and Past Environments, vol. 5 (eds. C. Caseldine, A. Russel, J. Hardardóttir and Ó. Knudsen), 319–334. Elsevier.

Hannon, G.E., Wastegård, S., Bradshaw, E., and Bradshaw, R.H.W. (2001). Human impact and landscape degradation on the Faroe Islands. Biology and Enviornment. *Proceedings of the Royal Irish Academy* 101B: 129–139.

Hannon, G.E., Arge, S.V., Fosaa, A.-M. et al. (2009). Faore islands. In: Encyclopedia of Islands (eds. R.G. Gillespie and D.A. Clague), 291–297. Berkeley: University of California Press.

Heaney, L.R. (2007). Is a new paradigm emerging for oceanic island biogeography? *Journal of Biogeography* 34: 763–757.

Hennion, F. and Walton, D.W.H. (1997). Ecology and seed morphology of endemic species from Kerguelen Phytogeographic zone. *Polar Bioogy* 18: 229–235.

Higgins, S.I., Nathan, R., and Cain, M.L. (2003). Are long-distance dispersal events in plants usually caused by nonstandard means of dispersal? *Ecology* 84: 1945–1956.

Hopkins, D.M. and Einarsson, T. (1966). Pleistocene glaciation on St. George, Pribilof Islands. *Science* 152: 343–345.

Icelandic Meteorological Office 2014. Unpublished data.

Jakobsson, S.P., Jónasson, K., and Sigurdsson, I.A. (2008). The three igneous rock series of Iceland. *Jökull* 58: 117–138.

Jensen, D.B. & Christensen, K.D. 2003. The biodiversity of Greenland – a country study. Technical Report No. 55. Pinngortitaleriffik, Grönlands Naturinstitut, Nuuk, 165 pp.

Jiménez-Mejias, P., Luceno, M., Lye, K.A. et al. (2012). Genetically diverse but with surprisingly little geographical structure: the complex history of the widespread herb *Carex nigra* (Cyperaceae). *Journal of Biogeography* 39: 2279–2291.

Jóhansen, J. 2000. *Föroysk Flora* (eds A.M. Fosaa & S. Rasmussen). Föroya Skúlabókagrunnur, 485 pp.

Johnson, P.N. and Campbell, D.J. (1975). Vascular plants of the Auckland Islands. *New Zealand Journal of Botany* 13: 665–720.

Koch, M.A., Kiefer, C., Ehrich, D. et al. (2006). Three times out of Asia Minor: the phylogeography of *Arabis alpina* L (Brassicaceae). *Molecular Ecology* 15: 825–839.

Krebs, C.J. (2001). Ecology. The Experimental Analysis of Distribution and Abundance, 5e, 695. San Fransisco: Benjamin Cummings.

Kreft, H., Jetz, W., Mutke, J. et al. (2008). Global diversity of island floras from a macroecological perspective. *Ecology Letters* 11: 116–127.

Kristinsson, H. (1996). Post-settlement history of Icelandic forests. *Búvisindi* 9: 31–35.

Kristinsson H. 2008. Checklist of the vascular plants of Iceland. Fjölrit Náttúrufræðistofnunar nr. 51. 58 pp.

Kristinsson, H. 2010. Checklist of vascular plants. Updates from the printed version 2008. Web version: http://www.floraislands.is/PDF-skjol/plontutal.pdf.

Kristinsson, H., Thorvaldsdóttir, E.G., and Steindórsson, B. (2007). Vöktun válistaplantna 2002-2006 (monitoring of red-listed plants 2002-2006). *Fjölrit Náttúrufræðistofnunar* 50: 86.

Landvik, J.Y., Brook, E.J., Gualtieri, L. et al. (2003). Northwest Svalbard during the last glaciation: ice-free areas existed. *Geology* 31: 905–908.

Larsen, G. and Eiríksson, J. (2008). Holocene tephra archives and tephrachronology in Iceland – a brief overview. *Jökull* 58: 229–250.

Lawson, I.T., Edwards, K.J., Church, M.J. et al. (2008). Human impact on an island ecosystem: pollen data from Sandoy, Faroe Islands. *Journal of Biogeography* 35: 1130–1152.

Lid, J. (1964). The Flora of Jan Mayen. University of Forlag 107 pp.

Lid, J. (1979). Norsk og Svensk Flora, 2e. Oslo: Det Norske Samlaget 808 pp.

Lid, J. and Lid, D.T. (2005). Norsk Flora (ed. R. Elven), 1230. Oslo: Samlaget.

Lomolino, M.V. (2001). The species-area relationship: new challenges for an old pattern. *Progress in Physical Geography* 25: 1–21.

Longton, R.E. (1988). Biology of Polar Bryophytes and Lichens, 391. Cambridge University Press.

Lubinski, D.J., Forman, S.L., and Miller, G.H. (1999). Holocene glacier and climate fluctuations on Franz Josef Land, Arctic Russian 80°N. *Quaternary Science Reviews* 18: 85–108.

MacArthur, R.H. and Wilson, E.O. (1967). The Theory of Island Biogeography, 224 pp. Princeton University Press.

McDowell, R.M. (2005). Falklands Islands biogeography: convergin trajectories in the South Atlantic Ocean. *Journal of Biogeography* 32: 49–62.

McGlone, M.S. (2002). The Late Quaternary peat, vegetation and climate history of the Southern Oceanic Islands of New Zealand. *Quaternary Science Reviews* 21: 683–707.

Meurk, C.D. (1984). Bioclimatic zones for the Antipodes – and beyond. *New Zealand Journal of Ecology* 7: 175–181.

Meurk, C.D., Foggo, M.N., and Bastow Wilson, J. (1994). The vegetation of sub-antarctic Campbell Island. *New Zealand Journal of Ecology* 18: 123–168.

Michaux, B. and Leschen, R.A.B. (2005). East meets west: biogeology of the Campbell Plateau. *Biological Journal of the Linnean Society* 86: 95–115.

Mitchell, A.D., Meurk, C.D., and Wagstaff, S.J. (1999). Evolution of Stilbocarpa, a megaherb from New Zealand's sub-antarctic islands. *New Zealand Journal of Botany* 37: 205–211.

Moore, D.M. (1968). The vascular flora of the Falkland Islands. *British Antarctic Survey Scientific Reports* 60: 202.

Nathan, R., Katul, G.G., Horn, H.S. et al. (2002). Mechanisms of long-distance dispersal of seeds by wind. *Nature* 418: 409–413.

NEEM community members (2013). Eemian interglacial reconstructed from a Greenland folded ice core. *Nature* 493: 489–494.

Nicholls, V.J. and Rapson, G.L. (1999). Biomass allocation in subantarctic island megaherbs, Pleurophyllum speciosum (Asteraceae) and Anisotome latifolia (Apiaceae). *New Zealand Journal of Ecology* 23: 87–93.

Nordal, I. (1987). Tabula rasa after all? Botanical evidence for ice-free refugia in Scandinavia reviewed. *Journal of Biogeography* 14: 377–388.

Norðdahl, H. and Ingólfsson, Ó. (2015). Collapse of the Icelandic iced sheet controlled by sea-level rise? *Arktos* 1: 13.

Norðdahl, H., Ingólfsson, Ó., Pétursson, H.G., and Hallsdóttir, M. (2008). Late Weichselian and Holocene environmental history of Iceland. *Jökull* 58: 343–364.

Norsk Polarinstitutt 1997, updated 2003. Natur-og kulturmiljöet på Jan Mayen. Norsk Polarinstitutt. Meddelelser nr. 144 Oslo 1997. See: http://www.jan-mayen.no/flora/janmayenflora.htm.

Nunn, P.D. (2009). Oceanic islands. In: Encyclopeida of Islands (eds. R.G. Gillespie and D.A. Clague), 689–696. Berkeley: University of California Press.

Ólafsson, J.S. (ed.) (1998). Íslensk Votlendi. Verndun Og nýting. (Icelandic Wetlands.

Conservation and Uses), 283. University of Iceland Press.

Oliver, C., Hollingsworth, P.M., and Gornall, R.J. (2006). Chloroplast DNA phylogeography of the arctic-montane species *Saxifraga hirculus* (Saxifragaceae). *Heredity* 96: 222–231.

Óskarsdóttir, A. (ed.) (2011). Náttúruvernd. Hvítbók Um löggjöf Til Verndar náttúru Íslands. (Nature Conservation. A White Paper on Legislation for the Conservation of Icelandic Nature), 477. Reykjavík: Nefnd um endurskoðun náttúruverndarlaga. The Ministry of the Environment and Resources.

Pan Arctic Flora Annotated checklist of the panarctic flora (PAF) vascular plants (editor-in-chief R. Elven) 2014. http://nhm2.uio.no/paf.

Raunkier, C. (1934). The Life Forms of Plants. Oxford: Oxford University Press.

Reisch, C. (2008). Glacial history of *Saxifraga paniculata* (Saxifragaceae): molecular biogeography of a disjunct arctic-alpine species from Europe and North America. *Biological Journal of the Linnean Society* 93: 385–398.

Ronikier, M., Schneesweiss, G.M., and Schönswetter, P. (2012). The extreme disjunction between Beringia and Europe in *Ranunculus glacialis* s.l. (Ranunculaceae) does not coincide with the deepest genetic split – a story of the importance of temperate mountain ranges in arctic-alpine phylogeography. *Molecular Ecology* 21: 5561–5578.

Rosenzweig, M.L. (2004). Applying the species–area relationship to conservation. In: Frontiers of Biogeography. New Directions in the Geography of Nature (eds. M.V. Lomolino and L.R. Heaney), 325–344. Sunderland, Mass: Sinauer Associate Inc.

Rundgren, M. and Ingólfsson, Ó. (1999). Plant survival in Iceland during periods of glaciation? *Journal of Biogeography* 26: 378–396.

Schönswetter, P., Paun, O., Tribsch, A., and Niklfeld, H. (2003). Out of the Alps: colonization of

Northern Europe by East Alpine populations of the Glacier Buttercup *Ranunculus glacialis* L. (Ranunculaceae). *Molecular Ecology* 12: 3373–3381.

Schönswetter, P., Elven, R., and Brochmann, C. (2008). Trans-Atlantic dispersal and large-scale lack of genetic structure in the circumpolar, arctic-alpine sedge Carex bigelowii s.l. (Cyperaceae). *American Journal of Botany* 95: 1006–1014.

Selkirk, P.M., Seppelt, R.D., and Selkirk, D.R. (1990). Subantarctic Macquarie Island: Environment and Biology. Cambridge University Press.

Selmi, S. and Boulinier, T. (2001). Ecological biogeography of Southern Ocean Islands: the importance of considering spatial issues. *The American Naturalist* 158: 426–437.

Shepherd, L.D., de Lange, P.J., and Ferrie, L.R. (2009). Multiple colonizations of a remote oceanic archipelago by one species: how common is long-distance dispersal? *Journal of Biogeography* 36: 1972–1977.

Sigurdsson, V., Sigurgeirsson, A., and Anamthawat-Jónsson, K. (1995). Identification of clones of the indigenous *Populus tremula* and introduced *P. trichocarpa* by RAPD techniques. *Icelandic Agricultural Science* 9: 145–152.

Sigurjónsson, A. (1958). Ágrip af gróðursögu landsins til 1880 (a summary of the vegetation history of the country to 1880). In: Sandgræðslan. Minnzt 50 ára starfs Sandgræðslu Íslands (ed. A. Sigurjónsson), 5–92. Reykjavík: Prentsmiðjan Edda.

Skrede, I., Eidesen, P.B., Portela, R.P., and Brochmann, C. (2006). Refugia, differentiation and postglacial migration in arctic-alpine Eurasia, exemplified by the mountain avens (*Dryas octopetala* L.). *Molecular Ecology* 15: 1827–1840.

Spiller, D.A. and Schoener, T.W. (2009). Species-area relationship. In: Encyclopedia of Islands (eds. R.G. Gillespie and D.A. Clague),

857–861. Berkeley: University of California Press.

Snorrason, A., Jónsson, T.H., and Eggertsson, Ó. (2019). Aboveground woody biomass of natural birch woodland in Iceland – Comparison of two inventories 1987–1988 and 2005–2011. *Icelandic Agricultural Sciences* 32: 21–29.

Steindórsson, S. (1962). On the age and immigration of the Icelandic flora. In: Rit Vísindafélags Íslendinga, vol. 35, 1–157. Vísindafélag Íslendinga: Reykjavík.

Steindórsson, S. (1963). Ice age refugia in Iceland as indicated by the present distribution of plant species. In: North Atlantic Biota and Their History (eds. Á. Löve and D. Löve), 303–320. Oxford: Pergamon Press.

Steindórsson, S. (1964). Gróður á Íslandi (Vegetation of Iceland), 186. Reykjavík: Almenna bókafélagið.

Streeter, R., Dugmore, A.J., Lawson, I.T. et al. (2015). The onset of the palaeoanthropocene in Iceland: changes to complex natural systems. *The Holocene* 25: 1662–1675.

Svendsen, J., Alexanderson, H., Astakhov, V. et al. (2004). Late Quaternary ice sheet history of Northern Eurasia. *Quaternary Science, Reviews* 23: 1229–1271.

Takhtajan, A. (1986). Floristic Regions of the World. (trans. T.J. Crovello and A. Cronquist), 522. Berkeley: University of California Press.

The flora of Svalbard: http://svalbardflora.net/index.php?id=1.

Thorarinsson, S. 1961. Uppblástur á Íslandi í ljósi öskulagarannsókna (Erosion in Iceland in the light of tephrochronology). *Ársrit Skógræktarfélags Íslands 1960–61*, 17–54.

Thordarson, T. and Höskuldsson, Á. (2008). Postglacial volcanism in Iceland. *Jökull* 58: 197–228.

Thórhallsdóttir, T.E. (1996). Áhrif búsetu á landið (The impact of inhabitation on the land, in Icelandic). In: Um landnám á Íslandi – fjórtán erindi (ed. G.Á. Grímsdóttir), 149–170. Reykjavík: Vísindafélag Íslendinga.

Thórhallsdóttir, T.E. (1997). Tundra ecosystems in Iceland. In: Tundra Ecosystems of the World (ed. F.E. Wielgolaski), 85–91. Holland: Elsevier.

Triantis, K.A., Mylonas, M., Lika, K., and Vardinoyannis, K. (2003). A model of the species-area-habitat relationship. *Journal of Biogeography* 30: 19–27.

Turner, P.A.M., Scott, J.J., and Rozefelds, A.C. (2006). Probable long-distance dispersal of *Leptinella plumosa* Hook.f. to Heard Island: habitat, status and discussion of its arrival. *Polar Biology* 29: 160–168.

UNESCO 2004, Natural system of Wrangel Island Reserve, http://whc.unesco.org/en/list/1023/ documents.

Van der Putten, N., Verbruggen, C., Ochyra, R. et al. (2010). Subantarctic flowering plants: pre-glacial survivors or post-glacial immigrants? *Journal of Biogeography* 37: 582–592.

Vickers, K., Erlendsson, E., Chruch, M.J. et al. (2011). 1000 years of environmental change and human impact at Stóra-Mörk, Southern Iceland: a multiproxy study of a dynamic and vulnerable landscape. *The Holocene* 21: 979–995.

Wagstaff, S.J., Breitwieser, I., and Ito, M. (2011). Evolution and biogeography of *Pleurophyllum* (Astereae, Asteraceae), a small genus of megaherbs endemic to the subantarctic islands. *American Journal of Botany* 98: 62–75.

Walker, D.A., Raynolds, M.K., Daniëls, F.J.A. et al. (2005). The circumpolar Arctic vegetation map. *Journal of Vegetation Science* 16: 267–282.

Wardle, P. (1991). Vegetation of New Zealand, 672. Cambridge: Cambridge University Press.

Wasowicz, P. and Heiðmarsson, S. (2019). A vascular plant red list for Iceland. *Acta Botanica Islandica* 16: 31–48.

Westergaard, K.B., Jörgensen, M.H., Gabrielsen, T.M. et al. (2010). The extreme Beringian/Atlantic disjunction in *Saxifraga rivularis* (Saxifragaceae) has formed at least twice. *Journal of Biogeography* 37: 1262–1276.

Westergaard, K.B., Alsos, I.G., Engelskjön, T. et al. (2011). Trans-Atlantic genetic uniformity in the rare snowbed sedge *Carex rufina*. *Conservation Genetics* 12: 1367–1371.

Westoby, M., Jurado, E., and Leishman, M. (1992). Comparative evolutionary ecology of seed size. *Trends in Ecology and Evolution* 7: 368–372.

Whittaker, R.J. and Fernández-Palacios, J.M. (2007). Island Biogeography. Ecology, Evolution, and Conservation, 401. Oxford University Press.

Wilson, P., Clark, R., Birnie, J., and Moore, D.M. (2002). Late Pleistocene and Holocene landscape evolution and environmental change in the Lake Sullivan area, Falkland Islands, South Atlantic. *Quaternary Science Reviews* 21: 1821–1840.

Witham, C.S., Oppenheimer, C., and Horwell, C.J. (2005). Volcanic ash-leachates: a review and recommendations for sampling methods. *Journal of Volcanology and Geothermal Research* 141: 299–326.

Wright, D.H. (1983). Species-energy theory: an extension of species-area theory. *Oikos* 41: 496–506.

Yurtsev, B.A. (1994). Floristic division of the Arctic. *Journal of Vegetation Science* 5: 765–776.

7

Quaternary Vertebrates from the North Atlantic Islands

Ole Bennike[1] and Bernd Wagner[2]

[1] *Geological Survey of Denmark and Greenland, Copenhagen, Denmark*
[2] *Institute of Geology and Mineralogy, University of Cologne, Cologne, Germany*

Introduction

This chapter is an updated version of an earlier review of Quaternary faunas of Greenland (Bennike 1997). That work dealt with Greenland only, whereas this chapter includes some notes on Iceland and the Faroe Islands.

The richest vertebrate faunas from the North Atlantic islands come from archaeological sites. However, in Iceland and the Faroe Islands, the archaeological record so far only extends back to the Viking age. In Greenland it goes back to the Saqqaq and Independence Cultures ~4500 cal. years BP. The faunas documented from archaeological sites are similar to modern faunas, which show that most if not all vertebrate species had arrived in Greenland by the Mid-Holocene. Vertebrate remains that pre-date the archaeological record are fairly rare; for example, no cave faunas are known. In Svalbard and the Canadian Arctic, raised beaches are often rich in remains of marine mammals, especially whales, but this is not the case in Greenland or Iceland, and in the Faroe Islands there are no raised beaches.

In northern Greenland robust bones may survive on the ground surface for millennia and surface finds have provided evidence about the history of large mammals.

The meagre record may also to some degree reflect that vertebrate remains have been ignored by most Quaternary scientists working on the North Atlantic islands. The Thule region is characterized by thick Holocene peat deposits that have accumulated below bird cliffs. These deposits as well as lake deposits in the area hold a potential for studies of bird and other vertebrate remains (Bennike et al. 2008a). In addition, ancient DNA holds a tremendous potential to study Quaternary vertebrate faunas (Hebsgaard et al. 2009; Schmidt 2011) and ancient DNA studies are currently undergoing a rapid development. However, ancient DNA is only present in vanishingly small quantities and samples can easily be contaminated; furthermore, the DNA must be amplified and the method is costly.

Several hundred bones from Greenland have been directly dated by radiocarbon age determination. A few selected ages are shown in Table 1.

Biogeography in the Sub-Arctic: The Past and Future of North Atlantic Biota, First Edition.
Edited by Eva Panagiotakopulu and Jon P. Sadler.

Table 1 Selected radiocarbon ages of vertebrate remains from Greenland.

Loc. no.[1]	Laboratory no.	Species	[14]C age (yr BP)	Calendar age[2] (cal. yr BP)	Ref.
1	LuS-6748	*Canis lupus*	6785 ± 100	7433–7836	A
2	K-3865	*Rangifer tarandus*	7980 ± 115	8540–9255	B
3	AAR-12025	*Ovibos moschatus*	4687 ± 46	5315–5574	C
4	COL-2862	*Odobenus rosmarus*	7165 ± 47	7167–7470	D
5	Lu-3701	*Monodon monoceros*	7730 ± 100	7616–8101	E
6	Ua-1346	*Canis lupus*	4745 ± 50	5325–5585	F
7	K-6096	*Balaenoptera physalis*	3630 ± 90	3412–3946	G
8	LuS-9183	*Ovibos moschatus*	1275 ± 50	1072–1292	H
9	K-5139	*Cygnus cygnus*	2140 ± 75	1943–2332	I
10	LuS-6443	*Balaena mysticetus*	8525 ± 50	8705–9152	J
11	K-4687	*Pusa hispida*	8680 ± 120	9092–9780	K

[1] Locality numbers refer to Figure 1.
[2] Calibrated according to the INTCAL20 and MARINE20 datasets. References: A: Bennike, et al., 1994b; B: Meldgaard, 1986; C: Campos, et al., 2010; D: B. Wagner and O. Bennike, unpublished, upper canine found at 81.58 °N, 16.41 °W and deposited at the Zoological Museum, Copenhagen, KNK 3807X; E: Hjort, 1997; F: C. Andreasen, unpublished; G: Weidick, et al., 1996; H: B. Wagner and O. Bennike, unpublished, sample collected at 72.21 °N, 23.68 °W; I: C. Hammer, unpublished; J: Bennike, 2008; K: Bennike, et al., 1989.

Radiocarbon ages have been calibrated to calendar years BP. This is fairly straightforward when dealing with terrestrial vertebrates, but more complicated for marine vertebrates, because marine organisms are influenced by the so-called reservoir effect. The reservoir age varies from region to region and, in addition to spatial variation, there have also been temporal variations in the past. Another complication arises because bones have been dated at many different laboratories that reported ages in different ways. Some of these issues were briefly discussed by Bennike (1997). A third problem is that migrating marine mammals may have lived in different water masses with different reservoir ages. In this paper we have used a reservoir age of 400 years for West Greenland and a reservoir age of 550 years for East and North Greenland. The location of finds listed in Table 1 and selected place names are shown in Figure 1 (see Plate section).

Fish

In Greenland and Iceland, littoral gravel and marine silt is commonly found above sea level because the glacio-isostatic rebound has surpassed the eustatic global sea level rise after the Last Glacial Maximum. At several localities in West Greenland raised silt deposits contain calcareous concretions, sometimes with fossils of marine organisms, including fish. Capelin (*Mallotus villosus*) is the most common species (Bendix-Almgreen 1976), but bones of this fish have also been reported from marine deposits found below lake sediments in lakes that were isolated from the sea as the land was uplifted (Bennike 1995; Sparrenbom et al. 2006). The oldest reported capelin remains are around 8000 cal. years old. A few specimens of red fish (*Sebastes* cf. *marinus*) have also been reported from Holocene concretions (Bendix-Almgreen 1976).

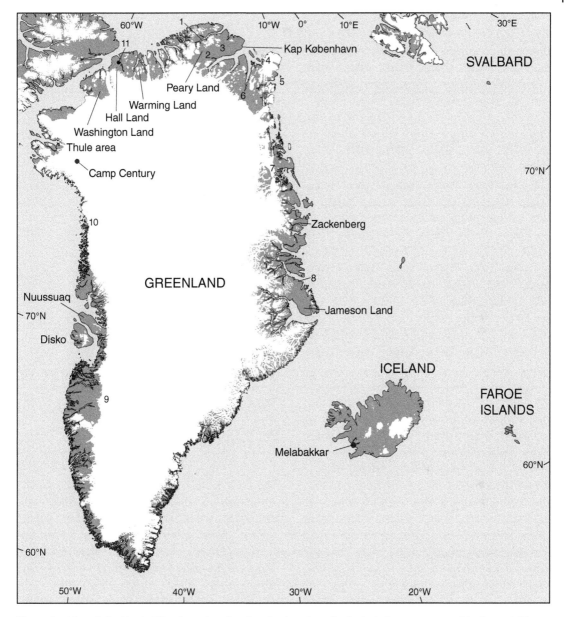

Figure 1 Map of the North Atlantic region showing the location of selected place names used in the text. The numbers refer to Table 1. (See colour plate section for colour representation of this figure.)

An otolith of Atlantic cod (*Gadus morhua*) was reported from the Early Quaternary Pátorfik beds on Nuussuaq and another otolith of Atlantic cod was found in Holocene deposits near Aassiat (Laursen 1944). The species is also reported from Mid-Holocene archaeological deposits (Meldgaard 2004). An otolith of Greenland cod (*Gadus ogac*) was found in an interglacial deposit on north-west Disko (Bennike et al. 1994a); the deposit is older than the last interglacial stage, the Eemian. Remains of polar cod (*Boreogadus saida*) have been found in Mid-Holocene deposits in West Greenland (Meldgaard 2004) and North Greenland (Kelly and Bennike 1992). Finally, there is a find of Arctic staghorn sculpin (*Gymnocanthus tricuspis*) from a Mid-Holocene deposit on Disko (Bennike et al. 1994a).

Bones of the small three-spined stickleback (*Gasterosteus aculeatus*) are often found in lake deposits, especially at the transition from marine to lacustrine deposits in isolation basins in Greenland (e.g. Fredskild 1983; Bennike 1995; Bennike et al. 2000a, 2011; Wagner and Melles 2002; Sparrenbom et al. 2006, 2013; Figure 2). In both East and West Greenland bones of *G. aculeatus* have been found in sediments from lakes that are located north of the northern range limit of the species (Fredskild 1985; Björck et al. 1994). These finds are from the Holocene thermal maximum, when many plant and animal species extended their ranges farther north than at present. The oldest finds of three-spined stickleback come from South Greenland and are dated to ~10400 cal. years BP (Bennike and Björck 2000). The documented fossil range of Arctic char (*Salvelinus alpinus*) extends back to the Mid-Holocene (Knuth 1967; Meldgaard 2004).

In Iceland there is a report of a hyoid bone of a cod (*Gadus* sp.) from a marine deposit near Hellisholtalækur in Hrunnamannahreppur, South-West Iceland (Símonarson 1981). The bone was found at an elevation of 175 m above sea level, which indicates a late glacial age.

Birds

In basal ice from the Camp Century ice core from North-West Greenland, short DNA molecule fragments of mammals and birds were reported by Schmidt (2011). The mammalian DNA was

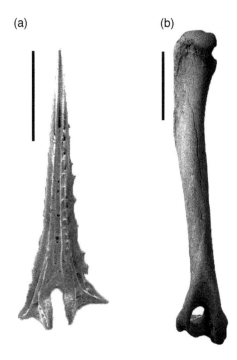

(a)   (b)

Figure 2 Two examples of vertebrate remains from Greenland. (a) A pelvic spine of a three-spined stickleback (*Gasterosteus aculeatus*) from Disko, West Greenland dated to ~5 cal. ka BP (Bennike 1995). Scale bar: 1 mm. (b) Left humerus of a wolf (*Canis lupus*) from North Greenland, dated to ~7.6 cal. ka BP (Bennike et al. 1994b). Scale bar: 5 cm.

identified as ox, pig and mouse and considered contamination of the ice. The bird DNA was assigned to Anatidae, which is a large family that includes ducks, geese and swans; this DNA was interpreted as non-contamination. The DNA from Camp Century may be around 1 million years old (Schmidt 2011).

There is only a single report of a bird bone from a deposit that pre-dates the oldest archaeological sites: a bone of little auk (*Alle alle*) was found in a Middle Pleistocene marine deposit in West Greenland (Bennike et al. 1994a).

Wagner and and Melles (2001) used the concentration of cadmium in sediments from a lake to reconstruct the former history of a little auk colony in East Greenland. They concluded that the colony was established at ~7500 cal. years BP.

There are some reports of fossil feathers from Greenland. Feathers and feather fragments were common in a peat deposit dated to 7100–5100 cal. years BP from North-West Greenland. The feathers could not be identified, but from the location of the peat deposit at high elevation, on a plateau near a cliff edge, it was suggested that they came from a puffin (*Fratercula arctica*) colony (Bennike et al. 2008a). This species is now rare so far north. Feathers may also be common in permanently frozen middens (Meldgaard 2004). A feather of a Lapland longspur (*Calcarius lapponicus*) was reported from a Mid-Holocene peat deposit in North Greenland, far north of the species current range (Bennike and Dyck 1986).

Burnham et al. (2009) reported on ages of bird guano and feathers from gyrfalcon (*Falco rusticolus*) nests from West and North-West Greenland. The oldest age was ~2500 cal. years BP, which shows that this raptor can use the same nest sites for millennia. Remains of a gyrfalcon, with bones, skin and feathers preserved, have been found in a cave in North-East Greenland; the find was radiocarbon dated to ~1100 cal. years BP (Moseley et al. 2019).

A carcass of a swan, probably a whooper swan (*Cygnus cygnus*) has been found in the ablation zone of the Greenland ice sheet in West Greenland; it was dated to 2000 cal. years BP (Table 1). Whooper swans are presently only rare visitors in Greenland, but the species was breeding in South-West Greenland until ~150 years ago (Winge 1899) and bones of swans have been found at Mid and Late Holocene archaeological sites in the region (Enghoff 2003; Gotfredsen and Møbjerg 2004. The oldest and northernmost swan remains come from Nipisat, a Palaeo-Eskimo site dated to ~4000–3000 cal. years BP. The swan bones may come from either whooper swan or tundra swan (*Cygnus colombianus*), but since whooper swans were breeding in South-West Greenland until quite recently, we consider it most likely that the bones represent this species. However, the possibility that the swan bones from Nipisat were tundra swans cannot entirely be ruled out (Gotfredsen and Møbjerg 2004).

The great auk (*Pinguinus impennis*) was hunted by people in Greenland for nearly 4500 years and the species occurred farther north along the west coast of Greenland ~4000 cal. years BP than in historical times (Meldgaard 1988). What may have been the last two birds on Earth of this flightless bird were killed in Iceland in 1844.

In the Melabakkar cliffs in western Iceland, Ingólfsson (1984) found a bone of a common eider (*Somateria mollissima*). The find is of late glacial age and marine shells in the area have been dated to ~13.7 cal. ka BP. The find is the oldest identified bird body fossil from Iceland, but there is also a report of tracks of birds in late glacial layers at Elliðaár near Reykjavik (Áskelsson 1953).

Pre-Holocene Mammal Remains

The occurrence of the extinct rabbit *Hypolagus* sp. and the extant hare *Lepus* sp. in member B of the Kap København Formation in North Greenland helped to constrain the age of the formation to 2–2.3 Ma (Repenning et al. 1987). *Hypolagus* is common in the mid-Pliocene Beaver Pond deposit on Ellesmere Island in High-Arctic Canada. The Beaver Pond deposit has yielded a unique vertebrate fauna that includes an extinct beaver, a primitive bear, a badger, a giant camel, a deerlet, a horse and an unusual shrew (Dawson and Harington 2007; Rybczynski et al. 2013). Given the proximity of Ellesmere Island to Greenland, it may be speculated whether these species also occurred in Greenland. It is possible that the Nares Strait that presently separates Canada from Greenland did not exist in the mid-Pliocene.

A find of an incomplete but articulated skeleton of a ringed seal (*Pusa hispida*) from the Pátorfik beds in central West Greenland is also of Early Quaternary age (Bennike 1997).

Finds referred more or less securely to the last interglacial stage include a fragment of a strongly weathered reindeer (*Rangifer tarandus*) antler found on the ground surface near Kap København and small droppings of lemming (*Dicrostonyx torquatus* (?)) from Warming Land in North Greenland (Meldgaard and Bennike 1989). Marine mammals are represented by bones of Greenland whale (*Balaena mysticetus*) from Jameson Land in East Greenland and from Saunders Ø in North-West Greenland (Hansen et al. 1994; Bennike 1997). From the latter locality a non-finite age of unidentified whale bones was also reported by Blake (1987). Finally, an ulna fragment of a ringed seal found in a till deposit in Jameson Land was probably reworked from last interglacial layers (Bennike 1997).

Holocene Marine Mammals

Many species of marine mammals probably followed the retreating glacier ice front and arrived in Greenland and the other North Atlantic islands in the Early Holocene or maybe during the late glacial period. However, most marine mammals die at sea and the bones usually end on the sea floor. Greenland whales are extremely fat and carcasses of this species can float for weeks or even months, so there is a good chance that such carcasses end up on beaches, which may be uplifted due to glacioisostatic rebound. Hence bones of Greenland whales are common on raised beaches in Arctic Canada and Svalbard, but for some reason not in Greenland or Iceland. Nevertheless, here are a number of finds of bones of marine mammals from raised marine and littoral deposits.

A skeleton of a ringed seal from raised marine deposits in Hall Land in central North Greenland has been dated to ~9.6 cal. ka BP (Bennike et al. 1989; Table 1); this is the oldest dated find

of mammal remains from Holocene deposits in Greenland. Ringed seal is the most cold-adapted marine mammal in the Arctic and may have been the first mammal to colonize Greenland after the Last Glacial Maximum.

The next species documented by a dated specimen is the Greenland whale (*B. mysticetus*), also known as bowhead in American English. A vertebra from Melville Bugt in North-West Greenland gave an age of ~9.1 cal. ka BP (Bennike 2008; Table 1; Figure 3). The bone was deposited in a marine bay and pushed up on land during the Little Ice Age when the Greenland ice sheet expanded. Similarly, during the Mid-Holocene, a Greenland whale died in Nioghalvfjerdsfjorden in North-East Greenland, and two fragments of ribs were deposited on a beach that was uplifted. At present, Nioghalvfjerdsfjorden is covered by a floating glacier, but the fjord must have been glacier-free during the Mid-Holocene, when whale bones and drift wood could strand along the shores of the fjord (Bennike and Weidick 2001). A number of other ages of bones of large whales from Greenland are also, with more or less confidence, identified as Greenland whale (Bennike 2008).

From Arctic Canada there are hundreds of radiocarbon ages of bones of Greenland whales and in this huge region the documented temporal range of the species goes back to the earliest Holocene (Dyke et al. 1996). The same presumably applies to West Greenland where Greenland whales from the eastern Canadian Arctic spend the spring time. In Svalbard, the documented history of the Greenland whale also extends back to the earliest Holocene, and the same presumably applies to North-East Greenland, although this is not documented by dated finds.

Next on the list is narwhale (*Monodon monoseros*), of which a specimen from a raised beach ridge in Holm Land in eastern North Greenland yielded an age of ~8 cal. ka BP (Hjort 1997; Table 1). To my knowledge, there are no other published dates

(a)

(b)

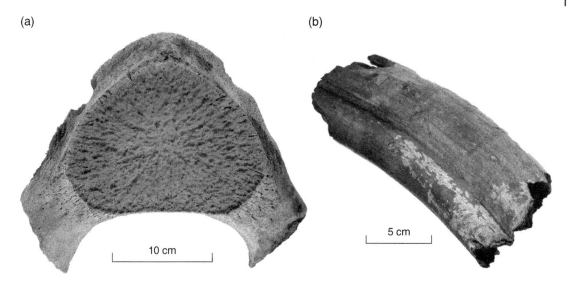

10 cm

5 cm

Figure 3 Two examples of remains of marine mammals from Greenland. (a) A vertebra of a Greenland whale (*Balaena mysticetus*) from Melville Bugt, North-West Greenland dated to ~9.1 cal. ka BP (Bennike 2008). (b) A tusk fragment of a walrus (*Odobenus rosmarus*) from Nuussuaq, West Greenland dated to ~3.1 cal. ka BP (Bennike and Andreasen 2007).

on narwhale finds from Greenland, but there is an undated find of a 2.2 m long tusk from near Kap Morris Jesup, the northernmost cape in Greenland (Grant 1969). Surprisingly, there are apparently no published stray finds of the third arctic whale species from Greenland, the white whale (*Delphinapterus leucas*).

The documented temporal range of walrus (*Odobenus rosmarus*) in Greenland also extends back to the Early Holocene, with the oldest dated specimen yielding an age of ~7.5 cal. ka BP (Wagner and Bennike, unpublished data; Bennike and Andreasen 2007; Table 1). Thirty-three walrus specimens from Greenland have been dated; most of them come from archaeological sites of Mid to Late Holocene age. An example of a stray find of a walrus tusk fragment is shown in Figure 3. In the Canadian Arctic Archipelago, the documented temporal range extends back to ~10.3 cal. ka BP (Dyke et al. 1999) and the species may also have arrived in Greenland during the earliest Holocene. Marine bivalves that could

have provided food for walrus were common all around Greenland in the Early Holocene.

In Greenland, walrus was eagerly hunted by Palaeo-Eskimos, Neoeskimos and Norsemen. The Norse that lived in Greenland from CE 985 to ~1450 hunted walrus north of their settlements and walrus ivory was an important element in the economy of the Norse in Greenland. Due to hunting many haul-out sites in Greenland have been abandoned and the population has decreased in central East Greenland and in South-West and West Greenland over the past century. Similarly, the range in walrus in Canada has been greatly reduced along the southern limit and the same is the case in northern Norway.

A recent study of walrus remains from Iceland that included radiocarbon dating of 34 bones shows that the history of the species can be traced back almost 9000 years (Keighley et al. 2019). The disappearance of walrus in Iceland coincided with the arrival of the Norse, as earlier suggested by Pierce (2009) and Frei et al. (2015).

A rib of a fin whale (*Balaenoptera physalis*) from North-East Greenland has been dated to ~3.8 cal. ka BP (Weidick et al. 1996; Table 1). This find is the only dated specimen of a fin whale from Greenland, but the find is also important because fin whales do not penetrate into the pack ice off North-East Greenland. The former presence of this species must mean that the pack ice was much more limited than at present in the Mid-Holocene. Furthermore, the find comes from a former strait that is now covered by an outlet glacier, Storstømmen, from the Greenland ice sheet.

Finally, it should be mentioned that there are only a few reported stray finds of bones of polar bear (*Ursus maritimus*) in Greenland and those dated gave Late Holocene ages (Bennike 1997, 2002). A specimen from the Thule region, supposed to be from an archaeological site, gave an age of ~5.8 cal. ka BP (Knuth 1978). This is older than expected and the find may not be related to the archaeological site. In North-East Greenland, the oldest dated find gave an age of ~3.8 cal. ka BP (Rasmussen 1996). In Iceland, a molar of a polar bear has been reported from marine deposits at Rondinni near Kopasker, north-east Iceland (Áskelsson 1938; Símonarson 1981). There is no direct dating of this find, but the deposit is around 15 cal. ka old (Ólafur Ingólfsson, personal communication, 2014). There are several finds of late glacial polar bear bones from North-West Europe (Ingólfsson and Wiig 2009) and it is not impossible that the species lived in Iceland during the late glacial time period.

Holocene Terrestrial Mammals

Bones of terrestrial mammals end on the ground after the animal dies, but most bones disappear fairly rapidly, unless they are buried. However, in North Greenland bones can survive on the ground surface for millennia if the ground is dry. Brain cases of adult male musk-oxen (*Ovibos*

moschatus) and antlers from reindeer are more resistant to erosion and decay than other bones. Sometimes bones or carcasses of terrestrial mammals are found on ice caps or on the Greenland ice sheet.

There are numerous direct dates of reindeer and musk-ox from Greenland. The oldest reindeer find is an eroded fragment of an antler from Jørgen Brønlund Fjord in North Greenland; it was dated to ~8.8 cal. ka BP (Meldgaard 1986; Table 1). At present, the reindeer in Greenland are confined to West and North-West Greenland, but reindeer bones and cast antlers can be found in almost all ice-free parts of Greenland, and the species lived in East Greenland until ~100 years ago (Figure 4, see Plate section). The first reindeer that arrived in Greenland were small animals with short legs, similar to those currently found in northernmost Canada and Svalbard. Larger animals with longer legs arrived ~4000 years ago, perhaps from Baffin Island, and spread in West Greenland (Meldgaard 1986).

The oldest musk-ox find also comes from North Greenland; it gave an age of ~5.4 cal. ka BP (Campos et al. 2010). The musk-ox expanded its range south in East Greenland and the oldest dated find from central East Greenland yielded an age of ~1.2 cal. ka BP (Table 1; Bennike and Andreasen 2005a). In North-West Greenland the oldest find is dated to ~2.2 cal. ka BP (Bennike and Andreasen 2005b; Bennike 2014). It is possible that the species crossed Nares Strait from Ellesmere Island and arrived in North-West Greenland south of the 100 km wide Humboldt Gletscher. In the Thule region the species was probably exterminated after the arrival of the Thule people around 800 years ago, whereas the species survived in Inglefield Land until around CE1850–1860 (Bennike 2014; Figure 4). Two dated skull fragments from Greenland are shown in Figure 5 (see Plate section).

The spread of musk-ox to Greenland from Beringia, where the species occurred during the

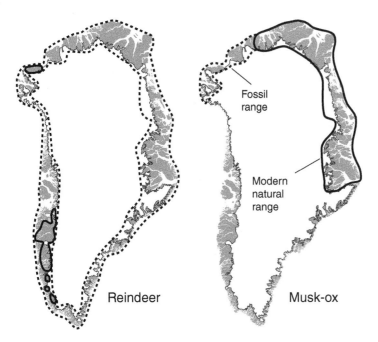

Reindeer

Musk-ox

Fossil range

Modern natural range

Figure 4 Maps of Greenland showing Holocene and modern natural geographical ranges of reindeer (*Rangifer tarandus*) and musk-ox (*Ovibos moschatus*). (See colour plate section for colour representation of this figure.)

Figure 5 Two examples of musk-ox (*Ovibos moschatus*) skull fragments. (a) A specimen of a female from Washington Land with the outer horny sheaths still present dated to 10–274 cal. years BP (K-5174; Bennike 2002). Note that BP = CE1950. (b) A strongly eroded specimen of a male from Olrik Fjord in the Thule area dated to ~2200 cal. years BP (Bennike 2014). (See colour plate section for colour representation of this figure.)

Last Glacial Maximum, can be followed from radiocarbon-dated finds. A bone from Banks Island has been dated to the Younger Dryas (MacPhee 2007) and a bone from Bathurst Island gave an age of ~7.6 cal. ka (Harington 2003).

Wolf (*Canis lupus*) may also have been widespread in Greenland in former times. There is some archaeological evidence that it has occurred in West Greenland, and it is also mentioned in 'The Kings mirror', which describes South-West Greenland and was written around 1260 (Bennike et al. 1994b). However, in the last centuries wolves have been confined to North and East Greenland. The oldest finds come from North Greenland and have been dated to ~7.6 and 5.5 cal. ka BP (Bennike et al. 1994b; Table 1). The finds indicate that wolves have been present in Greenland during large parts of the Holocene.

Droppings of collared lemmings have been found in a number of deposits in North and North-East Greenland (Bennike 1997, 2002; Bennike and Weidick 2001; Wagner et al. 2008). The oldest find has been dated to ~6.4 cal. ka BP (Bennike and Weidick 2001). Droppings of arctic hare (*Lepus arcticus*) from raised delta deposits at Zackenberg are dated to ~8.0 cal. ka BP (Christiansen et al. 2002). Figure 6 provides an overview of vertebrate finds from Greenland.

Discussion and Conclusions

For many years it has been debated whether vertebrates survived in ice-free refugia or if they immigrated after the Last Glacial Maximum to the North Atlantic islands. It has been suggested

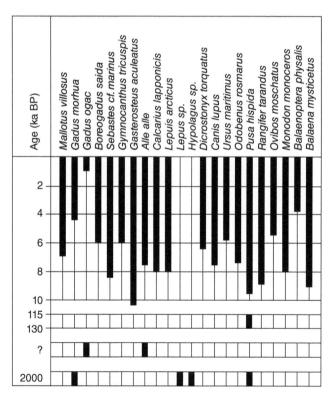

Figure 6 Temporal ranges of selected vertebrates from Greenland. *Source:* Modified and updated from Bennike (1997). Reprinted by permission of Elsevier.

that Peary Land in North Greenland was an ice-free refugium for wolves and other terrestrial mammals during the Last Glacial Maximum (e.g. Macpherson 1965; Nowak 1979, 1983). This idea may have been fostered because Koch (1928) showed that the Greenland ice sheet never covered northern Peary Land. However, the region was covered by a local ice cap (Kelly and Bennike 1992). Small non-glaciated alpine areas may have been present in Greenland during the Last Glacial Maximum, but ice core data show that temperatures were much lower than during the Holocene, and it seems highly doubtful if there was enough vegetation to support terrestrial vertebrates. Musk-ox survived in Beringia and spread eastward during the Holocene, and this may also hold for other species.

In contrast, marine vertebrates, especially fish, no doubt occurred in the northern North Atlantic during the last ice age. However, the continental shelves around Greenland and Iceland were glaciated during the Last Glacial Maximum (e.g. Andrews et al. 2000; Winkelmann et al. 2010; Slabon et al. 2016; Arndt et al. 2017; Laberg et al. 2017). The same may apply to the Faroe Islands, but so far we have no data from this region.

We suggest that most of the vertebrates currently living on and around the North Atlantic islands immigrated during the late glacial period and the Holocene. The fossil record only provides a glimpse of the fossil fauna.

Acknowledgements

The authors are grateful to Jeppe Møhl and Knud Rosenlund for identifications of bones and to C.R. Harington for discussions on Greenland Quaternary vertebrates. Ólafur Ingólfsson kindly provided information on Quaternary vertebrates from Iceland.

References

Andrews, J.T., Hardarsdóttir, J., Helgadóttir, G. et al. (2000). The N and W Iceland shelf: insights into the Last Glacial Maximum ice extent and deglaciation based on acoustic stratigraphy and basal radiocarbon AMS dates. *Quaternary Science Reviews* 19: 619–631.

Arndt, J.E., Jokat, W., and Dorschel, B. (2017). The last glaciation and deglaciation of the Northeast Greenland continental shelf revealed by hydro-acoustic data. *Quaternary Science Reviews* 160: 45–56.

Áskelsson, J. (1938). Um íslenzk dýr og jurtir frá jökultíma. *Náttúrufræðingurinn* 8: 1–16.

Áskelsson, J. (1953). Nokkur orð um íslenskan fornfugl og fleira. *Náttúrufræðingurinn* 23: 133–137.

Bendix-Almgreen, S.E. (1976). Palaeovertebrate faunas of Greenland. In: Geology of Greenland (eds. A. Escher and W.S. Watt), 537–573. Geological Survey of Greenland: Copenhagen.

Bennike, O. (1995). Palaeoecology of two lake basins from Disko, West Greenland. *Journal of Quaternary Science* 10: 149–155.

Bennike, O. (1997). Quaternary vertebrates from Greenland: a review. *Quaternary Science Reviews* 16: 899–909.

Bennike, O. (2000a). Palaeoecological studies of Holocene lake sediments from West Greenland. *Palaeogeography, Palaeoclimatology, Palaeoecology* 155: 285–304.

Bennike, O. (2002). Late Quaternary history of Washington land, North Greenland. *Boreas* 31: 260–272.

Bennike, O. (2008). An early Holocene Greenland whale from Melville Bugt, Greenland. *Quaternary Research* 69: 72–76.

Bennike, O. (2014). Radiocarbon dating of musk-ox (*Ovibos moschatus*) bones from the Thule region, Northwest Greenland. *Polar Record* 50: 113–118.

Bennike, O. and Andreasen, C. (2005a). New dates of muskox (*Ovibos moschatus*) remains from northwestern Greenland. *Polar Record* 41: 125–129.

Bennike, O. and Andreasen, C. (2005b). Radiocarbon dating of musk-ox (*Ovibos moschatus*) remains from Northeast Greenland. *Polar Record* 41: 305–310.

Bennike, O. and Andreasen, C. (2007). Radiocarbon dating of walrus (*Odobenus rosmarus*) remains from Greenland. *Polar Record* 43: 361–365.

Bennike, O. and Björck, S. (2000). Lake sediment coring in South Greenland in 1999. *Geology of Greenland Survey Bulletin* 186: 60–64.

Bennike, O. and Dyck, J. (1986). A subfossil Lapland Bunting *Calcarius lapponicus* feather from Vølvedal, North Greenland. *Ornis Scandinavica* 17: 75–77.

Bennike, O. and Weidick, A. (2001). Late Quaternary history around Nioghalvfjerdsfjorden and Jøkelbugten, North-East Greenland. *Boreas* 30: 205–227.

Bennike, O., Higgins, A.K., and Kelly, M. (1989). Mammals of central North Greenland. *Polar Record* 25: 43–49.

Bennike, O., Hansen, K.B., Knudsen, K.L. et al. (1994a). Quaternary marine stratigraphy and geochronology in central West Greenland. *Boreas* 23: 194–215.

Bennike, O., Meldgaard, M., Heinemeier, J., and Rud, N. (1994b). Radiocarbon dating of Holocene wolf (*Canis lupus*) remains from Greenland. *The Holocene* 4: 84–88.

Bennike, O., Björck, S., Böcher, J. et al. (1999). Early Holocene plant and animal remains from North-East Greenland. *Journal of Biogeography* 26: 667–677.

Bennike, O., Goodsite, M., and Heinemeier, J. (2008a). Palaeoecology of Holocene peat deposits from Nordvestø, North-West Greenland. *Journal of Paleolimnology* 40: 575–565.

Bennike, O., Wagner, B., and Richter, A. (2011). Relative sea level changes during the Holocene in the Sisimiut area, South-Western Greenland. *Journal of Quaternary Science* 26: 353–361.

Björck, S., Wohlfahrt, B., Bennike, O. et al. (1994). Revision of the early Holocene lake sediment based chronology and event stratigraphy on Hochstetter Forland, NE Greenland. *Boreas* 23: 513–523.

Blake Jr., W. 1987. Geological Survey of Canada radiocarbon dates XXVI. *Geological Survey of Canada,* Paper 86–7, 60 pp.

Burnham, K.K., Burnham, W.A., and Newton, I. (2009). Gyrfalcon *Falco rusticolus* post-glacial colonization and extreme long-term use of nest-sites in Greenland. *Ibis* 151: 514–522.

Campos, P.F., Willerslev, E., Sher, A. et al. (2010). Ancient DNA analyses exclude humans as the driving force behind late Pleistocene musk ox (*Ovibos*) population dynamics. *Proceedings of the National Academy of Sciences of the United States of America* 107: 5675–5680.

Christiansen, H.H., Bennike, O., Böcher, J. et al. (2002). Holocene environmental evidence from the Zackenberg Delta, NE Greenland. *Journal of Quaternary Science* 17: 145–160.

Dawson, M.R. and Harington, C.R. (2007). *Boreameryx*, an unusual new artiodactyl (Mammalia) from the Pliocene of Arctic Canada and endemism in Arctic fossil mammals. *Canadian Journal of Earth Science* 44: 585–592.

Dyke, A.S., Hooper, J., and Savelle, J.M. (1996). A history of sea ice in the Canadian Arctic archipelago based on the postglacial remains of the bowhead whale (*Balaena mysticetus*). *Arctic* 49: 235–255.

Dyke, A.S., Hooper, J., Harington, C.R., and Savelle, J.M. (1999). The Late Wisconsinan and Holocene record of walrus (*Odobenus rosmarus*) from North America: a review with new data from Arctic and Atlantic Canada. *Arctic* 52: 160–181.

Enghoff, I.B. (2003). Hunting, fishing and husbandry at the farm beneath the sand, Western Greenland. *Meddelelser om Grønland, Man and Society* 28: 105.

Fredskild, B. (1973). Studies in the vegetational history of Greenland. Palaeobotanical investigations of some Holocene lake and bog deposits. *Meddelelser om Grønland* 198 (4): 245.

Fredskild, B. (1983). The Holocene vegetational development of the Godthåbsfjord area, West Greenland. *Meddelelser om Grønland, Geoscience* 10: 28.

Fredskild, B. (1985). The Holocene vegetational development of Tugtuligssuaq and Qeqertat, Northwest Greenland. *Meddelelser om Grønland, Geoscience* 14: 20.

Frei, K.M., Coutu, A.N., Smiarowski, K. et al. (2015). Was it for walrus? Viking Age settlement and medieval walrus ivory trade in Iceland and Greenland. *World Archaeology* 47: 439–466.

Gotfredsen, A.B. and Møbjerg, T. (2004). Nipisat – a Saqqaq site in Sisimiut, central West Greenland. *Meddelelser om Grønland, Man and Society* 31: 243.

Grant, C.J. (1969). Mammalogy report. In: Joint Services Expedition North Peary Land 1969 (ed. J.D.C. Peacock), E1–E4. London: Ministry of Defence.

Hansen, L.A., Jørgensen, M.E., Houmark-Nielsen, M., and Kronborg, C. (1994). Late Pleistocene stratigraphy and depositional environments of the Fynselv area, Jameson Land, East Greenland. *Boreas* 23: 385–397.

Harington, C.R. (2003). Annotated Bibliography of Quaternary Vertebrates of Northern North America. Toronto: Toronto University Press.

Hebsgaard, M.B., Gilbert, M.T.P., Arneborg, J. et al. (2009). 'The farm beneath the sand' – an archaeological case study on ancient 'dirt' DNA. *Antiquity* 83: 430–444.

Hjort, C. (1997). Glaciation, climate history, changing marine levels and the evolution of the northeast water Polynia. *Journal of Marine Systems* 10: 23–33.

Ingólfsson, Ó. (1984). Æðarfuglsbein í Melabökkum. *Náttúrufræðingurinn* 53: 97–100.

Ingólfsson, Ó. and Wiig, Ø. (2009). Late Pleistocene fossil find in Svalbard: the oldest remains of a polar bear (*Ursus maritimus* Phipps, 1744) ever discovered. *Polar Research* 28: 455–462.

Keighley, X., Pálsson, S., Einarsson, B.F. et al. (2019). Disappearance of Icelandic Walruses coincided with Norse Settlement. *Molecular Biology and Evolution* 36: 2656–2667.

Kelly, M. and Bennike, O. (1992). Quaternary geology of western and central North Greenland. *Rapport Grønlands Geologiske Undersøgelse* 153: 34.

Knuth, E. 1967. Archaeology of the musk-ox way. *École Pratoque des Hautes Études, Contributions du Centre d'Études Arctiques et Finno-Scandinaves* 5, 70 pp.

Knuth, E. (1978). The 'old Nûgdlít culture' site at Nûgdlít peninsula, Thule District, and the Mesoeskimo site below it. *Folk* 19–20: 15–47.

Koch, L. (1928). Contributions to the glaciology of North Greenland. *Meddelelser om Grønland* 65: 181–464.

Laberg, J.S., Forwick, M., and Husum, K. (2017). New geophysical evidence for a revised maximum position of part of the NE sector of the Greenland ice sheet during the last glacial maximum. *Arktos* 3: 1–9.

Laursen, D. (1944). Contributions to the Quaternary geology of northern West Greenland especially the raised marine deposits. *Meddelelser om Grønland* 135 (9): 125.

MacPhee, R.D.E. (2007). Mammoths in the insular Nearctic? Some constraints on the existence of a Pleistocene megafaunal refugium in the Canadian Arctic Archipelago. *Quaternary International* 169–170: 29–38.

Macpherson, A.H. (1965). The origin of diversity of mammals in Canadian arctic tundra. *Systematic Zoology* 14: 153–173.

Meldgaard, M. (1986). The Greenland caribou – zoogeography, taxonomy, and population dynamics. *Meddelelser om Grønland, Bioscience* 20: 88.

Meldgaard, M. (1988). The great auk, *Pinguinus impennis* (L.) in Greenland. *Historical Biology* 1: 145–178.

Meldgaard, M. (2004). Ancient harp seal hunters of Disko Bay. *Meddelelser om Grønland, Man and Society* 30: 189.

Meldgaard, M. and Bennike, O. (1989). Interglacial remains of caribou (*Rangifer tarandus*) and lemming (*Dicrostonyx torquatus* (?)) from North Greenland. *Boreas* 18: 359–366.

Moseley, G.E., Rosvold, J., Gotfredsen, A.B. et al. (2019). First pre-modern record of the gyrfalcon (*Falco rusticolus*) in north-east Greenland. *Polar Research* 38: 3539.

Nowak, R.M. (1979). North American Quaternary Canis. In: Monograph of the Museum of Natural History, vol. 6, 154. University of Kansas.

Nowak, R.M. (1983). A perspective on the taxonomy of wolves in North America. In: Wolves in Canada and Alaska, *Canadian Wildlife Service, Report Series*, vol. 45 (ed. L.N. Carbyn), 10–19. Edmonton: Canadian Wildlife Service.

Pierce, E. (2009). Walrus hunting and the ivory trade in early Iceland. *Archaeologia Islandica* 7: 55–63.

Rasmussen, K.L. (1996). Carbon-14 datings from northern East Greenland. In: The Paleo-Eskimo Cultures of Greenland (eds. B. Grønnow and J. Pind), 188–189. Danish Polar Center: Copenhagen.

Repenning, C.A., Brouwers, E.M., Carter, L.D., Marincovoch Jr., L. & Ager, T.A. 1987. The Beringian ancestry of *Phenacomys* (Rodentia: Cricetidae) and the beginning of the modern Arctic Ocean borderland biota. *U.S. Geological Survey Bulletin* 1687, 31 pp.

Rybczynski, N., Gosse, J.C., Harington, C.R. et al. (2013). Mid-Pliocene warm-period deposits in the high Arctic yield insight into camel evolution. *Nature Communications* 4: 1550. https://doi.org/10.1038/ncomms2516.

Schmidt, A. 2011. Ice core genetics, uncovering biodiversity from ancient ecosystems in Greenland and Antarctica, 301 pp. PhD Thesis, Copenhagen University.

Símonarson, L.A. (1981). Íslenskir steingervingar. In: Náttúra Íslands (ed. V.T. Gíslason), 157–173. Reykjavik: Almenna Bókafélagid.

Slabon, P., Dorschel, B., Jokat, W. et al. (2016). Greenland ice sheet retreat history in the northeast Baffin Bay based on high-resolution bathymetry. *Quaternary Science Reviews* 154: 182–198.

Sparrenbom, C.J., Bennike, O., Björck, S., and Lambeck, K. (2006). Holocene relative sea-level changes in the Qaqortoq area, southern Greenland. *Boreas* 35: 171–187.

Sparrenbom, C.J., Bennike, O., Fedh, D. et al. (2013). Holocene relative sea-level changes in the inner Bredefjord area, southern Greenland. *Quaternary Science Reviews* 69: 107–124.

Wagner, B. and Melles, M. (2001). A Holocene seabird record from Raffles Sø sediments, East Greenland, in response to climatic and oceanic changes. *Boreas* 30: 228–239.

Wagner, B. and Melles, M. (2002). Holocene environmental history of western Ymer Ø, East Greenland, inferred from lake sediments. *Quaternary International* 89: 165–176.

Wagner, B., Bennike, O., Bos, J.A.A. et al. (2008). A multidisciplinary study of Holocene sediment records from Hjort Sø on Store Koldewey, Northeast Greenland. *Journal of Paleolimnology* 39: 381–398.

Weidick, A., Andreasen, C., Oerter, H., and Reeh, N. (1996). Neoglacial glacier changes around Storstrømmen, North-East Greenland. *Polarforschung* 64: 95–108.

Winge, H. (1899). Grønlands Fugle. *Meddelelser om Grønland* 21: 1–316.

Winkelmann, D., Jokat, W., Jensen, L., and Schenke, H.-W. (2010). Submarine end moraines on the continental shelf off NE Greenland: implications for Lateglacial dynamics. *Quaternary Science Reviews* 29: 1069–1077.

8

North Atlantic Insect Faunas, Fossils and Pitfalls

Eva Panagiotakopulu

School of GeoSciences, University of Edinburgh, UK

Introduction

One of Carl Lindroth's most notable quotes was his remark that the Quaternary record 'should engender a sense of fear in all biogeographers' as this would provide data against which hypotheses could be tested. This statement could not be more at home than with the North Atlantic insect fauna, the origin of which is a topic that has been debated for over a century by the scientific community. The theories range from human impact and biota wholly introduced by man (cf. Ostenfeld 1926) with survival of endemics through the past glaciation (Lindroth 1931, 1968) and immigration via a landbridge that connected the islands to the European mainland (Hallam 1973); aspects of this debate are still continuing. The main part of this discussion has to do with whether the island faunas are endemic and revolves around Lindroth's (1968) original well-argued yet conservative views – his original thesis dates from 1931 – concerning lack of speciation in the Icelandic fauna. Buckland et al. (1986) in his Darwin lecture provided an overview that built upon initially Lindroth's and later Coope's (1986) ice-rafting hypothesis. Years later, the debate,

survival in refugia versus postglacial introduction, continues and, although there are many more data, there are still questions to be answered.

The Discussion About Refugia

Part of the discussion about refugia revolves around theories of survival in the vicinity of hot springs in Iceland, on nunataks (Lindroth 1931, 1968) or debris-covered glacier surfaces (Fickert et al. 2007). Lindroth (1957) discussed the possibility of the small ground beetle *Bembidion grapii* Gyll. surviving in Iceland through the last glaciation. This is an animal that may be found on dry gravel, on moraines with very sparse vegetation (Larsson and Gígja 1959; Lindroth 1963) and is confined to above the treeline and high boreal coniferous and birch forest (Lindroth 1985). It has a circumpolar distribution, which sees it spread from northern Russia to Labrador and Newfoundland (Böcher 1988, Böcher et al. 2015). It is wing-dimorphic and may be found as short or long winged forms throughout Iceland and Greenland. Lindroth (1957, 1965) provided survival in glacial refugia as an explanation for differences in local distribution between the

Biogeography in the Sub-Arctic: The Past and Future of North Atlantic Biota, First Edition.
Edited by Eva Panagiotakopulu and Jon P. Sadler.
© 2021 John Wiley & Sons Ltd. Published 2021 by John Wiley & Sons Ltd.

two forms of the beetle and noted two refuges in Iceland along coastal areas around Eyjafjallajökull (south refuge) and Vatnajökull (southeast refuge) (Figure 1, see Plate section). Although he discussed this longer timeframe for *B. grapii*, this species currently has no fossil record from Iceland (Buckland and Panagiotakopulu 2010) and there is little evidence for long-term survival. In addition, the whole pattern discussed does not necessarily preassume this. The differential distribution of long

and short winged forms of another ground beetle, *Notiophilus biguttatus* (F.), in Newfoundland, also discussed by Lindroth (1957), was introduced in the post-medieval period, probably in sailing ships' ballast (Figure 2, see Plate section). In this case, instead of an indication of long-term survival, the differences observed probably relate to the clearance of its favoured habitat, woodlands and forest floor litter (Luff 1998). This provides another hypothesis for *B. grapii* and introduces

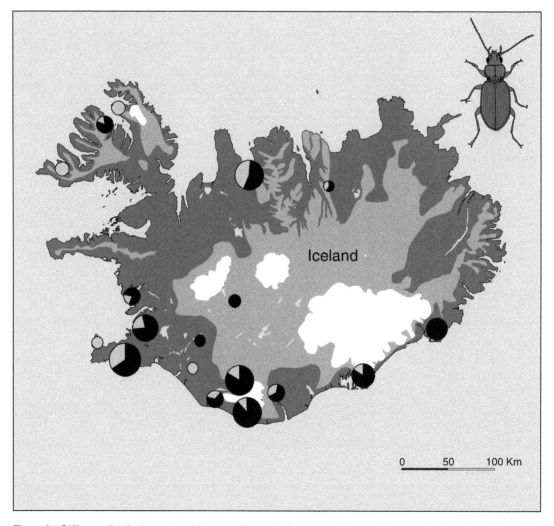

Figure 1 Different distribution patterns between long and short winged forms (= black parts of circles) of *Bembidion grapii* and the two refuges in Iceland in Eyjafjallajökull (south refuge) and Vatnajökull (southeast refuge) coastal areas. *Source:* Redrawn from Lindroth (1957). (See colour plate section for colour representation of this figure.)

the question as to whether the species was simply affected by expansion of habitat created by man-induced erosion, as opposed to genetic pressures on populations that survived the last glaciation.

This discussion has been extended to variations in form of other species. The minute rove beetle *Atheta groenlandica* Mahler (Böcher 1988) is closely related to the frequently parthenogenetic

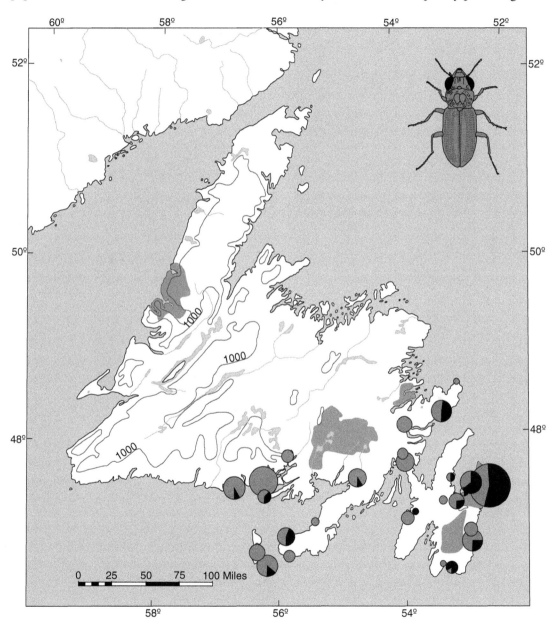

Figure 2 Map of distribution of the ground beetle *Notiophilus biguttatus* in Newfoundland, Canada which was introduced probably relatively recently in ballast (black parts of circles = short winged forms). *Source:* Redrawn from Lindroth (1957). (See colour plate section for colour representation of this figure.)

Atheta fungi (Grav.), which is found throughout the North Atlantic region. There is some discussion about *A. groenlandica* being endemic (Mahler 1988; Böcher 2015a), although this is a highly variable species group and the case might be that there is not enough justification for arguing for a distinct species. Part of the problem is limited taxonomic knowledge of a diverse species and DNA work may provide a definitive answer in the future. Similar examples are provided for the large ground beetle *Carabus problematicus* Herbst in the Faroe Islands, which was discussed by Lindroth (1968). Despite his espousal of the refugia hypothesis, he concluded that it represents a distinct morphological form rather than a distinct species. Similar arguments have been advanced for *Philonthus carbonarius* (= *varius*) var. *shetlandicus* Poppius from Shetland and Orkney and *Colymbetes dolabratus* (Payk.) has a subspecies *C. d. thomsoni* Sharp which is found only in Iceland (Lindroth et al. 1973).

To add to this debate, fossil finds from the previous interglacial period from Jameson Land in East Greenland and the Thule area in NW Greenland (Bennike and Böcher 1992, 1994; Böcher 2012, 2015b) has led to a renewed interest in theories of refugia and a hypothesis that micro-climate might have allowed species such as the seed bug *Nysius groenlandicus* (Zett.), which is now widespread in Greenland, to survive.

According to this hypothesis, taxa such as *Hydroporus morio* Aubé and *C. dolabratus*, *Byrrhus fasciatus* (Forst.) and *Simplocaria metallica* (Sturm), *Simplocaria elongata* Sahl., *Otiorhynchus arcticus* (F.) and *Otiorhynchus nodosus* (Müll.) could have also survived continuously in suitable micro-habitats since the previous interglacial period. However, there is little reason to assume continuity as opposed to a series of re-immigrations during warmer intervals after the previous near total extinction of the biota. This pattern of re-immigration with initial warming applies equally to the Lateglacial and Holocene (Buckland and Panagiotakopulu 2010; Panagiotakopulu 2014).

The discussion concerning endemics and amphiatlantic species also involves Diptera in Greenland, *Limnophora groenlandica* Malloch, *L. rotundata* Collin and *Dolichopus groenlandicus* Zett., all of which have been shown to have a wider distribution (Michelsen 2015; Pollet 2015). Taxonomic knowledge of several groups of flies, however, is rather limited and rather more research needs to take place to clarify any arguments of endemicity (Sadler and Skidmore 1995).

The Modern Faunas

Nearctic or Palaearctic

In his seminal works on North Atlantic faunas, Lindroth (1931, 1957) synthetically discussed the distribution of North Atlantic terrestrial, freshwater and littoral marine animals and also considered elements of the flora in an effort to explain biogeographic patterns. His overview includes insect species that inhabit the tidal zone, such as the staphylinid *Micralymma marinum* (Ström.), which is flightless and can survive regular submergence (Böcher 1988, Böcher et al. 2015). The affinity of this species to *Fucus* and other relevant seashore plants, under rocks (Kasule 1968), the fact that it can withstand high water levels and its amphiatlantic distribution had led Lindroth (ibid.) and others (e.g. Hicks 1990) to link its dispersal with the North Atlantic gyre. However, the species could equally have been effectively distributed in ships' ballast from port to port (Sadler 1991b; Panagiotakopulu 2014), spreading to both sides of the Atlantic (Figure 3, see Plate section). Two additional insect species also associated with seaweed, the hydrophilid beetle *Cercyon littoralis* (Gyll.) and the coelopid fly *Orygma luctuosum* Meigen, also

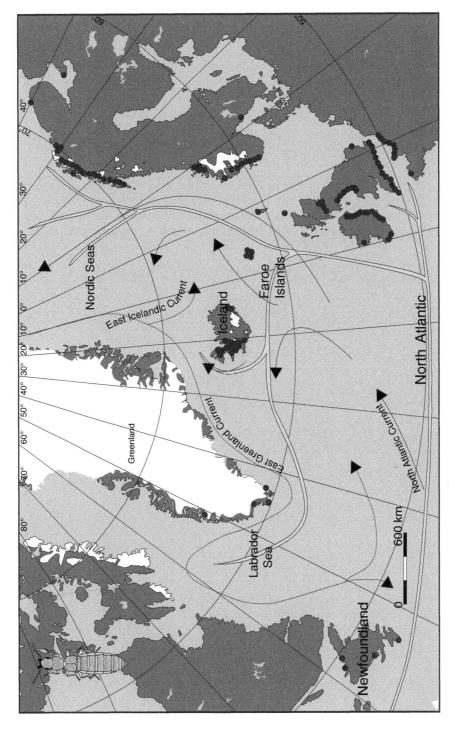

Figure 3 Map of distribution of the littoral rove beetle *Micralymma brevilingue* in the North Atlantic. It was probably introduced to Newfoundland via the cod fisheries based in SW English ports and the resultant large-scale movement of ballast across the North Atlantic for >300 years. *Source*: Redrawn from Lindroth (1957). (See colour plate section for colour representation of this figure.)

have an amphiatlantic distribution and a similar explanation would be appropriate.

This discussion about faunal distribution in the North Atlantic, and the mechanisms behind it, has been taken further by various researchers (Enckell 1989; Johansen and Hyttebom 2001; Gíslason 2005; Buckland 1988; Buckland and Panagiotakopulu 2008, 2010; Panagiotakopulu 2014).

Collation of data on modern insect faunas and relative percentages of Coleoptera and Diptera listed from the North Atlantic islands in terms of different biogeographic realms provides interesting information on distribution patterns. In terms of beetle taxa, where there are several species that are flightless or have limited flying ability, the affinities of the island faunas to the Palaearctic are in accordance with distance of the relevant islands from the mainland. Orkney has the highest percentage of Palaearctic species and the island further away, Greenland, the lowest (Sadler

and Skidmore 1995). Only one apparently exclusively Nearctic species, the byrrhid *Arctobyrrhus subcanus* LeC., has been recorded from Greenland; its taxonomic relationship to the North European *A. dovrensis* Münster would repay further investigation. The overview of modern beetle faunas from the islands provides a classic example of island biogeography theory (MacArthur and Wilson 2001), with a westward decrease in diversity of taxa and strongly indicates dispersal from east to west (Figure 4, see Plate section). In addition, the high arctic element in the beetle faunas is rather limited and *Gnypeta cavicollis* Sahl. is the only species that can be seen as truly representative of such environments (Lohse 1989).

The distribution of Diptera shows the exact opposite pattern with a very strong Nearctic element in the Greenlandic faunas and a large arctic component (Figure 5, see Plate section). Recent DNA research on non-biting midges has

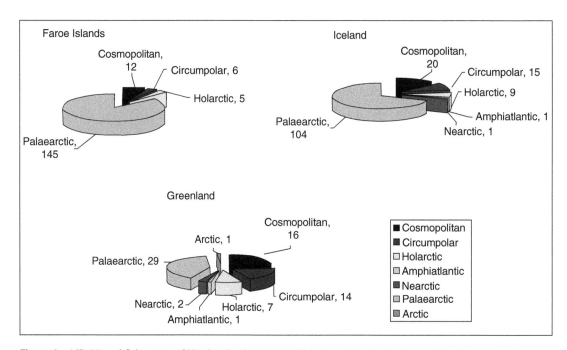

Figure 4 Affinities of Coleoptera of North Atlantic Islands which strongly indicate dispersal from east to west. *Source:* Redrawn from Sadler and Skidmore (1995). (See colour plate section for colour representation of this figure.)

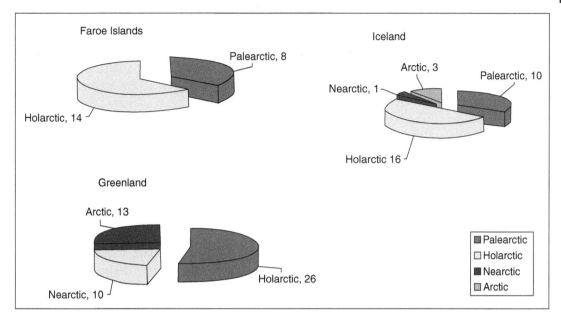

Figure 5 Affinities of Diptera in the North Atlantic islands. Atmospheric systems move from W to E so the bulk of the flies would come in from the Nearctic, reducing in numbers eastwards. *Source:* Redrawn from Sadler and Skidmore (1995). (See colour plate section for colour representation of this figure.)

confirmed affinities to both the Nearctic and the West Palearctic regions (Ekrem et al. 2018). Moving towards the west, Icelandic faunas show a Nearctic element and a small percentage of Arctic species, while for the rest of the islands Holarctic species dominate with Palaearctic elements encompassing the rest of the assemblages. This is the opposite of the pattern indicated by the Coleoptera and, as might be expected for active and passive fliers, dispersal of the modern dipterous fauna point to immigration via the aerial plankton following atmospheric patterns. A similar pattern is shown by the Lepidoptera (Downes 1966, 1988).

Timing and Mechanisms of Faunal Immigration

Even for the believers in endemics, the timing of the origins of the faunas, either survival of small numbers of species in refugia or earlier immigration from the European continent, is important for the debate. Survival from the previous interglacial was considered by Böcher (1988) on the basis of the Greenlandic fossil insect finds. Although the last interglacial was probably warmer than the recent one (Candy et al. 2016), the species that are proposed as endemics, survivors from the last interglacial, have very similar climatic requirements to the Holocene fauna, which is constrained and has few stenothermic taxa. There is little evidence in this respect for survival in refugia and, if this is the case, the question still stands as to when the faunas immigrated to the North Atlantic islands.

Early discussion about the origins of the biota considered the existence of Pleistocene 'land-bridges' (Lindroth 1963) although there is no evidence for connections even by island-hopping in the North Atlantic since the mid-Tertiary (Steindórsson 1963; Ægisdóttir and Þórhallsdóttir 2004). A discussion by Fridriksson (1969) about the ice cover of the Norwegian Sea during phases of the last glaciation, which would allow movement of the biota, is equally problematic as even if this hypothesis is accepted, low temperatures would have been a significant barrier for the biota. In addition, the paucity of true arctic elements in the faunas does not provide evidence for this argument.

Hypotheses on the immigration of flora in the North Atlantic islands also include dispersal on driftwood (Johansen and Hyttebom 2001). This would assume transport from the Palaearctic via the major Siberian rivers into the Arctic Ocean followed by a lengthy journey in the North Atlantic where waterlogging of the wood and salinity levels would prohibit survival of most invertebrates.

The other major mechanism of terrestrial faunal immigration is through drift ice moving westwards towards the North Atlantic islands during a period of climatic warming and reversal of the North Atlantic gyre (Rasmussen and Thomsen 2004; Rasmussen and Thomsen 2008). Coope's (1986) hypothesis of ice-rafted immigration favoured an early Lateglacial event that took place during the interstadial at the beginning of the Lateglacial. This is a probable scenario, preceded by a period of Atlantic Meridional Overturning Circulation (AMOC) and the freshening of the North Atlantic (Peltier et al. 2006), and any dispersal of biota on sediment-laden ice could have been accompanied by introductions of smaller taxa as part of the aerial plankton (Gislén 1948; Rundgren 1995, 2007).

However, climate cooling after the Lateglacial interstadial appears to have been sufficiently severe to lead to renewed glaciation on the North Atlantic islands (Denton et al. 2005; Broecker et al. 2010) and creation of another *tabula rasa*, a clean slate. One possible mechanism for the distribution of sea ice westwards in the Nordic Seas towards the North Atlantic Islands could be the catastrophic drainage of the Baltic Ice lake.

Although there has been debate about the amount of freshwater in the North Atlantic during warming events (Nesje et al. 2004; Thornalley et al. 2010, 2011; Murton et al. 2010), the recent varve data provide information for a relevant event that would have led to significant expansion of ice in the North Atlantic around 12 700 BP, which would perhaps be a trigger for the Younger Dryas (Muschitiello et al. 2016; Kelly and Passchier 2018). The climate of the Younger Dryas would have probably wiped the slate clean in terms of biota on the North Atlantic islands, for the whole process to be repeated at the beginning of the Holocene (Panagiotakopulu 2014). At around 11 700 cal. BP the ice damned Baltic Ice Lake (Andrén et al. 2011), which had probably reached a level of 25 m above the contemporary ocean (Lambeck 2001; Tikkanen and Oksanen 2002), drained catastrophically after the collapse of the ice barrier at Mount Billingen in southern Sweden (Figure 6, see Plate section). The resultant ice-rafted debris would have provided a matrix for dispersal of flora and fauna across the North Atlantic.

Comparison of faunas prior to the arrival of humans from the islands also points towards immigration of the biota at the beginning of the Holocene. The climatic envelopes of these assemblages are consistent with Holocene temperatures in Scandinavia (Panagiotakopulu 2014; Vickers and Buckland 2015). Even for Greenland the same patterns persist and the fossil record points towards immigration at the beginning of the current interglacial period.

Natural Faunas of North Atlantic Islands

Insect faunas on the Faroes, Iceland and Greenland, prior to the arrival of humans, have strong affinities with fossil assemblages from Lateglacial Scandinavia, the probable source area. Most of the taxa, which have been recovered from Scandinavian Lateglacial faunas, are also present in pre-Landnám samples from the North Atlantic islands and this perhaps points to dispersal from source Scandinavian populations (Table 1).

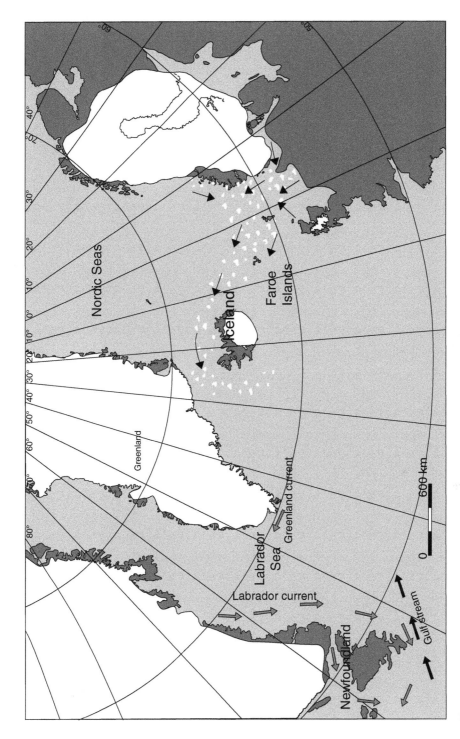

Figure 6 Map of the North Atlantic during the beginning of the Holocene showing the catastrophic drainage of the Baltic Ice Lake. Movement of ice in the North Atlantic towards the west is indicated. *Source*: Data on the Baltic Ice Lake are from Björck (1995) and Andrén et al. (2011). (See colour plate section for colour representation of this figure.)

Table 1 List of Coleoptera found on late-glacial sites on the Scandinavian coasts and pre-human settlement faunas from the Faroe Islands, Iceland and Greenland.

Taxonomy	Lateglacial Norway/Denmark	Faroe Islands	Iceland	Greenland
Carabus problematicus Hbst.		X		
Nebria rufescens (Ström.)	X	X	X	
Notiophilus aquaticus (L.)	X			
Trechus obtusus Er.	X	X		
Bembidion bipunctatum (L.)	X		X	
Bembidion grapii Gyll.				X
Patrobus septentrionis Dej.	X	X	X	X
Patrobus assimilis Chaud.	X			
Trichocellus placidus (Gyll.)		X		
Trichocellus cognatus (Gyll.)				
Pterostichus diligens (Sturm)		X		
Pterostichus rhaeticus Heer	X		X	
Calathus melanocephalus (L.)	X		X	
Calathus micropterus (Duft.)		X		
Amara quenseli (Schön.)	X		X	
Hydroporus palustris (L.)	X			
Hydroporus morio Aubé				X
Hydroporus pubescens (Gyll.)		X		
Hydroporus nigrita (F.)		X	X	
Stictotarsus griseostriatus (Deg.)	X			
Agabus biguttatus (Ol.)	X	X	X	
Colymbetes dolabratus (Payk.)	X			X
Gyrinus opacus Sahl.	X			
Hydraena britteni Joy			X	
Helophorus flavipes F.		X		
Coelostoma orbiculare (F.)		X		
Megasternum obscurum (Marsham)		X		
Anacaena globulus (Payk.)		X		
Micralymma marinum (Ström.)				X
Micralymma brevilingue Schöidte				X
Olophrum fuscum (Grav.)	X	X		
Eucnecosum brachypterum (Grav.)	X	X		
Lesteva heeri Fauvel		X		

Table 1 (Continued)

Taxonomy	Lateglacial Norway/Denmark	Faroe Islands	Iceland	Greenland
Lesteva longoelytrata (Goeze)	X		X	
Geodromicus longipes (Mann.)	X			
Stenus carbonarius Gyll.			X	
Stenus impressus Germ.			X	
Euaesthetus laeviusculus Mann.				X
Othius angustus Steph.		X		
Lathrobium brunnipes (F.)		X	X	
Quedius umbrinus Er.			X	
Quedius fellmanni (Zett.)				X
Boreophilia islandica (Kr.)				X
Gnypeta cavicollis Sahl.				X
Aleocharinae indet.	X	X	X	X
Bryaxis puncticollis (Denny)			X	
Hypnoidus riparius (F.)	X	X		
Simplocaria semistriata (F.)	X			
Simplocaria metallica (Sturm)	X			X
Simplocaria elongata Sahl.				X
Byrrhus fasciatus (Forst.)				X
Cytilus sericeus (Forst.)	X			
Corticaria linearis (Payk.)				X
Coccinella transversoguttata Fald.				X
Coccinella undecimpunctata L.	X			
Phratora polaris Schneid.				X
Apion haematodes Kirby		X		
Otiorhynchus arcticus (O. Fabricius)	X			X
Otiorhynchus nodosus (Müll.)	X		X	X
Tropiphorus obtusus (Bonsd.)		X		
Dorytomus taeniatus (F.)			X	
Dorytomus imbecillus Faust				X
Rutidosoma globulus (Hbst.)				X
Isochnus foliorum (Müll.)			X	
Nysius ericae groenlandicus (Zett.)				X
Chlamydatus pullus (Reut.)				X
Cacopsylla groenlandica (Sulc.)				X

For Greenland, this includes three species of Hemiptera. There is some discussion about *Nysius groenlandicus* for which there is an argument that it is a survivor from the previous interglacial, although this may be conspecific with the more widely distributed *N. ericae* (Schill.) (Böcher 2012).

The current lists include several uncertain identifications as there are limitations in the identification of fossil material, partly as a result of the way in which fossil insects are recovered, as disconnected sclerites, and partly as a result of a lack of taxonomic knowledge, particularly of dipterous puparia, and this inhibits taking the work further. Preservation is another parameter that plays a significant role as for several species, in particular small staphylinids, identification is not always possible without aedeagi; with more complete specimens, identification can often be taken to the species level. An interesting point about these faunas is that they include no dung beetles, which is a reflection of the lack of large herbivores on the islands. Greenland with both caribou (reindeer) and muskox similarly lacks a dung fauna. In terms of the Lateglacial Scandinavian faunas, this could be more a feature of sampling limitations as opposed to total lack of any relevant taxa. It is interesting, however, that the initial immigration of the biota is restricted to species that might be easily moved on sediment laden ice associated with marine littoral habitats and there is little evidence for any representatives of the dung fauna. Whilst in these island environments the mould beetle fauna would be able to exploit the relevant widespread habitats, any specific dung fauna would need to be introduced with or after their relevant pabula and the concordance of events, arrival of coprophiles and herbivores, may not have occurred until human introductions of both (e.g. Buckland et al. 1986; Panagiotakopulu et al. 2012).

There are differences in the faunas of Iceland and Greenland regarding species associated with *Salix*. Although the weevil *Dorytomus*

taeniatus (F.) with a European distribution which extends to Northern Scandinavia is present in Iceland in pre-Landnám assemblages, its congener *D. imbecillus* Faust is present in pre-Norse assemblages in South West Greenland. The latter is circumpolar and may have arrived from North America or directly from Siberia, although there are insufficient fossil assemblages to reconstruct effective models of dispersal.

There is a similar conundrum with the large ladybird *Coccinella transversoguttata* Fald. This is a eurytopic predator in Greenland, found on *Betula nana* L. and *Salix glauca* L. It appears to have an amphiatlantic distribution (Kovář 2005) and its presence in Greenland poses questions about the pathways by which it reached there. The Scandinavian records (Koch 1989) provide an indication of how it could have reached Greenland, although it should be noted that Kovář (ibid.) doubts the veracity of these records.

Human Impact and North Atlantic Faunas

The earliest evidence for insects associated with human activity on the North Atlantic islands comes from Greenland with the faunas recovered from samples from the archaeological excavations at Qeqertassusuk on Disko bay (Böcher and Fredskild 1993; Grønnow 2017). From this site we have evidence for human lice *Pediculus humanus* L. which must have arrived with the Saqqaq, whose ancestors migrated from Siberia across northern North America to Greenland (Gilbert et al. 2008), a route of dispersal that incidentally perhaps provides an explanation for some of the amphiatlantic species found in Greenland. In addition, from this site there is the first evidence for the presence of the cold tolerant dipteran *Heleomyza borealis* Bohe., christened the Viking house fly by the late Peter Skidmore, since its puparia are frequent fossils in Norse middens and living areas. The latter is probably a native species otherwise found in carrion and birds' nests (Block 2002), but able to exploit man-made habitats. The impact of the pre-Inuit in terms of introductions and changes in the faunas seem otherwise to be rather limited and the bulk of the changes are a result of human impact starting with the arrival of agropastoralists (Figure 7, see Plate section).

In the case of the Faroe Islands the date for initial colonization has recently been moved earlier by several centuries (Church et al. 2013) although there were no fossil insect assemblages from this particular site. In terms of the insect faunas from the Faroe Islands, most of the information recovered about introduced species comes from Toftanes (Edwards et al. 1998; Vickers et al. 2005). The faunas include a typically Norse package, with strongly synanthropic species such as *Xylodromus concinnus* (Marsh.), *Quedius mesomelinus* (Marsh.), *Omalium excavatum* Steph., and *Latridius minutus* (L.)/*pseudominutus* (Strand), all of which arrived with the Norse on the islands (Table 2). They are linked with hay-related activities, particularly its storage, and rely on the artificial warmth of the farms for their survival. There are various other species linked with Norse colonization. These are primarily mould feeders, such as *Typhaea stercorea* (L.), but also include species that arrived with trade in cereals, exotics such as the granary weevil, *Sitophilus granarius* (L.) and the saw toothed beetle, *Oryzaephilus surinamensis* (L.), although the earliest Faroese records are from the post-medieval period (Vickers and Buckland 2013). The dung beetle *Aphodius lapponum* Gyll. is a key species that became widespread post-Landnám in the Faroe Islands and Iceland, introduced with the domestic animals that arrived with the Norse on these islands (Buckland et al. 1986).

The species diversity on the Faroese islands post-Landnám increased, but there were casualties in the fauna. *Calathus micropterus* (Duft.) is a shade-loving ground beetle found in leaf litter

in forests and on moorland (Koch 1989). It was recovered from Holocene pre-Landnám deposits near Torshavn (Jessen and Rasmussen 1922) and from the Landnám farm at Toftanes (Vickers et al. 2005), although the latter probably entered the farm already fossil in peat.

Coelostoma orbiculare (F.), which prefers damp habitats, is found as a fossil pre-Landnám at Toftanes (Vickers et al. 2005) and in a natural sequence from Saksunardalur (Buckland et al. 1998); there are no more recent records. The same applies to the small rove beetle *Ochthephilus omalinus* (grp.), usually found on riverine sediment in the uplands (Lott 2008) and recorded as a fossil from Tjørnuvik (Buckland and Dinnin 1998).

A similar pattern is revealed from fossil insects in post-Landnám deposits in Iceland, which also includes ectoparasites. Human lice, *Pediculus humanus* L., human fleas, *Pulex irritans* L., which feed on the blood of their human hosts, and sheep keds, *Melophagus ovinus* (L.), feeding on the blood of sheep, have been recovered in considerable numbers from various farm sites in Iceland (Buckland and Perry 1989; Buckland et al. 1992, 2012). Research has indicated patterns of farm abandonment (Sveinbjarnardóttir 1992) and historical details from specific farms. The excellent dating framework, as a result of tephra isochrones, provides additional possibilities for fossil insect work in terms of understanding human impact and rates of change. From Iceland there are additional data for species that arrived in either ballast or dunnage and failed to establish. *Oxyomus sylvestris* (Scop.) from Bessastaðir (Amorosi et al. 1992) is found on dry manure and rotting hay and has a more southern modern distribution (Koch 1989). The flightless blind mould feeder *Aglenus brunneus* (Gyll.) was recovered in numbers from twelfth to thirteenth century deposits at Snorri Sturlusson's farm at Reykholt, perhaps originally imported in mouldy barley or malt to be used for Snorri's

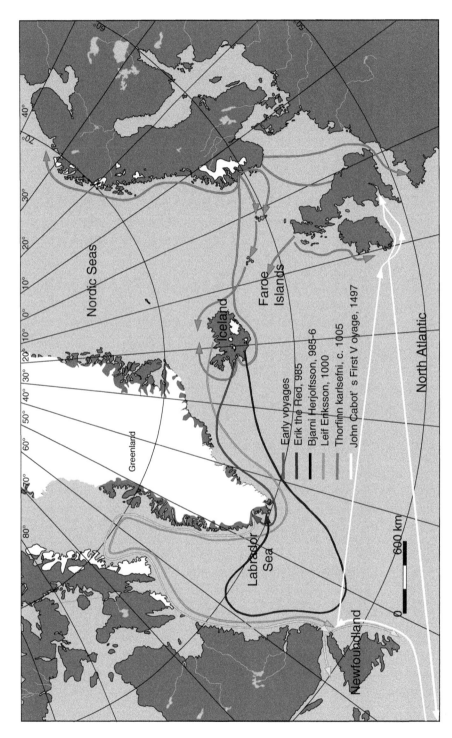

Figure 7 Map of the North Atlantic with early Norse colonization routes and John Cabot's first journey to Newfoundland, indicating movement of biota. (See colour plate section for colour representation of this figure.)

Table 2 Anthropochorous and synanthropic species (highlighted in grey) from the Faroe Islands, Iceland and Greenland.

Taxa	Faroe Islands	Iceland	Greenland
Laemostenus terricola (Hbst.)		X	
Cercyon melanocephalus (L.)		X	
Omalium rivulare (Payk.)	X	X	
Omalium excavatum Steph.	X	X	X
Xylodromus depressus (Grav.)	X	X	
Xylodromus concinnus (Marsham)	X	X	X
Othius angustus Steph.	X	X	X
Bisnius cephalotes (Grav.)	X	X	
Bisnius sordidus (Grav.)		X	
Quedius mesomelinus (Marsham)	X	X	X
Ocalea picata (Steph.)	X	X	X
Aleochara sparsa Heer		X	
Oryzaephilus surinamensis (L.)	X	X	
Cryptophagus scanicus (L.)		X	
Caenoscelis ferruginea (Sahl.)			X
Atomaria apicalis Er.		X	X
Latridius minutus (L.) (group)	X	X	X
Latridius pseudominutus (Strand)	X	X	X
Corticaria linearis (Payk.)		X	X
Typhaea stercorea (L.)		X	
Mycetaea subterranea (Marsham)		X	
Niptus hololeucus (Fald.)		X	
Tipnus unicolor (Pill. & Mitt.)		X	
Ptinus fur (L.)		X	
Aphodius lapponum Gyll.	X	X	
Aphodius fimetarius (L.)		X	
Aglenus brunneus (Gyll.)		X	
Callosobruchus maculatus (F.)		X	
Sitona sp.		X	
Sitophilus granarius (L.)	X	X	
Bovicola ovis (L.)		X	X
Linognathus stenopsis (Burmeister)			X
Haematopinus eurysternus (Nitzsch)			X
Pediculus humanus capitis Deg.			X

(Continued)

Table 2 (Continued)

Taxa	Faroe Islands	Iceland	Greenland
Pediculus humanus L.		X	X
Pulex irritans L.		X	X
Scathophaga furcata (Say)		X	X
Scathophaga sp.			
Heleomyza borealis Bohe.	X	X	X
Telomerina flavipes Meigen		X	X
Ischiolepta pusilla (Fallén)			X
Melophagus ovinus (L.)	X	X	X
Nabis flavomarginatus (Scholtz)			X
Macrosteles laevis Ribaut			X
Pthirus pubis (L.)		X	X

beer (Buckland et al. 2009). In the post-medieval period *Callosobruchus maculatus,* a pest of beans (Fox and Tatar 1994), and *Sitona* sp., a possible field pest of legumes, appear at the bishop's seat at Skalholt (Konráðsdóttir 2007; Konráðsdóttir et al. 2021). In addition, the Icelandic assemblages have produced interesting dipterous assemblages with large numbers of *H. borealis* from farmsteads and outhouses (Skidmore 1996). The sphaerocerid *Telomerina flavipes* Meigen requires artificially warm environments in the north. It also thrives in dark areas on high protein materials and has been found from Icelandic farms, together with species associated with herbivore dung such as *Scathophaga furcata* Say (Skidmore ibid.).

The spread of the synanthropic species in Iceland expands in the post-medieval period. However, during the same period there was at least one extirpation from the Icelandic fauna and other species have become increasingly rare. *Hydraena britteni* Joy is found in a range of habitats, including wetlands and edges of woodland (Koch 1989) and has been found in medieval and post-medieval deposits (e.g. Holt (Buckland et al. 1991b), Ketilsstadir (Buckland et al. 1983)

and Stóraborg (Panagiotakopulu et al. in preparation); thereafter it disappeared altogether from Iceland. It is possible that declining temperatures during the Little Ice Age contributed to its disappearance (Buckland et al. 1983; Vickers and Buckland 2015), although the clearance of woodland and disappearance of woodland pools must have contributed to its extinction from Iceland. In situations like this, it is difficult to differentiate the pressures of climate from the pressures of human impact and what was the final stroke that led to the disappearance.

In Greenland in terms of change as a result of human impact from the arrival of Norse farmers in the late tenth century a similar package was introduced of flora and fauna, including invertebrates. The excellent preservation in permafrost allowed for additional species of ectoparasites to be recovered, including the goat louse *Linognathus stenopsis* (Burm.) and the pig louse *Haematopinus suis* (L.) at Gården under Sandet. In terms of the flies as well as the warm loving *T. flavipes* there is evidence for the introduction of the synanthropic *Ischiolepta pusilla* (Fall.) from the same farm (Panagiotakopulu et al. 2007). In addition to the introduced Norse beetle and fly faunas it is possible that Hemiptera such as *Nabis flavomarginatus* (Scholtz) (Jensen and Christensen 2003) and perhaps *Macrosteles laevis* Ribaut, both of which were present immediately post-Landnám (Panagiotakopulu and Buchan 2015), were introduced by the Norse. These species remained in the landscape after their transporters had disappeared from Greenland. The spread of anthropochorous species includes a variety of species. For example, *H. borealis* is well represented with high numbers from both Eastern and Western settlement farms (Buckland et al. 2009; Panagiotakopulu et al. 2012), and Hemiptera, such as *N. groenlandicus*, were favoured by human activities, such as creation of hayfields. Iversen (1934) discussed the presence of large numbers of chrysalises of the moth *Eurois occulta* (L.) at Anavík in the Western Settlement, and surmised that a possible infestation of pasture may have been sufficiently destructive to have contributed to the demise of the Norse farmers. Recent thawing of permafrost has led to destruction of organics on the site and as a result no relevant fossils could be recovered. Currently destructive outbreaks of this moth may happen during warm summers. Further synanthropic species, which cannot survive without the warmth of human habitations were reintroduced in the early eighteenth century with Hans Egede and the beginnings of the second European colonization of western Greenland. There are, however, some interesting differences from the other North Atlantic islands. No cereal pests have been found in Norse deposits and dung beetles have not made it, although sheep, goat, pig and cattle were introduced (see, for example, Smiarowski et al. 2017). Perhaps this was a biogeographic accident, a result of the ability of the dung beetles to survive a lengthy journey in clinker-built boats or the stalling of stock and dung collection, which reduced the available habitat. Whatever the reasons, dung beetles never made it to Greenland.

Human impact on both settlements and deforestation led to local extinctions post-Landnám. Species related with willow, the weevils *Rutidosoma globulus* (Hbst.) and *D. imbecillus*, disappeared in the area around Tasiusaq immediately after Landnám (Panagiotakopulu and Buckland 2013). At the same time, the mould feeder *Corticaria rubripes* Mann. (= *linearis* (Payk.)), which in Europe is associated with decaying pine and oak (Alexander 2002) and is found under burnt bark and fire-killed trees (Kullingsjö 1999), appears in association with macroscopic charcoal, perhaps indicating burning in this landscape, although there are also records of this mould feeder from old hay in barns (Böcher 1988).

Whilst there are differences in terms of introduced faunas to the North Atlantic islands, they all share the fact that the common house fly *Musca domestica* L. did not make it to any of them. As this species had reached Alvastra in Southern Sweden by the Neolithic (Lemdahl 1995), it is interesting that it has not managed to spread out further together with the Norse, but perhaps the nature of the dunnage, wet and saline, during the journey played a significant role in its exclusion.

In terms of fossil faunas from other islands in the North Atlantic, such as those off the coast of Norway, there are several interesting points. The Norse faunas from Iceland and the Faroe Islands show strong similarities with those from medieval and post-medieval sites in the Lofoten group (Buckland et al. 2006). They share the same hay fauna and similar fly and ectoparasite assemblages. Norse material from Tuquoy (Sadler 1991a, in press; Skidmore 1996, Skidmore and Panagiotakopulu, in press) on Orkney is significantly different in this respect, although the nature of the feature studied, a manure pit, would have played a role in the assemblages recovered. There are elements of the hay fauna missing from this assemblage, such as *L. minutus/pseudominutus* and *Q. mesomelinus* from the beetles, and *H. borealis,* the Norse signature dipterous species, is also not present. From this particular assemblage from Orkney, there is some evidence that the faunas had perhaps a different origin from the ones on the Faroe Islands, Iceland, Greenland and Islands off the coast of Norway, but work on additional sites is needed to follow up this point further.

In terms of the modern faunas, global warming and the frequency of drier climate in the Arctic (Wrona et al. 2016) is perhaps the most significant change happening in the post-industrial era, with the progressive thawing of permafrost and destruction of its enclosed fossil record, which on some sites extends back into the late Tertiary (cf. Böcher 1995). In addition, the mechanisation of agriculture, the stress imposed by heavy farm vehicles (Humbert et al. 2009), the use of mineral fertilizers, as opposed to manuring the fields, and pesticides (Guðleifsson 2005; Geiger et al. 2010), and also monocultures to promote fodder grasses affect invertebrate habitats. Erosion as a result of overgrazing often results in reduction of richness in the insect faunas, as well as disappearance of many synanthropic farm habitats (cf. Buckland et al. 1991a). Introduction of insect species as a result of global trade and movement of commodities add to the complexities of the pressures on the native biota. Current change is unprecedented and although it may not ultimately be halted despite quarantine measures, monitoring of the insect faunas would provide a better understanding in order to conserve the indigenous taxa.

Conclusions

The historical biogeography of the North Atlantic insect faunas reveals the effect of climate change on the biota in terms of their immigration to the islands at the beginning of the Holocene. As a result of the later arrival of Europeans in the North Atlantic region, the fossil record also provides evidence about the extent of human impact and their impact on the biota. The disappearance of species as a result of woodland clearance, for example, and also the increase in diversity of the faunas with introduced species, provide a telling overview of changing biodiversity and species frequency and the reasons behind it. Some of the changes happened fast and are irreversible. Others are the effect of long-term processes with the gradual restriction of relevant habitats, globalization of the biota and industrialization of farming and storage.

References

Ægisdóttir, H.H. and Þórhallsdóttir, Þ.E. (2004). Theories on migration and history of the North-Atlantic flora: a review. *Jökull* 54: 1–16.

Alexander, K.N.A. (2002). The invertebrates of living and decaying timber in Britain & Ireland. A provisional annotated checklist. *Peterborough, English Nature Research Report* 467: 1–142.

Amorosi, T., Buckland, P.C., Ólafsson, G. et al. (1992). Site status and the palaeoecological record: a discussion of the results from Bessastaðir, Iceland. In: Norse and Later Settlement and Subsistence in the North Atlantic (eds. C.D. Morris and D.J. Rackham), 169–192. Department of Archaeology: University of Glasgow.

Andrén, T., Björck, S., Andrén, E. et al. (2011). The development of the Baltic Sea during the last 130 ka. In: The Baltic Sea Basin (eds. J. Harff, S. Björck and P. Hoth), 75–97. Berlin: Springer Verlag.

Bennike, O. and Böcher, J. (1992). Early Weichselian interstadial land biotas at Thule, Northwest Greenland. *Boreas* 21: 111–117.

Bennike, O. and Böcher, J. (1994). Land biotas of the last interglacial/glacial cycle on Jameson Land, East Greenland. *Boreas* 23: 479–487.

Björck, S. (1995). A review of the history of the Baltic Sea, 13.0–8.0 ka BP. *Quaternary International* 27: 19–40.

Block, W. (2002). Interactions of water, ice nucleators and desiccation in invertebrate cold survival. *European Journal of Entomology* 99: 259–266.

Böcher, J. (1988). The Coleoptera of Greenland. *Meddelelser om Grønland – Bioscience* 26: 100.

Böcher, J. (1995). Palaeoentomology of the Kap Kobenhavn Formation, a Plio-Pleistocene sequence in Peary Land, North Greenland. *Meddelelser om Grønland, Geoscience* 33: 1–82.

Böcher, J. (2012). Interglacial insects and their possible survival in Greenland during the last glacial stage. *Boreas* 41: 644–659.

Böcher, J. (2015a). Coeoptera. In: The Greenland Entomofauna: An Identification Manual of Insects Spiders and Their Allies, Fauna Entomologica Scandinavica, vol. 44. (eds. Böcher, N.P., Kristensen, T., Pape, and L. Vilhelmsen), 259–292. Brill: Leiden.

Böcher, J. (2015b). The Greenland entomofauna: zoogeography and history. In: The Greenland Entomofauna: An Identification Manual of Insects Spiders and Their Allies, Fauna Entomologica Scandinavica, vol. 44. (eds. Böcher, N.P., Kristensen, T., Pape, and L. Vilhelmsen), 21–36. Brill: Leiden.

Böcher, J. and Fredskild, B. (1993). Plant and arthropod remains from the palaeo-Eskimo site on Qeqertasussuk, West Greenland. *Meddelelser om Grønland – Geoscience* 30, 1–35.

Böcher, J., Kristensen, N.P., Pape, T., and Vilhelmsen, L. (eds.) (2015). The Greenland Entomofauna: An Identification Manual of Insects Spiders and Their Allies, Fauna Entomologica Scandinavica, vol. 44. Brill: Leiden.

Broecker, W.S., Denton, G.H., Edwards, R.L. et al. (2010). Putting the Younger Dryas cold event into context. *Quaternary Science Reviews* 29: 1078–1081.

Buckland, P.C. (1988). North Atlantic faunal connections – introduction or endemics? *Entomologica Scandinavica* 32: 7–29.

Buckland, P.C. (2012). (with Vickers, K. Panagiotakopulu, E., Sadler J.P., Buckland P.I.) insect remains. In: Reykholt. Archaeological Investigations at a High Status Farm in Western Iceland (ed. G. Sveinbjarnardóttir), 218–241. Reykjavík: Snorrastofa and National Museum of Iceland.

Buckland, P.C. and Dinnin, M. (1998). Insect faunas at Landnám: a palaeoentomological study at Tjørnuvík, Streymoy, Faroe Islands. *Fróðskaparrit* 46: 277–286.

Buckland, P.C. and Panagiotakopulu, E. (2008). A palaeoecologist's view of Landnám. A case still not proven? In: Símunarbók. Heiðursrit til Símun V. Arge á 60 ára degnum (eds. C. Paulsen and H.D. Michelsen), 31–41. Tórshavn: Faroe University Press.

Buckland, P.C. and Panagiotakopulu, E. (2010). Reflections on North Atlantic Island biogeography: a quaternary entomological view. In: Dorete – Her Book:– Being a Tribute to Dorete Bloch and to Faroese Nature, Annales Societatis Scientiarum Færoensis Supplementum, vol. 52 (eds. S.-A. Bengtson, P. Buckland, P.H. Enckell and A.M. Fosaa), 187–215. Tórshavn: Faroe University Press.

Buckland, P.C., Perry, D. 1989. Ectoparasites of sheep from Stóraborg, Iceland and their interpretation. Piss, parasites and people, a palaeoecological perspective. *Hikuin*, 15, 37–46.

Buckland, P.C., Perry, D., and Sveinbjarnardóttir, G. (1983). Hydraena britteni Joy (Coleoptera, Hydraenidae) fundin á Islandi í setlögum frá því seint á nútíma. *Náttúrufræðingurinn* 52: 37–44.

Buckland, P.C., Perry, D.W., Gíslason, G.M., and Dugmore, A.J. (1986). The pre-Landnám Fauna of Iceland: a palaeontological contribution. *Boreas* 15: 173–184.

Buckland, P.C., Dugmore, A., and Sadler, J.P. (1991a). Faunal change or taphonomic problem? A comparison of modern and fossil insect faunas from South-East Iceland. In: Environmental Change in Iceland Past and Present, pp. 127–146 (eds. J.K. Maizels and C. Caseldine). Dordrecht: Kluwer.

Buckland, P.C., Dugmore, A.J., Perry, D.W. et al. (1991b). Holt in Eyjafjallasveit, Iceland. A palaeoecological study of the impact of Landnám. *Acta Archaeologica* 61: 252–271.

Buckland, P.C., Sadler, J.P., and Sveinbjarnardóttir, G. (1992). Palaeoecological investigations at Reykholt, Western Iceland. In: Norse and Later Settlement and Subsistence in the North Atlantic (eds. C.J. Morris and D.J. Rackham), 149–168. University of Glasgow: Department of Archaeology.

Buckland, P.C., Edwards, K.J., and Sadler, J.P. (1998). Early Holocene investigations at Saksunardalur and the origins of the Faroese biota. *Fróðskaparrit* 46: 259–266.

Buckland, P.C., Panagiotakopulu, E., Buckland, P.I. et al. (2006). Insect faunas from medieval Langenes in Arctic Norway. In: Proceedings from the 8th Nordic Conference on the Application of Scientific Methods in Archaeology, Umeå 2001 (eds. R. Engelmark and J. Linderholm), 17–32. Umeå: Department of Archaeology and Sami Studies, University of Umeå.

Buckland, P.C., Panagiotakopulu, E., and Sveinbjarnardóttir, G. (2009). A failed invader in the North Atlantic, the case of *Aglenus brunneus* Gyll. (Col., Colydiidae) a blind flightless beetle from Iceland. *Biological Invasions* 11: 1239–1245.

Candy, I., White, T.S., and Elias, S. (2016). How warm was Britain during the last interglacial? A critical review of Ipswichian (MIS 5e) palaeotemperature reconstructions. *Journal of Quaternary Science* 31: 857–868.

Church, M.J., Arge, S.V., Edwards, K.J. et al. (2013). The Vikings were not the first colonizers of the Faroe Islands. *Quaternary Science Reviews* 77: 228–232.

Coope, G.R. (1986). The invasion and colonization of the North Atlantic islands: a palaeoecological solution to a biogeographical problem. *Philosophical Transactions of the Royal Society of London* B314: 619–635.

Denton, G.H., Alley, R.B., Comer, G.C. et al. (2005). The role of seasonality in abrupt climate change. *Quaternary Science Reviews* 24: 1159–1182.

Downes, J.A. (1966). The Lepidoptera of Greenland: some geographic considerations. *Canadian Entomologist* 98: 1134–1144.

Downes, J.A. (1988). The postglacial colonisation of the North Atlantic Islands. *Memoirs of the Entomological Society of Canada* 144: 55–92.

Edwards, K.J., Buckland, P.C., Craigie, R. et al. (1998). Landscapes at landnám: palynological and palaeoentomological evidence from Toftanes, Faroe Islands. *Fróðskaparrit* 46: 299–244.

Ekrem, T., Stur, E., Orton, M.G., and Adamowicz, S.J. (2018). DNA barcode data reveal biogeographic trends in Arctic non-biting midges. *Genome* 61 (11): 787–796. https://doi.org/10.1139/gen-2018-0100.

Enckell, P.H. (1989). When, how, and whence? A tentative background for the post-glacial immigration of terrestrial invertebrates of the Faroes. *Fróðskaparrit* 34–35: 50–67.

Fickert, T., Friend, D., Gruninger, F. et al. (2007). Did debris-covered glaciers serve as Pleistocene Refugia for plants? A new hypothesis derived from observations of recent plant growth on glacier surfaces. *Arctic, Antarctic and Alpine Research* 39: 245–257.

Fox, C.W. and Tatar, M. (1994). Oviposition substrate affects adult mortality, independent of reproduction, in the seed beetle *Callosobruchus maculatus*. *Ecological Entomology* 9: 108–110.

Fridriksson, S. (1969). The effects of sea ice on flora, fauna and agriculture. *Jökull* 19: 146–157.

Geiger, F., Bengtsson, J., Berendse, F. et al. (2010). Potential negative effects of pesticides on biodiversity and biological control potential on

'European farmland'. *Basic and Applied Ecology* 11: 97–105.

Gilbert, M.T., Kivisild, T., Grønnow, B. et al. (2008). Paleo-Eskimo mtDNA genome reveals matrilineal discontinuity in Greenland. *Science* 320 (5884): 1787–1789. https://doi.org/10.1126/science.1159750.

Gíslason, G.M. (2005). Origin of freshwater fauna of the North-Atlantic islands: present distribution in relation to climate and possible migration routes. *Verhandlungen des Internationalen Verein Limnologie* 29: 198–203.

Gislén, T. (1948). Aerial plankton and its conditions of life. *Biological Reviews* 23: 109–126.

Grønnow, B. (2017). The frozen Saqqaq sites of Disko Bay, West Greenland. Qeqertasussuk and Qajaa(2400–900 BC). *Studies of Saqqaq Material Culture in an Eastern Arctic Perspective.* Copenhagen, Museum Tusculanum Press.

Guðleifsson, B.E. (2005). Beetle species (Coleoptera) in hayfields and pastures in northern Iceland. *Agriculture, Ecosystems & Environment* 109: 181–186.

Hallam, A. (1973). Atlas of Palaeobiogeography. Amsterdam: Elsevier.

Hicks, B.J. (1990). Observations on the intertidal Staphylinid Micralymma marinum *Micralymma marinum* Stroem (Coleoptera: Staphylinidae) from Newfoundland. *The Coleopterists Bulletin* 44: 304–306.

Humbert, J.-Y., Ghazoul, J., and Walter, T. (2009). Meadow harvesting techniques and their impactson field fauna. *Agriculture, Ecosystems & Environment* 130: 1–8.

Iversen, J. (1934). Moorgeologische Untersuchungen auf Grönland. *Meddelelser fra Geologiske Foreningen* 8: 342–358.

Jensen, D.B. and Christensen, S.K. (2003). The Biodiversity of Greenland – A Country Study, 165. Grønlands, Naturinstitut, Nuuk: Pinngortitaleriffi k.

Jessen, K., Rasmussen, R. (1922). Et profil gennem en Torvemose paa Faeroerne. Danmarks geologiske undersogelse, 4R. Bd. 1, nr. 13, 32 pp.

Johansen, S. and Hyttebom, H. (2001). A contribution to the discussion of biota dispersal with drift ice and driftwood in the North Atlantic. *Journal of Biogeography* 28: 105–115.

Kasule, F.K. (1968). The larval characters of some subfamilies of British Staphylinidae (Coleoptera) with keys to the known genera. *Transactions of the Royal Entomological Scoiety of London* 120: 115–138.

Kelly, A.L. and Passchier, S. (2018). A sub-millennial sediment record of ice-stream retreat and meltwater storage in the Baltic Ice Lake during the Bølling-Allerød interstadial. *Quaternary Science Reviews* 198: 126–139.

Koch, K. (1989). Die Käfer Mitteleuropas. *Ökologie*, 1. Goecke & Evers, Krefeld, 440 pp.

Konráðsdóttir, H. (2007). An archaeoentomological contribution to the Skálholt project, Iceland. Thesis, Edinburgh, 88 pp.

Konráðsdóttir, H., Panagiotakopulu, E., Lucas, G (2021). A very curious larder - Insects from post-medieval Skálhot, Iceland, and their implications for interpreting activity areas. *Journal of Archaeological Science* https://doi.org/10.1016/j.jas.2020.105319.

Kovář, I. (2005). Revision of the Palaearctic species of the Coccinella transversoguttata species group with notes on some other species of the genus (Coleoptera: Coccinellidae). *Acta Entomologica Musei Nationalis Pragae* 45: 129–164.

Kullingsjö, O. (1999). The role of *Corticaria rubripes* (Coleoptera: Lathridiidae) in dispersal of fungi to burned forest. *Växtskyddsnotiser* 4.

Lambeck, K. (2001). Glacial crustal rebound, sea levels and shorelines. In: Encyclopaedia of Ocean Sciences, vol. 2 (eds. K.K. Turekian and S.A. Thorpe), 1157–1167. New York: Academic Press.

Larsson, S.G., Gigja, G. (1959). Coleoptera 1. Synopsis. *The Zoology of Iceland*, pp. 3(46a). Munksgaard, Copenhagen, Denmark.

Lemdahl, G. (1995). Insect remains from the Alvastra pile dwelling. In: Alvastra pile dwelling. Palaeoethnobotanical Studies.

(ed. H. Göransson), Theses and Papers in Archaeology, N.S. A6, 97–99. Lund University Press.

Lindroth, C.H. (1931). Die Insektenfauna Islands und ihre Probleme. *Zoologiska Bidrag från Uppsala* 13: 105–600.

Lindroth, C.H. (1957). The Faunal Connections between Europe and North America. New York: Wiley.

Lindroth, C.H. (1963). The problem of late land connections in the North Atlantic area. In: *North Atlantic Biota and Their History*. In: North Atlantic Biota and Their History (eds. A. Löve and D. Löve), 73–85. Pergamon: Oxford.

Lindroth, C.H. (1965). Skaftafell, Iceland, a living glacial refugium. *Oikos Suppl.* 6: 1–142.

Lindroth, C.H. (1968). The Icelandic form of Carabus problematicus Hbst. (Col. Carabidae) a statistic treatment of subspecies. *Opuscula Entomologica* 33: 157–182.

Lindroth, C.H. (1985). The Carabidae (Coleoptera) of Fennoscandia and Denmark. *Fauna Entomologica Scandinavica*, vol. 15, p. 1. E.J. Brill, Leiden.

Lindroth, C.H., Andersson, H., Bodvarsson, H. et al. (1973). Surtsey, Iceland – the development of a new fauna, 1963–1970. Terrestrial invertebrates. *Entomol. Scand. Suppl.* 5: 1–280.

Lohse, G.A. (1989). Gnypeta groenlandica sp. n., eine neue Staphylinide aus Grönland. *Entomologische Blätter* 85: 58–60.

Lott, D.A. (2008). The British species of *Ochthephilus mulsant* and Rey (Staphylinidae). *Coleopterist* 17: 17–22.

Luff, M.L. (1998). Provisional Atlas of the Ground Beetles (Coleoptera, Carabidae) of Britain. Monks Wood: Centre for Ecology & Hydrology.

MacArthur, R.H. and Wilson, E.O. (2001). The Theory of Island Biogeography. Princeton, N.J: Princeton University Press.

Mahler, V. (1988). A new species of *Atheta* Thomson, 1858, from Greenland (Coleoptera, Staphylinidae, Aleocharinae). *Steenstrupia* 14: 93–97.

Michelsen, V. (2015). Anthomyiidae, Fanniidae, Muscidae and Scathophagidae (the Muscidae family group). In: The Greenland Entomofauna: An Identification Manual of Insects Spiders and Their Allies, Fauna Entomologica Scandinavica, vol. 44. (eds. Böcher, N.P., Kristensen, T., Pape, and L. Vilhelmsen), 635–657. Brill: Leiden.

Murton, J.B., Bateman, M.D., Dallimore, S.R. et al. (2010). Identification of Younger Dryas outburst flood path from Lake Agassiz to the Arctic Ocean. *Nature* 464: 740–743.

Muschitiello, F., Lea, J.M., Greenwood, S.L. et al. (2016). Timing of the first drainage of the Baltic Ice Lake synchronous with the onset of Greenland Stadial 1. *Boreas* 45: 322–334. https://doi.org/10.1111/bor.12155. ISSN 0300-9483.

Nesje, A., Dahl, S.O., and Bakke, J. (2004). Were abrupt Lateglacial and early-Holocene climatic changes in Northwest Europe linked to freshwater outbursts to the North Atlantic and Arctic Oceans? *The Holocene* 14: 299–310.

Ostenfeld, C.H. (1926). The flora of Greenland and its origin. *Biologiske Meddelelser / Kongelige Danske Videnskabernes Selskab* 6: 1–71.

Panagiotakopulu, E. (2014). Hitchhiking across the North Atlantic – insect immigrants, origins, introductions and extinctions. *Quaternary International* 341: 59–68.

Panagiotakopulu, E. and Buchan, A.L. (2015). Present and Norse Greenlandic hayfields – insect assemblages and human impact in southern Greenland. *The Holocene* 25: 921–931.

Panagiotakopulu, E. and Buckland, P.C. (2013). Late Holocene insect faunas from Tasiusaq, South West Greenland. *Boreas* 42: 160–172.

Panagiotakopulu, E., Skidmore, P., and Buckland, P.C. (2007). Fossil insect evidence for the end of the western settlement in Norse Greenland. *Naturwissenschaften* 94: 300–306.

Panagiotakopulu, E., Greenwood, M.T., and Buckland, P.C. (2012). Irrigation and manuring in medieval Greenland. *Geografiska Annaler – Series A: Physical Geography* 94: 531–548.

Peltier, W., Vettoretti, G., and Stastna, M. (2006). Atlantic meridional overturning and climate response to Arctic Ocean freshening. *Geophysical Research Letters* 33 (L06): 713. https://doi.org/10.1029/2005GL025251.

Pollet, M. (2015). Dolichopodidae. In: The Greenland Entomofauna: An Identification Manual of Insects Spiders and Their Allies, Fauna Entomologica Scandinavica, vol. 44. (eds. Böcher, N.P., Kristensen, T., Pape, and L. Vilhelmsen), 635–657. Brill: Leiden.

Rasmussen, T.L. and Thomsen, E. (2004). The role of the North Atlantic drift in the millennial timescale glacial climate fluctuations. *Palaeogeography, Palaeoclimatology, Palaeoecology* 210: 101–116.

Rasmussen, T.L., Thomsen, E. 2008. Warm Atlantic surface water inflow to the Nordic seas 34–10 cal. kyr B.P. Paleoceanography 23 PA1201, doi:https://doi.org/10.1029/2007PA001453.

Rundgren, M. (1995). Biostratigraphic evidence of the Allerod-Younger Dryas-Preboreal oscillation in Northern Iceland. *Quaternary Research* 44: 405–416.

Rundgren, S. (2007). Glacial survival, post-glacial immigration, and a millennium of human impact: on search for a biogeography of Iceland. *Insect Systematics and Evolution Supplement* 64: 5–44.

Sadler, J.P. (1991a). Archaeological and palaeoecological implications of palaeoentomological studies in Orkney and Iceland. Unpublished PhD Thesis, University of Sheffield.

Sadler, J.P. (1991b). Beetles, boats and biogeography. *Acta Archaeologica* 61: 199–211.

Sadler, J. (in press) The insect fauna. In: Tuquoy, Westray: Home to a Norse Chieftain in the Orkney Earldom (ed. O. Owen), Archaeopress.

Sadler, J.P. and Skidmore, P. (1995). Introductions, extinctions or continuity? Faunal change in the North Atlantic Islands. In: Ecological Relations in Historical Times (eds. R. Butlin and N. Roberts), 206–225. Oxford: Institute of British Geographers, Blackwell.

Skidmore, P., (1996). A Dipterological perspective on the Holocene history of the North Atlantic area. Thesis, Sheffield, 469 pp.

Skidmore P., Panagiotakopulu, E. (in press) The Diptera. In: Tuquoy, Westray: Home to a Norse Chieftain in the Orkney Earldom (ed. O. Owen), Archaeopress.

Smiarowski, K., Harrison, R., Brewington, S. et al. (2017). Zooarchaeology of the Scandinavian settlements in Iceland and Greenland: diverging pathways. In: The Oxford Handbook of Zooarchaeology (eds. U. Albarella, M. Rissetto, H. Russ, et al.), 147–163. Oxford: Oxford University Press.

Steindórsson, S. (1963). Ice Age refugia in Iceland as indicated by the present distribution of plant species. In: North Atlantic Biota and Their History (eds. A. Löve and D. Löve), 303–320. Pergamon: Oxford.

Sveinbjarnardóttir, G. (1992). Farm Abandonment in Medieval and Post-Medieval Iceland: an Interdisciplinary Study. Oxford: Oxbow Monograph.

Thornalley, D.J.R., McCave, I.N., and Elderfield, H. (2010). Freshwater input and abrupt deglacial climate change in the North Atlantic. *Paleoceanography* 25: PA1201.

Thornalley, D.J.R., Elderfield, H., and McCave, I.N. (2011). Reconstructing North Atlantic deglacial surface hydrography and its link to the Atlantic overturning circulation. *Global and Planetary Change* 79: 163–175.

Tikkanen, M. and Oksanen, J. (2002). Late Weichselian and Holocene shore displacement history of the Baltic Sea in Finland. *Fennia* 180: 1–2.

Vickers, K. and Buckland, P.C. (2013). The Coleoptera remains from Toftanes. In: Toftanes. A Viking Age Farmstead in the Faroe Islands. Archaeology, Environment & Economy, vol. 84 (ed. S. Stumman Hansen), 157–174. Acta Archaeologica.

Vickers, K. and Buckland, P.I. (2015). Predicting island beetle faunas by their climate ranges: the tabula rasa/refugia theory in the North Atlantic. *Journal of Biogeography* 42: 2031–2048.

Vickers, K., Bending, J., Buckland, P.C. et al. (2005). Toftanes: the paleoecology of a Faroese Landnám farm. *Human Ecology* 33: 685–710.

Wrona, F.J., Johansson, M., Culp, J.M. et al. (2016). Transitions in Arctic ecosystems: ecological implications of a changing hydrological regime. *Journal of Geophysical Research: Biogeosciences* 121: 650–674. https://doi. org/10.1002/2015JG003133.

Section III

Human Impact

9

Landnám and the North Atlantic Flora

Kevin J. Edwards[1,2,3], Egill Erlendsson[4] and J. Edward Schofield[1]

[1] *Department of Geography and Environment, School of Geosciences, University of Aberdeen, Aberdeen, UK*
[2] *Department of Archaeology, School of Geosciences, University of Aberdeen, Aberdeen, UK*
[3] *Scott Polar Research Institute and McDonald Institute for Archaeological Research, University of Cambridge, Cambridge, UK*
[4] *Department of Geography and Tourism, Faculty of Life and Environmental Sciences, University of Iceland, Reykjavík, Iceland*

Introduction

The evolution of the flora of the North Atlantic prior to human colonization has been the subject of numerous contributions, which have been well summarized in the past (Húlten 1958; Dahl 1959; Löve and Löve 1963; Brochmann et al. 2003) and most recently within this volume. The aim of this chapter is to present the available evidence for the impact of people on vegetation around the time of the 'Scandinavian' settlement of the North Atlantic islands. The Norse/Viking *landnám* (land-taking) was enacted mainly by peoples of Norwegian origin, albeit with additional Scandinavians and probably even more occupants of the British Isles (Fitzhugh and Ward 2000; Helgason et al. 2001; Barrett 2003; Nordeide and Edwards 2019). Occurring from around 800 CE in the Faroe Islands, *landnám* saw its major push in Iceland beginning ca. 870 CE and in Greenland from 985 CE (Figure 1). The settlers introduced a system of northwest European-style agriculture, based around animal husbandry, into near-pristine landscapes (Dugmore et al. 2005).

The North Atlantic arena had been essentially uninhabited other than for the possible presence of anchorites (*papar*) in the Faroe Islands and Iceland, while southern Greenland had not been occupied for a millennium or so, and then by palaeo-Eskimo hunter-fishermen (Grønnow and Sørensen 2006), who probably had a minimal impact upon the local vegetation.

For the Faroes, Iceland and Greenland, we shall consider the existing baseline vegetation and the nature of anthropogenic impact upon the flora of each area, including related landscape and environmental impacts. The Atlantic areas of the British Isles were not immune to Scandinavian settlement, but as in Scandinavia, their biota had been subject to cultural depredations and transformations over thousands of years (Edwards 1996; Edwards et al. 2016) and thus they do not provide true comparanda for our purposes. Likewise, the already occupied Atlantic coast of North America only saw Norse occupation for a few years and the effects on vegetation may be barely detectable (Davis et al. 1988; Wallace 2008).

Biogeography in the Sub-Arctic: The Past and Future of North Atlantic Biota, First Edition.
Edited by Eva Panagiotakopulu and Jon P. Sadler.
© 2021 John Wiley & Sons Ltd. Published 2021 by John Wiley & Sons Ltd.

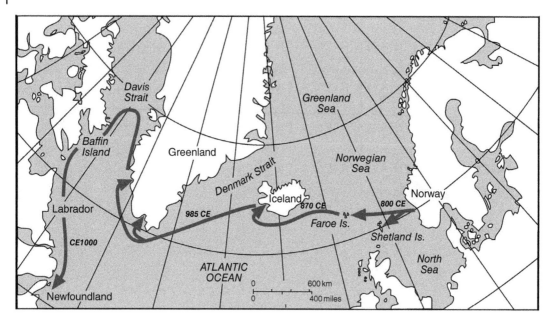

Figure 1 Map of the North Atlantic showing the pattern and approximate timing of Norse colonization.

A largely palynological perspective is presented here because pollen analysis has overwhelmingly produced most data for reconstructing historical floras at and around the time of Norse occupation. This means, regrettably, that various of the 'lower' plants must be neglected. Plant nomenclature follows Böcher et al. (1968), Kristinsson (1986), Jóhansen (2000) and Stace (2010) as appropriate.

The Faroe Islands

It is clear from pollen data that the Faroes archipelago (Figure 2) lacked an extensive woodland cover throughout the Holocene (e.g. Jóhansen 1985; Lawson et al. 2007a; cf. Figure 3). For the half millennium or so prior to the conventional Norse *landnám* of ca. 800 CE, the lowlands (below 200 m in altitude), which represent only around 30% of the land area, were probably dominated, as now, by temperate grasslands in which *Nardus stricta* (moor matgrass)*, Anthoxanthum odoratum*

(sweet vernal grass), *Agrostis capillaris* (common bent) and *Agrostis canina* (brown bent) were frequent (Hansen and Jóhansen 1982; Fosaa 2001). It is reasonable to assume that the greater part of these basaltic islands, with their extreme slopes, always had a low alpine vegetation which graded into arctic vegetation on the mountain tops and comprising snow-bed and fell-field communities typically featuring *Salix herbacea* (dwarf willow), *Carex bigelowii* (Bigelow's sedge), *Bistorta vivipara* (alpine bistort), and *Racomitrium lanuginosum* (woolly fringe-moss). Lowland areas with sufficient insolation have heathland communities featuring *Calluna vulgaris* (heather), *Empetrum nigrum spp. hermaphroditum* (mountain crowberry), *Vaccinium myrtillus* (bilberry), *Vaccinium uliginosum* (bog bilberry) and *Erica cinerea* (bell heather). The islands also lack ombrogenous blanket mire as opposed to soligenous and topogenous mires, and only about 1.3% of the land area is covered by peat (Edwards and Fosaa 2017). The landmark grass roofs of the Faroe Islands represent

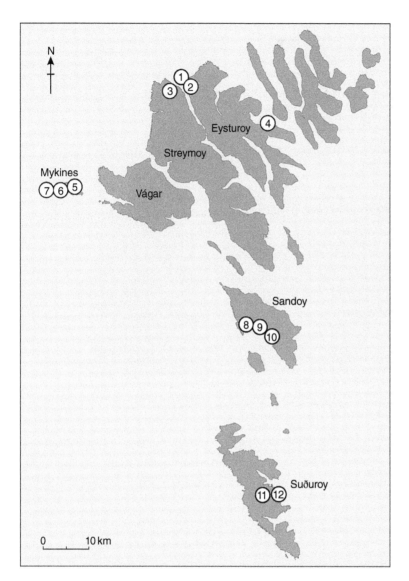

Figure 2 Sites and places within the Faroe Islands that are named in the text. Key to numbers: 1, Argisbrekka; 2, Eiði; 3, Tjørnuvík; 4, Toftanes; 5, Korkadalur; 6, North of Uldalíð; 7, Lambi; 8, Gróthusvatn; 9. Sandur; 10, Lítlavatn-20, Millum Vatna; 11, Hovsdalur; 12, Hov, Hovi B.

a highly variable type of habitat that is of great antiquity; the species composition of the turfs can be presumed to reflect initially the vegetation from which they were removed, usually from within the outfields or *hagi* (Ostenfeld 1905–1908; McMullen and Edwards 2007).

The coverage of this tundra-like flora would likely have been punctuated by low-density and low-stature woodland and shrubs at the time when humans arrived. *Juniperus communis ssp. nana* (*alpinum*) (juniper) was always ubiquitous, as undoubtedly were *Salix glauca* (grey willow)

Figure 3 Gróthusvatn viewed from the north. A storm beach separates the lake (centre) from the sea (top). *Source:* Photo: I.T. Lawson, August 2006.

and *Salix phylicifolia* (tea-leaved willow), but macrofossil finds at the shieling site of Argisbrekka, beside Eiðisvatn close to Eiði (Geikie 1880; Malmros 1994; Mahler 2007) and the Norse farm of Toftanes, Leirvík (Stummann Hansen 2013), both on Eysturoy, reveal that *Betula pubescens* (downy birch) was growing locally – and certainly so near Eiði. This is consistent with the pollen-morphological data from sites on Sandoy (Lawson et al. 2008) and is *contra* the assertion of Jóhansen (1985) that *Betula nana* (dwarf birch) was the only native taxon of the genus growing in the Faroes. The isolated grains of arboreal taxa such as *Pinus sylvestris* (Scots pine), *Alnus* (alder), *Quercus* (oak) and *Tilia* (lime) that are occasionally recorded in pollen diagrams are not from plants native to the Faroe Islands and are assumed to derive from long-distance airborne transport from continental areas.

It is now clear that the Norse settlers were preceded by people who apparently farmed in the vicinity of Sandur on the island of Sandoy, where archaeological evidence for barley cultivation and peat burning has been found (Church et al. 2013). These undertakings in the few centuries before ca. 800 CE are not assignable to any cultural group and might be placed alongside the sites from elsewhere in the archipelago that have produced early cereal-type pollen finds (see below). It seems unlikely that such activities had any major impact on the local vegetation, but soils seem to have been disturbed (Edwards and Borthwick 2008).

Reductions in birch, willow and juniper seen in pollen diagrams (cf. Figure 4) occur at many times both before and during the conventional *landnám* period and it is difficult to demonstrate human causation. There seems to be no

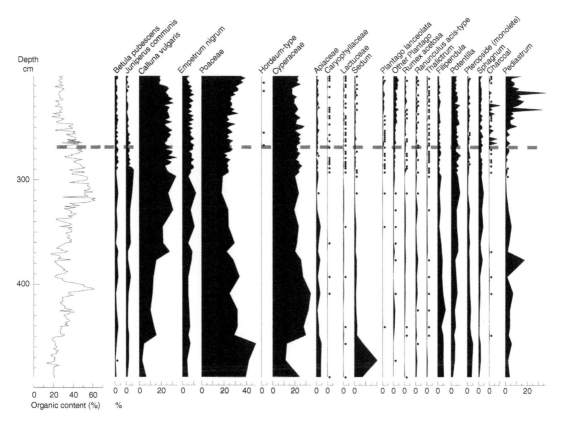

Figure 4 Selected taxa pollen diagram for Gróthusvatn, Sandoy. Depths are measured below the water surface; the sediment–water interface is at 183 cm. The line at 270 cm indicates the approximate level above which the data indicate anthropogenic activity. Black dots indicate the presence of pollen at frequencies below 0.5% TLP. *Source:* After Lawson et al. (2005). Reprinted with permission from Springer Nature.

support for the supposed decline of *Juniperus* at *landnám* as a result of browsing by goats introduced by the Norse (Small 1991; Edwards 2008) or as a consequence of its other uses (e.g. for ropes or as a flavouring agent; Larsen 1991). An interesting discovery is that of *Corylus avellana* (hazel), in the form of hazel nut shells and wood found at Toftanes (Stummann Hansen 2013) and Argisbrekka (Malmros 1994; Mahler 2007). Malmros suggests that *Corylus* was introduced as a food crop, but that cultivation only lasted for a relatively short time.

The frequencies of woodland and tall shrub pollen at *landnám* (often much less than 10%

of total land pollen [TLP]) are minimal in comparison with what is sometimes found in Iceland and Greenland. For the Faroe Islands, this means that any marked reduction in arboreal pollen representation cannot be expected, thus removing an otherwise useful palaeovegetational indicator. Therefore, is any anthropogenic palynological footprint in evidence, let alone a Norse one (Edwards et al. 2011a)? Most pollen diagrams display rather muted changes ascribable to human activity (Figure 4 and cf. Hannon and Bradshaw 2000; Edwards et al. 2005; Hannon et al. 2005; Lawson et al. 2005, 2008; Borthwick et al. 2006; Borthwick 2007) even though Jóhansen

(1985, p. 54), discussing the site of Tjørnuvík, maintained that 'The changes reflecting man's arrival are numerous'.

The pollen taxon, which has perhaps seen the greatest attention, is cereal-type, confidently assigned to the Cerealia by Jóhansen (Jóhansen 1979, 1985; cf. Hannon et al. 2001; Edwards and Borthwick 2010). Even *Elymus* (*Leymus*) *arenarius* (lyme-grass), and from which *Hordeum* (cf. barley) pollen is near-palynologically inseparable (Andersen 1979), is suggested as a possible human introduction by Jóhansen (1985, p. 55) – lyme-grass was grown as a corn crop in Iceland (Guðmundsson 1996), but it is a rare plant in the Faroes at present (Jóhansen 2000). It is perhaps instructive that assiduous searching for cereal-type pollen grains at Hov revealed none prior to ~550 CE (Borthwick 2007). Arguably, such examples of 'early' cereal-type pollen from conventionally pre-Norse contexts may signify colonization by *papar* or early Norse settlers (Edwards and Borthwick 2010). This suggestion has understandably received a boost with the early macrofossil finds of hulled barley on Sandoy (Church et al. 2013).

Rumex longifolius (northern dock) and *Rumex obtusifolius* (broad-leaved dock) were considered to be 'among the first anthropochor[e]s' (Jóhansen 1985, p. 55 and cf. Guldager Christiansen and Fosaa 2009) while *Rumex acetosa* (common sorrel) is noted as increasing from *landnám*. Palynologically, only *R. acetosa* is presented in several of Jóhansen's diagrams, where it is combined with *Oxyria digyna* (mountain sorrel). The latter is presumed to be the dominant pollen producer of the two, but both grew in lowland and mountain areas, and the pollen group (labelled collectively as *R. acetosa*) is shown to expand at Hovi B, Suðuroy, after *landnám,* as it did at Lambi, Mykines. The latter site, together with that of nearby North of Uldalíð, has just as much *R. acetosa* pollen prior to *landnám*. Tjørnuvík, on the island of Streymoy, does, however, have

a clear rise in (cf.) *R. acetosa* pollen at *landnám*. At the Sandoy sites of Gróthusvatn, Lítlavatn-20 and Millum Vatna, *R. acetosa* pollen has been well represented over the last >3500 years, although it expands in the time following *landnám* at the last of these (Lawson et al. 2008). Hannon et al. (2001) have enhanced representation of *Rumex* cf. *longifolius* pollen following *landnám* at Tjørnuvík, Eiði and Korkadalur.

Plantago lanceolata (ribwort plantain) has long been recognized as a key human indicator taxon in Europe (Iversen 1941; Godwin 1975; Behre 1981). Jóhansen (1986–1987) had seen the pollen grains of this 'weed' as indicating a prehistoric human presence as long ago as about 4300 BP. This is probably a misinterpretation of the records as the taxon is found in pre-settlement deposits in Iceland also (Hansom and Briggs 1989–1990). *P. lanceolata* was not found at the outset of *landnám* at Tjørnuvík (Jóhansen 1971), but it did occur regularly, if sporadically, thereafter and it also expands at Millum Vatna (Lawson et al. 2008). Jóhansen (1985, p. 55) considered it to be an input from long-distance transport, but it is commonly recorded elsewhere (Figure 4; Edwards et al. 2005; Lawson et al. 2008). At the Mykines sites of Lambi and North of Uldalíð, it is *Plantago maritima* (sea plantain) that increases and Jóhansen regarded it as an introduced species there along with *Avena* (oats) at Lambi. Sea plantain was evident long before this in other pollen profiles from the Faroe Islands (Jóhansen 1985) as was *Plantago major* (greater plantain; Lawson et al. 2008).

A common phenomenon around the time of *landnám* is the expansion in the pollen of Poaceae (grasses) and/or Cyperaceae (sedges). These ubiquitous taxa have frequent fluctuations and declines throughout the Holocene spectra and cannot, alone, be designated as providing anthropogenic 'footprints'. The expansion of grasses, though, is consistent with the development of hayfields, which are critical to the provision of winter fodder. This is apparent from *landnám* at

Hov (Edwards et al. 2005), as well as at Tjørnuvík and Korkadalur (Hannon et al. 2001). There are also less consistent increases in *Potentilla* (cf. *Potentilla erecta* [tormentil]) as at Hov and Argisbrekka (Hannon and Bradshaw 2007), Brassicaceae (perhaps reflecting *Capsella bursa-pastoris* [shepherd's purse]) at Lambi, and *Ranunculus acris*-type (meadow buttercups) and *Rhinanthus*-type (cf. yellow rattle) at Hov.

Some sites may feature increases in the abundance of herbs around *landnám*, but others are characterized by reductions in tall herbs, heaths and ferns. The sites of Hov/Hovi, for instance, witness falls in Apiaceae (carrot family), *Angelica archangelica* (garden angelica), *Angelica sylvestris* (wild angelica), *Filipendula ulmaria* (meadowsweet), *Caltha palustris* (marsh marigold), *Sedum/Rhodiala rosea* (roseroot), *Calluna vulgaris* (heather) and undifferentiated ferns (*Pteropsida* monolete indet.). Such plants are attractive to people or animals as well as being susceptible to grazing and trampling pressure. Many of these taxa were to be found in the archaeologically related pollen samples from Toftanes (Edwards et al. 1998, 2005; Vickers et al. 2005; Edwards 2013). Although such records should not be interpreted like those in the more consistent mire and lake sediment stratigraphic profiles, the Toftanes results are of interest in that the pollen spectra are likely to derive from habitation, infield and outfield areas, with palynomorphs arriving as a result of airborne pollen deposition in addition to being attached to feet and hooves, and being contained in peat brought to the site. It has been conjectured that an initial episode of grazing and small-scale cereal cultivation could have resulted in overgrazing (thereby decreasing flowering of grasses) or even some abandonment as other plants (e.g. sedges, thyme [Lamiaceae] and sorrel) invaded formerly grazed areas. An effort may then have been made to re-invigorate land-use and more charcoal was produced (either from burning of the land surface to encourage the renewed spread of grass and/or as a product of more domestic activity); this latest phase could also have seen further barley cultivation.

For the Faroe Islands, it would seem that the most helpful signs of cultural impacts on the past vegetational landscapes are to be seen at the level of the community and as reflected by suites of pollen and spores, combined where possible with records of microscopic charcoal, sedimentology and radiocarbon-dating (cf. Edwards et al. 2005; Edwards and Borthwick 2010). As yet, there are no studies involving coprophilous fungal spores (see below). At Gróthusvatn, increased abundances of the green alga *Pediastrum boryanum* would seem to add support to the inference of eutrophication following settlement, with the proxy indicating a rise in nutrient availability (Figures 3 and 4; Gathorne-Hardy et al. 2007; cf. Lawson et al. 2007b).

There are records for 'palynological richness' at both Hov and Hovsdalur but they do not suggest that the arrival of the Norse led to an increase in floristic diversity (Edwards et al. 2005). It might have been supposed that the development of an infield/outfield system and shielings would create environmental heterogeneity, resulting in an increase in plant habitat types. Instead, there are overall declines in diversity at the Suðuroy sites as tree, shrub, heath, tall herb, and some wetland taxa are reduced by grazing and drainage. Any anticipated increase in floristic diversity associated with the addition of anthropogenic taxa is offset by losses of tree and shrub components, and eventually heaths and the taller palatable herbs.

Iceland

The Norse settlement of Iceland (Figure 5) offered fresh opportunities for plants to migrate westwards with the wave of Norse-led colonists, resulting in the addition of a number of new species to the Icelandic flora. Þórhallsdóttir's (1996)

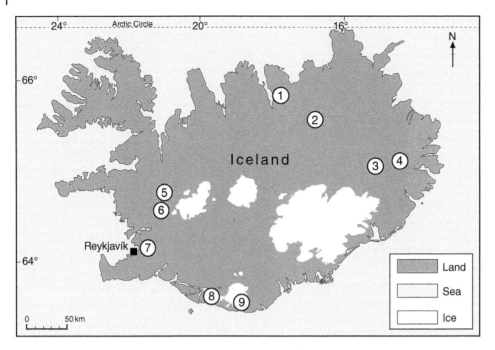

Figure 5 Sites and places within Iceland that are named in the text. Key to numbers: 1, Knarrarnes; 2, Mývantssveit; 3, Hrafnkelsdalur; 4, Helgutjörn; 5, Kjarardalur, Norðtungusel; 6, Reykholt, Reykholtsdalur; 7, Leiruvogur; 8, Eyjafjallahreppur, Stóra-Mörk; 9, Ketilsstaðir.

compilation of records from the botanists Steindór Steindórsson (1964) and Hörður Kristinsson (unpublished) suggests 62 possible post-settlement plant species based on their modern patterns of distribution and preferred habitats. Some of these plants are predominantly confined to farms, gardens and other nutrient-enriched areas and could be considered as likely anthropochores (i.e. not native and unintentionally introduced by people; sensu Behre 1988). Pollen analysis can confirm the post-settlement status of some but not all of these taxa. Of the 62 proposed candidates, only 11 are identifiable palynologically to species level, with others being 'invisible' in the pollen record for various taphonomic reasons, or only distinct at the level of genus, family or pollen-morphological type. Of those species that can be confidently identified, *Rumex acetosella* (sheep's sorrel) and *Polygonum aviculare* (knotgrass) are the most

frequently recorded in Icelandic pollen diagrams (Erlendsson 2007; Edwards et al. 2011a) and were almost certainly introduced after *landnám* (cf. Schofield et al. 2013). Also of interest in this context is *Achillea*-type (*Anthemis*-type of Moore et al. 1991), which for Iceland consists of four possible anthropochores (cf. Þórhallsdóttir 1996): *Tripleurospermum maritimum* (syn. *Matricaria maritima*; sea mayweed), *Leucanthemum vulgare* (syn. *Matricaria matricarioides*; oxeye daisy), *Achillea millefolium* (yarrow) and *Achillea ptarmica* (sneezewort). Although sporadic, the records of *Achillea*-type pollen are virtually confined to post-settlement sedimentary contexts, in south and west Iceland at least (Erlendsson 2007) and the same can be said for several other possible alien 'imports' such as *Urtica* (nettles), *Rumex longifolius*, and *Plantago major* (Hallsdóttir 1987; Erlendsson 2007).

Measurements of palynological richness at Ketilsstaðir and Stóra-Mörk in south Iceland and Reykholt in west Iceland, all indicate higher levels after settlement (Erlendsson 2007). Whether this resulted primarily from an enrichment of the flora with introduced elements or an increase in habitat heterogeneity (and thus wider opportunities for native plants) local to the settlements, where most of the pollen records were taken, is still difficult to ascertain. The post-settlement emergence of several of the taxa highlighted as possible anthropochores is demonstrated in a pollen diagram from the large Norse farm at Reykholt in Borgarfjörður, west Iceland (Figure 6), which records agricultural activities associated with the maintenance of a large estate, including evidence for the possible cultivation of barley (Sveinbjarnardóttir et al. 2007; Erlendsson et al. 2012). Assemblages of seeds recovered from archaeological contexts across Iceland also provide an indication

of which plants may have been introduced at, or shortly after, the time of settlement; in addition to those already named, these include *Stellaria media* (common chickweed), *Spergula arvensis* (corn spurrey) and *Ranunculus acris* (Guðmundsson 2010; Sveinbjarnardóttir 2012; Martin 2014). Another likely accidental introduction – possibly arriving in ship's ballast – is *Juncus gerardii* (saltmarsh rush). This species is found today in only two locations where the nearby place-names – Skiphóll ('Ship-hill'; Leiruvogur, southwest Iceland) and Knarrarnes ('Ship-peninsula'; Eyjafjörður, north Iceland – a Knörr being a Viking-age ship design) – indicate harbourages and/or the beaching of ships (Byock and Zori 2012).

Reconstructions of the pre-settlement vegetation of Iceland contrast markedly with the currently open and exposed character of the landscape. A key component of plant communities before and at the time of *landnám* was *Betula*

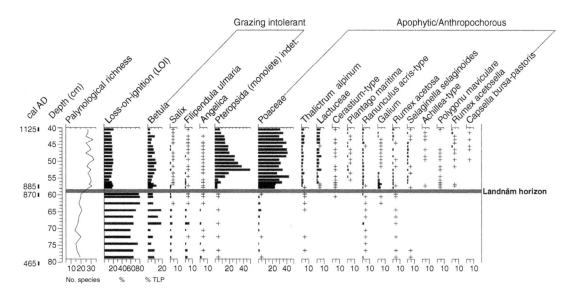

Figure 6 Percentage pollen diagram for Reykholtsdalur, west Iceland, showing selected taxa before and after *landnám*. Loss-on-ignition (a proxy for soil erosion) and palynological richness (a measure of the level of floristic diversity) are also displayed. Cal. AD dates are the mid-points of calibrated (2σ) radiocarbon age-estimates. + indicates representation at <1% TLP. *Source:* After Erlendsson (2007) and Erlendsson et al. (2012).

pubescens, the only species of tree in Iceland that forms continuous woodland (Caseldine 2001). Simulations of the potential distribution of *B. pubescens* under modern conditions (with anthropogenic factors excluded) show that downy birch could occupy ~25% of the island as woodland (>2 m height) and ~41% as scrub (Wöll 2008). It may be fair to assume that much of this potential range was realized towards the end of the ninth century CE, before the arrival of people. Yet the extent to which the first settlers were greeted with a landscape that supported woodland 'from mountain to seashore' – as Ari the Wise had written in the twelfth century *Íslendingabók* (Benediktsson 1968) – is debatable.

Even before the time of settlement, the spatial coverage of birch woodland had begun to shrink (Wastl et al. 2001; Eddudóttir et al. 2015, 2016). Palynological and macrofossil evidence suggests that during the time leading up to Norse settlement, birch trees had become smaller in stature, and were already sparse or absent in unfavourable habitats such as exposed coastal locations and some wetlands (e.g. Hallsdóttir and Caseldine 2005; Erlendsson 2007; Erlendsson et al. 2009, 2012; Gísladóttir et al. 2010). Closer inspection of the period from ~500 CE through to the time of settlement also shows that birch woodland was dynamic, expanding and contracting in accordance with fluctuations in the climate. At least two sites (Reykholtsdalur and Stóra-Mörk) demonstrate elevated frequencies of *B. pubescens* pollen between ~600 and 800 CE. This probably resulted from increased flowering and a greater spatial coverage and density of birch woodland as a consequence of a short-lived improvement in temperatures within a phase of longer-term cooler conditions (cf. Eiríksson et al. 2006; Erlendsson and Edwards 2009).

It is difficult to ascertain exactly where the tree line for birch stood at the time of settlement. Pollen and macrofossil analyses of lake sediments from the highland margin (413 m a.s.l.) in northwest Iceland show a gradual conversion from birch woodland to shrub and dwarf shrub heath from about 6700 cal. year BP, yet *B. pubescens* was still present in this elevated location at the time of settlement (Eddudóttir et al. 2016). Pollen records at two high altitude sites (395 and 425 m a.s.l.) in Hrafnkelsdalur, east Iceland, are probably representative of the plant communities above the altitudinal limit for *B. pubescens*. Assemblages reveal that *Salix*, *Juniperus communis* and *Betula nana* were prominent in these locations before *landnám* (Hallsdóttir 1982). Conceivably this low shrub vegetation graded into more exposed tundra in the interior highlands.

Upon their arrival in Iceland the colonists implemented a decentralized farming structure that required the clearance of fields for haymaking and, in some instances at least, cereal cultivation (Sveinbjarnardóttir et al. 2007; Zori et al. 2013). The clearance of woodlands is now well documented in pollen records and is evident stratigraphically (Figure 7). Marked reductions in the pollen of *Betula* and grazing-intolerant taxa, such as *Salix* and the tall, broad-leaved herbs *Angelica* and *Filipendula ulmaria*, coincide with expansions in grasses and exposure-loving, hardy herbs. The latter are usually considered to be apophytes (i.e. native taxa favoured and spread, either directly or indirectly, by cultural activity; sensu Behre 1988). Among the most commonly encountered palynologically are *Thalictrum alpinum*, *Rumex* spp., *Cerastium*-type, members of the Lactuceae (dandelions and hawkbits) and *Selaginella selaginoides* (lesser clubmoss) (e.g. Hallsdóttir 1987; Erlendsson 2007; Riddell et al. 2018). In south and southwest Iceland, the onset of these floristic changes is recorded between the Landnám tephra (877±1 CE) and the ash deposited ~920 CE following an eruption of Katla, thus emphasizing the speed at which vegetation changed in response to human settlement (Hallsdóttir 1987; Vickers et al. 2011). An exception to this pattern is Ketilsstaðir in

Landnám tephra

10 cm

Figure 7 Sediment profile from Mosfell in Mosfellsdalur, southwest Iceland, featuring pre-*landnám* remains of birch trees embedded in organic peat below the Landnám tephra from 877±1 CE. Light coloured, inorganic sediments above the tephra signify soil erosion after clearance of woodland around the site. *Source:* Photo: D. Zori, May (2011); Zori et al. (2013).

south Iceland, where pre-*landnám* birch pollen values were already low (typically <5%) and indicative of a location largely devoid of woodland. Consequently, the signal for human impact recorded in the pollen record for this site appears muted (Erlendsson et al. 2009), much like that observed for similar exposed, coastal landscapes across the Faroe Islands (e.g. Lawson et al. 2008; and see above).

Most of the pollen records available for locations in close proximity to Norse farms in Iceland demonstrate rapid changes in vegetation around the time of settlement, whereas palynological data from areas that were more remote tend to depict the continued presence of woodland into the late medieval period. At Mývatnssveit in northeast Iceland, Lawson et al. (2007b, 2010)

showed that *landnám* did not have any significant impact upon regional woodlands until after ~1300 CE, when birch and juniper were replaced by acidophilic taxa such as *Sphagnum* and *Empetrum nigrum*. A similar pattern has been reported from Reykholtsdalur in west Iceland, where pollen and plant macrofossil evidence suggest that woodland was present until ~1150–1300 CE, after which mires, grasslands and heaths developed in its place. The reduction in woodland appears to have been driven primarily by human agency as chironomids (a proxy used for establishing palaeo-temperatures) suggest that significant cooling resulting from the 'Little Ice Age' – which could potentially have also led to a decline in birch woodland – did not take place until ~1500 CE (Gathorne-Hardy et al. 2009; Erlendsson et al. 2018). The remaining scattered stands of native birch woodland show that the resource could be sustainably managed locally, a feature also suggested for Hofstaðir in Mývatnssveit on the basis of pollen analysis and the micromorphology of fire residues (Tisdall et al. 2018).

The removal of woodland reduced the habitat available for plants that form the field layer. Þórhallsdóttir (1996) lists 22 species for which the distribution and coverage probably diminished as a consequence of woodland destruction. These include *Melampyrum sylvaticum* (small cow-wheat) and the shade-loving *Oxalis acetosella* (wood sorrel). Several pteridophytes would also have suffered. *Gymnocarpium dryopteris*, *Athyrium filix-femina*, *Dryopteris filix-mas* and *Dryopteris expansa* (oak, lady, male, and beech fern, respectively) are today confined to refuges within woodland and shady, damp cracks in lava fields. Paradoxically, the representation of undifferentiated fern spores – Pteropsida (monolete) indet. – increases in some post-settlement deposits (Figure 6; e.g. Erlendsson et al. 2012). This is probably a taphonomic artefact rather than representative of real changes in abundance. Fern spores are highly resistant to deterioration and can survive for long periods in soils (Havinga 1985). An increase in their frequency following *landnám* seems likely to have resulted from the redeposition of soils eroded from areas where woodland had previously stood (e.g. Gathorne-Hardy et al. 2009).

Even though environmental degradation in Iceland had become severe by the late medieval period, it had not reached irreversible levels. Palaeo-environmental studies have shown that even relatively short-lived periods of reduced land use pressure led to discernible habitat recovery. A decrease in proxy evidence for soil erosion in south Iceland (Streeter et al. 2012) and increased values for birch pollen at Helgutjörn, east Iceland (Jónsson et al. 2012), have been linked to reductions in grazing and the intensity of land use as a consequence of the spread of plague in Iceland

after 1402–1404 CE. The disease may have killed between a quarter and a half of the Icelandic population and this inevitably resulted in (at least temporary) farm abandonment and reductions in numbers of livestock (Karlsson 1996; Callow and Evans 2016). At Kjarardalur, west Iceland, the impacts are apparent through the expansion of birch woodland around a shieling (at Norðtungusel) that was owned by the wealthy Reykholt church farm. The regeneration of woodland began shortly after ~1260–1400 CE, with high frequencies of birch pollen (60–80%) and low numbers of coprophilous spores recorded up to ~1500 CE, after which a permanent decline set in as climate deteriorated and populations of people and livestock returned to their previous levels.

Greenland

According to *Grœnlendinga Saga*, the Norse settlement of Greenland began around 985 CE following the arrival of colonists aboard 14 ships journeying from Iceland (Krogh 1967). The earlier Arctic indigenous inhabitants – Palaeo-Eskimos of the Dorset culture (McGhee 1981) – had left the area by the beginning of the first millennium CE (Grønnow and Sørensen 2006) and were hunter-gatherers who largely exploited marine resources. Consequently, their impact on the environment is likely to have been slight and ephemeral, leaving little (if any) legacy. The same argument probably applies for Inuit of the Thule culture (e.g. Panagiotakopulu et al. 2018) who spread into Greenland from eastern Canada after ~1200 CE (ibid.). By contrast, the environmental impacts of the Norse *landnám* were clearly significant with changes to vegetation, soils and landscape traceable through distinct and repeatable palynological 'footprints' preserved in peat and lake sediment profiles (Fredskild 1988; Edwards et al. 2011a).

It is important to note that data coverage for the period of interest is geographically uneven, with the number of sites providing palaeobotanical information from the Eastern Settlement (the primary concentration of Norse farms) far outweighing those from the Western and Middle Settlements (Figure 8). Indeed, at the time of writing, there is no Norse-age palynological information for the latter (Edwards et al. 2013). Much of

what follows will, as a consequence, focus upon events in the Eastern Settlement, the largest and most southerly (~60–61°N) of the three former Norse settlement areas.

In the Eastern Settlement, the character of the vegetation prior to *landnám* possibly resembled in many respects that present in Iceland

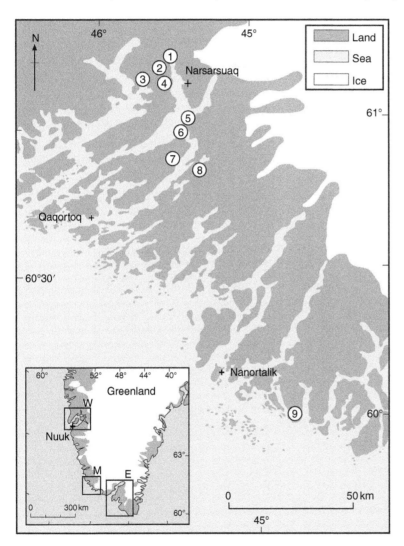

Figure 8 Sites and places within the Eastern Settlement of Greenland that are named in the text. Key to numbers: 1, Qinngua; 2, Qorlortoq valley; 3, Tasiusaq; 4, Qassiarsuk; 5; Lake Igaliku; 6, Igaliku; 7, Sissarluttoq; 8, Lake Vatnahverfi, Mountain Farm, Saqqaa, Saqqaata Tasia; 9; Sandhavn. Inset: the Norse Settlements in Greenland (boxed): E = Eastern; M = Middle; W = Western.

before its colonization in ca. 870 CE. Several inland farmsteads including those at Tasiusaq, Qinngua, Saqqaa and Saqqaata Tasia display mean frequencies of 20% or more for *Betula pubescens* pollen in assemblages immediately below the *landnám* horizon (Edwards et al. 2008; Schofield and Edwards 2011; Ledger 2013; Ledger et al. 2013, 2014a, 2014b). Similar values are also reported from lake basins such as Galium Kær (Fredskild 1973), Lake Igaliku (Gauthier et al. 2010) and Lake Vatnahverfi (Ledger 2013), which gather their pollen rain from much wider (regional) source areas. The patterns appear to indicate sparse or open birch woodland (Figure 9), although this community was possibly restricted to sheltered (valley) locations below 150 m a.s.l. and areas towards the (continental) interiors of the fjords, as is the case today (cf. Böcher 1979). Pollen from *Betula glandulosa* (American dwarf birch) is also common alongside *B. pubescens*

in many Eastern Settlement pollen records, and scrub woodlands containing both of these species and their hybrids (Sulkinoja 1990) may have formed copses of intermediate stature. Favourable temperatures during the 'Medieval Warm Period' (MWP) possibly encouraged an expansion in *Betula* in southern Greenland during the late first millennium CE. Palynological data from Tasiusaq provide supporting evidence for this with pollen values for both *B. pubescens* and *B. glandulosa* peaking at ~40% and ~60%, respectively, during the interval ~900–1000 CE.

In coastal, near-coastal, upland or otherwise exposed areas of the Eastern Settlement, the landscape prior to Norse settlement was probably more open in character than the interior. Dwarf shrub heath, or willow scrub of low stature, is likely to have been widespread. At Sissarluttoq, a farmstead occupying an exposed fjord-side location with an easterly aspect, *Betula*

Figure 9   Mixed birch-willow scrub and woodland covering sheltered valley slopes east of the airport at Narsarsuaq. The height of the vegetation exceeds 2 m in places. *Source:* Photo: J.E. Schofield, August 2004.

pollen is negligible (Edwards et al. 2011b) yet *Salix* approaches 20% TLP in pre-*landnám* assemblages indicating the local presence of open *S. glauca* heath or scrub. Similarly, pollen diagrams from the Western Settlement (Figure 10) – which lies north of the tree-line for *B. pubescens* and within a landscape that is today essentially treeless (Fredskild 1996) – indicate pre-*landnám* vegetation communities typically comprising scrub composed variously of *S. glauca*, *B. nana* and *Alnus crispa* (green alder) (Iversen 1953; Schofield et al. 2019). Pollen records suggest that a small population of *A. crispa* was also established across the interior of the Eastern Settlement, despite the plant rarely being encountered in Greenland today south of ~61°N (Ledger et al. 2015).

Following *landnám*, the majority of pollen diagrams from the settlement areas show a decline in tree and shrub pollen frequencies and an expansion in herbs (especially Poaceae) (Figure 11). This indicates a reduction in areas of woodland, scrub and heath and an expansion in grassland communities, including the hayfields that were vital for the production of fodder for the over-wintering of animals in the byre. One exception appears to have been at Qinngua, a large farm situated at the head of Tunulliarfik, where pollen values for *Betula* spp. remain high (~20%) throughout the period of settlement (Schofield and Edwards 2011), indicating that birch scrub and/or woodland was possibly being managed sustainably as a fuel resource in a similar manner to that observed in Eyjafjallahreppur in Iceland (Church et al. 2007). The presence of distinct charcoal layers at some Western Settlement farm sites, such as at Ujaragssuit – the Norse site

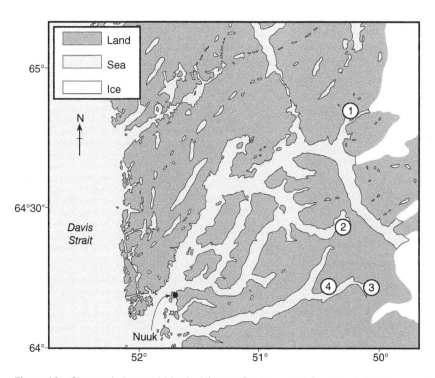

Figure 10 Sites and places within the Western Settlement of Greenland that are named in the text. Key to numbers: 1, Ujaragssuit; 2, Kapisigdlit; 3, Sandnes; 4, Niaquusat.

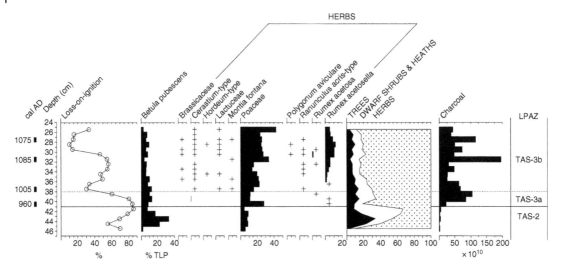

Figure 11 Percentage pollen diagram for Tasiusaq, Eastern Settlement of Greenland, showing selected taxa before and after *landnám* (the TAS-2/3a boundary). Soil erosion and burning are reflected by the values for LOI and concentrations of microscopic charcoal, respectively. Cal. AD dates are the mid-points of calibrated (2σ) radiocarbon age-estimates; + indicates representation at <1% TLP. *Source:* After Edwards et al. (2008).

known as *Anavík* (Iversen 1934) – and at Sandnes (Fredskild and Humle 1991), has led to the suggestion that the earliest settlers may have used fire to clear woody plant communities at *landnám*, presumably to create space for farms and their hayfields and to extend grazing areas. At Johs. Iversen Sø near Kapisigdlit, some 3 km from the ruins of the nearest Norse farmstead, Fredskild (1983) reports a dramatic increase in microscopic charcoal influx to the lake (from trace levels to ~900 particles per cm^2/year) that is contemporary with *landnám* and is seemingly representative of burning or land management on a wide scale. In the Eastern Settlement, discrete charcoal horizons have yet to be found in association with the *landnám* horizon, suggesting that clearance of scrub may have been undertaken manually (cf. Fredskild 1973, 1988). Subsequent high concentrations of microscopic charcoal in pollen profiles (especially at the individual farm sites) might then be largely explained as a consequence of fires set in domestic contexts for the purposes of heating and cooking (Edwards et al. 2008).

The activities of people and their domesticated animals (primarily sheep, goats and cattle) favoured the expansion of a range of native herbs and resulted in the introduction of others. By examining modern distributions, Ostenfeld (1926) considered that up to 13% of the flora of Greenland may have been introduced by the Norse, although Porsild (1932) later downscaled this 'Old Norse' element to (at most) 5%, while Feilberg (1984) regarded just eight of the 346 vascular plants found in the southernmost floristic province of Greenland – broadly equivalent to the Eastern Settlement – as having arrived with the Norse settlers. Palynological evidence provides a strong argument for the introduction of at least three plants (*Rumex acetosella*, *Polygonum aviculare* and *Achillea millifolium*) to southern Greenland following *landnám* (Schofield et al. 2013), but a case for others is more difficult to prove and this will continue to be the case unless more numerous macrofossil records are to be developed. Peat profiles from Qassiarsuk (Fredskild 1978) – the accepted location for Erik the Red's farm estate of *Brattahlið* – are the most useful in this sense as these demonstrate an increase in seeds from both annual and perennial 'weeds' within the settlement horizon, some of which the author considered as introduced 'beyond doubt' (e.g. *Stellaria media* and *Capsella-bursa pastoris*). The introduction of other species such as *Ranunculus acris* and *Potentilla anserina* (silverweed) was regarded as possible but less certain. Large numbers of seeds from *Montia fontana* (blinks) were recovered from the same contexts and point towards nutrient enrichment. Yet diatom records from Lake Igaliku (Perren et al. 2012) and a pond at Sissarluttoq (Edwards et al. 2011b) show little, if any, rise in the trophic status of surface waters at this time, indicating that elevated levels of key elements required for plant growth (N, P, K) are likely to have been restricted to the immediate areas around the farms where refuse disposal and manuring was taking place (e.g. Sandhavn; Golding et al. 2011).

A notable change to the flora of Greenland around the time of Norse settlement is the appearance and increase in *Rumex acetosella*. This plant seems to have been introduced to the Eastern Settlement at or around the 985 CE *landnám*, possibly amongst hay or within imported grass seed from Iceland. The herb became widespread in southern Greenland within a century of the arrival of the first Norse colonists and its pollen provides a useful biostratigraphic marker for human settlement (Schofield et al. 2013). Despite being native to the Western Settlement, just traces of *R. acetosella* pollen are recorded before the Norse arrival, and numbers of the plant appear to have expanded considerably during the Norse period (e.g. Iversen 1934, 1953; Fredskild 1983). Being of low stature and favouring disturbed acidic soils, the plant was possibly a key constituent of heavily grazed grasslands in eroding outfield or rangeland areas. The creation and expansion in suitable 'disturbed' habitats for the plant seem likely as Massa et al. (2012) note that soil erosion rates recorded

in a sediment core from Lake Igaliku had risen to double their pre-*landnám* levels by ~1180 CE, while from ~ 1150 CE onwards, enhanced microwear patterns on sheep's teeth demonstrate that soil ingestion was becoming more commonplace (Mainland 2006). This could indicate that the field layer was grazed close to the soil surface and/or was becoming patchy with some areas of unstable bare ground developing.

Most of the infield was presumably dedicated to the production of hay in support of pastoral farming, so the possible introduction and cultivation of arable crops to Greenland forms an interesting debate. *The King's Mirror* (Larson 1917) notes that some of the wealthiest farmers in Greenland had endeavoured to grow cereals, and although rare finds of cereal-type pollen from oats and barley (i.e. *Avena*-type and *Hordeum*-type) have been reported for the Eastern Settlement (e.g. Fredskild 1988; Edwards et al. 2008; Schofield and Edwards 2011), up until recently there was little firm evidence to corroborate this statement. The discovery of barley macrofossils – rachis fragments removed during threshing – in a midden at a farm in the Qorlortoq valley (Henriksen 2012) provides a stronger case for cereal cultivation, and also a cautionary note against dismissing all Norse-age *Hordeum*-type pollen records as deriving from the native grass *Elymus arenarius* (Figure 12), which grows vigorously around several of the Norse ruin groups today (Edwards 2014). Regarding other cultivated plants, traces of pollen and seeds of flax (*Linum usitatissimum*) have been reported from Niaquusat and Sandnes in the Western Settlement. Whether this plant was sown, or was simply a 'weed' introduced accidentally, is unclear (Fredskild and Humle 1991).

The abandonment of Greenland – possibly beginning as early as ~1350 CE in the Western Settlement (Barlow et al. 1997), but occurring slightly later (~1400 CE) in the Eastern Settlement – together with the onset of the 'Little Ice Age' (Grove 1988), led to further changes in

Figure 12 Lyme grass (*Elymus arenarius* L. spp. *mollis*) growing on the ruins of the Bishop of Greenland's farm and the cathedral at *Garðar* (Igaliku). *Source:* Photo: J.E. Schofield, September 2007.

the character of vegetation communities across southern Greenland. The reduced grazing pressure appears to have allowed the re-establishment of dwarf willow heath and scrub across the interior of the former settlement areas, as indicated by an increase in pollen of *Salix* in several post-abandonment assemblages (e.g. Fredskild 1973; Buckland et al. 2009). Pollen from *Betula* spp. is uniformly low at this time and, in contrast to the period preceding *landnám*, both tree and dwarf birches appear to have become minor components of the vegetation with the recovery of this genus presumably supressed by the cooler temperatures and perhaps the increased storminess (Dugmore et al. 2007a) that was a feature of the prevailing climate. A rise in Cyperaceae pollen is registered in all post-settlement assemblages and is suggestive of the development of tundra-like conditions in which

sedge-dominated steppe communities were widespread. The continued but sporadic appearance of pollen from Norse apophytes and anthropochores, such as *Rumex acetosella*, attests to the survival of 'Old Norse' plants into the post-settlement period, albeit in much reduced numbers.

Discussion

The Environmental Baseline

Moving west, as the first settlers did, between the Faroe Islands, Iceland and Greenland, significant fronts in both marine and atmospheric circulation patterns are crossed, which results in the environment taking on an increasingly arctic character (Dugmore et al. 2005). This is reflected by the transition from a humid but cool climate supporting oceanic heath in the Faroe Islands to drier and colder (subarctic) conditions in southwest Greenland that are, in sheltered places, suitable for the growth of scrub and woodland. This was presumably evident to the first settlers, who must have quickly recognized the contrast between the extremely 'open' landscapes that characterized the Faroe Islands – where woodland was probably never extensive (Jóhansen 1985) – and Iceland and the Eastern Settlement of Greenland where, on the basis of the pollen-analytical evidence, there appears to have been rather more birch-willow scrub and low stature woodland. This may have been viewed as an attractive resource as it potentially offered material for, amongst other things, light construction, firewood and charcoal burning (Schofield and Edwards 2011).

The coverage and density of pre-settlement woodland is difficult to estimate (cf. Hallsdóttir 1987). High frequencies (~35–40%) of *Betula pubescens* pollen are, for example, recorded immediately prior to *landnám* at several sites (e.g. Tasiusaq, Eastern Settlement [Edwards et al. 2008] and Stóra-Mörk, western Iceland [Erlendsson and Edwards 2009]). This seems to indicate significant coverage, yet this needs to be tempered by the knowledge that *B. pubescens* pollen is over-represented in pollen assemblages, with relative pollen productivity (RPP) estimated at four times that of Poaceae and Cyperaceae (based upon data from southwest Greenland; Schofield et al. 2007; Bunting et al. 2013). The abundance of *B. pubescens* pollen in pre-*landnám* assemblages from Iceland and Greenland still compares favourably against that reported for Faroese samples where frequencies below 5% are often typical (e.g. Sandoy; Lawson et al. 2005). At the local scale, topography may have played an important role in governing the distribution of woodland, with birch trees largely restricted to copses growing in sheltered valleys and/or areas with a protective winter snow cover (as is the current situation in Greenland).

Norse Impacts and Legacy

The relatively impoverished contemporary floras of the Faroe Islands, Iceland and Greenland – approximately 400, 440, and 500 vascular plants, respectively (Böcher et al. 1968; Kristinsson 1986; Jóhansen 2000) – mean that vegetation changes resulting from human impact at *landnám* appear less complex than in mainland regions with higher diversity (as Dugmore et al. 2005 first noted). Nevertheless, significant common changes are evident, most notably a general reduction in the overall woody vegetation cover – i.e. clearance; this being most obviously the case for Greenland and Iceland – and an expansion in plant communities representative of the hayfields and pastures that were such a crucial element of the subsistence (pastoral) farming system that the incoming people relied upon. Modes of clearance seem to have varied, with both manual removal (cutting/felling) and burning of in situ scrub vegetation, probably used to create space for farms and hayfields and to extend pastures. In this respect the introduction of domesticated herbivores must undoubtedly also have had a widespread impact on vegetation, with grazing by sheep and goats reducing the coverage of low scrub and hindering the regeneration of trees and shrubs. The drawdown on the protective cover that woody vegetation provided for soils appears to have led to increased soil erosion. This effect was probably compounded in the areas around farms where there was also stripping of turf to provide construction material for the walls and roofs of buildings (Roussell 1941; Edwards et al. 2011; Schofield and Edwards 2016).

Disturbance of natural vegetation communities and soils presented opportunities for the expansion of a suite of herbs (some native, others introduced), particularly around the farmsteads. Plants that are typically more visible and abundant after *landnám* include: *Achillea* spp.; *Capsella bursa-pastoris*; members of the Lactuceae; *Plantago lanceolata* (the Faroe Islands and Iceland only); *Polygonum aviculare*; *Rhinanthus*; *Rumex* spp.; and *Stellaria media*. In particular, *landnám* appears to have favoured the expansion of the Polygonaceae, some of which almost certainly arrived with the first Norse settlers and subsequently became naturalized (e.g. *Rumex acetosella* in the Eastern Settlement of Greenland; Schofield et al. 2013). There is no evidence for any extirpations from the floras, but a number of grazing sensitive herbs (e.g. *Angelica* spp., *Filipendula*) are less apparent in pollen records after *landnám* and may have suffered as a result of the appearance of domesticated animals.

There has been considerable debate (and it must be said, little overall agreement) amongst phytogeographers and palaeoecologists as to exactly which plants were introduced by the Norse settlers, and this may continue into the foreseeable future. Palynology is critical in providing the necessary historical perspective required for tracing the emergence and spread of 'Old Norse' elements in the North Atlantic flora, but one of the key limitations of the technique is that not all pollen types can be confidently identified to the species level. This leaves a degree of uncertainty in vegetation reconstructions. Plant macrofossil analysis potentially offers improved precision surrounding identifications but is not without its own limitations (Birks and Birks 1980). Macroscopic plant tissues (seeds, leaves, etc.) do not disperse far from source and may not be preserved in humified deposits/contexts that otherwise contain pollen and spores drawn from the surrounding vegetation. Ancient DNA of palynomorphs and sediments might be expected to advance taxonomic precision and floristic comprehensiveness in the future (cf. Parducci et al. 2013; Pedersen et al. 2013).

What Role for Climate?

One of the challenges that palaeoecologists often face when attempting to assign causality to vegetation changes is disentangling the effects of human impact from those of climate. The Norse *landnám* undoubtedly led to a significant and sustained impression on the vegetation communities of the Faroe Islands and large parts of Iceland and southwest Greenland (as this review has outlined). However, what discernible role, if any, did climatic changes play in shaping vegetation communities at the same time?

The Norse colonization of the North Atlantic islands coincided with an interval of generally improved temperatures – the 'Medieval Warm Period' (MWP), defined as covering the ninth to fourteenth centuries CE (sensu Hughes and Diaz 1994) – followed by a significant deterioration – the 'Little Ice Age' (LIA), conventionally the period 1550–1850 CE (Matthews and Briffa 2005) – although the timing of both episodes was geographically asynchronous (the effects of the LIA appear to have been felt much earlier in Greenland, for example, where it probably played an important role in the abandonment of the Western Settlement ca. 1350 CE; Barlow et al. 1997). The effects of the MWP are perhaps best reflected in the apparent healthy coverage of *Betula* woodland in Iceland and Greenland immediately prior to the arrival of people. As noted, woodland and scrub was to decline significantly following the arrival of the Norse, but the onset of a decrease in temperature from a nadir occurring around the turn of the second millennium CE (cf. Dugmore et al. 2007b) would also have been unfavourable for the persistence of North Atlantic birch woodlands over the longer term. Similarly, in the Faroe Islands, the gradual replacement of *Calluna* heathlands with grasslands as a consequence of intensive grazing was perhaps assisted by climatic deterioration (Dugmore et al. 2007a). Thus the consequences of climatic changes may, in certain cases, have been to contribute to humanly driven vegetation transformations, perhaps in rather subtle ways that are not easily measured or separated from anthropogenic signals.

Conclusions

The effects of Norse settlement on the vegetation of the Faroe Islands, Iceland and Greenland were first recognized in the outcomes presented by several pioneering pollen-analytical studies that addressed the subject (e.g. Thorarinsson 1944; Einarsson 1963; Fredskild 1973; Jóhansen 1985). These revealed evidence for woodland destruction, the expansion of graminoid plant communities, the appearance and proliferation of a suite of herbaceous taxa that might generically be categorized as 'weeds' and elevated levels of soil erosion (to list just some of the impacts following *landnám*). Over recent years, the number of palaeoecological investigations along the same theme has expanded and this has allowed ideas arising from the earlier investigations to be tested, confirmed and refined. Consequently, we now know that the impacts of *landnám* on vegetation do appear to have been broadly similar across that region of the North Atlantic featured in this review, yet when patterns are observed at a finer scale, as one might expect, there are subtle differences in the Norse 'footprint' (sensu Edwards et al. 2011a), which varied according to the interplay of the climatic, pedogenic, topographic and anthropogenic factors that characterized each location.

Acknowledgements

The authors thank the Leverhulme Trust, Rannís and the Universities of Aberdeen and Iceland for financial support, Ian Lawson and Davide Zori for providing photographs and Alison Sandison for assistance with artwork.

References

Andersen, S.T. (1979). Identification of wild grass and cereal pollen. *Danmarks Geologiske Undersøgelse, Årbog* 1978: 69–92.

Barlow, L.K., Sadler, J.P., Ogilvie, A.E.J. et al. (1997). Interdisciplinary investigations of the end of the Norse Western Settlement in Greenland. *The Holocene* 7: 489–499.

Barrett, J.H. (ed.) (2003). Contact, Continuity, and Collapse: The Norse Colonization of the North Atlantic. Turnhout: Brepols.

Behre, K.-E. (1981). The interpretation of anthropogenic indicators in pollen diagrams. *Pollen et Spores* 23: 225–245.

Behre, K.-E. (1988). The rôle of man in European vegetation history. In: Vegetation History (eds. B. Huntley and T. Webb III), 633–672. Dordrecht: Kluwer.

Benediktsson, J. (ed.) (1968) *Íslendingabók. Landnámabók* (*Book of Icelanders, Book of Settlements*). Íslenzk fornrit 1. Reykjavík: Hið íslenzka fornritafélag.

Birks, H.J.B. and Birks, H.H. (1980). Quaternary Palaeoecology. London: Edward Arnold.

Böcher, T.W. (1979). Birch woodlands and tree growth in southern Greenland. *Holarctic Ecology* 2: 218–221.

Böcher, T.W., Holmer, K., and Jakobsen, K. (1968). The Flora of Greenland. Copenhagen: P. Haase & Son.

Borthwick, D.M. 2007. The timing and impact of the Norse Landnám on the vegetation of Hovsdalur, Faroe Islands. Unpublished PhD Thesis, University of Aberdeen.

Borthwick, D.M., Edwards, K.J. and Cook, G. (2006). Shieling activity during the Norse period in the Faroe Islands: a palynological approach. In: J. Arneborg and B. Grønnow (eds), *The Dynamics of Northern Societies. Proceedings of the*

SILA/NABO Conference on Arctic and North Atlantic Archaeology, Copenhagen, 2004. Copenhagen: PNM, Publications from the National Museum, Studies in Archaeology and History, Vol. 10, pp. 299–306.

Brochmann, C., Gabrielsen, T.M., Nordal, I. et al. (2003). Glacial survival or tabula rasa? The history of North Atlantic biota revisited. *Taxon* 52: 417–450.

Buckland, P.C., Edwards, K.J., Panagiotakopulu, E., and Schofield, J.E. (2009). Palaeoecological and historical evidence for manuring and irrigation at *Garðar* (Igaliku), Norse Eastern Settlement, Greenland. *The Holocene* 19: 105–116.

Bunting, M.J., Schofield, J.E., and Edwards, K.J. (2013). Estimates of relative pollen productivity (RPP) for selected taxa from southern Greenland: a pragmatic solution. *Review of Palaeobotany and Palynology* 190: 66–74.

Byock, J. and Zori, D. (2012) The Mosfell Archaeological Project research report 2012. Unpublished report, Reykjavík, The Mosfell Archaeological Project.

Callow, C. and Evans, C. (2016). The mystery of plague in medieval Iceland. *Journal of Medieval History* 42: 254–284.

Caseldine, C. (2001). Changes in *Betula* in the Holocene pollen record from Iceland – a palaeoclimatic record or evidence for early Holocene hybridisation? *Review of Palaeobotany and Palynology* 117: 139–152.

Church, M.J., Dugmore, A.J., Mairs, K.A. et al. (2007). Charcoal production during the Norse and early Medieval periods in Eyjafjallahreppur, southern Iceland. *Radiocarbon* 49: 659–672.

Church, M.J., Arge, S.V., Edwards, K.J. et al. (2013). The Vikings were not the first colonizers of the Faroe Islands. *Quaternary Science Reviews* 77: 228–232.

Dahl, E. (1959). Amfiatlantiske planter. Problems of amphi-Atlantic plant distribution. *Blyttia* 16: 93–121.

Davis, A.M., McAndrews, J.H., and Wallace, B.L. (1988). Palaeoenvironment and the archaeological record at the L'Anse aux Meadows site, Newfoundland. *Geoarchaeology* 3: 53–64.

Dugmore, A.J., Church, M.J., Buckland, P.C. et al. (2005). The Norse *landnám* on the North Atlantic islands: an environmental impact assessment. *Polar Record* 41: 21–37.

Dugmore, A.J., Borthwick, D.M., Church, M.J. et al. (2007a). The role of climate in settlement and landscape change in the North Atlantic islands: an assessment of cumulative deviations in high-resolution proxy records. *Human Ecology* 35: 169–178.

Dugmore, A.J., Keller, C., and McGovern, T.H. (2007b). Norse Greenland settlement: reflections on climate change, trade, and the contrasting fates of human settlements in the North Atlantic islands. *Arctic Anthropology* 44: 12–36.

Eddudóttir, S.D., Erlendsson, E., and Gísladóttir, G. (2015). Life on the periphery is tough: vegetation in Northwest Iceland and its responses to early-Holocene warmth and later climate fluctuations. *The Holocene* 25: 1437–1453.

Eddudóttir, S.D., Erlendsson, E., Tinganelli, L., and Gísladóttir, G. (2016). Climate change and human impact in a sensitive ecosystem: the Holocene environment of the Northern Icelandic highland. *Boreas* 45: 715–728.

Edwards, K.J. (1996). A Mesolithic of the Western and Northern Isles of Scotland? Evidence from pollen and charcoal. In: The Early Prehistory of Scotland (eds. T. Pollard and A. Morrison), 23–38. Edinburgh: Edinburgh University Press.

Edwards, K.J. (2008). Juniper, goats and the Norse: did the decline of *Juniperus* in the Faroe Islands have a human cause? In: Símunarbók. Heiðursrit til Símun V. Arge á 60 ára degnum (eds. C. Paulsen and H.D. Michelsen), 58–71. Tórshavn: Fróðskapur, Faroe University Press.

Edwards, K.J. (2013). Pollen-analytical studies at Toftanes. *Acta Archaeologica* 84: 150–157.

Edwards, K.J. (2014). Early farming, pollen and landscape impacts from northern Europe to the North Atlantic: conundrums. In: Northern

Worlds – Landscapes, Interactions and Dynamics, vol. 22 (ed. H.C. Gulløv), 189–201. Copenhagen: PNM, Publications from the National Museum Studies in Archaeology & History.

Edwards, K.J. and Borthwick, D.M. (2010). The pollen content of so-called 'ancient' field systems in Suðuroy, Faroe Islands, and the question of cereal cultivation. In: Dorete – Her Book – Being a Tribute to Dorete Bloch and to Faroese Nature, Annales Societatis Scientiarum Færoensis, Suppl. 52. (eds. S.-A. Bengtson, P.C. Buckland, P.H. Enckell and A.M. Fosaa), 96–116. Tórshavn: Fróðskapur, Faroe University Press.

Edwards, K.J. and Fosaa, A.M. (2017). Faroe Islands. In: Mires and Peatlands of Europe. Status, Distribution and Nature Conservation (eds. H. Joosten, F. Tanneberger and A. Moen), 372–375. Stuttgart: Schweizerbart Science Publishers.

Edwards, K.J., Buckland, P.C., Craigie, R. et al. (1998). Landscapes at landnám: palynological and palaeoentomological evidence from Toftanes, Faroe Islands. *Fróðskaparrit* 48: 229–244.

Edwards, K.J., Borthwick, D., Cook, G. et al. (2005). A hypothesis-based approach to landscape change in Suðuroy, Faroe Islands. *Human Ecology* 33: 621–650.

Edwards, K.J., Schofield, J.E., and Mauquoy, D. (2008). High resolution paleoenvironmental and chronological investigations of Norse *landnám* at Tasiusaq, Eastern Settlement, Greenland. *Quaternary Research* 69: 1–15.

Edwards, K.J., Erlendsson, E., and Schofield, J.E. (2011a). Is there a Norse 'footprint' in North Atlantic pollen records? In: Viking Settlements and Society: Papers from the Sixteenth Viking Congress, Reykjavík and Reykholt, 16–23 August 2009 (eds. S. Sigmundsson, A. Holt, G. Sigurðsson, et al.), 65–82. Reykjavík: Hið íslenska fornleifafélag and University of Iceland Press.

Edwards, K.J., Schofield, J.E., Kirby, J.R., and Cook, G.T. (2011b). Problematic but promising ponds? Palaeoenvironmental evidence from the Norse Eastern Settlement of Greenland. *Journal of Quaternary Science* 26: 854–865.

Edwards, K.J., Schofield, J.E., Cook, G.T., and Nyegaard, G. (2013). Towards a first chronology for the Middle Settlement of Norse Greenland: ^{14}C and related studies of animal bone and environmental material. *Radiocarbon* 55: 13–29.

Edwards, K.J., Schofield, J.E., and Craigie, R. (2016). Norse landscape impacts: Northern Isles *versus* the North Atlantic islands. In: Shetland and the Viking World. Papers from the Seventeenth Viking Congress, Lerwick (eds. V.E. Turner, O.A. Owen and D.J. Waugh), 77–84. Lerwick: Shetland Heritage Publications.

Edwards, K.J., Stummann Hansen, S. and Bjarnason, B. (2011). A scalped peatscape on Nólsoy, Faroe Islands. *Fróðskaparrit* 59: 122–132.

Einarsson, T. (1963). Pollen-analytical studies on the vegetation and climate history of Iceland in late and post-glacial times. In: North Atlantic Biota and Their History (eds. A. Love and D. Love), 355–365. New York: Macmillan.

Eiríksson, J., Bartels-Jónsdóttir, H.B., Cage, A.G. et al. (2006). Variability of the North Atlantic current during the last 2000 years based on shelf bottom water and sea surface temperature along an open ocean/shallow marine transect in western Europe. *The Holocene* 16: 1017–1029.

Erlendsson, E. (2007) Environmental change around the time of the Norse settlement of Iceland. Unpublished PhD Thesis, University of Aberdeen.

Erlendsson, E. and Edwards, K.J. (2009). The timing and causes of the pre-settlement expansion of *Betula pubescens* in Iceland. *The Holocene* 19: 1083–1091.

Erlendsson, E., Edwards, K.J., and Buckland, P.C. (2009). Vegetational response to human colonisation of the volcanic and coastal environments of Ketilsstaðir, southern Iceland. *Quaternary Research* 72: 174–187.

Erlendsson, E., Vickers, K., Bending, J.M. et al. (2012). Late-Holocene environmental history of the Reykholt area, Borgarfjörður, western Iceland. In: From Nature to Script (eds. H. Þorláksson and Þ.B. Sigurðardóttir), 17–47. Reykholt: Snorrastofa.

Erlendsson, E., Edwards, K.J., Vickers, K. et al. (2018). The palaeoecology and cultural landscapes associated with Reykholt. In: Snorri Sturluson and Reykholt. The Author and Magnate, His Life, Works and Environment at Reykholt in Iceland (eds. H. Þorláksson and G. Sveinbjarnardóttir), 161–203. Copenhagen: Museum Tusculanum Press.

Feilberg, J. (1984). A phytogeographical study of South Greenland. Vascular plants. *Meddelelser om Grønland, Bioscience* 15: 1–70.

Fitzhugh, W.W. and Ward, E.I. (eds.) (2000). Vikings: The North Atlantic Saga. Washington: Smithsonian Institution.

Fosaa, A.M. (2001). A review of plant communities of the Faroe Islands. *Fróðskaparrit* 48: 41–54.

Fredskild, B. (1973). Studies in the vegetational history of Greenland. *Meddelelser om Grønland* 198: 1–245.

Fredskild, B. (1978). Palaeobotanical investigations of some peat deposits of Norse age at Qagssiarssuk, South Greenland. *Meddelelser om Grønland* 204: 1–41.

Fredskild, B. (1983). The Holocene vegetational development of the Godthåbsfjord area, West Greenland. *Meddelelser om Grønland, Geoscience* 10: 1–28.

Fredskild, B. (1988). Agriculture in a marginal area – South Greenland from the Norse *landnám* (985 A.D.) to the present (1985 A.D.). In: The Cultural Landscape – Past, Present and Future (eds. H.H. Birks, H.J.B. Birks, P.E. Kaland and D. Moe), 381–393. Cambridge: Cambridge University Press.

Fredskild, B. (1996). A phytogeographical study of the vascular plants of West Greenland (62°20′–74°00′ N). *Meddelelser om Grønland, Bioscience* 45: 1–157.

Fredskild, B. and Humle, L. (1991). Plant remains from the Norse farm Sandnes in the Western settlement, Greenland. *Acta Borealia* 1: 69–81.

Gathorne-Hardy, F.J., Lawson, I.T., Church, M.J. et al. (2007). The Chironomidae of Gróthúsvatn, Sandoy, Faroe Islands: climatic and lake phosphorus reconstructions, and the impact of human settlement. *The Holocene* 17: 1259–1264.

Gathorne-Hardy, F.G., Erlendsson, E., Langdon, P., and Edwards, K.J. (2009). Lake sediment evidence for climate change and landscape erosion in western Iceland. *Journal of Paleolimnology* 42: 413–426.

Gauthier, E., Bichet, V., Massa, C. et al. (2010). Pollen and non-pollen palynomorph evidence of medieval farming activities in southwestern Greenland. *Vegetation History and Archaeobotany* 19: 427–438.

Geikie, J. (1880). On the geology of the Faroe Islands. *Transactions of the Royal Society of Edinburgh* 30: 217–269.

Gísladóttir, G., Erlendsson, E., Lal, R., and Bigham, J.M. (2010). The effect of soil erosion on soil organic carbon and terrestrial resources over the last millennium in Reykjanes, Southwest Iceland. *Quaternary Research* 73: 20–32.

Godwin, H. (1975). The History of the British Flora: A Factual Basis for Phytogeography, 2e. Cambridge: Cambridge University Press.

Golding, K.A., Simpson, I.A., Schofield, J.E., and Edwards, K.J. (2011). Norse-Inuit interaction and landscape change in southern Greenland? A geochronological, pedological, and palynological investigation. *Geoarchaeology* 26: 315–345.

Grønnow, B. and Sørensen, M. (2006). Paleo-Eskimo migrations into Greenland: the Canadian connection. In: Dynamics of Northern Societies. PNM Studies in Archaeology and History, vol. 10 (eds. J. Arneborg and B. Grønnow), 59–74. Copenhagen: National Museum.

Grove, J. (1988). The Little Ice Age. London: Methuen.

Guðmundsson, G. (1996). Gathering and processing of lyme-grass (*Elymus arenarius* L.) in Iceland: an ethnohistorical account. *Vegetation History and Archaeobotany* 5: 13–23.

Guðmundsson, G. (2010). The plant remains. In: Hofstaðir: Excavations of a Viking Age Feasting Hall in North-Eastern Iceland, Institute of Archaeology Monograph Series, vol. 1 (ed. G. Lucas), 322–334. Reykjavík: Fornleifastofnun Íslands.

Guldager Christiansen, H. and Fosaa, A.M. (2009). Færøernes ældste kulturplanter. *Fróðskaparrit* 57: 128–149.

Hallsdóttir, M. (1982). Frjógreining tveggja jarðvegssniða úr Hrafnkelsdal. Áhrif ábúðar á gróðurfar dalsins. In: Eldur er í norðri (eds. H. Þórarinsdóttir, Ó.H. Óskarsson, S. Steinþórsson and Þ. Einarsson (eds)), 253–265. Reykjavík: Sögufélag.

Hallsdóttir, M. (1987) Pollen analytical studies of human influence on vegetation in relation to the Landnám tephra layer in southwest Iceland. Lundqua Thesis 18. Lund University.

Hallsdóttir, M. and Caseldine, C. (2005). The Holocene vegetation history of Iceland, state-of-the-art and future research. In: Iceland: Modern Processes and Past Environments (eds. C. Caseldine, A. Russel, J. Harðardóttir and Ó. Knudsen), 319–334. Amsterdam: Elsevier.

Hannon, G.E. and Bradshaw, R.H.W. (2000). Impacts and timing of the first human settlement on vegetation of the Faroe Islands. *Quaternary Research* 54: 404–413.

Hannon, G.E. and Bradshaw, R.H.W. (2007). Human impact and landscape change at Argisbrekka. In: Sæteren ved Argisbrekka – Økonomiske forandringer på Færøerne i vikingetid og tidlig middelalder. Annales Societatis Scientiarum Færoensis Supplementum, vol. 47 (ed. D.L. Mahler), 306–323. Tórshavn: Faroe University Press.

Hannon, G.E., Wastegård, S., Bradshaw, E., and Bradshaw, R.H.W. (2001). Human impact and landscape degradation on Faroe Islands. *Biology and Environment: Proceedings of the Royal Irish Academy* 101B: 129–139.

Hannon, G.E., Bradshaw, R.H.W., Bradshaw, E.G. et al. (2005). Climatic change and human settlement as drivers of late Holocene vegetation change in the Faroe Islands. *The Holocene* 15: 639–647.

Hansen, K. and Jóhansen, J. (1982). Flora and vegetation of the Faroe Islands. *Monographiae Biologicae* 46: 35–52.

Hansom, J.D. and Briggs, D.J. (1989–1990). Pre-landnám *Plantago lanceolata* in north-west Iceland. *Fróskaparrit* 38–39: 69–75.

Havinga, A.J. (1985). A 20-year experimental investigation into the differential corrosion susceptibility of pollen and spores in various soil types. *Pollen et Spores* 26: 541–558.

Helgason, A., Hickey, E., Goodacre, S. et al. (2001). mtDNA and the islands of the North Atlantic: estimating the proportions of Norse and Gaelic ancestry. *American Journal of Human Genetics* 68: 723–737.

Henriksen, P.S. (2012). Agriculture on the edge – the first finds of cereals in Norse Greenland. In: Northern Worlds – Challenges and Solutions (eds. H.C. Gulløv, P.A. Toft and C.P. Hansgaard), 174–177. Copenhagen: National Museum of Denmark.

Hughes, M.K. and Diaz, H.F. (1994). Was there a 'medieval warm period', and if so, where and when? *Climatic Change* 26: 109–142.

Húlten, E. (1958). The amphi-Alantic plants and their phytogeographical connections. *Kungl. Svenska vetenskapsakademiens handlingar*, Series 4 7: 1–340.

Iversen, J. (1934). Moorgeologische untersuchungen auf Grönland. *Meddelelser fra Dansk Geologisk Forening* 8: 341–358.

Iversen, J. (1941). Landnam i Danmarks stenalder (Land occupation in Denmark's Stone Age). *Danmarks Geologiske Undersøgelse*, Series II 66: 1–68.

Iversen, J. (1953). Origin of the flora of western Greenland in the light of pollen analysis. *Oikos* 4: 85–103.

Jóhansen, J. (1971). A palaeobotanical study indicating a pre-Viking settlement in Tjørnuvik, Faroe Islands. *Fróðskaparrit* 19: 147–157.

Jóhansen, J. (1979). Cereal cultivation in Mykines, Faroe Islands AD 600. *Danmarks Geølogiske Årbog* 1978: 93–103.

Jóhansen, J. (1985) Studies in the vegetational history of the Faroe and Shetland Islands. *Annales Societatis Scientiarum Færoensis Supplementum*, 11. Tórshavn: Føroya Fróðskaparfelag.

Jóhansen, J. (1986–1987). Joansokugras (*Plantago lanceolata*) og forsogulig buseting i Foroyum (*Plantago lanceolata* in the Faroe Islands and its significance as indicator of prehistoric settlement). *Fróskaparrit* 34–35: 68–75.

Jóhansen, J. (2000). Føroysk flora. A.M. Fosaa and S. Rasmussen (eds). Tórshavn: Føroya Skúlabókagrunnur.

Jónsson, S.A., Eggertsson, Ó., and Ingólfsson, Ó. (2012). Skógarsaga Fljótsdalshéraðs síðustu 2000 árin. *Náttúrufræðingurinn* 82: 87–97.

Karlsson, G. (1996). Plague without rats: the case of fifteenth century Iceland. *Journal of Medieval History* 22: 263–284.

Kristinsson, H. (1986). The Flowering Plants and Ferns of Iceland. Reykjavík: Örn og Örlygur.

Krogh, K.J. (1967). Viking Greenland. Copenhagen: National Museum of Denmark.

Larsen, A.-C. (1991). Norsemen's use of juniper in Viking Age Faroe Islands. *Acta Archaeologica* 61: 54–59.

Larson, L.C. (tr.) (1917). The King's Mirror (Speculum Regale – Konungs Skuggsjá). New York: American-Scandinavian Foundation.

Lawson, I.T., Church, M.J., McGovern, T.H. et al. (2005). Historical ecology on Sandoy, Faroe Islands: palaeoenvironmental and archaeological perspectives. *Human Ecology* 33: 651–684.

Lawson, I.T., Church, M.J., Edwards, K.J. et al. (2007a). Peat initiation in the Faroe Islands: climate or people? *Earth and Environmental Science Transactions of the Royal Society of Edinburgh* 98: 15–28.

Lawson, I.T., Gathorne-Hardy, F.J., Church, M.J. et al. (2007b). Environmental impacts of the Norse settlement: palaeoenvironmental data from Mývatnssveit, northern Iceland. *Boreas* 36: 1–19.

Lawson, I.T., Edwards, K.J., Church, M.J. et al. (2008). Human impact on an island ecosystem: pollen data from Sandoy, Faroe Islands. *Journal of Biogeography* 35: 1130–1152.

Lawson, I.T., Milek, K.B., Adderley, W.P. et al. (2010). The palaeoenvironment of Mývatnssveit during the Viking age and early medieval period. In: Hofstaðir. Excavations of a Viking Age Feasting Hall in North-Eastern Iceland, Institute of Archaeology Monograph Series, vol. 1 (ed. G. Lucas), 26–54. Reykjavík: Fornleifastofnun Íslands.

Ledger, P.M. (2013) Norse landnám and its impact on the vegetation of Vatnahverfi, Eastern Settlement, Greenland. PhD Thesis, University of Aberdeen.

Ledger, P., Edwards, K.J., and Schofield, J.E. (2013). Shieling activity in the Norse eastern settlement: palaeoenvironment of the 'mountain farm', Vatnahverfi, Greenland. *The Holocene* 23: 810–822.

Ledger, P.M., Edwards, K.J., and Schofield, J.E. (2014a). Vatnahverfi: a green and pleasant land? Palaeoecological reconstructions of environmental and land-use change. *Journal of the North Atlantic* 6: 29–46.

Ledger, P.M., Edwards, K.J., and Schofield, J.E. (2014b). A multiple profile approach to the palynological reconstruction of Norse landscapes in Greenland's Eastern Settlement. *Quaternary Research* 82: 22–37.

Ledger, P.M., Edwards, K.J., and Schofield, J.E. (2015). The biogeographical status of *Alnus crispa* (Ait.) Pursch in sub-Arctic southern Greenland: do pollen records indicate local populations during the past 1500 years? *Polar Biology* 39: 433–441.

Löve, Á. and Löve, D. (eds.) (1963). North Atlantic Biota and Their History. Oxford: Pergamon Press.

Mahler, D.L. (2007). Sæteren ved Argisbrekka – Økonomiske forandringer på

Færøerne i vikingetid og tidlig middelalder. Annales Societatis Scientiarum Færoensis Supplementum, 47. Tórshavn: Faroe University Press.

Mainland, I. (2006). Pastures lost? A dental microwear study of ovicaprine diet and management in Norse Greenland. *Journal of Archaeological Science* 33: 238–252.

Malmros, C. (1994). Exploitation of local, drifted and imported wood by the Vikings on the Faroe Islands. *Botanical Journal of Scotland* 46: 552–558.

Martin, S.L. (2014). The recovery and analysis of macrobotanical remains from Hrísbrú. In: Viking Archaeology in Iceland: The Mosfell Archaeological Project (eds. D. Zori and J. Byock), 193–206. Turnhout: Brepols.

Massa, C., Bichet, V., Gauthier, E. et al. (2012). A 2500 year record of natural and anthropogenic soil erosion in South Greenland. *Quaternary Science Reviews* 32: 119–130.

Matthews, J.A. and Briffa, K.R. (2005). The 'Little Ice Age': re-evaluation of an evolving concept. *Geografiska Annaler* 87A: 17–36.

McGhee, R. (2001). Ancient People of the Arctic. Vancouver: UBC Press.

McMullen, J.A. and Edwards, K.J. (2007). The vegetation of grass roofs in the Faroe Islands and the surrounding grassland vegetation – a study from Sandoy. *Fróðskaparrit* 55: 115–125.

Moore, P.D., Webb, J.A., and Collinson, M.E. (1991). Pollen Analysis, 2e. Oxford: Blackwell.

Nordeide, S.W. and Edwards, K.J. 2019. *The Vikings*. Leeds: Arc Humanities Press.

Ostenfeld, C.H. (1905–1908) *The land-vegetation of the Færöes, with special reference to the higher plants. Botany of the Færöes Based upon Danish Investigations*, 3. Copenhagen and Christiania: Gyldendalske Boghandel, Nordisk Forlag; London: John Weldon & Co., pp. 867–1026.

Ostenfeld, C.H. (1926). The flora of Greenland and its origin. *Biologiske Meddelelser Kongelige Danske Videnskabernes Selskab* 6: 1–70.

Panagiotakopulu, E., Schofield, J.E., Vickers, K. et al. (2018). Thule Inuit environmental impacts on Kangeq, southwest Greenland. *Quaternary International* 549: 176–190.

Parducci, L., Matetovici, I., Fontana, S. et al. (2013). Molecular- and pollen-based vegetation analysis in lake sediments from Central Scandinavia. *Molecular Ecology* 22: 3511–3524.

Pedersen, M.W., Ginolhac, A., Orlando, L. et al. (2013). A comparative study of ancient environmental DNA to pollen and macrofossils from lake sediments reveals taxonomic overlap and additional plant taxa. *Quaternary Science Reviews* 75: 161–168.

Perren, B.B., Massa, C., Bichet, V. et al. (2012). A palaeoecological perspective on 1450 years of human impacts from a lake in southern Greenland. *The Holocene* 22: 1025–1034.

Porsild, M.P. (1932). Alien plants and apophytes of Greenland. *Meddelelser om Grønland* 92: 1–85.

Riddell, S.J., Erlendsson, E., Gísladóttir, G. et al. (2018). Cereal cultivation as a correlate of high status in medieval Iceland. *Vegetation History and Archaeobotany* 27: 679–696.

Roussell, A. (1941). Farms and churches in the medieeval Norse settlements of Greenland. *Meddelelser om Grónland* 89: 1–342.

Schofield, J.E. and Edwards, K.J. (2011). Grazing impacts and woodland management in *Eriksfjord*: *Betula*, coprophilous fungi, and the Norse settlement of Greenland. *Vegetation History and Archaeobotany* 20: 181–197.

Schofield, J.E. and Edwards, K.J. (2016). Peat and people in Greenland. In: Shetland and the Viking World. Papers from the Seventeenth Viking Congress, Lerwick (eds. V.E. Turner, O.A. Owen and D.J. Waugh), 91–96. Lerwick: Shetland Heritage Publications.

Schofield, J.E., Edwards, K.J., and Christensen, C. (2008). Environmental impacts around the time of Norse *landnám* in the Qorlortoq valley, Eastern Settlement, Greenland. *Journal of Archaeological Science* 35: 1643–1657.

Schofield, J.E., Edwards, K.J., Erlendsson, E., and Ledger, P.M. (2013). Palynology supports 'Old Norse' introductions to the flora of Greenland. *Journal of Biogeography* 40: 1119–1130.

Schofield, E., Edwards, K.J., and McMullen, A. (2007). Modern pollen-vegetation relationships in subarctic southern Greenland with implications for the interpretation of fossil pollen data from the Norse *landnám*. *Journal of Biogeography* 34: 473–488.

Schofield, J.E., Pearce, D.M., Mair, D.W.F. et al. (2019). Pushing the limits: palynological investigations at the margin of the Greenland ice sheet in the Norse Western Settlement. *Environmental Archaeology,* https://doi.org/10.1080/14614103.2019.1677075.

Small, A. (1991). The juniper decline during the Norse landnam in the Faroe Islands. *Acta Borealia* 9: 3–6.

Stace, C. (2010). New Flora of the British Isles, 3e. Cambridge: Cambridge University Press.

Steindórsson, S. (1964). Gróður á Íslandi. Reykjavík: Almenna bókafélagið.

Streeter, R., Dugmore, A.J., and Vésteinsson, O. (2012). Plague and landscape resilience in pre-modern Iceland. *Proceedings of the National Academy of Sciences of the United States of America* 109: 3664–3669.

Stummann Hansen, S. (ed.) (2013). Toftanes. A Viking age farmstead in the Faroe Islands: archaeology, environment & economy. *Acta Archaeologica* 84 (1): 1–239.

Sulkinoja, M. (1990). Hybridization, introgression and taxonomy of the mountain birch in SW Greenland compared with related results from Iceland and Finnish Lapland. *Meddelelser om Grønland, Bioscience* 33: 21–29.

Sveinbjarnardóttir, G. (2012). Reykholt: Archaeological Investigations at a High Status Farm in Western Iceland. Publications of the National Museum of Iceland 29. Reykjavík and Reykholt: The National Museum of Iceland and Snorrastofa.

Sveinbjarnardóttir, G., Erlendsson, E., Vickers, K. et al. (2007). The palaeoecology of a high-status Icelandic farm. *Environmental Archaeology* 12: 197–216.

Thorarinsson, S. (1944). Tefrokronologiska studier på Island: Þjórsárdalur och dess förödelse. *Geografiska Annaler* 26: 1–217.

Þórhallsdóttir, Þ.E. (1996). Áhrif búsetu á landið. In: Um landnám á Íslandi – fjórtán erindi (ed. G.Á. Grímsdóttir), 149–170. Reykjavík: Vísindafélag Íslendinga.

Tisdall, E., Barclay, R., Nichol, A. et al. (2018). Palaeoenvironmental evidence for woodland conservation in Northern Iceland from settlement to the twentieth century. *Environmental Archaeology* 23: 205–216. https://doi.org/10.1080/14614103.2018.1437105.

Vickers, K., Bending, J., Buckland, P.C. et al. (2005). Toftanes: the paleoecology of a Faroese *landnám* farm. *Human Ecology* 33: 685–710.

Vickers, K., Erlendsson, E., Church, M.J. et al. (2011). 1000 years of environmental change and human impact at Stóra-Mörk, southern Iceland: a multiproxy study of a dynamic and vulnerable landscape. *The Holocene* 21: 979–995.

Wallace, B. (2008). L'Anse aux meadows, Leif Eriksson's home in Vinland. *Journal of the North Atlantic* 2: 114–125.

Wastl, M., Stötter, J., and Caseldine, C. (2001). Reconstruction of Holocene variations of the upper limit of tree or shrub birch growth in northern Iceland based on evidence from Vesturárdalur-Skíðadalur, Tröllaskagi. *Arctic, Antarctic, and Alpine Research* 33: 191–203.

Wöll, C. (2008) Treeline of mountain birch (Betula pubescens Ehrh.) in Iceland and its relationship to temperature. Unpublished MSc Thesis, Technical University Dresden.

Zori, D., Byock, J., Erlendsson, E. et al. (2013). Feasting in Viking age Iceland: sustaining a chiefly political economy in a marginal environment. *Antiquity* 87: 150–165.

10

Origin of the Northeast Atlantic Islands Bird Fauna

Scenarios of Ecosystem Development

Aevar Petersen[1] and Bergur Olsen[2]

[1] *Brautarland 2, Reykjavík, Iceland*
[2] *Faroe Marine Research Institute, Faroe Islands*

Introduction

During the Ice Age glaciations (Pleistocene) the Northeast Atlantic islands were ice-covered, with the final cold phase of the last Glacial period ending some 12–13000 years ago (cf. Gulliksen et al. 1998; Norðdahl et al. 2008). The Pleistocene period must have had a dramatic impact on the composition, abundance and distribution of island faunas, although in what way and how much has caused heated debates such as how geological formations and the extent of ice cover allowed colonization (Willis and Whittaker 2000) and speciation (Avise and Walker 1998). During times of maximum glaciation, the ice cover extended from southern Ireland across the North German Plain into western Russia; separate icecaps occupied more southerly mountains from Spain to the Caucasus (Figure 1, see Plate section). At its maximum, the North American Laurentide icesheet extended south into Illinois and New Jersey (e.g. Siegert 2001).

From the end of the last glacial period bird communities have evolved into present-day faunas.

During the last few centuries, the bird faunas on the Northeast Atlantic islands are mostly well understood while the detailed evolutionary processes of thousands of earlier years are poorly, or at best, fragmentarily known. In Iceland fossil bird remains hardly exist, mainly due to soils being of volcanic origin and low in carbonate (Símonarson 1981), and no fossils have been found in the Faroes.

Islands have definite borders and are therefore well suited for studies of faunal changes. The evolution of faunas is a continuous struggle of external and internal forces at the ecosystem, population and genetic levels (cf. Whittaker et al. 2008). This dynamic process is influenced by various local and global environmental factors. In historic times changes can also be due to direct or indirect anthropogenic stresses, which may necessitate specific conservation actions (see Chapter 14).

Diverse proxy data, abiotic and biotic, can be used to develop likely yet crude scenarios. Certain regions of the Northeast Atlantic islands are believed to have been ice-free during the

Biogeography in the Sub-Arctic: The Past and Future of North Atlantic Biota, First Edition.
Edited by Eva Panagiotakopulu and Jon P. Sadler.
© 2021 John Wiley & Sons Ltd. Published 2021 by John Wiley & Sons Ltd.

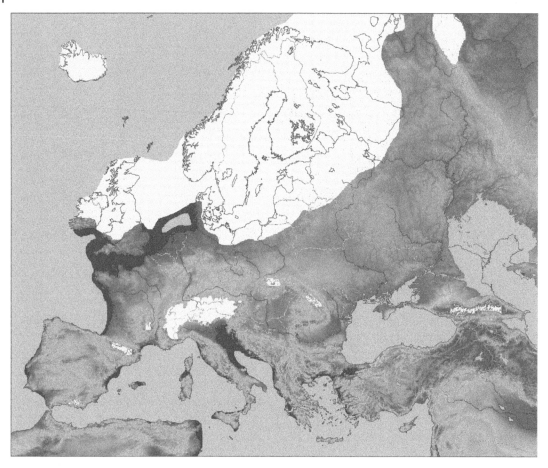

Figure 1 The extent of the Ice Age glaciation about 20 000 years ago. *Source:* San Jose, https://commons. wikimedia.org/wiki/File:Europe_topography_map.png. Licensed under CC BY-SA 3.0. (See colour plate section for colour representation of this figure.)

last Glacial Period, which dramatically changes the whole perspective of community evolution, but this is still debatable (see this volume, Chapter 6. The Faroe Islands were covered with its own ice cap with ice-free mountain tops (Humlum and Christiansen 1998).

The present chapter analyses the bird faunas on two Northeast Atlantic island groups, Iceland (103 000 km^2) and the much smaller Faroe Islands (1400 km^2). The state of knowledge of their evolution, or likely progress, is summarized.

Geological Overview and Climate Regimes

Geologically Iceland is noticeably young, with the oldest strata estimated to be ~16 million years old (Sæmundsson 1980). Coastal areas in West Iceland were the earliest to become ice-free after the last glacial period, 12–13 thousand years ago (Norðdahl et al. 2008). Since that time Iceland has undergone changes in climate (Ogilvie 1984;

Massé et al. 2008; Geirsdóttir et al. 2009), affecting both vegetation and fauna (Grímsson and Símonarson 2008). Bird populations have in turn been influenced by these processes, although both present-day floral and faunal communities are also formed through interactions of the biota (cf. Ellis 2005; Petersen 2009).

After the last Glacial Period, a generally warm period lasted for 5–6 millennia, followed by cooling and ice-cap developments, but with a warmer period again in the early Christian period. After the warm spell during the Settlement (Landnám) period, 1100 years ago, climate deteriorated with variably cold periods during the Little Ice Age 1300–1900 (Ogilvie 1990; Ogilvie and Jónsson 2001; Ogilvie, Hill and Demarée, Chapter 12 in this volume; Geirsdóttir et al. 2009; Ingólfsson et al. 2010). Climate amelioration was particularly rapid during the early twentieth century although this process started with fluctuations from around 1650 (Mann and Jones 2003).

Various geological events, such as land rise due to ice cap melting and volcanic eruptions, are likely to have influenced the development of the early biota. The overall climate has had probable similar influences in Iceland and the Faroe Islands but this theory is not so important concerning birds as e.g. plant communities. The most likely influencing factor on the development of the present-day fauna is, if parts of land were ice-free during the last glaciation period – a long-standing debate by scientists (Willis and Whittaker 2000). This was the case for Faroes while ice-free areas in Iceland have proved more debatable.

An environmental event following the end of the Ice Age was isostatic rise in Iceland. The Weichselian ice sheet put such pressure on land that this has ever since been rising (Caseldine et al. 2005). As the ice masses retreated, terrestrial habitats expanded; the extensive southern lowlands for instance were still water locked around

10 000 years ago (Norðdahl and Pétursson 2005; Geirsdóttir et al. 2009; Geirsdóttir 2011). Furthermore, due to the volcanic rift, created by plate tectonics, from the southwest to northeast, the area of Iceland expands by some 2.5 cm a year (USGS 2013). The increased size of terrestrial habitats through the ages probably did not affect the species structure of bird communities that much, rather the size of different bird populations, given similar diversity in habitats.

The Faroe Islands are geologically much older than Iceland. They were formed by volcanic activity during the Tertiary, about 50–60 million years ago (Rasmussen and Noe-Nygaard 1970). They consist of 18 islands with a total area of 1400 km^2 (only 1.3% of that of Iceland) located on a ridge between Scotland and Iceland. The distance to Shetland is 300 km, to Iceland 440 km and to Norway 585 km. During the last glacial period, the Faroe Islands were covered with an ice cap, distinct from the ice cap covering continental northern Europe and the ice cap covering Iceland and Greenland. Possibly the highest mountain peaks protruded from the ice, forming nunataks (Humlum 1996; Rasmussen 2002). These nunataks are thought to be refugia for some arctic plants, which were able to survive there (Fosaa 2001). In present times the climate is highly oceanic with cool summers and mild winters. It is humid, variable, and windy.

Since the termination of Tertiary volcanic activity, coastal erosion has gradually reduced the area of the islands, simultaneous with their slow sinking into the crust due to cooling and isostatic effects. A regional mapping of glacial striae indicates that several local ice caps accumulated in the Faroes during the Late Weichselian (25 000–13 000 BP), covering the landscape up to about 700 m above sea level in the north-central part of the islands and extending beyond the present coastline on to the surrounding shelf (Jørgensen and Rasmussen 1986).

During the Ice Age the sea level was 100–150 m lower than today and most of the shelf was above sea level (Humlum 1996). A postglacial sea level rise of about 125–130 m is assumed (Pirazzoli 1996), resulting in the productive Faroe Shelf waters, which now are the stronghold for Faroese seabirds in the breeding season. After the Ice Age the shoreline thus would have been much longer than today and during the sea level rose, the Faroe Shelf and the fjords would have been shallower and potentially better suited for sea-ducks and waders than today.

Origin of Bird Fauna

Birds are more mobile than most animal groups. To date, around 399 and 326 species have been recorded, respectively, in Iceland (per 2017) and the Faroes (per 2018), besides various subspecies.

The first Icelandic bird list stems from around 1590 (Einarsson 1971) and only mentions about 30 species. The first Faroese list dates from 1673 and mentions 28 species (Debes 1673). Figure 2 shows the number of bird species recorded in Iceland and the Faroe Islands since written sources became available. In the seventeenth century more birds were recorded in Iceland than in the Faroe Islands but from 1850 to 1950 more birds were recorded in the Faroe Islands. This reflects the higher ornithological activity and interest for new species in the Faroes in this period compared to Iceland (Salomonsen 1935). In Iceland, the greatest increase in numbers of recorded species took place during the past decades, when there was an exponential increase, so now there are recorded about 70 species more in Iceland than in the Faroe Islands. Even so, nowadays one or two new species are recorded each year in both island groups but due to the great difference in size more

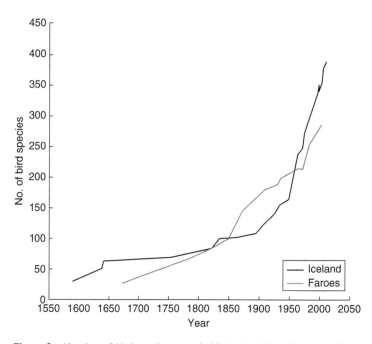

Figure 2 Number of bird species recorded in Iceland (black) and the Faroe Islands (grey) since written sources became available in the sixteenth and seventeenth century, respectively. The figure is from many diverse sources.

species are expected to be recorded in Iceland, which holds twice as many breeding species as the Faroe Islands.

A general knowledge of birdlife has escalated since the middle of the twentieth century, with increased numbers of birdwatchers and better opportunities to record and identify new species. Other reasons include species distributions abroad that have changed with time.

It has been hypothesized that most of the biota colonized Iceland after the last (Weichselian) glacial period (Sadler 1999, Kristinsson 2015). The vegetation history after this period is better known than that of the fauna (Norðdahl et al. 2008; Denk et al. 2011). The extent of glaciation and the size of refugia would have influenced the faunal development. During the Pleistocene, refugia are believed to have influenced the divergence of birds (Avise and Walker 1998). Great Black-backed Gulls *Larus marinus*[1] and Glaucous Gulls *L. hyperboreus* are known to have nested on glaciers and ice-cap bound nunataks in Iceland (Björnsson 1976, 2005; Friðriksson 1979). Therefore, even though the whole land mass was ice-covered, some bird species may have bred, as they could have foraged out at sea or scavenged along the glacial shoreline, both in the Faroe Islands and Iceland.

The current regular breeding birds in Iceland are largely of Temperate, Holarctic or Arctic origin (Petersen 1998). Of the 80 regular breeders in Iceland 53% are birds of European origin, 42% have a Holarctic-Arctic distribution, of which 14% show a more Nordic distribution and 10% Holarctic-Temperate origin, while the final 5% are of North American–Greenland origin. Even greater proportions of irregular breeders are of European origin than breeders, or 66%, with the second largest group 10% of European Arctic origin. Three irregular breeders are descendants of escapees from European waterfowl collections where they have established feral populations, one originally Asian (Bar-headed Goose *Anser indicus*) and two North American (Canada Goose

Branta canadensis, Ruddy Duck *Oxyura jamaicensis*). Although vagrants are Holarctic, the fourth irregular breeder was of the North American subspecies (Black Tern *Chlidonias niger surinamensis;* Ólafsson 1983). Some vagrants have been transported to nearby countries from where they have found their way to Iceland, e.g. the Australian Black Swan *Cygnus atratus* and the South American Chilean Flamingo *Phoenicopterus chilensis*. Other vagrants are believed to have been imported (illegally), species such as the Black-throated Green Warbler *Dendroica virens* and the White-crowned Sparrow *Zonotrichia leucophrys*.

By 2018 a total of 326 species and 17 subspecies have been recorded in the Faroe Islands (Olofson and Sörensen 2018), and 79 of them have bred. Forty species with a population larger than 20 pairs breed regularly while 39 species have less than 20 pairs, most of them breeding irregularly. Thirteen species have been introduced or are escaped pets. One of them, the Barnacle Goose, has established a feral population. As in Iceland, the current regular breeding birds in the Faroe Islands are largely of Temperate, Holarctic or Arctic origin. Of the regular breeders, 50% are birds of European origin and 30% have a Holarctic-Arctic distribution. An even greater proportion of the irregular breeders are of European origin, 85%, and the rest are of European–North American and Holarctic–Arctic distribution.

Colonization and Evolution

General Principles of Island Biogeography

The details whereby island communities evolve are subject to general principles of island biogeography; islands generally have fewer species, less competition and greater predation rates (MacArthur and Wilson 2001). Island bird species generally exhibit broader habitat preferences than birds in mainland biota, which thus have greater diversity of ecologically related species. As examples, in Iceland common open land species such as Meadow Pipit *Anthus pratensis* and Snipe *Gallinago gallinago* also occupy shrubs, while Tree Pipit *Anthus trivialis* and Woodcock *Scolopax rusticola* are found in such habitats on the European mainland. The latter species is a very rare breeder in Iceland. Rock Ptarmigan *Lagopus muta* is found from coast to mountains but is elsewhere confined to mountains where Willow Ptarmigan *L. lagopus* occupy lowlands.

According to evolutionary theory island populations are more vulnerable than mainland ones, and species are theoretically more likely to go extinct. Yet no examples exist of extinctions from pre-Landnám in Iceland or the Faroe Islands although this may have taken place. Fossil and sub-fossil bird remains, or evidence are exceedingly rare (Símonarson 1981); the only known from Iceland are gull footprints ca. 5300 years old (Áskelsson 1953) and ca. 12000 years old Common Eider *Somateria mollissima* bones (Ingólfsson 1984). In 2005 sub-fossil bird bones were discovered in Northwest Iceland. They have neither been identified to species nor dated, but Arctic Fox *Vulpes lagopus* bones found at same site, which was a closed cave, were ^{14}C dated to around 3400 years old (Hersteinsson et al. 2007). The bird bones are therefore presumably of similar age. In the Faroes no bird fossils have been found.

Development of the Island Bird Communities

With fossil records hardly existing, the dynamic development of the island bird communities is rather speculative. Evolution of different habitat types is probably important in steering this evolutionary process, be that through speciation or colonization. Through the past millennia the types and magnitude of different habitats have changed, with undoubtedly corresponding changes in the bird fauna.

Development of vegetation communities during the warmer part of the early Holocene following the end of the Ice Age appear to have been slow. Plant cover was discontinuous, developing grasslands at first, then scrub, with open birch woodlands by around 6000 years ago; wetlands forming in the latter part of Holocene (Norðdahl et al. 2008). This scene is not much different from the scene during past centuries, although the extent of the various habitat types may have been different, even variable, through the ages.

Archaeological excavations of middens, with the finding of bird bones, have pushed the knowledge of occurrence of birds further back than available written materials, in Iceland as far back as the Settlement Period, c. 874 (e.g. McGovern 2009) and in the Faroes to the ninth–twelfth centuries (Brewington and McGovern 2008). In the Faroes, bones especially of Puffins *Fratercula arctica* (77%) and Guillemots *Uria* spp. (20%) were found. New archaeological finding in the Faroes places human colonization in the fourth–sixth centuries (Church et al. 2013) but no bird bones have been found from that period. In Iceland dozens of careful excavations from various time periods have revealed around 30 identified bird species (Guðmundsdóttir Beck 2013). The most common ones are Puffin, then Common Guillemots *Uria aalge* or Brünnich's Guillemots *Uria lomvia* (the species could not be separated). Moreover, various geese species are commonly found, as well as domestic geese, also Common Eiders.

Much can be learnt about colonization from Surtsey, an island in Iceland formed by an eruption starting in 1963. Seabirds such as Kittiwakes *Rissa tridactyla* started using the island immediately it surfaced and now around a hundred bird species have been recorded. By 2008 14 bird species had been recorded breeding; at first there were only seabirds but later terrestrial birds arrived when vegetation communities started to develop, and a pair of Ravens *Corvus corax* moved in as a terrestrial omnivore representative (Petersen 2009).

The structure of the ancient bird fauna on the Northeast Atlantic islands may not have changed much. However, the fact that nearly 40% of recorded Icelandic breeders have first bred during the last 100 years indicates that the bird fauna has not been as species-rich as at present times. There are some 43 new species but most of them have not established regular breeding populations. The group of species with the highest proportion of new breeders is the songbirds (Passeriformes), with about 67% of the breeding species present. Of the different bird groups seabirds include the fewest new breeders, with just nearly 30% recently and some species most likely to have survived the glacial period.

The reasons for immigration are varied. Most of the seabirds (seven) are gulls, which have shown huge range changes in their traditional breeding areas in Europe, mostly due to human influences. Humans have also played a major part by creating different habitats, e.g. urban and plantation habitats, mostly favoured by passerines. Better observations are also important here as especially irregular breeders are likely to have attempted to colonize in centuries past without being observed. There is also the establishment of feral populations in neighbouring countries that have 'spilled over' to Iceland.

The various bird groups may have colonized the country at different times after the Last Glaciation. The physical and biological processes involved suggest the following scenario: seabirds colonized first (some may never have left during the glacial period), followed by open dry land species, such as the Golden Plover *Pluvialis apricaria*. With the increase of scrub, northern passerine species, e.g. the Redwing *Turdus iliacus*, may have arrived. Lastly, with the increase in mire areas, the freshwater waterfowl and waders were probably the last bird groups to colonize the islands. Although much the same species as at present may have been involved in traditional habitats, the different populations may have varied in size with time.

Unique Identities

In contrast to the much older Pacific islands, the Northeast Atlantic islands have no endemic bird species (Sadler 1999). No new bird species are known to have evolved from the times Iceland and the Faroes became ice-free from the glacial ice shields. The time period is possibly too short, although many species, water birds as well as land birds have been resident sufficiently long to evolve some unique identities. Usually the island subspecies tend to be larger than mainland ones (see, for example, Salomonsen 1935; Engelmoer and Roselaar 1998).

Icelandic Subspecies

These have been described for a number of regular breeders, e.g. the Iceland Falcon (subspecies *islandicus*), Merlin (*subaesalon*), Rock Ptarmigan (*islandorum*), Oystercatcher (*malagophaga*), Golden Plover (*altifrons*), Common Ringed Plover (*psammodroma*), Whimbrel (*islandicus*), Black-tailed Godwit (*islandica*), Common Redshank (*robusta*), Common Snipe (*faeroensis*), Common Puffin (*arctica*), Razorbill (*islandica*), Black Guillemot (*islandicus*), Wren (*islandicus*), Wheatear (*leucorhoa*), Redwing (*coburni*), Redpoll (*islandica*), and Snow Bunting (*insulae*). Some of these subspecies are restricted to Iceland, or the Faroe Islands and Iceland, sometimes even further afield in the neighbouring countries, both Greenland and Scandinavia. The status and difference from mainland races are still questionable for many of these subspecies, awaiting more rigorous scrutiny using modern methodologies and evolutionary ideas. Subspecies *Carduelis flammea islandica* of the Redpoll, for instance, have been considered synonymous with mainland *rostrata*, although they tend to have a smaller bill and paler plumage (Herremanns 1990). Other subspecies of, for example, the Black-tailed Godwit *Limosa limosa*, Redshank *Tringa totanus*, Wren *Troglodytes troglodytes* and Redwing are identifiable in the field, using colouration and size. Subspecies separation in the Puffin is highly questionable, as their difference in size represents a cline rather than clearly separated entities (Petersen 1976). A recent study on the Icelandic Redwing (subspecies *coburni*) indicates that separation from the European nominate race (*iliacus iliacus*) took place after the last glacial period (Vignisson 2012). Although considered of the same subspecies, the Icelandic Goosander *Mergus merganser*, is genetically different from mainland birds, and should therefore be delineated as a separate population (Hefti-Gautschi et al. 2009). Thies et al. (2018) have recently confirmed the validity of the Icelandic subspecies of Common Ringed Plover (*Charadrius hiaticula psammodroma*). Evolution towards speciation is clearly quite variable from species to species.

Faroese Subspecies

The Faroese bird fauna is in many instances like that in Iceland, with some species belonging to the same subspecies and populations. Due to the much larger area of habitats in Iceland, the breeders here make up most of the common populations. Species that occur with distinct subspecies in Iceland and the Faroes include the Common Snipe (*faeroeensis*), Whimbrel (*islandicus*), Common Redshank (*robusta*), and Redwing (*coburni*). The European Oystercatcher on these islands is also sometimes considered a separate subspecies (*malacophaga*), although not generally recognized by some present workers (van de Pol et al. 2014). The resident species in the Faroes, Eider (*faeroeensis*), Black Guillemot (*faeroeensis*), Wren (*borealis*) and Starling (*faroensis*), are all considered as Faroese subspecies.

Immigration

Seabirds have most likely been the first birds to colonize the Northeast Atlantic islands, if some of them were not present during the Ice Age. Some gulls may have bred on nunataks while others like the Kittiwake, Common Guillemots, Puffins and Eiders probably started to breed as soon as some coastlines became ice free. The history of the immigration and colonization is only known during the last centuries and although the islands have been ice-free for thousands of years new bird species are still immigrating. It therefore seems that immigration was relatively slow at the beginning and the bird fauna not as variable as today. For the gulls it is interesting to see that some species, such as the Lesser Black-backed Gull *Larus fuscus* and Herring Gull *Larus argentatus*, have immigrated to the Faroes at least hundreds of years before they colonized Iceland, which suddenly received four regular gull species and three irregular ones during the last century. The most impressive increase and spread is that of the Northern Fulmar *Fulmarus glacialis*, which only lay one egg and first start to breed at an age of about 10 years. The great spread started in Iceland in the middle of the eighteenth century and then to the Faroes in the early nineteenth century, Scotland, followed by Ireland and southern Britain (Fisher 1952). This pattern suggests Fulmars immigrated from the north. Currently the Fulmar is the most common breeding species both in Iceland and the Faroes, competing only with the Common Puffin (Petersen 1998, 2000; Garðarsson et al. 2019; Jensen et al. 2005).

Immigration of Breeders in Iceland since 1900

During the first half of the twentieth century no less than seven Temperate bird species joined the regular Icelandic breeding fauna: the Starling *Sturnus vulgaris*, Short-eared Owl *Asio flammeus*, Shoveler *Anas clypeata*, Tufted Duck *Aythya fuligula*, Black-headed Gull *Chroicocephalus ridibundus*, Herring Gull, and Lesser Black-backed Gull (Guðmundsson 1951).

During the further 30 years (1950–1980) three more species established breeding populations: the Common Gull *Larus canus*, Barnacle Goose

Branta leucopsis and Curlew *Numenius arquata*. A second invasion of the Starling colonized Iceland with a time difference of some 25 years (Evans 1980; Þórisson 1981; Petersen 1998).

In the next three decades (1980–2010) no less than seven new bird species colonized Iceland to become regular breeders: the Shelduck *Tadorna tadorna*, Woodcock, Long-tailed Skua *Stercorarius longicaudus*, Long-eared Owl *Asio otus*, Blackbird *Turdus merula*, Goldcrest *Regulus regulus*, and Crossbill *Loxia curvirostra*. The populations are still small and vulnerable, except for the Shelduck, Blackbird and Goldcrest.

During the last 10 years (2011–2020) colonization has continued with species such as the Common Crane *Grus grus*, Little Gull *Hydrocoloeus minutus* and Waxwing *Bombycilla garrulus*. It still remains to be seen whether these species form stable breeding populations.

The Barn Swallow *Hirundo rustica* has nested annually in recent years, while earlier nesting was irregular and an Icelandic population has not developed, rather a constant influx. Other irregular breeders include the Coot *Fulica atra* and the House Martin *Delichon urbica*. Nearly 30 additional species have bred one or more times but have not established breeding populations.

An interesting chain of events started when Herring Gulls colonized Iceland and started breeding around 1925 (Ingólfsson 1970). Soon they began to hybridize with Glaucous Gulls, to which they had been allopatric for a long time, and numerous intermediate individuals currently exist (Vigfúsdóttir et al. 2008; Pálsson et al. 2009). Looking back several decades, Herring Gulls have spread westwards from their core eastern Iceland nesting area both along the northern and southern Iceland coasts. The core nesting area for Glaucous Gulls is North-West Iceland, which has been progressively approached by nesting Herring Gulls (Petersen 1998) and there is a real danger that the entire Glaucous Gull population becomes mixed (Petersen et al. 2014, 2015).

Immigration of Breeders in the Faroes

The Fulmar immigrated to the Faroes from Vestmannaeyjar in Iceland (Fisher 1952). It started to breed in the southernmost island, Suðuroy, but at an uncertain date. According to Aksal Poulsen (personal communication) the first chick was seen on Sumba on 1812 and according to Patursson (1926) the first pairs were breeding in 1816. Wolley (1850) says that Fulmars were breeding for the first time somewhere around 1839 near Hvalba on Suðuroy and that is the year most often cited (cf. Patursson 1946; Fisher 1952; Jensen 2012). Already in 1845 it was breeding on Stóra Dímun and Skúvoy and soon it was found on most of the islands. By the 1920s and early 1930s no less than 80 000 young were taken for food each year in the Faroe Islands (Patursson 1926; Fisher 1952). The enormous increase in the breeding population and the number of young taken indicate that there must have been many immigrants and a long-lasting immigration (Patursson 1926).

Many of the bird species that immigrated to Iceland after 1900 were already established breeders in the Faroes long before. The Starling was known from before 1673, the Lesser Black-backed Gull and the Herring Gull were common breeders in 1781 (Svabo 1976), the Black-headed Gull started to breed in 1848, and the Common Gull about 1890 (Holm 1848; Salomonsen 1935).

Two pairs of the Tree Sparrow *Passer montanus* immigrated to Skúvoy in 1866 where they bred twice that year and were very numerous about 1884 (Andersen 1901). One colony that doubtless originated from the Skúvoy stock also existed on Kunoy in the early twentieth century (Williamson 1945a). These islands remained the sole breeding places with a few irregular breeders, but early in the twentieth century they suddenly decreased and disappeared (Salomonsen 1935). Since then the Tree Sparrow has been a rare guest with one breeding in 2013 (Olofson and Sörensen 2018).

The House Sparrow *Passer domesticus* was a very rare vagrant, in fact having only been recorded once, in 1900 (Andersen 1901; Salomonsen 1935), before its colonization in 1935–1936. They first settled in Vágur on Suðuroy and the original birds are said to have arrived there on a vessel (Williamson 1945b). It was a common breeding bird in some of the islands in 1951 (Nørrevang 1955) and now it occurs abundantly in built-up areas throughout the Faroe Islands (Bengtson et al. 2004).

The Icelandic Redwing *Turdus iliacus coburni* is a common passage visitor. The species immigrated as a breeding bird in 1869 and bred occasionally in the gardens of Tórshavn. On account of the rather large plantation in Tórshavn, it commenced to breed regularly there in 1928 but the total breeding population is still only about 5-10 pairs (Jensen and Sørensen 2015).

Leach's Petrel *Oceanodroma leucorrhoa* was found breeding in a small colony on Mykineshólmur in 1934 (Salomonsen 1935) and has been breeding there ever since. According to Williamson (1945b) and Nørrevang (1955), the bird, however, was known by the locals long before that, so it should maybe not be treated as a new immigrant.

The Redshank *Tringa totanus robusta* is stated to have bred in the Faroes before 1935, but without proof (Salomonsen 1935). In the middle of the twentieth century, it was a very rare breeder (Holm Joensen 1966) and now the population is about 15 pairs (Jensen et al. 2005).

The Blackbird started to breed in the mid-twentieth century after being a regular autumn, winter and spring visitor (Nørrevang 1955) and is now a common breeder.

The Greylag Goose *Anser anser* that became locally extinct in the early 1800s started to breed again in the middle of the 1900s. At first there were only a few pairs (Nørrevang 1955; Olsen 1994), but now the population has reached such a size that the farmers are complaining that the geese reduce their crop, and they want to lift the protection that has been effective since 1928. Since 2014 it has been possible for landowners to ask for permission to shoot Greylag Geese on their cultivated areas.

The Goldcrest has been a common visitor and during the last decades it has become a common breeder.

Stragglers

Stragglers, which are not part of the regular breeding fauna, reach islands through different avenues or causes. Weather is by and large the most significant factor; direction, strength and sustained winds determine the numbers (cf. Pétursson and Skarphéðinsson 1978). The levels of magnitude in various species are also determined by their migratory urge, timing of migration and numbers, which again depend on productivity and survival (cf. Petersen 1983). This means that species exhibit different likelihoods of becoming stragglers, but the species, subspecies or populations that have the shortest distance to go are, however, not necessarily the most likely to hit the islands, as exemplified in *Phylloscopus* warblers (Björnsson 1979). Some species, e.g. the Crossbill and Waxwing are irruptive, i.e. disperse in large numbers outside their usual range at irregular intervals in search of food. The smaller birds, not the least passerines, are mostly weather-dependent. Larger non-Icelandic birds, like swan, goose, and duck species, sometimes join in the groups during the regular migration of native species. Then smaller birds and birds of prey are known to make use of ships for staging, e.g. during inclement weather.

Some species have been stragglers for as long as records extend, but cases exist of birds colonizing Iceland due to unusually large numbers at the same time. One such example is the Starling, which in autumn 1959 reached Iceland in flocks. Having survived the subsequent winter the birds started breeding in spring 1960, and ever since

Starlings have increased and spread in the country (Þórisson 1981; Petersen 1998). In the Faroe Islands the Starling was mentioned in a ballad, probably written before 1500, and it has presumably been breeding for centuries as it has evolved its unique identities as *Sturnus vulgaris faroensis*. The Starlings that immigrated to Iceland did not come from the Faroes but belonged to the subspecies *vulgaris* from the British Isles, Scandinavia, or the central European continent.

Analysis of Colonization

Colonization has been researched for only a few species in more detail than just their general region of origin. Tiedemann et al. (2004) in a genetic analysis concluded that colonization of Common Eiders in Iceland started in continental Europe through the Faroe Islands.

Fisher (1952) proposed a sole Icelandic source for the Fulmar colonists during the nineteenth century. This has been genetically tested on museum collections and support was found for Fisher's hypothesis as the patterns of genetic diversity suggest an Icelandic origin for the pre-1940 samples (Burg et al. 2014).

A DNA analysis of White-tailed Eagle *Haliaetus albicilla* populations across the Arctic and Temperate regions from Greenland in the west to Japan in the east revealed that climate changes impacted the demography and distribution of this species (Hailer et al. 2007). Results indicate that colonization of Iceland took place from Europe, possibly through the Faroe Islands.

The Garganey *Anas strepera* is a relative newcomer to the Icelandic breeding fauna. Faber (1822) is thought to be the first to record it breeding in Iceland, in 1819. Peters et al. (2008), analysing the phylogeography of this species, including samples from Iceland, concluded that North American Garganey originated from Eurasia. Icelandic Garganey are most likely of

European origin, to where they migrate in winter (Petersen 1998).

Studying the geographic variation in Horned Grebe *Podiceps auritus*, Fjeldså (1973) concluded that the Icelandic birds of subspecies *P. a. arcticus* would have originated from North Norway. An ongoing study is looking into a possible metapopulation connection consisting of Icelandic, Scottish and North Norwegian Horned Grebes, on the premise that these populations now show zig-zag population changes, implying exchanges between countries (cf. Ewing et al. 2013).

In a study of Dunlins *Calidris alpina* the Iceland subspecies *C. a. schinzii* and *arctica* in East Greenland are found to be closely related and cannot easily be separated genetically (Marthinsen et al. 2007, 2008). The *schinzii* subspecies has affinities to southern Scandinavia, the British Isles and the Baltic, from where the Icelandic birds most probably originated.

In a study of the colonization history of the Pink-footed Goose *Anser brachyrhynchus*, Ruokonen et al. (2005) concluded that the breeding populations in Svalbard, Greenland and Iceland were founded from one refugial population in Northwest Europe, separated less than 10 000 years ago. This fits well with the end of the last Glacial Period. Ploeger (1968) suggested Pink-footed Geese even had a glacial refugium in Northwest Iceland.

Thies et al. (2018) recently proposed that the Icelandic subspecies of the Common Ringed Plover (*psammodroma*) orginated from Eurasia after the last glacial period, after splitting of two earlier subspecies (*tundrae* and *hiaticula*).

Extinction in Iceland

Three species are known to have become extinct as breeders in the last few centuries in Iceland. One of them also became globally extinct in 1844, the Great Auk *Pinguinus impennis*. Human persecution and climate changes are believed to have sealed its fate (Bengtson 1984; Petersen 1995). The Water Rail *Rallus aquaticus* is last known to have bred in 1973 and the Little Auk *Alle alle* in 1997 (Petersen 1998; Skarphéðinsson and Þorleifsson 1998). The last two species were in Iceland clearly at the edge of their global breeding distribution, while the Great Auk bred on remote islands in a band across the Atlantic.

The extinction of the Water Rail and Little Auks as breeders in Iceland are subject to alternative explanations. Originally the former species is believed to have declined due to extensive wetland drainage, while the feral Mink *Neovision vison* turned out to be even more dangerous adversary (Skarphéðinsson and Þorleifsson 1998). Little Auks always were at the extreme southern limits of their breeding range in Iceland, and the population is believed never to have been more than a few hundred pairs. During the twentieth century, the population steadily declined, probably due to amelioration of the climate (Guðmundsson 1951).

Bird extinctions in Iceland have therefore come about for different reasons, indirectly human (Water Rail, Great Auk), while climate change is likely to have been the factor in other instances (Little Auk, Great Auk).

Extinction in the Faroes

It is very doubtful whether the Great Auk ever bred in the Faroes (cf. Salomonsen 1935). All seems to indicate that it was only an irregular visitor both in winter and summer. It was already mentioned in the Faroe ballads from the Middle Ages. It was especially observed on the low skerries or rocks along the coast and was captured there together with Common Guillemots.

A few place names and rumours indicate that the White-tailed Eagle may have been breeding in the Faroes in older times (Salomonsen 1935; Svabo 1976). There are, however, no proofs but in a description from 1592 it is stated that no eagles were in the Faroes (Claussøn Friis 1632).

The Great Cormorant *Phalacrocorax carbo* was breeding on several islands in former times, but towards the end of the nineteenth century it decreased considerably (Salomonsen 1935; Svabo 1976) and no breeding birds have been recorded since the middle of the twentieth century. On Nólsoy it was expelled by Fulmars (Andersen 1898) but persecution has probably also had a negative effect on the population. The Cormorant has been protected since 1954 (Dam 1974) and in recent years they have been seen more regularly.

The Raven *Corvus corax varius* consisted in older times of two phases in the Faroes, the normal black, which was the commonest, and a pied, white-speckled mutant, known from the Faroes already in the Middle Ages (Niels á Botni 1952; van Grouw 2014). The latter, however, is extinct, the last record being from 1902 (Salomonsen 1935; Bloch 2012). The cause of this extinction was severe persecution as it was sent to museums in large numbers as a curiosity. Also, its special gene was recessive, so that it could never have been particularly numerous (Salomonsen 1935).

The Greylag Goose was in earlier times (first recorded in 1592) breeding in large numbers in meadowland near freshwaters. About 1750 it began to decrease in numbers, primarily on account of persecution by man, but also because the Great Skua *Stercorarius skua* robbing its eggs (Svabo 1976). About 1800 it had become very rare (Landt 1800) and it was totally exterminated as a Faroese breeding bird about 1832 (Müller 1862; Salomonsen 1935). About 130 years later the Greylag Goose started to breed again on the islands and is now a common breeder.

The Great Skua was nearly extinct in the nineteenth century. Formerly they bred in large numbers but declined in the eighteenth and nineteenth centuries so only four pairs were left when it was protected in 1897. In the twentieth century the population increased and now it is about 500 pairs (Jensen et al. 2005). The reason for its rapid decrease was the violent persecutions by man, partly because its nestlings were killed in great numbers and used for food and in part on account of the damage it was supposed to cause to other birds and lambs (Svabo 1976). The Great Skua is recorded as a Faroese bird as early as in 1604 and the first good description of this species originates from the Faroes (Brünnich 1764). On Skúvoy, the type of locality of the Great Skua, 6000 young were said to have been captured annually around 1700 (Svabo 1976), but this is presumably far too high an estimate.

Bird extinctions in the Faroes have therefore mostly come about because of persecution by man but may also have been affected by climate change.

Climate Change

Many of the variations in colonization and population sizes are believed to be due to climate change. Looking back over the millennia since the end of the Ice Age, with temperature and habitat changes, similar changes have more than likely taken place in the Icelandic and Faroese bird fauna. In Norway, both the Northern Fulmar and Northern Gannet *Morus bassanus* seem to have been present but become extinct thousands of years BP, as indicated by zooarchaeological materials (Montevecchi and Hufthammer 1990).

Birds from other places are steady visitors to the Northeast Atlantic islands. These species are mostly vagrants, which arrive singly or in small numbers during the non-breeding season and do not establish breeding populations. Some manage to become irregular breeders, but usually a long time elapses before viable breeding populations develop, if that happens at all. One example is the Goldcrest, which is a newly established breeder in both Iceland and the Faroes. This species was known as one of the most common vagrants for a long time. The Curlew, as another example, had

been a winter visitor for centuries before starting to nest on both islands. The immigration history of the House Sparrow is totally different. In Iceland, the first record was a nesting pair and, in the Faroes, it was only recorded once before breeding. The fact that passerines are the group of birds with the highest proportion of new breeders in Iceland may be a result of a warmer climate and recent man-made habitats.

Although certain bird species have been breeding for centuries it is possible that steady immigration has maintained these populations, at least to some extent. Local conditions depend on whether colonizations are successful. As examples, Water Rail are still seen annually in Iceland, although they have been extinct as breeders since 1973. At least in some years Scandinavian Redwings (different subspecies from the Icelandic one) have been recorded and, similarly, Blackbirds and Fieldfares *Turdus pilaris*. Influx of conspecific breeders is difficult to establish, but there is no reason to doubt that a similar influx continuously takes place, even though they have established breeding populations. The Faroese Gannet population, which has been harvested for centuries but is still stable or increasing, is presumably supplemented by receiving immigrants from other colonies (Nelson 2002).

Probably the most extensive effects of climate change on the bird fauna involves the seabirds (e.g. Anon 2008, 2010). Wide-ranging changes have taken place in the marine fauna, invertebrates and vertebrates alike (e.g. Harris et al. 2007; Hátún et al. 2009).

Two sentinel fish species in Icelandic waters are Sandeels *Ammodytes* spp. and Capelin *Mallotus villosus*, which are important food species for seabirds (Lilliendahl et al. 2013, Pálsson et al. 2014). Declines in these are related to major breeding failure and serious population declines in a number of seabirds in Iceland, some even as far back as 1995 but more widely after 2003 (Garðarsson 2006; Hansen et al. 2008;

Garðarsson 2010; Petersen 2010; Garðarsson et al. 2011, 2013).

Conservation Problems Concerning Birds

Iceland

Prior to Landnám ca. 870, Iceland is not believed to have been influenced much by humans. Knowledge of the biota prior to the Settlement is a prerequisite for estimating the impacts of humans on the environment (Dugmore et al. 2005). Rapid environmental changes started amazingly soon after humans settled the country, with the destruction of birch and willow scrubs through grazing and cutting, resulting in erosion problems and desertification (Sveinbjarnardóttir et al. 1982; Dugmore et al. 2009). As a result, terrestrial habitats changed, scrub declining until in present times it has only 1.2–1.5% coverage (Snorrason et al. 2007; Traustason and Snorrason 2008) and increased open moorlands. Birch woodland is estimated to have covered 27% of the country at Landnám (Sigurðsson 1977), while the extent of willow scrub does not appear to have been estimated.

Corresponding changes are likely to have taken place in the bird fauna, although direct information is not available. With declining scrub, populations of passerines, such as the Redwing and Wren, would probably have decreased. On the other hand, waders, e.g. the Golden Plover, Purple Sandpiper *Calidris maritima* and Whimbrel *Numenius phaeopus*, which are birds of the open country, may have benefited. These changes would have resulted in the situation of present-day Iceland, which is a globally important breeding station for waders (cf. Gunnarsson et al. 2006; Gunnarsson 2010; Jóhannesdóttir et al. 2019a).

Different but even more rapid and significant changes of the landscape took place after the start of modern agricultural practices about a century ago, with the making of hayfields and large-scale drainage of wetlands (cf. Jóhannesdóttir et al. 2019b). Nowadays most of the wetlands, once 55–75% of lowland Iceland (Óskarsson 1998), have been changed. Most extensive changes have taken place on the southern lowlands, with over 97% of the wetlands drained or improved for agriculture or afforestation (Þorleifsson 1998). The effects of these changes on the bird fauna has often been emphasized (Garðarsson 1975; Ólafsson 1998). Examples do exist of birds disappearing, such as the Water Rail mentioned previously, as result of drainage of lakes or ponds and nearby land drying up. Although individual nesting sites have been destroyed, this, however, is not the most likely reason for its extinction as a breeder, which is rather the feral Mink.

In general, the most important effect by agricultural practices is probably on local distributions, rather than population size. The two primary freshwater wetland bird groups are waterfowl (swans, geese, ducks) and waders. It seems the effects of these changes on the bird fauna, such as the waders, have been somewhat exaggerated in the past. Consistent with island biogeography theory, Icelandic wetland birds, such as the Black-tailed Godwit and Snipe, do have broad habitat preferences. Hence, contrary to expectations, Godwits increased and spread into new breeding regions contemporaneous with agricultural changes (see Guðmundsson 1951), and this spread is still taking place (Gunnarsson 2004; Gunnarsson et al. 2007). The periphery of agricultural fields and other drained areas are used significantly by waders for nesting, while feeding conditions may have been improved. Although invertebrate faunas in improved land become less diverse in species (Guðleifsson and Bjarnadóttir 2004, 2008; Guðleifsson 2005), they may reach greater densities in cultivated hayfields (Bengtson et al. 1975), or at least variable influence on different invertebrate groups (Guðleifsson 1998). Thus, negative effects on the birds by changes in habitats are probably balanced by other environmental factors, positive for at least some bird species. Drainage is likely to have had much greater influence on the composition of vegetation communities (Þórhallsdóttir 1998).

Other land use changes are associated with increased human population, with matching infrastructures, townships, road systems, capture of geothermal and hydro-power energy, etc. Little quantitative information exists on the overall influence of these factors on the Icelandic bird fauna. One relatively new threat lies in the greatly increased forestry plans, which will eventually change the composition of the current bird fauna (Gunnarsson 2006). These have already started, where woodland species have replaced open moorland species (Nielsen 2003; Jónsson et al. 2006; Elmarsdóttir et al. 2008; Elmarsdóttir et al. 2011). As plantations of non-native trees have matured, these have created new habitats not only for various passerine birds, which until recently have only been stragglers, e.g. the Goldcrest, Crossbill and Siskin *Carduelis spinus*, but also the Woodcock and Long-eared Owl (Snæþórsson and Pétursson 1992; Óskarsson 1995a, 1995b; Sigurðsson and Magnússon 2004; Bergmann 2005; Stefánsson and Bjarnadóttir 2005). Traditionally the Icelandic bird fauna in a scrub habitat has been generally poor in species although density may be high (Bengtson 1970; Wink 1973; Nielsen 1979). In centuries past, with the decline in this type of habitat within human habitation there would have been a faunal switch to the open land species we know at present.

Another recent threat to the Icelandic flora and fauna is the use of the introduced Nootka Lupin *Lupinus nootkatensis* and Cow Parsley *Anthriscus sylvestris* for revegetation purposes. Although Lupin may have positive effects when used for re-vegetating desolate, eroded areas, in the sense that plant growth and breeding bird fauna is increased (Gunnarsson and Indridadottir 2009),

both plant species colonize areas of native flora, which retreat (Magnússon et al. 2003; Arnalds and Runólfsson 2004). The bird fauna on the island of Hrísey (North Iceland) is believed to have suffered due to spread of these introduced plant species (Þorsteinsson and Thorstensen 2014).

Still another recent agricultural change is the use of cereals besides the more traditional hay making. Geese and Whooper Swans *Cygnus cygnus* have for a long time been considered to have caused damage to agriculture (Kear 1967). This has been an ongoing problem, but the most recent aspect is damage by these birds to the recent practice of growing cereals, not the least by swans. This change in crop may affect both distribution of birds and size of wintering populations, although these in turn are heavily influenced by winter temperatures and related climate variables. Some cultivation of cereals occurs for the sole purpose of hunting geese (swans are fully protected).

Mink was introduced in the 1930s, and with its spread throughout lowland Iceland, this has resulted in faunal changes (Skírnisson and Petersen 1980; von Schmalensee 2010; Stefánsson et al. 2016). Mink was considered a serious threat to the diverse, and internationally important, waterfowl community at Lake Mývatn in the 1960s (Guðmundsson 1963). The indigenous Arctic Fox has been a human adversary since Settlement times, predating on sheep and ravaging Common Eider colonies. The lasting influence of foxes on the native fauna has been debated for a long time, but systematic and quantitative studies are regrettably lacking. Recent studies have shown that fox and Mink predation can influence local Red-throated Diver *Gavia stellata* breeding productivity and distribution (unpublished).

Destruction of scrubland, overgrazing and volcanic eruptions, with resulting soil erosion, are considered the greatest overall environmental problems in Iceland (cf. Arnalds 2008). How much the bird fauna has been affected is a matter of conjecture and has been little studied. In its most advanced form indisputably soil erosion influences the composition, density, and distribution of the bird fauna, while their effects, and extent, would be variable depending on the species. Erosion has been most problematic in highland regions where the bird fauna is poorest anyway due to elevation, both in species and density, at least under the present-day climate regime. Some species, like the Golden Plover, are species of the open land, where vegetation cover is not necessarily complete. Another species that prefers less than 100% vegetated area is the Common Ringed Plover, which breeds on land of sparse, sandy vegetation, both coastal and inland. Unfortunately, in recent years much of this habitat has been destroyed when surplus hay, Lupin, and woodland species have been used to re-vegetate such areas, without total conservation planning.

Through the ages volcanic eruptions have affected both lowland and highland regions, with a variable impact depending on the location, type of volcanic material and volume. Lavas have sometimes covered large land areas. In historical times the largest is the immense one at Skaftáreldar in 1783 (Gunnlaugsson et al. 1984). Lava fields are generally poor habitats for breeding birds with low density populations, especially if devoid of vegetation or primarily moss-covered (Wink 1973). Eruptions, as well as overgrazing and erosion, have in the long run had negative local influences on the bird fauna.

Hunting has been carried out since the times of the Settlement, as archaeological excavations have shown (McGovern et al. 2006, 2007), and is reflected in the Icelandic legislation from as early as the twelfth century (Grágás 1997; Jónsbók 2004). How much impact this has had on bird populations is largely unknown. It can be pointed out that for most of historic times hunting equipment was rather primitive (Kristjánsson 1986) and not likely to have caused significant damage. The possible exception is descending seabird cliffs for eggs and snaring of breeding auks. Annual, and repeated, visits in the spring may have affected the populations. It is known that some small bird cliffs are at present devoid of the typical birds, that were harvested. Against this is the argument that not the entire cliff face was covered. On some cliffs, parts were considered 'heathen', i.e. not deemed safe for harvesting as these cliff parts were believed to be occupied by trolls or other superstitious beings, keeping people away. The truth is that these cliff parts were more dangerous for descending, both due to sharp edges and the danger of rock falls. It was not until the introduction of guns that in general more effective hunting could take place. In the nineteenth century there are examples of the use of nets for capturing breeding Common Puffins at a colony, even destroying colonies (Petersen 1998). This method was effective and clearly unsustainable, which led to the introduction of a different, and not as destructive, method, the triangular net (fleygastong) from the Faroe Islands (Jónsson 1896; Petersen 2005). The use of floating boards to catch auks on the sea in the neighbourhood of bird cliffs was also practised but is now banned (Petersen 2005).

Examples of individual conservation problems are numerous, and one of the more striking was the earlier killing of White-tailed Eagles (Skarphéðinsson 1992, 2003). This was both directly and indirectly through fox poisoning, starting in the late 1800s as they were ravaging Common Eider colonies, killing sheep, and even taking children. In only a few decades the Icelandic eagle population crashed, leading to the species being declared formally protected in 1913, the first country in the world to do so. Despite full protection the eagle population did not recover for the next half a century. The reason was that Arctic Foxes were poisoned with strychnine and being scavengers, numerous eagles were killed. The eagle population did not start to recover until after 1964 when a ban on strychnine was introduced.

Another example is the Great Auk. This species became extinct in 1844 when the last birds were killed, having become so rare that museums or individuals were willing to pay handsomely for specimens. Although excessive exploitation by humans is the popular explanation for the Great Auk extinction, Bengtson (1984) believed climate change had influenced the population long before substantial human impact became important. However, one explanation does not rule out the other. Humans at least gave the Great Auks the final blow and the population was still pretty strong around 1500 when the main human exploitation began (Petersen 1995).

At present Northern Gannets breed in nine colonies around the coasts of Iceland, the largest of which is on the island of Eldey in the southwest (Garðarsson 1989, 2019; Gíslason et al. 2019). For centuries Gannet young have been taken for food, and by Icelandic law this is still legal where harvesting has been a tradition. Formerly the colonies were considered overharvested (Garðarsson 1995). The last harvesting trip to Eldey in 1939 was cut short by inclement weather and hundreds of killed young birds were left behind. This caused an outcry, leading to formal protection of the island and its birds (Einarsson 1959), the first bird sanctuary in Iceland to be protected.

A more recent conservation problem that can be mentioned is the bycatch of birds in fishing gear. Around the year 2000 between 100 and 200 thousand birds were estimated to be killed per year in the Icelandic fishing industry (Petersen 2002). This mortality has greatly declined because of different fishing gear, legal restrictions, and general seabird decline of the most common bycaught species (Christensen-Dalsgaard et al. 2019). Yet a real, systematic up-to-date survey is greatly needed, analysing the effects on populations of different bird species and looking at mitigation measures.

Another conservation problem is the death of birds in traffic ('roadkill'). Tens of thousands of birds are killed each year by colliding with cars. This problem has undoubtedly increased with growing human population, numbers of cars, better roads, and greater speeds. So far, this problem has not been carefully evaluated in Iceland.

Bird populations have also benefited from humans. Goose and swan populations have, for instance, greatly increased in numbers due to agricultural practices, both on the breeding and wintering grounds. So, did some of the gull species in the early twentieth century, presumably from greatly increased food availability from humans, such as open rubbish tips and the fishing industry (Guðmundsson 1951, 1954) providing offal from fishing vessels (Boswall 1977), but fishery discards are now banned, with negative effects on some scavengers, such as Glaucous Gulls *Larus hyperboreus* and Northern Fulmar.

In recent years debates on climate change with global implications have dominated international environmental discussions. Related to this are changes in food supplies and major declines in certain seabird populations in the Northeast Atlantic (Anon 2008, 2010). In Iceland, these changes have become most apparent during the past 20 years (Garðarsson 2006; Garðarsson et al. 2013) but have varied with species, temporally as well as spatially (cf. Petersen 2010).

Other conservation problems that originate outside Iceland are of a different nature. Gulls in general increased noticeably in densely populated countries in Europe during the twentieth century (see, for example, Harris 1970). This led to population explosions and corresponding distribution expansions, such as into Iceland. The colonization of the Herring Gull in the early twentieth century led to hybridization with the indigenous Glaucous Gull. Should the expansion in breeding range by Herring Gulls continue in the future, the High Arctic Glaucous Gull is in danger from total mixing with the Temperate Herring Gull (Petersen et al. 2014, 2015). This can become a real conservation problem, corresponding to the hybridization of the introduced North American Ruddy Duck with the European White-headed Duck *Oxyura leucocephala* (Muñoz-Fuentes et al. 2007), a conservation problem of man-made nature relating to escapees. For centuries man has introduced live birds into Europe for waterfowl collections, some of the species originating as far as Asia, North America or Australia (cf. Long 1981). Several such escaped birds of different species have been found as vagrants in Iceland, and even bred, such as the Ruddy Duck and Bar-headed Goose *Anser indicus*. The most imminent problem related to the Ruddy Duck was potential competition, rather than mixing, with such native species as Barrow's Goldeneye *Bucephala islandica* and Horned Grebe (Nielsen 1994; Petersen 1998). This potential threat has not been observed for at least some 20 years.

The first legal bird conservation action dates from 1787, when in a trade resolution Eiders were protected from shooting. The first general hunting legislation stems from 1849, while the first overall bird protection and hunting act is from 1882. This was revised in 1903 and more so in 1913, when many previously unprotected species became fully protected, e.g. the Whooper Swan, passerines (except the Raven), divers, and waders. General bird acts were later revised in 1954 and 1966, while the present general legislation stems from 1994, in which all bird species are fully protected unless their protection is lifted in regulations for hunting and harvesting purposes or pest control.

Although various environmental changes have been taking place over the centuries, it is only in the last decades that the necessary studies have come forward to evaluate some of these changes. However, in most cases country-wide assessments are lacking although available studies give some indications.

Faroe Islands

Since people arrived on the Faroe Islands in the fourth–sixth centuries (Church et al. 2013) they have affected the bird populations, although it must have been very local at the beginning. Hunting has probably had the most severe effect, while changes to the environment, due to grazing by sheep, wetland drainage, and cultivation, have been less important. During the first centuries all kinds of available birds were hunted and only during the last few centuries have birds been protected and the hunting restricted to certain species.

Birds that competed with economic interests were previously violently pursued and slaughtered. In the first place, it was birds that were injurious to sheep-farming by killing weak sheep or lambs, and birds that to a great extent lived on seabird eggs (Salomonsen 1935). The Raven had the worst reputation and there was an ancient custom that every man who was 'able to row a boat' had the duty to hand over a beak of one Raven to the authorities once a year (Debes 1673), a so-called 'bill-tax'. If they were not able to deliver a Raven bill, they had to pay a fine. As this custom was not always respected it became a statutory provision in 1741. Every man between the ages of 15 and 50 was obliged each year to submit one beak of the White-tailed Eagle or a Raven to the authorities, or two beaks of Hooded Crows *Corvus cornix* or Great Black-backed Gulls. Later, Great Skua was also included. The tax was discontinued in 1881, after which men were paid for the beaks (Bjørk 1963). Records of the beaks exist from 1741 until 1934 with about 800 beaks annually. Most of the beaks were from Hooded Crows and 150–250 from Ravens. White-tailed Eagles were not breeding in the Faroes, but were rare visitors (Svabo 1976), and no beak was reported for this species (Bloch 2012).

The first protection of seabirds against shooting in the colonies and on the neighboring seas is from 1741, when two areas on Vágoy were protected (Nørrevang 1977a). The Eider was the first species to be protected in the whole country when it was protected against shooting and disturbance in 1784. The first hunting and conservation law dates from 1854 and according to this law and some additions in 1891, birds at most of the seabird colonies and the sea below were protected against shooting (Dam 1974). A new law came into force in 1897, revised in 1928, protecting, among others, Starlings, and all smaller birds. A new law in 1954 mentions only those bird species on which hunting was allowed while all other birds were protected. Hunting is allowed on Fulmars, Puffins, Common Guillemots, Razorbills *Alca torda*, Manx Shearwater *Puffinus puffinus* chicks, Gannets, Shags *Phalacrocorax aristotelis*, and gulls. Even nowadays, Ravens, Hooded Crows, Arctic Skuas *Stercorarius parasiticus*, and Great Skuas can be killed. In 2014 an announcement stated that landowners may reduce the numbers of Greylag Geese in their hayfields. The hunting of Common Guillemots, Razorbills, Puffins and Shags is restricted to an open season in the winter, while Puffins also may be taken in the summer with the traditional 'fleygastong'. This hunting equipment is a 3.5 m long pole with a triangular net at the end and the birds are picked out of the air as they fly along the coast. Shags taken are probably all of Faroese origin while Razorbills from Iceland, Guillemots from Britain and Puffins from Norway inhabit Faroese waters in winter and are subject to hunting (Olsen et al. 2000). The Greylag Goose and the Great Cormorant were eradicated by hunting in the 1830s and 1950s, respectively. It was 130 years before the Greylag Goose started to breed again (Olsen 1994) and Cormorants still do not breed although it is more regularly seen nowadays. There has been a severe decline in the population of Guillemots, Razorbills, Puffins and Kittiwakes in the last decades, but this is mainly caused by natural variations in the forage fish populations, especially Sandeels (Olsen 2007; Anon 2010; Eliasen et al. 2011). Already in 1859 it was assumed that lack of Sandeels was the reason for the bad Puffin fowling that year and that

a lot of dead Puffins were found the previous winter (Müller 1862).

Mice *Mus musculus domesticus* were probably introduced very early in the Settlement Period as they were already common early in the sixteenth century (Claussøn Friis 1632) and are now found on most of the islands. They mostly live indoors or close to humans but may also be found in the seabird colonies in the summer (Bloch and Fuglø 1999) but have not had any noticeable effect on bird populations. Also, the Black Rat *Rattus rattus* was formerly found in Tórshavn and in the 1630s it reached Vágoy, the only two places where they were known in 1782 (Svabo 1976). Although they were considered pests by people, nothing is mentioned about their effect on birds. Now the Black Rat is only seen occasionally as it has been displaced by the larger Brown Rat *Rattus norvegicus*. The Brown Rat, on the other hand, has had a dramatic negative impact on birds (Patursson 1939), especially the burrow-nesting species, such as Storm Petrels *Hydrobates pelagicus*, Manx Shearwaters and Puffins, by taking eggs, chicks and even nesting birds. The first Brown Rats were observed in 1768 on Suðuroy and are considered to have come from a shipwreck (Svabo 1976). The subsequent year they were found in Tórshavn on Streymoy and during the next 10 years they colonized Eysturoy and later Vágoy. Then more than a century passed until in the early twentieth century they invaded the northern islands of Kunoy, Borðoy and Viðoy (Kyrjarheygg 2002). Genomic analysis has revealed three independent introductions of the Brown Rat to the Faroe Islands (Puckett et al. 2020). No range expansion has taken place since then. Solitary rats have, however, been seen on some rat-free islands, without establishing themselves. One of the most challenging conservation problems is to secure the remaining islands free from rat invaders since the connection between islands has improved with car ferries and subsea tunnels (Olsen 2006, 2010; Hammer 2011). In 2023, the largest rat-free island, Sandoy, will be connected by a subsea tunnel to the rat-infested Streymoy.

Feral cats have been held to keep mice and rats at bay in the settlements, but they have also reduced the numbers of Wrens and other small birds as they still do today. Already in the eighteenth century, feral cats were living away from built-up areas (Svabo 1976) and may have survived on birds, as still happens locally.

Mink has not been living in the wild although a few animals escaped from fur farms in the late twentieth century. Now there are no Mink farms, but there is still a threat from those that arrive on ships, as happened in 2011 when one was shot in Tórshavn harbour.

Pet birds or birds that escaped from parks in Europe are occasionally seen in the Faroe Islands, but they rarely breed and become a problem for the local birds. A pair of Canada Geese that had been ringed in England in 1983 started to breed on Sandoy in 1985 (Jensen 1987). A population was quickly established and there was some inbreeding with Greylag Goose (Jensen 1990), but the population was restricted to a few pairs and is now extinct. In 1989 a pair of Barnacle Goose started to breed, and the population is now 48 pairs (Hammer et al. 2017).

The Whooper Swan is a common migrant and a few are resident in the Faroe Islands, often birds in poor condition. Some have been cared for and bred in captivity (Leivsson 2004). In recent years, these birds and their offspring have been set free and have bred in the wild, causing concern as they are overly aggressive on their breeding areas and drive other birds away.

Bycatch of Fulmars on longline is a problem and it is estimated that some 5000–25 000 birds are taken unintentionally in the Faroes each year (Olsen 2008). The birds are caught mainly during line-setting while snatching bait from the hooks or scavenging for offal (Dunn and Steel 2001). The birds benefit indirectly from humans as fishing boats discharge offal and the trawlers bring up fish that can be picked up by seabirds, especially Fulmars, Kittiwakes, Gannets, and gulls. Garbage and leftovers from fish factories was common food for gulls, Hooded Crows and Ravens, but the garbage is taken care of and the discharge from fishing boats is now used more efficiently or not thrown overboard, so this is a declining food source for birds.

Sheep are grazing free on all the Faroe Islands, keeping grass and other plants short, but it is unknown how this affects birds. Only a small part of the islands is cultivated; fields are 7.8% of the area and these are only partly cultivated, especially as hay fields (Djurhuus 2013). In many places the old hay fields are not used any more. A few farmers with dairy cattle have a more intensive agriculture where they sow and manure their hayfields. These hayfields are particularly attractive to geese, in such a concentration that hay production is reduced according to the farmers (Vang 2014; Vang and Jensen 2016). These farmers are now allowed to shoot Greylag Geese on their hayfields. During the last century, introduced trees, bushes and plants have been planted giving more shelter for migrating passerines and breeding areas for some new species. The tourist industry is increasing and sightseeing on boats to the bird cliffs is one of the most popular trips arranged for tourists. There are no rules protecting the birds against any potential disturbances from boats, e.g. how often a cliff can be visited or how close the boats can go. Walking in breeding bird areas may also become a problem with increasing tourism, but landowners have the right to invoke controls if needed.

Economic Importance of Birds

Iceland

Recorded observations of Icelandic bird life hardly exist from the first centuries of human settlement around 1100 years ago. Trade in wild birds was first mentioned in a written account for the year 1169 when a Gyrfalcon *Falco rusticolus* was sold to the King of England (Diplomatarium Islandicum 1911–1921). The trade in Gyrfalcons became quite lucrative until it came to an end in 1810 (Petersen 1998). Archaeological studies in middens have recently started to reveal the presence of various bird species, where bone and egg data give indications of utilization (e.g. McGovern 2009). Breeding status or commonness may not be confirmed, but these materials can be used as proxies to allow comparisons of relative abundance through time, reflecting abundance or economic interest.

The Icelandic bird fauna is relatively well known during the last five centuries. Many species are also mentioned in Snorra-Edda's bird mantra from the thirteenth century (Sturluson 1848), many of which are common breeders at present times. Mostly the same species have dominated as nowadays although there may have been fluctuations in individual populations, new breeders have become established and others disappeared. The strength of the present-day Icelandic bird fauna lies in seabirds, waterfowl and waders (Petersen 1982, 1998, 2005). The first written account of the bird fauna dates from c. 1590 (Einarsson 1971). Since then various manuscripts or published works with information of birds are available, although it was not until 1822 that the first real bird book was printed, *Prodromus der isländischen Ornithologie, oder Geschichte der Vögel Islands* by Faber (1822).

Among the earliest written accounts on birds in Iceland include the old law books of the twelfth century – Grágás, Járnsíða and Jónsbók – which indicate species of economic importance (Júlíusson 1981; Grágás 1997; Jónsbók 2004). By and large the same species were harvested as utilized nowadays, or recently have been, such as various seabirds, e.g. the Common Eider, Arctic Tern *Sterna paradisaea* and auks, waterfowl

such as geese, ducks and swans, as well as Rock Ptarmigan. Golden Plovers and Whimbrels are also mentioned as potential game, and eggs from 'edible birds' could be taken for food. Birds with talons (birds of prey) were stated not to be eaten; these include Ravens as well as White-tailed Eagles, Gyrfalcons and Merlins *Falco columbarius*. They were already at those times considered pest species, which should be eradicated at all costs. This view is further reflected in the Icelandic sagas and annals. Gyrfalcons were already valuable for falconry in the twelfth century, becoming even more so in later centuries. Archaeological studies have shown that the use of birds has also been much the same species over the period since the Settlement over 1100 years ago. Middens at various study locations have shown different profiles of bones and eggs, mostly reflecting the local fauna, although a certain amount of trade also took place between districts, even between countries (cf. Harrison et al. 2008). Quantitatively seabirds have been most important in the bird harvest. Rock Ptarmigan is widespread inland and often represented in inland middens, while duck eggs were a local source in limited areas, of which Lake Mývatn is notably the most important. A number of other species provided more irregular and minor harvests (McGovern et al. 2006; McGovern 2009).

Seabirds were mostly caught at colonies during the spring and summer months, until guns came into general ownership and hunting at sea became common. The bird cliffs included various auk species, Kittiwake, and during the recent centuries also Fulmar. In many areas, birds killed by rock fall in spring were collected from below bird cliffs, in competition with Arctic Foxes which also scavenge on the shore and provide an important source of food for them (Hersteinsson and Macdonald 1996). Besides the meat, seabirds provided feathers for bedding, which in later centuries was exported. Fulmars became more and more common over some 250 years and were continually increasing until very recently. They also became an important source of food in some regions, especially in southern Iceland and the Vestmannaeyjar islands. During the 1930s a disease (*psittacosis*) in the Fulmar population resulted in a ban in 1940 on taking Fulmars for food, as this was transmitted to humans. Although the ban was lifted in the 1950s, utilization of this species for food never really caught on again, mainly due to major societal changes after the World War II. Nowadays, taking of Fulmar chicks is only practised locally on a limited scale.

In earlier times, and into the twentieth century, Whooper Swans were taken for food, both cygnets and adults, during the flightless period in late summer. As writing became more and more common from the middle ages onwards, swan quills for pens came into demand. Feathers from wild swans were collected at moulting sites, something that is no longer practised (Theódórsson 1936; Petersen 1998). Whooper Swans were first protected in 1903 during the breeding period but they have enjoyed full annual protection since 1953.

Common Eiders have played a particularly important role for most of the period since the Settlement. In the early centuries, their eggs were the main yield, with some harvest of birds, but since the sixteenth century their down has been the main product (Theódórsson 1936, Petersen 1998). The Icelandic literature on Common Eiders and its husbandry is extensive and forms a substantial part of all written materials on birds in Iceland (see, for example, Jónsson 2001; Goryashko 2020).

Falconry was a royal sport for centuries and Gyrfalcons from Iceland were in great demand (van Oorschot 1974). Written records exist of the falcon export from the end of the seventeenth century until formally abolished in 1810, with a maximum of over 200 birds exported per year in 1764 (Petersen 1998).

By the eighteenth century, Icelanders had more or less stopped hunting small waders, such as Golden Plovers and Purple Sandpipers. The reason for this is possibly by and large the availability of larger and more abundant prey, such as seabirds and waterfowl, but inland Ptarmigan was, and still is, a preferred game species. Hunting of waders remained legal until 1882, when they were protected during the breeding season, and were accorded full protection from 1913. Besides, larger birds were available, the reasons were probably that these birds were harbingers of spring and the end of winter, especially Golden Plovers. However, foreign travelers often indulged in such killings, for sport or food, as many travel books from the nineteenth century disclose, much to the general dislike of Icelanders.

Wild birds provided food in the form of meat or eggs. Miscellaneous devices have been invented for catching the birds. Guns did not become common in Iceland until the nineteenth century, although the first guns are reported from the fifteenth century (Friðriksson 1996). Other methods were employed, different depending on the species (cf. Kristjánsson 1986). Colonial cliff-nesting birds were caught, and eggs gathered when the bird cliffs were descended on a rope, a particularly hazardous occupation that has claimed many lives through the ages. From at least the seventeenth until the mid-twentieth century floating boards with leg nooses were used to catch auks offshore from colonies, esp. Drangey and Grímsey islands in the North. Formerly, Puffins and Black Guillemots *Cepphus grylle* were mostly harvested in hauling young from burrows using hooks of three different lengths. Since around 1950 the Puffin harvest has been nearly all full-grown birds. Gannet, Shag and Great Cormorant chicks, and previously also Great Auks, and even gull chicks, were clubbed at their colonies. Adult Kittiwakes and Arctic Terns were sometimes caught using baited traps, especially by young boys, and Common Eiders were in earlier centuries taken in baited, floating nets. Formerly Ptarmigan were captured in snares, but later guns were employed as they came into common use. According to the present legislation, guns are the main hunting equipment. Most other kinds of equipment are illegal in accordance with the Bern Convention and have been so since 1954. There are exceptions: the use of pole nets for catching Puffins and clubs to take young of Shag, Cormorant and Gannet. Young of some species, such as Fulmar and gulls, are taken by hand.

Little is known of the impact of utilization on different bird populations in past centuries. Examples exist from the nineteenth century about impacts on Puffin colonies. On Vestmannaeyjar around 1850 the unfortunate method of covering colonies with nets to capture the breeding birds was begun. This resulted in a clear population decline, leading to a ban on using nets and the start of using pole nets (Jónsson 1896; Petersen 2005). Mainly during recent decades some insight has been gained into the impact of hunting, but not on all species, only some economically and culturally important ones like the Ptarmigan and Puffin (Brynjarsdóttir and Nielsen 2017; Vigfúsdóttir et al. 2007). Hunting statistics can be used to estimate the likely effect on bird populations. Such statistics were collected on harvested species in the period 1889–1939; down from Common Eider, and the birds themselves in the case of the Fulmar, Gannet, Auks, Puffin, Kittiwake, Black Guillemot and Ptarmigan. It was not until 1995 that hunting records were introduced again, giving a valuable insight into the 29 bird species that can be hunted, either for food or as pests (two now fully protected are the Greenland White-fronted Goose *Anser albifrons flavirostris* and Black Guillemot). By numbers, Puffins and Ptarmigan are the most common quarry species. These two species accounted for over half of the recorded hunt around 1995, but their proportion has declined since then due to population declines and resulting hunting restrictions. Egg collecting is, however, still exempted from the hunting reports.

Faroe Islands

Seabirds are the most numerous birds in the Faroes. It is most likely that they were also the most important birds for the first settlers in the fourth–sixth centuries CE (Church et al. 2013). Puffins, Common Guillemots and Kittiwakes have probably dominated the bird fauna. Eggs, chicks and adults were taken for food and the feathers for bedding as well as export (Williamson 1945a; Svabo 1976; Nørrevang 1977a), while guano-rich turves from Puffin colonies may have been used to supplement soils for cereal cultivation (Buckland and Panagiotakopulu 2008). The Fulmar immigrated in the early 1800s and after only about 100 years they had become one of the most important birds. While other bird species leave the colonies after breeding, Fulmars can still be hunted throughout most of the winter.

Hunting techniques had been poor in the beginning, but in the breeding period eggs and chicks could be collected by hand from ground breeding species. The cliff nesters were more difficult, although some of these birds probably bred in more accessible areas than now, as the Faroe Islands had no ground predators.

All evidence shows that the fowling methods have remained almost unchanged during the past 300 years (Nørrevang 1986). Birds that nest in burrows, e.g. Puffins and Manx Shearwaters, were taken from their burrows by hand or by a stick with a hook. If the birds could not be reached in this way, they were dug out. In older times dogs were also used to find and bring young to their owner (Nørrevang 1951, 1977b). Since the middle of the twentieth century Manx Shearwater chicks have been dazzled with a torch at night as they are sitting in the entrance or in front of their burrows (Nørrevang 1977b; Olsen and Nørrevang 2005). Since 1928 it has been banned to take Puffins in their nests, but it can be allowed by license. Another more sophisticated method for catching Puffins is the 'fleyg' where birds are taken as they fly along the colony edges. For this the fowler uses a 'fleygingarstong', a pole about 3.5 m with a triangular net at the end. This is an old Faroese method that has been used for hundreds of years (cf. Nørrevang 1977a; Jensen 2010). It is not as harmful to the population as taking breeding birds from the burrows because many of the birds taken by fleyg are non-breeding immatures. By these two methods at least 250 000 Puffins were caught in the late nineteenth century and 150 000 in the 1930s. In the 1930s about 15% of the birds were taken from the nests (Patursson 1939). With fleyg alone 10 000–100 000 Puffins were taken each year in the late twentieth and early twenty-first century (Olsen and Nørrevang 2005; Jensen 2010). However, due to many years of breeding failure the bag has declined to almost zero (Olsen 2007; Jensen 2010), so now most of the landowners have decided to stop hunting until the population recovers.

The breeding cliffs for Common Guillemots are the most difficult to reach. The fowlers must climb up on the breeding ledges or descend from above using a long rope. Eggs were collected in some places while adult birds were taken in others, but only every third year. The adults were taken with a 'fyglingarstong' that was stronger and with a bigger net than the fleygingarstong used for Puffins. The birds were not taken in air but from the ledges. Many breeding birds were taken in this way and therefore it was considered a harmful method and thus banned in 1954, but at that time the use of this method already had come to an end in most places. The fleygingarstong was also used for guillemots in some places in the same way as for Puffins. Another method, imported from Iceland in the 1920s, was the 'snara', a floating board with nooses placed on the water beneath guillemot colonies. This method was banned in 1980. The average catch of guillemots in the early and middle twentieth century was estimated at about 60 000 (Salomonsen 1935) and 55 000 (Nørrevang 1977a), but the maximum for the biggest Faroese Common

Guillemot colony on Skúvoy was about 70 000 around 1920 (Nørrevang 1977a).

The only Gannet colony in the Faroes has been known since 1673 (Debes 1673). This colony has been particularly important for the locals on the remote island of Mykines, who have exploited the colony as long as is known – and still do. According to Svabo (1976) about 200 adults and 200 full grown chicks were taken annually around 1782, but in the last decades around 500 full grown chicks have been taken each year. Although the colony has been harvested for centuries it has increased slowly during the last hundred years (Olsen and Permin 1972; Nelson 2002), which is an indication of immigration from surrounding colonies (Nelson 2002).

For the Kittiwake, eggs, nearly fledged chicks and adults have been taken but not of the same importance as Puffins, Common Guillemots and Fulmars. Flying adults were taken with the fleygingarstong and the full-grown chicks were often taken from the lowest nests that could be reached without climbing.

Fulmars have been taken ever since the population became well established in the nineteenth century. At first it was mostly chicks that were taken but since the early twentieth century adults have also been taken with the fleygingarstong. In the early twentieth century about 80 000 chicks were taken from nests (Salomonsen 1935), but now the newly fledged chicks are taken on the sea. At that stage they are too heavy to fly and can be picked up from boats with a hand-held net. In total 50 000–100 000 chicks may be taken each year (Olsen and Nørrevang 2005).

Full-grown chicks of Shags have been taken from nests and also together with adults when sleeping on the rocks at the foot of bird cliffs. However, the population is small and only a few birds were taken. Black Guillemot chicks were also taken from their nests in some places before they were protected in 1928. Chicks of gulls and Great Skuas have also previously been taken for food. On the island of Skúvoy in ancient times 6000 Great Skua chicks were said to be taken each year, but this figure seems much too high, as in 1782 hardly 10 pairs were breeding on the island (Svabo 1976). The oily chicks of Storm Petrels have been used earlier for illumination on Mykines in the seventeenth century. They were dried to be lit in winter (Salomonsen 1935).

Eiders were hunted and their eggs taken until they became protected in a rescript from 1784. Svabo (1976) argued in 1782 for their protection, as he saw great economic value in the down, but the colonies never reached a size large enough for economic down exploitation as in Iceland.

In earlier times the feathers from Puffins, Common Guillemots and Kittiwakes were of high value, and in the middle of the nineteenth century feathers from about 270 000 seabirds were exported. Added to this are the feathers used by the locals (Nørrevang 1977a). Wings were also sewed together and used as brooms (Svabo 1976).

Shooting from boats started in the eighteenth century and became common from the early nineteenth century onwards. As the hunting on the sea was free for everyone it was a good opportunity for those who did not have fowling rights on land, but shooting has never had any economic importance compared to the other hunting methods. In the middle of the twentieth century shooting became more intense and the hunting pressure increased at the same time as the Common Guillemot population was declining (Olsen 1982). Shooting of Common Guillemots and Razorbills was therefore banned during the breeding season and is now only allowed in winter.

Birds, especially Kittiwakes but also Black Guillemots, have been used as bait for fishing. Before freezers became common, it was difficult to store Herring and other baits, and therefore birds were commonly shot for bait at the beginning of fishing trips (Patursson 1948).

In total 374 000 birds were hunted around the middle of the twentieth century (Patursson 1946), corresponding to 12 birds for each inhabitant, which indicates the economic importance of the birds at that time. The fowling rights on land are restricted to the landowners, while at sea hunting is free for everyone. Shooting birds and capturing Fulmar chicks at sea has therefore been popular by those who have no access to seabird colonies. As the production of Puffin chicks has failed for more than a decade and Puffin fleyg has terminated at least temporarily, Fulmar chicks are now the most important harvest. The seabirds and the seabird cliffs also have a high recreational value, and as there are plans to attract many more tourists to the islands, the importance of the birds may be seen to shift from hunting to provide a recreational value.

Note

1 Scientific name is given when species is mentioned first.

References

Anon [Ekker, M.] (ed.) (2008). West-Nordic seabirds in a pressed marine ecosystem. (What is the status of seabird populations in the Nordic countries? Which effects endanger the populations? To which measures can be taken?) *TemaNord* (2008), 573:100 pp. (Norwegian, English summary).

Anon [Sollie, J. and Einarson, S.] (eds) (2010). Action plan for seabirds in Western-Nordic areas. Report from a workshop in Malmö,

Sweden, 4–5 May 2010. *TemaNord* 587: 143.

Avise, J.C. and Walker, D. (1998). Pleistocene phylogeographic effects on avian populations and the speciation process. *Proceedings of the Royal Society of London B* 265: 457–463.

Andersen, K. (1898). Information on the Faroese birds. *Videnskabelige Meddelelser fra den naturhistorisk Forening i Kjøbenhavn* 10: 315–332. (Danish).

Andersen, K. (1901). Information about the Faroese birds. From written information from P. F. Petersen, Nolsø, and S. Niclassen, Mykines. *Videnskabelige Meddelelser fra Dansk Naturhistorisk Forening* 53: 253–294. (Danish).

Arnalds, Ó. (2008). Soils of Iceland. *Jökull* 58: 409–421.

Arnalds, A., Runólfsson, S. (2004). The role of Nootka Lupin (*Lupinus nootkatensis*) for revegetation in Iceland, pp. 94–96. In: E. van Santen (ed.), *Wild and Cultivated Lupins from the Tropics to the Poles, Proceedings of the 10th International Lupin Conference, Laugarvatn, Iceland, 19–24 June 2002.* Department of Agronomy and Soils, Alabama Agricultural Experiment Station and Auburn University, USA, i–xvi + 382 pp.

Áskelsson, J. (1953). A few words, including on an Icelandic fossil bird. *Náttúrufræðingurinn* 23 (3): 133–137. (Icelandic).

Bengtson, S.-A. (1970). Densities of passerine bird communities in Iceland. *Bird Study* 17 (3): 260–268.

Bengtson, S.-A. (1984). Breeding ecology and extinction of the Great Auk (*Pinguinus impennis*): anecdotal evidence and conjectures. *Auk* 101 (1): 1–12.

Bengtson, S.-A., Nilsson, A., Nordström, S., and Rundgren, S. (1975). Habitat selection of lumbricids in Iceland. *Oikos* 26 (3): 253–263.

Bengtson, S.-A., Eliasen, K., Jacobsen, L.M., and Magnussen, E. (2004). A history of colonization and current status of the House Sparrow (*Passer domesticus*) in the Faroe Islands. *Fróðskaparrit* 51: 237–251.

Bergmann, D. (2005). First confirmed breeding of Long-eared Owl in Iceland. *Bliki* 26: 47–50. (Icelandic, English summary).

Bjørk, E.A. (1963). Beak tax and more recent Faroese laws to control predatory birds. *Fróðskaparrit* 12: 7–52. (Faroese, English summary).

Björnsson, H. (1976). Bird life in the Öraefi area, S.E. Iceland. *Náttúrufræðingurinn* 46 (1–2): 56–104. (Icelandic, English summary).

Björnsson, H. (1979). Willow Warblers and Chiffchaffs, vagrants in Iceland: their frequency of occurrence, and times of arrival. *Náttúrufræðingurinn* 49 (2–3): 163–174. (Icelandic, English summary).

Björnsson, S. (2005). The Máfabyggðir nunatak, pp. 274–277. In: S. Ægisson (ed.). *[Diversities.] Anniversary volume for Helgi Hallgrímsson natural historian at his 70 years birthday, 11 June 2005.* Hólar. 479 pp. (Icelandic).

Bloch, D. (2012). Beak tax to control predatory birds in the Faroe islands. *Archives of Natural History* 39: 126–135.

Bloch, D. and Fuglø, E. (1999). Wild Nordic mammals. Tórshavn: Føroya Skúlabókagrunnur. (Faroese).

Bloch, D., Skårup, P., and Van Grouw, H. (2010). The Faroese White-speckled Raven. Tórshavn: Náttúrugripasavnið. 51 pp (Faroese, Danish).

Boswall, J. (1977). The use by seabirds of human fishing activities. *British Birds* 70 (2): 79–81.

Brewington, S.D. and McGovern, T.H. (2008). Plentiful Puffins. Zooarchaeological evidence for early exploitation in the Faroe Islands. In: Símunarbók. Heiðursrit til Símun V. Arge á 60 ára degnum (eds. C. Paulsen and H.D. Michelsen), 23–30. Tórshavn: Fróðskapur - Faroe University Press.

Brünnich, M.T. (1764). *Ornithologia Borealis, sistens collectionem avium ex omnibus, imperio Danico subjectis, provinciis, insulisque Borealibus Haniæ factam, cum descriptionibus novarum, Havniæ.* (8)+80+(2) pp. (Latin and Danish).

Brynjarsdóttir, J. and Nielsen, Ó.K. (2017). Estimating trends in Ptarmigan numbers. Chapter 9. In: Applied Raptor Ecology: Essentials from Gyrfalcon Research (eds. D.L. Anderson, C.J.W. McClure and A. Franke), 171–181. Boise, Idaho, USA: The Peregrine Fund 308 pp.

Buckland, P.C. and Panagiotakopulu, E. (2008). A palaeoecologist's view of Landnám. A case still not proven? In: *Símunarbók Heiðursrit til Símun V. Arge á 60 ára degnum* (eds C. Paulsen and H.D. Michelsen), 31–41. Tórshavn: Fróðskapur, Faroe University Press.

Burg, T.M., Bird, H., Lait, L. et al. (2014). Colonization pathways of the Northeast Atlantic by Northern Fulmars: a test of James Fisher's 'out of Iceland' hypothesis using museum collections. *Journal of Avian Biology* 45 (3): 209–218. https://doi.org/10.1111/j.1600-048X.2013.00262.x.

Caseldine, C., Russell, A., Hardardóttir, J., and Knudsen, O. (2005). *Iceland – Modern Processes and Past Environments*. Amsterdam: Elsevier, 420 pp.

Christensen-Dalsgaard, S., Anker-Nilssen, T., Crawford, R. et al. (2019). What's the catch with Lumpsuckers? A North Atlantic review of seabird bycatch in Lumpsucker gillnet fisheries. *Biol. Cons.* 240: 108–278. https://doi.org/10.1016/j.biocon.2019.

Church, M.J., Arge, S.V., Edwards, K.J. et al. (2013). The Vikings were not the first colonizers of the Faroe Islands. *Quaternary Science Reviews* 77: 228–232.

Claussøn Friis, P. (1632). A truthful description of Norway and surrounding islands. København. (Danish).

Dam, O.N. (1974). The hunting legislation. Tórshavn. 35 pp. (Faroese).

Debes, L. J. (1673), A Description of the Faroe Islands and the Inhabitants. København. (Danish).

Denk, T., Grímsson, F., Zetter, R., Símonarson, L.A. (2011). The biogeographic history of Iceland – The North Atlantic land bridge revisited. In: Late Cainozoic Floras of Iceland: 15 million years of vegetation and climate history in the Northern North Atlantic. *Topics in Geobiology* 35:647–668. doi: 10.1007/978-94-007-037-8_12. Springer Science+Business Media B.V.

Diercke International Atlas. http://www.diercke.com/kartenansicht.xtp?artId=978-3-14-100790-9&stichwort=modern%20man&fs=1. Downloaded 4 January 2015.

Diplomatarium Islandicum (1911–1921) 1169. Report on the sale of hawks and an Icelandic Gyrfalcon to Henry II, King of England. pp. i–xxviii + 917. Reykjavik, Iceland. (Icelandic).

Djurhuus, R. (2013). Use of the Faroese landscape, agriculture and sheep pasture. *Frøði* 2: 22–23. (Faroese).

Dugmore, A.J., Church, M.J., Buckland, P.C. et al. (2005). The Norse *landnám* on the North Atlantic islands; an environmental impact assessment. *Polar Record* 41 (216): 21–37.

Dugmore, A.J., Gísladóttir, G., Simpson, I.A., and Newton, A. (2009). Conceptual models of 1200 years of Icelandic soil erosion reconstructed using tephrochronology. *J. North Atlantic* 2: 1–18.

Dunn, E. and Steel, C. (2001). The Impact of Longline Fishing on Seabirds in the North-East Atlantic: Recommendations for Reducing Mortality. RSPB, NOF, JNCC and BirdLife International. 108 pp.

Einarsson, T. (1959). The last harvesting trip for Gannet young to the island of Eldey in 1939. *Blik* 20: 86–96. (Icelandic).

Einarsson, O. (1971) (written around 1585). *An account of Iceland*. Bókaútgáfa Menningarsjóðs, Reykjavík. 164 pp. (Icelandic).

Eliasen, K. Reinert, J., Gaard, E., et al. (2011). Sandeel as a link between primary production and higher trophic levels on the Faroe shelf. *Mar. Ecol. Prog. Ser.* 438: 185–194. https://doi.org/10.3354/meps09301.

Ellis, J.C. (2005). Marine birds on land: a review of plant biomass, species richness, and community composition in seabird colonies. *Plant Ecology* 181: 227–241.

Elmarsdóttir, Á., Fjellberg, A., Halldórsson, G., Ingimarsdóttir, M., Nielsen, Ó.K., Nygaard, P., Oddsdóttir, E.S., Sigurðsson, B. D. (2008) Effects of afforestation on biodiversity. In: G. Halldórsson, E.S. Oddsdóttir & B.D. Sigurðsson (eds). AFFORDNORD: Effects of afforestation on ecosystems, landscape and rural development. *TemaNord* 562, 37–48, 120 pp.

Elmarsdóttir, Á., Sigurðsson, B.D., Oddsdóttir, E.S. et al. (2011). Effects of afforestation on species richness. *Náttúrufræðingurinn* 81 (2): 69–81. (Icelandic, English summary).

Engelmoer, M. and Roselaar, C.S. (1998). *Geographical Variation in Waders*. Dordrecht, Boston, London: Kluwer Acad. Publ. i–xi + 331 pp.

Evans, P.G.H. (1980) Population genetics of the European Starling *Sturnus vulgaris*. University of Oxford, DPhil Thesis. 640 pp.

Ewing, S.R., Benn, S., Cowie, N. et al. (2013). Effects of weather variation on a declining population of Slavonian Grebes *Podiceps auritus*. *Journal für Ornithologie* 154: 995–1006. https://doi.org/10.1007/s10336-013-0967-y.

Faber, F. (1822). *Prodromus der isländischen Ornithologie, oder Geschichte der Vögel Islands*. Kopenhagen. 112 pp. (German).

Fisher, J. (1952). *The Fulmar*. London: Collins. i–xv + 496 pp.

Fjeldså, J. (1973). Distribution and geographical variation of the Horned Grebe *Podiceps auritus* (Linnaeus, 1758). *Ornis Scandinavica* 4 (1): 55–86.

Fosaa, A.M. (2001). A review of plant communities of the Faroe Islands. *Fróðskaparrit* 48: 41–54.

Friðriksson, S. (1979). Investigation of Black-backed Gull's nesting on Kvíárjökull 2 June, 1977. In: *Surtsey. Technical Progress Report of Biological Research on the Volcanic Island Surtsey and Its Environs for the Period 1965–1978*, pp. 86–102. Report to Department of Energy, Washington DC. Contract no. EY-76-C-02-3531,113 pp.

Friðriksson, Ó.E. (1996). *Hunting with Gun in Icelandic Nature*. Reykjavík: Iðunn. 440 pp. (Icelandic).

Garðarsson, A. (1975) The birds of Icelandic wetlands. In: *Wetlands. Rit Landverndar* 4: 100–134. Landvernd, Reykjavík. 238 pp. (Icelandic, English summary)

Garðarsson, A. (1989). A survey of Gannet *Sula bassana* colonies in Iceland. *Bliki* 7: 1–22. (Icelandic, English summary).

Garðarsson, A. (1995). Numbers of Gannets (*Sula bassana*) in Iceland 1989–94. *Náttúrufræðingurinn* 64 (3): 203–208. (Icelandic, English summary).

Garðarsson, A. (2006). Recent changes in numbers of cliff-breeding seabirds in Iceland. *Bliki* 27: 13–22. (Icelandic, English summary).

Garðarsson, A. (2010). *Icelandic cliff-nesting seabirds*. Hafrannsóknastofnunin. Málstofa 24.09.2010. Presentation, summary on website. (Icelandic).

Garðarsson, A. (2019). Icelandic colonies of the Northern Gannet in 2013-2014. *Bliki* 33: 69–71. (Icelandic, English summary).

Garðarsson, A., Guðmundsson, G.A., and Lilliendahl, K. (2011). Numbers of Northern Fulmar *Fulmarus glacialis* in Iceland: notes on early records, and changes between 1983-86 and 2005-09. *Bliki* 31: 1–10. (Icelandic, English summary).

Garðarsson, A., Lilliendahl, K., and Guðmundsson, G.A. (2019). Northern Fulmar *Fulmarus glacialis* breeding in Iceland surveyed in 2013–15. *Bliki* 33: 1–14. (Icelandic, English summary).

Garðarsson, A., Guðmundsson, G.A., and Lilliendahl, K. (2013). Numbers of Kittiwakes in Iceland in 2005–2009 and recent changes. *Bliki* 32: 1–10. (Icelandic, English summary).

Geirsdóttir, Á. (2011). Pliocene and Pleistocene Glaciations of Iceland: a brief overview of the glacial history. In: *Developments in Quaternary Science*, vol. 15 (eds J. Ehlers, P.L. Gibbard and P.D. Hughes), 199–210. Elsevier, Amsterdam, the Netherlands. 1108 pp.

Geirsdóttir, Á., Miller, G.H., Axford, Y., and Ólafsdóttir, S. (2009). Holocene and latest Pleistocene climate and glacier fluctuations in

Iceland. *Quaternary Science Reviews* 28 (21–22): 2107–2118.

Gíslason, S., Ragnarsdóttir, S.B., Vignisson, S.R., and Halldórsson, H.P. (2019). Using drones in seabird colony census. *Náttúrufræðingurinn* 89 (1–2): 22–33. (Icelandic, English summary).

Goryashko, A. (2020). *A Wild Bird and a Cultured Man (The Common Eider and Homo sapiens Fourteen Centuries Together)*. Alexandra Goryashko and Alexander Kondratyv (eds), St. Petersburg. 496 pp.

Grágás. The collection of laws of the Icelandic Commonwealth (1997) Mál og menning, Reykjavík. i–xxxv + 567 pp. (Icelandic)

Grímsson, F. and Símonarson, L.A. (2008). Upper Tertiary non-marine environments and climatic changes in Iceland. *Jökull* 58: 303–314.

Guðleifsson, B.E. (1998) The effect of hayfield cultivation on soil invertebrates. *Ráðunautafundur* 1998: 190-198. (Icelandic).

Guðleifsson, B.E. (2005). Beetle species (Coleoptera) in hayfields and pastures in northern Iceland. *Agriculture, Ecosystems and Environment* 109: 181–186.

Guðleifsson, B.E. and Bjarnadóttir, B. (2004). Spider (*Araneae*) populations in hayfields and pastures in northern Iceland. *Journal of Applied Entomology* 128 (4): 284–291.

Guðleifsson, B.E. and Bjarnadóttir, B. (2008). Springtail (*Collembola*) populations in hayfields and pastures in northern Iceland. *Icelandic Agricultural Sciences* 21: 49–59.

Guðmundsdóttir Beck, S. (2013). Exploitation of wild birds in Iceland from the Settlement Period to the 19th century and its reflection in archaeology. *Archaeologia Islandica* 10: 28–52.

Guðmundsson, F. (1951). The effects of the recent climatic changes on the bird life of Iceland. *Proceedings of the International Ornithological Congress* 10: 502–514.

Guðmundsson, F. (1954). Icelandic birds X. The Great Black-backed Gull (*Larus marinus* L.). *Náttúrufræðingurinn* 24 (4): 177–183. (Icelandic, English summary).

Guðmundsson, F. (1963). Problems of bird preservation in Iceland. *ICBP Bulletin* IX: 145–149.

Gulliksen, S., Birks, H.H., Possnert, G., and Mangerud, J. (1998). A calendar age estimate of the Younger Dryas-Holocene boundary at Kråkenes, western Norway. *The Holocene* 8 (3): 249–259.

Gunnarsson, T.G. (2004). Population increase of Black-tailed Godwits in Önundarfjörður and Dýrafjörður in NW-Iceland between 1979 and 2003. *Bliki* 25: 61–65. (Icelandic, English summary).

Gunnarsson, T.G. (2006). Icelandic moorland birds and forestry. *Fuglar* 3: 46–52. (Icelandic).

Gunnarsson, T.G. (2010). Shorebirds and wetlands. *Náttúrufræðingurinn* 79 (1–4): 75–86. (Icelandic, English summary).

Gunnarsson, T.G. and Indridadottir, G.H. (2009). Effects of sandplain revegetation on avian abundance and diversity at Skogasandur and Myrdalssandur, South-Iceland. *Conservation Evidence* 6: 98–104.

Gunnarsson, T.G., Gill, J.A., Appleton, G.F. et al. (2006). Large-scale habitat associations of birds in lowland Iceland: implications for conservation. *Biological Conservation* 128 (2): 265–275.

Gunnarsson, T.G., Appleton, G., Sutherland, W.J., Petersen, A., and Gill, J.A. (2007). Changes in breeding distribution and abundance of the Icelandic Black-tailed Godwit. *International Wader Study Group Annual Conference: La Rochelle, France, 28 September–1 October 2007*. Abstract.

Gunnlaugsson, G.Á., Guðbergsson, G.M., Þórarinsson, S. et al. (1984). *The Skaftáreldar eruption 1783–1784*. Reykjavík: Mál og menning. 442 pp. (Icelandic).

Hailer, F., Helander, B., Folkestad, A.O. et al. (2007). Phylogeography of the White-tailed Eagle, a generalist with large dispersal capacity. *Journal of Biogeography* 34 (7): 1193–1206.

Hammer, S. (2011). Distribution of rats. *Frágreiðing* 2011:3. Umhvørvisstovan, Argir. 19 pp. (Faroese).

Hammer, S., Joensen, H., and Jensen, J.-K. (2017). The history of Barnacle Geese in the Faroe Islands. *Dansk ornitologisk forenings tidsskrift* 111: 76–78.

Hansen, E.S., Bogason, V., Egilsson, K., Garðarsson, A., Jónsson, P. M., Lilliendahl, K., Petersen, A., Sigurðsson, I.A., Sigurðsson, I.A. (2008). The effects of Sandeel availability, Puffin harvest and climate change on the Vestmannaeyjar Atlantic Puffin population. *Raunvísindaþing* 14.-15.03.2008. Poster: 172.

Harris, M.P. (1970). Rates and causes of increases of some British gull populations. *Bird Study* 17 (4): 325–335.

Harris, M.P., Beare, D., Toresen, R. et al. (2007). A major increase in Snake Pipefish (*Entelurus aequoreus*) in northern European seas since 2003: potential implications for seabird breeding success. *Marine Biology* 151 (3): 973–983.

Harrison, R., Roberts, H.M., and Adderley, W.P. (2008). Gásir in Eyjafjörður: international exchange and local economy in medieval Iceland. *Journal of the North Atlantic* 1: 99–119.

Hátún, H., Payne, M.R., Beaugrand, G. et al. (2009). Large bio-geographical shifts in the northeastern Atlantic Ocean: from the subpolar gyre, via plankton, to Blue Whiting and Pilot Whales. *Oceanography* 80 (3–4): 149–162.

Hefti-Gautschi, B., Pfunder, M., Jenni, L. et al. (2009). Identification of conservation units in the European *Mergus merganser* based on nuclear and mitochondrial DNA markers. *Conservation Genetics* 10: 87–99.

Herremanns, M. (1990). Taxonomy and evolution in Redpolls *Carduelis flammea-hornemanni*; a multivariate study of their biometry. *Ardea* 78 (3): 441–458.

Hersteinsson, P. and Macdonald, D.W. (1996). Diet of Arctic Foxes (*Alopex lagopus*) in Iceland. *Journal of Zoology* 240: 457–474.

Hersteinsson, P., Nyström, V., Jóhannsson, J.H. et al. (2007). The oldest known remains of Arctic Foxes in Iceland. *Náttúrufræðingurinn* 76 (1–2): 13–21. (Icelandic, English summary).

Holm, P.A. (1848). Ornithological contributions to the Faroese fauna. *Naturhistorisk Tidsskrift*, 2nd series 2 (5): 465–525. (Danish).

Holm Joensen, A. (1966). *The birds of the Faroe Islands*. Copenhagen: RHODOS. 185 pp. (Danish).

Humlum, O. (1996). The principal forms of the landscape, Funningur, Slættaratindur. In: *The Faroe Islands Topographic Atlas* (ed. R. Guttesen), 38–41. Copenhagen: Det Kongelige Danske Geografiske Selskab og Kort og Matrikelstyrelsen. (Danish).

Humlum, O. and Christiansen, H.H. (1998). Mountain climate and periglacial phenomena in the Faeroe Islands. *Permafrost and Periglacial Processes* 9: 189–211.

Ingólfsson, A. (1970). Hybridization of Glaucous Gulls *Larus hyperboreus* and Herring Gulls *L. argentatus* in Iceland. *Ibis* 112 (3): 340–362.

Ingólfsson, Ó. (1984). Late glacial bird remains from the Melabakkar cliffs, Western Iceland. *Náttúrufræðingurinn* 53 (3–4): 97–100. (Icelandic, English summary).

Ingólfsson, Ó., Norðdahl, H., Schomacker, A. (2010). Deglaciation and Holocene Glacial History of Iceland. In: A. Schomacker, J. Krüger & K.H. Kjær (eds). The Mýrdalsjökull Ice Cap, Iceland. Glacial processes, sediments and landforms on an active volcano. *Developments in Quaternary Sciences* 13, pp. 51–68. Elsevier. 211 pp.

Jensen, J.-K. (1987). Interesting observations. *Frágreiðing frá Føroya Fuglafrøðifelag*. Tórshavn. pp. 1–3. (Faroese).

Jensen, J.-K. (1990). Interesting observations in 1989. *Frágreiðing frá Føroya Fuglafrøðifelag*. Tórshavn, p. 2–6. (Faroese).

Jensen, J.-K. (2010). *Puffin fowling - a fowling day on Nólsoy, Faroe Islands*. Føroya Skúlabókagrunnur, Tórshavn. 88 pp.

Jensen, J.-K. (2012). *The Fulmar on the Faroe Islands*. Tórshavn: Prenta, 102 pp. (Danish, English summary).

Jensen, J.-K., Bloch, D., Olsen, B. (2005). List of Birds Seen in the Faroe Islands. Føroya Náttúrugripasavn. Tórshavn. 18 pp.

Jensen, J-K., Sørensen, S. (2015). Birds of the Faroe Islands – Facts and Numbers. Forlagið í Støplum. Tórshavn, 363 pp. (Danish, English summary).

Jóhannesdóttir, L., Gill, J.A., Alves, J.A., and Gunnarsson, T.G. (2019a). Icelandic meadow-breeding waders: status, threats and conservation challenges. *Wader Study* 126 (1): 19–27.

Jóhannesdóttir, L., Gill, J.A., Alves, J.A. et al. (2019b). Interacting effects of agriculture and landscape on breeding wader populations. *Agriculture, Ecosystems and Environment* 272: 246–253.

Jónsbók. The Icelandic law code approved at the Althing in year 1281 and updated around mid-14th century but printed first in year 1587. 2004. Háskólaútgáfan, Reykjavík. 383 pp. (Icelandic).

Jónsson, Þ. (1896). Bird hunting in the Westman Islands. *Eimreiðin* 2: 165–169. (Icelandic).

Jónsson, J. (2001) *The Common Eider and eider husbandry in Iceland*. Mál og Mynd, Reykjavík. 528 pp. (Icelandic).

Jónsson, J.Á., Sigurðsson, B.D., and Halldórsson, G. (2006). Changes in bird life, surface fauna and ground vegetation following afforestation by Black Cottonwood (*Populus trichocarpa* Torr. & Gray). *Icelandic Agricultural Sciences* 19: 33–41.

Jørgensen, G. and Rasmussen, J. (1986). *Glacial Striae, Roches Moutonnées and Ice Movements in the Faeroe Islands*: DGU series C, no. 7.

Júlíusson, K. (1981) Hunting rights. Skotveiðifélag Ísland, Reykjavík. 87 pp. (Icelandic).

Kear, J. (1967). Feeding habits of the Greylag Goose *Anser anser* in Iceland, with reference to its interaction with agriculture. *Congr. Biol. du Gibier* 7: 615–622.

Kristinsson, H. (2015). Distribution patterns and age of the Icelandic flora. *Náttúrufræðingurinn* 85(3–4): 121–133. (Icelandic, English summary).

Kristjánsson, L. (1986). The use of Icelandic seabirds. In: *Icelandic Sea Culture V*, 113–316. Reykjavík: Bókaútgáfa Menningarsjóðs. 498 pp. (Icelandic, English summary).

Kyrjarheygg, J.M. (2002). Letter from J.M. Kyrjarheygg. *Frágreiðing frá Føroya Fuglafrøðifelag*. Tórshavn. pp. 6–7. (Faroese).

Landt, J. (1800). Attempt to a description of the Faroe Islands.. Copenhagen. (Danish).

Leivsson, T. (2004). 2004 – a memorable year in Faroese natural history. *Frágreiðing frá Føroya Fuglafrøðifelag*, Tórshavn. pp 16–22. (Faroese).

Lillienthal, K., Hansen, E.S., Bogason, V., et al. (2013). Recruitment failure of Atlantic Puffins *Fratercula arctica* and Sandeels *Ammodytes marinus* in Vestmannaeyjar islands. *Náttúrufræðingurinn* 83(1–2): 65–79. (Icelandic, English summary).

Long, J.L. (1981). *Introduced birds of the world: The worldwide history, distribution and influence of birds introduced to new environments*. Newton Abbot, London: David & Charles. 528 pp.

MacArthur, R.H. and Wilson, E.O. (2001). *The Theory of Island Biogeography*. Princeton Univ. Press. i–xv + 203 pp. Thirteenth printing and first Princeton Landmarks in Biology edition, with a new preface by E.O. Wilson.

Magnússon, B., Magnússon, S.H., and Sigurðsson, B.D. (2003). Effects of introduced Nootka Lupin (*Lupinus nootkatensis*) on plant succession in Iceland. *Náttúrufræðingurinn* 71 (3–4): 98–111. (Icelandic, English summary).

Mann, M.E. and Jones, P.D. (2003). Global surface temperatures over the past two millennia. *Geophysical Research Letters* 30: 1820–1823. https://doi.org/10.1029/2003GL017814.

Marthinsen, G., Wennerberg, L., and Lifjeld, J.T. (2007). Phylogeography and subspecies taxonomy of Dunlins (*Calidris alpina*) in western Palearctic analysed by DNA microsatellites and amplified fragment length polymorphism markers. *Biological Journal of the Linnean Society* 92 (4): 713–726.

Marthinsen, G., Wennerberg, L., Pierce, E.P., and Lifjeld, J.T. (2008). Phylogeographic origin and genetic diversity of Dunlin *Calidris alpina* in Svalbard. *Polar Biology* 31 (11): 1409–1420.

Massé, G., Rowland, S.J., Sicre, M.A. et al. (2008). Abrupt climate changes for Iceland during the last millennium: evidence from high resolution sea ice reconstructions. *Earth and Planetary Science Letters* 269: 565–569.

McGovern, T.H. (2009). The Archaeofauna. In: *Hofstaðir (Excavations of a Viking Age Feasting Hall in North-Eastern Iceland)* (ed. G. Lucas), 168–252. Reykjavik: Institute of Archaeology, Monograph No. 1. i–xxiii + 440 pp.

McGovern, T., Perdikaris, S., Einarsson, Á., and Sidell, J. (2006). Coastal connections, local fishing, and sustainable egg harvesting: patterns of Viking Age inland wild resource use in Mývatn District, Northern Iceland. *Environmental Archaeology* 11 (1): 187–206.

McGovern, T.H., Vésteinsson, O., Friðriksson, A. et al. (2007). Landscapes of settlement in Northern Iceland: historical ecology of human impact and climate fluctuation on the millennial scale. *American Anthropologist* 109 (1): 27–51.

Montevecchi, W.A. and Hufthammer, A.K. (1990). Zooarchaeological implications for prehistoric distributions of seabirds along the Norwegian coast. *Arctic* 43 (2): 110–114.

Müller, H.C. (1862). The Faroese birds with remarks on the bird hunting. *Meddelelser fra den naturhistoriske Forening i København*, pp. 2–78. (Danish).

Muñoz-Fuentes, C., Vilà, C., Green, A.J. et al. (2007). Hybridization between White-headed Ducks and introduced Ruddy Ducks in Spain. *Molecular Ecology* 16: 629–638.

Nelson, B. (2002). *The Atlantic Gannet.* 2ed. Norfolk: Fenix Books Limited. 396 pp.

Niels á Botni (1952). Ideas concerning the White- spackled Raven (*Corvus corax varius*). *Fróðskaparrit* 1: 114–121. (Faroese).

Nielsen, O.K. (1979). Research into density of moorland birds in Mývatnssveit 1978 and in Önundarfjörður and Dýrafjörður in 1979. University of Iceland, Unpublished thesis. 55 pp. (Icelandic)

Nielsen, O.K. (1994). The Ruddy Duck (*Oxyura jamaicensis*) in Iceland. *Oxyura* 7: 67–73.

Nielsen, O.K. (2003). Project SKÓGVIST: Moorland and woodland birds at Hérað, E-Iceland, 2002. Náttúrufræðistofnun Íslands NÍ03010. 21 pp. (Icelandic)

Norðdahl, H., Ingólfsson, Ó., Pétursson, H.G., and Hallsdóttir, M. (2008). Late Weichselian and Holocene environmental history of Iceland. *Jökull* 58: 343–364.

Norðdahl, H. and Pétursson, H.G. (2005). Relative sea-level changes in Iceland: New aspects of the Weichselian Deglaciation of Iceland. In: *Iceland – Modern Process and Past Environments* (eds C. Caseldine, A. Russel, J. Harðardóttir and Ó. Knudsen), 25–78. Amsterdam: Elsevier. 397 pp.

Nørrevang, A. (1951). Manx Shearwater (*Puffinus puffinus* (Brünn.)) and its Catching in the Faeroe Islands. *Dansk Ornith. Foren. Tidsskr.* 45: 96–101. (Danish, English summary).

Nørrevang, A. (1955). Changes in the bird fauna of the Faeroes in relation to the climatic changes in the North Atlantic region. *Dansk Ornithologisk Forenings Tidsskrift* 49: 206–229. (Danish, English summary).

Nørrevang, A. (1977a). *Fowling in the Faroe islands.* København: Rhodos. 275 pp. (Danish).

Nørrevang, A. (1977b). Catching of Manx Shearwater chicks in the Faroes. *Folk og Kultur. Årbog for Dansk Etnologi og Folkemindevidenskab* (1977): 41–61. (Danish).

Nørrevang, A. (1986). Traditions of sea bird fowling in the Faroes: An ecological basis for sustained fowling. *Ornis Scandinavica.* 17: 275–281.

Ogilvie, A.E.J. (1984). The past climate and sea-ice record from Iceland, part 1: Data to A.D. 1780. *Climatic Change* 6 (2): 131–154.

Ogilvie, A.E.J. (1990). Climatic changes in Iceland A.D. c. 865 to 1598. *Acta Archaeologica* 61: 234–251.

Ogilvie, A.E.J. and Jónsson, T. (2001). 'Little Ice Age' research: a perspective from Iceland. *Climatic Change* 48: 9–52.

Ólafsson, E. (1983). The Black Tern *Chlidonias niger* breeding in Iceland. *Bliki* 2: 48–55. (Icelandic, English summary).

Ólafsson, J.S. (ed.) (1998). *Icelandic wetlands: Conservation and utilization*. Háskólaútgáfan, Reykjavík. 283 pp. (Icelandic, English summary)

Olofson, S.K.K. and Sörensen, S. (2018). List of the Faroese birds – with special reference to the rare species. http://www.jenskjeld.info/ artikler/ Faeroliste_udg.14c.pdf. (Danish).

Olsen, B. (1982). Some reasons for the decline in the Faroese guillemot population estimated from the pattern of decline and ringing results. *Viltrapport* 21: 24–30. (Danish).

Olsen, B. (1994). Has the population of Greylag Geese become too large? *Frágreiðing frá Føroya Fuglafrøðifelag*. Tórshavn, pp. 20–25. (Faroese).

Olsen, B. (2006). The subsea tunnel to Sandoy threatens the birds due to rats. *Frágreiðing frá Føroya Fuglafrøðifelag*. Tórshavn, pp. 24–25. (Faroese).

Olsen, B. (2007). The seabird populations are declining. *Frøði*, Føroya Fróðskaparfelag, Tórshavn. 1: 10–15. (Faroese).

Olsen, B. (2008). Fulmars bycatch on longlines. *Sjóvarmál*, Fiskirannsóknarstovan. Tórshavn. pp. 6–9. (Faroese).

Olsen, B. (2010). Rats threatening the world largest Storm Petrel colony, and it is our responsibility. *Frøði*, Føroya Fróðskaparfelag, Tórshavn. 2: 22–24. (Faroese).

Olsen, B. and Nørrevang, A. (2005). Seabird fowling in the Faroe Islands. In: *Traditions of Seabird Fowling in the North Atlantic Region,* 162–180. Isle of Lewis: The Islands Book Trust. Port of Ness. 215 pp.

Olsen, B. and Permin, M. (1972). The population of Gannet *Sula bassana* on Mykineshólmur 1972. Dansk Ornith. Foren. Tidsskr. 68: 38–42. (Danish).

Olsen, B., Jensen J.-K. and Reinert, A. (2000). Populations of Guillemots, Razorbills and Puffins in Faroese Waters as documented by ringed birds. GEM Report, No. C22–161. 33 pp.

Oorschot, J.M.P. van (1974). Royal birds and falconeers from Valkenswaard. *Bijdragen Tot de Geschiedenis van het Zuiden van Nederland*, xxix. i–xxxix + 329 pp. (Dutch).

Óskarsson, Ö. (1995a). First breeding record of Siskin *Carduelis spinus* in Iceland. *Bliki* 15: 57–59. (Icelandic, English summary).

Óskarsson, Ö. (1995b). First breeding attempt of Crossbill *Loxia curvirostra* in Iceland. *Bliki* 15: 59–60. (Icelandic, English summary).

Óskarsson, H. (1998). Wetland draining in Western Iceland. In: *Icelandic Wetlands (Preservation and Utilization)* (ed. J.S. Ólafsson), 121–129. Reykjavík: Háskólaútgáfan. 283 pp. (Icelandic, English summary).

Pálsson, S., Vigfúsdóttir, F., and Ingólfsson, A. (2009). Morphological and genetic patterns of hybridization of Herring Gulls (*Larus argentatus*) and Glaucous Gulls (*L. hyperboreus*) in Iceland. *Auk* 126 (2): 376–382.

Pálsson, Ó.K., Gíslason, A., Gunnarsson, B. et al. (2014). Ecosystem structure in the Iceland Sea and recent changes in the Capelin (*Mallotus villosus*) population. *Náttúrufræðingurinn* 84 (1–2): 4–18. (Icelandic, English summary).

Patursson, S. 1926. *Fulmarus glacialis* on the Faroe Islands. Naturen Bergen 50: 97–104. (Norwegian).

Patursson, S. (1939). Report on the Faroese Puffin population. Tórshavn. 27 pp.

Patursson, S. (1946). Bird populations on the Faroe Islands. *Naturen*: 179–186. (Norwegian).

Patursson, S. (1948). *The birds are of great value for the country*. Tórshavn: Landnám. 40 pp. (Faroese).

Peters, J.L., Zhuravlev, Y.N., Fefelov, I. et al. (2008). Multilocus phylogeography of a Holarctic duck: colonization of North America from Eurasia by Gadwall (*Anas strepera*). *Evolution* 62 (6): 1469–1483.

Petersen, A. (1976). Size variables in Puffins *Fratercula arctica* from Iceland, and bill features as criteria of age. *Ornis Scandinavica* 7 (2): 185–192.

Petersen, A. (1982). Icelandic seabirds. pp. 15–60. In: *Birds*. Reykjavík. 216 pp. (Icelandic, English translation available)

Petersen, A. (1983). An influx of Short-eared Owls *Asio flammeus* in Iceland, autumn 1982. *Bliki* 1: 12–16. (Icelandic, English summary).

Petersen, A. (1995). Some aspects of the history of the Great Auk in Iceland. *Náttúrufræðingurinn* 65 (1–2): 53–66. (Icelandic, English summary).

Petersen, A. (1998). *Icelandic Birds*. Vaka-Helgafell, Reykjavík. 312 pp. (Icelandic).

Petersen, A. (2000). Monitoring Icelandic seabirds. *Náttúrufræðingurinn* 69 (3–4): 189–200. (Icelandic, English summary).

Petersen, A. (2002). Seabird bycatch in fishing gear in Iceland. *Náttúrufræðingurinn* 71 (1–2): 52–61. (Icelandic, English summary).

Petersen, A. (2005). Traditional seabird fowling in Iceland. In: *Traditions of Sea-Bird Fowling in the North Atlantic Region. Conference Sept. 9–11, 2004*, 194–215. Isle of Lewis, Scotland. The Islands Book Trust, Isle of Lewis. 215 pp.

Petersen, A. (2009). Formation of a bird community on a new island Surtsey, Iceland. *Surtsey Research* 12: 131–145.

Petersen, A. (2010). The Kittiwake *Rissa tridactyla* in Breiðafjörður (NW-Iceland): Colony distribution, population changes, historical perspectives, and census techniques. *Náttúrufræðingurinn* 79 (1–4): 45–56. (Icelandic, English summary).

Petersen, A., Thorstensen, S., and Þórisson, B. (2014). Distribution and changes in numbers of Glaucous Gulls *Larus hyperboreus* breeding in Iceland. *Náttúrufræðingurinn* 84 (3–4): 133–143. (Icelandic, English summary).

Petersen, A., Irons, D., Gilchrist, H.G. et al. (2015). The status of Glaucous Gulls *Larus hyperboreus* in the Circumpolar Arctic. *The Arctic* 68 (1): 107–120.

Pétursson, G. and Skarphéðinsson, K.H. (1978). Vagrant birds in SW-Iceland, autumn 1977. *Náttúruverkur* 5: 10–31. (Icelandic, English summary).

Pirazzoli, P.A. (1996). Sea-level changes: the last 20,000 years. *Coastal Morphology and Research Bibliography*: 175–196.

Ploeger, P.L. (1968). Geographical differentiation in Arctic Anatidae as a result of isolation during the Last Glacial. *Ardea* 56 (1–2): 1–159.

Puckett, E.E., Magnussen, E., Khlyap, L.A. et al. (2020). Genomic analyses reveal three independent introductions of the invasive Brown Rat (*Rattus norvegicus*) to the Faroe Islands. *Heredity* 124: 15–27.

Rasmussen, J. (2002). The Faroe-Shetland gateway: late Quaternary water mass exchange between the Nordic seas and the northeastern Atlantic. *Marine Geology* 188: 165–192.

Rasmussen, J. and Noe-Nygaard, A. (1970). *Geology of the Faroe Islands*. Danmarks Geologiske Undersøgelse I, 25: Copenhagen.

Ruokonen, M., Aarvak, T., and Madsen, J. (2005). Colonization history of the High-Arctic Pink-footed Goose *Anser brachyrhynchus*. *Molecular Ecology* 14 (1): 171–178.

Sadler, J.P. (1999). Biodiversity on oceanic islands: a palaeoecological assessment. *Journal of Biogeography* 26 (1): 75–87.

Salomonsen, F. (1935). Aves, volume 3, pp. 1–277. In: Jensen, A. D. S., Lundbeck, W., Mortensen, Th., Spärck, R. (eds), *The Zoology of the Faroes*. A.F. Høst & Søn, Copenhagen.

von Schmalensee, M. (2010). Ecosystems in peril, part two: alien and invasive species in Iceland. *Náttúrufræðingurinn* 80 (3–4): 84–102. (Icelandic, English summary).

Siegert, M.J. (2001). Ice Sheets and Late Quaternary Environmental Change. Chichester: Wiley.

Sigurðsson, S. (1977). Propagation and condition of birch woodlands in Iceland. In: H. Ragnarsson, H. Guðmundsson, I. Þorsteinsson, J. Jónsson, S. Blöndal and S. Sigurðsson (eds), *Woods in Iceland*. Edda hf, Reykjavík, pp. 146–172, 281 pp. (Icelandic).

Sigurðsson, B.D. and Magnússon, B. (2004). Woodcock (*Scolopax rusticola*) found breeding in

Icelandic woodland. *Skógrœktarritið* (1): 14–17. (Icelandic, English summary).

Símonarson, L.A. (1981). Icelandic fossils. In: *Icelandic Nature*, 2 ed., changed and extended. Almenna Bókafélagið, Reykjavík, pp. 157–173. 475 pp. (Icelandic).

Skarphéðinsson, K.H. (1992). *Damage of White-tailed Eagles to Common Eider colonies.* Ministry for the Environment – Náttúrufræðistofnun Íslands. 88 pp. (Icelandic).

Skarphéðinsson, K.H. (2003) Sea Eagles in Iceland: population trends and reproduction. In: B. Helander, M. Marquiss and B. Bowermann (eds), *Sea Eagle 2000. Proceedings from an International Conference at Björkö, Sweden, 13–17 September 2000.* Swedish Society for Nature Conservation/ SNF & Åtta.45 Tryckeri AB. Stockholm, pp. 31–38.

Skarphéðinsson, K.H. and Þorleifsson, E. (1998). Water Rail – an extinct breeder in Iceland. In: Árnason, G. S. (ed.), *The Book on the Farm Kvísker. Publication in Honour of the Family at Kvísker.* Sýslusafn Austur-Skaftafellssýslu, Höfn í Hornafirði, pp. 266–296, 303 pp. (Icelandic).

Skírnisson, K. and Petersen, A. (1980). Mink in Iceland. In: Einarsson, Á. (ed.), *Wild Mammals in Iceland.* Rit Landverndar 7. Reykjavík, pp. 80–94. 119 pp. (Icelandic).

Snæþórsson, A.Ö. and Pétursson, J.G. (1992). Birds and forestry. *Skógrœktarritið*: 99–108. (Icelandic, English summary).

Snorrason, A., Harðardóttir, V.B., and Kjartansson, B.Þ. (2007). Status on surveys of the natural birch woodlands in Iceland. *Rit Frœðaþings Landbúnaðarins*: 572–574. (Icelandic).

Stefánsson, R.A. and Bjarnadóttir, S. (2005). The distribution of Goldcrest in W-Iceland. *Bliki* 26: 5–10. (Icelandic, English summary).

Stefánsson, R.A., von Schmalensee, M., and Skorupski, J. (2016). A tale of conquest and crisis: invasion history and status of the American Mink (*Neovison vison*) in Iceland. *Acta Biologica* 23: 88–100.

Sturluson, S. ≈1220 (1848). *Edda Snorra Sturlusonar eða Gylfaginning, Skáldskaparmál og Háttatal.*

Published by Sveinbjörn Egilsson, Reykjavík. i–viii + 252 pp. (Icelandic).

Svabo, J.C. (1976). Report from a journey in the Faroe Islands 1781 and 1782. København: Selskabet til udgivelse af færøske kildeskrifter og studier. 497 pp. (Danish).

Sveinbjarnardóttir, G., Buckland, P.C., and Gerrard, A.J. (1982). Landscape change in Eyjafjallasveit, Southern Iceland. *Norsk Geologisk Tidsskrift* 36 (1): 75–88.

Sæmundsson, K. (1980). Outline of the geology of Iceland. *Jökull* 29: 7–28.

Þorleifsson, E.Ó. (1998). Effects of drainage on wetlands birds in South Iceland. In: *Icelandic Wetlands (Preservation and Utilization)* (ed. J.S. Ólafsson), 173–183. Reykjavík: Háskólaútgáfan 283 pp. (Icelandic, English summary).

Þorsteinsson, Þ. and Thorstensen, S. (2014). Birds of Hrísey island in Eyjafjörður (Census in summer 2014 compared to Censuses in 1994 and 2004). Printed report for Akureyri Environmental Committee. 63 p. (Icelandic).

Þórhallsdóttir, Þ.E. (1998). The restoration of wetland. In: *Icelandic Wetlands (Preservation and Utilization)* (ed. J.S. Ólafsson), 273–283. Reykjavík: Háskólaútgáfan, 283 pp. (Icelandic, English summary).

Þórisson, S. (1981). Starlings in Iceland: immigration, distribution, and population size. *Náttúrufrœðingurinn* 31 (4): 145–163. (Icelandic, English summary).

Theódórsson, J. (1936). Whooper Swans and swan feathers. *Eimreiðin* 42 (3): 236–238. (Icelandic).

Thies, L., Tomkovich, P., dos Remedios, N. et al. (2018). Population and subspecies differentiation in a high latitude breeding wader, the Common Ringed Plover *Charadrius hiaticula*. *Ardea* 106 (2): 163176.

Tiedemann, R., Paulus, K.B., Scheer, M. et al. (2004). Mitochondrial DNA and microsatellite variation in the Eider Duck (*Somateria mollissima*) indicate stepwise postglacial colonization of Europe and limited current long-distance dispersal. *Molecular Ecology* 13: 1481–1494.

Traustason, B. and Snorrason, A. (2008). Spatial distribution of forests and woodlands in Iceland in accordance with the CORINE land cover classification. *Icelandic Agricultural Sciences* 21: 39–47.

USGS (2013). Understanding plate motions. http://pubs.usgs.gov/gip/dynamic/understanding.html. Downloaded 19.10.2013.

van Grouw, H. (2014). Some black-and-white facts about the Faeroese White-speckled Common Raven *Corvus corax varius. Bulletin of the British Ornithologists' Club* 134 (1): 4–13.

van de Pol, M., Atkinson, P., Blew, J. et al. (2014). A global assessment of the conservation status of the nominate subspecies of Eurasian Oystercatcher *Haematopus ostralegus ostralegus. International Wader Studies* 20: 47–61.

Vang, H.B.M. (2014). Faroese Greylag Goose population: population status and effects on Faroese agriculture. Aarhus University. Unpublished MSc Thesis.

Vang, H.B.M. and Jensen, J.-K. (2016). Changes in Greylag Goose population management in the Faroe Islands. GooseNews 15: 8–10.

Vigfúsdóttir, F., Kolbeinsson, and Y., Jónasson, J.P. (2007). Puffin catch records in Iceland: do they reflect past population fluctuations? Waterbird Soc. Meeting, Barcelona. October 2007. Poster. 1 pp.

Vigfúsdóttir, F., Pálsson, S., and Ingólfsson, A. (2008). Hybridization of Glaucous Gull (*Larus hyperboreus*) and Herring Gull (*Larus argentatus*) in Iceland: mitochondrial and microsatellite data. *Phil. Trans. R. Soc. B.* 363: 2851–2860. https://doi.org/10.1098/rstb.2008.0042.

Vignisson, S.R. (2012) Evolutionary identity of Icelandic Redwing, studied in cytochrome. University of Iceland. BS Thesis. 23 pp. (Icelandic, English summary).

Whittaker, R.J., Triantis, K.A., and Ladle, R.J. (2008). A general dynamic theory of oceanic island biogeography. *Journal of Biogeography* 35: 977–994.

Williamson, K. (1945a). The economic importance of sea-fowl in the Faeroe Islands. *Ibis* 87: 249–269.

Williamson, K. (1945b). Some new and scarce breeding species in the Faeroe Islands. *Ibis* 87: 550–558.

Willis, K.J. and Whittaker, R.J. (2000). The refugial debate. *Science*, New Ser., 287 (5457): 1406–1407.

Wink, M. (1973). Siedlungsdichteundetersuchungen in Heidebiotopen und Lavafeldern Nord-Islands. *Die Vogelwelt* 94 (2): 41–50. (German, English summary).

Wolley, J. (1850). Some observations on the birds of the Faroe Islands. *Jardine's Contributions to Ornithology*: 106–117.

11

Human Impact on North Atlantic Biota

Farming and Farm Animals, Fishing, Sealing and Whaling

Ingrid Mainland and Jennifer Harland

Archaeology Institute, University of the Highlands and Islands, Orkney College, Kirkwall, UK

Introduction

Throughout prehistory the world's oceans have acted not as a barrier but rather a pathway for the seafaring communities who live around their rims, bringing to the many islands and island groups in these oceans successive waves of human activity of differing intensity, duration and impact, from short-lived exploratory contacts to full colonization and settlement (Rainbird 2007; Rick et al. 2013). The arrival of humans modified island ecosystems through the introduction of vertebrate faunas for farming and hunting, clearance of forest and other vegetation for agriculture and grazing animals, and the harvesting and predation of indigenous species for food and other resources. Alongside these are the unintentional effects of the diverse commensal and parasitic species who travel along with humans and their domesticates, rodents (Searle et al. 2009; Cucchi et al. 2014), insects (Sadler and Panagiotakopulu in the Introduction to this book) and even pathogens (Rick et al. 2013). The North Atlantic islands are no exception to this. Today these islands, from Iceland in the west to Shetland and Orkney in the east, are synonymous with sheep and the products

these provide: this species, however, which is so iconic of and for the island communities in the North Atlantic, is not indigenous to these islands. Sheep were introduced along with other domesticates through the establishment of farming communities in the North Atlantic islands, a process that began during the Neolithic (c. 3500 BCE) for Orkney and Shetland and culminated in the ninth and tenth centuries CE with the colonization of the North Atlantic by the Norse, a Scandinavian people originating mainly from Norway (Fitzhugh and Ward 2000).

In this chapter, we explore the profound impact of farming on North Atlantic vertebrate biota, reviewing evidence for the introduction of domesticated faunas and of the irrevocable changes to the island landscapes and environments effected in particular by pastoralism and the exploitation of marine resources. Over the last two decades, there has been sustained research on the historical ecology of the North Atlantic (Dugmore et al. 2012), which whilst demonstrating how Norse farming communities modified the terrestrial ecosystems they encountered, has also begun to question the widely held assumption that this process was necessarily maladaptive

Biogeography in the Sub-Arctic: The Past and Future of North Atlantic Biota, First Edition.
Edited by Eva Panagiotakopulu and Jon P. Sadler.

and unsustainable; after all, farming communities existed for nearly 500 years in Greenland and continue until the present day in Iceland, the Faroes and the Northern Isles. Dugmore et al. (2007, 2012) have recently presented a comprehensive review of the environmental impact of Norse farming practices on Iceland, Greenland and the Faroes and have highlighted various examples of terrestrial ecosystem management, soils (Adderley and Simpson 2006), avian faunas (McGovern et al. 2006), caribou (Dugmore et al. 2012) and pasture management (Simpson et al. 2001, 2004; Thomson et al. 2005). These, it is argued, reflect a successful response and adaptation to northern and sub-arctic environments that are moreover of relevance for a future response to climate change (Dugmore et al. 2007, 2012). Here we extend coverage of the impact of farming to include the easternmost Atlantic islands settled by the Norse, Orkney and Shetland, and go on to explore the argument for sustainable management through a specific case study, Norse grazing management systems for domestic ungulates. An area that has received less attention in a North Atlantic context has the potential of marine historical ecology for understanding marine resource use. Recent research on fishing in Orkney and Shetland is brought together to explore the value of centennial–millennial perspectives on human–fish interaction in northern waters.

History of Settlement: Introduction, Exploitation and Modification of Vertebrate Biota

The North Atlantic islands have different settlement histories. There is a continuous record of farming communities in Orkney and Shetland from the mid third millennium BCE onwards (Downes et al. 2005). Evidence for earlier, hunter–gatherer populations suggest pre-farming occupation of the islands but little is known about the nature of terrestrial fauna prior to the advent of farming due to a lack of faunal assemblages from this period (ScARF 2012). By c. 3500 BCE at Knap of Howar, the earliest dated Neolithic site in Orkney, cattle, sheep, goat and dog were present along with red deer (Noddle 1983). Pine marten, Orkney vole, field mouse and otter are also attested elsewhere in Orkney during the Neolithic, as is fox (McCormick and Buckland 1997; Mainland and Simpson 2005; Nicholson et al. 2005; Cucchi et al. 2014). Sheep and goats, which are not native to Europe, will have been introduced to the islands. Domestic cattle are also likely to have been imports as there is currently little evidence to support indigenous domestication of this species within a British context (Viner 2011). However, aurochs DNA in Late Neolithic cattle from the Links of Notland in Westray does raise interesting questions about the potential presence of aurochs and indeed other large herbivores in the islands prior to the first farmers (Fraser et al. 2017). Cucchi et al. (2014) have argued that Orkney voles were transported along with the first farmers and it is possible that such groups were also responsible for the introduction of other non-domesticates (cf. Serjeanston 1990). This well-documented phenomena of 'transported landscapes' is, however, also evidenced in some hunter-gatherer groups (Zeder 2011; Rick et al. 2013).

A second wave of species introductions is apparent at the end of the first millennium BCE/early first millennium CE, i.e. during the Atlantic Iron Age. The domestic cat appears in the archaeological record in the late first millennium BCE (Mainland et al. in preparation; Smith 1994; Bond 2007; Cucchi et al. 2014) and horse is first recorded at a similar date (Mainland et al. in preparation; Bond 2007). It is generally assumed that these represent gift exchange and other contacts between the Northern Isles and Iron Age communities further to the south; earlier pre-Norse Scandinavian contact should not, however, be precluded (e.g. Church et al. 2013). Fox may also have been introduced, or re-introduced, at this time (Fairnell and Barrett 2007; Cucchi et al. 2014). House mouse is first recorded in Shetland during the Middle Iron Age at Old Scatness (c. 350 BCE–CE20) (Nicholson et al. 2005), but has not been found in Orkney before the ninth to tenth century CE, the Viking/ Norse period (Harland 2012). Genetic studies have shown that the subsequent expansion of this species across into the Faeroes, Iceland and Greenland can be attributed to the colonization of these islands by the Norse, but with the founder populations originating in the Northern Isles rather than Norway (Searle et al. 2009; Jones et al. 2012).

The arrival of the Vikings in the Northern Isles was a period of major social, cultural and genetic change, with the introduction of a new material culture and permanent settlement from the late eighth/ninth century CE by incoming settlers from Scandinavia, concomitant with a take-over of existing farms and estates (Barrett et al. 2000; Dockrill et al. 2010, p. 95). Whether this process reflects a relatively peaceful integration or more violent process is still debated but most researchers have envisaged a continuation of Iron Age practices, citing little evidence for substantial change to farming systems (Bond 2007; Cussans and Bond 2010; Dockrill et al. 2010; Mainland et al. 2016) or livestock (Cussans et al. 2007). Given a documented movement of domestic livestock from Norway to other of the North Atlantic islands (see below), it seems probable, however, that some livestock were also being brought into, and indeed out from, Orkney and Shetland, especially as cattle and horses were of high status at this period (Mainland and Halstead 2005; McGovern et al. 2009; Mainland et al. 2016). That zooarchaeological studies have so far failed to identify such introduction or to demonstrate significant change in practice may merely reflect methodological limitations (e.g. equifinality resulting from

the influence of environmental, genetic and dietary factors on body size; Cussans 2010). Isotopic and genetic studies are beginning to enable more nuanced understanding of husbandry practices (Telldahl et al. 2011; Jones et al. 2012), as well as the scale of animal movements through exchange, tribute and prestige networks, in prehistoric and early historic periods (Viner et al. 2010; Becker and Grupe 2012), and will likely make a significant contribution to the nature of farming practices across the Pictish/Viking transition in the future). Red deer disappear from the archaeological record in Orkney during the Norse period, as does fox, perhaps reflecting a change in attitude to and eradication of these species by the incoming Norse. The importance of antler as a raw material and the social significance of hunting in the Norse world (Holstein et al. 2014), together with evidence for sustainable management of 'wild' deer and caribou populations by Norse settlers in both Greenland (Dugmore et al. 2012) and the Hebrides (Mulville 2010), may, however, better support arguments for an earlier population collapse in the Late Iron Age (Smith 1994; Mainland et al. 2016).

The movement of Norse settlers further east, conventionally dated to the mid- to late eighth century for the Faroes and Iceland and c. 1000 CE for Greenland (Fitzhugh 2000), was accompanied by the translocation and introduction to these islands of the full suite of domestic species, evident in farming communities in coastal Norway and the Northern Isles: cattle, sheep, goats, pigs, horse, dog and cat, along with a commensal vertebrate species, the house mouse (Jones et al. 2012). Here the Norse farmers encountered island landscapes with diverse avian faunas (Petersen and Olsen, Chapter 10 in this volume), which were largely devoid of humans and of indigenous terrestrial mammals: caribou and musk oxen in Greenland and arctic fox and polar bear in Iceland (Bennike and Wagner, Chapter 7 in this volume). Greenland and Iceland were likely uninhabited but a pre-Viking settlement of the Faroes dating to between the mid-fourth–mid-sixth centuries has recently been confirmed at Á Sondum on the island of Sandoy (Church et al. 2013). Although currently unproven, it has been argued on the evidence of indicators of disturbance in the palynological record (Hannon et al. 2005) and the eighth century CE writings of Dicuil, an Irish monk, that sheep had already been introduced to the Faroes prior to the Norse:

> There are many other islands in the ocean to the north of Britain which can be reached from the northern isles of Britain ... now because of the Northmen pirates they are emptied of anchorites, and are filled with countless sheep (Dicuilis 1976, pp. 75–77, quoted in Arge 2000).

Pigs are found in Landnám faunas in Iceland and Greenland, but apparently did not thrive, and are not evident in deposits later than the eleventh century. A Faroese population survived until the late medieval period (Arge et al. 2009) and a small, high-backed, coarse bristled 'native' breed was common in the Northern Isles until the early twentieth century (Fenton 1978, pp. 496–497).

The 'native' breeds of sheep found across the North Atlantic islands today, the Icelandic, the Faroese, the Shetland and the North Ronaldsay, are all 'Northern short-tails', a breed that also includes other primitive Scandinavian breeds such as the Gute and the Spael (Ryder 1983; Tapio et al. 2005). Morphologically distinct from long-tailed breeds in having a shortened tail of 10–14 vertebrae, the breed is adapted to the harsh environments of the North Atlantic and performs well on low-intensity grassland management systems (Austrheim et al. 2008). Modern Greenlandic sheep, and also Northern short-tails, derive from a twentieth century re-introduction of sheep from Iceland and the Faroes (Feilberg and Høegh 2008), all domesticates introduced by the

Norse having died out sometime after the Norse settlements were abandoned in the fifteenth century (Dugmore et al. 2012). Microsatellite genotyping confirms the Northern short-tails as a genetically distinctive group with greatest affinity seen between the North Atlantic breeds and Norwegian short-tails, reflecting the origin of these breeds in the Viking/Norse expansion (Tapio et al. 2005, 2010). Retroviral DNA also points to the distinctiveness of a Scandinavian group and demonstrates connection to other British native breeds, such as the Soay and the Herdwick (Chessa et al. 2009; Bowles et al. 2014). This is again attributed to the early medieval Scandinavian migrations, though the direction of movement between the Scottish island populations (Soay, Hebridean, North Ronaldsay, Shetland) and the Nordic groups had not yet been established. Likewise, genetic analysis of Icelandic cattle (Edwards et al. 2011; Felius et al. 2011) and Icelandic horse demonstrates genetic affinities with Scandinavian breeds, as does the Shetland pony (Petersen et al. 2013), the native horse of the Northern Isles. Whilst also genetically part of the Nordic group of cattle, the genetic history of the native Faroese cattle is complicated by recent historic breeding programmes with the Norwegian Red (Li et al. 2005). The genetic history of the North Atlantic breeds has, with only few exceptions (e.g. Edwards et al. 2003), been addressed using modern animals; this data will be affected by breed improvements and herd restocking from the post-medieval period onwards as well as other factors such as local herd population crashes and extinctions in all periods. The potential for ancient DNA to illuminate the origins and spread of mammalian species across the North Atlantic, and with this the diverse connections between human populations living in these islands, is shown by a DNA research in rodent species (Searle et al. 2009; Jones et al. 2012; Cucchi et al. 2014). A future research priority must be to extend such research to the domesticated species brought into the North Atlantic by the Norse and Neolithic farmers, or by even earlier colonists.

Unlike in Orkney, there is no evidence for extinction of the indigenous Icelandic or Greenlandic terrestrial mammalian fauna during the Norse settlement. Rather, it has been argued that in Greenland the continued presence of caribou, a species that is susceptible to overhunting over the duration of the Norse settlement in Greenland (500 years), indicates successful and sustainable management practices (Dugmore et al. 2012). In Iceland, arctic fox were exploited for furs by the Norse but continue to the present day, albeit being heavily controlled as vermin in historic times leading to their near extinction between the 1950s and 1970s (Mellows et al. 2012); polar bear were likely only a transitory and seasonal presence in any case. A more sustained use and substantial impact on marine mammal resources is indicated, though usage is not always easy to assess due to processing away from settlement sites. Whale bone is a common find on archaeological sites, but its frequent modification into artefacts and its difficulty of identification makes it hard to provide more than a presence/absence checklist. That said, the historical exploitation of whales through the recent past has been well documented (Szabo 2008), particularly in the pilot whale hunt in the Faroe Islands, an important social event involving much of the community that probably originates during the early years of the Norse settlement (Dugmore et al. 2007, p. 27). Seal remains have likewise been a ubiquitous find in the Norse North Atlantic, providing food for humans and dogs (Harland 2012, p. 145) as well as fur and other materials; in Iceland, the Faroes and the Northern Isles these have been sustainably managed until the present day. In Greenland, exploitation of seals, the migratory harp and hooded seals, as well as the common seal, became an increasingly important dietary resource through time, but again over-exploitation of this resource is not evidenced (Ogilvie et al. 2009). In Iceland, however, place names on

the Rekyanes coastline indicative of a once resident breeding walrus population on Iceland may point to extinction of this species at the time of settlement (Dugmore et al. 2012; Frei et al. 2015).

Farming communities have thus transformed mammalian biodiversity within the North Atlantic islands, with at least nine species introductions definitely identified during the Holocene. Three separate phases of introduction are apparent: cattle, sheep, goat and pig and Orkney vole to Orkney and Shetland during the initial 'Neolithic' spread of farming into Northwest Europe in the fourth millennium BCE; a secondary introduction of cat, horse and perhaps fox, to Orkney and Shetland at the end of the first millennium BCE; and of the full suite of European domesticates along with the house mouse to Iceland, Greenland and the Faroes during the first and early second millennium CE as part of the colonization of the North Atlantic by the Norse. Today the North Atlantic 'native' breeds of cattle, sheep and horse, although closely related to Scandinavian breeds, are genetically distinct from European populations, reflecting their relative isolation and adaptation to the demands placed on pastoral farming by the northern and sub-arctic environments (e.g. length of growing season, limitations on overwintering, marginal for cereal fodder production, etc.). These breeds represent an important genetic resource for future farming in this region and are widely recognized to be worthy of conservation (Anstraheim et al. 2007; Dýrmundsson and Niżnikowski 2010; Li et al. 2005; Tapio et al. 2010). Few episodes of extermination are documented, the only clear examples being red deer and fox in Orkney and potentially walrus in Iceland, but few mammal species were present prior to human settlement in any case. Moreover, farming will have impacted extant biota significantly in other ways, through restriction of range by human presence and modification of the landscape and genetic pool through predation (Mellows et al. 2012; others in this volume).

Ovigenic Landscapes or Adaptive Grazers?

It is undoubtedly through the introduction of grazing livestock, and in particular sheep and goats, that farming has had its greatest impact on North Atlantic ecosystems, with clearance of indigenous woodland and burning of moorland for grazing and fodder production (Edwards et al. 2008), overgrazing and accelerated soil erosion (Dugmore et al. 2007); it has been estimated, for example, that up to 40% of Icelandic soils have been lost since settlement (Simpson et al. 2001). The Norse established a decentralized farming system in the islands, comparable to that evident in Late Iron Age Norway (Albrethsen and Keller 1986; Øye 2005, 2013; Thomson et al. 2005; Lucas 2008; Dugmore et al. 2012; Ledger et al. 2013; Vickers and Sveinbjarnardóttir 2013) in which three basic elements can be identified, an infield (*innan gardr*, Øye 2005) around the farmstead for arable cultivation where this was climatically feasible and/or hay fodder production, an outfield (*utan gardr*, Simpson et al. 2004; Øye 2005; Vickers and Sveinbjarnardóttir 2013) for grazing livestock likely separated from the infield by a boundary, and saeters, or sheilings, seasonally occupied settlements located in the outfield zone for the summer grazing of livestock, milk production as well as other activities such as iron working and hunting (Lucas 2008; Øye 2013). The outfield zone was also used for extensive rangeland grazing, a resource that became increasingly important from the twelfth to thirteenth centuries onwards, with the demise of the sheiling system and a shift towards specialized wool production; this is the dominant management system in the uplands today (Simpson et al. 1995; Austraheim et al. 2007). Øye (2005, p. 366) has argued for a 'transfer of whole farming structures and systems, not only elements' into the islands with the Norse, but due to limited excavation of structures and boundaries associated with animal husbandry in the wider landscape there remains some uncertainty over dating and arguably even the function and derivation of farming systems. Mahler (1991), for example, has argued that an infield/outfield system is a later, twelfth/thirteenth century introduction into the Faroes; sheilings appear to be evident in Iceland (Lucas 2008; Vickers and Sveinbjarnardóttir 2013) and perhaps Greenland (Albrethsen and Keller 1986; Ledger et al. 2013) from the settlement period, but physical evidence for these in Orkney is currently lacking and place name evidence is equivocal because of uncertainty over the etymology of *saeter/setr* (Thomson 1995; Sandnes 2010; contra Øye 2005). Ownership of the outfield and access to common grazing is a further area which requires clarification (Lucas 2008; Øye 2013), as does the antiquity of Norse land management systems in the Northern Isles and the potential contribution of earlier pre-Norse systems to farming practices (Dockrill and Bond 2009; Barrett et al. 2012; Mainland et al. 2016), both in these islands and as imported practice across the island groups (Lucas 2008; Vickers and Sveinbjarnardóttir 2013). This lack of clarity over form, function and timing of development has implications for understanding scale and intensity of impact at both regional and local levels (Mainland 2006; Madsen 2012).

In the more recent past, overgrazing by domestic livestock, and in particular sheep, has been identified as a major issue for the North Atlantic islands (Austraheim et al. 2007; Hannon and Bradshaw 2013). This is particularly acute in Iceland, where desertification is apparent over vast areas of the interior and uplands (Austraheim et al. 2007) but is also evident in Greenland, where increased erosion is apparent with re-introduction of sheep farming in the 1920s (Feilberg and Hoegh 2008; Gauthier et al. 2010; Madsen 2012). Equally, in the Northern Isles, loss of biodiversity through livestock grazing in the moorland and uplands is of concern (Simpson et al. 1995; Amar et al. 2011; García et al. 2013). A series of restrictive measures have been put in place to limit impact, from systematic slaughtering of sheep in Iceland (Thórhallsdóttir et al. 2007) to regulations on winter feeding in Greenland (Feilberg and Hoegh 2007) and grazing quota systems throughout the islands (Austrheim et al. 2007). For most of the twentieth century archaeologists and historians drew heavily on these modern parallels, applying the term 'ovigenic landscapes' (e.g. Buckland 2000; Hannon and Bradshaw 2013) to emphasize the role that humans and their livestock had in transforming 'pristine' climax willow/birch shrub woodland to the treeless, grass, heath and moorland dominated landscapes we see today. Overgrazing and pasture degradation was moreover seen as being instrumental in land and farm abandonment as the climate worsened during the later medieval period with the onset of the Little Ice Age (LIA) and was identified as a significant factor in the abandonment of the Norse colony in Greenland in the fifteenth century (Keller 1990; McGovern 1992; Buckland et al. 1996; Amorosi et al. 1997).

Recent research, however, is showing that historically impact is not so simple and clearcut. Rather it is now argued that Norse farmers were responsive to overgrazing with evidence of regulatory mechanisms in place in the Faroes and Iceland from at least the twelfth century to prevent overgrazing of summer grazing areas. Modelling of resource availability has shown that there was sufficient biomass in the Norse period to support estimated stocking densities, even with the deteriorating climate from the fourteenth century (Simpson et al. 2001; Thomson et al. 2005), while specific responses to periods of overgrazing through reduction in grazing density and soil enhancement have been documented in Iceland and Greenland using sediment accumulation rates and micromorphology (Simpson et al. 2004; Gauthier et al. 2010; Ledger et al. 2013. Thus, while recognizing that overgrazing and soil erosion is apparent from settlement onwards (Simpson et al. 2001, 2004; Mainland 2006; Edwards et al. 2008), it is becoming clear that this will be spatially and temporally variable, dependant on local landscape, terrain and growing conditions as well as stocking ratios and herding goals. Whether overgrazing occurs will ultimately depend on the decision of individual farmers and herders, which in turn reflects political and social influences operating in the wider community and the Norse world as a whole, the potential role of social mechanisms such as feasting in driving stocking densities (Zori et al. 2013; Mainland and Batey 2019) and the development of regional and long-distance trade networks in wool and other animal products.

At the same time, in a modern context there is growing recognition that across the North Atlantic uplands, heaths and moorland are a product of long interaction between 'natural' ecosystems, humans and their livestock, i.e. that these landscapes are *utan gardr* and not wilderness, and hence that conservation and management of these areas should take into account the historical dimension (Hjelle et al. 2012; Austraheim et al. 2007; Birks 2012). Restriction of grazing in moor/heath and semi-natural grassland has, for example, been shown in several studies to reduce rather than enhance biodiversity (of birds, insects, vascular plants) and has led to a reintroduction of recent historic grazing practises as a management tool (e.g. Ryland et al. 2012; Crossley 2013; García et al. 2013). Austrheim et al. (2007), writing largely from an agricultural and ecological perspective, have argued that a sustainable system for sheep management in these islands requires 'A more developed evidence-basis of the long term effects of different grazing regimes (varying density, breed, season and habitat productivity) involving both management and research' (Austrheim et al. 2007, p. 7) and should take into account both natural and cultural factors. This echoes Simpson et al. (2001), who suggest the interdisciplinary perspective afforded by historical ecology, which looks at long-term trajectories of change incorporating archaeological, historical and ecological evidence, enables a more nuanced understanding of livestock management and farming systems, both past and present. Not only does the past provide case studies for human control of and response to grazing conditions, but these exemplars will represent 'closed experiments' allowing analysis of impact arising from specific local conditions of terrain and climate over differing time depths – decadal, centennial, etc. – as well as insight into cultural and other reasons behind breaching or non-application of grazing regulations (profit, distance managers, etc.) and the lasting effects of these. Yet, actual application of such integrated approaches to the development of modern livestock management strategies are limited, perhaps reflecting lack of awareness from agriculturalists and conservationists of research in this area and vice versa (Birks 2012). Given the apparent interest in applying traditional grazing systems within conservation areas, there is arguably a need to better evaluate their potential through further targeted interdisciplinary studies across the North Atlantic islands that bring together conservationists and agriculturalists with historians, environmental archaeologists and palaeoecologists (cf. Birks 2012) to focus on temporal trends in grazing management at a local scale. It is at this level that human decision-making and its impact can best be observed and understood, as has been aptly demonstrated by Simpson et al. (2001, 2004) for Mývatnssveit and Ejyafjallajökull in Iceland.

Northern Fisheries

Establishing a marine historical ecology of the North Atlantic using archaeological and historical data to reconstruct some of the ways people have interacted with the sea over the past few millennia is of primary importance to marine conservation. Such an approach would provide a long-term history of human interactions with the sea, and should indicate when, and to what extent, humans start to have an impact on the sea. This would also have to take into account factors like environmental change – both anthropogenic and otherwise – in order to understand chronological and social changes in fishing, fish consumption and marine mammal exploitation through time. Within historical ecology, humans are seen as a driving force for environmental change, separate from natural selection or natural patterns of climate change because of their potential for large-scale modification to the landscape (Crumley 2003; Balée and Erickson 2006). Such modifications and management decisions need not always be construed negatively (at least when considering terrestrial historical ecology), although the recent history of our interactions with the sea makes for desultory and depressing reading (e.g. Roberts 2012).

This section of the paper will discuss some of the ways people have exploited the seas around the North Atlantic islands from the arrival of the Vikings onwards, thus focusing on the centuries in which humans have had a long-lasting and sustained impact on the fauna of the sea. The history of the North Atlantic fisheries during the Norse and later medieval periods has been extensively reviewed (Perdikaris 1999; Barrett et al. 2004; Perdikaris and McGovern 2007; Perdikaris and McGovern 2008; Barrett et al. 2011; Dugmore et al. 2012) and will not be repeated here. Rather, fish bones from selected sites in Orkney and Shetland will be presented as a case study to show a geographically targeted, local–regional scale time sequence in fish exploitation. This will be used in two ways: firstly, to tell the story of fishing and its impact using both archaeological and historical interpretations using methods suggested by historical marine ecology and, secondly, to introduce the idea of contrasting archaeological data with modern data on fish populations.

If we can establish a 'baseline' ecological pattern from a time prior to large-scale human impact on the oceans, we could establish far-reaching and sustainable conservation goals for the future (Erlandson and Rick 2010). It can be simplistic, however, to view one particular time as an idealized 'baseline', because of ongoing natural climactic and geologic changes (Bailey et al. 2008), but equally it is important not to disregard ocean ecology prior to detailed scientific record keeping. 'Shifting baselines' have long been a problem in the study of oceans' past. The current generation is loath to believe their grandfathers' stories of plentiful, large fish in the sea, just as those grandfathers did not believe stories of prior generations. However, using historical and photographic data just from the nineteenth and twentieth century it is possible to see decreasing catches, decreasing sizes and changing availability of species (Roberts 2007).

'Fishing down the food web' is a phenomenon observed repeatedly when exploring the history of marine ecosystems. In the past – be it the recent past in living memory or one only visible archaeologically – humans often targeted apex species (including walruses and whales), and as those got smaller and rarer other taxa were targeted, often those that were not as high up the food chain and/or those that were available in plentiful numbers (Pauly et al. 1998). As those in turn were increasing fished out, particularly in the very recent past, those at the bottom of the food chain are all that remain. This phenomenon has been identified archaeologically and historically in numerous locations and it can be used to interpret the archaeological evidence from the North Atlantic.

The main difficulty of establishing an historical ecology of the North Atlantic is the problem of combining data from different disciplines. Fish bones recovered archaeologically can tell us what fish were eaten and in what proportions, how big (and thus approximately how old) they were, if they were preserved or traded and approximately

when they were likely deposited. Analogy can be used to estimate fishing areas, boating technologies and fishing methods, while the importance of marine protein in human diets can be studied using carbon and nitrogen isotopic evidence from human bones of a relevant date. Comparisons between archaeological sites can indicate past distributions of taxa, from a simple presence/absence to relative abundance, while temporal changes can be related to environmental factors (e.g. water temperature declines driving fish south) or changes in fishing methods and preferences linked to complicated anthropogenic factors. In contrast, fisheries ecology is focused on a seasonal or year resolution of catch sizes, mathematical modelling of fish stocks and future predictions based on very short time scales of a few decades at best.

> There is much to be done … to bridge the gaps between archaeological, historical, and ecological data often collected in very different spatial and temporal scales. At this point, any methodology for measuring human impacts across prehistoric, historic, and recent times must be considered a work in progress, given that historical ecology is a young discipline and interaction between archaeologists and marine scientists is still relatively limited.
>
> *Erlandson and Rick 2010, p. 180*

Fish and marine mammal bones have long been found in midden deposits in the North Atlantic. Bones from Skara Brae and other Neolithic sites testify to their contribution as food and as raw materials for decorative beads (Harland and Parks 2009), yet contemporary isotopic evidence from human remains indicates marine protein has only a slight to negligible contribution to the diet (Schulting and Richards 2009). A wide range of fish were exploited, from inshore (saithe and rocklings) to deeper water (cod and ling) and included potential freshwater sources for salmon and eels. Sharks, dogfishes, rays, Atlantic herring, conger eels, European seabass, sea breams, wrasses, Atlantic mackerel, blennies, gurnards, sea scorpions, turbots, halibuts and angler fish – these and many others – have been found associated with human habitation. The millennia that led up to the Viking Age present a similar pattern: varying degrees of small-scale exploitation of marine resources, without any particular focus and without a significant contribution to dietary protein.

The arrival of the Viking Age in Orkney and Shetland changed this pattern dramatically. Fish middens became a feature of the landscape, built out of remains of hundreds of thousands of fish bones and shells from bait, along with some marine mammals, sea birds and varying quantities of domestic mammal remains. These fish middens are densely packed with cod and saithe, as well as ling, haddock and other members of the cod family. Other fish taxa typically represent fewer than 5% of identified bones (Harland 2006, Table 5.1). The creation of these fish middens is linked to the larger 'Fish Event Horizon', the sudden and widespread deposition of marine fish throughout western European sites in the years following CE 1000 (Barrett et al. 2004). Human diets changed during this time, with $\delta^{13}C$ isotopic measurements showing a peak in marine protein consumption. During the early years of the Viking Age in Orkney, prior to c.1000 CE, between 10 and 30% of human dietary protein came from the sea. A dramatic increase to include values up to and exceeding 50% of marine protein occurred c. 1000 CE, a trend that lasted for about three centuries before declining to levels of between 20 and 40% (Barrett and Richards 2004).

In Orkney and Shetland, fish middens fell out of use in the thirteenth and fourteenth centuries, when intensive fishing was no longer undertaken (matching the decline in marine protein contributions to the human diet; Barrett and Richards 2004). Two Viking Age and medieval settlement sites in Orkney have produced large quantities of fish bones: Quoygrew, Westray (Barrett 2012; Harland and Barrett 2012) and Stackelbrae, Eday (Brend 2010; Harland 2013). At Quoygrew and other sites, like Stackelbrae, fish were still consumed and fish bones were still frequently found after the thirteenth and fourteenth centuries, but these tended to be smaller saithe (Figure 1), a trend that continued through to recent centuries. Cod were still caught, but they became less important than saithe in terms of quantities, and they were smaller and younger (Figure 2). Why? One conclusion would be that 'fishing down the food web' had already started to remove the largest fish from the sea, thus leaving only those smaller ones available for exploitation in any quantity. However, before drawing such a simplistic conclusion, we need to examine the evidence in more detail, including the various climatic, social and economic factors that affected fishing and fish consumption at the time.

The fish remains from Quoygrew and Stackelbrae were both analysed by the author (Harland) and both sites used similar recovery methods, thus removing one potential source of variation in quantification and sizing. Stackelbrae is important as it is the first later medieval and early modern site in Orkney to have produced fish bones in quantity. Even if it is not (yet) precisely dated, contemporary historical records can be used to help interpretation. At Quoygrew, the end of the 'fish event horizon' is illustrated by comparing the eleventh to thirteenth century deposits with those of a later date. At some point between the thirteenth and fifteenth centuries, saithe began to be caught in larger quantities than cod for the first time. Those cod that were caught became smaller, but so too did the saithe. The latter show a steady decrease in size through time. This is particularly apparent by the mid-seventeenth to early nineteenth century at Stackelbrae, where over 90% of saithe were less than 30 cm in total length.

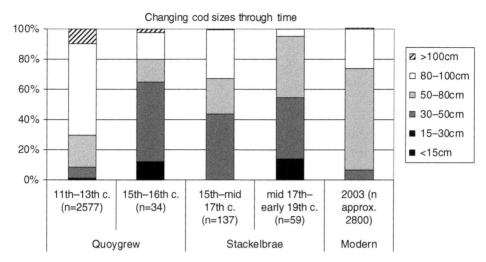

Figure 1 Cod sizes from Quoygrew and Stackelbrae (Viking Age and medieval sites in Westray and Eday, Orkney), sieved dataset, compared with modern cod sizes caught off Shetland in 2003. Archaeological sizes are estimated for routinely identified cranial and appendicular elements, based on comparison with reference material of known size. All from deposits sieved to 2 mm, with very good preservation. Some highly fragmented elements may be recorded twice, but broad size patterns are confirmed by regression data for selected, non-duplicating elements. *Source:* Harland (2006), Harland and Barrett (2012, pp. 123–125), Figure 7.3; Harland (2013). Modern data derived from cod caught on two fishing voyages around Shetland in 2003. Data were presented as quantities of fish caught per hour of trawling, with fish sizes presented in 10 cm increments; gaps in the data did not allow complete reconstruction of actual fish sizes and quantities, but nevertheless the proportions of different fish sizes are directly comparable to those recovered archaeologically. Fishing gear and landing requirements meant very few fish of less than 32 cm total length were caught. *Source:* Cotter et al. (2004), Figure 3d.

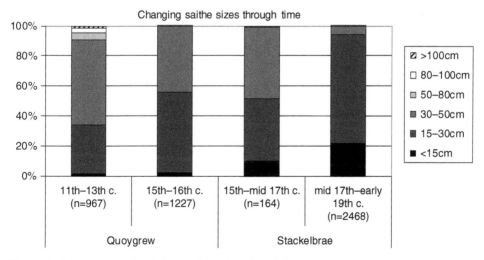

Figure 2 Quoygrew and Stackelbrae saithe sizes, sieved dataset.

Fishing for large cod and related species was a specialized, high-risk activity, one that relied on excellent knowledge of the seas and its dangers (Barrett 2012), whereas fishing for small, young saithe could be undertaken from the shore or from inshore waters, using smaller boats on shorter fishing trips and with considerably less risk (Fenton 1978). The latter could be undertaken in conjunction with the routines surrounding arable and pastoral agriculture, but deep, open water fishing requires a considerable investment in time and labour. There appears to have been a significant shift towards fishing inshore, shallow waters which do not have the larger cod and related species, but which contain plentiful quantities of juvenile saithe and other small taxa. The mid-seventeenth to early nineteenth century phase at Stackelbrae shows an intensification of this shift. There, small saithe were eaten and deposited to the exclusion of almost all other species.

At the height of fish midden creation in the Northern Isles, large cod and related species were dried and preserved in quantities, much for domestic consumption later (as at Quoygrew) but some for trade and payment in kind. Earl's Bu, a high-status site on mainland Orkney, contains the remains of preserved, imported cod and haddock that were prepared elsewhere and consumed on site (along with many fish consumed fresh). Imports tended to date from the later phases of occupation, towards the latter half of the late ninth to early thirteenth century (Batey and Morris 1992; Harland 2006). The preserved fish trade was of increasing importance throughout the North Sea, but, within Orkney, there is little evidence for it beyond the thirteenth century: fish middens ceased to be created, cod became less important and fish sizes decreased. The fourteenth century was a period of economic decline and contraction, and not just in Orkney: the effects of the plague, climatic deterioration, crop failures, sand blows, land abandonment, famine and other crises were felt throughout the North

Atlantic (Thomson 2008; Barrett 2012). These all contributed towards Orkney's growing political and economic isolation from activities that were increasingly centred on southern Scotland or the more northern parts of the North Atlantic (Thomson 2008).

Iceland and Arctic Norway continued to produce preserved fish, with huge deposits of fish bones recovered archaeologically long after Orkney's fish middens ceased accumulating (Perdikaris and McGovern 2008). These areas were probably becoming increasingly specialized, thus out-competing Orkney and, slightly later, Shetland (Barrett 2012). Hanseatic merchants traded directly with Shetland as early as the fifteenth century, and likely traded with Faroe and Iceland at the same time. Hanseatic laws dating from the late thirteenth century required all trade from the North Atlantic to go directly through Bergen (Friedland 1983), which may have disadvantaged Orkney compared to other archipelagos capable of large-scale preserved fish production.

Changing climatic conditions are another factor to consider: they may have contributed to the shift towards low-risk, inshore fishing in Orkney. A favourable climate likely characterized the Norse expansion across the North Atlantic, with low levels of storminess, good summer temperatures and little sea ice during the 'Medieval climate anomaly' of c. 800–1200 CE. However, the onset of the Little Ice Age in the thirteenth or fourteenth century (Perdikaris and McGovern 2008; Surge and Barrett 2012; dates vary according to area and proxy indicators) introduced cooler, less predictable weather patterns with increased storminess and sea ice, which would have affected fishing both directly and indirectly. Fish distributions are known to shift in response to water temperatures (Cheung et al. 2013), making traditional ecological knowledge less predictable, while fishing itself became more risky in the worsening and unpredictable weather. Storms were known to increase in both frequency and intensity in the fifteenth century, producing a 'significantly more hostile North Atlantic marine environment' (Perdikaris and McGovern 2008). The seventeenth century temperature extremes were probably the worst of the Little Ice Age for the North Atlantic (Cullen 2010). Shetland suffered greatly in the late seventeenth century because of storms, inundations, sand blows, famine and fishing failures – probably because cooler Arctic waters pushed fish stocks south (Cullen 2010). This was a problem throughout the northern North Atlantic; Iceland suffered greatly at this time, with the additional problem of sea ice preventing access to the fish that had not migrated to warmer waters (Grove 1988). With a worsening climate and a decreased population, a focus on terrestrial farming may have taken on an increased priority in Orkney to the detriment of its fishing traditions.

Recovery from the ravages of the Little Ice Age, famines and failures would not have been easy. Repeated cooler years and cooler waters would have sporadically affected fish stocks throughout the North Atlantic until the early nineteenth century (Grove 1988). Historical accounts from the sixteenth and early seventeenth century showed that fish (largely in the form of oil) provided only a very small contribution to Orkney's economy (Anderson 2012, pp. 52, 54), suggesting that although Iceland and Shetland had to return to fishing for subsistence, Orkney chose to rely primarily on terrestrial resources. Orkney and Shetland waters *were* fished commercially in the late sixteenth and early seventeenth centuries, when taxes were extracted from fishing boats visiting from mainland Scotland and the Netherlands (Thomson 2008), but with little local involvement. Tellingly, a taxation agreement in 1594 forbade outsiders fishing 'between the islands' in Orkney, except for bait (Thomson 2008), possibly a recognition that the inshore and coastal fishery was of importance to the local subsistence economy but that fisheries in deeper waters around Orkney were available to any who wanted to fish there.

This is certainly the pattern seen from the saithe and cod at Stackelbrae in the mid-seventeenth to early nineteenth century: almost all fish consumed there were small saithe caught from the shore or in shallow waters. If local people were involved in early commercial fisheries (and a few certainly were by the 1841 census), then they may not have been eating any of the products (Harland 2013).

Orkney struggled to regain a commercial fishery in the eighteenth and nineteenth centuries, despite several references to the wealth of fish in Orkney waters and various attempts by merchants to raise required capital (Barry 1805; Low 1813; Thomson 2008). A lack of investment in boats, landings, storage buildings and the high cost of preserving salt all contributed towards the problem and deeper water fishing knowledge seems to have been lost to locals in the hard centuries of decline. Kelp-making (burning seaweed to make potash and soda) became a new and, for a while, very lucrative industry in Orkney during the late eighteenth and nineteenth centuries, one that drew people away from fishing (Barry 1805). The herring boom in the nineteenth century created some jobs and opportunities locally, yet the final layers at Stackelbrae contain virtually no herring despite being contemporary (Harland 2013).

Taken at face value, the shift away from fishing large cod at the end of the 'fish event horizon' could be interpreted as 'fishing down the food web', moving from high tropic level predators to smaller but more numerous lower-level fish because the larger ones have been over-exploited and are simply not present in adequate quantities. However, the example from Orkney is not so simple, as we have seen: climate deterioration, shifting fishing grounds, increased risk and a lack of commercial investment all drove people away from deeper water fishing but the fish themselves were there in considerable quantities.

Having unravelled the archaeological evidence for fishing over the last millennium, is it possible to use data from the heyday of Norse fishing in

Orkney in a modern context? Despite the plethora of information available to modern fisheries scientists, comparison with archaeological data is often difficult. Fish weights and year classes are often of importance now, but archaeologically is it fish *lengths* that are important: calibrating the two are not easy, but it has been attempted here. The modern data derive from a single fishing vessel which undertook two voyages in autumn 2003 (Cotter et al. 2004). A trawl net was used that allowed smaller fish of less than 40 cm total length to slip free. In this modern sample, cod of 50–80 cm total length were most common, representing about two thirds of all cod caught. Fish of 80–100 cm represented about a quarter of all caught, while only 1% were greater than 100 cm. This is in stark contrast with the cod from eleventh to thirteenth century Orkney. There, almost three quarters of all cod were at least 80 cm in length, with only a fifth between 50 and 80 cm in length. Very large cod of over 100 cm contributed substantially to the diet (certainly in terms of flesh provided, even if less in terms of actual quantities of fish).

Although fishing gears are not directly comparable with the hand-lines or long-lines used in the past, the fishing grounds themselves are relatively similar, although likely to have been modified by decades of intensive fishing pressure. It is also more likely the Orkney fishers exploited grounds closer to home and as they fished without minimum landing size requirements, they could have landed smaller fish if desired. However, the Norse fishermen were clearly able to target large and very large fish in substantial quantities despite their small vessels and lack of fish finding equipment. Even if viewed simplistically, it is possible to see that modern cod have a dramatically different size composition (and thus they are a much younger population) compared to those fished centuries ago. If the state of the fisheries seen during the Norse arrival in Orkney could be considered as relatively free of fishing pressures, then the modern results indicate the extent to which the older, larger and most fertile year classes have

been reduced. Future work to establish growth rates and ages of archaeological material would be of great importance to further understand the year-class structure of ancient populations.

Several factors need to be explored in order to fully understand the changes in cod and saithe sizes and abundance in the North Atlantic. Prior to the Norse arrival in the North Atlantic, people would have had little impact on the sea: fish, whales, seals and other marine mammals were certainly used for food (and for tools, clothing, lighting, raw materials, etc.), but the small human population sizes and lack of focused fishing effort meant that the North Atlantic approximated to an ecosystem without anthropogenic modification in the early years of the second millennium CE. Despite difficulties, it is worth trying to combine archaeological datasets with modern fisheries research in an attempt to develop a marine historical ecology of the North Atlantic islands. This case study has used selected archaeological information from fish sizes to examine changes in exploitation of cod and saithe through time, but it would be worth extending these methods to explore the complex interplay of archaeological and modern data. Many papers have discussed the possibilities of these datasets to inform fisheries policies, but few have successfully put ideas into practice (MacKenzie et al. 2011).

Although there is no way to completely reverse the massive changes to marine ecosystems of the recent past, it is possible to use archaeological and historical data to establish conservation goals for fish stocks and marine mammal populations. Fish bones can indicate relative proportions of species and age profiles of stocks, which can be contrasted with modern data, while marine mammal ranges and population sizes from the past can inform areas for reintroduction and careful management. Rather than setting conservation goal 'baselines' using twentieth century data – as is currently done – archaeological data from a thousand years ago must be considered (e.g. Ólafsdóttir et al. 2017) if we are to consider not just the recent future, but the next thousand years of interaction with the marine environment and all its potential resources.

Conclusions

The transformative impact that farming communities have had on the biota of the North Atlantic islands is undeniable. The introduction of farming to these islands has expanded the range of species present with the introduction of two, perhaps three, top-predators, a commensal rodent, voles (in Orkney), several large terrestrial grazing/browsing species along with pigs into island ecosystems that had previously supported relatively few endemic terrestrial vertebrates and, with the exception of Greenland, had no native ungulates. Moreover, the distinctive treeless landscapes of the North Atlantic islands are largely a product of the farming practices associated with the management of these imported domestic livestock. It is the grazing of livestock and exploitation of marine resources, however, that has underpinned the sustainability of these island communities through the last millennia, economically and culturally. Pastoral farming and fishing were vital to subsistence and trade as well as being core to island and community identity and continue to be so. Furthermore, they have created the open landscapes, fishing villages and unique culinary traditions that now attract tourism to these islands. For these reasons, we have argued that future conservation management practices in these islands should adopt the interdisciplinary approach afforded by historical ecology. Whilst this perspective is hardly new (Dugmore et al. 2007, 2012; McGovern et al. 2007), there are still few actual examples in which the past has been used to inform present-day management through a genuine collaboration of fishery scientists, agriculturalists, ecologists, etc., with archaeologists and palaeoecologists. The challenge for the future will be for these disciplines to actively engage with each other's research agendas and move beyond rhetoric to explore more rigorously how modern practice can be grounded in a solid scientific understanding of long-term trajectories of change.

References

Adderley, W.P. and Simpson, I.A. (2006). Soils and palaeo-climate based evidence for irrigation requirements in Norse Greenland. *Journal of Archaeological Science* 33: 666–1679.

Albrethsen, S.E. and Keller, C. (1986). The use of the sæter in Medieval Norse farming in Greenland. *Arctic Anthropology* 23: 91–128.

Amar, A., Davies, J., Meek, E. et al. (2011). Long-term impact of changes in sheep *Ovis aries* densities on the breeding output of the hen harrier *Circus cyaneus*. *Journal of Applied Ecology* 48: 220–227.

Amorosi, T., Buckland, P., Dugmore, A. et al. (1997). Raiding the landscape: human impact in the Scandinavian North Atlantic. *Human Ecology* 25: 491–518.

Anderson, P. (2012). *The Stewart Earls of Orkney*. Edinburgh: John Donald.

Arge, S.V. (2000). Vikings in the Faroes Islands. In: Vikings. The North Atlantic Saga (eds. W.W. Fitzhugh and E.I. Ward), 154–163. Washington and London: Smithsonian Press.

Arge, S.V., Church, M.J., and Brewington, S. (2009). Pigs in the Faroe islands: an ancient facet of the islands' paleoeconomy. *Journal of the North Atlantic* 2 (1): 9–32.

Austrheim, G., Asheim, L.-J., Bjarnason, G. et al. (2008). Sheep Grazing in the North-Atlantic Region. A Long Term Perspective on Management, Resource Economy and Ecology (Norges Teknisk-Naturvitenskapeligeuniversitet Vitenskapsmuseet Rapport Zoologisk

Serie 2008-3). Trondheim: Norges Teknisk-naturvitenskapelige Universitet Vitenskapsmuseet Seksjon for Naturhistorie.

Bailey, G., Barrett, J., Craig, O., and Milner, N. (2008). Historical ecology of the North Sea Basin. In: Human Impacts on Ancient Marine Ecosystems: A Global Perspective (eds. T.C. Rick and J.M. Erlandson), 215–242. Berkeley: University of California Press.

Balée, W. and Erickson, C.L. (2006). Time, complexity, and historical ecology. In: Time and Complexity in Historical Ecology: Studies in the Neotropical Lowlands (eds. W. Balée and C. Erickson), 1–20. New York: Columbia University Press.

Barrett, J.H. (2012). Being an Islander. In: Being an Islander: Production and Identity at Quoygrew, Orkney, AD 900–1600 (ed. J.H. Barrett), 275–291. Cambridge: McDonald Institute for Archaeological Research.

Barrett, J.H. and Richards, M. (2004). Identity, gender, religion and economy: new isotope and radiocarbon evidence for marine resource intensification in early historic Orkney, Scotland, UK. *European Journal of Archaeology* 7: 249–271.

Barrett, J., Beukens, I., Ashmore, P. et al. (2000). What was the Viking Age and when did it happen? A view from Orkney. *Norwegian Archaeological Review* 33: 1–39.

Barrett, J.H., Locker, A.M., and Roberts, C.M. (2004). The origin of intensive marine fishing in medieval Europe: the English evidence. *Proceedings of the Royal Society B* 271 (2004): 2417–2421.

Barrett, J.H., Orton, D., Johnstone, C. et al. (2011). Interpreting the expansion of sea fishing in medieval Europe using stable isotope analysis of archaeological cod bones. *Journal of Archaeological Science* 38: 1516–1524.

Barrett, J.H., Farr, L.R., Redhouse, D. et al. (2012). Quoygrew and its landscape context. In: Being an Islander: Production and Identity at Quoygrew, Orkney, AD 900–1600 (ed. J.H. Barret),

25–46. Cambridge: McDonald Institute for Archaeological Research.

Barry, G. (1805). The History of the Orkney Islands. Edinburgh: Archibald Constable and Company.

Batey, C.E. and Morris, C.D. (1992). Earl's Bu, Orphir, Orkney: excavation of a Norse horizontal mill. In: Norse and Later Settlement and Subsistence in the North Atlantic (ed. D.J. Rackham), 33–41. Glasgow: University of Glasgow, Department of Archaeology.

Becker, C. and Grupe, G. (2012). Archaeometry meets archaeozoology: Viking Haithabu and medieval Schleswig reconsidered. *Archaeological and Anthropological Sciences* 4: 241–262.

Birks, H.J.B. (2012). Ecological palaeoecology and conservation biology: controversies, challenges, and compromises. *International Journal of Biodiversity Science, Ecosystem Services and Management* 8: 292–304.

Bond, J.M. (2007). The bioarchaeological evidence. In: The Excavations at Pool Sanday (ed. J. Hunter), 169–286. Kirkwall: The Orcadian Press.

Bowles, D., Carson, A., and Isaac, P. (2014). Genetic distinctiveness of the Herdwick sheep breed and two other locally adapted hill breeds of the UK. *PLoS One* 9 (1): e87823. https://doi.org/10.1371/journal.pone.0087823.

Brend, A. 2010. Stackelbrae, Eday excavation: Data Structure Report, ORCA unpublished report.

Buckland, P.C. (2000). The North Atlantic environment. In: Vikings. The North Atlantic Saga (eds. W.W. Fitzhugh and E.I. Ward), 164–153. Washington and London: Smithsonian Press.

Buckland, P.C., Amorosi, T., Barlow, L.K. et al. (1996). Bioarchaeological and climatological evidence for the fate of Norse farmers in medieval Greenland. *Antiquity* 70: 88–96.

Chessa, B., Pereira, F., Arnaud, F. et al. (2009). Revealing the history of sheep domestication using retrovirus integrations. *Science* 324: 532–536.

Cheung, W.W.L., Watson, R., and Pauly, D. (2013). Signature of ocean warming in global fisheries catch. *Nature* 497: 365–368.

Church, M.J., Arge, S.V., Edwards, K.J. et al. (2013). The Vikings were not the first colonizers of the Faroe Islands. *Quaternary Science Reviews* 77: 28–232.

Cotter, J., van der Kooij, J., Satchell, C. et al. (2004). Report on Catches of Saithe, Cod and Haddock in the Northern North Sea by FV Farnella in Autumn 2003. Lowestoft: Fisheries Management Group Report, CEFAS.

Crossley, J.E. 2013. Loch of Isbister and the Loons Site of Special Scientific Interest and Special Area of Conservation: National Vegetation Classification Survey and Site Condition Monitoring of Basin Fen (Scottish Natural Heritage Commissioned Report No. 564). www.snh.org.uk/pdfs/publications/commissioned_reports/564.pdf, consulted 8/10/14.

Crumley C.L. 2003. Historical ecology: integrated thinking at multiple temporal and spatial scales. Presented at *World System Historical Global Environmental Change Conference*, Lund University, Sweden.

Cucchi, T., Barnett, R., Martınkova, M. et al. (2014). The changing pace of insular life: 5000 years of microevolution in the Orkney vole (*Microtus arvalis Orcadensis*). *Evolution* 68: 2804–2820.

Cullen, K.J. (2010). Famine in Scotland: The 'Ill Years' of the 1690s. Scottish Historical Review Monograph. Edinburgh: Edinburgh University Press.

Cussans, J. E. 2010. Changes in the size and shape of domestic mammals across the North Atlantic Region over time. Unpublished PhD Thesis, University of Bradford.

Cussans, J. and Bond, J.M. (2010). The mammal bone. In: Excavations at Old Scatness, Shetland Volume 1: The Pictish Village and Viking Settlement (eds. S. Dockrill et al.), 132–155. Lerwick: Shetland Heritage Publications.

Cussans, J.E., Bond, J.M., and O'Connor, T. (2007). Biometry and population change: metrical analysis of the mammal bone. In: The Excavations at Pool Sanday (ed. J. Hunter), 242–262. Kirkwall: The Orcadian Press.

Dockrill, S. and Bond, J.M. (2009). Sustainability and resilience in Prehistoric North Atlantic Britain: The importance of a mixed Paleoeconomic system. *Journal of the North Atlantic* 2 (1): 33–50.

Dockrill, S., Bond, J.M., Turner, V.E. et al. (2010). Excavations at Old Scatness, Shetland Volume 1: The Pictish Village and Viking Settlement. Lerwick: Shetland Heritage Publications.

Downes, J., Foster, S.M., and Wickham-Jones, C.R. (eds.) (2005). The Heart of Neolithic Orkney World Heritage Site Research Agenda. Edinburgh: Historic Scotland.

Dugmore, A.J., Keller, C., and McGovern, T.H. (2007). Norse Greenland settlement: reflections on climate change, trade, and the contrasting fates of human settlements in the North Atlantic Islands. *Arctic Anthropology* 44: 12–36.

Dugmore, A.J., McGovern, T.H., Vésteinsson, O. et al. (2012). Cultural adaptation, compounding vulnerabilities and conjunctures in Norse Greenland. *PNAS* 109: 3658–3663.

Dýrmundsson, Ó. and Niżnikowski, R. (2010). North European short-tailed breeds of sheep: a review. *Animal* 4: 1275–1282.

Edwards, C.J., Connellan, J., Wallace, P.F. et al. (2003). Feasibility and utility of microsatellite markers in archaeological cattle remains from a Viking Age settlement in Dublin. *Animal Genetics* 34: 410–416.

Edwards, K.J., Schofield, E., and Mauquoy, D. (2008). High resolution paleoenvironmental and chronological investigations of Norse landnám at Tasiusaq, Eastern Settlement, Greenland. *Quaternary Research* 69: 1–15.

Edwards, C.J., Ginja, C., Kantanen, J. et al. (2011). Dual origins of dairy cattle farming – evidence from a comprehensive survey of European Y-chromosomal variation. *PLoS One* 6 (1): e15922. https://doi.org/10.1371/journal.pone.0015922.

Erlandson, J.M. and Rick, C. (2010). Archaeology meets marine ecology: the antiquity of maritime cultures and human impacts on marine fisheries and ecosystems. *Annual Review of Marine Science* 2: 165–185.

Fairnell, E.H. and Barrett, J.H. (2007). Fur-bearing species and Scottish islands. *Journal of Archaeological Science* 34: 463–484.

Feilberg, J. and Høegh, K. (2008). Greenland. In: Sheep Grazing in the North-Atlantic Region. A Long Term Perspective on Management, Resource Economy and Ecology, Norges Teknisk-Naturvitenskapeligeuniversitet Vitenskapsmuseet Rapport Zoologisk Serie 2008-3 (eds. G. Austrheim et al.), 44–53. Trondheim: Norges Teknisk-naturvitenskapelige Universitet Vitenskapsmuseet Seksjon for Naturhistorie.

Felius, M., Koolmees, P.A., Theunissen, B. et al. (2011). On the breeds of cattle. Historic and current classifications. *Diversity* 3: 660–692.

Fenton, A. (1978). The Northern Isles. Edinburgh: John Donald.

Fitzhugh, W.W. (2000). Puffins, ringed pins and runestones. In: Vikings. The North Atlantic Saga (eds. W.W. Fitzhugh and E.I. Ward), 11–25. Washington and London: Smithsonian Press.

Fitzhugh, W.W. and Ward, E.I. (2000). Vikings. The North Atlantic Saga. Washington and London: Smithsonian Press.

Fraser, S., Elsner, J., Hamilton, W.D. et al. (2017). Matrilines in Neolithic cattle from Orkney, Scotland reveals complex husbandry patterns of ancestry. *Journal of Archaeological Science: Reports* 14: 46–54.

Frei, K.M., Coutu, A.N., Smiarowski, K. et al. (2015). Was it for walrus? Viking Age settlement and medieval walrus ivory trade in Iceland and Greenland. *World Archaeology* 47: 439–466.

Friedland, K. (1983). Hanseatic merchants and their trade with Shetland. In: Shetland and the Outside World 1469–1969 (ed. D.J. Withrington), 86–95. Aberdeen: University of Aberdeen.

García, R.R., Fraser, M.D., Celaya, R. et al. (2013). Grazing land management and biodiversity in the Atlantic European heathlands: a review. *Agroforestry Systems* 87: 19–43.

Gauthier, E., Bichet, V., Massa, C. et al. (2010). Pollen and non-pollen palynomorph evidence of medieval farming activities in southwestern Greenland. *Vegetation History and Archaeobotany* 19: 427–438.

Grove, J.M. (1988). The Little Ice Age. Routledge.

Hannon, G.E. and Bradshaw, R.H.W. (2013). Long term consequences for vegetation of ungulate introductions to North Atlantic islands. *Boreal Environment Research* 18: 4–12.

Hannon, G.E., Bradshaw, R.H.W., Bradshaw, E.G. et al. (2005). Islands, climate change and human settlement as drivers of late-Holocene vegetational change in the Faroe. *The Holocene* 15: 639–647.

Harland, J.F. 2006. Zooarchaeology in the Viking Age to Medieval Northern Isles, Scotland: An investigation of spatial and temporal patterning. Unpublished PhD Thesis, University of York.

Harland, J.F. (2012). Animal husbandry: the mammal bone. In: Being an Islander: Production and Identity at Quoygrew, Orkney, AD 900–1600 (ed. J.H. Barrett), 135–154. Cambridge: McDonald Institute for Archaeological Research.

Harland, J.F. 2013. Technical Report: The fish remains from Stackelbrae, Orkney. Reports from the Centre for Human Palaeoecology, University of York, 2013/01, 39 pp.

Harland, J.F. and Barrett, J.H. (2012). The maritime economy: fish bone. In: Being an Islander: Production and Identity at Quoygrew, Orkney, AD 900–1600 (ed. J.H. Barrett), 115–138. Cambridge: McDonald Institute for Archaeological Research.

Harland, J. and Parks, R. (2009). The fish remains. In: On the Fringe of Neolithic Europe: Excavation of a Neolithic Chambered Cairn on the Holm of Papa Westray, Orkney (ed. A. Ritchie), 94–140. Edinburgh: Society of Antiquaries of Scotland.

Hjelle, K.L., Kaland, S., Kvamme, M. et al. (2012). Ecology and long-term land-use, palaeoecology and archaeology – the usefulness of interdisciplinary studies for knowledge-based conservation and management of cultural landscapes. *International Journal of Biodiversity Science Ecosystem Services & Management* 8: 321–337.

Holstein, I.C.C., Ashby, S., van Doorn, N.L. et al. (2014). Searching for Scandinavians in pre-Viking Scotland: molecular fingerprinting of early medieval combs. *Journal of Archaeological Science* 41: 1–6.

Jones, E.P., Skirnisson, K., McGovern, T.H. et al. (2012). Fellow travellers: a concordance of colonization patterns between mice and men in the North Atlantic region. *BMC Evolutionary Biology* 12: 35. http://www.biomedcentral.com/1471-2148/12/35.

Keller, C. (1990). Vikings in the West Atlantic: a model of Norse Greenlandic Medieval Society. *Acta Archaeologica* 61: 126–141.

Ledger, P.M., Edwards, K.J., and Schofield, E. (2013). Sheiling activity in the Norse Eastern settlement: palaeoenvironment of the 'Mountain Farm', Vatnahverfi, Greenland. *The Holocene* 23: 810–822.

Li, M.H., Sternbauer, K., Haahr, P.T., and Kantanen, J. (2005). Genetic components in contemporary Faroe islands cattle as revealed by microsatellite analysis. *Journal of Animal Breeding and Genetics* 122: 309–317.

Low, G. (1813). Fauna Orcadensis or the Natural History of the Quadrupeds, Birds, Reptiles, and Fishes of Orkney and Shetland. Edinburgh: Archibald Constable and Company.

Lucas, G.M. (2008). Pálstóftir. A Viking age shieling in Iceland. *Norwegian Archaeological Review* 41: 85–100.

MacKenzie, B.R., Ojaveer, H., and Eero, M. (2011). Historical ecology provides new insights for ecosystem management: eastern Baltic cod case study. *Marine Policy* 35: 266–270.

Madsen, C. K. 2012. Pastures found. Farming in Greenland, (re)introduced: pp. 142–166. In: Gulløv, H.C., Toft, P.A. and Hansgaard, C.P. (eds), *Challenges and Solutions. Report from Workshop 2 at the National Museum, 1 November 2011*. Rosendahls – Schultz Grafisk: Copenhagen. http://nordligeverdener.natmus.dk/fileadmin/user_upload/temasites/nordlige_verdener/nordlige_verdener/Workshop_2_Challenges_and_Solutions/Challenges_and_solutions.pdf.

Mahler, D.L. (1991). Argisbrekka: new evidence of shielings in the Faroe Islands. *Acta Archaeologica* 61 (1990): 60–72.

Mainland, I. (2006). Pastures lost? A dental microwear study of ovicaprine diet and management in Norse Greenland. *Journal of Archaeological Science* 33: 238–252.

Mainland, I. (ed.). (in preparation) The animal bone. In: Downes, J. and Card, N. (eds), *Excavations at Mine Howe*.

Mainland, I. and Batey, C. (2018). The nature of the feast: commensality and the politics of consumption in Viking Age and Early Medieval Northern Europe. *World Archaeology* 50 (5): 781–803.

Mainland, I. and Halstead, P. (2005). The economics of sheep and goat husbandry in Norse Greenland. *Arctic Anthropology* 43: 103–112.

Mainland, I. and Simpson, I.A. (2005). The formation and utilisation of the landscape. In: The Heart of Neolithic Orkney World Heritage Site Research Agenda (eds. J. Downes, S.M. Foster and C.R. Wickham-Jones), 87–95. Edinburgh: Historic Scotland.

Mainland, I., Towers, J., Ewens, V. et al. (2016). Toiling with teeth: an integrated dental analysis of sheep and cattle dentition in Iron Age and Viking-Late Norse Orkney. *Journal of Archaeological Science: Reports* 6: 837–855.

McCormick, F. and Buckland, P.C. (1997). Faunal change. In: Scotland. Environment and Archaeology, 800 BC-AD 1000 (eds. K.J. Edwards and I.B.M. Ralston), 83–103. Chichester: Wiley.

McGovern, T.H. (1992). Bones buildings and boundaries: palaeoeconomic approaches to Norse Greenland. In: Norse and Later Settlement in the North Atlantic (eds. C.D. Morris and J.D. Rackham), 193–230. Glasgow: University of Glasgow.

McGovern, T.H., Perdikaris, S., Einarsson, A., and Sidell, J. (2006). Coastal connections, local fishing, and sustainable egg harvesting, patterns of Viking Age inland wild resource use in Mývatn district, northern Iceland. *Environmental Archaeology* 11: 102–128.

McGovern, T.H., Fridriksson, A., Church, M. et al. (2007). Landscapes of settlement in northern Iceland: historical ecology of human impact and climate fluctuations on the millennial scale. *American Anthropologist* 109: 27–51.

McGovern, T.H., Perdikaris, S., Mainland, I. et al. (2009). Chapter 4: The archaeofauna. In: Hofstadir: Excavations of an Age Feasting Hall in North-Eastern Iceland, Institute of Archaeology Reykjavik Monograph 1 (ed. G. Lucas), 168–252. Reykjavik: Fornleifastofnun Islands (Institute of Archaeology, Iceland).

Mellows, A., Barnett, R., Dalén, L. et al. (2012). The impact of past climate change on genetic variation and population connectivity in the Icelandic arctic fox. *Proceedings of the Royal Society Series B: Biological Sciences* 279: 4568–4573.

Mulville, J. (2010). Wild things? The prehistory and history of Red Deer on the Hebridean and Northern Isles of Scotland. In: Extinctions and Invasions: A Social History of British Fauna (eds. T. O'Connor, N. Sykes and N.J. Sykes), 43–50. Oxford: Windgatherer Press.

Nicholson, R., Barber, P., and Bond, J.M. (2005). New evidence for the introduction of the house mouse, *Mus musculus domesticus* Swartz & Swartz and the field mouse, *Apodemus sylvaticus* (L.) to Shetland. *Environmental Archaeology* 10: 143–151.

Noddle, B. 1983. Animal bones at Knap of Howar, pp. 92–100. In Ritchie, A. (ed.), *Excavations at a Neolithic Farmstead at Knap of Howar, Papa Westray*. PSAS 113, pp. 40–121.

Ogilvie, A.E.J., Woollett, J.M., Smiarowski, K. et al. (2009). Seals and sea ice in Medieval Greenland. *Journal of the North Atlantic* 2: 60–80.

Ólafsdóttir, G.Á., Pétursdóttir, G., Bárðarson, H., and Edvardsson, R. (2017). A millennium of north-east Atlantic cod juvenile growth trajectories inferred from archaeological otoliths. *PLoS One* 12 (10): e0187134. https://doi.org/10.1371/journal.pone.0187134.

Øye, I. 2005. Farming and farming systems in Norse societies of the North Atlantic, pp. 359–370. In Mortensen, A. and Arge, S. (eds), *Viking and Norse in the North Atlantic*. Select Papers from *Proceedings of the Fourteenth Viking Congress Tórshavn*, 19–30 July 2001 (Annales Societas Scientiarium Færoensis Supplementum XLIV). The Faroese Academy of Sciences: Tórshavn.

Øye, I. (2013). Technology, land use and transformations in Scandinavian landscapes, c. 800–1300. In: Economic Archaeology: From Structure to Performance in European Archaeology (eds. T. Kerig and A. Zimmermann), 295–309. Bonn: Habelt.

Pauly, D., Christensen, V., Dalsgaard, J. et al. (1998). Fishing down marine food webs. *Science* 279: 860–863.

Perdikaris, S. (1999). From chiefly provisioning to commercial fishery: long-term economic change in Arctic Norway. *World Archaeology* 30: 388–402.

Perdikaris, S. and McGovern, T. (2007). Cod fish, walrus and chieftains. In: Seeking a Richer Harvest, Studies in Human Ecology and Adaptation, vol. 3 (eds. T.L. Thurston and C.T. Fisher), 193–216. Springer US.

Perdikaris, S. and McGovern, T. (2008). Codfish and kings, seals and subsistence: Norse marine resource use in the North Atlantic. In: Human Impact on Ancient Marine Ecosystems (eds. T.C. Rick and J.M. Erlandson), 187–214. Berkley and Los Angeles: University of California Press.

Petersen, J.L., Mickelson, J.R., Cothran, E.G. et al. (2013). Genetic diversity in the modern horse illustrated from genome-wide SNP data. *PLoS One* 8 (1): e54997. https://doi.org/10.1371/journal.pone.0054997.

Rainbird, P. (2007). The Archaeology of Islands. Cambridge: Cambridge University Press.

Rick, T., Kirch, P.V., Erlandson, J.M., and Fitzpatrick, S.M. (2013). Archaeology, deep history and the human transformation of island ecosystems. *Anthropocene* 4: 33–45.

Roberts, C. (2007). The Unnatural History of the Sea: The Past and Future of Humanity and Fishing. Washington: Island Press.

Roberts, C. (2012). Ocean of Life: How our Seas Are Changing. London: Allen Lane.

Ryder, M. (1983). Sheep and Man. London: Duckworth.

Ryland, K., Mucklow, C. and Lock, L. 2012. Management for choughs and coastal diversity in Cornwall, RSPS South West Regional Office Report. https://www.birdwatch.rspb.org.uk/Images/Management_for_choughs_and_coastal_biodiversity_tcm9-330224.pdf [accessed 8/10/2014].

Sandnes, B. 2010. *From Starafjall to Starling Hill. An Investigation of the Formation and Development of Old Norse Place-Names in Orkney.* E-book publisher: Scottish Place-Name Society. www.spns.org.uk.

ScARF 2012. Saville, A and Wickham-Jones, C (eds), Palaeolithic and Mesolithic Panel Report, Scottish Archaeological Research Framework: Society of Antiquaries of Scotland. Available online at: http://tinyurl.com/d86dgfq.

Schulting, R. and Richards, M. (2009). Radiocarbon dates and stable isotope values on human remains. In: On the Fringe of Neolithic Europe: Excavation of a Neolithic Chambered Cairn on the Holm of Papa Westray, Orkney (ed. A. Ritchie), 66–74. Edinburgh: Society of Antiquaries of Scotland.

Searle, J.B., Jones, C.S., Gündüz, I. et al. (2009). Of mice and (Viking?) men: phylogeography of British and Irish house mice. *Proceedings of the Royal Society B* 276: 201–207.

Serjeanston, D. (1990). The introduction of mammals to the Outer Hebrides and the use of boat in animal management. *Anthropozoologica* 13: 7–18.

Simpson, I., Scott, L., Kirkpatrick, A.H., and MacDonald, A.J. (1995). Sheep grazing on the moorland landscapes of Orkney and its implications for nature conservation. In: Landscape Ecology: Theory and Application. International Association for Landscape Ecology (ed. G.H. Griffiths), 40–48. Aberdeen: Aulla.

Simpson, I.A., Dugmore, A.J., Thomson, A., and Vésteinsson, O. (2001). Crossing the thresholds: human ecology and historical patterns of landscape degradation. *Catena* 42: 175–192.

Simpson, I.A., Guðmundsson, G., Thomson, A.M., and Cluett, J. (2004). Assessing the role of winter grazing in historic land degradation, Mývatnssveit, Northeast Iceland. *Geoarchaeology* 19: 471–502.

Smith, C. (1994). Animal bone report. In: Howe, Four Millennia of Orkney Prehistory (ed. B. Ballin Smith), 139–153. Edinburgh: Society of Antiquarians of Scotland Monograph.

Surge, D. and Barrett, J.H. (2012). Marine climatic seasonality during medieval times (10th to 12th centuries) based on isotopic records in Viking Age shells from Orkney, Scotland. *Palaeogeography, Palaeoclimatology, Palaeoecology* 350–352: 236–246.

Szabo, V. (2008). Monstrous Fishes and the Mead-Dark Sea: Whaling in the Medieval North Atlantic. Leiden: Brill Academic Publishers.

Tapio, M., Tapio, I., Grislis, Z. et al. (2005). Native breeds demonstrate high contributions to the molecular variation in northern European sheep. *Molecular Ecology* 14: 3951–3963.

Tapio, M., Ozerov, M., Tapio, I. et al. (2010). Microsatellite-based genetic diversity and population structure of domestic sheep in northern Eurasia. *BMC Genetics* 11: 76. http://www.biomedcentral.com/1471-2156/11/76.

Telldahl, Y., Svensson, E., Götherström, A., and Storå, J. (2011). Typing late prehistoric cows and bulls – osteology and genetics of cattle at the Eketorp Ringfort on the Öland Island in Sweden. *PLoS One* 6 (6): e20748. https://doi.org/10.1371/journal.pone.0020748.

Thomson, W. (1995). Orkney farm-names; a re-assessment of their chronology. In: Scandinavian Settlement in Northern Britain (ed. B. Crawford), 42–63. Leicester: Leicester University Press.

Thomson, W.P.L. (2008). The New History of Orkney, 3e. Birlinn: Edinburgh.

Thomson, A.M., Simpson, I.A., and Brown, J.L. (2005). Sustainable rangeland grazing in Norse Faroe. *Human Ecology* 33: 737–761.

Thórhallsdóttir, A.G., Jónsdóttir, I.S., and Magnússon, B. (2007). Iceland. In: Sheep Grazing in the North-Atlantic Region. A Long Term Perspective on Management, Resource Economy and Ecology, Norges Teknisk-Naturvitenskapeligeuniversitet Vitenskapsmuseet Rapport Zoologisk Serie 2008-3 (eds. G. Austrheim et al.), 22–43. Trondheim: Norges Teknisk-naturvitenskapelige Universitet Vitenskapsmuseet Seksjon for Naturhistorie.

Vickers, K. and Sveinbjarnardóttir, G. (2013). Insect invaders, seasonality and transhumant pastoralism in the Icelandic shieling economy. *Environmental Archaeology* 18: 165–177.

Viner, S. (2011). Cattle and pig husbandry in the British Neolithic. In: Dynamics of Neolithisation in Europe. Studies in Honour of Andrew Sherratt (eds. A. Hadjikoumis, E. Robinson and S. Viner), 313–352. Oxbow: Oxford.

Viner, S.J., Evans, J., Albarella, U., and Parker Pearson, M. (2010). Cattle mobility in prehistoric Britain: strontium isotope analysis of cattle teeth from Durrington Walls (Wiltshire, Britain). *Journal of Archaeological Science* 37: 2812–2820.

Zeder, M. (2011). The origins of agriculture in the near east. *Current Anthropology* 52: 221–235.

Zori, D., Byock, J., Erlendsson, E. et al. (2013). Feasting in Viking Age Iceland: sustaining a chiefly political economy in a marginal environment. *Antiquity* 87: 150–165.

Section IV

Conservation in a Warming World

12

A Fleet of Silver

Local Knowledge Perceptions of Sea Ice from Iceland and Labrador/Nunatsiavut

Astrid E.J. Ogilvie[1,2], Brian T. Hill[3] and Gaston R. Demarée[4]

[1] *Stefansson Arctic Institute, Akureyri, Iceland*
[2] *Institute of Arctic and Alpine Research (INSTAAR), University of Colorado, Boulder, CO, USA*
[3] *Institute for Ocean Technology, National Research Council, Canada*
[4] *Royal Meteorological Institute of Belgium, Brussels, Belgium*

Introduction

Ertu kominn, landsins forni fjandi?
Fyrstur varstu enn að[1] sandi,
fyrr en sigling, sól og bjargarráð.
Silfurfloti, sendur oss að kvelja!
situr ei í stafni kerling Helja,
hungurdiskum hendandi yfir gráð

Have you come, our country's ancient enemy?
You arrived upon the sandy shore
Before sailing ship, sun and urgent help.
A fleet of silver, come to torment us!
Is that not the goddess Hel sitting in the bow?
Bringing us plates of hunger ...

Hafísinn/The Sea Ice, Matthías Jochumsson
(Translated by Astrid Ogilvie
and Níels Einarsson)

This paper draws upon ongoing work on the past sea-ice record for Iceland, as well as research on sea-ice records for the Labrador Sea and considerations of current issues of sea-ice impacts in Labrador/Nunatsiavut[2]. The main focus of this paper is to show that, although recent variations in sea ice show similar patterns across the North Atlantic Arctic, including in the records from Labrador and Iceland, the attitude towards sea ice in these two locations is very different. In Iceland, the ice has traditionally been regarded as an enemy, now seemingly being vanquished, while elsewhere, Arctic and Subarctic peoples, including those of Labrador, are mourning the loss of an old friend who is no longer faithful, but who has become fickle and unreliable (Gearheard et al. 2013). However, it should be noted that this paper lays no claims to being a detailed, in-depth analysis but seeks merely to highlight and to comment on this great difference, and some similarities, between two North Atlantic cultures.

The context of the paper is sea-ice variations from ca. 1815 to the present and the role of sea ice as experienced by two Arctic/Subarctic populations, that of the island of Iceland and coastal Labrador/Nunatsiavut, both geographically situated in the northern North Atlantic Ocean. The two locations make for an interesting comparison in that their respective relationships with ice could scarcely be more different. The Inuit and

Biogeography in the Sub-Arctic: The Past and Future of North Atlantic Biota, First Edition.
Edited by Eva Panagiotakopulu and Jon P. Sadler.
© 2021 John Wiley & Sons Ltd. Published 2021 by John Wiley & Sons Ltd.

other Indigenous groups in Labrador have been honing their sea-ice skills for centuries, while for Icelanders, sea ice was a deadly peril to be avoided at all costs. Nonetheless, there are excellent reasons for choosing these two locations for comparative study. Both have an economy that, in recent times, has been based to a large extent on fishing and other marine activities. In Labrador/Nunatsiavut there still exist permanent communities and fishing stations – as was the case in Iceland in the past, but there the old fishing stations have either been abandoned or have become small towns. Both locations have a burgeoning tourist industry and are seeking to attract tourists by advertising the quality and purity of their natural landscapes and the excellent opportunities for whale watching. In Iceland, tourism has now overtaken fisheries as the primary industry and some 20% of all visitors go on whale-watching tours (http://icewhale.is). Both countries are developing hydro-electric power and are involved in the delicate balance between preserving unspoilt nature and in developing industries for much-needed revenue. Iceland and Labrador/Nunatsiavut have relatively low population densities of approximately 340 365 for Iceland as of June 2019 (http://www.worldometers.info/world-population/iceland-population; Statistics Iceland 2019) and 27 197 for Labrador according to the 2016 census (Statistics Canada 2018 www.stats.gov.nl.ca/Statistics/Census2016) with a total population of 528 817 in 2018 for the combined province of Newfoundland and Labrador (http://canadapopulation2018.com/population-of-newfoundland-and-labrador-2018.html).

Apart from this, they have interesting historical connections in that Icelanders and Greenland Norse undoubtedly visited the coast of Labrador around the year 1000, and named the land they saw *Markland,* meaning 'Forest-land' (Ogilvie et al. 2000). The name 'Labrador' derives from the late-fifteenth century Portuguese explorer João Fernandes Lavrador. The Inuit self-governing region of the northern coastal area of Labrador is called *Nunatsiavut*, meaning 'our beautiful land', and was established in 2005 with the signing of the Labrador Inuit Land Claims Agreement and the establishment of the Nunatsiavut Government. This region includes the settlements of Nain, Natuashish, Hopedale, Postville, Rigolet and Makkovik. Part of Labrador is also the ancestral homeland of the Innu peoples, who call it *Nitassinan* ('our land'). Labrador is highly culturally diverse (thus, for example, the community of Makkovik was settled in the 1890s by a Norwegian from Begnadalen in Oppland, Norway). However, the focus here is on the Inuit, who call themselves the 'sea-ice people' or *Sikumiut* in Inuktitut, the Inuit language (Borlase 1993; Clarke 1999). As for Iceland, there were no native peoples there when it was settled in the late-ninth century onwards by colonizers who came primarily from Norway and the northern British Isles. As well as the similarities between Iceland and Labrador noted above, clearly great differences also exist, for example in terms of culture and language, and not least in their relationship with coastal sea ice. To Icelanders in the past, the ice that drifted to its coasts with the East Greenland Current brought with it famine and hardship. The recent trend towards a lack of ice is thus regarded as most fortunate in Iceland but, as elsewhere in the Arctic, it is causing numerous difficulties for the people of Labrador/Nunatsiavut.

Arctic Climate Change

Dramatic changes are occurring in the Arctic and Subarctic. These include: increasing temperatures, reductions in extent and thickness of sea ice, ice sheet and glacier mass; reduced snow extent and duration; thawing permafrost; and a general overall 'greening' of the Arctic (see, for example, ACIA 2005; Arctic Report Card 2018). Of all these changes, sea-ice loss is perhaps the most evident

(Maslanik et al. 2007; Serreze et al. 2007, 2009, 2016; Stroeve et al. 2007, 2008, 2012; SWIPA 2011; Serreze and Stroeve 2015). Recent sea-ice losses are significant. Thus, for example, in the 2007 melt season, Arctic sea ice reached its lowest level since satellite measurements began in 1979. In 2008, it dropped to the second lowest level (Stroeve et al. 2008). From 2008 through 2010 '... sea-ice extents remained substantially below the 1979–2000 average .... In 2011, Arctic sea ice nearly tied the 2007 record low' (http://nsidc.org/cryosphere/sotc/sea_ice.html). The Arctic sea ice September minimum extent also reached a new record low in 2012. 'The last six years (2007–2012) have seen the six lowest minimum extents in the satellite record (since 1979). Over the last 11 years, a new record was set four times (2002, 2005, 2007, and 2012) and several other years saw near-record lows, particularly 2008 and 2011' (http://nsidc.org/arcticseaicenews/2011/09). Over the summer of 2013, Arctic sea-ice loss was somewhat held in check due to relatively cool and stormy conditions. As a result, there was more ice at the end of summer, compared to the record low extent of 2012. Overall, the 2014 Arctic maximum was the fifth lowest in the 1978–2014 record (http://nsidc.org/arcticseaicenews/2014/04). On February 25 2015 'Arctic sea ice likely reached its maximum extent for the year, at 14.54 million square kilometers (5.61 million square miles). The maximum ice extent of the year described (2015) was the lowest in the satellite record, with below-average ice conditions everywhere except in the Labrador Sea and Davis Strait' (http://nsidc.org/arcticseaicenews). Arctic sea-ice extent for March 2018 averaged 14.30 million square kilometres, the second lowest in the 1979 to 2018 satellite record (http://nsidc.org/arcticseaicenews). At the end of May 2019, Arctic sea ice daily extent stood at the second lowest in the 40-year satellite record (https://nsidc.org/arcticseaicenews).

Not only will the melting of sea ice lead to seasonal opening of potentially important marine transportation routes, but the reduced sea-ice extent and duration will cause significant changes in surface reflectivity, cloudiness, humidity, exchanges of heat and moisture, and ocean circulation (Fabricius et al. 1995; Wadhams and Munk 2004). These, and other, changes will, in turn, affect global climate. Clearly, human and animal populations are also impacted, and the voices of Indigenous and stakeholder populations all over the circumpolar Arctic are to be heard expressing their concerns regarding the threat of diminishing sea ice to their traditional ways of life and what is occurring with *sila* – the Inuktitut word that means 'climate and all things that surround human beings' (see, for example Huntington et al. 2001; Fox 2003; AHDR 2004, 2015; Bravo 2010; Krupnik et al. 2010). In this regard, coastal communities in Labrador/Nunatsiavut are no different.

Sea Ice and Locations of Iceland and Labrador

The island of Iceland is located in a climatologically sensitive area close to major and contrasting features of the Northern Hemisphere's atmospheric and oceanic circulations – at the intersection of cold Polar air and warmer Atlantic air, and the relatively warm Irminger current and the colder East Iceland current (Ogilvie 1984, 2020b; Hanna et al. 2004). Because of this, Iceland is very sensitive to minor fluctuations in the strength of these different air masses and ocean currents. This is one of the main causes of the variability of the climate of Iceland on all time scales, and Iceland's vulnerability to climate impacts in the past, and potentially in the future, is due, in large part, to this variability of the climate (Bergthórsson 1969; Ogilvie 1984a, 1991, 1992a, 1984b, 2001, 2005, 2010, 2017; Ogilvie and Jónsdóttir 2000; Ogilvie and McGovern 2000; Ogilvie and Jónsson 2001). Iceland is also situated at the seasonal boundary of the Arctic sea ice, which is another important feature of the climate (Ogilvie and Jónsson 2001; Miles et al. 2014). The ice is carried southward by the East Greenland Current and its extent varies considerably. Apart from the anomalous 'sea-ice years' of 1965–1971 (Dickson et al. 1988) there has been little sea ice in evidence off the coasts of Iceland during the twentieth century and up to the present time (2021). In the past, it occurred most frequently off the coasts from late winter to early spring, but during severe seasons it could remain far into the summer and even the autumn. The months April and May were likely to have the greatest extent of ice and September to December the least. The presence or absence of the ice has a considerable influence on the climate of Iceland, both directly because of its nature as a heat sink, and indirectly through the influence of sea ice on the atmospheric circulation over a much wider region. The proximity of the ice to Iceland's coasts is associated with a fall in both land and sea temperatures.

The coast of Labrador and the east coast of the island of Newfoundland are exposed to the cold Labrador Current, resulting in a cold moist climate. The Labrador Current is the southerly component of the Labrador Sea gyre, which mixes the West Greenland Current from the east side of the sea with the Polar Water of the Canadian Current flowing down from the Arctic channels to the north, and the fresher water flowing out from Hudson Bay through Hudson Strait at the northern tip of Labrador. It is this cold current that distributes sea ice and icebergs across the Grand Banks of Newfoundland and into the North Atlantic Ocean (see Figure 1). Ice appears through local formation and drift from further north off the Labrador coast in late autumn. In the past, drift ice could close off the harbour of St John's in February and, in severe years, reach its greatest extent in late March or early April in a latitude of about 45°N. Ice in the Gulf of St Lawrence forms in situ in autumn and by

January can start drifting out through the south side of Cabot Strait between Newfoundland and Cape Breton. Its greatest extent is normally about mid-March and, in the most severe years, can extend along the Scotian Shelf as far as Halifax, Nova Scotia, to the southwest, or about 43° north latitude to the south. In extreme ice-years, the island of Newfoundland can be almost totally enclosed by sea ice, with ice from the gulf extending as far east as the French islands of St Pierre and Miquelon, about mid-point along the south coast of Newfoundland, and by ice drifting with the Labrador Current and curling westward along the south coast to almost the same point. Ice is driven far on the Grand Banks by the cold winter northwesterly winds and is associated with high North Atlantic Oscillation (NAO) index values.

Impacts of Sea-Ice Variations in Iceland and Labrador

Broadly speaking, the impact of sea-ice variability on human life can be traced back to the role of the NAO – the Atlantic component of the Arctic Oscillation (AO) – and potentially a forcing mechanism in the high Arctic climate system (Dickson et al. 2000). A positive NAO implies an anomalous low pressure over Iceland, leading to cold northwesterly winds over the Labrador Sea and warm easterly winds over the Greenland Sea. Under such circumstances the Labrador Sea will have more than average sea ice, its ports will be icebound and its climate will be colder than usual. The warm easterly winds will push back the East Greenland ice westward, keeping the coasts of Iceland ice-free (see, for example, Vinje et al. 1998). The Norwegian Atlantic Current will be stimulated, keeping the west side of Spitsbergen ice-free and warmer than usual. A negative NAO will have opposite effects.

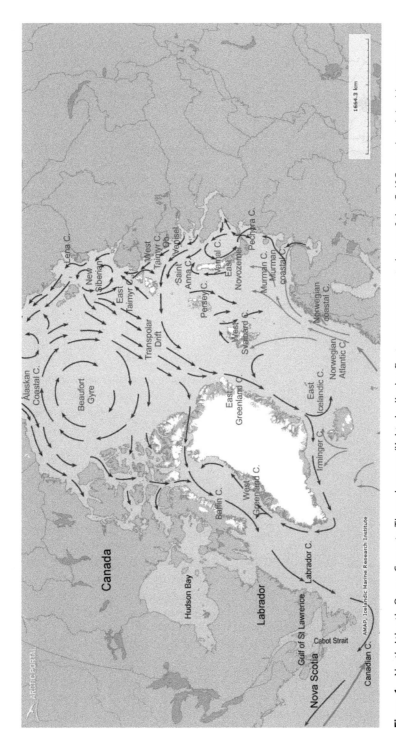

Figure 1 North Atlantic Ocean Currents. The red arrows (light shading) reflect warmer currents (arms of the Gulf Stream) and the blue arrows dark shading colder currents as marked. *Source:* Figure courtesy of Holmgrímur Helgason and Arctic Portal, http://arcticportal.org.

Historical Sea-Ice Data for Iceland and Labrador

Prior to the era of systematic meteorological records and satellite data, information concerning sea-ice variations in North Atlantic/Arctic regions is available from documentary records and other climate proxy data. Three diverse but excellent sources of data that have been used in our reconstructions are described here. These are: the records related to Moravian missionaries to Labrador, the Hydrographic Bulletins of the US Hydrological Office and official governmental reports from Iceland. These are described in brief below.

Moravian missionaries established settlements in many parts of the world, including among the Inuit in Labrador (Demarée and Ogilvie 2008). These mission stations were usually given names with Biblical associations, and in Labrador included: Hopedale (1782), Zoar (1865), Nain (1771), Okak (1776), Hebron (1830) and Ramah (1871). Moravian culture and trade have significantly shaped northern Labrador and the lives of Inuit and settlers living there. The Moravian church is still a religious force in the region with approximately 2500 members in four churches: Nain, Hopedale, Makkovik and Happy-Valley-Goose Bay (Rollmann 2009). The missionaries appear to have been greatly interested in what might be termed natural history, and many of the historical documents they produced contain not only information pertaining to religious matters but also give details on climate, weather and related topics. Of particular interest is the fact that the missionaries also undertook instrumental meteorological observations (Demarée and Ogilvie 2008, 2011, 2021; Demarée et al. 2010, 2018, 2020). The historical legacy of the Moravian missionaries is to be found in records scattered throughout a number of European libraries and archives and has been the subject of tireless research by Gaston Demarée of the Royal Meteorological Office, Belgium, in collaboration with Astrid Ogilvie, and is proving to be a valuable source of climatic information.

Notable among the records are the missionary journals that were published as a way of keeping contact between the missionaries abroad and their churches and followers in Europe. Through the journals, funding was raised and gifts were collected for the missionaries far away. For the interest of the reader, the journals also provided secular information on the state of the country where the missions were stationed, including on geography, weather and climate. It is clear that information concerning the climate in northerly countries such as Labrador and Greenland was considered to be extremely interesting by contemporary readers and may be seen in the context of the preoccupation with Arctic exploration in Britain and Europe in the nineteenth century (Potter 2007). The manuscripts of the journals travelled to Europe by means of the Moravian vessel that visited the Labrador stations in the summer of each year. For this reason, the information is organized in 'ship-years'; this means roughly July of one year to August of the next. The exact day in which this period began or ended depended on many conditions, among them the sea ice and the meteorological conditions encountered crossing the Atlantic Ocean.

The annual voyage from London was made every summer for 156 years between 1770 and 1926. Of the 12 ships involved, five were named the *Harmony*. The voyage generally involved a stop at Stromness in the Orkney islands of Scotland to pick up a crew and, for many years, the *Harmony*'s captain (Marr 2010). The journals provide detailed information on the presence or absence of sea ice during the journey, and near the Labrador coast. This occurrence of ice along the coast was one of the main constraints regarding the safe arrival of the ship. The presence of the ice could make the journey dangerous and could potentially delay the arrival of the ships, and the missionary accounts contain many descriptions of heavy ice years. A notable year is 1816, the 'Year Without a Summer', which followed the massive eruption of Mount Tambora on 10 April 1815, on the island of Sumbawa in what is now Indonesia. The effects were felt in Labrador as elsewhere, and included extensive drift ice along the coast (Harrington 1992; Newell 1992; Hill 1998). In the year before, at the time that our series start, 1815 (see Figure 2), severe ice conditions are also described: 'On the 19 July 1815, the Lord unexpectedly led the missionary vessel *Jemima* hither in safety, through the drift ice which had for a long time encircled our coast' (Periodical Accounts 1790–1889).[3]

Another significant source of data for the Labrador/Newfoundland region is to be found in copies of *The Weekly Hydrographic Bulletin of the U.S. Hydrographic Office, 1889–1954*, located in the US National Archives in Washington, DC. Information from these bulletins have been extracted by Brian Hill (together with Alan Ruffman). These bulletins had the object of placing 'within reach of mariners, at no expense to them, such useful information as cannot be collected profitably by any private individual, but which the Government can readily gather, without any additional cost, through agencies already established.' This information included mainly hazards to navigation, such as the location of wrecks and derelicts, ice and icebergs, and, during war and post-war years, the location of mines. Other meteorological and scientific observations were often included as well (Hill 1998, 2008; Hill et al. 2002, 2008).

Iceland is well known for its rich literary tradition, which includes a wealth of historical records containing accounts of climate and weather (Ogilvie and Jónsson 2001; Ogilvie 2005, 2008,

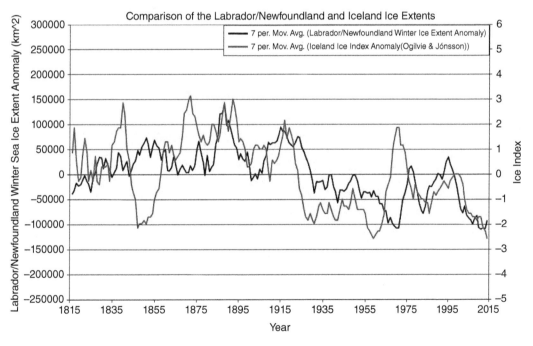

Figure 2 Comparison of Labrador/Newfoundland (blue/dark shading) and Iceland (red/light shading) Ice Extents 1815–2014.

2010, 2015, 2020, 2021; Hartman et al. 2017). The early part of the sea-ice record for Iceland used here is based on historical data and particular use has been made of a valuable legacy from Danish rule (which lasted in effect from ca. 1536 to 1944) in the form of official reports describing conditions in Iceland and covering the period ca. 1700 to 1894. The reports were written one to three times a year by Icelandic officials known as *Sýslumenn* (Sheriffs) and *Amtmenn* (District Governors) and sent to the *Stiftamtmaður* or *Landshöfðingja* (Governors of Iceland). They are in manuscript form and are written in Danish, in Gothic handwriting. They were produced for all of the counties of Iceland (23), thus enabling comparison of conditions in different areas. The reports contain information on climate (especially temperature and precipitation) and sea-ice variations, as well as socio-economic information. They thus form a goldmine of climatic, environmental and historical information. They are located in the National Archives in Iceland and are currently being analysed by Astrid Ogilvie (Ogilvie 2005, 2008, 2015). As in Labrador, 1815 and 1816 were severe years in Iceland (Ogilvie 1992b) and a translation of a letter regarding the sea-ice year of 1815 is given below.

Local and Indigenous Knowledge Systems

In recent times, the value of what is referred to as Indigenous Local Knowledge Systems[4] or Traditional Ecological Knowledge (TEK) has been realized. This refers to local and Indigenous perceptions of environmental change, stability and variability. TEK may be constructed as data sets that can be analysed quantitatively and linked with scientific records, data and concepts for modelling. Incorporating TEK in scientific research is mutually beneficial and enriching. It can provide valuable information important to scientific research and enable researchers to communicate better and to share scientific findings. However, it may be noted that the gathering of TEK is no easy task. There is no single way to do it and many perspectives are involved. In this regard it is very different from the traditional scientific method (see, for example, Huntington 2005) and TEK can generally be defined as a: '... system of knowledge, practice and belief acquired through interaction with the environment and transmitted across generations' (Berkes 2008). For the purpose of this paper, no complex modelling or statistical analyses of TEK have been undertaken. However, a foundation for such analyses was made during meetings with members of local communities in Labrador/Nunatsiavut in the spring of 2007, and later in May and August 2011. These provided anecdotal local-knowledge evidence regarding recent changes in sea-ice conditions. TEK also forms an invaluable perspective on the study of human ecodynamics and long-term change in social-ecological systems (Fitzhugh et al. 2019).

Another aspect of TEK, less frequently emphasized, may be found in the writings of local people describing their environment through the medium of written documents. In this regard, the written records of highly literary cultures such as that of Iceland provide a unique form of TEK from the past (Ogilvie 2005). Iceland possesses a very rich store of historical records that describe weather and climate from early settlement times onwards (Ogilvie 1982 *et seq.*), one form of which is described below.

A Perspective from the Past: Iceland

> ... the winter was among the best, but the spring was very cold, especially after the sea ice, which lay here for some time, had embraced the coasts. In the similarly cold summer, the grass growth was thus very

poor. The hay harvest, which began in mid August, was hindered by frost, fog and cold chills as well as much snow on occasion, especially around 18 August and again on 19 to 26 September. It was also difficult to harvest the hay in the constant and severe rain in late September and early October .... In the spring the inhabitants caught several sharks, and in the autumn a considerable number of cod and halibut .... However, on 19 October the fishing stopped due to encroaching drift ice. The two whales washed up in the jurisdictional areas of Broddanes and Bær by the sea ice in June, helped much in preventing hunger deaths in the dearth at that time.

(Extract from letter written by Sheriff Jón Jónsson, dated 3 January 1816, Bær, Hrútafirði, Strandasýsla. Translated by Astrid Ogilvie)

It is possible that Iceland owes its name to the presence of sea ice (Ogilvie 2005) and this reflects the importance of sea ice for the country from earliest times. It is recorded in an early historical source that the first would-be settler, Flóki Vilgerðarson, gave it this name in a moment of pique and disappointment when he observed sea ice off the shores after a hard spring, some time around 865 CE, when his cattle died of hunger after he had neglected to gather hay to feed them over the winter (Benediktsson 1968). However, if the story became known among subsequent potential settlers in the late-ninth century it did not dissuade them! The early colonists brought with them an economy based on animal husbandry, primarily sheep and cattle, with supplementary fishing and marine-mammal hunting, and this remained the main economic pattern until fishing became a major industry in the late-nineteenth century (Karlsson 2007). For the most part, the climate of Iceland has not been suitable for grain-growing and, until recent times, the main crop has been the grass upon which the livestock were dependent for winter fodder (Ogilvie 1984b, 2001; Júlíusson 2001, 2018; Júlíusson and Jónsson 2013).

The story about Flóki, whether apocryphal or not, is interesting, not least because the presence or absence of sea ice off the coasts does have a major impact on grass-growth. This is because the proximity of sea ice has the effect of lowering temperatures on land. Colder temperatures mean poor grass growth, and hence a resulting lack of hay to feed livestock over the winter. If a shortage of fodder became acute, the animals would die of starvation over the winter. As they were dependent on milk and meat products for survival, this could result further in loss of human life (Friðriksson 1969; Ogilvie 1984b, 2001, 2010, 2015; Ogilvie and Jónsdóttir 2000). The presence of the ice off the coasts also led to other difficulties, such as the prevention of fishing and access by trading vessels.

However, the proximity of sea ice could also have some positive effects. Useful products such as driftwood and marine mammals could accompany the ice. In stark prose, the report quoted at the start of this section describes several of these elements. A more literary description of sea ice may be found in the famous (in Iceland) poem entitled *Hafísinn* ('The Sea Ice') by the Icelandic poet Matthías Jochumsson (1835–1920). He composed the poem just before Easter in 1888 after a series of severe years with much sea ice (Guðmundsson 1916; Ogilvie 2015). He was then residing in Akureyri, situated on Iceland's longest fjord, Eyjafjörður, in the north of Iceland, and apparently began to write the poem on seeing the ice glide into the fjord. The first verse of this poem is given at the start of this paper. A metaphor evoking beauty, stateliness and abundance is used, *a fleet of silver* (in Icelandic 'silfurfloti'), but this is deceptive, for the ice has come, not to delight, but to torment, for the fleet does not bring food, or useful goods, like normal trading vessels, but *plates of hunger* ('hungurdiskum'). The reference is to pancake ice, which also resembles empty plates, and is ironically suggestive of the fact that pancake ice brings, not sustenance, but starvation. Chief among all scourges, the ice is the worst – it is 'the country's ancient enemy' – and, in referring to Hel, the name of the Norse goddess of the underworld, it evokes the one enemy that can never be defeated – death.

A Perspective from the Present: Labrador/ Nunatsiavut

> If the ice is treacherous, just walk lightly ....
>
> *(Anonymous informant in Makkovik)*

As is well documented, sea ice reaching the shores of Iceland is now rare, and the current climate forms a backdrop to a life for modern Icelanders that is very different to the past. The lack of ice may appear to be a great blessing. However, in other Arctic and Subarctic regions the picture is very different. This has been documented extensively (Huntington et al. 2001; Gearheard et al. 2006, 2013; Krupnik et al. 2010; Lovecraft 2013). Discussions with local informants in Labrador/Nunatsiavut illustrate a similar story to those told in Greenland, Alaska and other parts of northern Canada. In this section, rather than give quotations from different informants, a general narrative that typifies the anecdotal evidence for drastic changes in sea-ice cover over the past 30 years or so is given below. Invariably, it was stated that over the last 20–30 years 'the winters have been different'. In past times it would usually get cold at the end of October or beginning of November, and then there would be a steady increase in the cold. In the last 10–15 years 'there has not even been proper freezing until January'. There has been no long steady cold that makes the ice hard. One informant noted that if

you get snow on top of the ice, it acts as insulation to keep it frozen hard. This happens less now. Another informant said: 'The snow is no good now – no good for making snow houses – my children and grandchildren don't know how to do it. Thirty years ago people would go out to the *sina*, the ice edge, all the time. This has changed: We are not seeing the heavy pack ice as before. This could stay to the first week in July. The ice used to extend for 80 to 90 miles, but not now. We used to go out on the ice for days, looking for seals. Now we don't trust the ice anymore. People used to be able to look at the ice and see if it was safe to walk on. An elder is mentioned who said, if the ice was treacherous, "just walk lightly". Apparently people would even walk on loose ice, as long as the wind stayed on shore. In recent times many tragedies have occurred, with people falling through the ice. Perhaps the old friend is fast becoming an enemy, as the old ways are being lost. In the old days people had knowledge of the land but now they have GPS.'

Overview of Recent Sea-Ice Variations

Perhaps the most striking aspect of the diagram in Figure 2 is the great variability that can be seen over the period ca. 1815 to 2014, almost 200 years, in both regions, but particularly for Iceland. For the most part, however, the diagram suggests relative agreement between the two locations. The early part of the period shows heavy ice conditions for both Iceland and Labrador. From 1840 to 1854 there was little ice off the Icelandic coasts. However, in contrast, there continued to be relatively heavy ice concentrations in the Labrador/Newfoundland area. The latter part of the nineteenth century saw some very severe sea-ice years in Iceland, particularly in the 1860s and 1880s. The 1880s, specifically the period from 1881 to 1888, were unusually severe climatically, and they have come to be known as the 'Dire Years'

(Ponzi 1995). Sea ice was present in 1881, 1882, 1883, 1886, 1887, and 1888. A succession of poor summers caused consecutive hay-crop failure and Iceland suffered its last great subsistence famine. During these years many people in Iceland emigrated to the United States and Canada. The reasons for this were complex, but undoubtedly the severe weather played a part. A Sheriff's report describing the period November 1880 to April 1881 reads as follows:

> The extremely severe weather that began in earnest in the middle of November (1880) lasted until the beginning of April (1881). It was the general opinion that no one now living had experienced such long-lasting and severe frost ... There was frequent fog due to the sea ice, and the bay of Húnaflói was full of sea ice. The spring was cold and dry and the grass growth was of the poorest quality. The summer was also cold and dry and there was night frost.
>
> *(Extract from letter written by Sheriff Lárus Blöndahl, dated 1 October 1881, Kornsá, Húnavatnssýsla. Translated by Astrid Ogilvie)*

Severe sea-ice conditions may also be noted in Figure 2 for the same periods in the Labrador region. To further illustrate the human dimension, an extract is also given here from an account written on 3 August 1888 (a few months after Matthías Jochumssen wrote his poem on sea ice) by the Reverend Benjamin La Trobe who had then reached Labrador with the missionary ship the *Harmony*.

> It is six weeks all but a day since we left London. We might have reached Hopedale three days ago, for we were within eighty miles. But a dense fog made it impossible to venture among the islands, where drift ice might be added to the dangers of rocks. So we were driving to and fro for the last three days and nights over a high sea, studded with icebergs hidden from us by a thick white mist, which made everything wet and cold. It has been the least pleasant and most anxious part of our voyage hitherto. This morning the fog cleared away, and we could see how good the Lord had been to us, for the icebergs were still surrounding us, but had never been permitted to come nigh our vessel. (Not till later did we know how well He had not only protected but piloted us. Drift ice beset the whole coast, but during those three days it cleared away southward. Nor could we have reached Hopedale by the usual southerly route, past the Gull Island, even on August 3rd. The course by which we were taken, *nolens volens*, was the only one open).
>
> As morning wore on our swift progress brought us to the outer islands, bare bleak rocks, at whose base the sea was breaking terrifically. The first was Ukalek (the hare), about equal distance from Nain, Zoar, and Hopedale. We turned southward, our good ship speeding along before a favourable breeze and rolling heavily. Many icebergs of all shapes and sizes were visible around our now widened horizon. Tremendous waves were beating against their gleaming white sides, and sending the spray high towards their towering pinnacles, in one case clean over a huge berg perhaps 150 feet high.
>
> *(La Trobe 1888, p. 2).*

From around 1903, sea ice falls off dramatically in Iceland and a corresponding pattern is seen in the Labrador/Newfoundland area. The twentieth-century decline in sea ice was interrupted in the Iceland area by the so-called 'ice-years' of the period 1965–1971. This period is also known as the 'Great Salinity Anomaly' (Dickson et al. 1988). A 'lag' effect is seen in the Labrador region. After this time the two records seem to be in agreement, doubtless to some extent due to the better data coverage available with the advent of satellite data. The decline in sea-ice extent of the early twenty-first century is also to be seen in both graphs.

Conclusions

As outlined above, for the most part, sea ice was considered a deadly enemy in Iceland and a 'friend' in the Labrador/Nunatsiavut region, at least by the Inuit, if not by the Europeans who voyaged there by sea. However, as with most human/environment relations, the situation is complex. When ice reached the coasts of Iceland in the past, it did sometimes bring positive benefits, and, for example, seal hunting on the ice was by no means unknown (Kristjánsson 1980; Ogilvie et al. 2009) and now, with diminishing sea ice in the Arctic, it is becoming far less of a friendly entity for those who live there. The broader context here is that human settlements and natural ecosystems in Arctic/Subarctic regions are currently experiencing the impacts of environmental change resulting from global warming. Syntheses of environmental and human systems research in these regions hold the potential to provide both a theoretical and practical understanding of how people have developed adaptive systems in response to environmental change, stability and variability in the past, and to develop tools for decision-making in the future. As these regions support a rich marine and terrestrial habitat surrounded by relatively densely populated nations, the rapid climate change and high inter-annual variability currently occurring in these areas (with greater changes predicted in the future; ACIA 2005; Wigley 2005; IPCC 2013; Arctic Report Card 2018) means that it is a matter of urgency to assess the impacts of global change on humans and ecosystems in these areas. The documentary historical data highlighted here serve to provide a context for such changes, as do the comments of those who are currently living with changing patterns of sea-ice distribution.

Acknowledgements

The authors acknowledge US National Science Foundation awards 0629500, 0638897 and 0902134. The work in this paper on Iceland is also supported by, and contributes to, the NordForsk-funded Nordic Centre of Excellence project (Award 76654) *Arctic Climate Predictions: Pathways to Resilient, Sustainable Societies (ARCPATH)*. There are too many friends and colleagues in Labrador/Nunatsiavut who deserve thanks to name them all here, but especial thanks go to Martha MacDonald and Tim Borlase, of the Labrador Institute, for their 'introduction to Labrador' in 2007, and Susan Felsburg of Goose Bay and Mud Lake for assistance on many occasions and her friendship. Susan Crate, George Mason University, is thanked for her collaboration and for companionship on fieldwork in 2011. Níels Einarsson, Director of the Stefansson Arctic Institute, collaborated on the translation from *Hafísinn*. In addition, our many conversations around the general topics discussed are greatly valued. Ingibjörg Jónsdóttir, of the University of Iceland, friend and colleague in sea ice, is thanked for her collaboration. Special thanks go to Trausti Jónsson of the Icelandic Meteorological Office for sharing data and for climate collaboration and friendship for many years. Brian Hill thanks Alan Ruffman for his collaboration. The map showing ocean currents in Arctic regions was provided courtesy of Hólmgrímur Helgason and the Arctic Portal (http://arcticportal.org). Last, but not least, Astrid Ogilvie thanks her local informants in Labrador/Nunatsiavut who gave willingly of their time to discuss the issue of sea ice that is so important to them.

Notes

1 The Icelandic alphabet includes the letters ð (upper case Ð) pronounced like the 'th' in 'clothe' and þ (upper case Þ) pronounced like the 'th' in 'thank'.

2 An earlier version of this paper was published online following a presentation at the 6th Open Assembly of the Northern Research Forum held in Hveragerði, Iceland, in September 2011. Permission has been granted to publish this revised version here. Another online tale of 'sea-ice stories' is a brief representation of the situation described in this paper: https://bifrostonline.org/sea-ice-stories-from-iceland-and-labrador. This also features Shari Gearheard speaking on Inuit knowledge and climate changes.

3 Quotations from the Moravian missionary accounts have been translated by Gaston Demarée when the original is not in English.

4 http://www.unesco.org/new/en/natural-sciences/priority-areas/links/related-information/what-is-local-and-indigenous-knowledge.

References

ACIA (Arctic Climate Impact Assessment) (2005). *Impacts of a Warming Climate: Arctic Climate Impact Assessment.* New York: Cambridge University Press.

AHDR (2004). *Arctic Human Development Report* (eds. N. Einarsson, J. Nymand Larsen, A. Nilsson and O.R. Young). Akureyri: Stefansson Arctic Institute.

AHDR (2015). *Arctic Human Development Report: Regional Processes and Global Linkages* (eds. J. Nymand Larsen and G. Fondahl). Nordic Council of Ministers.

Arctic Report Card, 2018. http://www.arctic.noaa.gov/reportcard. Retrieved 8 June 2019.

Benediktsson, J. 1968. Íslendingabók. Landnámabók. *Íslenzk Fornrit* I. Reykjavik: Hið Íslenzka Fornritafélag.

Bergthórsson, P. (1969). An estimate of drift ice and temperature in 1000 years. *Jökull* 19: 94–101.

Berkes, F. (2008 [1999]). *Sacred Ecology: Traditional Ecological Knowledge and Resource Management.* Philadelphia: Taylor & Francis.

Borlase, T. (1993). *The Labrador Inuit, Labrador Studies.* Labrador Integrated School Board.

Bravo, M.T. (2010). The humanism of sea ice. In: *SIKU: Knowing Our Ice: Documenting Inuit Sea Ice Knowledge and Use* (eds. I. Krupnik, C. Aporto, S. Gearheard, et al.). Dordrecht, The Netherlands, pp. 457–464: Springer.

Clarke, B. (1999). *The Labrador Inuit, Newfoundland Museum Notes.* St John's Newfoundland.

Demarée, G.R. and Ogilvie, A.E.J. (2008). The Moravian missionaries at the Labrador Coast and their centuries-long contribution to instrumental meteorological observations. *Climatic Change* 91: 423–450.

Demarée, G.R. and Ogilvie, A.E.J. (2011). Climate related information in Labrador/Nunatsiavut: evidence from Moravian missionary journals. *Bull. Séanc. Acad. R. Sci. Outre-Mer Meded. Zitt K. Acad. Overzeese Wet (Royal Academy for Overseas Sciences, Belgium)* 57 (2–4): 391–408.

Demarée, G.R. and Ogilvie, A.E.J. (2021). Early meteorological observations in Greenland: the contributions of David Cranz, Christian Gottlieb Kratzenstein and Christopher Brasen. In: *Christianities in the Trans-Atlantic World, Legacies* of David Cranz's 'Historie von Grönland' (1765), (eds. F.A. Jensz and C. Petterson). Palgrave, 141–164.

Demarée, G.R., Ogilvie, A.E.J., and Csonka, Y. (2010). The Inuit of Labrador/Nunatsiavut, the Moravian Brethren and connections with French-speaking Switzerland. *Journal of the North Atlantic* 3: 24–30. https://doi.org/10.3721/037.003.0106.

Demarée, G.R., Ogilvie, A.E.J., and Kusman, D. (2018). Historical records of earthquakes for Greenland and Labrador in Moravian Missionary Journals. *Journal of Seismology* https://doi.org/10.1007/s10950-018-9796-z. Online 4 October 2018.

Demarée, G.R., Ogilvie, A.E.J. and Mailier, P. (2020). Early meteorological observations in Greenland and Labrador in the 18th century: a contribution of the Moravian Brethren, In: *Proceedings of the 35th International Symposium on the Okhotsk Sea and Polar Oceans 2020*, pp. 16–19 February 2020, Mombetsu, Hokkaido, Japan, Okhotsk Sea and Polar Ocean Research Association (OSPORA), C5, pp. 35–38.

Dickson, R.R., Meinke, J., Malmberg, S.A., and Lee, A.J. (1988). The great salinity anomaly in the Northern North Atlantic. *Progress in Oceanography* 20: 103–151.

Fabricius, J.S., Frydendahl, K. and Frich, P. (1995). Polar sea ice off West Greenland – A review. In: *Proceedings of the 14th International Conference on Offshore Mechanics and Arctic Engineering*, Nixon, W.A, Sodhi, D.S. and Sinha, N.K.(eds). Book No. H00942, 265–272.

Fitzhugh, B., Butler, V.L., Bovy, K.M., and Etnier, M.A. (2019). Human ecodynamics: a perspective for the study of long-term change in socioecological systems. *Journal of Archaeological Science* 23: 1077–1094. https://doi.org/10.1016/j.jasrep.2018.03.016.

Fox, S. (2003). *When the Weather Is Uggianaqtuq: Inuit Observations of Environmental Change.* Boulder, CO: University of Colorado Geography Department Cartography Lab.

Distributed by National Snow and Ice Data Center. CD-Rom.

Friðriksson, S. (1969). The effects of sea ice on fauna, flora and agriculture. *Jökull* 19: 146–157.

Gearheard, S., Matumeak, W., Angutikjuag, I. et al. (2006). "It's Not That Simple": a collaborative comparison of sea ice environments, their uses, observed changes, and adaptations in Barrow, Alaska, USA and Clyde River, Nunavut, Canada. *Ambio* 35 (4): 204–212.

Gearheard, S., Kielsen Holm, L., Huntington, H.P. et al. (eds.) (2013). *The Meaning of Ice: People and Sea Ice in Three Arctic Communities.* Hanover: International Polar Institute, 412 pp.

Guðmundsson, S. (1916). Matthías áttræður. *Skírnir* 90: 1–16.

Hanna, E., Jónsson, T., and Box, J.E. (2004). An analysis of Icelandic climate since the nineteenth century. *International Journal of Climatology* 24: 1193–1210. Published online in Wiley InterScience (http://www.interscience.wiley.com), https://doi.org/10.1002/joc.1051.

Harrington, C.R. (ed.) (1992). *The Year without a Summer? World Climate in 1816.* Ottawa: Canadian Museum of Nature.

Hartman, S., Ogilvie, A.E.J., Ingimundarson, J.H. et al. (2017). Medieval Iceland, Greenland, and the new human condition: a case study in integrated environmental humanities. *Global and Planetary Change* 156: 123–139. https://doi.org/10.1016/j.gloplacha.2017.04.007.

Hill, B.T. (1998). Historical Record of Sea Ice and Iceberg Distribution around Newfoundland and Labrador, 1810–1958. In: *Conference and Workshop of Arctic Climate Systems Study: Sea Ice Charts of the Arctic, Seattle*, 1998. WMO/TD No. 949; IAPO Informal Report No. 3, pp. 13–15. National Research Council Canada Institute for Marine Dynamics Laboratory Memorandum LM-1998-02. Also available at: http://www.icedata.ca/Pages/NL_IceExtent/NL_index.php.

Hill, B.T. (2008). Recent Sea-ice Records from Newfoundland and Labrador. In: *International*

Congress on the Arctic Social Sciences (ICASS VI), Nuuk, Greenland, 22–26 August 2008. Available at: http://www.arctichost.net/ICASS_VI/#_Toc206827757.

Hill, B. T., Ruffman, A. and Drinkwater, K. (2002). Historical Record of the Incidence of Sea Ice on the Scotian Shelf and the Gulf of St. Lawrence. In *Proceedings of 16th International Association of Hydraulic Engineering and Research, International Symposium on Ice*, Dunedin, New Zealand, 2002 Vol. 1, 313–320.

Hill, B. T., Ruffman, A. and Ivany, K. (2008). Historical Data added to the Grand Banks Iceberg Database. Icetech08. In: *International Conference and Exhibition on Performance of Ships and Structures in Ice*, Banff, Alberta, 20–23 July 2008.

Huntington, H.P. (2005). We dance around in a ring and suppose: academic engagement with traditional knowledge. *Arctic Anthropology* 42: 29–39.

Huntington, H.P., Brower, H. Jr., and Norton, D.W. (2001). The Barrow symposium on sea ice, 2000: evaluation of one means of exchanging information between subsistence whalers and scientists. *Arctic* 54 (2): 201–204.

IPCC, (2013). Climate Change 2013: The Physical Science Basis. Contribution of Working Group I to the *Fifth Assessment Report of the Intergovernmental Panel on Climatic Change*, p. 1535, Cambridge, UK, and New York, NY, USA.

Júlíusson, Á.D. (2001). The environmental effects of Icelandic subsistence farming in the late middle ages and early modern period. In: *Aspects of Arctic and Sub-Arctic History* (eds. I. Sigurðsson and J. Skaptason), 279–288. Reykjavík: University of Iceland Press.

Júlíusson, Á.D. (2018). *Af Hverju Strái: Saga af Byggð, Grasi og Bændum 1300–1700*. Reykjavík: Háskólaútgáfan.

Júlíusson, Á.D. and Jónsson, J. (2013). *Landbúnaðarsagan Íslands* 1-4 ("Agricultural History of Iceland"). Reykjavík: Skrudda.

Karlsson, G. (2007). *Lífsbjörg Íslendinga frá 10. öld til 16. aldar*. Reykjavík: Háskólaútgáfan.

Kristjánsson, L. (1980). *Íslenzkir sjávarhættir 1*. Reykjavik: Bókaútgáfa Menningarsjóðs.

Krupnik, I., Aporto, C., Gearheard, S. et al. (eds.) (2010). *SIKU: Knowing our Ice: Documenting Inuit Sea Ice Knowledge and Use*. Netherlands, Dordrecht: Springer.

La Trobe, B. (1888). *With the Harmony to Labrador: Notes of a Visit to the Moravian Mission Stations on the North-East Coast of Labrador*. London: Moravian Church and Mission Agency.

Lovecraft, A.L. (2013). The human geography of Arctic sea ice. Special Issue. *Polar Geography* 36: 1–4.

Marr, Rebecca. (2010). *Harmony: The Moravian link between Orcadians and Canada's Inuit*. University of the Highlands and Islands, Assignment 3: Historical and Cultural perspectives of the North Atlantic Rim, December 2010, 15 pp.

Maslanik, J., Drobot, S., Fowler, C. et al. (2007). On the Arctic climate paradox and the continuing role of atmospheric circulation in affecting sea ice conditions. *Geophysical Research Letters* 34 https://doi.org/10.1029/2006GL028269.

Miles, M.W., Divine, D.V., Furevik, T. et al. (2014). A signal of persistent Atlantic multidecadal variability in Arctic Sea ice. *Geophysical Research Letters* 41 https://doi.org/10.1002/2013GL058084.

Newell, J.P. (1992). The climate of the Labrador Sea in the spring and summer of 1816, and comparisons with modern analogues. In: *The Year Without a Summer? World Climate in 1816* (ed. C.R. Harrington), 245–254. Ottawa: Canadian Museum of Nature.

Ogilvie, A.E.J., 1982. *Climate and Society in Iceland from the Medieval Period to the Late Eighteenth Century*. Unpublished PhD Thesis, School of Environmental Sciences, University of East Anglia, Norwich, UK.

Ogilvie, A.E.J. (1984a). The past climate and sea-ice record from Iceland. Part 1: data to AD 1780. *Climatic Change* 6: 131–152.

Ogilvie, A.E.J. (1984b). The impact of climate on grass growth and hay yield in Iceland: AD 1601 to 1780. In: *Climate Changes on a Yearly to Millennial Basis* (eds. N.A. Mørner and W. Karlen), 343–352. Dordrecht: Reidel.

Ogilvie, A.E.J. 1991. Climatic changes in Iceland AD c. 1500 to 1598. In: *The Norse of the North Atlantic* (Presented by G.F. Bigelow), *Acta Archaeologica*, Vol. 61–1900, Munksgaard, Copenhagen, 233–251.

Ogilvie, A.E.J. (1992a). Documentary evidence for changes in the climate of Iceland, A.D. 1500 to 1800. In: *Climate Since A.D. 1500* (eds. R.S. Bradley and P.D. Jones), 92–117. London and New York: Routledge.

Ogilvie, A.E.J. (1992b). 1816 - a year without a summer in Iceland? In: *The Year Without a Summer? World Climate in 1816* (ed. C.R. Harrington), 331–354. Ottawa: Canadian Museum of Nature.

Ogilvie, A.E.J. (2001). Climate and farming in northern Iceland, ca. 1700-1850. In: *Aspects of Arctic and Sub-Arctic History* (eds. I. Sigurðsson and J. Skaptason), 289–299. Reykjavík: University of Iceland Press.

Ogilvie, A.E.J. (2005). Local knowledge and travellers' tales: a selection of climatic observations in Iceland. In: *Iceland - Modern Processes and Past Environments, Developments in Quaternary Science 5*. Series Editor Jim Rose (eds. C. Caseldine, A. Russell, J. Harðardóttir and O. Knudsen), 257–287. Amsterdam-Boston-Heidelberg-London: Elsevier.

Ogilvie, A.E.J. (2008). *Bréf sýslumanna til stiftamtmanns og amtmanns*: environmental images of nineteenth-century Iceland from official letters written by district sheriffs. In: *The Discovery of Nineteenth-Century Scandinavia* (ed. M. Wells), 43–56. Norwich: Norvik Press.

Ogilvie, A.E.J. (2010). Historical climatology, *Climatic Change*, and implications for climate science in the 21st century. *Climatic Change* 100: 33–47.

Ogilvie, A.E.J. (2015). An ancient enemy observed: images of sea ice in selected narratives of Iceland from the settlement to the late nineteenth century. In: *Långa linjer och många fält: Festskrift till Johan Söderberg*, Acta Universitatis Stockholmensis: Stockholm University, *Studies in Economic History 65* (eds. M. Gustavsson and D. Retsö), 137–155. Stockholm.

Ogilvie, A.E.J. (2017). A brief description of sea ice. In: *Out of Ice* (ed. E. Ogilvie), 88–90. London: Black Dog Publishing.

Ogilvie, A.E.J. (2020). Famines, mortality, livestock deaths and scholarship: environmental stress in Iceland ca. 1500-1700. In: *The Dance of Death. Environmental Stress, Mortality and Social Response in Late Medieval and Renaissance Europe* (eds. A. Kiss and K. Prybil), 9–24. London: Routledge. Online 2019 at: https://doi.org/10.4324/9780429491085.

Ogilvie, A.E.J. (2021). Stormy weather: climate and sea-ice variations in the North Atlantic (Iceland sector). In: *German Voyages to the North Atlantic Islands (1400–1700), Northern World series* (ed. N. Mehler). Leiden: Brill. In press.

Ogilvie, A.E.J. and Jónsdóttir, I. (2000). Sea ice, climate and Icelandic fisheries in historical times. *Arctic* 53 (4): 383–394.

Ogilvie, A.E.J. and Jónsson, T. (2001). Little Ice Age' research: a perspective from Iceland. *Climatic Change* 48: 9–52.

Ogilvie, A.E.J. and McGovern, T.H. (2000). Sagas and science: climate and human impacts in the North Atlantic. In: *Vikings: The North Atlantic Saga* (eds. W.W. Fitzhugh and E.I. Ward), 385–393. Washington: Smithsonian Instititution Press.

Ogilvie, A.E.J., Barlow, L.K., and Jennings, A.E. (2000). North Atlantic climate c. A.D. 1000: millennial reflections on the Viking discoveries of Iceland, Greenland and North America. *Weather* 55 (2): 34–45.

Ogilvie, A.E.J., Woollett, J.M., Smiarowski, K. et al. (2009). Seals and sea ice in medieval Greenland. *Journal of the North Atlantic* 2: 60–80.

Periodical Accounts related to the Missions of the Church of the United Brethren (1790–1889 and 1890–1930), London.

Ponzi, F. (1995). *Ísland fyrir aldamót: harðindaárin 1882–1888. Iceland: the dire years: 1882–1888, úr ljósmyndum og dagbókum Maitland James Burnett og Walter H. Trevelyan.* Brennholt: Mosfellsbær.

Potter, R.A. (2007). *Arctic Spectacles: The Frozen North in Visual Culture 1818–1875.* Seattle and London: University of Washington Press.

Rollmann, H. (2009). *Moravian Beginnings in Labrador: Papers from a Symposium held in Makkovik and Hopedale.* An Occasional Publication of Newfoundland and Labrador Studies, No. 2. St. John's, Newfoundland and Labrador: Faculty of Arts Publications, 2009.

Serreze, M. and Stroeve, J. (2015). Arctic Sea-ice trends, variability and implications for seasonal forecasting. *Philosophical Transactions of the Royal Society A* 373: 20140159. https://doi. org/10.1098/rsta.2014.0159.

Serreze, M.C., Holland, M.M., and Stroeve, J. (2007). Perspectives on the Arctic's shrinking sea-ice cover. *Science* 315 (5818): 1533–1536.

Serreze, M.C., Barrett, A.P., Stroeve, J.C. et al. (2009). The emergence of a surface-based Arctic amplification. *The Cryosphere* 3: 11–91.

Serreze, M.C., Stroeve, J., Barrett, A.P., and Boisvert, L.N. (2016). Summer atmospheric circulation anomalies over the Arctic Ocean and their influences on September Sea-ice extent: a cautionary tale. *Journal of Geophysical Research-Atmospheres* 121 (19): 11,463–11,485. https://doi. org/10.1002/2016JD25161.

Statistics Canada. (2018). www.stats.gov.nl.ca/ Statistics/Census2016. Retrieved 10 June 2019.

Statistics Iceland, 2019. http://www.statice.is. Retrieved 10 June 2019.

Stroeve, J., Holland, M.M., Meier, W. et al. (2007). Arctic Sea ice decline: faster than forecast. *Geophysical Research Letters* 34: L09501. https:// doi.org/10.1029/2007GL029703.

Stroeve, J., Serreze, M., Drobot, S. et al. (2008). Arctic Sea ice plummets in 2007. *Eos* 89 (2): 13–14.

Stroeve, J.C., Kattsov, V., Barrett, A. et al. (2012). Trends in Arctic Sea ice extent from CMIP5, CMIP3 and observations. *Geophysical Research Letters* 39: L16502. https://doi. org/10.1029/2012GL053676.

SWIPA, 2011. http://amap.no/swipa. Retrieved 10 June 2019.

Vinje, T., Nordlund, N., and Kvambekk, A. (1998). Monitoring ice thickness in Fram Strait. *Journal of Geophysical Research* 104 (C5): 10437–10449. Available at: http://onlinelibrary.wiley.com/ doi/10.1029/97JC03360/abstract.

Wadhams, P. and Munk, W. (2004). Ocean freshening, sea level rising, sea ice melting. *Geophysical Research Letters* 31: L11311. https:// doi.org/10.1029/2004GL020039.

Wigley, T.M.L. (2005). The climate change commitment. *Science* 307: 1766–1769.

13

Biodiversity Conservation in the Faroe Islands Under Changing Climate and Land Use

Anna Maria Fosaa[†]

Faroese Museum of Natural History, Tórshavn, Faroe Islands

Introduction

The Faroe Islands is a treeless archipelago situated on the border between the arctic and boreal environment, between 61° 20′ N and 62° 24′ N and between 6° 15′ W and 7° 41′ W. The climate in the Faroe Islands is strongly influenced by the warm North Atlantic Current and by the proximity to storm tracks in the North Atlantic region. Consequently, the climate is humid, variable and windy. The warmest months are July and August, with a mean temperature of 11 °C (lowland), and the coldest is February, with a mean of 4 °C (lowland). The mean precipitation is 1500 mm annually (lowland). The precipitation reflects the topography of the islands, such that the coastal areas receive around 1000 mm per year, increasing to more than 3000 mm in the central parts (Cappelen and Laursen 1998). The nearest neighbour, the Shetland Islands, lies 345 km to the south-east. The Faroe Islands consist of 18 islands separated by narrow fjords with a total land area of 1400 km² and a distance from north to south of 113 km and from east to west of 75 km. The highest mountain peak is 882 m above sea level (m a.s.l.)

[†]Deceased.

Changes in Flora since the Last Ice Age

The main impact on the vegetation since the last glaciation has been related first to fluctuating climate (Jóhansen 1985; Humlum and Christiansen 1998), and, second, later, to the impact of humans. When the ice melted after the last ice age 10 000–12 000 years ago, the islands were bare rocks with almost no plants. The flora colonized the islands with the wind, by sea currents, birds, and people.

Not all plants growing in the Faroe Islands today arrived after the ice age. Some arctic species, such as Mountain Poppy, *Papaver radicatum*, and Dwarf Cudweed, *Omalotheca supina*, probably survived the last ice age on ice-free nunataks. The first period (ca. 10000–9000 BP) is characterized by unstable and raw soils. Plant species like Hairy Stonecrop, *Sedum villosum*, Mountain Sorrel, *Oxyria digyna*, and Fir Clubmoss, *Huperzia selago*, thrived. These species were growing together with dwarf shrubs like Dwarf Birch, *Betula nana*, and Dwarf Willow, *Salix herbacea*. In the beginning of this period the composition of the flora shows a cold, almost arctic, climate, Dwarf Birch in particular indicating this climate.

Biogeography in the Sub-Arctic: The Past and Future of North Atlantic Biota, First Edition.
Edited by Eva Panagiotakopulu and Jon P. Sadler.
© 2021 John Wiley & Sons Ltd. Published 2021 by John Wiley & Sons Ltd.

As the climate warmed (ca. 9000–7000 BP), the Dwarf Birch disappeared and the climate became oceanic. In the lowlands up to 300 m, Juniper, *Juniperus communis*, and Willow shrubs grew together with Meadowsweet, *Filipendula ulmaria*, Garden and Wild Angelica, *Angelica archangelica* and *A. sylvatica*, and species of tall ferns. Later (ca. 7000–1100 BP), grasses and sedges became richly represented and this period is the most stable period in the vegetation history. The soil became wetter, poorer and more acid with time. The distribution of Heather, *Calluna vulgaris*, increased and the damp climate resulted in declines of Juniper and Willow. This trend was more pronounced after human settlement.

Changes in the vegetation indicate that there have been two phases of settlement in the Faroe Islands. The first settlement was about CE 650 and the second CE 850. Investigations show that the people were growing oats, *Avena* sp., and barley, *Hordeum* sp. Many new plant species were introduced to the islands during the settlements, e.g. Common Nettle, *Urtica dioica*, White Clover, *Trifolium repens*, Tufted Vetch, *Vicia cracca*, and Ribwort Plantain, *Plantago lanceolata*. Before the settlement, tall herbs and bushes were much more common everywhere in the lowland. When people arrived with their livestock, the vegetation was changed to the short vegetation we know today. Only in steep areas, in crevices inaccessible to grazing sheep, do we find native relatively undisturbed vegetation today that were not influenced by human settlement (Jóhansen 1985; Hannon and Bradshaw 2000, 2007).

The Vegetation and Flora

As the islands are sparsely vegetated and almost treeless, the vegetation has a tundra-like appearance. About 70% of the land area of the islands is above 200 m a.s.l. and the vertical vegetation zonation from this point upwards is low alpine,

grading into alpine on the mountain tops. At high elevations, grassland vegetation is found on both south- and north-facing slopes. The alpine area is dominated by Fringe-moss, *Racomitrium* heaths, some snow-bed vegetation in areas with late-lying snow and fell-field vegetation. Common species in this area are Dwarf Willow, Stiff Sedge, *Carex bigelowii*, Alpine Bistort, *Polygonum viviparum*, and Woolly Fringe-moss, *Racomitrium lanuginosum*. The predominant vegetation on north-facing slopes is grassland from sea level up to the mountain tops (Figure 1, see Plate section).

The lowland vegetation (below 200 m a.s.l.) is usually classified as the northern boreal vegetation zone. The dominant species in the lowland grassland are Mat grass, *Nardus stricta*, and Sweet vernal Grass, *Anthoxanthum odoratum*, together with Common and Velvet Bent, *Agrostis capillaris*, and *A. canina*, which are common from low to high altitudes. Heathland vegetation is only found on the larger islands on warm south- and west-facing slopes up to 200 m a.s.l., where this vegetation type disappears. The heathland is mixed with many grasses, herbs and mosses. The dominant plant species are Heather, Crowberry, *Empetrum hermaphroditum*, Bilberry and Bog Bilberry, *Vaccinium myrtillus*, and *V. uliginosum*, and rarer Bell Heather, *Erica cinerea*. Of the herb species that are found in the heathland, Tormentil, *Potentilla erecta*, Slender St John's wort, *Hypericum pulcrum*, and Common Milkwort, *Polygala serphylla*, are worthy of note. The limiting factor for the growth of heathers is probably too little sun, but the heavy sheep grazing and proximity to the northern limit of Heather could also have a negative effect on their distribution.

Three types of mires are found in the islands: topogenic mires, which are overgrown lakes, sologenic mires, which are found on hills and slopes, and ombrogenic mires, which are found in valleys and called 'blanket mires'. Raised bogs are not found. Common species in these

Figure 1 From the top of Sandfelli (790 m a.s.l.) in the northern part of Eysturoy with Kalsoy and Kunoy in the background. (See colour plate section for colour representation of this figure.)

wetland areas are Heath Rush, *Juncus squarrosus*, Deergrass, *Scirpus cespitosus*, and sedge species such as Common Sedge, *Carex nigra*, and Carnation Sedge, *Carex panicea*, as well as Spike-Rush *Eleocharis* species. Common herbs are Common Butterwort, *Pinguicula vulgaris*, and Starry Saxifrage, *Saxifraga stellaris*. There are a great many lakes on the islands, which support several genera of submerged water plants including Quillwort *Isoetes* and Pondweed *Potamogeton*, along with algae such as *Chara* and phytoplankton. Species richness is poor in the lakes, most likely due to the low nutrient content and the substrate, which is often stony.

The coastal cliffs are covered in algae at and below sea level, as well as crustose lichens such as *Verrucaria*, foliose lichens, *Xanthoria*, and species of *Ramalina* higher up. Eelgrass, *Zostera marina*, is recorded in one of the fjords, on the southernmost island, Suðuroy. Where coarse-textured soil has built up in crevices formed by weathering,

some species that can tolerate constant salt spray survive. These include Thrift, *Armeria maritima*, Common Scurvygrass, *Cochlearia officinalis*, and Sea Plantain, *Plantago maritima*. In more protected localities of the inner fjords, salt marshes are found around the mouths of small streams. Common species are Sea Arrowgrass, *Triglochin maritima*, Common Saltmarsh grass, *Pucinellia maritima*, and Common Bent, *Agrostis capillaris*. Sand dunes are found only on Sandoy, which is the island with the lowest relief. The characteristic species for these dunes are Marram, *Ammophila arenaria*, and Lyme-grass, *Leymus arenarius*. On the flat sand beach, closest to the sea, Arctic Sea Rocket, *Cakile arctica*, and Sea Sandwort, *Honckenya peploides*, are found. Behind the sand dunes away from the sea, the species diversity is higher, with species such as Heath Spotted Orchid, *Dactylorhiza purpurella*, Frog Orchid, *Coeloglossum viride*, and Scots Lovage, *Ligusticum scoticum*.

Impacts on the Flora

The main impacts on the vegetation in the Faroe Islands can be divided into agriculture (sheep grazing, draining and fertilization), climate change and the threat from new invasive species.

Effects of Grazing

Grazing pressure on the islands is pronounced with 70 000 grazing sheep, and most likely accounts for the major impact on nature. No long-term experiment with grazing has been done in the islands, but palynological research (e.g. Jóhansen 1985) has shown that the occurrence of ferns was reduced dramatically after people settled in the Faroes with their domestic animals. Tall herbs and bushes were much more common everywhere in the lowland before settlement. When people came to the islands, the vegetation was changed to the short tundra-like vegetation that occurs today. Thus, sheep grazing has undoubtedly reduced the diversity of species as we only find native relatively undisturbed vegetation today in steep areas and in crevices inaccessible to the sheep.

In small short-term sheep exclosure experiments it can be seen that sheep grazing has affected the vegetation significantly both in the lowland and in the alpine zone (Fosaa and Olsen 2007). In the exclosures, both vegetation cover and leaf length increase significantly, with the largest changes in the lowland. In the lowland, Mat grass and Carnation Sedge had significantly higher frequency in grazed plots compared to ungrazed plots. In ungrazed plots, palatable grasses like Velvet Bent and the herb Tormentil had significantly higher frequencies. At the alpine site, the frequencies of species like Wavy Hair-grass, *Deschampsia cespitosa*, Alpine Bistort and Dwarf Willow increased in ungrazed plots. After 10 years of exclosure in the alpine zone, Alpine Bistort, Dwarf Willow and graminoids had increased leaf length significantly and the frequency of graminoids and bryophytes continued

to increase while the frequency of Dwarf Willow decreased. Ten years may well be a much too short period to study the succession in grazing exclosure and many more years are needed to tell how the vegetation will change.

Effects of Climate Change

Recent research has shown that the Faroese vegetation is vulnerable to changing climate and the temperature range of plant species is narrow. The vertical vegetation distribution has changed due to warmer and colder climate periods during the last century. Three vegetation zones were defined by quantitative analysis (Fosaa 2004): temperate zone 0–200 m a.s.l., the low alpine zone 200–400 m a.s.l. and the alpine zone 400–882 m a.s.l. In the 1930s, Böcher (1937) found these zones at considerably higher altitudes. At that time, the temperature in the area was 0.25 °C warmer than in the newer study. Although these two studies are not directly comparable, a temperature difference of 0.25 °C is sufficient to lower the vegetation zones about 30 m with a lapse rate of 0.8 °C.

Dwarf shrubs such as Heather and Crowberry, *Empetrum hermaphroditum*, which are characteristic for the temperate zone, are found to have a temperature optimum of 12–13 °C. Dwarf Willow and Alpine Bistort, characteristic for the alpine zone, have a temperature optimum of less than 6 °C, and it is also found that a temperature change of 1–2° C is sufficient to change the distribution of these species (Fosaa 2004). Increased warming will therefore affect the alpine species more severely, as an upward migration can result in their extinction. In the lowland, more new and invasive species will thrive in a warmer climate and can be a threat to the local biodiversity.

Research in flowering phenology (Fosaa et al. 2011; Oberbauer et al. 2013) has shown that warming of alpine species can accelerate the flowering time by a week. This result was found in an ITEX (International Tundra Experiment) warming experiment in a mountain area in the islands.

The flowering phenology of Moss Campion, *Silene acaulis* was studied during the summer time for 10 years in open top chambers (OTCs) acting like small greenhouses. Phenology changes can result in problems with reproduction of insect-pollinated flowers as mismatches may occur.

New and Invasive Species

Several new species of plants and animals have invaded and are established in the islands (Fosaa et al., 2000b). Some of these have become invasive and are a threat to the local flora of the islands. Most of the new plant species that we find in the wild today are species that have been imported to be planted in gardens from whence they have escaped and spread into the natural environment.

One of the most conspicuous is Monkeyflower, *Mimulus guttatus*. It was brought into the islands in the 1920s to be planted in gardens. Today, it is widespread throughout the islands where it grows along river banks, and seems to thrive. Monkeyflower is originally from North America and is found in the Faroe Islands in several varieties. One of the newest species that has escaped from gardens is Lady's mantle, *Alchemilla mollis*. It has also been brought in as a garden plant and during the last decade, it has spread to many of the islands and is especially common along the roadsides. It is spreading vigorously and will undoubtedly be a problem in the future. Creeping Willowherb, *Epilobium komarovianum*, is also one of the newest arrivals. It was registered for the first time in the islands in 2005 and has spread vigorously both in the wild and in gardens. We do not know exactly how this species came to the islands, but it could have been brought in with horse fodder.

In 1976, an expedition to Patagonia brought several new species to the islands, which were planted in an arboretum. One of the species is Hummingbird Fuchsia, *Fuchsia magellanica*. This species has occasionally been found in the wild and will undoubtedly become more widespread in the future (Højgaard et al. 1989).

Status of the Flora and Fauna

Red-Listed Vascular Plants

In 2004, a preliminary red-list for vascular plant species in the islands was made, where 74 vascular plant species were grouped into five International Union for Conservation of Nature (IUCN) categories (Fosaa et al. 2005). The list was based on information in floras (Jóhansen 2000), as well as information from the Museum of Natural History in Tórshavn and the Botanical Museum in Copenhagen. This procedure was used because no regular monitoring of the vegetation has yet been established in the area. Therefore, 25 species were categorized as Data Deficient, as there was insufficient information for these species. In Figure 2, it is seen how the species are distributed in the five categories.

The red-listed plant species were divided into the following biotopes: alpine areas, ravines, heathland, wetland, freshwater and seashores/sea. Most of the red-listed species were found in wetland/freshwater, whereas the other biotopes had similar occurrences of red-listed species. The major part of the threatened species was found

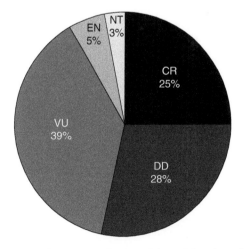

Figure 2 The distribution of the red-listed species in the five IUCN categories. VU: Vulnerable, EN: Endangered, NT: Near threatened, CR: Critical and DD: Data deficient.

in the lowland (Fosaa et al. 2005). Which factors affected the plants was also investigated and it was found that the major impacts were from sheep grazing and agriculture, as well as other human activities and climate change.

Alpine Areas

Fellfields and Racomitrium Heaths

Alpine vegetation is found in the area from about 400 m altitude upwards. It covers about 25% of the total land area. Due to the harsh conditions, the alpine vegetation is sparse and mainly includes species from the lowland Arctic or the high-altitude alpine zones (Fosaa et al. 2004). This area includes the pointed mountains that are covered with the greyish Woolly Fringe-moss, *Racomitrium lanuginosum*, and the flat mountaintops that form the sparsely vegetated 'fell fields'. Such plateau-like areas are exposed to strong winds and the substrate freezes and thaws repeatedly. Most of these areas consist of a mosaic of cliff surfaces with moss and lichens, and a few higher plants (Figure 3).

Some of the red-listed species are only found on the highest mountains and are therefore vulnerable to climate change; these are Arctic Poppy, *Papaver radicatum*, Dwarf Cudweed,

Omalotheca supina, and Scottish Asphodel, *Tofieldia pusilla*. Others that are also found lower in the mountains are Trailing Azalea, *Loiseleuria procumbens*, Arctic Willow, *Salix arctica*, Slender snow Saxifrage, *Saxifraga tenuis*, and Alpine Speedwell, *Veronica alpina*.

Lowland and Low Alpine Areas

Heathland and Grassland

Outside the settled area, the most common vegetation is heath and grassland, from sea-level up to the low alpine area at 200 m altitude (Figure 3). Of red-listed species, Mountain Avens, *Dryas octopetala*, was originally found in five localities (Hansen 1972) but today probably only one locality remains. Interrupted Clubmoss, *Lycopodium annotinum*, was first found in 1897 (Ostenfeld 1905–1908) but after that it was not found again by until 2007 (Fosaa et al. 2008). Soft Downy-rose, *Rosa mollis*, was originally found in three localities, but in the 1980s, it was found in a new locality whilst it is almost extinct in the original localities. Alpine Saw-wort, *Saussurea alpina*, was first found in 1999 with only a few specimens (Fosaa et al. 2000a). Other red-listed species in the heathland and grassland are Alpine Cinquefoil, *Potentilla crantzii,* and Harebell, *Campanula rotundifolia*.

Lakes

Most Faroese lakes are small, less than 100 m^2, and poor in nutrients. A total of 33 species of aquatic plants are found in the Faroe Islands, which is 10% of the total 0f 330 species of wild flowers. The plants have different life-forms: some float on the water surface and others grow on the lake bottoms. In shallow water on the lake shores, Shoreweed often hides the bottom like a mat. Fifteen of the 33 species of water plants are very rare and are in the preliminary red-list. Seven of the eight species of Pondweed are very rare and only Bog Pondweed, *Potamogeton polygonifolius*, is common. Most of these red-listed species

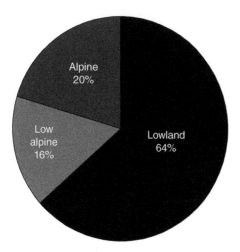

Figure 3   The distribution of the red-listed species in the lowland, the low-alpine and the alpine areas.

grow in the lowland where the threat is greatest, due to eutrophication from agriculture, pollution and as a result of building activities. Greater Bladderwort, *Utricularia vulgaris*, was only known to grow in two localities until one of the localities was destroyed due to building activity in the 1970s. Another example is Red Pondweed, *Potamogeton alpinus*, which disappeared from its only known locality due to hydropower construction early in the 1980s, but it has since been found again in two other lakes (Schierup et al. 2002).

Mires

The appearance of the mires is a mosaic of several species of *Sphagnum* mosses that show a wide range of colours, from light yellow to scarlet. Mires cover 1.4% of the total area of the Faroe Islands and most of it is distributed in the lowland. Similar to the lakes, most of the mires are very small. The greatest threat is drainage from agriculture. In places where *Sphagnum* grows, the nutritional value is low, but two of the three Faroese carnivorous plants are found here: Common Butterwort and Round-leaved Sundew, *Drosera rotundifolia*

(Figure 4, see Plate section). The last mentioned is red-listed and only found in four localities.

The rarest of the mire species are Common Marsh Bedstraw, *Galium palustre*, and the two orchids Bog Orchid, *Hammarbya palludosa*, and Lesser Twayblade, *Listera cordata*. Other red-listed mire species are Bog Pimpernel, *Anagallis tenella*, Marsh Cinquefoil, *Potentilla palustris*, and the two species of sedge, Oval Sedge, *Carex ovalis*, and Tawny Sedge, *C. hostiana*.

Ravines

Here, the vegetation is luxuriant and varied, and surveys have shown that the plants have lived in these locations for a long time – precisely because they were out of the reach of sheep and people. Great Wood rush, *Luzula sylvatica*, which is characteristic for the ravines, is seen covering large areas like a mat with the green new leaves and the brown dead leaves and the long brown inflorescence. In this mat of leaves, we often find the purple flowers of Wood Crane's-bill, *Geranium sylvaticum*, which also thrives well in the ravines. Roseroot, *Rhodiala rosea*,

Figure 4 Round-leaved Sundew, *Drosera rotundifolia*, is one of the red-listed plants growing in mires. (See colour plate section for colour representation of this figure.)

Figure 5 Oysterplant, *Mertensia maritima*, is one of the threatened plant species on the Faroese seashore. (See colour plate section for colour representation of this figure.)

Meadowsweet, Stone Bramble, *Rubus saxatilis*, and Red Campion, *Silene dioica*, are also richly represented in the ravines. Many kinds of ferns can be found in steep terrain. Most prominent are the big Male-fern, *Dryopteris filix-mas*, and the almost equally large Lady-fern, *Athyrium filix-femina*. Of the 15 species of ferns growing in the islands, eight are red listed. These are Beech Fern, *Phegopteris connectilis*, Black and Maidenhair Spleenwort, *Asplenium adianthum nigrum* and *A. trichomanes*, Oak Fern, *Gymnocarpium dryopteris*, Holly Fern, *Polystichum lonchitis*, and Alpine Lady Fern, *Athyrium distentifolium*. The two species of Hairy Fern, *Oreopteris limbosperma* (Jensen and Fosaa 2014), and Hart's-Tongue Fern,

Asplenium scolopendrium (Jensen et al. 2008), are species new to the Faroese flora.

Seashores

On the few places with sand beaches and the one locality with sand dunes, we find the red-listed Marram, Baltic Rush, *Juncus balticus*, Curved Sedge, *Carex maritima*, and Oysterplant, *Mertensia maritima* (Figure 5, see Plate section). Close to the seashore, occur the two species Spring Squill (*Scilla verna*) and Buck's-horn Plantain, *Plantago coronopus*. The biggest threat for these species is human activities, including plant collectors, disturbance of the land and oil pollution.

References

Böcher, T.W. (1937). Nogle studier over Færøernes alpine vegetation. *Botanisk Tidskrift* 44: 154–201.

Cappelen, J. and Laursen, E. V. (1998). The climate of the Faroe Islands – With Climatological Standard Normals, 1961–1991. Danish Meteorological Institute. Technical report 98–14.

Fosaa, A.M. (2000a). Wildflowers in the Faroe Islands/Vilde planter på Færøerne – checklist – Føroya Náttúrugripasavn.

Fosaa, A.M. (2000b). A review of plant communities of the Faroe Islands. *Fróðskaparrit* 48: 41–54.

Fosaa, A.M. (2004). Altitudinal distribution of plant communities in the Faroe Islands. *Fróðskaparrit* 51: 200–211.

Fosaa, A.M. (2013). Lívfrøðiligt margfeldi hjá plantum í Føroum. Tema. Lívfrøðiligt margfeldi og lendisnýtsla, pp. 4–7. Frøði.

Fosaa, A.M. and Olsen, E. (2007). The impact of grazing on mountain vegetation and the arbuscular mycorrhizal symbiont. *Fróðskaparrit* 55: 177–187.

Fosaa, A.M., Lawesson, J.E., and Sykes, M. (1999). *Saussurea alpina* (L.) DC. Subsp. *alpina* (Asteraceae) -alpine Saw Wort – a new record from the Faroe Islands. *Fróðskaparrit* 47: 153–157.

Fosaa, A.M., Lawesson, J.E., Sykes, M.T., and Gaard, M. (2004). Potential effects of climate change on the vegetation in the Faroe Islands. *Global Ecology and Biogeography* 13: 427–437.

Fosaa, A.M., Gaard, M., and Hansen, J. (2005). Reyðlistar. Frágreiðing um reyðlistaflokking av plantum og fuglum. Føroya Náttúrugripasavn.

Fosaa, A.M., Olsen, E., Simonsen, W. (2008). Eiði-2. Environmental Impact Assessment. *Føroya Náttúrugripasavn.*

Fosaa, A.M., Danielsen, O., and Nyholm Debess, H. (2011). The influence of experimental warming on flowering phenology of Moss Campion, *Silene acaulis. Fróðskaparrit* 59: 104–112.

Hannon, G.E. and Bradshaw, R.H.W. (2000). Holocene vegetation dynamics and impact of human settlement on the Faroe Islands. *Quaternary Research* 54: 404–413.

Hannon, G.E. and Bradshaw, R.H.W. (2007). Human impact and landscape change at Argisbrekka. In: Saeteren ved Argisbrekka (ed. D.L. Mahler). Torshavn: Froðskapur pp. 306–323.

Hansen, K. (1972). Vertical vegetation zones and vertical distribution types in the Faeroes. *Botanisk Tidskrift* 67: 33–63.

Højgaard, A., Jóhansen, J. and Ødum, S. (1989). A century of tree-planting in the Faroe Islands. Tórshavn: *Annales Societatis Scientiarum Færoensis*, Supplementum 14. Føroya Fróðskaparfelag.

Humlum, O. and Christiansen, H.H. (1998). Mountain climate and Periglacial phenomena in the Faroe Islands, SE North Atlantic Ocean. *Permafrost and Periglacial Processes* 9: 189–211.

Jensen, J.K. and Fosaa, A.M. (2014). Dúnhærdur fjallakampur *Oreopteris limbosperma* er nýggjur trøllakampur í Føroyum. *Frøði* 19 (1): 16–17.

Jensen, J.-K., Jespersen, D., and Patursson, A. (2008). Hjortetunge – en ny færøsk bregne. *URT* 32 (1): 22–23.

Jóhansen, J. (1985). Studies in the vegetational history of the Faroe and Shetland Island. *Annales Societatis Scientiarum Færoensis*, Supplementum 11. Føroya Fróðskaparfelag.

Jóhansen, J. (2000). *Føroysk Flora* (Flora of the Faeroe Islands) (eds. A.M. Fosaa and S. Rasmussen). Føroya Skúlabókagrunnur.

Oberbauer, S.F., Elmendorf, S., Troxler, T.G. et al. (2013). Phenological response of tundra plants to background climate variation tested using the international tundra experiment. *Philosophical Transactions of the Royal Society* 368: 1, 20120481–13. https://doi.org/10.1098/rstb.2012.0481.

Ostenfeld, C.H. (1905-1908). The land vegetation of the Faeroes with special reference to higher plants. *Botany of the Faeroes* 3: 867–1026.

Schierup, H.H. Mjelde M., Bagger, J. (2002). Aquatic Macrophytes in Six Faroese Lakes. *Annales Societatis Scientiarum Færoensis,* Supplementum 36. Føroya Fróðskaparfelag.

14

Biodiversity Conservation in Iceland Under Changing Climate

Erlingur Hauksson

Fornistekkur 14, Reykjavík, Iceland

Introduction

Before the industrial revolution, farmers and fisherman lived with Nature and used its goods for their own and their families' livelihood; rarely was there any concern for the finite nature of resources. Modern man now wants to protect and conserve nature as it was in the time of their ancestors, establishing some kind of 'status quo' in nature of their liking or according to a picture in their mind, which may or may not be realistic. Climate change is a complicating issue, because coordinated ecological experiments based on international collaboration are needed to address problems at regional and global scales in order to understand ecological patterns and processes, and to develop solutions for environmental management based on sound scientific data (Sternberg and Yakir 2015). Investigating global change by methods of global ecology demands very big ecological research projects, so big that it is very difficult to carry them through. For big ecology to result in great science, ecologists must become informed, aware and engaged in the advocacy and governance of large ecological projects (Schimel and Keller 2015).

There is little literary information on the natural world in Iceland before the post-medieval scientific revolution. Research about Icelandic nature was very limited, and one must depend on information about various aspects from eccentric amateur scientists such as Jón Guðmundsson lærði[1] (Hallgrímsson 2013). In the sixteenth century very little research took place in Iceland and resident scholars who were mostly educated at Danish universities had their knowledge from books, not by doing research of their own (Thoroddsen 1892). It was necessary to protect nature against anthropogenic mischief, overhunting, overfishing, overgrazing and pollution, fight against disappearances of species and their habitats but the realization of human impact was slight. Often, however, humans cannot just produce an environment to their liking by protecting and conserving nature, the processes of nature being too complex for humans to control. There might be natural oscillations, unrealized by people, even in quite healthy predator–prey systems and host–parasite systems, or even whole ecosystems that are still evolving towards a climax state after natural perturbations decades ago (Marcogliese 2001; Scheffer et al. 2001; Kausrud

Biogeography in the Sub-Arctic: The Past and Future of North Atlantic Biota, First Edition.
Edited by Eva Panagiotakopulu and Jon P. Sadler.

et al. 2008). Predator–insect-vectored plant pathogen interactions can be very complicated with unexpected results, such as increased predator diversity not influencing plant infection rates (Long and Finke 2015). The effect of temperature increase on the total metabolic rate of ectotherms remains not too clear. The activity metabolic rate may respond quite differently to temperature increase than resting metabolic rate does, which is usually the basis for estimating temperature coefficients (Halsey et al. 2015).

A 'revolution' has occurred in research on natural phenomenon in Iceland in the last 70 years, as can be seen in the compiled work by Snorri Baldursson about the living nature of Iceland (Baldursson 2014). Plausible predictions of regional temperature and precipitation trends in Iceland have been developed in the international project Nordic Climate Solutions, based on a combined ocean–ice–atmosphere system. In comparison with 1961–1990, the project scenario predicts a warming of 2.8 °C and a 6% increase in precipitation by 2071–2100. The increases in temperature and precipitation vary according to season, both being higher for winter than summer (Björnsson 2009; Björnsson et al. 2018). One of the clearest climate changes in Iceland, affecting the freshwater and terrestrial ecosystem the most, is the shrinking of glaciers observed in recent decades. Ice is collected on the glaciers during the cold season, spring, winter and late autumn and melts away during the summer. This is a sensitive balance that has in recent decades been unfavourable for most of the glaciers in Iceland. Hofsjökull and Vatnajökull glaciers are expected to lose 25% of their present volume within half a century and Langjökull glacier to lose 35% of its volume in 50 years and disappear after 150 years. Melt-water runoff is expected to increase accordingly and with the disappearance of the glaciers, glacial rivers turn into freshwater rivers discharging exclusively precipitation (Björnsson 2009).

The sea-level has risen 3 mm annually in the world oceans in recent times. Sea-ice cover in summer in the Arctic Sea was in year 2012 the smallest ever recorded. It is even prognosed that in the Arctic Sea there will be no ice-cover in the autumn by 2020. The temperature of the surface layers of the world ocean has increased by 0.6 °C and pH has increased by 0.1, but the most dramatic changes have occurred in polar waters, where the temperature has recently increased by 3.5 °C in comparison with the period 1951–1980. The marine ecosystem is highly sensitive to climate variation, increasing the amount of CO_2 in the atmosphere and in the ocean, and warmer climates are causing synergic change of the condition in the sea, such that productivity has decreased, the oceanic food-webs are changing, marine species are dispersing farther north and northwest and coral-reefs formations are diminishing in distribution (Baldursson 2014). Boreal marine fauna are invading the Arctic Ocean (Andrews et al. 2019). In Iceland this has been demonstrated by abundance and distribution changes of many species during the warm period in the 1930s, the cold period in the late 1960s and warming observed during recent years (Astthorsson et al. 2007; Björnsson et al. 2018). More recent data on the hydrographic situation in north and northeastern waters of Iceland may even suggest a downward trend in the sea temperature over the shallow continental shelf (Björnsson et al. 2018). It has been demonstrated that the weight of adult capelin in winter is related to the hydrographic conditions over the shelf north of Iceland in spring the previous year. It has also been demonstrated that the weight of cod was related to the size of the capelin stock. Local atmospheric conditions have an important effect on timescales, from days to at least to the seasons. On longer timescales, the large-scale atmospheric circulation (blockings) and large-scale dynamics of the sub-polar gyre and the Arctic Ocean play the major roles in the hydrographic condition in this area (Astthorsson and Vilhjalmsson 2002). Another case worth considering, in North Atlantic waters, is the changes in the distribution of mackerel (*Scomber scombrus*) in the Norwegian Sea and Icelandic and East Greenlandic waters. The Northeast Atlantic mackerel is a highly migratory, dynamic and widely distributed pelagic fish species, and plays a key ecological role in coastal and oceanic ecosystems and are one of the most valuable fish stocks in the North Atlantic. They are effective schooling predators on zooplankton and smaller fish, feeding competitors for other pelagic fish and prey species for larger fish, seabirds and marine mammals. The estimated mackerel abundance shows about a fivefold increase in the period 2007–2016 and the stock has also nearly tripled its feeding areas in the same period, mainly towards northern and western regions of the Nordic Seas, and the mean density has also doubled in these seven years, increasing the possibility for increased intra-specific competition and density dependent growth. The available habitat with acceptable temperatures (>6–7 °C) for mackerel has also increased in the Northeast Atlantic during the last 10–15 years, providing mackerel with larger feeding areas. The main reason for the greatly expanding feeding areas for mackerel is probably due to a record high stock size, linked to available prey concentrations. Five of the strongest year-classes throughout the entire time series have come after year 2000. Mackerel spawns from January to July over an enormous area, which results in a high probability for successful annual spawning (Björnsson et al. 2018). The temperature-sensitive Atlantic mackerel has been observed as far north-west as Greenland after 2009. This may be related to the fact that summer temperatures have been at a record high. In this way mackerel has increased the size of its potential habitat enormously and its seasonal duration in this area. The recent population of the potential habitat in Greenland occurred during a general geographic expansion of mackerel in the Northeast Atlantic, possibly initiated by density-related processes. This may, however, not have been a recent phenomenon as suggested by the most recent observations. Temperature data dating back to 1870 indicate that the current fishing area for mackerel has had suitable sea-temperatures (>8.5 °C) during most summers. In less remote parts of the same water mass, north and west of Iceland, mackerel had been observed back to 1900 (Björnsson et al. 2018). Two other major players in this contest are the blue whiting (*Micromesistius poutassou*) and herring (*Clupea harengus*). The mackerel could have regulatory effects on the population of Norwegian Sea herring through predation (Bachiller et al. 2015a) and also via competition for food which the herring would probably lose in higher latitudes, at least the autumn spawning herring depending on light and eyesight for catching prey (Nash and Geffen 2015). Diet studies in the Norwegian Sea indicate that mackerel and herring take similar prey. In the spring to summer the dominance of copepods in their guts was partially replaced by relatively larger prey like krill and amphipods. Blue whiting overall had a different diet composition, typically ingesting relatively larger prey than the other species and therefore suggesting a low level of interaction with mackerel and herring in the same area (Bachiller et al. 2015b). If stock size continues to increase, sea temperatures will not prevent mackerel summer feeding range from expanding further westward into the Labrador Sea, or further northeast into the Barents Sea ecosystem (Olafsdottir et al. 2016). The sub-polar gyre limb in the Irminger Sea is a major source of nutrients for the sub-polar Atlantic, and the vigorous vertical convection there induces high primary productivity and zooplankton abundances, making this area an attractive feeding region for the mackerel and other fish. The sub-polar gyre has weakened much since the mid-1990s, allowing warm, saline and nutrient poor eastern waters to spread poleward, and the nutrient concentrations and zooplankton abundances in the Norwegian Sea have declined in a similar fashion. One likely hypothesis would be that the presently declining nutrient levels in the North Atlantic might have been the driving force for the westward expansion of the mackerel stock, which directed it stepwise towards the main nutrient sources in the Irminger Sea (Hátún et al. 2016). Taking this nutrient depletion further, Holst (2015) argued that the strong increase in sea temperature in the period 1995–2008 in the Norwegian Sea had a favourable effect on recruitment of the herring, mackerel and blue whiting stocks of the area – the pelagic complex. The pelagic stocks soared with detrimental effects on the zooplankton stocks. Upward and downward cascading effects have, amongst others, been seen through the collapse in plankton-dependent seabirds, like the kittiwake (*Rissa tridactyla*) and a strong increase in seabird feeding on pelagic fish like gannets (*Sula bassana*). Among other suggested effects are collapses in sprat (*Sprattus sprattus*) stocks in Norwegian fjords, in European and Icelandic salmon (*Salmo salar*) stocks and large-scale shifts in the distribution of large whales between the Norwegian Sea and the Barents Sea. During the last decade, mackerel stock size increased 170% and size-at-age declined about 25%. In 2013 the average mackerel was 4 cm shorter and weighted 175 g less than the average individual in 2002. Mackerel condition (weight-at-length) continually declined during the last five years, whereas cohort growth has continually declined for the last 11–25 cohorts investigated. Growth rate of the latest cohort was 34% of the maximum growth rate. Mackerel condition was negatively affected by stock size of both mackerel and Norwegian spring-spawning herring, but positively affected by average sea surface temperature in the mackerel summer feeding area. Density-dependent growth among mackerels was likely mediated via higher forage cost and intensified intra-specific competition associated with higher mackerel density. Negative effects of herring stock size on mackerel growth suggest inter-specific

competition for limited food resources. Carrying capacity of the Norwegian Sea and adjacent areas for plankton feeding fish stocks has probably been reached in recent years. However, compounding effects of a less productive Norwegian Sea during the 30-year period cannot be excluded (Olafsdottir et al. 2016).

Another case from the North Atlantic waters was the recently observed recruitment failure in seabird species on the south coast of Iceland and in the North Sea, probably due to recruitment failure of the lesser sand eel (*Ammodytes marinus*) in the areas (Frederiksen et al. 2007; Lilliendahl et al. 2013). Fisheries are hardly to blame as there was a fishery for sand eels in the North Sea, but in Icelandic waters there has never been any fishery for sand eels. There is no evidence for climate change causing this recruitment failure and a state shift in this predator–prey system: seabird ← sand eel or mackerel ← sand eel → sea bird food chain. This sand eel recruitment failure has affected not only seabirds but also other fish-species, seals and whales in Icelandic waters, and even the terrestrial arctic fox (*Alopex lagopus*) (Vikingsson et al. 2014; Elmhagen et al. 2014; Hauksson unpublished; Unnsteinsdóttir unpublished).

In the freshwater ecosystem of Iceland, some observations related to climate change have been made. Þingvallavatn has got warmer, with an increase in nitrate concentration and also an abundance increase of phytoplankton following. This could have a negative effect on stickle-backs (*Gasterosteus aculeatus*) and Arctic char (*Salvelinus alpinus*) varieties in the water. Arctic char has also decreased in abundance in Elliðavatn and the river Eyjafjarðará; trout (*Salmo trutta*), on the other hand, increased in abundance. An invasive warm water fish species, flounder (*Platichthys flesus*) has been frequently found in the estuaries on the south coast of Iceland, as well as a parasitic Sea lamprey (*Petromyzon marinus*). Distribution and occurrence of those have also increased to the north part of Icelandic waters (Björnsson et al. 2018). Pink salmon (*Oncorhynchus gorbuscha*) has also occurred more frequently in recent years (Baldursson 2014).

In Iceland's terrestrial ecosystem in the twenty-first century, about 55 species of invertebrates have been found as invaders, due to climate change. Most of them are not causing any problems and are considered even as an interesting addition to the poor invertebrate fauna of the country. However, a few are probably invasive and harmful to the indigenous fauna and flora (http://www.ni.is/poddur). Vegetation has been changing, scrubs, grass and flowering plants are on the increase, but moss and lichens are on the decrease. Scrub grows increasingly higher up in the mountains and overall vegetation reaches higher altitudes. Special high mountain arctic flowering plant species could vanish, and vegetation adapted to survival for a long time under cover of snow and to reproduce late in summer or even in the autumn may disappear. By December 2012 a total of 153 foreign new species from the plant and animal kingdom had been found in Iceland, of which seven are clearly invasive. Nine bird species, nesting in trees, were included with the 153 (Baldursson 2014).

Conservation of Biodiversity in Iceland

Icelanders were one of the last people in Europe to set laws especially for conserving nature. The reason was probably, being few habitants per area, slow growth in technological progress and few conservation disasters, except the recognized deforestation and soil erosion following colonization of the country by Norwegian Vikings and farmers (Guttormsson 1974). Iceland is also a volcanic island and, as the historical record indicates, eruptions caused frequent destruction of vegetated land, including inhabited farmed land. The volcanic eruption, called the Skaftár

Fires (Laki), from the Grímsvötn volcanic system in South Iceland produced one of the largest basaltic lava flows in historical times; in 1783–1785 a total of $7200\,km^2$ of land was affected and a total of $15\,km^3$ of lava and pyroclastics was spread across the land. The release of sulphurous gases produced a haze that spread widely and had considerable climatic effects in the Northern Hemisphere. The haze and its environmental effects led to a famine that reduced the human population of Iceland by 22%. One third of the two districts closest to the eruption were deserted and survivors moved from the inland to the fishing districts to start a new livelihood (Rafnsson 1984; Thórðarson 1990). There is earlier anecdotal evidence for destruction of farms by volcanic activity under the icecap of Vatnajökull, in the south and southeast parts of Iceland (Björnsson 2009).

In 1787 the Icelandic Parliament put forward a law for the total protection of reindeer (*Rangifer tarandus*), which had been imported from Norway at that time to establish a reindeer herding system, as was practiced by the Sámi in Northern Scandinavia. -The reindeers were a gift from a Norwegian businessman to the poor people of Iceland, who at that time were suffering from bad winters and volcanic eruptions. People starved and over the next one and a half centuries, many people left the country for a better life in North America. A total of 17000 Icelanders is believed to have left the country in the period 1855–1920, or about one-fifth part of the population (Guðmundsson 2001). The reindeer herding plan, however, did not materialize and in Iceland reindeer run wild and population management is by hunting. Perhaps no one had the initiative to carry the scheme through; farming in Iceland largely relied on cattle, sheep and horses. Ewes and rams roamed the mountains and valleys of the Icelandic wilderness, lambs were gathered in the autumn for slaughter and adult sheep were stalled for feeding and stocking. Horses were left outside to fend for themselves, except for a few taken into the stable in the winter, to be used as riding and work horses. Some were slaughtered each year for meat, consumed fresh, smoked and salted. Consuming horsemeat was an early tradition, banned by the Catholic Church until 1600, but allowed again after the Lutheran Reformation. Cows (*Bos taurus*) were few and used for domestic milk production. There appears to be no contemporary warnings about overgrazing, deforestation and soil erosion.

In 1849, laws were passed and rules made for limiting egg-collecting and forbidding fishing with nets inside the 60 fathoms area from the shore, for all people except the landowner. Special laws were also passed about sealing rights, making it possible only for the landowner to catch seals on his land and out to 60 fathoms. There were even laws for protection of woodland and Lyme grass (*Leymus arenarius*), a sturdy grass used to fight soil erosion in Iceland. These laws were all signed by the Danish King, the monarch of Iceland at that time. Even though the first statute for conservation of nature in Iceland did not come into effect until 1956, some laws had come into force much earlier for taking care of special conservation issues that in the opinion of the Icelandic authorities required control. Few animal species were protected and laws had been in existence from the early seventeenth century concerning the hunting of wildlife for food. These laws, however, did not save the great auk (*Pinguinus impennis*) from extinction by the year 1844. This was also the last stand for the great auk on a world scale and it disappeared from the face of the Earth. Even though the great auk survived longest in Iceland, it was not an honour for conservation for Iceland to take a final part in its disappearance. Perhaps drawing on this, a nationwide funding appeal was made in 1971 to buy at auction, for a price of £9300 (about the same cost as a three room apartment in Reykjavik at this time), a stuffed great auk for display at the Natural History Museum, which, at that time,

owned only one egg and a skeleton made out of several birds (INH 2000; Petersen 1995).

After Iceland got home rule in 1904, which included the first prime minister, laws were established about forestry and for protecting land from soil erosion. At this time the Icelandic Government had to deal with the threat of land being destroyed by large-scale soil erosion due to the non-sustainable scale of grazing on wild Icelandic vegetation by sheep, which had been going on since the colonization of the country. In addition, the results of earlier volcanic eruptions led to erosion by coarse volcanic ash blowing in the wind and settling on vegetated areas, covering and damaging the vegetation. A major step in conservation was taken in year 1913, when general laws about the protection of birds were legislated. They incorporated a special rule for the total protection of the white-tailed eagle (*Haliaeetus albicilla*) in Iceland, which had nearly been eradicated by putting out poison bait in winter when food was sparse. Ostensibly this was aimed at arctic foxes, but it was more often taken and eaten by white-tailed eagles due to its scavenging habits. This constant fighting against the arctic fox by Icelandic farmers, using any means, still goes on today, by shooting and trapping to reduce the fox population and especially to killing foxes that have taken to attacking sheep; some arctic foxes turn to sheep predation, particularly predating on lambs in early summer (Thorsteinsson 1948). Killing of foxes was also deemed necessary for protecting nesting eider ducks (*Sommateria mollisima*), ptarmigans (*Lagopus mutus*) and wild birds in general. The total protection of the white-tailed eagle started on 1st January 1914, and from that date putting out poisoned bait was totally banned. This was a milestone date in the history of the conservation of nature in Iceland, since putting out poisoned bait to kill foxes was a very unselective method, killing many more animal species than it was intended for, killing gulls, ravens, mice, dogs, cats, etc. The next milestone in conservation in

Iceland was the law for establishing the national park at Thingvellir in 1930. The same year a big gathering was held at Thingvellir to discuss the future of democracy in Iceland, although Iceland did not become a free democratic state until 1944, when in a national and parliamentary meeting at Thingvellir the first president, Sveinn Björnsson, was elected. More national parks were to come, and now there are four; Skaftafell in 1967, which became Vatnajökull national park a decade ago when it was increased enormously in area (Parliament of Iceland 2007), Jökulsárgljúfur national park in 1973 and Snæfellsjökull national park in 2001. Several 'public land' regions and several nature reserves have also been established, for example Hornstrandir Nature Reserve in northwest Iceland, Landmannalaugar 1979, which in 2011 the Icelandic Government proposed as a UNESCO Heritage site. In Iceland, there are now two UNESCO Heritage sites: Thingvellir National Park for its historical significance and the island of Surtsey for its geological formation and biota, and as a research site (Ólafsson and Ásbjörnsdóttir 2014).

Overall legislation for conservation of Icelandic nature was first put forward in 1956, and in it were rules made for protecting not only special geological features, plant and animal species per se, but also habitats of plants and animals, or areas of land or lakes of significance. Laws for making national parks and special land areas were strengthened in this legislation. In 1973, this legislation was revised and signed by the Minister of the Environment. Later these laws were modified and put under the jurisdiction of the Ministry of the Environment, when it was established in year 2002; the Ministry of the Environment became the Ministry for the Environment and Natural Resources (MENR) in 2012. All this legislation was heavily debated in the parliament and also outside of it. As in earlier times there was often a big difference between the views of farmers and the city-dwellers, the farmer being the land user and land protector, and the citizen being the land viewer or tourist. Associations and societies were established by amateurs interested in conservation of Icelandic nature and lobbying for protection of nature, and often for animal rights as well. The Icelandic Environment Association (Landvernd) was established in 1969; SUNN, the Society for Conservation in the northern part of Iceland in 1970, then NAUST for conservation in the East-fjords and NSVE for the southwest part of Iceland were established a little later and now every part of Iceland has an amateur conservation society. They, and other organizations, became members of The Icelandic Environment Association. In 1997 all those small already established societies were brought together into one big umbrella organization for conservation work, the Icelandic Nature Conservation Association. This probably increased the 'punch' for conservation, which was needed against strong opponents, such as those lobbying for agriculture, fisheries and the energy sector, who had a strong influence in the Icelandic parliament. Later, in 1996, this became more official and the Nature Conservation Agency (NCA) was established.

In 1904, Iceland had only one government minister, but ministers increased in number as time passed and in 1990 an environmental minister and an environmental ministry were established. The legislation for conservation and protection of nature was revised once more in the parliament, and the laws in force now date from 1994. It included measures for the conservation of marine biota and marine habitats, and also a requirement for the Minister of the Environment to put together a new plan for conservation of Icelandic nature every fifth year. Therefore, in the year 2003 a new plan was published to further strengthen conservation and protection of plants, animals and their habitats. The last act on protection of nature in Iceland was put forward by the Government on 10th April 2013, revising the older laws (Parliament of Iceland 2013a). The debate continues between conservationists and the energy sector, which wants to make dams and drill holes to utilize hydraulic and geothermal power for producing electricity, to make roads and raise pylons and masts for electrical lines across the wilderness of the country and for new industry in almost every part of the country. Conservation is still a hot issue in Iceland. Tourism has been growing exponentially until just recently and can itself be a problem. Tourists want to witness the solitude and the undisturbed views of 'the real Icelandic wilderness'. There is an increasing possible conflict between growing tourism and the need to utilize the rivers and hydrothermal fields for producing electricity. An unlimited flow of tourists to the most popular tourist sites can also ruin those sites and devalue the nature, solitude and tranquillity for which they are popular. Off-road driving by tourists, causing damage to natural phenomena, is also an increasing problem in Iceland.

Environmental Legislation in Iceland

Laws number 52/1989, the Environmental Responsibility Act 55/2012, Climate Change Act 70/2012 and acts concerning use of renewable energy in transportation on land have their impact upon the natural world. These laws are about minimizing environmental pollution, use of one-time drinking containers, bottles and cans, laws and rules for paints, about making stakeholders responsible for damage to the environment by their activities or if they cause damage, making them responsible for repairing or paying for reconstruction of the environment, and about reducing the output of greenhouse gases by Iceland in economic and practical ways. The last also considers the increase in storage of CO_2 from the atmosphere, adaptation to the effects

of climate change and increases the possibilities for the Icelandic Government to fulfil international agreements. All these acts have jurisdiction inside Iceland and the Icelandic Economic Zone (IEZ), but the last also applies to aircraft operated by Icelandic airlines in accordance with the European Economic Community (EEC) agreement. The third act has the purpose to increase the use of reusable energy in transportation on land and by so doing decrease the output of greenhouse gases to the atmosphere, in an economic and controlled manner

The Fishery Management Act (Ministry of Fisheries) (38/1990 and 79/1997), Act for Taxation of Fishing Rights (74/2012) and Act on Responsible Utilization of Fish Stocks (Ministry of Fisheries), and later the Act of Management of Marine Fisheries, are mostly economic, but also ensure the sustainability of Icelandic marine fisheries. They include definitions about what is a commercially exploitable population, be they marine animals or plants. However, they do not include seals and whales, where there are special laws in separate acts. In these laws there are very exact rules about where you can and cannot fish, and what gear can be used. In effect, this has made some coastal areas into protected areas, at least for fishing-gear operated on the seabed. Here the Act for Increasing the Culturing of Molluscs in Saltwater could be mentioned (Parliament of Iceland 2011a), which also incorporates cultivation of echinoderms, tunicates and marine gastropods. The acts (74/2012 and 145/2018) describe how fishing rights in Icelandic waters should be taxed and how the income should be spent by the Government, whether allotted to research, inspection or control. The purpose of these laws is to ensure sustainability in utilizing commercial invertebrate and fish stocks, so that yields from their utilization can be maximized for the Icelandic people for the future. The main rule is to bring to shore all catch, but the fishery minister can, however, make exceptions, for example catch infested by disease, damaged by seals or by other means, and those alive and too small for utilization. Trash fish, intestines, heads and other non-usable visceral organs produced by processing onboard can also be thrown overboard at sea. The Directory of Fisheries enforces the legislation in this act in the name of the Minister of Fisheries. In an amendment to the older laws with an act (116/2006), it enforces the law that commercially important fish stocks inside the IEZ are the property of the people of Iceland. However, the fishing quota handed to firms and individuals do not represent a gift or represent an infinite use commodity by the parties and can be taken back without any compensation (Parliament of Iceland 2006a).

Laws exist for protecting the sea against pollution (61/1996), amendments to the older laws (32/1986), and widening their jurisdiction to international waters, in accordance with international agreements that Iceland has signed. However, the laws apply only to ships flying the Icelandic flag. In short, throwing waste overboard at sea is prohibited, apart from those that the Institute for Human Health can allow, which are: material from digging out harbours and shipways for making them deeper, natural inert materials, which have not been treated chemically and do not include soluble materials, and for the sea and fish waste from fish-processing plants and fish-processing ships.

The Protection and Hunting of Wild Species Act (64/1994) legislation concerns conservation, protection, hunting, management of game and birds, damage caused by wild animals and definition of habitat by law, with birthing time of the arctic fox set as 1st May to 31st July. It also includes the definition of an area close to shores of lakes and the sea belonging to the land and its owner, taking also to island and rocks, of an area of land as a property to the landowner or landlord, community or the state, with the definition of a wild animal being all birds and mammals, other than pinnipeds, cetaceans, pets and livestock on farms. The purpose of this legislation is to ensure natural biodiversity, manage hunting of game and recognizing that wild animals can cause damage. They only apply inside the IEZ and MENR supervises this legislation. Reindeer is a special case, where the minister has established an advisory board for managing the reindeer population by establishing a hunting quota each summer. The minister also hires a biologist for operating on his/her behalf in matters of management of wild animal populations, especially those that cause damage, such as the arctic fox and the introduced mink (*Mustela vision*). It is prohibited to hunt wild animals with poison, sleeping drugs, explosives, petrol or other flammable liquids for making gas or smoke. It is also unlawful to hunt with rocks, clubs, swords, harpoons and spires, or similar objects. It is also prohibited to catch birds in nets, e.g. fishing-nets. Seabirds caught in fishing-nets cannot be sold, given or taken as a gift. The law bans wild animal hunting by using baited hooks or loops. Foot traps and other such traps for holding wild animals can only be used on rats, mice, mink and fox yearlings at the den. Electric devices that kill or knock out animals, light and aiming lights, mirrors for blinding, night-vision devices, automatic and semiautomatic firearms and any firearms with a magazine for more than two shots are unlawful. It is also prohibited to use live animals as decoys and dogs to run after and catch wild animals, except mink. Individuals are not permitted to hunt from a motor vehicle, except boats on the sea and lakes, which do not exceed the nine nautical miles per hour speed limit. Cars and four wheelers, and six wheelers for that matter, can be used for transportation on roads and tracks, but not to shoot game from. Shotguns and rifles should be unloaded in the vicinity of vehicles, closer than 250 m. The minister has rights to bend the laws if needed, after seeking advice from his advisors. Finally, every person who wants to hunt wild animals, except rats and mice, need to buy a hunting card each year, which s/he should carry on their person while hunting. On this card it says what animals s/he has a right to hunt, which depends on what kind of firearms s/he has a licence to use after taking appropriate training courses, usually operated by the sheriff of the county. There are special cards for farmers utilizing the wild animals' goods on his land. Hunters shooting reindeer must pass a special test before going hunting each season and take part in a draw for a reindeer. In this legislation there are special chapters about the arctic fox, mink, reindeer, rats and mice, polar bears (*Ursus maritimus*), which are protected in Iceland, and birds. The legislation protects every wild animal in Iceland, except those the minister allows the Icelanders to hunt by special permit. Protection, conservation and sustainability are in the spirit of the law.

A separate act has been passed on the Protection of Breiðafjörður (54/1995), with the purpose to protect the fiord Breiðafjörður in West Iceland (Figure 1, see Plate section), adjacent to Snæfellsnes National Park. The protection takes in geological features, biota and cultural heritage. The sea bottom is not included, at least the parts outside the jurisdiction of local farms. The MENR oversees this act and the Institute of the Environment has the role of supervision. The minister assembles an advisory board of seven people on matters of Breiðafjörður, mostly local people but also scientists from the Icelandic Institute of Natural History (INH) in Reykjavík. The minister appoints the chairman of this group. The communities and landowners around Breiðafjörður must put their building plans or projects to this advisory board for approval and take into consideration the conservation plan existing for land, island and rocks. The INH is obligated to do research on the biota in Breiðafjörður, which this legislation applies to. Costs are met by the Government, with a sum presented in the governmental annual budget.

The Genetically Modified Organisms Act (18/1996) has the purpose of protecting Icelandic nature, ecosystems, plants and health of humans and animals from the negative effects of genetically modified organisms. This act should ensure that production and use of genetically modified organisms is carried out using morally and socially secure methods, based on a basic rule of sustainability. It also deals with the disposal of waste from such production and the escape of genetically modified organisms. This act does not include anything about breeding, in a natural way or by insemination. The MENR has charge of this act and puts together an advisory board of nine persons.

An Act for Conservation of Icelandic Nature (60/2013) is the responsibility of MENR (Parliament of Iceland 2013a) and its purpose is to protect for all future the diversity of Icelandic nature, biodiversity, geodiversity and geographic diversity. As far as possible the laws should ensure the development of Icelandic nature on its own terms and conserve what is spectacular and historical, as well as reclaim disturbed ecosystems and promote increasing resilience of Icelandic ecosystems to natural disasters and climate change. The spirit of the act is the conservation and sustainable utilization of Icelandic natural resources. The act aims at making interaction between people and nature non-destructive and to facilitate encounters of the public with nature and to educate them about Icelandic nature and cultural remains. It also increases the public right to walk in nature and enjoy it without destruction, encouraging public access to wild nature. This act incorporates many issues, such as walking, riding, biking and off-road driving. The red list of organisms and other natural phenomena, its constant re-evaluation and on what terms, conservation issues, classification of conservation areas including the coastal waters off Iceland, foreign invasive species, control and monitoring, and establishing a nature conservation fund is also included.

An Afforestation Act (3/1955) is supervised formally by the MENR. In Iceland viable 'forests' of

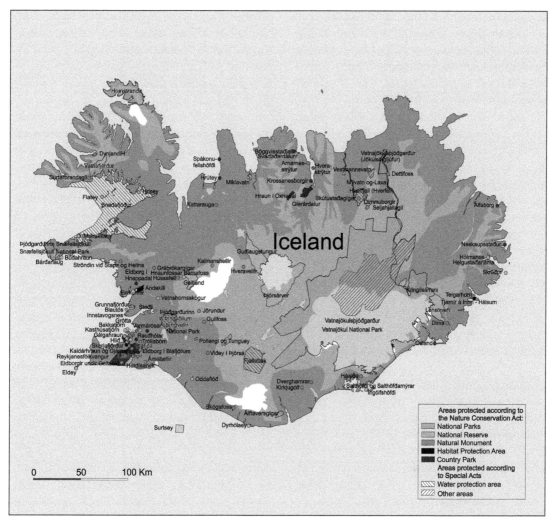

Figure 1 Map of protected areas in Iceland using data from the Environment Agency of Iceland. *Source:* Data from Environment Agency of Iceland. https://gis.ust.is/geoserver/web/wicket/bookmarkable/org.geoserver.web.demo. MapPreviewPage?1 (See colour plate section for colour representation of this figure.)

tree birch (*Betula pubescens*) are still to be found. This act ensures their protection and preservation, but also tries to increase forestry in the country, planting commercial forest and forest strips for shelterbelt protection from winds. A special plan will be enforced to make this happen, for the good of farmers and other inhabitants of various parts of the country. The Minister of Agriculture

previously took charge of this act, which is now in the charge of the MENR. Three types of forests are mentioned in the act: commercial forest for timber production, forest strips for shelterbelts and forests on wasteland, sand and soil, to reduce soil erosion, and forests for land-protection, afforestation, beauty and tourism. The cost is met by the government. Recent results of a study of the distribution of birch forests in Iceland indicate that they are gaining ground, have been increasing in the last 25 years and now cover 1.5% of Island's area (Institute of the Environment 2007), but at the Settlement of Iceland it is believed that birch covered 25% of the country (Thorgilsson 1968). The reason for this decrease in cover of birch can hardly be blamed on climate change; rather it was caused by the colonizing of the country and farming, and, in addition, a lot of land has been destroyed by eruptions and ash fall. The Norwegians colonizing Iceland were used to burning wood for cooking and warmth and kept on doing so until they had cleared land for agriculture, and even longer. Only woods high up in the mountains or in remote places such as valleys between glaciers, or behind a glacier river difficult to cross, were not eradicated. After deforestation, the inhabitants of Iceland had to rely on peat, seaweed or dung for fires for cooking and warming their homes. This had an enormous influence on housing. High standing wooden houses became uncommon and were replaced by low houses made of rock and turf, with walls over a metre thick. Timber, usually driftwood, was only noticeable on the inside in the roof and on the outside in facing the main wall. A few of these old farmhouses are still standing and are protected. Forestry enthusiasts have recently got a helping hand from an unexpected direction, the silica production industry, which uses a lot of industrial tree waste for burning in the production ovens. The silica production industry would buy the tree waste from timber-cutting companies of the industrial forests and sponsor expanding forestry on Icelandic bare ground. Sustainable timber production for industrial purposes can also be a good way to stop soil erosion in Iceland, close to towns and cities, at the least.

The Public Lands Act from the Prime Minister's Office (58/1998) describes three forms of land: private, public and pastures for sheep and horses. Public land is defined as a land area outside privately owned land, even though persons, communities and societies may have limited ownerships there; this is land where the public can walk and rest, without many restrictions. Tents can be put up but not permanent houses. If, say, a hiking group wants to build a house for its members, it must ask the Prime Minister of Iceland for permission. Public land is often in the wilderness. There is an ongoing debate about where the private land ends and the wilderness begins, and many lawsuits are still in the courts.

An Act on Research and Use of Underground Resources (57/1998) concerns mining rights of ores, chemical compounds and energy underground, and on the bed of lakes and the ocean, inshore, within the jurisdiction of farms and governmental land. It does not matter in what state they occur, solid, liquid or gas, and at what temperatures they would be mined. This legislation also incorporates the research and utilization of micro-organisms found in geothermal waters in hot springs. However, here cooperation is required with the MENR, as well as the INH. To do research and mining according to these laws, the Act for Conservation of Nature also applies, as well as other legislation about research and utilization of land and land resources. It is the Minister of Industries and Innovations (MII) who oversees these laws. The Institute of Energy operates on behalf of the Minister in charge of control of research and eventual mining. The Law of Conservation of Nature also applies in many cases, and rules about confidentiality also apply. Landowners cannot hinder research to be done on their land. If the owner and the researcher are partners, they are obligated to make sure there is no pollution to the environment as a result of the research. If the mining rights do not go to the landowners, they can demand payments for damage caused by the research and the mining. If the landowners' demands are too high according to valuation of the goods and fair settlements are not reached, the area can be purchased even though the landowner does not want to sell. This is done in the courtroom and the landowner usually has a say in how payments are made, one sum in the beginning or in parts annually, but they cannot influence the amount of compensation. The government can do as it pleases with land owned by it, but in the case of national land (land owned by the Icelandic people), other laws may restrict the process of mining.

The Environmental Impact Assessment Act (106/2000) has the purpose to secure that, before any permission is granted for any kind of building project, its effect on the environment shall be assessed, also to involve stakeholders in cooperation, aim to solve any environmental damage of their doing and to publicly announce effects of particular building projects on the environment and proposed solutions, making it possible for the public to have a say before the impact and the project start. This act applies to land, sea and air inside the IEZ. In every case the Icelandic National Planning Agency (INPA) makes its own assessment of the effect of the building projects on the environment. In this act the term environment is defined as incorporating people, animals, plants and other parts of the biocoenosis, soil, geological formations, water, air, weather and landscape, communities, health, culture, cultural heritage, jobs and material goods. There is also a clause on the scale of damage to the environment, the greatest effect being irreversible damage to the environment that cannot be repaired with any counteractions. The MENR is involved as well as the INPA. Of course, not all building processes need to be investigated for effect on the environment and it depends on the size and magnitude and placement, but it is the duty of the INPA to make decisions concerning the implementation of this act.

The Regulation establishing the Ministry for the Environment (77/1990) was the forerunner of the act for establishing its major institute, the Institute of the Environment Act (90/2002). The Institute of the Environment takes care of the issues formerly in the jurisdiction of the Institute of Public Health, that is health and pollution control, poisonous and dangerous materials (Parliament of Iceland 1988), protection against pollution of the ocean (Parliament of Iceland 1986), genetically modified organisms (Parliament of Iceland 1996), restaurants and guesthouses, hostels and hotels, fighting the use of tobacco, prohibiting development, production, collection, use and destruction of chemical weapons. It also takes over the issues supervised by the former Governmental Natural Conservation Board, special conservation of Lake Mývatn and the river Laxá, burning grassland and use of fire in the wilderness, which was the Act on Restriction of Fires in Open Landscape (61/1992), laws against burning of grassland for agricultural purposes and setting rules about special permits for starting a fire, which can only be given by the sheriff of the county. Fire (75/2000) legislation, which is about protection of life, health and property of people against fire, also incorporates protecting the environment against fire, in any form or source. It also considers pollution accidents and getting pollution agents out of the environment by cleaning them up. Later these issues were put under the Act of the Institute of the Environment, with protection, conservation and hunting of wild birds and mammals, protection of Breiðafjörður, control of pollution of the ocean, control of poison and dangerous materials, legislation about the INH, together with its implementation around the country, organization of tourism issues, control of genetically transformed organisms, and takes care of the hunting officer incorporated in the law about protection, conservation and hunting of wild birds and mammals. It incorporates the advisory board for hunting of reindeer, which is incorporated into the act about protection, control and hunting of wild birds and mammals, with later amendments to all these legislations (Parliament of Iceland 1994).

Legislation has been enacted for the power and jurisdiction of the INH Acts (60/1992 and

169/1998). In the later laws the power of the director of the INH was increased. However, in the case of determining the value of or need for protection of nature and organisms, the director is obligated to seek advice and cooperate with the Governmental Natural Conservation Agency. Later, INH was put under the jurisdiction of MENR. The Nature Conservation Agency Act (93/1996) is the legislation about conservation of nature and is purposely to ensure that humans and nature interactions operate in a sustainable manner and that the sea, water and air systems are not polluted by the activity of the people in Iceland. This act ensures the development of Icelandic nature as far as is possible on its own terms and protects what is special and historical. The legislation should make it easier for Icelanders to observe natural phenomena and get acquainted with nature. This act takes to and describes, by law, special natural phenomena, protected areas, national parks and areas where people can freely move around, public land and geological natural phenomenon, which are put on the Icelandic red-list. Protected areas can be on dry land and in the sea, which can be protected by other Icelandic laws, related to nature or landscape. Natural artefacts for protection can be miscellaneous, from areas, phenomena, organisms, habitats of living organisms and whole ecosystems. The MENR takes care of all aspects of conservation of the Icelandic nature and the IIE organizes the way matters are treated. In the process of policy making the minister should seek advice from the institutes of Natural Conservation Agency of Iceland and the Advisory Board on Conservation of Nature in Iceland. The INH based in Reykjavík liaises with farmers and other users of land, communities around Iceland and societies for natural conservation established by amateurs, as is regarded as fit in each case.

The Act about Treatment of Waste Material (55/2003) and the Act about Chemicals (61/2013) have the purpose to ensure proper management and treatment of waste, so that it cannot cause harm to health of humans and animals, and the environment is not degraded, that noise and smell pollution does not occur, there is no destruction of landscape or places of importance, to ensure that waste management is done in an organized and economic manner and that each sort of waste gets proper treatment. Sustainable use of resources is enforced by using proper methods and by education concerning minimizing waste. Utilization of waste is to be increased and those who produce waste should pay for its treatment or destruction. This legislation incorporates almost any waste material, but not gases, old landfills, natural soil dug up on a building site and used again on that site, radioactive materials, old dynamite and such demolition material taken out of use, waste material and its use in agriculture and forestry or to produce energy. Methods of its utilization should be harmless to the environment and health of people, such as sewage, most by-products from animals and animal corpses from those that have not entered slaughterhouses, e.g. corpses of animals killed to hinder spreading of animal diseases. In these laws are definitions to be found about remote districts, best available technique, incineration station, reuse, reutilization, and production from waste, waste separation and classification, transportation of waste material and more. The act about chemicals and mixture of compounds has also the aim to preclude chemicals in affecting health of humans and animals and polluting the environment, but it is mostly about commercial issues and the EES agreement (Parliament of Iceland 2013b).

The Act about the Marine and Freshwater Research Institute (MFRI) in Iceland (112/2015) takes care of the marine and freshwater ecosystems and marine and freshwater fisheries in Iceland. This act is the responsibility of MII. It also takes care of aquaculture projects in the ocean and freshwaters, research and control, but there are special laws about aquaculture in

Iceland (Parliament of Iceland 2008a) and even as a Governmental institution it can act as a private contract research institute.

The Freshwater Fisheries Act (61/2006) and the Freshwater Fish Cultivation Fund (72/2008) are about fishing rights in freshwaters and sensible, economic and sustainable utilization of resources and conservation of freshwater fish populations. In this act there are definitions about special areas on land and in lakes, which have different fishing rights. Also, the difference between fish cultivation and aquaculture in freshwaters and ocean fish farming is highlighted, and the differences between local fish and anadromous migrating fish from the sea into rivers and lakes and wild fish population. A farm cannot be deprived of its fishing rights to the advantage of one of the farm's products. The minister can, however, allow such action if it is advised by the Icelandic Fisheries Directorate. In this legislation there is also a very interesting chapter about seals (pinnipeds), since it is an allowance for the owner of the fishing rights to cull seals or harass them in estuaries, rivers and lakes. In case of a situation when fishing rights and sealing rights are not in the same hands, the culling and harassment of seals can be allowed by the Icelandic Fisheries Directorate, on advice from the MFRI and the INH. If the sealing rights are valuable to the other party, compensations are to be made by the fishing rights owner (Parliament of Iceland 2006b). Just recently an amendment has been made to this act, the 11th paragraph, which makes it possible for the Minister of Fisheries to protect seals in the waterways if the MFRI recommends that. The freshwater fish cultivation fund is an independent fund owned by the Icelandic Government and is the responsibility of the MII. Its purpose is to lend money to or fund fish cultivation projects, improving the fishing environment, research projects in rivers and lakes and maximizing catch from rivers and lakes (Parliament of Iceland 2008b).

Domestic Laws for Conservation of Species, Habitats and 'Ecosystems'

Terrestrial, Water and Estuarine Biota

The water resource act (36/2011) has the purpose to conserve water and the water ecosystem, to hinder reduction of water quality and to ensure sustainability in water utilization as a resource. This encompasses making plans for sustainability in water use and monitoring water use in the country. This legislation encompasses surface waters, groundwater, estuaries and adjacent coastal waters (defined as surface water on the land side of a line drawn one nautical mile outside of the 115 m limit from the shore belonging to the landowner) with their ecosystems and adjacent ecosystems connected to their waters systems (Parliament of Iceland 2011b).

The environment of Mývatn and the river Laxá has been protected with new laws from 9th June 2004, which are similar to the older laws, but with more emphasis on conservation of biological diversity in this area (Parliament of Iceland 2004a). Thingvallavatn and river systems were protected with a special act (Parliament of Iceland 2005), which forbids any spoiling of surface water and groundwater with pollution. The main purpose of this law is to protect and conserve habitat and spawning grounds of the varieties of arctic char (*Salvelinus alpinus*) and sub-populations of trout (*Salmo trutta*) that now inhabit the lake and its river system. Agriculture on the lake bank is permitted if it does not pollute the water; however, aquaculture in the lake is generally forbidden and those interested must apply for a special permit to the MENR. The spirit of the law implies that such a permit would be very hard to get. There are old dams and electrical power stations with fish gangways in the river system of Thingvallavatn, which date from the early 1960s. This did cause lowering of the water level in the system seasonally each year and differently each year in relation to the status of the water budget in the lake. This had an impact on the trout population in the river system (Skarphéðinsson 1996). This act takes cares of this and limits how low the water level can go.

The Red List for Plants

At least 235 terrestrial plants have been protected everywhere they survive in the wild, according to rule 23 of Act 47/1971 (INH 1996). In the red list plants are classified in endangered categories, which also includes lower plants, such as lichens, mosses and algae (https://www.ni.is/midlun/utgafa/valistar/plontur). In this web report there are images of plants and distribution charts pointing out finding sites. Iceland's most experienced botanists compiled this list with fine systematic drawings. The red list for plants is under constant re-evaluation and in 2018 there were 56 endangered plants according to IUCN classifications.

Invertebrates

In 1998, a new endemic family of subterranean gammaridean amphipod (Crustacean) was discovered in Thingvallavatn, representing a new species and genus to science, *Crymostygius thingvallensis*, found in spring inlets feeding the lake. This was the first report of a stygobiont freshwater amphipod from Iceland and the northernmost report of a stygobiont species in Europe. In 2000 another new species to science, *Crangonyx islandicus*, was discovered also in Lake Thingvallavatn. There are indications that this species may have survived the Quaternary glacial period in sub-glacial refuges, e.g. in the groundwater of the porous lava, and even that they have persisted in Iceland for millions of years. These relict amphipods from the Ice Age in the lake will be especially protected when Thingvellir National Park is made a UNESCO site (Jónasson and Hersteinsson 2002).

Fish, the Red List for Birds and Mammals

No marine fish species are totally protected by Icelandic laws, but the giant variety of Thingvallavatn trout is probably going to be protected in the future (Jónasson and Hersteinsson 2002; Skarphéðinsson 1996).

Several bird species have been protected besides the white-tailed eagle, Water rail (*Rallus aquaticus*), Grey Phalarope (*Phalaropus fulicarius*) and local stocks of Barnacle Goose (*Branta leucopsis*) in Breiðafjörður, Skaftafellssýslur and Skagafirði. In total there are 41 bird species endangered according to the IUCN classification (https://www.ni.is/midlun/utgafa/valistar/fuglar). Almost all birds are protected during the nesting period and hunting only allowed during autumn (https://www.ust.is/einstaklingar/veidi/veiditimabil). Migrating goose species such as Brent (*Branta bernicla*) and White-fronted (*Anser albifrons*) are protected from hunting while they stay In Iceland. Seabirds are generally not totally protected, and there is a hunting period for most species except Leach's Petrel (*Oceanodroma leucorrhoa*), Storm Petrel (*Hydrobates pelagicus*), Manx Shearwater (*Puffinus puffinus*), Sooty Shearwater (*Puffinus griseus*), Gannet (*S. bassana*) and Little Auk (*Alle alle*). The major threats to each species are presented in the list as well as information on the biology of the species, population size and distribution, conservation measures and monitoring programmes in Iceland. The status of each species in a regional and international context is discussed and references made to relevant international conventions and commitments. In Iceland the Red List is considered an important tool for fulfilling obligations undertaken by the Government through various international and regional conventions on the conservation of threatened species and their habitats. The Red List is also crucial for the effective monitoring of the most vulnerable biota and forms a basis for sustainable use and the conservation of biological diversity (INH 2000).

Five mammal species were classified as endangered in the Red List of year 2018 (https://www.ni.is/midlun/utgafa/valistar/spendýr). The grey whale (*Eschrichtius robustus*) is extinct (RE) in Icelandic waters. The North Atlantic right whale (*Eubalaena glacialis*) and the harbour seal (*Phoca vitulina*) are classified as CR, the grey seal (*Halichoerus grypus*) and the blue whale (*Balaenoptera musculus*) are classified as VU. No terrestial mammal of Icelandic origin is totally protected. There are special permits for reindeer hunting, sealing is allowed unless the Minister of Fisheries decides otherwise, but the landowner has solely the right to hunt seals on his land and 115 m out to sea. Whales in Icelandic waters are protected by International laws, which Iceland has signed. Iceland is a long-time member of the International Whaling Commission (IWC) and the whale-catching quotas are set in cooperation with IWC. Only minke whales (*Balaenoptera aqutorostrata*) and fin whales (*B. physalus*) are caught and there are special laws regarding whaling in Iceland (26/1949) such that whales are not included in the act about protection and hunting of wild birds and mammals in Iceland (64/1994). The MII gives permission to catch whales to those who fulfil stringent conditions set by the legislation about whaling in Iceland. Most whale species are protected inside the IEZ, because Iceland is a member of the IWC and CITES. Until 1978 sealing for harbour seals pups was a profitable undertaking for many farmers living by the sea. After the demand for sealskin dropped at the skin markets in Europe and prices fell, this was no longer a well-paid undertaking. For counteracting this and keeping the sealing going, organizations of the fishing industry in Iceland started paying for caught seals in 1982, first for all types of seals for utilizing in the feed-production for fur-animals (fox and mink), but after 1989 only for grey seal and skin of harbour seal pups. The skins were utilized in fur coats for the domestic and international market. This was done in cooperation with the Seal Farmers Association of Iceland, which wanted to uphold the traditional sealing and utilization of sealskin, −meat and fat. After 1995 this project was ended and lately all promotion of sealing in Iceland has ended. Polar bears do not reside in Iceland but they sometimes come visiting and are protected on Icelandic ground by the Act of 94/1994, and only shot when the sheriff and IIE agree that they are dangerous to humans and livestock. However, Icelanders may shoot polar bears in self-defence and need to report the kill afterwards (Haraldsson and Hersteinsson 2004).

Marine Biota

Presently there are 21 coastal areas protected around Iceland by the Act of Conservation of Icelandic Nature: seven islands, three pits, eleven littoral and sub-littoral zones and nine areas close to the sea (The Ministry of Fisheries 2004). Protected areas around pits, coasts and islands usually reach only 115 m out to sea, but three islands have protected areas around them that reach as far out as two kilometres; those are the islands of Eldey, southwest Iceland, Surtsey (Figure 2, see Plate section), south Iceland, and Melrakkaey, in Grundarfjörður, West Iceland. In the agreement on the Icelandic Economic Zone in 1901 fishing by trawl was banned inside this zone; Faxafjörður was not part of this agreement then, but when the Icelandic Economic Zone was increased out to the four nautical mile limit in 1952, this fjord was also included in the trawl-free zone. Other laws, such as 81/1976 and 79/1997, made it possible to further protect small and young fish by area closure for a short or long period of the year. The latter laws also banned all foreign fishing fleets entering the IEZ, unless they had a special permit issued by the Icelandic Government. Such agreements have usually been bilateral and issued only to people of the Faroe Islands and Norway.

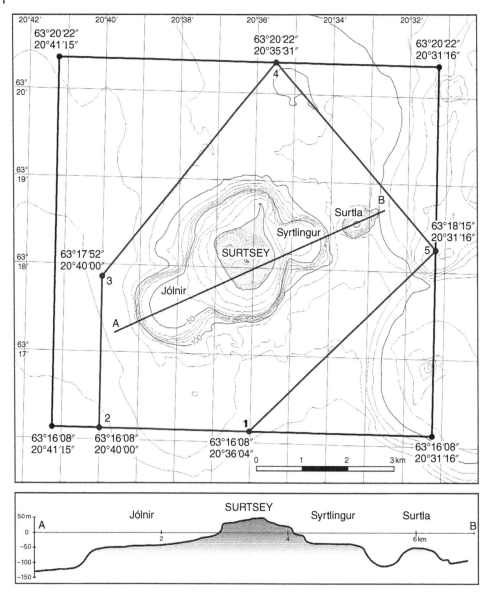

Figure 2 The preservation area in Surtsey. *Source:* The map is courtesy of the Icelandic Institute of Natural History, supplied by The Surtsey Research Society. (See colour plate section for colour representation of this figure.)

Iceland has a National Programme of Action for the protection of the marine environment from land-based activities (Ministry for the Environment 2006a). Recently, there have been plans drawn up for establishing the first underwater marine nature reserve, south of Reykjanes and reaching as far to the east as the glacial river Markarfljót and including Vestmannaeyjar as far south as the island of Surtsey (Baldursson 2014). Undersea hot water vents were found about 15 years ago in the fjord Eyjafjörður and were protected by the Act on Conservation of Icelandic Nature and the Minister of Fisheries in 2001 (Ministry of Fisheries 2004). Deep water corals are particularly vulnerable to bottom trawling, due to sensitivity to physical damage and slow growth. According to Ragnarsson et al. (2018), there are cold water corals in two different colours, found within a 40 km^2. area at a depth of 200–500 m, at several sites around Iceland. No sunlight reaches the coral, so they filter their nutrition from ocean currents. It takes several hundred thousands of years for a coral reef to develop. In that time, it creates a special habitat for other organisms. Corals are very sensitive organisms and their existence has widely been jeopardized through demersal fishing, with serious consequences for the biota that inhabit it. Around 1970, 11 coral grounds were distributed between Víkuráll (NW) and Rósagarður (SE), normally close to the shelf break. Within the distribution area otterboard trawling effort was considerable during 1991–2002. Out of 11 coral grounds existing at around 1970, only four still remain. Some relatively large coral grounds have vanished: one on the Reykjanes Ridge (36 km^2) and two near the Öræfagrunn bank (68 and 30 km^2 in area, respectively). Since then new coral grounds have been found. Considerable corals exist on the Reykjanes Ridge, within an area protected from bottom trawling, and relatively large areas of coral probably still exist in the Hornafjarðardjúp deep (12 km^2) and in the Lónsdjúp deep (38 km^2). Other coral grounds are small (commonly around 1 km^2). It is proposed that coral areas should be closed for bottom trawling, giving priority to coral grounds adjacent to high fishing effort areas (Steingrímsson and Einarsson 2004). The coral areas that have previously been discovered around Iceland are protected as nature reserves and the goal is for the other more recently discovered corals to also be preserved (Anon 2014).

International Laws, Agreements and Treaties About the Environment and Wild Organisms That Iceland Has Signed

The Icelandic Government has agreed on several international rules for conservation of nature and protection of wetlands. Protection was afforded to Thjórsárver in 1990 and Grunnafjörður and Borgarfjörður in 1996. Part of Mývatn and Laxá had already been protected in 1977, with the Ramsar and Bern agreements concerning protection of wild plants and animals and marine habitats. In the United Nations (UN) agreement on combating climate change, desertification, along with climate change and the loss of biodiversity were identified as the greatest challenges to sustainable development. This led to the 1992 *Rio Earth Summit and Convention on Biological Diversity*. Policy making and carrying the Rio treaty through was agreed by the Icelandic Government in 2008 and great emphasis was put on the special nature of the Icelandic environment and on the need for more research and monitoring of terrestrial, freshwater and marine ecosystems, to fight against all kinds of pollution, intrusive foreign species, recovering natural diversity and improving the rules about the use and distribution of genetically changed organisms, as well as increasing education about nature and natural processes and the protection of biodiversity. Sigurjónsdóttir (2014) has emphasized the use of the littoral biocoenosis as a teaching ground for all students from kindergarten, elementary schools, high schools, colleges and universities. International cooperation plays a key role in environmental affairs since most aspects have shared relevance to more than one nation, and the nature of many is global in scope. The MENR administers multifaceted Nordic collaboration and supervises the implementation of international environmental protection agreements in which

Iceland takes part. The ministry participates in the environmental efforts of many multinational organizations, such as the UN, the Council of Europe and the OECD. The ministry also handles the environmental and food aspects of the Agreement of the European Economic Association (EEA). Emphasis on the environmental affairs of the Northern Hemisphere has grown in recent years and the Stefánsson Arctic Institute, based in Akureyri, works on issues in this field. The international offices of two projects under the auspices of the Arctic Council, which sees to the protection of the biosphere (CAFF) and marine conservation (PAME), are also located in Iceland.

The Atmosphere

The *Vienna Convention for the Protection of the Ozone Layer*, including the Montreal Protocol on Substances that Deplete the Ozone Layer, is an international treaty designed to reduce the production and consumption of ozone depleting substances in order to reduce their abundance in the atmosphere, and thereby protect the Earth's fragile Ozone Layer. Iceland became partner of this treaty on 29th August 1989, a few months before this treaty came into action on 27th November 1989 and recognized later amendments, made in London on 29th June 1990, Copenhagen on 25th November 1992 and in Montreal on 17th September 1997. In Iceland, policy, execution, participation in meetings and elucidation are in the hands of the MENR, in cooperation with The Environment Agency of Iceland.

The *Convention on Long-Range Transboundary Air Pollution* (LRTAP) is designed to protect people and the environment against air pollution. It is a geographically limited treaty under control of The General Secretary of the UN and the Economic Commission of Europe (ECE), 51 nations have signed this treaty, amongst them USA, Canada and Israel. The General Secretary of ECE prepares

the agenda and invitations to the meetings of the Executive Body. It was signed in 1979 and became valid on 16th March 1983. Iceland signed and validated it on 5th May 1983 and it became operational in Iceland on 3rd August that year. Later conventions are many and Iceland is a member of a few of them. In Iceland one EMEP station is in operation at Írafoss, South Iceland, for measuring sulphur dioxide (SO_2); however, nitrogen dioxide (NO_2) and ozone (O_3), which are also measured on such stations in Europe, are not measured.

The *United Nations Framework Convention on Climate Change* (UNFCCC) is an international treaty under the control of the Secretary General of the UN, with 186 member nations including the EEC. It was agreed in New York on 9th May 1992 and took effect on 21st March 1994. Iceland validated it on 16th June 1993 and it came into effect in Iceland on 21st March 1994. The most important agreement in relation to UNFCC is The Kyoto Protocol, which is an international agreement, which commits its parties to set internationally binding emission reduction targets. Recognizing that developed countries are principally responsible for the current high levels of Green House Gas (GHG) emissions to the atmosphere as a result of more than 150 years of industrial activity, the Protocol places a heavier burden on these under the principle of 'common but differentiated responsibilities'. The Kyoto Protocol was adopted in Kyoto, Japan, on 11th December 1997 and entered into force on 16th February 2005. The detailed rules for the implementation of the Protocol were adopted at COP 7 in Marrakesh, Morocco, in 2001, and are referred to as the 'Marrakesh Accords'. Its first commitment period started in 2008 and ended in 2012. The Kyoto Protocol from 11th December 1997 has no international jurisdiction, with only 74 members in June 2002. Iceland validated it on 23rd May 2002. In Doha, Qatar, on 8th December 2012, the 'Doha Amendment to the Kyoto Protocol' was adopted. The amendment includes: New commitments for

Annex I Parties to the Kyoto Protocol who agreed to take on commitments in a second commitment period from 1st January 2013 to 31st December 2020. A revised list of greenhouse gases to be reported on by parties in the second commitment period was published, with amendments to several articles of the Kyoto Protocol which specifically referenced issues pertaining to the first commitment period and which needed to be updated for the second commitment period. On 21st December 2012, the amendment was circulated by the Secretary General of the UN, acting in his capacity as Depositary, to all Parties to the Kyoto Protocol in accordance with Articles 20 and 21 of the Protocol. During the first commitment period, 37 industrialized countries and the European Community committed to reduce GHG emissions to an average of 5% against 1990 levels. During the second commitment period, parties committed to reduce GHG emissions by at least 18% below 1990 levels in the eight-year period from 2013 to 2020; however, the composition of parties in the second commitment period was different from the first. Under the Protocol, countries must meet their targets primarily through national measures. However, the Protocol also offers them an additional means to meet their targets by way of three market-based mechanisms. The Kyoto mechanisms are: International Emissions Trading, Clean Development Mechanism (CDM) and Joint Implementation (JI). Iceland is a full member of the Paris agreement on climate change, made in 2017.

Conservation of Biota, Habitats and Ecosystems

The *International Convention for the Protection of Birds* is an international treaty, whose aim is to protect wild birds; however, it is now mostly invalid, being superceded by the Bernar treaty. It is under the control of the Government of France and there are only 10 member countries. Agreed in Paris on 18th October 1950 and enforced from 17th January 1953, Iceland became a member and validated the treaty on 28th January 1956. It includes the following: (a) all wild birds shall be protected. The Icelandic Government can make exceptions from the general rule for science and education and in the case of vermin-birds. (b) Member countries are obligated to: (i) protect wild birds while nesting, (ii) protect migratory birds on their way to their nesting-places, (iii) protect wild birds against extermination the whole year round, (iv) prohibit gathering of eggs, eggshells and young birds, (v) prohibit some special hunting methods, (vi) make a list of birds that it is allowed to hunt or take, (vii) take precautions against destruction of birds by water pollution, electrical lines, pesticides and other poisons, (viii) educate children and the public about the necessity to protect birds and (ix) establish nature reserves for nesting birds. In Iceland the policy is executed by the MENR in cooperation with the INH. Execution, participating in meetings and elucidation of information is included with the Bernar treaty.

The *Convention on Wetlands of International Importance*, especially as Waterfowl Habitat (Ramsar Convention), is an international convention under the protection of UNESCO, agreed at Ramsar in Iran on 2nd February 1971 and fully validated on 21st December 1975; on 22nd June 2001 there were 124 nations as partners. Iceland became a full member on 2nd April 1978. The Ramsar Convention Bureau is linked to UNEP and IUCN. In Iceland, policy is in the hands of the MENR and in cooperation with the Environment Agency of Iceland it oversees execution of the convention and participation in meetings and reports information together with INH. Under the 'three pillars' of the Convention, the Contracting Parties commit to: (a) work towards the wise use of all their wetlands, (b) designate suitable wetlands for the list of Wetlands of International Importance (the 'Ramsar List') and ensure their effective management and (c) cooperate internationally on transboundary wetlands, shared wetland systems and shared species. There are over 2000 Ramsar Sites in the territories of over 160 Ramsar Contracting Parties across the world. In Iceland there are now six sites (three that have recently been nominated by Iceland: Mývatn-Laxá (Garðarsson and Einarsson 1991), Thjórsárver and Grunnafjörður.

The *Convention on the Conservation of European Wildlife and Natural Habitats* is a treaty geographically limited to Europe and adjacent countries that share the same animal species. It is under the jurisdiction of the Council of Europe and was signed by 45 member nations in Bern on 19th September 1979, coming into force on 1st June 1982. It came into effect in Iceland on 1st October 1993. The convention aims to ensure conservation of wild flora and fauna and their habitats. Special attention is given to endangered and vulnerable species, including migratory species, specified in appendices. There are four appendixes: (a) a list of rare plants, which need protection together with their habitats and (b) a list of mammals, birds, reptiles, fish, insects and other invertebrates, which need protection together with their habitats. It especially prohibits hunting, gathering of eggs and disturbances in their nesting areas, especially during the mating- and breeding seasons. It also prohibits the selling of products from these organisms if that helps conservation of the species. Resting places for migratory animals on the red list should also be protected. The last two appendixes consist of (c) a list of mammals, birds and reptiles, which need protection together with their habitats and (d) a list of hunting methods that should be banned.

The *Convention on Biological Diversity* (CBD) is an international convention under the aegis of the Secretary General of the UN, and by year 2010 a total of 193 nations had validated it and put it into their own laws and legislations. The policy is to protect and enforce sustainability in utilization of natural resources and defend biodiversity by using planning and legislation. It will effectively control and inspect the use and release of genetically modified organisms, increase research and monitoring of biological diversity, increase education and knowledge of biodiversity and put into legislation monitoring of environmental factors and anthropogenic factors affecting biodiversity negatively. It will also enforce sustainability in the use of biological diversity. The exchange of scientific information will assist underdeveloped countries in living up to the convention. There is a growing recognition that biological diversity is a global asset of tremendous value to present and future generations. The convention was opened for signature on 5th June 1992 at the *UN Conference on Environment and Development* (the Rio 'Earth Summit'). It remained open for signature until the 4th June 1993, by which time it had received 168 signatures. The convention entered into force on 29th December 1993, which was 90 days after the 30th ratification. Iceland fully incorporated it into Icelandic legislation on 11th December 1994. The amendment of the Cartagena Protocol on Biosafety was agreed in Montreal on 29th January 2000 and was validated on 11th September 2003, with the agreement of 157 nations.

The *Convention on International Trade in Endangered Species of Wild Fauna and Flora* (CITES) is an international agreement between governments. Its aim is to ensure that international trade in specimens of wild animals and plants does not threaten their survival. Because the trade in wild animals and plants crosses borders between countries, the effort to regulate it requires international cooperation to safeguard certain species from over-exploitation. CITES was drafted as a result of a resolution adopted in 1963 at a meeting of members of the IUCN (The World Conservation Union). The international treaty was proposed by Switzerland, but agreed in Washington, USA, on 3rd March 1973, and brought into force on 1st June 1975. Iceland became a member on 3rd

January 2000 and in Iceland this treaty was fully validated, with the Bonn (22nd June 1979) amendment on 2nd April 2000. The Ministry of Foreign Affairs has the duty to inform about CITES in Iceland. There are three appendixes: (a) endangered species, international trade only allowed in exceptional cases, both import and export papers need to be in order, (b) possibly endangered species if international trade with them is not controlled, export papers need to be in order to say the least (like Appendix a in some countries) and (c) species that are protected in some of the party nations and those wanting other parties to assist in banning international trade in these species. International trade is therefore banned unless the protective nation allows it.

The *United Nations Convention to Combat Desertification in those Countries Experiencing Serious Drought and/or Desertification*, particularly in Africa (UNCCD), is an international treaty under the aegis of the Secretary General of the UN, with 195 party nations in 2001. Agreed in Paris on 17th June 1994 and validated on 26th December 1996, Iceland fully validated it on 1st September 1997. Execution in Iceland is by the Soil Conservation Service of Iceland (SCSI) and the Icelandic International Development Agency (ICEIDA). The MENR has the duty to publish information. There are five appendixes, one for each international area: Africa, Asia, South America and the Caribbean, North Mediterranean and the Middle East, and Europe. In the 10-Year Strategy of the UNCCD (2008–2018), which was adopted in 2007, parties to the convention further specified their goals: 'to forge a global partnership to reverse and prevent desertification/land degradation and to mitigate the effects of drought in affected areas in order to support poverty reduction and environmental sustainability'. The UNCCD is particularly committed to a bottom-up approach, encouraging the participation of local people in combating desertification and land degradation. The UNCCD secretariat facilitates cooperation between developed and developing countries, particularly around knowledge and technology transfer for sustainable land management. As the dynamics of land, climate and biodiversity are intimately connected, the UNCCD collaborates closely with the other two Rio Conventions, CBD and UNFCCC.

Pollution of the Sea

There are three conventions regarding prevention of pollution of the sea that Iceland has validated with its membership. It is important but not totally about conservation of wild biota, being more connected with transport. The relevant conventions are: *International Convention for the Prevention of Pollution from Ships 1973*, as modified by the Protocol of 1978 relating thereto (MARPOL 73/78), *Convention on the Prevention of Marine Pollution by Dumping of Wastes and Other Matter* (London Convention 1972), *International Convention on Oil Pollution Preparedness, Response and Co-operation* (OPRC), 'Nordisk aftale om samarbejde vedrørende bekæmpelse af forurening af havet med olie and andre skadelige stoffer' (Nordic cooperation for keeping oil and chemical pollution in the sea down), *International Convention Relating to Intervention on the High Seas in Cases of Oil Pollution Casualties* (Intervention Convention), Protocol to Amend the *International Convention on Civil Liability for Oil Pollution Damage 1969* as amended in 2000, *International Convention on the Establishment of an International Fund for Compensation for Oil Pollution Damage* (FUND), *Basel Convention on the Control of Transboundary Movements of Hazardous Wastes and their Disposal* (Basel Convention) and *Stockholm Convention on Persistent Organic Pollutants* (Stockholm Convention on POPs).

The *Convention for the Protection of the Marine Environment of the North-East Atlantic* (OSPAR Convention) is designed to prevent pollution of the Northeast Atlantic Ocean, monitor conditions in the sea and conservation of ecosystems and biodiversity. The convention has been signed and ratified by all of the Contracting Parties: Belgium, Denmark, the European Union, Finland, France, Germany, Iceland, Ireland, the Netherlands, Norway, Portugal, Spain, Sweden, the United Kingdom of Great Britain and Northern Ireland, Luxembourg and Switzerland. Iceland fully validated it on 18th July 2001. The most important issues taken care of by the convention is the dumping of hazardous, even radioactive, waste from ships and oil-drilling platforms, also the burning of waste at sea and the treatment of sewage from ships. A convention limited geographically, under the aegis of France, with 16 participating nations was agreed in May 2001, signed in Paris on 22nd September 1992 and validated by Iceland on 25th March 1998. Decisions are made at annual meetings of the OSPAR. The subcommittees are: Head of delegations (HOD), Environmental Assessment and Monitoring committee (ASMO), Trends and Effects of Substances in the Marine Environment (SIME), Biodiversity Committee (BDC) and Point and Diffuse Sources (PDS). Execution in Iceland is the duty of the Environment Agency of Iceland and the MFRI. Contained within the OSPAR Convention are a series of Annexes, which deal with the following specific areas: (a) prevention and elimination of pollution from land-based sources; (b) prevention and elimination of pollution by dumping or incineration; (c) prevention and elimination of pollution from offshore sources; and (d) assessment of the quality of the marine environment. The first Ministerial Meeting of the OSPAR Commission at Sintra, Portugal, in 1998 adopted Annex V to the Convention, to extend the cooperation of the Contracting Parties to cover all human activities that might adversely affect the marine environment of the Northeast Atlantic. In 2000, to fulfil obligations under Annex IV to the OSPAR Convention, the OSPAR Commission published the first comprehensive Quality Status Report on the quality of the marine environment of the OSPAR maritime area.

UNESCO Heritage Sites in Iceland

The Thingvellir UNESCO heritage site is the National Park where the Althing, an open-air assembly representing the whole of Iceland, was established in 930 and continued to meet until 1798. The Althing has deep historical and symbolic associations for the people of Iceland (Figure 1). Thingvellir is a natural wonder on an international scale, with the geologic history and the biosystem of Lake Thingvallavatn forming a unique entity. The Thingvellir area is part of a fissure zone running through Iceland, being situated on the tectonic plate boundaries of the Mid-Atlantic Ridge. Thingvellir National Park was designated by a special law on the protection of the area, passed by the Althing on 7th May 1928. New legislation about the National Park at Thingvellir was passed on Althing on the 1st June 2004 (Parliament of Iceland 2004b). Thingvellir was accepted on the World Heritage list for its cultural values in 2004 at a World Heritage Committee meeting in China (http://www.thingvellir.is/world-heritage.aspx).

The Surtsey UNESCO heritage site, a volcanic island approximately 32 km from the south coast of Iceland, is a new island formed by volcanic eruptions that took place from 1963 to 1967. Surtsey (www.surtsey.is) was inscribed as a natural property on UNESCO's World Heritage List during the 32nd session of the World Heritage Committee in July 2008. One of the ruling factors was that the island '...has been protected since its birth, providing the world with a pristine natural laboratory. Free from human interference, Surtsey has been producing unique long-term information on the colonization process of new land by plant and animal life'. Owing to the scientific research projects that are carried out on Surtsey, the island was declared a nature reserve in 1965 by the Environment and Food Agency. This declaration of preservation was renewed in 1974 with reference to new nature conservation legislation. The declaration was again renewed in January 2006. The renewed declaration now covers the entire volcano, whether above the surface of the sea or underwater, including the craters of Jólnir, Syrtlingur and Surtla, together with a specified area of ocean around the island (Figure 2). The objective of declaring Surtsey a protected area is to ensure that development of the island will be in keeping with the principles of nature itself. The purpose of conservation is to ensure that colonization by plants and animals, biotic succession and the shaping of geological formations will be as natural as possible, and that human disruption will be minimized. The arrival of seeds carried by ocean currents and the appearance of moulds, bacteria and fungi were followed in 1965 by the first vascular plant, of which there were 10 species by the end of the first decade. By 2004, they numbered 60 together with 75 bryophytes, 71 lichens and 24 fungi. Eighty-nine species of birds have been recorded on Surtsey, 57 of which breed elsewhere in Iceland. The island is 141 ha in size and is also home to 335 species of invertebrates (Ólafsson and Ásbjörnsdóttir 2014). The following rules apply in the Surtsey Nature Reserve (information on sanctions for violation of these rules can be found in the nature conservation act from years 1999 and 2013 (60/2013)). (1) It is prohibited to visit Surtsey without a permit from the Surtsey Research Society, which manages all scientific research conducted on the island. The Environment and Food Agency has authorized the Surtsey Research Society to supervise all activity on Surtsey. (2) It is prohibited to disturb anything on Surtsey. In order to build permanent facilities, a permit from the Environment and Food Agency is required. (3) It is prohibited to transfer living animals, plants, seeds or plant parts to the island. (4) It is prohibited to leave any form of waste on or near the island. (5) All use of firearms is prohibited within 2 km from the island.

RAMSAR Sites in Iceland

The fiord Grunnafjörður became a Ramsar site (no. 854) on 24th June 1996 and is 1470 ha in size. In Iceland it is classified as a Nature Reserve. It consists of a river mouth, estuary and sea bay consisting of mudflats rich in invertebrates, supporting mussel banks and salt marsh vegetation. The site is an important staging, wintering and breeding area for large numbers of various species of water birds (Figure 1). Andakíll, Hvanneyri, became a Ramsar Site (no. 2129) on 18th February 2013, classified as a Protected Nature Reserve and Habitat Area in Borgarfjarðarsýsla and is 3086 ha in size. It is a complex wetland located at the estuary of the fjord Borgarfjörður, with two rivers, Hvítá and Andakílsá, and the lake Vatnshamravatn, as well as alluvial floodplains, marshes and managed hayfields. The shallow and rich freshwater lake hosts numerous species of water birds, among them Shelducks (*Tadorna tadorna*) and the White-Tailed Sea Eagle. When the tide is low, extensive mud, sand and gravel bars provide important feeding grounds for water birds. There is a peninsula into the fjord that consists of rows of rocky outcrops and extensive freshwater bogs. Along the river Hvítá there are alluvial plains created by regular floods containing high sediment loads and providing an important resting, feeding and breeding area for many wetland birds and a resting place for the migratory Greenland White-fronted Goose (*Anser albifrons flavirostris*). On the other side of the peninsula, the floodplains of the river Andakílsá include extensive wetlands and marshes. Within the site there is a wetland centre for research and for visitors (Figure 1).

Thjórsárver, became a Ramsar site (no. 460) on 20th March 1990 and is 37 500 ha in size (Figure 1). This nature reserve, the upper part of the Thjórsa

River, consists of tundra meadows dissected by numerous glacial and spring-fed streams; the site includes abundant pools and lakes and extensive marshland dominated by sedges. The site is surrounded by a desert composed of volcanic sand. It is the most important nesting area in Iceland for the Pink-Footed Goose (*Anser brachyrhynchus*), supporting about 10 000 pairs.

Gudlaugstungur, located in Austur-Húnavatnssýsla, the Nature Reserve became Ramsar Site no. 2130 on 18th February 2013. It is 40 160 ha in size. One of the most extensive wetland areas in the central highlands of Iceland, it comprises an extensive mosaic of sedge fens, palsa mires and drier heathland. The site is crossed by small streams and glacial rivers, and small ponds are abundant. The wetland area is surrounded by species-rich dwarf willow scrub heath land with high cover of mosses and lichens, which provide diverse habitats for plants, animals and birds. Guðlaugstungur wetland hosts the largest breeding colony of the Pink-Footed Goose in the world, estimated at 13 600 pairs in 2002 or over 25% of the national and 18–21% of the world population of this species (Figure 1).

A part of the whole area of Lake Mývatn and River Laxá became a Ramsar site (no. 167) on 2nd December 1977 and is 20 000 ha in size. The area has been protected since 1973 by special legislation and is now protected under the terms of Act 97/2004. The protection ensures that all constructional activity and other disturbances of the natural environment is prohibited or subject to approval by the Environment Agency of Iceland. The site supports freshwater marshes, a rich submerged flora, algal communities, *Betula* woodland, bog and moorland. The bottom fauna in Mývatn has a productivity that is 8–30 times greater than that of other lakes at the same latitude. The ecosystem is being intensively studied and the most recent findings indicate that its cyclic populations are shaped by unusual population dynamics. More than 40 species of midges occur along the lake and river; the name of the lake, *Mývatn*, derives from the vast numbers of midges that emerge from the lake, forming impressive mating swarms on its shores. The American blackfly (*Simulium vittatum*) has one of its largest known populations in the world in this area. Since Mývatn is a shallow lake (maximum 4 m, except for the part where siliceous sediments [diatomite] have been extracted), enough sunlight penetrates to sustain rich bottom vegetation, including lake balls that are a rare variety of green algae (*Aegagropila linnaei*). Mývatn and Laxá have one of the world's richest populations of breeding aquatic birds, which owes its presence to the abundant supply of nutrients in the lake, with its abundant primary production and huge quantities of insects and other small creatures, providing rich feeding for birds and fish (Guðni Guðbergsson 2018). In all, 115 species of birds have been recorded in the area, including 28 species of duck, of which 15 species breed in the area regularly. The most common ducks are tufted duck (*Aythya fuligula*), scaup (*Aythya marila*) and wigeon (*Anas penelope*). Other common ducks are Barrow's goldeneye, red-breasted merganser (*Mergus serrator*), common scoter (*Melanitta nigra*) and mallard (*Anas platyrhynchos*). Three of the breeding ducks are rare elsewhere in Iceland. Mývatn along with its immediate surroundings is the only known breeding area for Barrow's goldeneye in Europe, and the harlequin duck (*Histrionicus histrionicus*) has its easternmost breeding area here. In addition to ducks, over 300 pairs of Slavonian grebes (*Podiceps auritius*) breed here. Other water birds include whooper swans (*Cygnus cygnus*), red-necked phalaropes (*Phalaropus lobatus*), great northern divers (*Gavia immer*) and red-throated divers (*Gavia stellata*) (Garðarsson and Einarsson 1991) (Figure 1).

Snæfell and Eyjabakkar, National Park, habitat/species management area and Nature Reserve area in Snæfells- and Eyjabakkar, and Norður-Múlasýsla became Ramsar Site no. 2131 on

18th February 2013, a total of 26 450 ha in size, on the northeastern boundaries of the Vatnajökull icecap, in the outwash plain formed by the river Jökulsá í Fljótsdal, where it flows through the depression to the north of Eyjabakkajökull glacier. Small ponds and lakes, sedge and sandy fens, palsa mires, moist sedge and moss heath are the main habitat types. The site is a key area for moulting of the Pink-Footed Goose during summer. The most common breeding birds of the Eyjabakkar wetlands and surrounding heath lands are Whooper Swan, Golden Plover (*Pluvialis apricaria*), dunlin (*Calidris alpina*) and Snow Bunting (*Plectrophenax nivalis*) (Figure 1).

Sites Submitted on the Tentative List of UNESCO Heritage Site Because of Natural Phenomena

Breiðafjörður Nature Reserve, submitted as a Ramsar site first in 2011 and resubmitted in 2014, after some changes were made to the protection regulations. Breiðafjörður is a large shallow bay located in Western Iceland, with an exceptional combination of natural features and cultural and historical heritage. It is approximately 50 km wide and 125 km long, encircled by mountains, including the volcano Snæfellsjökull on the Snæfellsnes peninsula on the south side and the Western Fjords peninsula to the north (Figure 1). The coast is a narrow strip interspersed with farms and small urban areas. The spectacular land- and seascape consists of shallow bays, small fjords and inlets, with the inner part consisting of extensive intertidal areas dotted with about 3000 islands, islets and rocks. The area contains about half of Iceland's intertidal area and over one-third of its coastline. Tides of six metres, unique for Iceland, contribute to the diverse land- and seascapes, with several geothermal sites, some visible only at low tide. The area has diverse flora and fauna with substantial proportions of the Icelandic population of several bird and mammal species, and an intertidal zone high in biodiversity and productivity with extensive algal 'forests' and other important habitats for invertebrates and fish, essential to the food chain. The area supports 230 recorded species of vascular plants and around 50 regular breeding bird species. It is the main habitat for the white-tailed eagle in Iceland and important for the eiderduck. There are important habitats of red listed species, such as the white-tailed eagle and the grey-phalarope (*Phalaropus fulicarius*). The two Icelandic seal species, the harbour seal and the grey seal, have their haul-outs on the islands and rocks (Figure 1). The area is an internationally important staging site for the High-Arctic Brent goose (*Branta benicla*) and knot (*Calidris canutus*). The natural and cultural heritage of the area is protected under the terms of the Breiðafjörður Conservation Act (54/1995). Cultural monuments are also protected under the terms of the National Cultural Heritage Act (107/2001).

Mývatn and Laxá in the RAMSAR area was submitted on the tentative list of UNESCO heritage sites in the year 2011, because of natural phenomena.

Thingvellir National Park is located on the northern shore of Lake Thingvallavatn, about 240 km^2 in size and its protection is based on the Thingvellir Conservation Act dating back to 1928. The national park was enlarged and the conservation status improved through better conservation and management with new legislation in 2004 by Act 47/2004 on Thingvellir National Park. The old national park, part of the current national park, was inscribed on the World Heritage List in 2004 as a cultural landscape (Figure 1). Birch woodland is characteristic of the Thingvellir area, indicated by the original name of the area in Icelandic: Bláskógar (literally 'Blue Woods'). In the National Park, 172 species of higher plants have been found or about 40% of the Icelandic flora. Birch, dwarf birch and willow, plants of the heath family, transform the appearance of Thingvellir in autumn. Thingvallavatn is the largest natural lake in Iceland with a surface area of approximately 84 km^2, mean depth of 34 m and maximum depth of 114 m and ca. 3 km^3 in volume. The lake is crystal clear, oligotrophic in nature and with nitrogen as a limiting factor for primary production. The lake outlet, River Efra-Sog, is one of Europe's largest spring-fed rivers, flushing about 100 tons of water every second. The retention time of water in the lake is about one year. The great diversity of life in Thingvallavatn can be traced back to these processes, as algae and plants, food for invertebrates, make use of the abundant nutrients in the water. The lake is particularly fertile and rich in vegetation, despite the very cold temperatures. A third of the bottom area down to a depth of 10 m is covered by epiphytic diatoms whereas between 10 and 20 m depth there is a zone of up to 50 cm and dense stands of charophytes. Thingvallavatn is abundant in fish, and three of the five species of freshwater fish found in Iceland, brown trout, Arctic char and three-spine stickleback (*Gasterosteus aquleatus*) live in the lake. The presence of four Arctic charr morphs in the lake, representing one of the most spectacular examples of resource polymorphism among fish in the Subarctic, gives the lake a special status. Recent studies on sticklebacks also show that two different morphs of this species exist in the lake. Generally, 52 bird species live by the lake while 30 others come and go. The most notable bird is the great northern diver, which nests in a few places by the lake (Jónasson and Hersteinsson 2002).

Vatnajökull National Park, Iceland, is situated in the eastern part of the country and stretches coast to coast from south to north. It is the largest national park in Europe, covering a total area of 12 850 km^2 or almost 13% of Iceland. Key features are Vatnajökull, the largest ice cap by volume in Europe, and several highly active volcanic systems within and outside of the ice cap. The Vatnajökull ice cap covers roughly two-thirds of the National Park and large areas surrounding the glacier have been protected by national legislation for over

35 years. The interplay of ice and fire has created in one place a huge range of volcanic, geothermal and geomorphologic features. The National Park was established and protected by regulation no. 608/2008 based on the Vatnajökull National Park Act (60/2007). It entails two older national parks, Skaftafell National Park and Jökulsárgljúfur National Park. Its cultural heritage is protected by the National Heritage Act (107/2001). Within Vatnajökull National Park there are vast areas of uninhabited, pristine land. The park covers lowland as well as highland areas, the highest peak in Iceland and complete systems of features created by volcanic activity, glacial activity or the interaction between the two, such as long hyaloclastite ridges and single mountains, extensive lava fields, geothermal areas, glacial rivers, canyons and *sandur* (large sandy sediment areas of glacial rivers).

The Torfajökull Volcanic System/Fjallabak Nature Reserve and geothermal pool Landmannalaugar cover an area of approximately 600 km^2 of rhyolite massif at an altitude of 600–1200 m above sea level in the south-central Icelandic highlands. The conservation value of the area is indisputable and a part of the Torfajökull area, the Fjallabak Nature Reserve (446 km^2), is a popular place for tourism and hiking. A part of the Torfajökull area is the Fjallabak Nature Reserve and this has been protected under the Nature Conservation Act since 1979. The landscape is spectacular, mountainous, screes are abundant, and the effects of volcanic activity are dominant. Craters, lava and hyaloclastite characterize the northern part of the area, but light-coloured rhyolite dominates the Torfajökull caldera to the south. The high-temperature geothermal field associated with Torfajökull is the largest and most powerful in the country and the terrain inside the caldera is typified by immense geothermal activity. Fumaroles and hot springs are widespread and steam plumes are visible in many places. These conditions create different habitats for the biota, which is diverse, especially when considering the high elevation. Diverse and unique thermophilic bacteria and archaea are found in the geothermal area at Torfajökull. The weather, soil and animal life determine the extent of the vegetation; however, because of the cold climate in the Nature Reserve, the vegetation's growing period is only about two months every year and the formation of soil is very slow. The soil is deficient in fully rotted and weathered minerals and is therefore rough and incoherent; wind and water transport are easy. Sandstorms, common in large parts of the area, as well as volcanic eruptions, cover the Nature Reserve with lava and ash. If all these conditions are borne in mind, together with the region being heavily grazed over the years, it does not come as a surprise that vegetation is scarce in the Nature Reserve, and the largest and greenest vegetated areas are close to rivers and lakes. The acidic rhyolite bedrock is largely barren, but the hyaloclastite formations are often clothed in moss from top to bottom. About 150 types of flowering plants, ferns and allies have been identified. Least willow (*Salix herbacea*) is common on dry sands and lava, and cotton grass (*Eriophorum scheuchzeri*) in marshes. Lowland vegetation is found next to the geothermal area at Landmannalaugar with common sedge widespread and marsh cinquefoil pleasing to the eye. The Icelandic Government agreed in 2011 to apply for a UNESCO Heritage site for this area around the glacier Torfajökull.

Climate Change Strategy, Long-Term Vision 2007–2050

This Strategy sets forth a long-term vision for the reduction of net emissions of greenhouse gases by 50–75% by the year 2050, using the 1990 emissions figures as a baseline. Emphasis is placed on reducing net emissions by the most economical means possible, including the introduction of new technology, economic measures, carbon sequestration in vegetation and soil, and financing of measures adopted abroad (Ministry for the

Environment 2007). Iceland's Fourth National Communication on Climate Change under the UN Framework Convention on Climate Change and Iceland's Report on Demonstrable Progress under the Kyoto Protocol was released in 2006 (Ministry for the Environment 2006) and its national strategy of sustainable development statistical indicators was also released in the year 2006. The publication (2002) entitled *Welfare for the Future* had the aim to make key facts on burning issues accessible and comprehensible. When examined together, these statistical indicators should give some idea of the state of the environment, the pressures on nature and the governmental response to these (Ministry for the Environment 2006b). More recent developments in the climate change issues, which the Icelandic Government has to address, were put forward by Norwegian scientists and one of an Icelandic origin, Professor Rögnvaldur Hannesson, to the Prime Minister of Norway, Erna Solberg (https://www.klimarealistene.com/2019/04/05/apent-brev-til-statsminister-erna-solberg).

Future Trends in Conservation and Protection of Biodiversity in the Icelandic Environment

A new version of the conservation and protection of wild animals (64/1994) is lying in the paperpile to be taken care of by the Icelandic Parliament – it had been waiting there for years. There were several issues unresolved there and one of special interest for the conservation discussion in Iceland: the marine mammals, whales and seals. Whales are conserved in the Icelandic marine environment by special laws, which allow a catch of whales in accordance with international maritime laws and rules and regulations of IWC, of which Iceland is an active member. Minke and fin whales are caught in Icelandic waters by Icelandic whalers. This has been an international issue and a source of constant disputes between the Icelandic

Government and the Minister of Foreign Affairs in the United States of America (USA). The USA is threatening boycotts of Icelandic import goods to the States. This boycott has, however, not been realized, but now there is the issue of a bycatch of marine mammals in fishing gear. Seals do not have special protection as those of the whales, but they are not outside laws and jurisdiction in Iceland. Several old laws about hunting and use of land by farmers include seals as an important subsidiary, but seals are unprotected in estuaries of salmon and trout rivers, and can be pursued there to conserve the fish, under the Freshwater Fisheries Acts (29/1937 and 61/2006). This could now be about to end as the Icelandic Parliament has legislated an amendment to act 61/2006, paragraph 11, which makes it possible for the Minister of Fisheries to protect seals from harassment and hunting, on the MFRI advice. Opponents to this protection of seals are people from the fisheries and fish merchant organizations in Iceland, because seals are the final host for sealworm, whose larvae infest commercial fish as well as non-commercial fish species (McClelland 2002). Many farmers too want to keep seals and seal hunting as an important asset.

Another issue relating to the new version of the act on protection, conservation and hunting of wild animals and farmers in Iceland is the increased protection of the arctic fox in Iceland spelled out there. Arctic foxes are seen by farmers as vermin, causing damage especially to eider duck rookeries, where farmers can collect eiderdown from the birds' nests, providing a good subsidiary income for many farmers in Iceland (Jónsson 2001). A small portion of the arctic fox population in Iceland is predatory and kills lambs in the mountains, when they are grazing there over the summer months. Many farmers look upon arctic foxes as enemies to all birdlife and want to eradicate it, on their land at least. This has been constantly argued by the organization of Icelandic farmers to governmental

officials, which take care of the payment farmers get for each foxtail they turn in to sheriffs. The situation in one area in the northwestern part of Iceland, the Hornstrandir Nature Reserve, has been criticized by neighbouring farmers, for all hunting of foxes is illegal and until recently the fox population there had been increasing. However, in the last arctic fox population survey there shows that the stock had declined, reproduction was low and the condition of the animals was bad (Unnsteinsdóttir unpublished). Nature as it seems has taken over and foxes are now suffering from the food shortage experienced by their most important prey, the sea-birds nesting in the cliffs of this area, which has experienced a collapse in reproduction due to recruitment failure of the lesser sand eel stock (Lilliendahl et al. 2013). Harbour seals have also been observed to be in a bad condition in this north-western area (Hauksson et al. unpublished). Now an interesting question has emerged, how can wildlife be protected or conserved from nature itself? Sand eel seems to be the keystone species in Icelandic waters, what has caused its collapse? Did a volcanic eruption with following flooding of the coast with glacial water spoil its spawning grounds on the south coast of Iceland? Or did the sand eel stock, which is based on short-lived fish and few year-classes to sustain it, collapse in the same way as the capelin (*Mallotus villosus*) stock did previously? This is also a short-lived fish with only a few year-classes, due to environmental changes (Jakobsson 1992; Vilhjálmsson 1994). Why this natural phenomenon happened no-one yet knows. Probably the sand eel stock will rise again. Recruitment of Arctic tern (*Sterna paradisaea*) also shows failures, at least in some coastal areas, probably due to lesser sand eel scarcity, but now it seems that some arctic tern rookeries are doing better, or is it the fate of the lesser sand eel stock going to be the same as the fate of the Icelandic herring stock, the spring spawning part? In the Surtsey eruption it seems the spawning area of this part of the herring population was destroyed and this herring has never recovered (Jakob Jakobsson personal communication), or can we blame this on climate change? Another case worth considering, as mentioned before, is the changes in the distribution of mackerel in the Norwegian Sea and Icelandic and East Greenlandic waters. Two other major players in this contest are the blue whiting and the herring. It will be interesting to follow its further development in the North Atlantic waters.

The shrinkage of glaciers (Björnsson 2009) uncovers a new land which can be colonized by plants and animals. Glacial river deltas can be very productive, if they are not flooded for a prolonged period. Density of the vegetation on Skeiðarársandur (glacial river moraines and clay), southeast Iceland, has increased enormously in recent years (Thórhallsdóttir unpubl.). The increasing cover and distribution of birch forests in Iceland can also probably be 'blamed' on climate change, but is this bad? The moral being that we cannot protect or conserve nature to a state of our liking, if the overall natural processes, colonization and succession are not going in that direction. Processes, as predation and competition, are not on hold even if climate change is occurring. The studies of natural processes may be too limited to detect whether the cause is climate change or other factors.

On the increase in species richness on dry land, which the increase in arthropod terrestrial fauna is evident, the author can be quite positive. I am enjoying the beautiful song of blackbirds in my garden in Reykjavík, which just a few years ago started nesting there and in adjacent gardens. However, there is a problem; some of the invaders are invasive species doing harm to the ecosystems that they enter (Baldursson 2014).

One case study by Gunnarsson and Hauksson (2009) has studied the colonization and succession of marine algae and invertebrates on the rocky bottom around Surtsey for years with underwater photographic methods. The succession has not gone in the direction towards climax state, which is found in the littoral and sub-littoral of neighbouring islands in the Vestmannejyar archipelago that for some years we have been waiting for! What has caused this is not climate change, and the most likely explanation is the constant removal of pieces of the shore of Surtsey by heavy swells, making a constantly new substrate for the algae and invertebrates to colonize, and by this keeping the succession at an earlier stage than the climax.

Another case, illustrating the variability of natural processes, the air temperature and temperature of ocean surface waters are increasing in a linear relationship due to climax change, with increasing CO_2 in the air and water. That is the theory, but this is not reflected in the marine ecosystem around Iceland, where great climate variability has been the case observed over the last 100 years (Astthorsson and Vilhjalmsson 2002; Björnsson et al. 2018). The ocean is no pond. Frontal zones in the oceans play a decisive role in how and why all kinds of variability occur in the sea spatially. In Iceland there was a warm period 1925–1945, a cold period 1965–1971 and another warm period 1996 to now, and so there is probably going to be another cold period soon (Pall Bergthorsson unpublished). This had profound influences on the ecosystem in Icelandic waters, hardly to be related simply to climate change. In Iceland and surrounding waters, the effects of climate change seem not to be linear and simple, but rather non-linear, variable and complex.

Concluding Remarks

Iceland has come a long way in nature conservation since the end of the Second World War. It has adopted many international and regional treaties on conservation, biodiversity and sustainable use of natural resources. These treaties can be a financial burden for a small country with a low governmental budget and a small economic system. It helps that Iceland has many things to gain from not spoiling the environment. As a fish-producing country, we want to keep the ocean clean and we want to keep our wilderness intact for the increasing tourism. The most controversial issue is energy production and its effect on the natural environment spatially. We need to make dams and windmills for producing electric power and to construct structures for harnessing geo-thermal energy, for industrial and domestic use, including the increasing use of electricity in private transportation. Energy-production in Iceland is 'green', and all the energy Icelanders produce for the international industry, which would otherwise be produced elsewhere by burning oil and coal, makes the world a greener place. This has not, in my opinion, always been realized by the international forum, talking energy issues of the world and putting up restrictions internationally, which Icelanders are also supposed to abide by. Indigenous whaling should not be a big issue internationally, only a few minke and fin whales are taken annually, only as part of a surplus, under a strict quota set by the Icelandic Government in accordance with the rules of the IWC. We are also working hard to solve the seabird and marine mammal bycatch issue in the fisheries.

Acknowledgements

In this chapter many references are made to Icelandic laws, which are in Icelandic of course and can be found in the Icelandic laws collection made available on the website of the Icelandic parliament (http://www.alþingi.is/lagasafn). They can by addressed by number and year system used throughout in the text NO/YEAR. Also available are very limited translations into English (http://www.loc.gov/law/help/guide/nations/iceland.php#constitution). Google translates Icelandic law texts very poorly(!), so it is not recommended. In the References the author has tried to translate into English the main issues that each Icelandic law is about.

Thanks for language help goes to the editors of the book on *North Atlantic Island Biota: Aspects of the Past, Choices for the Future*.

The map of protected areas in Iceland is by courtesy of the Environment Agency in Iceland and the map of Surtsey protected area is by courtesy of the INH. The websites of Icelandic Institutions and Ministries were very helpful in giving information, even in English.

The views and opinions expressed in this paper are the author's own. He is not the spokesman for environmental issues of the institution where he worked and he has now retired!

Note

1 John the Learned (1574–1658).

References

Andrews, A.J., Christiansen, J.S., Bhat, S. et al. (2019). Boreal marine fauna from the Barents Sea disperse to Arctic Northeast Greenland. *Scientific Report* 9: 5799–5807.

Anon (2014). New Coral Reefs Discovered in Iceland. Reykjavík: Iceland Review on Line.

Astthorsson, O. and Vilhjalmsson, H. (2002). Iceland shelf LME: decadal assessment and resource sustainability. In: Large Marine Ecosystems of the North Atlantic. Changing States and Sustainability (eds. K. Sherman and H. Skjoldal), 219–243. Amsterdam: Elsevier Science.

Astthorsson, O., Gislason, A., and Jonsson, S. (2007). Climate variability and the Icelandic marine ecosystem. *Deep-Sea Research II* 54: 2456–2477.

Bachiller, E., Skaret, G., Nöttestad, L., and Slotte, A. (2015a). Seasonal Differences in the Diet of Mackerel, Herring and Blue Whiting in the Norwegian Sea. Reykjavík: Marine Research Institute in Reykjavík.

Bachiller, E., Skaret, G., Langöy, H., and Stenevik, E. (2015b). Mackerel Predation on Herring Larvae during Summer Feeding in the Norwegian Sea. Reykjavík: Marine Research Institute in Reykjavík.

Baldursson, S. (2014). *Lífríki Íslands. Vistkerfi lands og sjávar* [the Biota of Iceland. Terrestrial and Marine Ecosystems], 1e. Reykjavík: Bókaútgáfan Opna og Forlagið.

Björnsson, H. (2009). *Jöklar á Íslandi* [Glaciers of Iceland], 1ste. Reykjavík: Bókaútgáfan Opna.

Björnsson, H., Sigurðsson, B.D., Davíðsdóttir, B., Ólafsson, J., Ástþórsson, Ó.S., Ólafsdóttir, S., Baldursson, T. & Jónsson, T. 2018. Loftslagsbreytingar og áhrif þeirra á Íslandi – Skýrsla vísindanefndar um loftslagsbreytingar (Climate change and its effect in Iceland – Report from a scientific committee). Veðurstofa Íslands (The Meteorologic Office of Iceland), Reykjavík.

Elmhagen, B., Hersteinsson, P., Norén, K. et al. (2014). From breeding pairs to fox towns: the social organisation of arctic fox populations with stable and fluctuating availability of food. *Polar Biology* 37: 111–122.

Frederiksen, M., Furness, R., and Wanless, S. (2007). Regional variation in the role of bottom-up and top-down processes in controlling sandeel abundance in the North Sea. *Marine Ecology Progress Series* 337: 279–286.

Garðarsson, A. and Einarsson, Á. (1991). *Náttúra Mývatns* [Lake Myvatn], 1ste. Reykjavík: HÍN.

Guðbergsson, G. (2018). Silungurinn í Mývatni – Veiðinýting Og Stofnsveiflur 1986–2016. *Náttúrufræðingurinn* 88: 85–102.

Guðmundsson, B. (2001). *Bréf Vestur-Íslendinga I* (Letters from Icelanders Migrating to North America). Reykjavík: Mál og menning.

Gunnarsson, K. and Hauksson, E. (2009). Succession and benthic community development in the sublittoral zone at the recent volcanic island. *Surtsey Research* 12: 161–166.

Guttormsson, H. (1974). *Vistkreppa eða náttúruvernd* (Ecocrisis or Conservation of Nature). Reykjavík: Mál menning.

Hallgrímsson, H. (2013). Náttúrufræðingurinn Jón lærði (The naturalist John the learned). In: Í spor Jóns lærða (ed. H. Guttormsson), 83–104. Reykjavík: Hið íslenska bókmenntafélag.

Halsey, L., Matthews, P.G.D., Rezende, E.L. et al. (2015). The interactions between temperature and activity levels in driving metabolic rate: theory, with empirical validation from contrasting ectotherms. *Oecologia* 177: 1117–1129.

Haraldsson, Þ. and Hersteinsson, P. (2004). Hvítabjörn [Polar bear]. In: Islensk spendýr (ed. P. Hersteinsson), 344. Reykjavík: Vaka – Helgafell.

Hátún, H., Lohman, K., Matei, D. et al. (2016). An inflated subpolar gyre blows life toward the northeastern Atlantic. *Progress in Oceanography* 147: 49–66.

Holst, J. (2015). Poleward Shift of the Pelagic Complex, an Effect of Overgrazing of the Pelagic Ecosystem? An Alternative Hypothesis to the Temperature Hypothesis. Reykjavík: Marine Research Institute in Reykjavík.

INH (1996). Red List of Threatened Species in Iceland, Red List 1, Plants. Garðabær.

INH (2000). Red List of Threatened Species in Iceland, Red List 2, Birds. Garðabær.

Institute of the environment [IIE] (2007). Vernd og endurheimt íslenskra birkiskóga. Skýrsla og tillögur nefndar (Protection of and increasing the cover of birch forests in Iceland. Report and recommendations). Umhverfisráðuneytið mars 2007. Reykjavík.

Institute of the environment [IIE] (2015). *Veiðidagbók* (Hunting diary for year 2015), Reykjavík.

Jakobsson, J. (1992). Recent variability in the fisheries of the North Atlantic. *ICES Marine Science Symposium* 195: 291–315.

Jónasson, P. and Hersteinsson, P. (2002). *Þingvallavatn, undraheimur í mótun* (Lake Thingvallavatn). Reykjavík: Mál og menning.

Jónsson, J. (2001). Hættur og vanhöld (Danger and bad conditions experienced by eiderducks). In: Æðarfugl og æðarrækt á Íslandi (ed. J. Jónsson), 149–165. Mál og mynd: Reykjavík.

Kausrud, K., Mysterud, A., Steen, H. et al. (2008). Linking climate change to lemming cycles. *Nature* 456: 93–97.

Lilliendahl, K., Hansen, E.S., Bogason, V. et al. (2013). Viðkomubrestur lunda og sandsílis við Vestmannaeyjar (Recruitment failure of puffins and sand eels off Westmann Isles). *Náttúrufræðingurinn* 83: 65–79.

Long, E. and Finke, D. (2015). Predators indirectly reduce the prevalence of an insect-vectored plant pathogen independent of predator diversity. *Oecologia* 177: 1067–1074.

Marcogliese, D. (2001). Implications of climate change for parasitism of animals in the aquatic environment. *Canadian Journal of Zoology* 79: 1331–1352.

McClelland, G. (2002). The trouble with sealworm (*Pseudoterranova decipiens* species complex, Nematoda): a review. *Parasitology* 124: 183–203.

Ministry for the environment (2006a). Iceland's fourth national communication on climate change. Under the United Nations framework convention on climate change and Iceland's report on demonstrable progress under the Kyoto protocol, Reykjavik.

Ministry for the environment (2006b). Iceland's National Programme of action for the protection of the marine environment from land-based activities, Reykjavik.

Ministry for the environment (2006c). Welfare for the future. Iceland's national strategy for sustainable development. Statistical indicators 2006, Reykjavik.

Ministry for the environment (2007). *Iceland's Climate Change Strategy*, Reykjavik.

Ministry of Fisheries 2004. Friðun viðkvæmra hafsvæða við Ísland (Protection of vulnerable underwater areas off Iceland), Reykjavik.

Nash, R. and Geffen, A. (2015). The Future in Store for Autumn-Spawning Herring: From the Frying-Pan into the Fire? Reykjavík: Marine Research Institute in Reykjavik.

Olafsdottir, A., Slotte, A., Jacobsen, J.A. et al. (2016). Changes in weight-at-length and size-at-age of mature Northeast Atlantic mackerel (*Scomber scombrus*) from 1984 to 2013: effects of mackerel stock size, herring stock size. *ICES Journal of Marine Science* 73: 1255–1265.

Ólafsson, E. and Ásbjörnsdóttir, L. (2014). *Surtsey í sjónmáli* (he Island of Surtsey), 1ste. Reykjavík: Edda.

Parliament of Iceland (1986). Lög um varnir gegn mengun sjávar (Legislation about protecting the sea against pollution). Reykjavík.

Parliament of Iceland (1988). Lög um eiturefni og hættuleg efni (Legislation about poisonous and dangerous chemicals). Reykjavík.

Parliament of Iceland (1996). Lög um erfðabreyttar lífverur (Legislation about genetically modified organisms). Reykjavík.

Parliament of Iceland (2004a). Lög um verndun Mývatns og Laxár í Suður-Thingeyjarsýslu (Legislation about conservation of lake Myvatn and river Laxa). Reykjavík.

Parliament of Iceland (2004b). Lög um Thjóðgarðinn á THingvöllum (Legislation about the National Park of Thingvellir). Reykjavík.

Parliament of Iceland (2005). Lög um verndun Þingvallavatns og vatnasviðs þess (Legislation about conservation of lake Thingvallavatn and adjacent waters). Reykjavík.

Parliament of Iceland (2006a). Lög um stjórn fiskveiða (Legislation about Icelandic marine fisheries). Reykjavík.

Parliament of Iceland (2006b). Lög um lax-og silungsveiði (Legislation about freshwater fisheries). Reykjavík.

Parliament of Iceland (2007). Lög um Vatnajökulsþjóðgarð (Legislation about the National Park of the glacier Vatnajökull). Reykjavík.

Parliament of Iceland (2008a). Lög um fiskeldi (Legislation on aquaculture). Reykjavík.

Parliament of Iceland (2008b). Lög um Fiskræktarsjóð (Legislation about the fish culture fund). Reykjavík.

Parliament of Iceland (2011a). Lög um skeldýrarækt (Legislation about culturing molluscs). Reykjavik.

Parliament of Iceland (2011b). Lög um vatnamál (The water act). Reykjavik.

Parliament of Iceland (2013a). Lög um náttúruvernd (Legislation about nature conservation). Reykjavík.

Parliament of Iceland (2013b). Efnalög (The chemical act). Reykjavík.

Petersen, Æ. (1995). Brot úr sögu geirfuglsins [on the history of the great auk]. *Náttúrufræðingurinn* 65: 53–66.

Rafnsson, S. (1984). Búfé og byggð við lok Skaftárelda og Móðuharðinda (Lifestock and inhabitants after the Laki eruption). In: Skaftáreldar 1783–1784 (eds. G. Gunnlaugsson et al.), 163–178. Reykjavík: Mál og menning.

Ragnarsson, S. Á., Burgos, J. M., & Ólafsdóttir, S. H. (2018). Overview of the contribution of the Marine and Freshwater Research Institute to the Coral fish project (2008–2012). HV 2018–38.

Scheffer, M., Carpenter, S., Foley, J.A. et al. (2001). Catastrophic shifts in ecosystems. *Nature* 413: 591–596.

Schimel, D. and Keller, M. (2015). Big questions, big science: meeting the challenges of global ecology. *Oecologia* 177: 925–934.

Sigfússon, A. (2015). Icelandic geese – monitoring breeding success. Stykkishólmur, Conference of the Icelandic Ecological Society 2015.

Sigurjónsdóttir, H. (2014). The seashore – a place to experience biodiversity. *Náttúrufræðingurinn* 84: 141–149.

Skarphéðinsson, Ö. (1996). *Urriðadans* (The Giant Trout). Reykjavík: Mál og menning.

Steingrímsson, S. and Einarsson, S. (2004). *Kóralsvæði á Íslandsmiðum. Mat á ástandi og tillaga um aðgerðir til verndar þeim* (Deep Sea Corals in Icelandic Waters, Conditions and Conservation). Reykjavík: MRI.

Sternberg, M. and Yakir, D. (2015). Coordinated approaches for studying long-term ecosystem responses to global change. *Oecologia* 177: 921–924.

Thórðarson, Þ. (1990). *Skaftáreldar 1783–1785* (The Laki Eruptions 1783–1785). Reykjavík: University of Iceland.

Thorgilsson, A. (1968). *Islendingabók Landnámabók* (The Colonization of Iceland). Reykjavík: Hið íslenska fornritafélag.

Thoroddsen, Þ. (1892). *Landfræðisaga Íslands. Hugmyndir manna um Ísland, náttúruskoðun þess og rannsóknir, fyrr og síðar* (Geographic History of Iceland), 1ste. Reykjavík: Hið íslenska bókmenntafélag.

Thorsteinsson, K. (1948). *Úr bygðum Borgarfjarðar II* (Historical accounts from the land of Borgarfiord, West-iceland). Reykjavík: s.n.

Valdimarsson, H. (2015). Hydrographic Variability in Icelandic Waters in the Last Decades. Reykjavik: Marine Research Institute of Iceland.

Vikingsson, G., Elvarsson, B.Þ., Ólafsdóttir, D. et al. (2014). Recent changes in the diet composition of common minke whales (*Balaenoptera acutorostrata*) in Icelandic waters. A consequence of climate change? *Marine Biology Research* 10: 138–152.

Vilhjálmsson, H. (1994). The Icelandic capelin stock. Capelin *Mallotus villosus* (Müller) in Iceland – Greenland – Jan Mayen area. *Rit Fiskideildar* 13: 1–281.

15

The Natural Environment and Its Biodiversity in Greenland During the Present Climate Change

Ib Johnsen and Henning Heide-Jørgensen

Department of Biology, University of Copenhagen, Copenhagen, Denmark

Introduction

Greenland is, as the rest of the world, experiencing the effects of man-induced climate change, closely related to the massive human emissions of carbon dioxide during the past century. The implications are dramatic for Greenland, as outlined by Briner et al. (2020). This chapter deals with the background to, and some of the present main observations of the biological response related to the increasing greenhouse effect and stratospheric ozone depletion. The emphasis is on terrestrial plant ecology.

The recent IPCC report (Larsen et al. 2014) presents the following statements concerning climate change in the Arctic and Antarctic, appending levels of confidence in each statement:

> The impacts of climate change, and the adaptations to it, exhibit strong spatial heterogeneity in the Polar Regions because of the high diversity of social systems, biophysical regions, and associated drivers of change (high confidence). For example, the tree line has moved northward and upward in many, but not all, Arctic areas

(high confidence) and tall shrubs and grasses have increased their distribution significantly in many places (very high confidence).

Climate change is affecting terrestrial and freshwater ecosystems in some areas of Antarctica and the Arctic. This is due to ecological effects resulting from reductions in the duration and extent of ice and snow cover and enhanced permafrost thaw (very high confidence), and through changes in the precipitation–evaporation balance (medium confidence).

Shifts in the timing and magnitude of seasonal biomass production could disrupt matched phenologies in the food webs, leading to decreased survival of dependent species (medium confidence). If the timing no longer matches the primary and secondary production to the timing of spawning or egg release, survival is likely to decrease, with cascading implications to higher trophic levels. This impact would be exacerbated if shifts in timing occur rapidly (medium confidence). Climate change will increase the vulnerability of terrestrial ecosystems to invasions by non-indigenous species, the majority likely to

Biogeography in the Sub-Arctic: The Past and Future of North Atlantic Biota, First Edition.
Edited by Eva Panagiotakopulu and Jon P. Sadler.

arrive through direct human assistance (high confidence).

Ecosystems in Greenland are under massive pressure during these years of climate change due to increasing greenhouse effect and depletion of the stratospheric ozone layer.

Greenland (Figure 1, see Plate section) is the largest island in the world, with an area of 2 184 000 km². However, ice covers more than 77% of this area, which reaches a maximum height of 3238 m ASL (above sea level), and most of the ice sheet is at an elevation greater than 2000 m. This ice sheet has naturally a tremendous impact on the climate of the ice-free coastal zone of the island. The ice sheet also acts as a migration barrier to both plants and animals, not only

Figure 1 Map of Greenland with ice cap borderline shown and name of localities mentioned in the chapter. (See colour plate section for colour representation of this figure.)

cross-country, but also along the coastal zone, since the ice reaches the sea over long stretches of coastline in several places. The south to north distance of 2670 km from Kap Farvel to Oodaap Qeqertaa (near Kap Morris Jesup) extends from 59°47′N to 83°40′N, the most northern land point on Earth. From east to west, Greenland extends over 1000–1200 km in the central part of the country. The highest mountain is Gunnbjørn Fjeld, 3693 m, in East Greenland.

Because of the vast extent of the country, there is a gradual change from a subarctic climate in the south to a high arctic climate in the north. Despite the lesser extent of the ice-free coastal zone, limited to a maximum of 200 km, a gradient from an oceanic climate near the coast to a more continental climate near the ice sheet also exists. The prevailing scenarios for global climate change may strongly, and at probably unprecedented rates, alter the present climatic conditions in Greenland in several directions, causing both structural changes to ecosystems and changes in biodiversity.

The extent of sea ice and heat transport by sea currents are also important factors for establishing climatic gradients in Greenland. As a mountain-rich country, local climate is highly variable. General information on geology, topography, climate, and on plant and animal distribution and ecology are published in Danish in Nørrevang and Lundø (1981) and Böcher (2001); in Greenlandic, Danish and English in Berthelsen et al. (1990) and Bernes (1996). Böcher (1975) further describes the vegetation. Similar information in English, including regional descriptions and references for further reading, are found in Böcher and Petersen (1997), Born and Böcher (2000) and Jensen and Christensen (2003). Vibe (1967) published a comprehensive study of animal life in relation to climatic fluctuations.

Four main phytogeographical elements are present in Greenland today: circumpolar, North American, Eurasian and amphi-atlantic

(Bay 1993). The main immigration route for the High Arctic element of the first two groups is across the Nares Strait, as it has been for animals and humans (Böcher 1975; Fredskild 1973; Funder 1987; Heide-Jørgensen and Johnsen 1997). There are about 45 km between Inglefield Land and Ellesmere Island and about 20 km across Robeson Channel, which birds, large terrestrial mammals and even some wind-dispersed seeds easily cross. An example of recent immigration via this route is *Pedicularis albolabiata*, which most likely was transported to its only known Greenlandic locations at Qaanaaq from Ellesmere Island by the lesser snow goose (Bay 1993; Heide-Jørgensen and Johnsen 1997). Likely examples of early immigrants via the Nares Strait route are *Salix arctica* and *Cassiope tetragona*, which according to pollen records (Fredskild 1985), had arrived at Inglefield Land before 7200 BP and then spread along the coast. Low Arctic North American and some amphi-atlantic species most likely immigrated across the broader Davis Strait from Labrador, while other amphi-Atlantic and Eurasian species immigrated via Iceland with birds or, in a few cases, as floating seeds. An example of a recent immigration of this sort is *Trientalis europaea*, which was first observed in Greenland north east of Narsaq, in the floristically well investigated South Greenland (Bay 1993).

Recent Climate – The Last Hundred Years

Putnins (1970) provides a comprehensive treatment of the general climate of Greenland and general information on the recent climate is also available in Vibe (1967), Danks (1981), Fristrup (1981), Ohmura (1987), Ohmura and Reeh (1991), Berthelsen et al. (1990), Nielsen and Rasmussen (1993), Chernov (1995) and Böcher and Petersen (1997). Regional surveys are available for the Kangerlussuaq Sisimiut

(Sdr. Strømfjord Holsteinsborg) area (Hasholt and Søgaard 1978) and for Jameson Land (Thingvad and Kern-Hansen 1989). Automatic monitoring of climate parameters has been running at the scientific stations at Qeqertarsuaq (Disko) since 1992 and at Zackenberg since 1995. The ZERO programme at Zackenberg is a full-scale monitoring of both climatic and biological parameters (Meltofte and Thing 1996, 1997). The Danish Meteorological Institute (DMI) publishes yearly reports on the climate of Greenland and runs a number of automatic climate stations, as well as some manual (synoptic) stations. The selection of stations secured the best comparability between the climate data. Systematic meteorological observations began in Greenland in 1873, but uninterrupted records that were made far back exist for only a few stations like Nuuk (Godthåb).

Climate characterization takes place at different levels. The general climate of Greenland as a region is based on data suitable for synoptic interpretation. Major vegetation features, like the tree line, extent of deserts, etc. often relate well to such large-scale climate descriptions. Local climate (mesoclimate) is local variations superimposed on the regional pattern (Danks 1981). Such variations can greatly modify conditions for life, as defined by the general/regional climate, from one valley to the next, depending on effects related to topography.

Most of Greenland is located within the arctic climate zone (Fristrup 1981; Putnins 1970). According to the definition of Arctic Climate, the mean temperature is below 10 °C for July, the warmest month. The low July temperature is associated with a short growing season and the two factors together prevent the development of true forests in the arctic climate zone. Winter temperature is not a factor in delimiting arctic climate zones and mean temperatures for the winter months vary far more than summer temperatures. The present authors subdivide the Arctic Climate zone into three: High Arctic, Low Arctic

and, in the southern-most part of Greenland, the Subarctic, where conditions also allow copses of *Betula* sp. and *Salix* sp. to develop (Feilberg 1984). Off the coast, sea ice cover and sea temperatures influence the delimitation of the different climate zones.

The lack of a warming effect of solar radiation during winter generates permafrost in all areas of Greenland. In most areas, permafrost is continuous and the southern limit may be related to a mean annual air temperature around −4 °C in coastal areas (Fristrup 1981). On the continents, the southern boundary of continuous and discontinuous permafrost roughly corresponds to −8.5 °C and −1 °C mean annual air temperature, respectively. In southern Greenland both discontinuous and sporadic permafrost occur. Above the permanently frozen ground, which at Pituffik (Thule Air Base) is 500 m thick, an active layer thaws every summer. The depth of this layer is 0.5–1.5 m. The permafrost layer becomes thinner and disappears near the sea, larger rivers and lakes (Fristrup 1981). In the southern-most lowland, sporadic permafrost occurs mainly as ice lenses of 0.5–1 m thickness on north exposed slopes. At higher elevations, permafrost is widespread also in the south (Fristrup 1981), where vegetation shades the ground and thus preserves or enhances permafrost. However, permafrost may also weaken or destroy vegetation, since it reduces soil temperature, drainage, aeration and root depth (Danks 1981).

A large number of soil development phenomena depend on permafrost-related processes, and four phenomena, which occur mainly in regions with continuous permafrost, are relevant (Billings et al. 1982). Thermokarst structures may be formed where the vegetation is sufficiently damaged, e.g. by vehicle traffic and herbivory, to permit localized thawing of ground ice. The result is an uneven thermokarst topography including mounds, sinkholes, tunnels, caverns, short ravines, lake basins and circular lowland structures (Danks 1981). In the wettest soil types, with the highest accumulation of organic matter, contraction during heavy frost in winter may lead to the formation of crevices. During thaw periods, these crevices become water filled and, when refrozen, form more or less permanent ice lenses or ice wedges. These ice wedges may in turn change local hydrology and mineralization to the detriment of plant growth and community structure. In sloping areas, the often water saturated active layer may form solifluction deposits, moving downslope under gravity. On more planar soils, sorting of material results in formation of stone polygons and other patterns. The instability of such soils generally impedes plant growth, which may be restricted to stabilized edge zones.

Since ice covers about 82% of Greenland, this ice sheet, often called the Inland Ice, has a profound influence on the climate of the ice-free coastal areas on both a general and a local level. Greenland is partly located in the predominantly west to east pathway of low-pressure systems and, due to the elevation of the country, with 87% of the ice sheet above 1200 m, a pronounced orographic effect is exerted on atmospheric low-pressure cells. Shallow lows are often delayed and move northwards along the west coast. Some are split in two by the southern tip of Greenland, one part following its usual course along the west coast, while the other moves east or northeast. The results are more precipitation on the west coast than the east coast (apart from the SE corner), large exchanges of air masses of southern origin and interdiurnal temperature changes as large as 30 °C over the ice sheet. Lowland coastal stations on the east coast have lower annual precipitation than stations on the west coast. Over the northern part of the ice sheet, nearly permanent but shallow high-pressure cells dominate (Diamond 1958; Putnins 1970).

A pronounced phenomenon related to the ice sheet is the almost permanent surface temperature inversion. It is created by the strong cooling effect of snow and ice surfaces on the lowermost air layer. The atmospheric inversion layer is thickest in winter and may reach 1.5 km in height. The lowest air temperature observed directly on the ice sheet is almost −70 °C, but a minimum thermometer has measured −80 °C during winter (Fristrup 1981). Diamond (1958) and Ohmura (1987) constructed maps of annual mean temperatures over the ice sheet. The cold air sinks from higher elevations at the centre of the ice sheet towards the periphery. It is then deflected to the right and circulates clockwise near the coast as a 'glacial anticyclone'. The cold outflow also produces vertical air circulation near the coast and if a low-pressure system is present at sea, terrifying storms, equal in strength to tropical typhoons, can develop. Such storms are called katabatic winds, and wind speeds of up to 90 m/s are known. The katabatic winds have several local names, like piteraq in the Tasiilaq (Ammassalik) area. After a storm, temperatures may fall by up to 20 °C (Fristrup 1981; Putnins 1970). In summer, the katabatic winds are weak. Temperatures may exceed the melting point and occasionally rain occurs in areas remote from the coast (Putnins 1970).

Despite unfavourable temperature conditions, the ice sheet is not without life. Where mineral and organic dust are concentrated and absorb heat radiation, so-called cryoconite holes are formed. Mainly algae, rotifers and tardigrades inhabit these holes. The tardigrades are wind dispersed and have been found in highest abundance 20 km from the ice margin, in cryoconite holes 15 cm deep at an altitude of 1000 m (cf. Böcher and Petersen 1997).

The length of the growing season relates strongly to the number of degree-days above 0 °C and an expected north–south gradient exists. The year-to-year variability is greatest at coastal stations along the west coast and in the south. Here, more than 100% variation occurs in both positive and negative degree-days. The variability in winter temperature (negative degree-days) is a greater threat to animals than to plants, although plant productivity and seed production may be strongly reduced in years low in positive degree-days. Consecutive years with unfavourable low positive or negative degree-days can cause disasters on both the species and ecosystem levels.

Precipitation decreases with increasing latitude and at the same latitude, precipitation tends to amount to less at lowland west coast stations, where the maximum falls in late summer, than on the east coast, where the maximum is in winter. Values from Ohmura and Reeh (1991) show a marked difference in amounts of yearly precipitation in the south over the short distance between the west coast station at Ivittuut-Qaqortoq (Julianehab) of about 850–900 mm and the east coast station at Torgilsbu-Ikerasassuaq (Prins Christian Sund) of about 1930–2500 mm. On the west coast, a maximum yearly mean total precipitation of 1000–1300 mm falls within the latitude corresponding to the position of Ivittuut. On the east coast, the maximum precipitation falls in a similar narrow zone between 60°N and 62°N.

On the ice sheet, the distribution of total precipitation and accumulation of solid precipitation is opposite to the situation at coastal stations, except south of 65°N. North of this latitude, total precipitation in water equivalent on the west side is two to three times that on the summit and the east side of the ice sheet (Bernes 1996; Diamond 1958; Ohmura and Reeh 1991). In the ice-free areas of North Greenland, precipitation is mostly less than 100 mm/year. Annual precipitation varies widely between years. Inland areas, like Kangerlussuaq (Sdr. Strømfjord), are the most stable with an annual variation rarely >100%, while a 3–400% variation occurs at the coastal stations. Throughout Greenland, thunderstorms are very rare, occurring at a rate of 0–3 in 25 years.

The vast extension of Greenland, with the north located in the frozen polar region and the south in the Atlantic influenced by the drift of sub-tropical air masses towards the pole, is the main reason for the existence of different sub-types of arctic climate in Greenland. As mentioned above, three main types of climate occur: subarctic, low arctic and high arctic. The main types may be further sub-divided into oceanic (maritime) and continental climate sub-types. Due to the complicated orography of Greenland, the main types and sub-types form a mosaic at the local level, as described for South Greenland in Feilberg (1984).

The north–south climatic gradient is particularly marked with respect to winter temperature, degree-days, precipitation, and of course day-length. Mean temperatures for the coldest winter months vary from −3.4 °C in January at Nanortalik to about −33 °C in March at Station Nord. Variations in temperature and day length result in a gradient in the length of the growth season from five months in the south to two months in the north. In the extreme south, the climate is maritime, with a yearly mean precipitation of about 2500 mm at Ikerasarsuaq (Prins Christian Sund).

Generally, the climate of the arctic deserts in the north is strongly continental, though characterized by very low summer temperatures. Other characteristics are very little precipitation and strong wind erosion due to föhn activity. The strong wind erosion and evaporation causes salt crustations and salt lakes.

Freezing begins very suddenly in the autumn, and thawing equally suddenly in spring. There are few days with alternate freezing and thawing. Precipitation is rarely more than 100–125 mm per year and may be considerably less (range: 25–285 mm). Although most of the precipitation falls as snow, the strong winds prevent a continuous snow-cover from developing (Fristrup 1952). The redistribution of snow means that almost no precipitation is available for plant growth in certain areas, except what may be available when the active layer thaws. The mean number of frost-free days decreases from south to north, from about 150 days at Narsarsuaq (61°09′ N, 045°25′ W) to about 70 days at Danmarkshavn (76°46′ N, 018°40′ W) and 50–60 days at Station Nord (81°36′ N, 16°40′ W). In general, the frost-free period begins earlier and lasts longer towards the south. Due to the decidedly continental climate of Peary Land, the frost-free period there is relatively long.

There are differences in the latitudinal gradient of the west coast as compared to the east coast. On the west coast, open water occurs in July–August to Inglefield Bredning at approximately 75°N. In September, the southern boundary of the polar ice on the east coast has retreated only to 70°N near Ittoqqortoonniit (Scoresbysund). At the same latitude on the west coast, ocean freezing does not start until November–December (Petersen 1935). The west coast is somewhat warmer in the summer, with a growing season a few weeks longer than the east coast at the same latitude. However, the 0 °C annual isothermal line hits the west coast about 62°N, but not until 65°N on the east coast. At higher latitudes, annual mean temperatures are nearly similar on the two coasts (Ohmura 1987).

In general, temperatures rose in the Arctic, including Greenland, in the first half of the last century. At Svalbard, the increase in mean air temperature was about 6.5 °C in the period 1895–1934 (Brázdil 1988). Since the 1940s and 1950s, temperatures have declined, notably in the central Greenland-Svalbard area, but also in the north (Danks 1981). In the mid-1970s air temperature was about 2.5 °C lower than in 1934. Mean July temperature at Pituffik (Thule Air Base) changed from 8 °C in 1947–1963 to 5.6 °C in 1964–1974 (Danks 1981). The magnitude of this temperature decrease varies considerably between stations. At Nuuk (Godthåb), the fall in yearly mean temperature began around 1939 with an increasing rate since 1962, so the running mean temperature (Gauss filter, 9) had fallen 1.4 °C in the early 1990s to −2.1 °C. That is almost to the same temperature as a hundred years ago. However, the temperature fall appears less drastic when comparing 25- and 30-year means. DMI has recently published a comprehensive report on the climatic development in Greenland based on weather data from 1784 until today (Cappelen 2014).

The overall assumption of the recent IPCC reports (Larsen et al. 2014; Watson et al. 1996) is that increases in atmospheric CO_2 will lead to atmospheric warming. Greater warming than the global average is predicted for the Arctic and sub-Arctic regions. However, the climate in Greenland may partly behave differently due to changes in thermohaline circulation in the North Atlantic Sea. At least for southern Greenland the present climatic trend is a decrease in temperature and an increase in precipitation.

An increase in the mean yearly temperature of 1.8–3.6 °C at the end of the present century is predicted for Greenland and the greatest increase is expected at mid and high latitudes in West Greenland. The increase will primarily be in winter temperatures. The maximum predicted increase in the July temperature is about +2 °C for Ilulissat (Jakobshavn). The IPCC predicts the highest temperature increase at the most northerly latitudes. This, however, may only apply to truly continental regions, e.g. parts of Canada and Siberia, and not to the coastal region of Greenland. The most continental inland localities may be comparable to central west coast stations with a yearly temperature rise of up to 4 °C, mainly through a rise in winter temperature.

The rate of change in temperature and precipitation is expected to be nearly linear, so half the change will be accomplished within the next 40–50 years. Other consequences of climate change include lengthening of the snow-free season by a month or more (mostly at southern latitudes), a deepening of the active soil layer and a northward movement of the permafrost boundary (Maxwell 1992). Loss of permafrost would have a drastic impact on the vegetation, resulting in waterlogging or dry surface soils, depending on topography, soil water retention capacity, precipitation, etc. A further effect could be an enhanced release of CO_2 and CH_4 from peat deposits (Christensen and Cox 1995; Street and Melnikov 1990). Since winter temperatures expect to increase the most, a slight increase in the length of the growing season by one to two weeks is expected. Changes in wind systems are uncertain.

In the soil, climate warming is expected to affect hydrology through the development of an unfrozen zone, or talik, between the seasonal frost and permafrost layers. This in turn may alter surface hydrology by increasing soil moisture storage, improving subsurface drainage and thus decreasing the amount of moisture in the soil profile. Generally, a permafrost layer is relatively impermeable due to the presence of ice. This leads to a water-saturated zone in the active layer following snowmelt and major rain falls. The presence of permafrost may even guarantee that a saturated layer will prevail throughout the growing season. The predicted warming will increase the heat transfer to the soil, increase the thickness of the active layer and decrease the thickness of the permafrost layer. The change in active layer thickness will occur within decades, but degradation of permafrost will take centuries (Kane et al. 1992). The authors have modelled near-surface soil temperatures after 50 years of 4 °C surface climatic warming. The greatest soil warming will occur during the winter. During summer, the soil may be about 3 °C warmer, while the difference from present temperatures in October will be about 1 °C only.

Soil microbial activity and hence decomposition and soil mineralization rates are expected to increase with temperature, improving conditions for plant growth and net primary production (Nadelhoffer et al. 1992). Increased air temperature may not affect soil nutrient mineralization, unless soil temperature also rises (Jonasson and Michelsen 1996). In permafrost areas with continuous vegetation cover, this may happen with considerable delay.

The depletion of the stratospheric ozone layer above the North Pole region appears until recently to continue at a rate of about 1% yearly, thereby increasing UV-B radiation to the biosphere (Gates 1993; Prinn 1994). Apparently, redistribution of ozone from the stratosphere to the troposphere takes place. Increased tropospheric ozone tends to decrease UV exposure, but according to Tsay and Stamnes (1992), the opposite may happen at low solar elevations, as is the case in the High Arctic. Stratospheric aerosols have a similar effect, while arctic haze results in a decrease in the UV dose rate. Arctic stratus clouds of ice or water droplets provide a substantial shield against direct UV radiation, but in the Arctic, diffuse UV radiation is as important as direct radiation. The UV albedo of snow and ice may be particularly high and can be 4–5 times the value for open water or tundra (Grenfell and Warren 1994). The increasing UV-B irradiance trend in the Arctic may harm both lichens and higher plants in the future (Heide-Jørgensen and Johnsen 1995, 1998) as well as marine ecosystems.

The Biology of Greenland with Emphasis on Terrestrial Ecosystems

Greenland, almost entirely situated within the arctic climate zone, has a relatively low species diversity. This is mainly due to climatic consequences of the still persisting ice sheet and difficult immigration routes. Among plants, several globally large families are absent or scarce. Among animals, the small number of species is to some extent compensated for by a great number of individuals. For general descriptions of flora and fauna in Greenland, the following literature may be consulted: Böcher (1975), Böcher et al. (1978), Muus et al. (1990), Nørrevang and Lundø (1981), Feilberg et al. (1984), Moeslund and Ravn-Nielsen (1987), Gensbøl (1996), Böcher and

Petersen (1997), Born and Böcher (2000), Jensen and Christensen (2003) and Böcher et al. (2015). In the following sub-sections, a short survey of the major groups of terrestrial and freshwater organisms is given.

Microorganisms, like bacteria, cyanobacteria, algae, and saprophytic and parasitic microfungi, are important for decomposition and mineralization of organic matter in arctic soils and fresh waters. They experience harsh conditions in an environment largely governed by permafrost, moisture extremes, from waterlogging to drought, and frequent anaerobic conditions. Arctic soils are therefore expected to contain a number of microorganisms uncommon or absent in temperate or tropical soils. However, many of these arctic microorganisms, particularly bacteria, are not yet described or classified. Extraordinarily high diversity has been demonstrated among phytoplankton in Alaska, although many species seem to be nutrient limited in the north (Danks 1981).

In Greenland nearly 700 macromycete fungi (mainly Agaricales) are known, including some excellent edible though unexploited fungi (Dissing and Lange 1987). Generally, in the Arctic, the number of macromycete species is lower, the individual species more sporadic in occurrence and the ratio of litter decomposers to mycorrhiza-forming species is lower than in temperate forests (Petersen 1977). Much of the belowground fungal biomass appears to be mycorrhizal (Miller and Laursen, in Danks 1981). The cold Arctic environment provides extreme conditions for the establishment and functioning of mycorrhiza symbiosis (Gardes and Dahlberg 1996). Nonetheless, mycorrhiza association is regarded as a major mechanism by which plants acquire nutrients in cold-dominated environments (Michelsen et al. 1996).

From the limited surveys of mycorrhizal associations in the Arctic, the following appear. (a) Typical arbuscular mycorrhizal associations known from both graminoids and woody perennials are ubiquitous in Low Arctic areas. (b).

Root colonization by mostly unidentified fungi having dark septate hyphae is common (e.g. in Cyperaceae), but the ecological significance of this is still unknown. (c) A large number of ectomycorrhizal fungi (e.g. members of the genera *Cortinarius*, *Hebeloma*, *Inocybe*, *Lactarius*) are present as symbionts of relatively few, widely distributed shrubs (e.g. *Betula nana*, *Salix* spp., *Dryas octopetala*, *Arctostaphylos* spp.) and herbaceous plant species (e.g. *Kobresia myosuroides*, *Polygonum viviparum*). (d) Ericaceous genera (e.g. *Cassiope*, *Vaccinium*, *Empetrum*), with ericoid mycorrhiza, dominate large areas covered by heath communities. (e) Non-mycorrhizal, widespread plants from the families Cyperaceae, Juncaceae, Brassicaceae, Polygonaceae and Caryophyllaceae predominate in certain arctic plant communities (Gardes and Dahlberg 1996). The same species may have mycorrhiza in one but not in another plant community (Michelsen et al. 1996).

Petersen (1977) studied macromycete fungi in the Qeqertarsuaq (Godhavn) area over a three-year period. The peak season occurred in the first half of August. Fructification correlated strongly with solar irradiance and soil temperature. Low soil temperature may delay growth and development of macromycete mycelia so much that there is insufficient time for fructification before the definitive decrease in soil temperature in autumn. Locally, the brevity of the frost-free period, as well as low soil moisture, may be limiting to fructification in some years.

Lichens and mosses are better represented at high latitudes than vascular plants. The lichen flora is particularly diverse and well developed in Greenland and other Arctic regions. Lichens are well adapted to snow and ice, since arctic species remain productive at low temperatures and some species are photosynthetically active even at −10 °C. They also resist drought and can take up water from snow and ice (Kappen 1993). *Neuropogon sulphureus* is even active at −18.5 °C at low light intensities. The optimum temperature in this species for low light photosynthesis is about 0 °C, increasing to 5 °C at higher light intensities (OL Lange in Christiansen 1981). In Greenland, more than a thousand species of lichens are known. Most of the species have an Arctic circumpolar distribution, others are North American and still others amphi-Atlantic (Hansen 1987). Lichens dominate the vegetation, the more extreme the environmental conditions become. According to Matick (1953), the ratio of the number of lichen species to the number of vascular plant species increases from 0.48 in Germany to 0.95 in Sweden and 2.0 in Greenland. A similar increasing ratio from south to north exists within Greenland. A guide to 300 Greenland macro- and microlichens is available (Hansen and Andersen 1995).

Lichens grow slowly and depend on the exchange of nutrients between two symbiotic organisms, a fungus and a photosynthetic alga. In general, lichens are highly tolerant of certain environmental stress factors, like low moisture, low nutrient availability and extreme temperatures, while very sensitive to others, like some air pollutants (Ahmadjian 1993). There are indications that lichens are also sensitive to changes in the radiation climate, such as increases in UV-B radiation (Heide-Jørgensen and Johnsen 1995, 1998). A dormant propagule bank of species requiring a warmer climate for development has been demonstrated for Antarctic soils (Kennedy 1996) and is no doubt present in Arctic and Greenland soils as well.

Substrates suitable for lichens include everything from soil to stones, dead plant material, bark, bones, dry faeces and shells. A number of species may grow on stones right up to the edge of the glacial ice. Since lichens grow so slowly, a zone of naked stones in front of a glacier indicates the ongoing retreat of the glacier (Figure 2, see Plate section). In Greenland, more than a

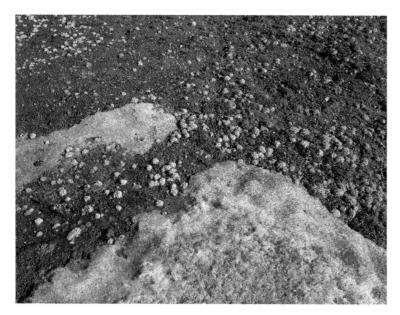

Figure 2 Retreating ice sheet permitting the first pioneer lichens (*Stereocaulon* sp.) to form small cushions on the barren, newly exposed soil in the High Arctic. July, Thule District, Greenland. *Source:* Ib Johnsen. (See colour plate section for colour representation of this figure.)

hundred epiphytic species are known from shrubs and dwarf shrubs (Hansen 1987). Among the soil resident species, reindeer-lichens (*Cladonia* spp., subgenus *Cladina*) are particularly important as winter food for caribou and may dominate certain lichen heaths. Most lichens have very modest nutrient requirements, but a special flora develops on stones and cliffs near colonies of nesting sea birds. Characteristic Greenland bird cliff lichens include species and genera like *Haematomma ventosum, Xanthoria elegans, Rhizoplaca* spp. and *Umbilicaria* spp., though most species in the last genus are not particularly nutrient demanding and grow on other cliffs and stones as well.

Climatic parameters, like temperature, moisture, snow-cover and light, as well as substrate qualities and nutrient availability influence the distribution of a single lichen species. However, ambient temperature has little relevance to the actual temperatures experienced by lichens on the ground. Kershaw (1985) and Longton (1988) give comprehensive treatments of the microclimate around lichens. In Greenland, species distribution patterns reflect the oceanic continental climate gradient with longer snow-cover, more moisture and lower summer temperatures near the coast and shorter snow-cover, warmer and drier summer climate at the head of the long fiords. Reindeer lichens, *Cladonia* spp., form the most dense and thick mats in an intermediate zone where they obtain shelter from dwarf shrubs and are covered by snow during winter. The present short and cool summers in the north restrict many lichens to southern Greenland, while other species avoid warm summers; *Dactylina arctica,* a possible Tertiary relict, for example, has a High Arctic distribution (Christiansen 1981).

In less severe habitats, lichens are replaced by faster-growing moss species, which can compete with vascular plants. From a biomass point of view, mosses may be considered the most important plant group in Greenland, with more than 700 species known, including over 130 liverworts

and about 25 *Sphagnum* species. Schuster and Damsholt (1974) produced a monograph on the 136 species from 41 genera of liverworts (Hepaticae) in central West Greenland. A similar high species diversity in the Arctic is only known from Alaska and possibly Svalbard. The high diversity is ascribed to the combination of the varied geology, the oceanic-continental climate gradient and the occurrence of both a northern, High Arctic, and a southern floral element in the region.

Excluding liverworts, only 18% of the mosses occur in all parts of Greenland; 49% are most common in the south, while 7% have an exclusively High Arctic distribution. Other distributional types confined to the extreme north, the Westcoast, the East coast, bicentric West and East coast, the South East coast and the extreme South range between 0.7 and 8% (Mogensen 1987). The low diversity of soil types in the north, as opposed to a more severe climate, explains the low representation of mosses in the north compared to southern Greenland (Holmen and Mogensen 1981). The majority of mosses are also common in boreal and temperate regions, including alpine areas. About 80% of arctic mosses and 70% of lichens are circumpolar, and a few species are bipolar (Longton 1988). A moss flora of Arctic North America, including Greenland, and distribution maps, are available (Mogensen 1985, 1986, 1987).

Mosses resemble lichens in that both groups cover a wide ecological spectrum, while most species have rather specific requirements within their given habitat. Although most mosses are distributed according to substrate type, some mosses are also distributed by climatic parameters. *Kiaeria glacialis,* confined to gneiss areas, is such an example. It is absent from northern gneiss areas because of low precipitation. *Sphagnum lindbergii, S. compactum* and *Pleurozium schreberi* have a similar distribution for the same reason. Several of the more widely distributed species become rare north of 81°N, near their northern climatic boundary. The relatively few High Arctic mosses tolerate strong frost and some, like *Racomitrium lanuginosum*, tolerate desiccation as long as water is periodically available. A study of the total distribution of species like *Mnium hornum*, *Rhodobryum roseum*, *Sphagnum papillosum*, and others occurring in southern-most Greenland, indicates that these species depend on warm growing seasons (Holmen and Mogensen 1981).

The vascular plant flora comprises about 514 species, though this number varies; according to what rank some of the more problematic taxa have at the time of counting, this number fluctuates. Only a few are endemic species. Most of these are apomictic and not always recognized as species, though *Saxifraga nathorstii* and *Sisyrinchium groenlandicum* deserve mention (Böcher 1981a). Of the 514 species, about 9% occur from North to South in Greenland (based on maps in Bay 1992), although a few may be absent from parts of either the west or east coasts. Several other distributional types are recognized, including High Arctic, Low Arctic, western, eastern, boreal, oceanic, continental and bicentric mid-latitude. These and further subdivisions of distributional types are described by Böcher (1975), Feilberg (1984), Bay (1992) and Fredskild (1996).

Some northern species become alpine and occur only at high elevations in the southern part of their range. Disjunct distribution of the type with a major distribution in either the north or the south and an isolated occurrence in the Qeqertarsuaq (Disko)-Nunavik (Svartenhuk) area is the result of geological conditions. A number of species avoid the acidic soil on gneiss prevailing in the Melville Bay area and in the Sisimiut-Ilulissat area (Holsteinsborg-Jakobshavn); see, for example, the geological map (Escher and Pulvertaft 1995). A few recently immigrated species have very limited distribution (Pedersen 1972). Böcher et al. (1959) classified the vascular flora according to the global distribution of species. Feilberg (1984),

Bay (1992) and Fredskild (1996) made more contributions that are recent. The South East coast up to Ittoqqortoormiit (Scoresbysund) has a higher percentage of indigenous species of the eastern than western types, while the percentage of western type species is highest on all of the west coast and increases dramatically towards the north (Böcher et al. 1959). Despite the lack of information on East Greenland, the main immigration route must be across the Nares Strait.

Several very detailed regional and local floristic and vegetation descriptions exist (e.g. Bay 1992; Böcher 1963, 1975, 1981a, 1981b; Feilberg 1984; Fredskild 1996; Porsild 1920; Sørensen 1933, 1941; for older contributions, see Bay 1992 and Fredskild 1996). Well-illustrated surveys are found in Böcher (1975), Feilberg et al. (1984), Gensbøl (1996) and Heide-Jørgensen and Johnsen (1997). Greenland comprises a number of floristic districts, and the occurrence of each species in these districts is included in the flora by Böcher et al. (1978). Although 514 species is high compared to the nearest land, Ellesmere Island, with about 150 species, it is low compared to both the near 1200 species found in the continental Nunavut of Canada (Danks 1981) and the about 500 species on the much smaller Iceland (Love 1983). Several large families that are well represented in temperate and sub-Arctic regions are almost absent in arctic Greenland and even more so in North Greenland. This applies to gymnosperms, represented only by *Juniperus communis* spp. *nana* (common juniper) in Southern Greenland, the pea family (two species, one of which is introduced), umbelliferous plants (two species), and orchids (five species). Pteridophytes, such as club mosses, horsetails and ferns, are also poorly represented, with about 32 species in all of Greenland.

Vascular plants in Greenland, to a larger extent than lichens and mosses, distribute themselves according to regional climatic parameters, with

Figure 3 Photo from July in the high arctic near Thule. The more favourable life conditions on the right slope are due to higher exposure from the sun. Probably, such conditions become more widespread due to climate change. *Source:* Ib Johnsen. (See colour plate section for colour representation of this figure.)

length of the growing season, summer temperature and soil moisture being the more important distributional factors (Figure 3, see Plate section). Many otherwise widely distributed species live at the edge of existence in Greenland and have their northern distributional limit there. *Koenigia islandica*, *Arnica angustifolia*, *Arenaria humifusa* and *Carex ursina* have only an isolated occurrence in the extreme north or North West (further examples are the dwarf shrubs *Ledum palustre* spp. *decumbens* and *Vaccinium vitis-idaea* spp. *minus*). A much smaller number of High Arctic circumpolar species, including *Erysimum pallasii* and *Ranunculus sabinei*, have their southern limit in Greenland at about 76°N. In North Greenland, most plants are limited to sheltered lowland habitats where the winter snow-cover provides freezing and drought protection and secures water availability at least at the beginning of the growing season (Bay 1992; Heide-Jørgensen and Johnsen 1997, 1998). Only about a dozen species can grow at altitudes higher than 3–400 m ASL, *Luzula confusa* being one of the most height-tolerant plants.

Distribution of Plant Communities in the North

The border between the southern High Arctic, continental and southern High Arctic, oceanic vegetation zones around 76°N in West Greenland is a most distinct one with regards to the number of vascular plant species that have either their northern or southern limit in this area (Bay 1992; Heide-Jørgensen and Johnsen 1997, 1998). Of the 162 species in Avanersuaq (Thule district), 39 species have their absolute northern Greenlandic distribution boundary and a further 29 their west Greenlandic boundary in the district, while 10 species have their most southern occurrence here. Four species have their only Greenlandic occurrence in the district. Figure 4 (see Plate section) shows a landscape typical for the Thule district.

Ninety-nine species in Thule district are circumpolar. Forty-one or one fourth is western, primarily occurring in North America, while only two are eastern, with a main distribution area in Eurasia. Seventeen are amphi-Atlantic,

occurring on both sides of the Atlantic Ocean. Of the 39 species with an isolated occurrence in the Thule district, 15 or one-third are Western and of the four only occurring in this district, the two louseworts, *Pedicularis langsdorfii* and *P. albolabiata*, are western, while *Androsace septentrionalis* and the grass *Dupontia fisheri* are circumpolar. The presence of several isolated species in the Thule district may reflect the presence of two main physical dispersal barriers, namely the Humboldt glaciers to the north and a number of wide glaciers in the Melville Bay area to the south (Heide-Jørgensen and Johnsen 1997, 1998).

Several species of dwarf shrubs from the heaths have their northern distribution boundary in the Thule floristic district. These are *Rhododendron*

Figure 4 July landscape in the Thule area. The border of the Greenland ice cap (Indlandsisen) is seen in the background. *Source:* Ib Johnsen. (See colour plate section for colour representation of this figure.)

lapponicum, Empetrum nigrum spp. *hermaphroditum, Vaccinium vitisidaea* (cowberry), *Ledum palustre* spp. *decumbens* and *Diapensia lapponica*. Another five dwarf shrub species including *Betula nana* have their northern boundary just south of Melville Bay. The herbs in the heaths include some of the few hemiparasitic plants in Greenland, like species of *Pedicularis*. A large number of lichens, including *Cladonia* spp. (reindeer lichens), are also important in the heaths and *Racomitrium lanuginosum* is the dominant moss. North of 70°N, heaths on relatively nutrient-rich basic soils are dominated by grasses like *Poa abbreviata, Poa hartzii, Deschampsia brevifolia* and *Alopecurus alpinus*.

Plants, which in their southern distribution area are often calcicole, extend their pH range to neutral or even acidic soils in the High Arctic climate zone. The explanation is partly a lack of competition in the more species-poor northern plant communities. Examples are *Equisetum variegatum, Lesquerella arctica, Arenaria humifusa, Rhodendron lapponicum* and *Juncus triglumis* (Heide-Jørgensen and Johnsen 1997, 1998).

The number of ecosystems in Greenland is relatively few, with low species diversity and hence a simpler structure than at more southern latitudes. From the distribution of species outlined in the preceding section, it seems appropriate to distinguish between High and Low Arctic ecosystems. Differences in continentality justify a distinction between coastal and inland heath and fen ecosystems. In general, terrestrial ecosystems in the Arctic are characterized by a greater below-ground than above-ground productivity. For plants, up to 98% of the phytomass may be below ground and almost all nitrogen and phosphorous are bound in plants and soil microorganisms. Mycorrhiza are important throughout the Arctic (Callaghan and Jonasson 1995a, 1995b). As above-ground flora and fauna, the soil flora and fauna are poor in species but rich in numbers of

individuals (Chemov 1995). Nematodes tolerate adverse conditions and are considered a relatively important part of arctic ecosystems, though they may avoid the wettest habitats (Danks 1981).

Consequences of Climate Change at the Ecosystem Level

Studies of individual species are the basis for predicted changes at the community and ecosystem level because of climate change. Although very useful, such studies are far from sufficient for understanding or predicting how arctic ecosystems might respond to a changing climate. This is because species not only respond directly to a variety of interacting climatic parameters but also at all stages in the life cycle they respond to biotic interactions controlled by the environment. Studies of complete ecosystems are very few and predictions of an ecosystem response rely on extrapolation from the individual and population levels, where processes act on shorter time scales than at the ecosystem level (Jonasson 1997; Oechel and Billings 1992). Hence, at present, a high degree of uncertainty exists.

The difficulty in projecting results at the species level to ecosystems is evident from the field study of *Eriophorum vaginatum* in tussock tundra in Alaska by Tissue and Oechel (1987). They did not observe increased productivity as a response to enhanced CO_2 above ambient, even though increased photosynthesis is a normal response in laboratory studies. The low response in the field was probably due to limitation by nutrients, rather than CO_2, when *E. vaginatum* grew in its natural community. Therefore, as emphasized by Jonasson (1997), increased growth as a response to increased temperature and CO_2 only occurs when nutrient availability also increases.

Because the most widespread communities in the Arctic have low species diversity, the loss of even a few species would dramatically alter community structure. Walker and Jones (1996) suggest considering the following three hypotheses, each having a spatial, a genetic and a time component, when discussing ecosystem response to climate change:

1) Species will exhibit individualistic responses to increased summer temperature, but there will be high similarity of response within groupings of species, genera or functional types (ecotypes).
2) Because of the long-term interaction between climate and site conditions and local populations, and because of similarities in both the sets of climate and site conditions and the local populations throughout the Arctic, there will be consistent patterns of response relative to climate and site conditions.
3) In both 'warm' (Low Arctic) and 'cold' (High Arctic) sites, a short-term response is primarily a function of the physiology of the individual species. In warmer sites, however, there will be a greater possibility for short-term transient phenomena and long-term indirect effects.

Concluding Remarks

The major ecological consequences of climate change in Greenland result from the increasing greenhouse effect. The adverse effect of depletion of stratospheric ozone has diminished over the last decades due to an international effort to reduce emissions of halogenated hydrocarbons.

The increased greenhouse effect will be most apparent in the High Arctic, which is going to experience particularly strong increases in winter temperatures. The melting depth of the permafrost layer will increase and result in strong paludification as well as higher mineralization rates on well-drained soils. Boreal and Low Arctic species will extend their distribution range towards the north and a few high arctic species may become confined to the very far north, eventually to vanish completely.

Nature in Greenland is highly vulnerable and many recent interactions between human activities and the environment have enormous potential for devastating effects. This is true whether the focus is on the Greenland population itself or on the highly industrialized world on the arctic doorstep.

References

Ahmadjian, V. (1993). The Lichen Symbiosis. New York: Wiley. 250 pp.

Bay, C. (1992). A Phytogeographical Study of the Vascular Plants of Northern Greenland – North of 74° Northern Latitude, Meddelelser om Grønland: Bioscience, vol. 36, 1–102. Kommissionen for videnskabelige undersøgelser i Grønland, København.

Bay, C. (1993). Taxa of vascular plants new to the flora of Greenland. *Nord. J. Bot.* 13: 247–252.

Bernes, C. (1996) The Nordic Arctic environment – unspoilt, exploited, polluted. *Nord* 1996(26):1–240.

Berthelsen, C., Mortensen, I.H., and Mortensen, E. (eds.) (1990). Kalaallit Nunaat. Greenland. Atlas. Pilersuiffik: Greenland Home Rule.

Billings, W.O., Luken, J.O., Mortensen, D.A., and Peterson, K.M. (1982). Arctic tundra: a source or sink for atmospheric carbon dioxide in a changing environment? *Oecologia* 53: 7–11.

Böcher, T.W. (1963). Phytogeography of Middle West Greenland. *Meddr. Grønl.* 148 (3): 1–289.

Böcher, T.W. (1975). Det Grønne Grønland. København: Rhodos, 256 p.

Böcher, T.W. (1981a). Grønlands karplanteflora. In: *Danmarks Natur* 11: *Grønland* (eds. A. Nørrevang and J. Lundø), 342–365. København: Politikens Forlag.

Böcher, T.W. (1981b). Hovedtræk af Grønlands plantegeografi. In: *Danmarks Natur* 11: *Grønland* (eds. A. Nørrevang and J. Lundø), 350–365. København: Politikens Forlag.

Böcher, J. (2001). Insekter og andre smådyr i Grønlands fjeld og ferskvand. Nuuk & Copenhagen: Atuagkat.

Böcher, J. and Petersen, P.M. (1997). Greenland. In: Polar and Alpine Tundra, *Ecosystems of the World*, vol. 3 (ed. F.E. Wielgolaski), 685–720. Amsterdam: Elsevier.

Böcher, T.W., Holmen, K., and Jakobsen, K. (1959). A synoptical study of the Greenland flora. *Meddr. Grønl.* 163: 1–32.

Böcher, T.W., Fredskild, B., Holmen, K., and Jakobsen, K. (1978). Grønlands Flora. Kebenhavn: P. Haase & Søns Forlag, 326 pp.

Böcher, J., Kristensen, N.P., Pape, T., and Vilhelmsen, L.B. (eds.) (2015). The Greenland Entomofauna: An Identification Manual of Insects Spiders and Their Allies, *Fauna Entomologica Scandinavica*, vol. 44. Leiden: Boston.

Born, E.W. and Böcher, J. (2000). The Ecology of Greenland. Nuuk: Ministry of Environment and Natural Resources.

Brázdil, R. (1988). Variation of air temperature and atmospheric precipitation in the region of Svalbard and of Jan Mayen. In: Recent Climatic Change (ed. S. Gregory), 53–68. London: Belhaven Press.

Briner, J.P., Cuzzone, J.K., Badgeley, J.A. et al. (2020). Rate of mass loss from the Greenland Ice Sheet will exceed Holocene values this century. *Nature* 586: 70–74.

Callaghan, T.V. and Jonasson, S. (1995a). Arctic terrestrial ecosystems and environmental change. *Philos. Trans. R. Soc. Lond. A* 352: 259–276.

Callaghan, T.V. and Jonasson, S. (1995b). Implications for changes in arctic plant biodiversity from environmental manipulation experiments. In: Arctic and Alpine Biodiversity: Patterns, Causes and Ecosystem Consequences, *Ecological Studies (Analysis and Synthesis)*, vol. 113 (eds. F.S. Chapin and C. Körner), 151–166. Springer, Berlin, Heidelberg.

Cappelen, J. (2014) Greenland – DMI Historical Climate Data Collection 1784–2013. Technical Report 14-04, DMI, Copenhagen. 90 pp.

Chernov, Y.I. (1995). Diversity of the Arctic terrestrial fauna. In: *Arctic and Alpine Biodiversity: Patterns, Causes and Ecosystem Consequences, Ecological Studies (Analysis and Synthesis)*, 113 (eds. F.S. Chapin and C. Körner), 81–95. Springer, Berlin, Heidelberg.

Christensen, T.R., Cox, P. (1995) Modelling the response of methane emission from arctic tundra to climatic change: an overview of relevant controlling factors. In: Callaghan, T.V. (ed.), *Global Change and Arctic Terrestrial Ecosystems. Proceedings of papers contributed to the International Conference*, 21–26 August 1993, Oppdal, Norway. Ecosystem Research Report 10 (EUR 15519 EN), pp. 296–304.

Christiansen, M.S. (1981). Laverne. In: *Danmarks Natur* 11: *Grønland* (eds. A. Nørrevang and J. Lundø), 394–405. København: Politikens Forlag.

Danks, H.V. (1981). Arctic Arthropods – A Review of Systematics and Ecology with Particular Reference to the North American Fauna. Canada: Entomological Society, 608 pp.

Diamond, M. (1958) Air temperature and precipitation on the Greenland ice cap. US Army SIPR Establishment Report 43, pp. 1–9.

Dissing, H. and Lange, M. (1987) Grønlands svampe. URT 1987(4): 47–52. Dansk Botanisk Forening, København.

Escher, J.C. and Pulvertaft, T.C.R. (1995). Geological Map of Greenland 1:2,500,000. Copenhagen: Geological Survey of Greenland.

Feilberg, J. (1984). A phytogeographical study of South Greenland. Vascular plants. *Meddr. Grønl. Biosci.* 15: 1–70.

Feilberg, J., Fredskild, B., and Holt, S. (1984). Grønlands Blomster/Flowers of Greenland. Ringsted: Flensborgs Forlag.

Fredskild, B. (1973). Studies in the vegetational history of Greenland. *Meddr. Grønl.* 198 (4): 1–245.

Fredskild, B. (1985). The Holocene vegetational development of Tugtuligssuaq and Qeqertat, Northwest Greenland. *Meddr. Grønl. Geosci.* 14: 1–20.

Fredskild, B. (1996). A phytogeographical study of the vascular plants of West Greenland (62°20'N-74°00'N). *Meddr. Grønl. Biosci.* 45: 1–157.

Fristrup, B. (1952). Wind erosion within the arctic deserts. *Geogr. Tidsskr.* 52: 51–65.

Fristrup, B. (1981). Klimatologi. In: *Danmarks Natur* 11: *Grønland* (eds. A. Nørrevang and A. Lundø), 170–179. København: Politikens Forlag.

Funder, S. (1987). Fra skov til tundra – glimt af bevoksningens historie. *URT* 1987: 1–10.

Gardes, M. and Dahlberg, A. (1996). Mycorrhizal diversity in arctic and alpine tundra: an open question. *New Phytol.* 133: 147–157.

Gates, D.M. (1993). Climate Change and Its Biological Consequences. Sunderland: Sinauer Associates, Inc., 280 pp.

Gensbøl, B. (1996). Grønlands natur – en rejsehåndbog. København: GAD, 448 pp.

Grenfell, T. and Warren, S.G. (1994). Spectral albedo of Antarctic snow. *J. Geophys. Res.* 99: 18,669–18,684.

Hansen, E.S. (1987). Grønlands laver. *URT* 1987 (4): 27–38.

Hansen, E.S. and Andersen, J. (1995). Greenland Lichens. Copenhagen: Rhodos. 124 pp.

Hasholt, B. and Søgaard, H. (1978). Et forsøg på en klimatisk hydrologisk regionsinddeling af Holsteinsborg kommune (Sisimiut). *Geogr. Tidsskr.* 77: 72–92.

Heide-Jørgensen, H.S. and Johnsen, I. (1995). Analysis of surface structures of *Cladonia mitis podetia* in historic and recent collections from Greenland. *Can. J. Bot.* 73: 457–464.

Heide-Jørgensen, H.S. and Johnsen, I. (1997). Høj-Arktisk vegetation i NV-Grønland. *Naturens Verden* 1997: 208–223.

Heide-Jørgensen, H.S., Johnsen, I. (1998) Ecosystem vulnerability to climate change in Greenland and the Faroe Islands. *Miljønyt* 33, Ministry of Environment and Energy, Danish EPA, Copenhagen. 266 pp.

Holmen, K. and Mogensen, G.S. (1981). Mosserne. In: *Danmarks Natur* 11: *Grønland* (eds. A. Nørrevang and J. Lundø), 388–394. København: Politikens Forlag.

Jensen, D.B. and Christensen, S.K. (2003). The Biodiversity of Greenland – A Country Study. Nuuk: Pinngortitaleriffik, Grønlands Naturinstitut.

Jonasson, S. (1997). Buffering of arctic plant responses in a changing climate. In: Global Change and Arctic Terrestrial Ecosystems, *Ecological Studies*, vol. 124 (eds. W.C. Oechel, T.V. Callaghan, T. Gilmanov, et al.), 365–380. New York: Springer.

Jonasson, S. and Michelsen, A. (1996). Nutrient cycling in subarctic and arctic ecosystems, with special reference to the Abisko and Torneträsk region. *Ecol. Bull.* 45: 45–52.

Kane, D.L., Hinzman, L.D., Ming-ko, W., and Everett, K.R. (1992). Arctic hydrology and climate change. In: Arctic Ecosystems in a Changing Climate. An Ecophysiological Perspective (eds. F.S. Chapin III, R.L. Jefferies, J.F. Reynolds, et al.), 35–57. San Diego: Academic Press.

Kappen, L.K. (1993). Plant activity under snow and ice, with particular reference to lichens. *Arctic* 46: 297–302.

Kennedy, A.D. (1996). Antarctic fellfield response to climate change: A tripartite synthesis of experimental data. *Oecologia* 107: 141–150.

Kershaw, K.A. (1985). Physiological Ecology of Lichens. Cambridge: Cambridge University Press, 293 pp.

Larsen, J.N., Anisimov, O.A., Constable, A. et al. (2014). Polar regions. In: Climate Change 2014: Impacts, Adaptation, and Vulnerability. Part B: Regional Aspects. Contribution of Working Group II to the Fifth Assessment Report of the Intergovernmental Panel on Climate Change (eds. V.R. Barros, C.B. Field, D.J. Dokken, et al.), 1567–1612. Cambridge, United Kingdom and New York, NY, USA: Cambridge University Press.

Longton, R.E. (1988). The Biology of Polar Bryophytes and Lichens. Cambridge: Cambridge University Press, 393 pp.

Love, A. (1983). Flora of Iceland. Reykjavik: Almenna B6kafólagid, 403 pp.

Matick, F. (1953). Lichenologische Notizen: 1. Der Flechten-Koëfftzient und seine Bedeutung für die Pflanzengeographie. *Ber. Dtsch. Bot. Ges.* 66: 263–269.

Maxwell, B. (1992). *Arctic climate: Potential for change under global warming. In: Arctic Ecosystems in a Changing Climate, An Ecophysiological Perspective* (eds. F.S. Chapin et al.), 11–34. San Diego, CA: Academic Press, Inc.

Meltofte, H., Thing, H. (eds.) (1996) ZERO. Zackenberg Ecological Research Operations, 1st Annual Report, 1995. Danish Polar Center, Copenhagen, 64 pp.

Meltofte, H., Thing, H. (eds.) (1997) ZERO. Zackenberg Ecological Research Operations, 2nd Annual Report 1996. Danish Polar Center, Copenhagen, 80 pp.

Michelsen, A., Schmidt, I.K., Jonassen, S. et al. (1996). Leaf 15N abundance of subarctic plants provides field evidence that ericoid, ectomycorrhizal and non- and arbuscular mycorrhizal species access different sources of soil nitrogen. *Oecologia* 105: 53–63.

Moeslund, S. and Ravn-Nielsen, J.O. (eds.) (1987). Grønlands planteverden. *URT* 1987 (4): 1–96.

Mogensen, G.S. (ed.) (1985). Illustrated moss flora of Arctic North America and Greenland. I. Polytrichaceae. *Meddr. Grønl. Biosci.* 17: 1–57.

Mogensen, G.S. (ed.) (1986). Illustrated moss flora of Arctic North America and Greenland. 2. Sphagnaceae. *Meddr. Grønl. Biosci.* 18: 1–61.

Mogensen, G.S. (ed.) (1987). Illustrated moss flora of Arctic North America and Greenland. 3. Andreaeobryaceae – Tetraphidaceae. *Meddr. Grønl. Biosci.* 23: 1–36.

Muus, B., Salomonsen, F., and Vibe, C. (1990). Grønlands Fauna. Fisk, Fugle, Pattedyr. København: Gyldendal, 464 pp.

Nadelhoffer, K.J., Giblin, A.E., Shaver, G.R., and Linkins, A.E. (1992). Microbial processes and plant nutrient availability in Arctic soils. In: Arctic Ecosystems in a Changing Climate. An Ecophysiological Perspective (eds. F.S. Chapin III, R.L. Jefferies, J.F. Reynolds, et al.), 281–300. San Diego: Academic Press.

Nielsen, N.W. and Rasmussen, L. (1993). Grønlands klima og vejr. *Naturens Verden* 1993 (3): 81–96.

Nørrevang, A. and Lundø, J. (eds.) (1981). *Danmarks Natur* 11: Gronland. København: Politikens Forlag, 587 pp.

Oechel, W.C. and Billings, W.D. (1992). Effects of global change on the carbon balance of Arctic plants and ecosystems. In: Arctic Ecosystems in a Changing Climate. An Ecophysiological Perspective (eds. F.S. Chapin III, R.L. Jefferies, J.F. Reynolds, et al.), 139–168. San Diego: Academic Press.

Ohmura, A. (1987). New temperature distribution maps for Greenland. *Z. Gletscherkd. Glazialgeol.* 23: 1–45.

Ohmura, A. and Reeh, N. (1991). New precipitation and accumulation maps for Greenland. *J. Glaciol.* 37: 140–148.

Pedersen, A. (1972). Adventitious plants and cultivated plants in Greenland. *Meddr. Grønl.* 178 (7).

Petersen, H. (1935). Das Klima der Küsten von Grönland. *Handb. Klimatol.* 2 (1): 33–65.

Petersen, P.M. (1977). Investigations on the ecology and phenology of the macromycetes in the Arctic. *Meddr. Grønl.* 199 (5): 1–72.

Porsild, M.P. (1920). The flora of Disko island and the adjacent coast of West Greenland. *Meddr. Grønl.* 58 (1): 1–156.

Prinn, R.G. (1994). The interactive atmosphere: global atmospheric biospheric chemistry. *Ambio* 23: 50–61.

Putnins, P. (1970). The climate of Greenland. In: Climates of the Polar Regions – World Survey of Climatology, vol. 14 (ed. S. Orvig), 3–127. New York: Elsevier Publishing Company Inc., 375 pp.

Schuster, R.M. and Damsholt, K. (1974). The hepaticae of West Greenland from ca. 66°N to 72°N. *Meddr. Grønl.* 199 (1): 1–373.

Sørensen, T. (1933). The vascular plants of East Greenland from 71°00′ to 73°30′N lat. *Meddr. Grønl.* 101 (3): 1–177.

Sørensen, T. (1941). Temperature relations and phenology of the Northeast Greenland flowering plants. *Meddr. Grønl.* 125 (9): 1–305.

Street, R.B. and Melnikov, P.L. (1990). Seasonal snow cover, ice and permafrost. In: Climate Change. The IPCC Impact Assessment (eds. W.J.M.G. Tegart, G.W. Sheldon and D.C. Griffiths), 7.1–7.33. Canberra: Australian Government Publishing Service.

Thingvad, N., Kern-Hansen, C. (1989) Klima. Jameson Land. Del I+II. Nuna Tek rapport.

Sektionen for Hydrotekniske Undersøgelser. 43 pp and 123 pp.

Tissue, D.T. and Oechel, W.C. (1987). Response of *Eriophorum vaginatum* to elevated CO_2 and temperature in the Alaskan arctic tussock tundra. *Ecology* 68: 401–410.

Tsay, S.-C. and Stamnes, K. (1992). Ultraviolet radiation in the Arctic: the impact of potential ozone depletions and cloud effects. *J. Geophys. Res.* 97: 7829–7840.

Vibe, C. (1967). Arctic animals in relation to climatic fluctuations. *Meddr. Grønl.* 170 (5): 1–227.

Walker, M.D. and Jones, M.H. (1996). A circumpolar comparison of tundra response to temperature manipulation: a synthesis of International Tundra Experiment data. In: 7th ITEX Workshop 26–29 April 1996. Book of Abstracts (eds. P. Mølgaard and T.B. Berg), 28–29. Copenhagen: Royal Danish School of Pharmacy.

Watson, R.T., Zinyowera, M.C., and Moss, R.H. (eds.) (1995). *Climate Change – Impacts, Adaptations and Mitigation of Climate Change:* Scientific-Technical Analyses, 879. IPCC: Cambridge University Press, Cambridge.

Index

Biogeography in the Sub-Arctic: The Past and Future of North Atlantic Biota, First Edition.
Edited by Eva Panagiotakopulu and Jon P. Sadler.
© 2021 John Wiley & Sons Ltd. Published 2021 by John Wiley & Sons Ltd.

Colour Illustrations for the Plate Section

Chapter 1 Upton

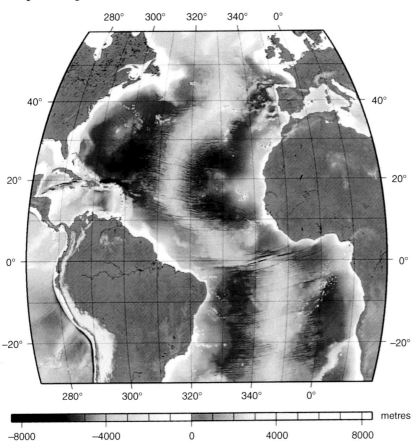

Figure 1 The bathymetry of the North Atlantic, based on satellite sea-surface altimetry, model DNSC08. The symmetrical disposition of the mid-Atlantic ridge relative to the bounding continents is well exhibited. *Source:* Based on Anderson, O.B. & Knudsen, P. 2009.

Biogeography in the Sub-Arctic: The Past and Future of North Atlantic Biota, First Edition.
Edited by Eva Panagiotakopulu and Jon P. Sadler.
© 2021 John Wiley & Sons Ltd. Published 2021 by John Wiley & Sons Ltd.

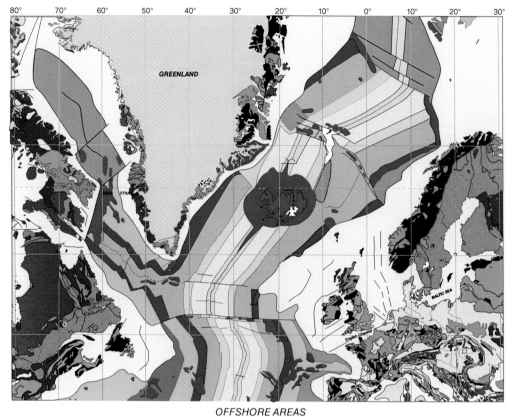

OFFSHORE AREAS

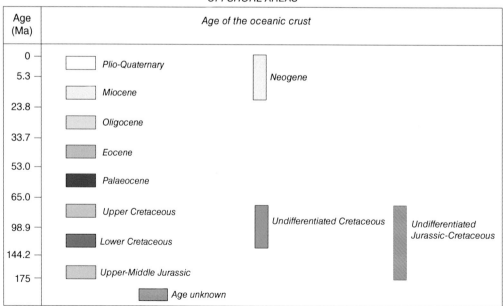

Age (Ma)	Age of the oceanic crust
0 —	Plio-Quaternary
5.3 —	Miocene
23.8 —	Oligocene
33.7 —	Eocene
53.0 —	Palaeocene
65.0 —	Upper Cretaceous
98.9 —	Lower Cretaceous
144.2 —	Upper-Middle Jurassic
175 —	Age unknown

Neogene

Undifferentiated Cretaceous

Undifferentiated Jurassic-Cretaceous

Figure 2 The pattern of magnetic stripes in the North Atlantic, 2005. Geological Map of the World. Scale: 1:50 000 000. *Source:* Published by CGMW & UNESCO.

Figure 3 (a) Conglomerate from a 2–3 m thick stratum separating Cretaceous shales from the base of the overlying plateau lavas on Wollaston Forland, East Greenland (75° N). Cobbles are of quartzite and muscovite granite. (b) Aerial photograph of the same (white) stratum on Kap Broer Ruys, East Greenland (73°30′N). Well-stratified dark grey Cretaceous shales beneath and brown/black lavas above. *Source:* B.G.J. Upton.

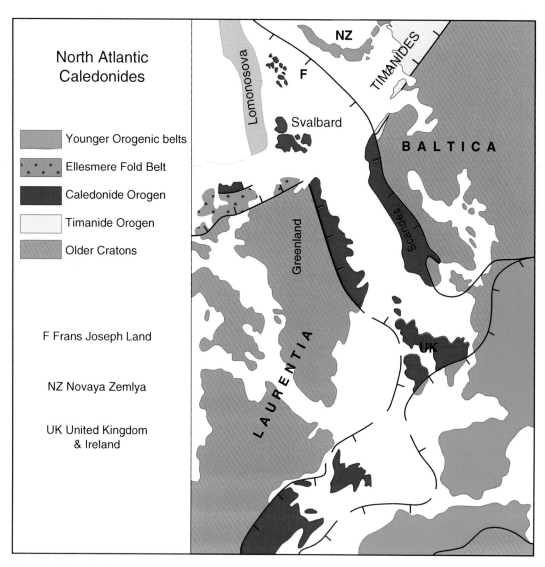

Figure 5 Map showing the orogenic belts on either side of the North Atlantic. Note that between Greenland and Norway the North Atlantic is approximately bilaterally symmetrical through the Caledonian Orogenic belt. *Source:* Gee et al. 2008.

Figure 6 A coastal section on Cape Searle Island, Baffin Island, Canada, showing a succession similar to that of parts of the East Greenland coast. Palaeocene non-marine sediments form the basal third, with white sandstones and dark coals and organic-rich shales. The central part (pale brownish and not well stratified) is of sub-aqueous volcanic rocks (picritic hyaloclastites and pillow breccias). The upper third consists of subaerially erupted picritic lavas. *Source:* B.G.J.Upton.

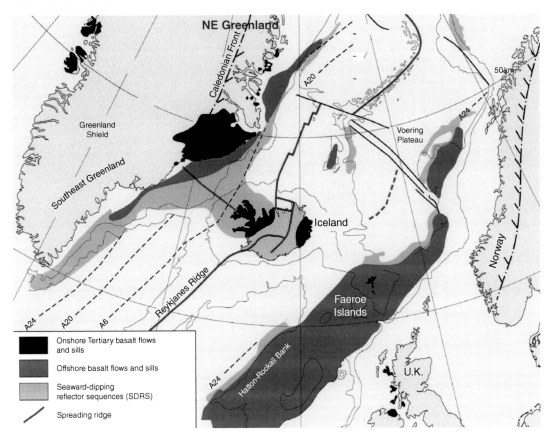

Figure 8 Distribution of the early Paleogene lavas, subaerial and submarine. The current spreading centres are marked in red. *Source:* Based on Larsen et al. (1994).

Figure 9 (a) Flat-lying basalts of the Geikie Plateau Formation, Gåseland, East Greenland, looking towards 1980 m summit. *Source:* Photo by W.S. Watt. (b) View of the steep east coast of Greenland (the Blosseville coast) between ca. 67° and 69° N, composed of horizontal basalt lavas, west of the seaward flexing. *Source:* Photo by B.G.J. Upton.

Figure 10 Kap Hammer on the East Greenland coast (67°40′N), within the zone showing maximum seaward flexing. The cliffs here consist almost entirely of dykes, thus composing a 'sheeted complex'. Since the flexure here is eastwards, the dykes have a corresponding westward dip. The greater the inclination, the older the dyke. A few (young) near-vertical dykes are seen in the near cliffs. *Source:* Photo by B.G.J. Upton.

Figure 11 Sub-aerial (picritic) lavas on the Svartenhuk peninsula, West Greenland (71° 30′N). These lie within the flexed zone, dipping westwards towards the Baffin Bay spreading centre. Such 'seaward-dipping reflectors' are generally sunk below sea-level but in this instance they are well seen sub-aerially. *Source:* Photo by T.C.R. Pulvertaft.

Figure 12   Dark ash layers contrasting with white diatomite sediments on the island of Fur, Limfjord, Jutland. Originally deposited sub-horizontally, the sequence was later severely deformed by Pleistocene ice sheets. *Source:* Photo by B.G.J. Upton.

Figure 13   Lava fountaining along a fissure (Krafla volcano) northern Iceland 1980, during an episode of extension and rift opening. *Source:* Photo by Halldór Ólafsson.

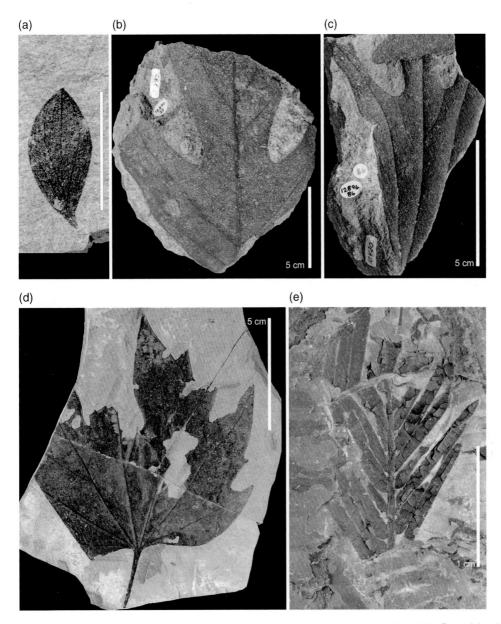

Figure 3   Palaeocene fossil leaves from West Greenland (Agatdalen, Atanikerluk) and the Faroe Islands (Mykines). (A) Small acrodromous leaf from Upper Atanikerluk B, MGUH 6443 [as *Paliurus pusillus* Heer in Heer (1883; Pl. LXXXI, figs 9 and 10)]. (B) *Liriodendron* sp., from Agatdalen, MGUH 10393 [as cfr. *Liriodendron* sp. in Koch (1963; Pl. 16, fig. 1)]. (C) *Sassafras* sp., from Agatdalen, MGUH 10420 [as *Lauraceaephyllum stenolobatus* Koch in Koch (1963; Pl. 30, fig. 2)]. (D) Large actinodromous leaf from Upper Atanikerluk B, MGUH 6435 [as *Cissites steenstrupi* Heer in Heer (1883; Pl. LXXXI, fig. 1)]. (E) *Metasequoia occidentalis* (Newb.) Chaney, from Mykines (Beinisvørð Formation), S134471.

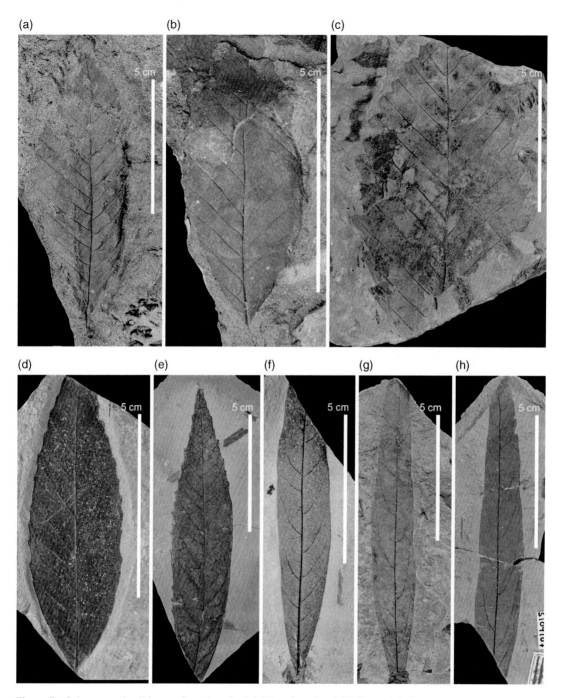

Figure 5 Palaeocene fossil leaves from Atanikerluk, West Greenland. (A) *Fagopsiphyllum groenlandicum* (Heer) Manchester, from Upper Atanikerluk A, MGUH 6894 [as *Fagus castaneaefolia* Ung. in Heer (1868; Pl. XLVI, fig. 3a)]. (B) *Fagopsiphyllum groenlandicum* (Heer) Manchester, from Upper Atanikerluk A, MGUH 6269 [as *Castanea ungeri* Heer in Heer (1883; Pl. LXIX, fig. 3)]. (C) *Fagopsiphyllum groenlandicum* (Heer) Manchester, from Upper Atanikerluk A, MGUH 6270 [as *Quercus grönlandica* Heer in Heer (1883; Pl. LXIX, fig. 4)]. (D) *Eotrigonobalanus* sp., from Upper Atanikerluk B, MGUH 6349 [as *Quercus laharpii* Gaud. in Heer (1883; Pl. LXXV, fig. 2)]. (E) *Eotrigonobalanus* sp., from Upper Atanikerluk B, MGUH 6372 [as *Pterocarya denticulata* Web in Heer (1883; Pl. LXXVI, fig. 1)]. (F) *Eotrigonobalanus* sp., from Upper Atanikerluk B, MGUH 6390 [as *Laurus reussii* Ettingsh. in Heer (1883; Pl. LXXVII, fig. 7)]. (G) *Eotrigonobalanus* sp., from Upper Atanikerluk B, S109006 [as *Laurus primigenia* Ung. in Heer (1880; Pl. III, fig. 8a)]. (H) *Eotrigonobalanus* sp., from Upper Atanikerluk B, S109107.

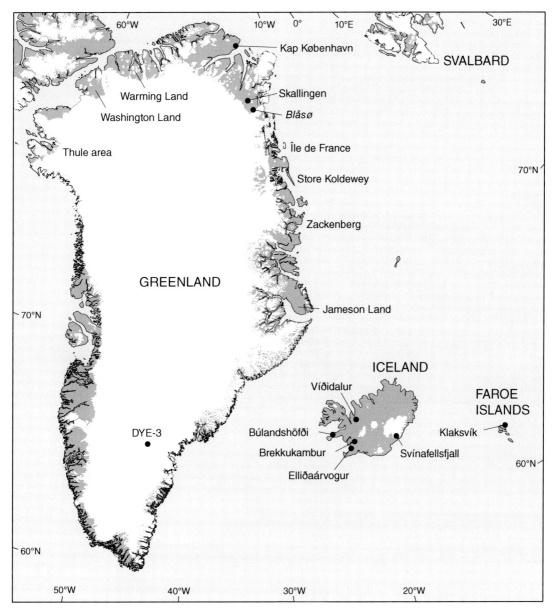

Figure 1   Map of the North Atlantic region showing the location of place names used in the text.

Figure 3 (a) Mt. Stöð with an outcrop of the Búlandshöfði Formation showing lagoonal mud overlain by deltaic sandstones. (b) Svínafell with the Svínafellsfjall Formation showing exposed lake sediments. *Source:* Photographs kindly provided by Friðgeir Grímsson.

Figure 5 (a) A log of *Larix* sitting in sandy deposits of the Kap København Formation (member B) in North Greenland. The light part has been bleached by the sun. Note the contrasting modern treeless landscape. (b) Organic-rich layers of the Kap København Formation (member B). (c) Excavation of last interglacial deposits on Jameson Land, central East Greenland. (d) Sandy interglacial deposits on Jameson Land with organic-rich sediments in the bottom of a trough. (e) Archaeological excavation of a Mid-Holocene midden in central West Greenland.

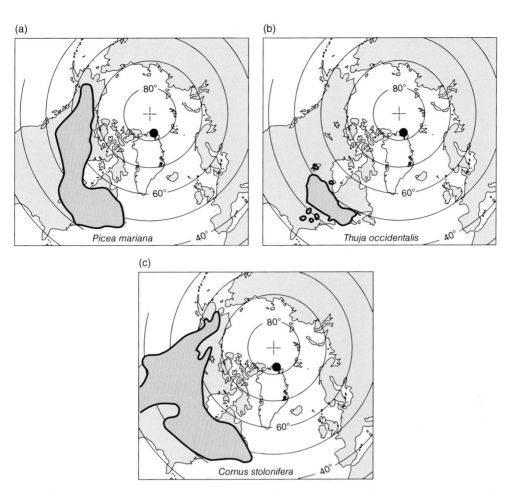

Figure 8 Maps of the northern parts of the Earth, showing present geographical ranges of *Picea mariana* (a), *Thuja occidentalis* (b) and *Cornus stolonifera* (c). Remains of these species have been found in the Kap København Formation (black dot in North Greenland). *Source:* From Bennike (1990).

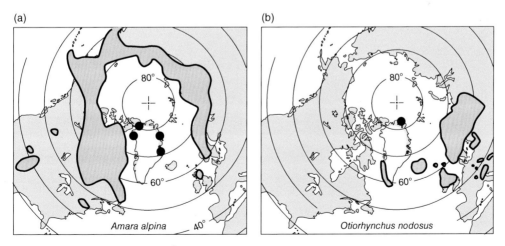

Figure 12 Maps of the northern part of the Earth, showing the present-day range of the ground beetle *Amara alpina* and the weevil *Otiorhynchus nodosus*. The dots show fossil finds in Greenland, assumed to come from the last interglacial. Modern distributions according to Böcher (1989) and Bennike and Böcher (1994).

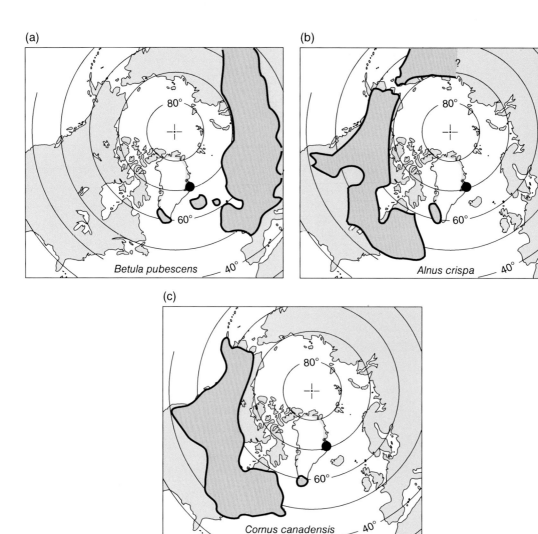

Figure 13 Maps of the northern parts of the Earth, showing the present-day geographical ranges of (a) *Betula pubescens*, (b) *Alnus crispa* and (c) *Cornus canadensis*. Remains of these species have been found in layers from the last interglacial stage in Jameson Land, East Greenland (black dots). *Source:* From Bennike and Böcher (1994; 1996).

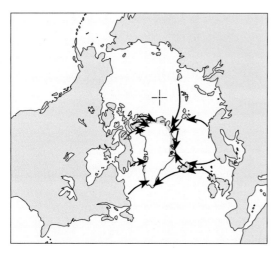

Figure 15 Maps of the Earth's northern parts with arrows that show immigration routes to the North Atlantic islands. The routes are mainly suggested from the modern-day geographical ranges of the species. However, we know from historical sources that Norse people sailed to the North Atlantic islands from North-West Europe and hunters travelled with their families to Greenland from Canada as late as the 1860s. In 1937 large flocks of migrating fieldfares *Turdus pilaris* were blown from Norway to Greenland where they established a small breeding population. Surprisingly many species have colonized the North Atlantic islands from North-West Europe. The distance between the islands is long, but the islands form stepping stones along the route *Source:* From Bennike (1999).

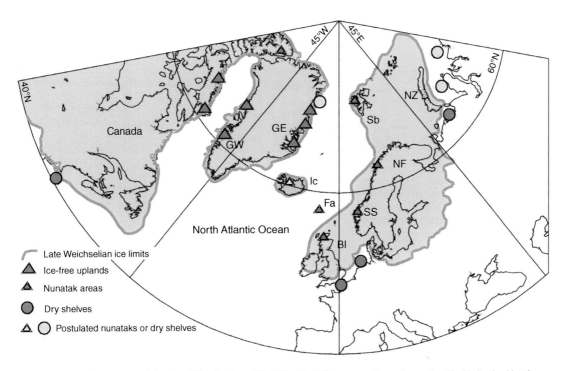

Figure 1   Reconstruction of the Late Weichselian (25 000–10 000 years ago) maximum ice limits in the North Atlantic region. Ice-free areas are indicated (red symbols: strong geological evidence). The nine Atlantic subregions analysed for endemism are indicated: GW – Greenland, West and South (SE to Lindenowfjord); GE – Greenland, East (N of Lindenowfjord); Sb – Svalbard including Bear Island and Franz Josef Land; NZ – Novaya Zemlya (excl. Vaigach); Ic – Iceland; Fa – The Faroes; BI – Northern British Isles; SS – Scandes, southern part; NF – Fennoscandia, northern part including the Kola Peninsula. A nunatak may also have existed in Jan Mayen, but there are no recent studies of glaciation in this island. Reproduced with permission from Brochmann et al. (2003).

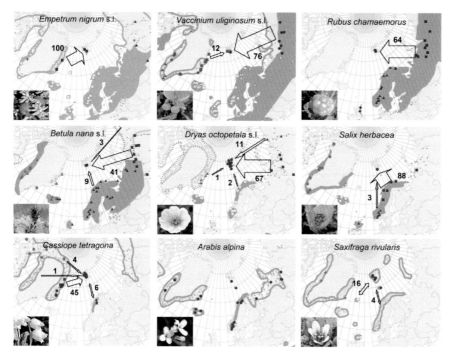

Figure 2 Colonisation of the Svalbard archipelago with source regions inferred from statistical assignment analyses of AFLP multilocus genotypes. The geographical distribution of each species is shaded (that of closely related species is indicated by dotted lines for *Betula nana* (*B. exilis*) and *Dryas octopetala* (*D. integrifolia*). Colours represent main genetic groups and symbols represent subgroups. Numbers on the arrows indicate the percentage allocation of Svalbard genotypes to a source region (using a log-likelihood difference of 1; i.e. 10 times as likely from that source region as from any other source regions). For *C. tetragona*, the direction of dispersal between Svalbard and Scandinavia is uncertain because of low diversity in Scandinavia. The source for the Svalbard populations of *A. alpina* could not be determined because of lack of genetic variation. In *S. rivularis*, the highest levels of genetic variation and most private markers were observed in the Svalbard populations, which also were clearly separated from the two amphi-Atlantic genetic groups. Thus, survival in Svalbard during the last glacial maximum cannot be excluded for this high-arctic species. Reproduced with permission from Alsos et al. (2007).

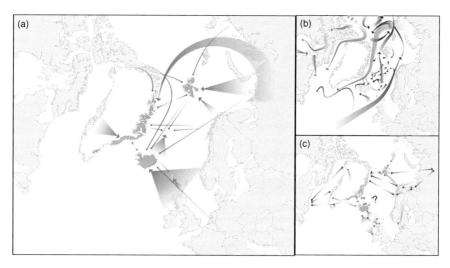

Figure 3 (a) Main (thick arrows) and additional (thin arrows) long-distance dispersal routes of plants in the North Atlantic area inferred from genetic and floristic data (cf. Figure 1). (b) Sea surface circulation patterns in the North Atlantic area (blue: cold water, red: warm water). (c) Main migration routes for geese species (thick blue arrows) and the supposedly efficient seed disperser *Plectrophenax nivalis* (snow bunting, thin red arrows) in the North Atlantic area. Reproduced with permission from Alsos et al. (2015).

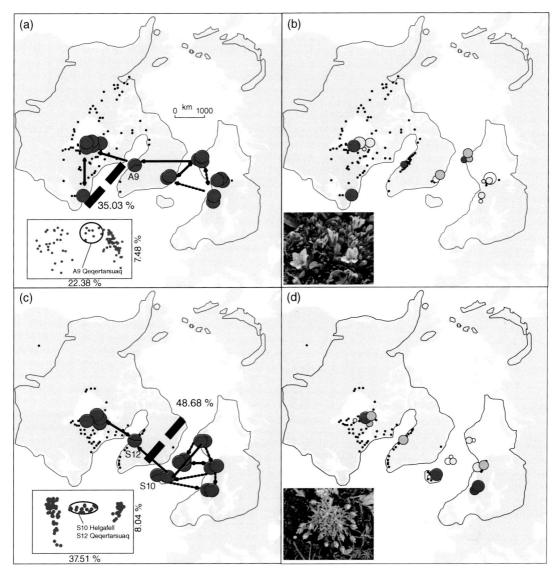

Figure 4 Genetic patterns detected in two west-arctic species, providing quite convincing evidence of glacial persistence in East Greenland/Svalbard (*Arenaria humifusa*) and southern Scandinavia (*Sagina caespitosa*). Each species contains two distinct genetic (AFLP) groups, one East Atlantic (red) and one West Atlantic (blue), excluding with reasonable certainty postglacial dispersal from North America as an explanation for their rare European occurrences. The maps show total geographical distribution (black dots), sampling sites and the Last Glacial Maximum ice extent (blue line). Reproduced with permission from Westergaard et al. (2011). (a, c) Genetic groups (blue and red) identified by structure analysis; pie diagrams with both colours indicate mixed ancestry, probably resulting from postglacial long-distance dispersal. Arrows represent dispersal routes inferred from assignment to geographic regions. The dashed black line shows division between the two main groups with the percentage of genetic variation assigned to between-group variation. The variation among all individual plants analysed, coloured according to genetic group, are depicted in the ordination analysis placed in the lower left corner of each map. (b, d) Geographical distribution of genetic diversity and distinctiveness. The size of the circles is proportional to gene diversity within populations, and the colours of the circles represent the four quartiles of genetic distinctiveness measured by occurrence of rare alleles (red – upper quartile, orange and yellow – intermediate quartiles, white – the lower quartile). The geographical positions of Svalbard (S) and Jan Mayen (JM) are indicated in (d). Photos: I. G. Alsos (*A. humifusa*; Svalbard, Bockfjorden) and K. I. Flatberg (*S. caespitosa*; S Norway, Knutshø Mts).

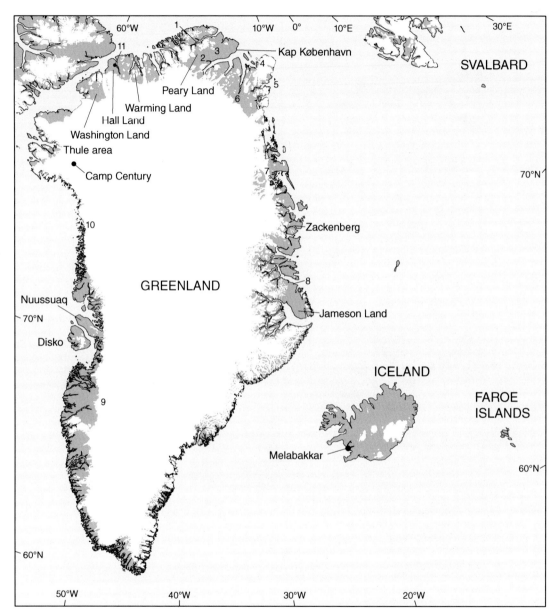

Figure 1 Map of the North Atlantic region showing the location of selected place names used in the text. The numbers refer to Table 1.

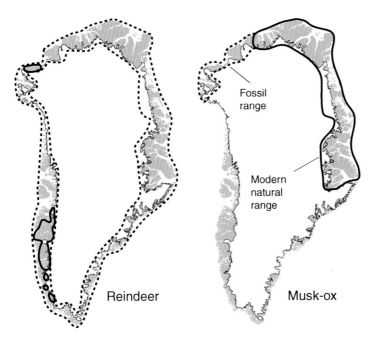

Figure 4 Maps of Greenland showing Holocene and modern natural geographical ranges of reindeer (*Rangifer tarandus*) and musk-ox (*Ovibos moschatus*).

Figure 5 Two examples of musk-ox (*Ovibos moschatus*) skull fragments. (a) A specimen of a female from Washington Land with the outer horny sheaths still present dated to 10–274 cal. years BP (K-5174; Bennike 2002). Note that BP = CE1950. (b) A strongly eroded specimen of a male from Olrik Fjord in the Thule area dated to ~2200 cal. years BP (Bennike 2014).

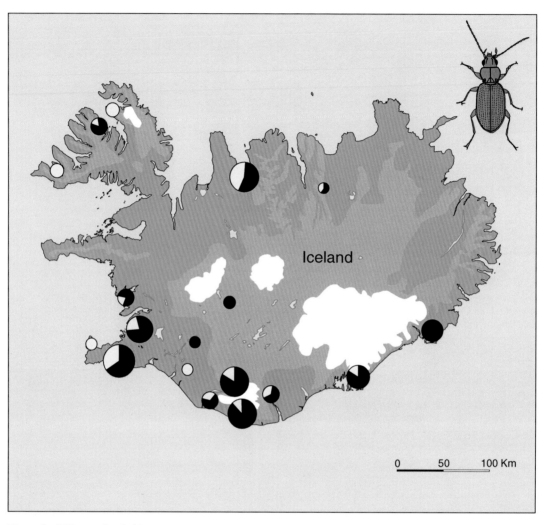

Figure 1   Different distribution patterns between long and short winged forms (= black parts of circles) of *Bembidion grapii* and the two refuges in Iceland in Eyjafjallajökull (south refuge) and Vatnajökull (southeast refuge) coastal areas. *Source:* Redrawn from Lindroth (1957).

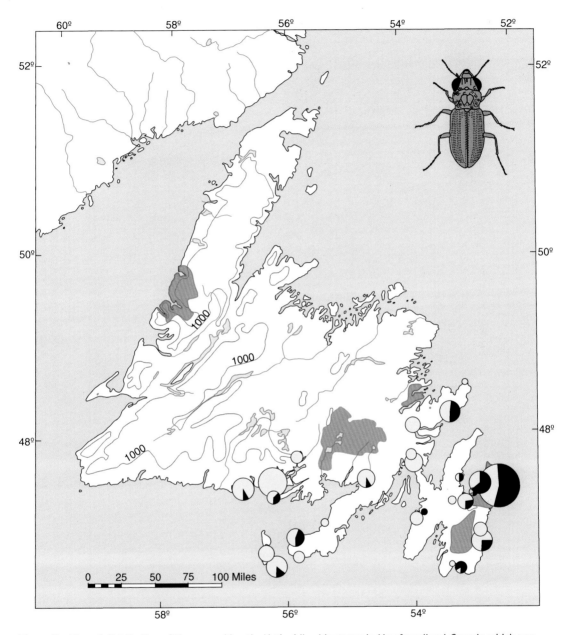

Figure 2 Map of distribution of the ground beetle *Notiophilus biguttatus* in Newfoundland, Canada which was introduced probably relatively recently in ballast (black parts of circles = short winged forms). *Source:* Redrawn from Lindroth (1957).

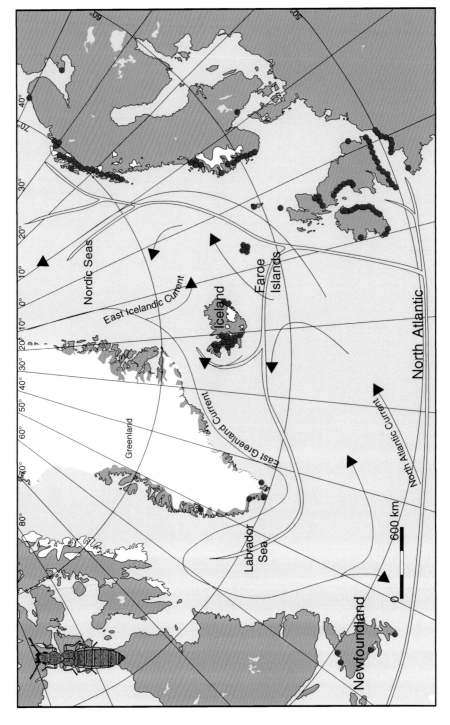

Figure 3 Map of distribution of the littoral rove beetle *Micralymma brevilingue* in the North Atlantic. It was probably introduced to Newfoundland via the cod fisheries based in SW English ports and the resultant large-scale movement of ballast across the North Atlantic for >300 years. *Source:* Redrawn from Lindroth (1957).

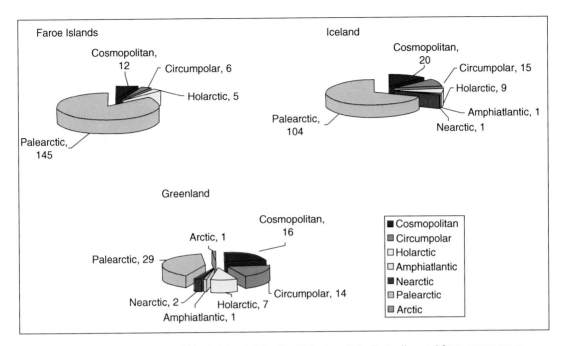

Figure 4 Affinities of Coleoptera of North Atlantic Islands which strongly indicate dispersal from east to west. *Source:* Redrawn from Sadler and Skidmore (1995).

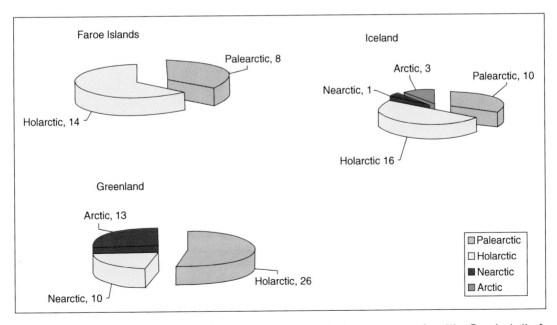

Figure 5 Affinities of Diptera in the North Atlantic islands. Atmospheric systems move from W to E so the bulk of the flies would come in from the Nearctic, reducing in numbers eastwards. *Source:* Redrawn from Sadler and Skidmore (1995).

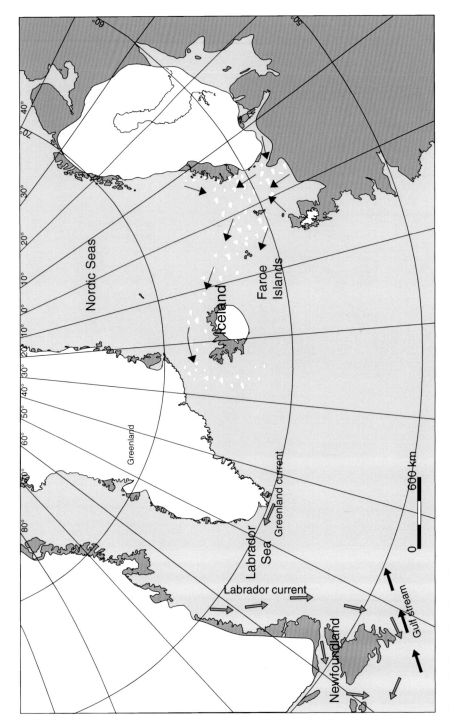

Figure 6 Map of the North Atlantic during the beginning of the Holocene showing the catastrophic drainage of the Baltic Ice Lake. Movement of ice in the North Atlantic towards the west is indicated. *Source*: Data on the Baltic Ice Lake are from Björck (1995) and Andrén et al. (2011).

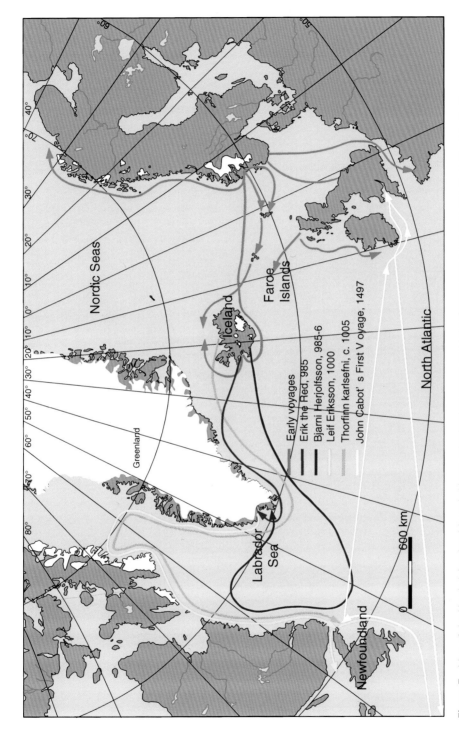

Figure 7 Map of the North Atlantic with early Norse colonization routes and John Cabot's first journey to Newfoundland, indicating movement of biota.

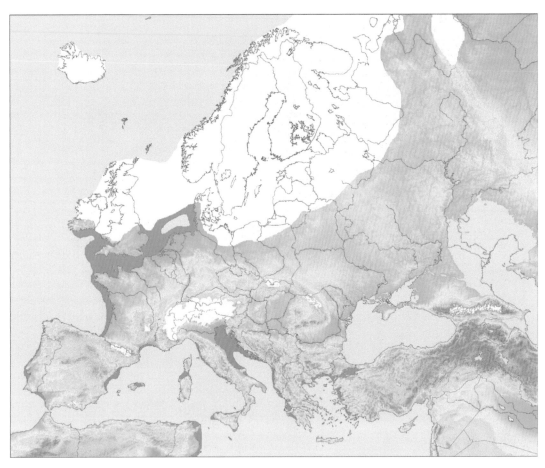

Figure 1   The extent of the Ice Age glaciation about 20 000 years ago. *Source:* San Jose, https://commons. wikimedia.org/wiki/File:Europe_topography_map.png. Licensed under CC BY-SA 3.0.

Figure 1 From the top of Sandfelli (790 m a.s.l.) in the northern part of Eysturoy with Kalsoy and Kunoy in the background.

Figure 4 Round-leaved Sundew, *Drosera rotundifolia*, is one of the red-listed plants growing in mires.

Figure 5 Oysterplant, *Mertensia maritima*, is one of the threatened plant species on the Faroese seashore.

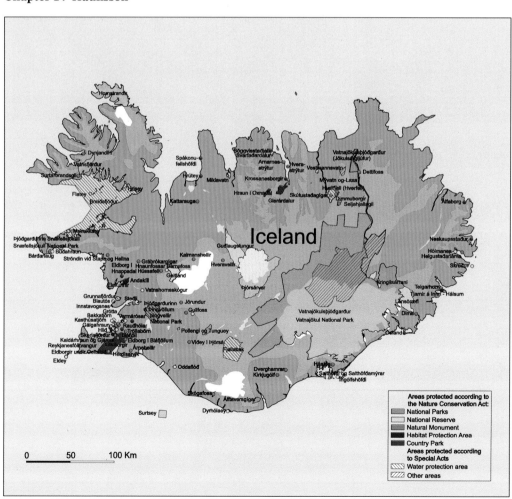

Figure 1 Map of protected areas in Iceland using data from the Environment Agency of Iceland. *Source:* Data from Environment Agency of Iceland. https://gis.ust.is/geoserver/web/wicket/bookmarkable/org.geoserver.web.demo. MapPreviewPage?1

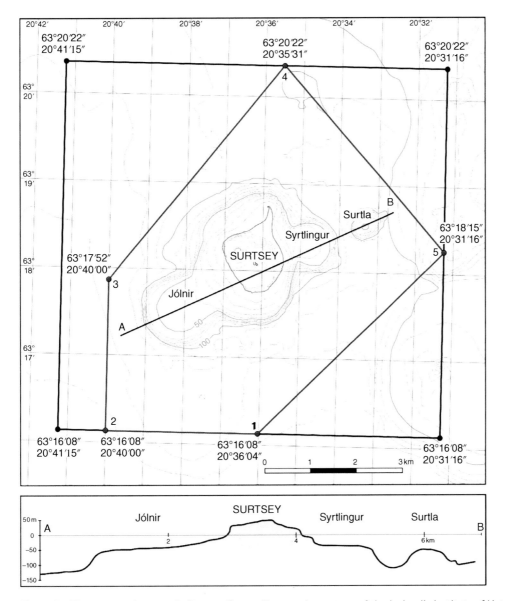

Figure 2 The preservation area in Surtsey. *Source:* The map is courtesy of the Icelandic Institute of Natural History, supplied by The Surtsey Research Society.

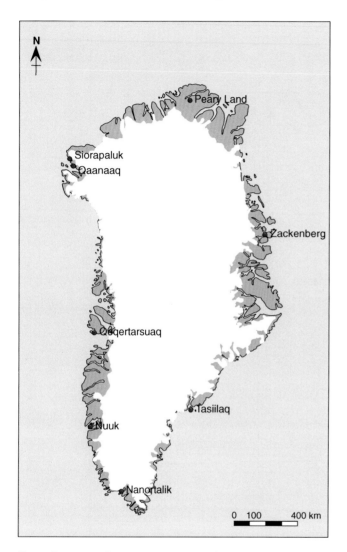

Figure 1 Map of Greenland with ice cap borderline shown and name of localities mentioned in the chapter.

Figure 2 Retreating ice sheet permitting the first pioneer lichens (*Stereocaulon* sp.) to form small cushions on the barren, newly exposed soil in the High Arctic. July, Thule District, Greenland. *Source:* Ib Johnsen.

Figure 3 Photo from July in the high arctic near Thule. The more favourable life conditions on the right slope are due to higher exposure from the sun. Probably, such conditions become more widespread due to climate change. *Source:* Ib Johnsen.

Figure 4 July landscape in the Thule area. The border of the Greenland ice cap (Indlandsisen) is seen in the background. *Source:* Ib Johnsen.